GRIMSBY TOWN

A COMPLETE RECORD 1878-1989

GRIMSBY TOWN

A COMPLETE RECORD 1878-1989

LES TRIGGS with DAVID HEPTON and SID WOODHEAD

Breedon Books Sport

First published in Great Britain by
The Breedon Books Publishing Company Limited
45 Friar Gate, Derby DE1 1DA
1989

ISBN 0 907969 46 1

Printed by Butler and Tanner Limited, Frome.
Jacket designed by Graham Hales and printed by Arkle Print, Northampton.

Contents

Photographic Acknowledgements

Photographs have been supplied by Birmingham Public Libraries, Colorsport, *Grimsby Evening Telegraph*, Grimsby Public Library.

Introduction and Acknowledgements

The statistics contained in this volume are the result of several years' research by the compilers, during which many hundreds of match reports have been perused, in most cases twice, with any discrepancy being checked a third time.

The compilers, however, would not be presumptious enough to claim that the work is without error. Early reporting of football matches was somewhat haphazard. Separate reports of the same match sometimes gave different line-ups and the same goal is sometimes attributed to different players.

Often it is not made clear who scored a goal, 'the ball was rushed over the line in a scrimmage' being the total account.

No official attendance records exist before 1925 and figures for these years, where given, are gleaned from match reports. From 1925 to 1950 attendances are taken from official records at Football League headquarters. Those from 1951 to the present time are as given in the *Grimsby Evening Telegraph.* These may vary slightly from those at Lytham St Annes.

Over the years assistance has been sought from fellow members of the Association of Football Statisticians. These are too numerous to name individually, although special mention should be made of Douglas Lamming, that doyen of football statisticians, whose book the *Who's Who of Grimsby Town FC* has proved a valuable source of reference. Our thanks are due to them all.

Thanks is also due to Graham Kelly, the former secretary of the Football League, for permitting access to League archives at Lytham St Annes and the secretaries of Aston Villa FC and Blackpool FC.

Pat Glover, Grimsby Town's greatest centre-forward, holder of several club records for goalscoring and international appearances.

The Grimsby Town Story

THE first seed from which grew Grimsby Town Football Club was sown when members of the Worsley Cricket Club were bemoaning the bleak prospects of the winter months ahead, after stumps were drawn at the close of the 1878 season. Someone suggested that the cricketers should form a football club and a meeting was called.

At the Wellington Arms, Freeman Street, on Friday, 20 September 1878, Grimsby Pelham FC was formed. Local worthies, Sir John Astley and John Winteringham, were elected president and vice-president respectively. Each subscribed a sovereign and, with £2.00 in hand, the history of the Mariners commenced. C.Horn was elected captain and club colours of white jerseys with blue hoops were chosen.

The Wellington Arms in Freeman Street, where Grimsby Pelham FC was formed in 1878. Well over a century later, the public house is still serving thirsty Grimbarians.

Possibly because of the severe winter of 1878-9, only two matches were played, both against Brigg Brittania. For the away fixture the club could muster only ten players (12 were normally used in those days) and Pelham lost 2-0. The team for this first match was: C.Horn, J.C.Coates, A.Ousley, S.Huxley, R.Chapman, W.Bridge, F.Long, A.Mountain, F.Charlton and S.Haddlesey.

By the time of the first annual general meeting, the club's funds had grown to £3 18s 5d and the name of the club was changed to Grimsby Town FC.

In the 1879-80 season, the fixture list grew and, of 15 matches played, six were won and three drawn, 21 goals were scored and 15 conceded. The following season, Grimsby Town's ambition grew to the point where they took a lease on their own ground at Clee Park (see *The Mariners' Grounds.*)

Grimsby Pelham FC, photographed in 1878. Back row (left to right): W.T.Lamming, R.C.Hall, Bob Lincoln, G.Atkinson, H.Evans, W.Ashling, A.H.Read. Front row: S.Noble, J.Warner, T.Atknison, H.Monument, J.Fanthorpe.

A significant development came in 1881-2, with the formation of the Lincolnshire Football Association and the inauguration of the Lincolnshire Cup. Town's first-ever truly competitive match was against Brigg Ancholme at Brigg, where the Grimsby side won 6-3.

In 1882, the important decision was taken to enter the FA Cup, then known as the English Cup. In those days, teams from Scotland, and even Ireland, also competed for the Cup and great excitement was aroused when Grimsby were drawn to play the renowned Glaswegian club, Queen's Park, at Clee Park. The Scotsmen, however, did not fancy the trip south and scratched.

Thus, Grimsby Town's first encounter in the Cup was against the Rotherham works side, Phoenix Bessemer, and resulted in a 9-1 thrashing for the Mariners. The financial return from the exorbitant entrance fee of 6d was scant reward. In 1884, the club's colours were changed to chocolate and blue quarters with white shorts.

On 13 March 1886, what is thought to be Town's first-ever 5,000-plus attendance assembled at Clee Park to witness the semi-final of the Lincolnshire Cup against Lincoln City. After 90 minutes, the score stood at one goal apiece. Grimsby demanded extra-time, Lincoln refused and referee Sam Omerod, because of the excitable nature of the crowd, decided not to continue. Appeals by Grimsby to both the Lincolnshire and the English Football Associations resulted in a ruling that the match be replayed. Grimsby protested vehemently and were summoned before a special meeting of the Football Association.

Dr Morley of Blackburn was of a mind to mete out Draconian punishment and proposed that the club be given until the first month of the following season to replay the match and that in default they be suspended from the Association permanently. Fortunately, a counter-proposal from the Grimsby Town representative, H.S.Mundahl — that the club were innocent of blame and that they should be

Grimsby Town FC, photographed in 1885. Back row (left to right): J.H.Taylor, W.Asling, H.Taylor. Middle row: W.T.Lamming (honorary secretary), R.C.Hall, G.Kimpson, H.S.Mundahl. Front row: S.Noble, T.Garnham, R.Raynes, H.Monument, A.H.Read.

awarded the match — was carried by an overwhelming majority. The cup, however, was withheld, after Lincoln Lindum were beaten in the Final.

On 12 January 1889, came a black day in the history of Grimsby Town. Derbyshire club, Staveley, were the visitors to Clee Park. Dan Doyle, the Grimsby left-back, and William Cropper, of the Staveley side and a promising county cricketer for Derbyshire, went for a high ball. Doyle's knee caught Cropper in the stomach and Cropper was carried from the field without it being realized how seriously he had been injured. Despite medical attention, his condition deteriorated overnight and he died the following day from a ruptured bowel. An unfortunate aftermath was that, although the incident was a complete accident, feeling against Grimsby was so intense in the Sheffield area that Sheffield Wednesday thought it prudent to cancel both fixtures against the club.

During the 1888-9 season, Grimsby had participated in an abortive attempt to form a league known as the 'Combination'. Lack of any proper organisation resulted in the failure of this competition and it was dissolved after one season, the Football Alliance being formed to replace it. Prime movers were clubs like Sheffield Wednesday and Birmingham St George's who, incensed at the virtual closed shop of the Football League — they had refused to sanction a Second Division — opted to form their own competition. Because the clubs were mainly from the Midlands, there was some objection to teams from further away — which involved a lot of travelling — being admitted. In order to overcome these objections, Grimsby Town had to undertake to pay half of all visitors' travelling expense. Sunderland Albion, even further out on a limb, were asked to pay three-quarters. Sunderland withdrew their application rather than pay up.

At the close of the 1888-9 season, the lease on the Clee Park ground expired and the club moved to Abbey Park, then on the south-west outskirts of the town. The opening match, on 7 September 1889, was a friendly against West Bromwich Albion, which Town won 6-1. The first competitive match was an Alliance game against Newton Heath, now better known as Manchester United, which again resulted in a win for the Town, this time by 3-1

In 1892, Town at last achieved Football League status when Alliance members formed the Second Division, although Nottingham Forest and Sheffield Wednesday were elected straight into Division One. Town joined Division Two, along with clubs like Small Heath (later Birmingham), Lincoln City, Ardwick (Manchester City) and Sheffield United.

The Grimsby club was improving in stature, with players like Jimmy Whitehouse, Sandy Higgins and Harry Fletcher starring. On 5 February 1895, Notts County won by the only goal at Abbey Park. The Town were not to suffer another defeat at home until 13 March 1897, a run of 31 League and three Cup games without defeat. In fact, in the three seasons 1894-5 to 1896-7, they dropped only seven out of a possible 90 points in front of their own supporters. In those three seasons they finished fifth, third and third again.

Their stay at Abbey Park was a brief one. Landlord Edward Heneage was developing housing in the area and his correspondence to his solicitor shows that he was regretting his association with the club, considering the conduct of the players less than gentlemanly. After a decade the lease was terminated and Town moved to their present home at Blundell Park. Luton Town were the visitors in the opening match on 2 September 1899 and drew 3-3.

The change seemed to suit Grimsby Town, for the following season was to be the most successful, thus far, in their history. 'Enthusiast,' the football writer for the *Grimsby News*, opined that the Second Division clubs were a ragged lot and if Grimsby Town were ever going to reach the top flight, now was their chance. The team was centred around a half-back line of Griffiths, Gray and Nelmes which, apart from the legendary Hall, Betmead and Buck middle line of the inter-war period, was probably the greatest half-back line in the club's history. George Harris opened the season in goal, but was later ousted by Rab MacFarlane. Mountain, and Leiper were the full backs. Harry Fletcher had returned from Trent Bridge, then the home of Notts County, to join Leigh and Mellor in the attack.

At first, Town's form showed little indication that the season was to be any different from previous campaigns but by the end of November, they shared top place with Blackpool and for some weeks the two clubs vied for top position. On 19 January 1901, a 5-0 reverse at New Brighton sent Grimsby down to third position. The team was strengthened by the signing of Welsh international Alfred Watkins from Aston Villa. Promotion hopes took a turn for the better and in the next eight games, only two points were dropped. Only two points were gained from the next four matches, however, and Town lost first place to Small Heath. The last two games of the season produced a home win against Glossop and a goalless draw at Middlesbrough, whilst Small Heath gained only two points out of their last three games. The Mariners, therefore, won the Second Division championship by one point and secured promotion to the top flight.

In preparation for the First Division, a new stand was built on the Harrington Street side of the ground, this structure still forming the basis of the present main stand. Attempts were made to strengthen the team, notably, by signing no less than five players from Southern League club Queen's Park Rangers (Ronaldson, Bellingham, Skinner, Clutterbuck and Alex McConnell). Alfred Dean arrived from Nottingham Forest, Andrew Gardner from Clyde, George Harper from Wolves, and former goalkeeper Walter Whittaker returned from Blackburn. With a greatly enlarged squad of players, Grimsby formed a reserve team which was entered in the Midland League.

Derby County were the visitors to Blundell Park in the opening match of the 1901-02 season and the result was a creditable 1-1 draw. The next week, at Sheffield Wednesday, despite being reduced to ten men after an injury to McConnell in the first ten minutes, the Town led 1-0 at half time, thanks to a goal by Dean. Trying to retain this lead, they pulled everyone back into defence and held on until ten minutes from time. Wednesday's persistence, however, paid off and three goals were conceded in the final minutes.

From then on, Grimsby's fortunes went mostly downhill, due in part to an appalling crop of injuries. For the rest of 1901, only nine more points were picked up from 15 games and the club were next to bottom of the division. On Christmas Day, the team was strengthened by the acquisition of 'Cockles' Appleyard from local football. A 3-1 revenge defeat of Sheffield Wednesday on 4 January heralded a run of 16 games to the end of the season, of which nine were won, three drawn and only four lost. Town finished fifth from bottom and, despite further signings, the following season was even worse, starting on a bad note when the Football Association suspended, for a week, the entire team that had taken part in an unpleasant match at Stoke at the end of the previous season. Fortunately, Nottingham Forest agreed to a postponement of the opening match, which was eventually lost 1-0 to set the pattern for the season.

By the turn of the year, only two matches had been won. A point at Aston Villa on 27 December and the first away victory of the season, at Bolton on 3

The Mariners' playing staff in 1902-03. Back row (left to right): G.Craddock (trainer), W.Whittaker. Fifth row: Mr S.Withers (director), A.McConnell, A.Nelmes, P.Gray, H.N.Hickson (secretary), Mr A.Burnham (director). Fourth row: P.Paterson, Mr W.Page (director), Ben Hall, D.R.Gardener, E.Bromley, T.H.Blyth, H.Colbrook (assistant trainer). Third row: J.Bellingham, M.Spendiff, A.Dunn, A.Glen, W.E.Hemmingfield, Mr J.Brusey (director). Second row: Mr Chris White, D.Ronaldson, J.Long, T.Atherton, G.Harper, H.B.Singleton, Mr W.H.Bellamy (hon financial secretary). Front row: G.Mountain, W.Appleyard, H.Fletcher.

January, did little to lift the club from the relegation zone. They struggled for the rest of the season but, when the end eventually came, it was especially bitter as it was generally thought that Town had been the victim of some match-fixing. Blackburn Rovers, also in the frame for relegation, won surprisingly at Everton by three clear goals.

Opinion on both sides of the Pennines suspected all was not fair and an appeal was made to the Football League. The verdict of the enquiry was: 'We are of the opinion that Mr J.Walmsley, the secretary of Blackburn Rovers FC, endeavoured to arrange that Rovers should be allowed to win the match. There was no evidence that their players had been approached, so no action will be taken against Everton.' Walmsley was suspended for life from holding any post in football and the result was allowed to stand. Blackburn thus escaped relegation at Grimsby's expense.

This was the beginning of the first serious slump in Grimsby Town's fortunes. After being relegated, the club released many of their best players and, despite having the great Charlie Roberts (later to captain the first of Manchester United's championship teams) at centre-half, they could finish no higher than sixth. For the rest of the decade, the team struggled as the directors failed to establish a regular side. For several seasons, Grimsby diced with re-election, only late season rallies pulling them clear of the danger spot. In 1907-08, they failed to pull themselves clear, but were re-elected. The plunge continued until 1909-10, when rock-bottom was reached. A contemporary critic reported that it looked as though 'the management of the team had gone to a rummage sale in the hopes of a bargain'.

By the turn of the year, only three wins and two draws had been gained out

Grimsby Town players in 1908. Back row (left to right): S.Wheelhouse, I.Owens, C.G.Henderson, A.A.Hull, W.Scott, T.S.Lonsdale, A.G.Rudd, A.Hatton. Third row: A.Lee, W.Forster, A.C.Davidson, J.C.Bisby, T.Coxon, W.Bidmead, E.Glennon. Second row: H.Salter, P.Stokes, A.Kilbourne, M.Bradley, J.D.L.Burkinshaw, H.Leonard, A.E.Appleton. Front row: T.Raybould, W.Hargreaves, C.G.Bacon.

Tommy Coxon, who was a regular member of the Mariners' Second Division team between 1908 and 1910. Coxon, an outside-left, scored on his League debut, against Stockport County on the opening day of the 1908-09 season. His last game was in the 7-0 victory over Barnsley in April 1910, but the win came too late to save Grimsby from being voted out of the Football League.

of 20 games; Town had scored 17 goals and conceded 48. By the end of the season, they were next to bottom, having lost 23 out of 38 games. Once again the directors went cap in hand to the Football League. This time, however, they were unlucky and were ousted in favour of Huddersfield Town.

During this decade, Town changed their colours with almost chameleon-like regularity. In 1904-05 and 1905-06, the shirts were salmon pink and the shorts white; in 1906-07, 1907-08 and 1908-09, they wore white shirts with red collars and cuffs and black shorts. In 1909-10, they reverted to the chocolate and blue quarters with white shorts; and for their season in the non-League football, Town wore for the first time, the now familiar black and white stripes, albeit still with white shorts.

In 1910-11, the first team took the Reserves' place in the Midland League. The shock of losing Football League status must have proved a lesson for the directors, for they assembled one of the best teams that supporters had seen for some seasons. Tony Arrowsmith came in at left-back to join Sid Wheelhouse and Tommy Lonsdale in a solid defence while Jimmy Gordon was centre-half. As the season progressed, 'Ranji' Hubbard, from Norwich, and Gus Huxford, from local football, helped bolster the forward line. After a shaky start, Town climbed to third position in the table, a place which they held consistently, despite having games in hand. By April it was evident that the Midland League championship was there for the taking if the outstanding games could be won. On Good Friday, Grimsby met the leading side, Sheffield Wednesday Reserves, at Blundell Park and won 2-0, thanks to goals from Hobson and Young. A point dropped at Rotherham Town on 18 April proved a slight hiccup and the last game of the season came nine days later, when Rotherham County were the visitors to Blundell Park. Two points would ensure the title and a hat-trick from Chris Young and a further goal from Hubbard, without reply, gave them victory and the title. The Mariners were re-elected to the Football League.

Most of the championship side were retained and amongst the notable players brought in to strengthen the team were 'Pecker' Mountney from Preston, Frank Martin from Hull and, as the season progressed, Tommy Mayson and 'Pip' Rippon joined the club.

The season started in an unspectacular manner. Then, on 7 October 1911, Chelsea visited Blundell Park. With three minutes remaining, the visitors led by the only goal and the spectators were streaming from the ground. A ball from Mountney sent Gus Huxford on a run. Eluding the defence, the little winger placed the ball past Whitley in the Chelsea goal. From the restart the ball once again found Huxford, a run down the wing and an inch-perfect pass found Staniforth clear — and once again Whitley was beaten. The match ended amidst scenes of great jubilation, but many left the ground convinced that the game was lost.

Another sensation occurred on 6 January, when Leicester Fosse were the visitors. The match was played in appalling conditions. By the time the Fosse were three down, they complained about the state of the pitch and two of them refused to play any further. By full time another four had left the field and a gallant five men held Grimsby to a 4-0 scoreline. A better second half of the season enabled Town to finish in a respectable ninth position.

Amongst the new players to join the club during the 1912-13 season was the Irish international, William Andrews, from Glentoran. Andrews was, in fact a native of Kansas City and was probably the first North American to play in League football. Town began the season badly and by Christmas had won only four games. Over the holiday period, however, wins at Leeds, Huddersfield and Fulham and a home victory against Bury heralded the start of a reasonable second half of the season and a respectable ninth place was achieved.

Amongst the signings for 1913-14 was goalkeeper Martin Spendiff, who had been first-choice 'keeper for two seasons between 1903 and 1905. His transfer from Millwall was disputed by Bradford City, who claimed that his registration was held by them and he was only on loan to Millwall. Grimsby also broke their transfer record by paying Hamilton Academical £400 for Willis Rippon. The season was however not a good one and the Town finished 15th in Division Two.

With war clouds gathering, the 1914-15 season opened as it was generally expected that the war would be quickly over and that League football would be unaffected. After early setbacks on the Marne, the matter was re-considered but it was decided to complete the season. With a poor forward line, and with Sid Wheelhouse suffering a long bout of injury, the team plunged towards the bottom of the table. Dwindling attendances placed the club in a parlous financial position and they had to apply to the League for assistance. They also asked the players to accept reduced terms but allowed them to accept employment during the week. By February, many players had joined the Forces and Grimsby finished fourth from bottom.

At the end of the season, it was realized that the war would not be over as quickly as had been thought. It was felt that football could not continue on a full-time basis but that the game should be retained in some form as a morale booster, especially for troops at home on leave from the horrors of the front line and for munitions workers. The Football League, the FA Cup and the County Cup were all abandoned and professionalism suspended.

Football was regionalized and clubs were allowed to select teams from whichever players were available in the area. Grimsby played in the Midland Region, a competition consisting of a primary tournament, usually of 30 games played from September to March, and a subsidiary tournament of six games played in March and April. Although many of the Town's former professionals put in regular appearances, there was an amazing turnover of players and in 1917-18, Grimsby used 87 different players in only 34 matches. On 18 November, they arrived at

Bradford with no goalkeeper and trainer Tommy Holden was pressed into service. Grimsby were defeated 9-0. Another unusual feature of wartime football was the return of left-back Jack Butler, who had played a decade previously. In 1916-17 he played 20 games, eight of them with his son, W.Butler, as a teammate. Amongst players who were not to return from the war were Ralph Thompson, amateur international Harold Springthorpe and the outstanding pre-war full-back Sid Wheelhouse.

When professionalism was reinstated in 1919, veteran Martin Spendiff was in goal, Harry Storer (later to shine with Derby County and England and to manage Coventry twice, Birmingham and Derby), was at centre-forward. Frank Martin, David Kenny and Tommy Spink had all played for the club before the war. George Affleck and Arthur Wainwright were acquired in the auction that followed the collapse of Leeds City.

The season was a disaster. By the start of February only four wins and three draws had been gained from 25 games. Attempts to strengthen the team, notably by the signing of Wilf Gillow from Preston North End, failed to stem the tide and Town finished next to bottom of the Second Division and failed to gain re-election, Cardiff City being admitted to the League instead.

A life-line, however, was thrown when the League voted to incorporate the Southern League as a Third Division, a decision possibly influenced by the fact that the Southern League clubs had been poaching League players without the inconvenience of having to pay transfer fees.

In preparation for the new season, the Grimsby directors took the unprecedented step of appointing a team manager. Selection and the signing of new players had hitherto been the prerogative of the board. Haydn Price, the former Welsh international, was the first to occupy the Blundell Park managerial chair.

If Grimsby thought that they were in for an easy ride they received a rude awakening. They opened the season well enough, beating Northampton Town in front of 12,000 spectators at Blundell Park and two more points against Southend United in midweek gave them a brief spell at the top of the table.

This form, however, did not last and Town began to slide down the table. A visit to The Dell in December, however, produced a surprise. Southampton, thus far unbeaten at home that season, were beaten by a single goal. It was the first time that season that the Saints had failed to score at home. Ironically, Town were now managerless, Haydn Price having resigned the previous week after having been informed that he had lost the confidence of board, players and supporters. Town eventually finished 13th in the table.

The following season, a Northern Section to the Third Division was formed and Grimsby Town transferred to that section, with former Lincoln City boss, George Fraser, in charge. Hopes for a quick return to the Second Division were high, but the acquisition of centre-forward James Miller, from Morton, was not an immediate success and only seven points were picked up from the first seven games. Local lad, Tommy Talks, was then tried and Town picked up full points from all their games in November.

It was not until just before Christmas 1921, however, when George Fraser heeded repeated pleas from the local Press to try Jimmy Carmichael at centre-forward, that Town's fortunes began to soar. Carmichael scored four times in his first game in that position and by the end of the season had netted 37 League goals, equalling the club's individual record for a season as well as becoming the Football League's leading scorer. It was not quite enough to lift Town into the Second Division, however. Stockport County took the title, whilst Town were pipped for second place by Darlington on goal-average.

Once again the Town's fortunes went into decline. The following season, despite

Joe Robson (on ground), one of Wilf Gillow's first signings after he became player-manager, puts the Clapton Orient defence under pressure during a match at Blundell Park.

a promising start, they could finish no higher than 14th. The 1923-4 season was little better and in March, George Fraser quit the managership. Grimsby finished 11th in the Northern Section. This season black shorts were worn for the first time to complete the present strip.

It was then that the board made the move that laid the foundations for the golden era of Grimsby Town Football Club. They promoted Wilf Gillow from the ranks to become player-manager. Unfortunately, most of the squad for the 1924-5 season had been signed before Gillow was appointed and, although Joe Robson was amongst the new signings and Joe Cooper joined as the season progressed, Gillow's first season in charge was a continual struggle to maintain a respectable placing. Town eventually finished 11th.

In 1925-6, the full impact of Gillow's stewardship took effect. Amongst the new signings were Hughie Jacobson from Blyth Spartans, Charlie Wrack from local football and John Pugsley from Cardiff. What a season it turned out to be for the home supporters. The only home point dropped was on 14 November, when Wigan managed to hold the Mariners to a 1-1 draw. Despite a moderate away record, therefore, Town approached the last match of the season needing two points to ensure the Third Division North championship. A draw might have sufficed, unless Bradford had a big win at Wigan.

Town threw everything they had at New Brighton, but for 80 minutes the score sheet remained blank, with Mehaffy in the visitor's goal performing wonders. With the minutes ticking away, up popped Jimmy Carmichael to snatch the vital second point. It was as well he did, for news came through that Bradford had hammered Wigan 6-1. Second Division football, though, had returned to Blundell Park.

On 28 August 1926, Grimsby Town started their Second Division campaign at Barnsley, fielding the same team which had clinched the championship. It was a disappointing beginning, for Charlie Wilson was taken off injured in the first half and McKenna followed him as Town went down 2-1.

Wilson did not play again until January and, by Christmas, only four games had been won. By mid-January, rock-bottom had been reached and in six games, Town conceded 26 goals. Goalkeeper Archibald was made the scapegoat and never played for the first team again. Despite all this, Town managed to finish in 17th place, four points clear of relegation, and ended the season by thrashing Wolves 6-0, with Robson netting four of them.

There followed another moderate season with an appalling home record, including a 6-0 defeat at the hands of West Bromwich Albion. This was countered by an above-average away record which ensured 11th spot in the table.

Town entered their Golden Jubilee season of 1928-9 with the knowledge that, off the field at least, great improvements had been made. Through the generosity of club director Alderman Frank Barrett, Grimsby Town now owned Blundell Park and a new stand had been named in honour of the good alderman.

Alderman Frank Barrett, a Mayor of Grimsby and the director of the club. His financial help enabled Grimsby Town to purchase Blundell Park. A new stand was named after him to mark his generosity.

Mariners' goalkeeper Read pushes the ball around the post as Plymouth Argyle's Briggs leaps over him. Grimsby won this game 2-0 at Home Park in February 1934, a victory which helped them towards the Second Division championship that season.

Grimsby Town players and officials in 1929-30, the season Town finished 18th in Division One. Back row (left to right): H.Woods (trainer), H.Swaby, T.Bell, J.Preistley, J.Prior, Williams, T.Poskett, T.Read, C.H.Wilson, W.Gillow (manager), H.Jacobson, W.M.Powell, A.Bateman, J.Calderwood, F.Wattam, M.Golightly (assistant trainer). Front row: A.Hall, H.Barley, S.Coglin, J.Bestall, E.Coleman, J.Robson, E.Munnings, E.Glover, J.Cooper, W.Marshall, J.Wright, C.Wrack.

Notable amongst the new signings was half-back Jock Priestley from Chelsea. The season opened with reasonable promise, but in the second half of December, three successive 4-1 defeats, two of them at home, meant that the halfway stage of the season saw Town in a mid-table position. The second half of the season, however, produced 16 wins from the last 21 games, including a 100 per cent home record. By 23 April, promotion was assured, but failure in the last two away games — at Bradford and Middlesbrough — meant that the championship was missed. Centre-forward Joe Robson, with 32 goals in 36 games, was one of several success stories.

Town found it difficult to adjust to First Division football. With no notable new signings, the season opened promisingly with a 3-1 win at Bramall Lane, but the campaign was, for the most part, a struggle to avoid immediate relegation. Only a strong finish, in which five wins and a draw were gained from the last seven games, secured 18th place. Most decisive of these games was a 4-2 win against fellow strugglers Everton at Goodison Park, where Joe Robson scored all four.

After three seasons in the First Division, however, it was apparent that Grimsby's team was not good enough and, inevitably, the 1931-2 season saw them relegated. There were some particularly bleak moments — like a 7-0 thrashing at Villa Park — but also some highlights, including a 5-1 home win over Liverpool (Coleman scored a hat-trick) and a remarkable 6-5 win at West Brom in the penultimate game of the season, when Max Holmes, a centre-forward from the Spalding area, netted three and Jimmy Dyson, the former Oldham Athletic player, also grabbed a hat-trick.

Back in Division Two, Town were now managed by ex-Birmingham full-back Frank Womack, who had replaced Gillow at the close of the relegation season. Grimsby were to stay in Division Two only for two seasons. By 1933-4, the trainers had developed such a peak of fitness that seven players appeared in all 42 games and only 18 were used all season. It was this consistency that enabled Town to move immediately to the top of the table, winning four out of the first five games. September and October saw a slight hiccup but a 3-0 home defeat of Lincoln City on 11 November regained them top spot and the Mariners could not be dislodged for the remainder of the season.

Their victories included a 7-3 win over Manchester United on Boxing Day and

Goalkeeper George Tweedy in action agianst Chelsea at Stamford Bridge in the 1939 FA Cup quarter-final.

Tom Galley scores from the penalty spot for Wolves against the Mariners in the 1939 FA Cup semi-final.

a 7-0 hammering of Blackpool (Holmes scoring three) at the end of April. They scored 103 goals altogether, of which Pat Glover netted 42 in only 39 League appearances, a figure which remains a club record.

Back in the First Division, Grimsby Town's glory days continued. Consistent home form saw them undefeated until 23 February, when a hat-trick from Hughie Gallacher gave Derby County a 3-1 win at Blundell Park. Town finished fifth in Division One, the best League performance in the history of the club. Once again the ability to field a regular team no doubt helped. Four players appeared in all 42 games and a further two missed only one each. Pat Glover scored his 100th League goal for Grimsby, on Boxing Day at White Hart Lane.

Following their successful return to the top flight, Town found the 1935-6 season something of a disappointment and the side struggled all season to stay out of the relegation zone; it was not until 18 April, with three games remaining, that a 4-1 defeat of Derby County ensured First Division survival. It was some consolation that, for the first time, Town made a good impression in the FA Cup.

After being held to a goalless draw at Hartlepool, the Mariners won the replay convincingly. Port Vale (away) and Manchester City (home) were eliminated and the Mariners entered the sixth round for the first time. Middlesbrough were drawn to play at Blundell Park and, although the Mariners won an exciting tussle 3-1, a dark cloud fell over the proceedings when centre-half Harry Betmead clashed both verbally and physically with his former teammate Tim Coleman and both were sent-off. Whether Betmead's enforced absence in the semi-final at Leeds Road made any difference to the result is open to speculation, but it was Arsenal who went through to Wembley by the only goal.

Despite a bright start to 1936-7, which saw Town in second place during October, inconsistent form saw them finish in mid-table, albeit a slight improvement on the previous season. It was a blow, then, when Frank Womack was appointed manager of Leicester City.

His successor was Charlie Spencer, who did not enjoy the easiest of starts. It was not until the sixth game of the season that Town recorded their first victory. This was the story throughout the season and the Mariners were never out of the bottom six. Only by winning their last three games did they avoid relegation and it was not until Chelsea were beaten on the last day of the season that survival was ensured. The inability to score was the main problem. Despite 12 appearances by veteran Scottish international Hughie Gallacher, who had been signed as cover for the injury-prone Glover, the pair of them only managed seven goals between them in 19 outings.

Town were certainly not finding life in the First Division easy, despite a strong defence and the legendary Hall, Betmead and Buck half-back line. The departure of old favourites such as Bestall and Craven from the forward line and the fact that Glover was now past his prime, meant a lack of fire power. In an attempt to rectify this, Scottish international Jimmy Boyd had been signed from Dundee and the experienced Thomas Jones from Blackpool. As the season progressed, ex-Liverpool and Manchester City centre-forward Fred Howe joined Grimsby. They helped the club to a respectable tenth place, whilst another good run in the FA Cup made the last pre-war season one of the more satisfying in Town's history.

When they met Wolves at Old Trafford in the semi-final, however, fate dealt them a cruel blow. With goalkeeper George Tweedy sidelined, George Moulson had been drafted in as deputy. After more than holding their own in the opening quarter of the game, the Mariners saw their chances disappear when, after a collision with the Wolves inside-left Dorsett, Moulson was carried off with concussion and took no further part in the game. Jack Hodgson took over in goal and Wolves were held to a two-goal lead at the interval. A penalty just after half-time, and

Grimsby Town 1949-50. Back row (left to right): P.Johnston, F.Fisher, K.Moody, B.Bircham, D.Harnby, J.Duthie, Mr T.Dawson (trainer). Front row: S.Lloyd, J.Shearer, J.Briggs, W.Cairns, J.McStay, D.McMillan. Insets: W.Chisholm, G.Hair, L.MacKenzie.

Veteran forward Billy Cairns, seen here in action against Blackburn Rovers.

two goals in the final three minutes finally dashed Town's Wembley hopes, as Wolves won 5-0. The attendance of 76,962 that day, remains a record for Old Trafford.

The comparative success of the 1930s was due, in no small amount, to the depth and strength of Town's playing staff. The club ran four teams and, for most of the decade, Grimsby Town Reserves were the outstanding team in the Midland League. In the 11 seasons from 1928-9 to 1938-9 inclusive, they amassed a total of 1,456 goals in 478 matches, an average of just over three goals per game; and in 1932-3 they scored 189 in 42 games, averaging 4.1 per game. Between 1931 and 1934 the Reserves took the championship three times, losing out in 1931-2, only after a play off with Bradford. The 'worst' seasons were the last two before the war, when they could manage only fifth place on each occasion.

With the outbreak of World War Two, the 1939-40 League season was abandoned and a regional competition operated until 1946-7, although the FA Cup resumed in 1945-6, on a two-legged basis up to and including the sixth round. As in World War One, Grimsby relied on several 'guest' players.

When League football began again in 1946, Grimsby Town found themselves with an ageing squad. Most of the players were well past their prime and the only speculation in football circles as to relegation was who would go down with Grimsby. The season started badly. Until the middle of October, Town were not out of the bottom four but an unbeaten run of seven games in October and November lifted them to mid-table and a bright end to the season, with 4-1 wins over Middlesbrough and Sunderland, ensured First Division survival.

The 1947-8 season was arguably the worst in the history of Grimsby Town. Pre-war veterans Betmead, Hodgson and Tweedy were still with the club and, despite the previous season's struggle, only a raw Tommy Briggs had been added to the squad. The rest is history. Only fifteen points at home and seven away were picked up. Town conceded 111 goals and scored only 45. They remained firmly in bottom place for the last 18 games and were relegation certainties well before the end of the season. For the first time in their history, Grimsby Town finished as wooden-spoonists.

Any illusions that the Blundell Park faithful may have had about an early return to the top flight were quickly dispelled when Fulham, visiting on the first day of the season, went in at half-time leading 3-0 and, despite a fighting finish by the Town, won 3-2. Town took only one point from their first four home games, but five out of eight on their travels to maintain a reasonable position, which they maintained throughout the season to finish just in the top half, a performance that was repeated the following season.

As the 1950-51 season opened, manager Charlie Spencer was taken seriously ill and the club sent him away for treatment. Initially, George Tweedy took over as caretaker manager and, later in the season, Frank Womack returned on a temporary basis. Spencer's illness proved an omen for the season to come and it was not until the tenth game of the season that maximum points were gained. Grimsby never recovered from this bad start, were never out of the bottom five and, despite a fighting finish, they once again finished as bottom of the pack.

Charlie Spencer, still far from well, resigned as manager at the close of the season and, back in the Third Division North after an interval of 26 years, Grimsby Town had a new manager, Bill Shankly. He promised that his players would work hard and play entertaining football and, even in his early days in management, displayed the talent that was to make him one of the most respected team bosses in the history of the game.

In his autobiography, Shankly recalls that, had he arrived at Blundell Park a little earlier, some of the players whom the club had released would have been retained. Their identities can only be speculated upon, but amongst his signings were Jimmy Hernon from Bolton Wanderers, Bill Brown from Elgin City and Wally Galbraith from New Brighton. The latter two formed the full-back pairing, with Duncan McMillan, Reg Scotson and Paddy Johnston as half-backs and Hernon joining Stan Lloyd, Jimmy Bloomer, Billy Cairns and Alex McCue, who came with Shankly from Carlisle, as forwards.

The season opened disastrously. Following defeat at Chesterfield, Town lost goalkeeper Stan Hayhurst with a broken finger and Alex McCue with a broken leg in the opening home game against Lincoln City and, despite two goals from veteran Billy Cairns, went down 2-3. Cairns, then aged 39, was rated by Shankly as still the best header of a ball in the game.

To replace Hayhurst, Shankly brought out of retirement another veteran, George Tweedy. So well did the manager blend his players that soon the club looked a good bet for an immediate return to Division Two. With a team that Shankly recalled was 'pound for pound and class for class the best football team I have seen in England since the war', the Town achieved some remarkable results. Halifax were thrashed 8-1 in December and when promotion rivals Stockport County visited Blundell Park on 11 April, the gates were locked as nearly 27,000 spectators saw the Mariners triumph 4-0.

In the end, though, those fateful injuries in the opening home game decided the promotion issue. Although the Town collected 66 points, the championship went to Lincoln City with 69. Had the Mariners had 11 fit men back in August, those vital two points would most probably have gone the other way and Town might have collected enough to overtake their Lincolnshire rivals.

With basically the same team, prospects looked good when Town opened the following season with a nine-game undefeated run which took them to the top of the table. They remained in the top three throughout the season until a run of four defeats, starting on Easter Saturday, saw them drop to sixth. Although they recovered to win the last two matches, the chance of promotion was gone.

Town received a severe blow in October 1953 when Bill Shankly left to manage Workington, who were struggling for survival. Strangely, the board seemed in no hurry to appoint a replacement and the club remained managerless for most of the season. It certainly showed in the results. The team struggled all season and attendances fell. Blundell Park 'gates' topped 10,000 on only seven occasions, which in the 1950s was considered pretty poor. The arrival of Billy Walsh as manager in March was too late to prevent Grimsby from finishing a disappointing 17th.

Walsh was not the first to discover that managing a League football club is no easy way to earn a living. Despite opening with a promising win at Rochdale, Town struggled for most of the 1954-5 season and with the prospect of relegation imminent, Walsh paid the price when he was dismissed after only a year in office. The story of Walsh's reign, however, could have been altogether different, had a bold and imaginative move by the club not foundered upon the rocks of bureaucracy.

In November 1954, it was decided to appoint a coach. Amongst the applicants was one Emilio Berkessy. Berkessy, a Transylvanian by birth, had fled to Hungary on the establishment of the Romanian state and had proved himself as a major force in the game in his host country, joining the legendary Ferencváros club and making 17 international appearances for his country before the war. He then joined the national coaching staff, where under his tutelage came such names as Puskas, Hidegkuti, Kocsis and Boscis.

Upon the establishment of the communist state in Hungary, Berkessy had once again become a refugee and had taken coaching jobs in Italy and Spain. In 1954 he was performing this duty with the Barcelona club, Zaragosa, but went to England to try and break into the English game. Upon the recommendation of Villa coach, Jimmy Hogan, Berkessy was appointed to the Blundell Park staff.

Grimsby Town 1953-4. Back row (left to right): Bill Brown, Duncan McMillan, Jimmy Bloomer, Clarrie Williams, Ray Robson, Pat Johnston. Front row: Derek Stroud, Reg Scotson, Dick Conner, Archie Wright, Jimmy Maddison.

After only two days the local police informed the club that, as Berkessy had no work permit, he could not continue coaching. Town applied for the permit but on 1 December, learned that their application had been refused. Despite an appeal, the decision was final. There was much speculation that both the FA and the PFA had influenced the Minister of Labour. Whatever the reasons, Berkessy had to return to Spain. Thus the privilege of being the first English club to employ a continental coach was denied Grimsby Town, a loss not only to them but, possibly to English football as a whole.

In no mood to dally this time, the board approached Manchester United and acquired the services of centre-half Allenby Chilton as player-manager. Chilton arrived too late to fend off the humiliation of the club once again having to apply for re-election. The following season, however, he was to help create a little bit of footballing history.

During the close season, Chilton set about reshaping the team and on the opening day of the 1955-6 campaign, there were five new faces in the side. What a change Chilton had wrought. Built around himself at the centre of defence, he had created a team that after, a draw against Rochdale in the first home match, were to win the next 12 games at Blundell Park, a run ended by Workington Town at the end of January. Lincolnshire neighbours, Scunthorpe United, were the only other team to succeed at Blundell Park and 41 out of 46 available points were picked up. Coupled with an away form that produced 11 wins and five draws, Town won the championship with three games still to play, when 23,000 fans saw Southport defeated 2-0 at Blundell Park. Once again, the ability to field a consistent side was a key factor, with nine players appearing in over 40 of the 46 games.

The Mariners prepare to leave for their close-season tour of Czechoslovakia in 1957.

With all the promotion side retained, the only strengthening for the Second Division campaign was the arrival of Chilton's former teammate from Old Trafford, right winger Johnny Scott. A player of considerable talent, he found himself unable to command a place amongst the legendary 'Busby Babes'.

Once again, the club found it difficult to adjust to the higher grade of football and spent the season in the lower half of the table. Even the arrival of the free-scoring Ron Rafferty in mid-season did little to improve the Mariners' position. Chilton had given up playing after only a few games and his experience was sadly missed in defence as 62 goals were conceded. The 1957-8 season was little better, despite a bright start that saw the club in the top six places until mid-October. Thereafter, they hovered around the middle of the table until February-March, when a goal dearth which saw them score only once in six games left them in the bottom quarter of the division. That one goal was scored by Tommy Briggs on his return debut at Blundell Park. Another arrival, from Old Trafford, was Geoff Whitefoot, a wing-half of considerable talent, who found Blundell Park too small a stage on which to perform and who, after less than a season, left for the City Ground where he gained an FA Cup winners' medal with Nottingham Forest. In his season at Blundell Park, he saw Grimsby finish in mid-table.

Despite the importing of new players, the 1958-9 season proved to be another poor campaign in which only nine games were won, seven in the first half of the season. Despite the fact that this lack of success was due to bad luck and a crop of injuries, Allenby Chilton paid the usual sacrifice of managers and left before the end of the season. Town finished 21st and were back in the Third Division, which was by now de-regionalized. One highlight of the season was the visit of Prague Dynamo for a friendly. No-one who was present will forget the mighty clearance by Doeljst in the Prague goal. The ball soared the length of the field, landed in front of the advancing Malcolm White in the Grimsby goal and bounced over his head into the empty net.

Once again the directors seemed in no hurry to fill the managerial vacancy and the last season of the decade opened with trainer Bill Lambton in charge of team affairs, assisted by ex-Mariner Billy Cairns. It was not until the season was nearly over that Tim Ward arrived to fill the vacancy.

In view of this situation, Grimsby had a remarkably successful season in the newly-formed Third Division. Lambton's only addition had been Ralph Hunt from Derby County, who was to form, with 'Chips' Rafferty, a potent striking partnership that produced 57 goals that season. Altogether, Town scored 87 goals but that was countered by 70 conceded and Town could finish no better that fourth.

The 1960s dawned like a new era at Blundell Park. New floodlights, a new manager and a new strip — the black and white stripes having been abandoned for white shirts with a black 'vee' neck and, most controversial of all, red shorts. This move was not well received by the die-hard traditionalists among the supporters. Ward's first season turned out to be one of those that 'nearly was'. The side were one of the strongest in the division and were never out of the top four until the end of March. A dreadful loss of form during April, when they won only three of the last seven games, dissolved all hopes of promotion. Perhaps if Jimmy Fell had not been allowed to leave for Goodison Park, then things might have been better. One can only speculate on the 'might-have-beens'.

The 1961-2 season proved to be a reverse of the previous one. A moderate first half saw Grimsby reach the turn of the year in 12th place in the Third Division. On 6 January, a 3-0 defeat of Bournemouth at Blundell Park heralded the start of a second half to the season that was to see only another six points dropped. Town crept up the table and went to Griffin Park on the last day of the season in second place, needing one point to ensure that Queen's Park Rangers could not overhaul them. Goals from Ron Rafferty and Cliff Portwood made promotion safe, and the Mariners were once again in the Second Division.

There was no notable team strengthening for the return to the higher division, but once again a change of manager had seen Tim Ward depart for Derby County, to be replaced by Tom Johnston who moved from a similar position at Rotherham.

It was the same old story, with Town finding it difficult to adjust to a higher

Ralph Hunt is outnumbered by two Chesterfield defenders at Blundell Park in August 1960.

grade of football. The entire season was spent in the bottom six of the table and, despite attempts to bolster the side by new signings, notably striker Rod Foster and goalkeeper Charlie Wright, only the fact that Grimsby lost only one of the last eight games preserved the Second Division status.

This reprieve was only temporary. Despite the acquisition of Matt Tees, who was to become another of Grimsby's legendary strikers, the 1963-4 season was to be a repeat performance of the previous campaign. This time there was no last-minute revival and the club found themselves back in Division Three, albeit only by 0.045 of a goal. The fact that the team were back in the familiar black and white stripes was of little consolation to the supporters.

The 1964-5 season opened promisingly and by early October the Mariners topped the Third Division. They received a severe jolt when Tom Johnston left to take over at Huddersfield. Jimmy McGuigan, who was managing Crewe after over 200 appearances as a player at Gresty Road, was the new Grimsby boss. Town remained in the promotion frame until just before Christmas but on 19 December, a 4-1 defeat at Exeter heralded the start of a 17-match run without a win, although nine were drawn. As a result of this unexplained slump, Town finished ninth in the table.

As the 1965-6 season approached, economy was the watchword at Blundell Park and the decision was made not to run a reserve side. With substitutes being allowed in League football, initially as an experiment, Ray Lancaster made club history by replacing Matt Tees at Bootham Crescent in the third game of the season. Home form was of promotion standard and it was not until Good Friday that the visitors took both points at Blundell Park, when Scunthorpe won a local derby 3-0, Town's

Grimsby Town, 1965. Back row (left to right): Clarrie Williams, Jim Bloomer, Angus Davidson, Harry Wainman, John Wilkinson, Perry Thompson, David Morgan, Jim McCoy. Front row: Jimmy Charlton (mascot), Trevor Haynes, Brian Kerry, George Taylor, David Boylen, Peter Beckers.

A young supporter has his team group autographed by members of Grimsby's first-team squad.

misery being compounded the following day when Mansfield Town also won. These were the only two home defeats, as 36 out of 46 points were picked up.

Away form was, however, a disaster, with only two wins early in the season. The last 18 away games produced only six points. A good run in the League Cup, in which Bolton and Preston were beaten and West Ham held to a 2-2 draw before winning a fifth round replay, was some consolation. It would seem likely that the mid-table position was due to the lightweight squad and the folly of not running a reserve team was abandoned the following season.

Not that any improvement in the club's fortunes materialized. What was proceeding as a mediocre season turned into one of disaster, as the twin strike force of Rod Green and Matt Tees were transferred to Charlton, a deal which incensed the Blundell Park faithful. After a struggle to keep out of the relegation zone, Town finished 17th, their worst end-of-season placing for a decade. Highlight of the season was a 7-1 defeat of Scunthorpe at Blundell Park, the unfortunate goalkeeper for the Iron being a young Ray Clemence.

Jimmy McGuigan's services were not retained and 1967-8 saw a luckless Don McEvoy in charge. McEvoy was on a hiding to nothing, with the club on a downward spiral, dwindling attendances and little or no money to strengthen the squad. In fact, only one outfield player, Terry Bartlett, made his League debut, with a solitary appearance against Tranmere Rovers. With the club hovering in the danger zone, Don McEvoy paid the price after only six months and was replaced by Bill Harvey.

Harvey could do nothing to reverse the downward plunge and, despite a brave struggle, the players went to Swindon on the last day of the season, knowing that they had to win 3-0 and Mansfield lose by at least 2-0 to stay in the Third Division. Mansfield obliged by going down 3-0 and Town got the required three goals.

Unfortunately, Swindon replied with two and the Mariners were in the Fourth Division for the first time by 0.008 of a goal. The downward spiral was to continue and by the halfway stage of the 1968-9 season, only five victories had been achieved.

Following the usual pattern, the manager carried the can and Bill Harvey left. Again the board opted for a player-manager and once again looked towards the city of Manchester, this time obtaining the services of wing-half Bobby Kennedy from Maine Road. Once more the managerial change came too late in the season to have any significant effect.

The managerless few weeks between mid-January and mid-March had seen a five-game run which produced but a single point. Indeed, between Boxing Day and Easter Monday, in a run of 17 games, only three were won and the Mariners were comprehensively thrashed on several occasions. The outcome was inevitable and Grimsby Town reached the nadir of its League existence by finishing 23rd in the Fourth Division and having to apply once again for re-election to the Football League.

For a while it seemed as though the decade was going to end on a brighter note as the 1969-70 season started well and at the end of August, Town topped the Fourth Division. This early promise proved a flash in the pan and soon the familiar slide down the table began again. Although a mid-table position was maintained for a good part of the season, a poor finish, in which four out of the five last games were lost, saw them finish 16th.

An unenviable record was set up this season when Graham Rathbone felt the brunt of a disciplinary clampdown and was suspended for two months after having been sent-off in the local Derby against Scunthorpe. Regrettably, the same standards were not applied when some well-known names with First Division clubs appeared before disciplinary hearings. With attendances hovering around the 3,000 mark and little prospect of any substantial signings, the future at Blundell Park looked grim.

Indeed, when the 1970-71 season opened there were only 14 professionals on the books, hardly the makings of a promotion-seeking squad. The side struggled once again and even a shrewd move by Bobby Kennedy, in bringing Matt Tees back to Blundell Park, had little effect other than to almost double the attendance to well over 7,000 for his return debut. As the end of the season approached, another plea for re-election seemed inevitable, but an end-of-season revival, which produced 17 points out of 22 in the 11-game run in, pulled Town clear of the bottom four. Despite this Houdini act, the die was already cast and Bobby Kennedy became yet another manager to pay the price of failure.

A Messiah was, however, waiting in the wings in the form of one Lawrie McMenemy, who had incurred the wrath of the Doncaster Rovers directors, where he was manager. A 4-1 thrashing of Scunthorpe United on the opening day of the 1971-2 season raised the fans' hopes and they were further bolstered with another four goals at Exeter. So the pattern was set. Grimsby hovered near the top of the table all season and were assured of promotion well before the end. They met Exeter at Blundell Park on 2 May, needing only a point to clinch the title. There was no question of negative play to save the draw and goals from Matt Tees, Mike Hickman and Lew Chatterley brought a 3-0 victory. Club secretary Mrs Dorothy Edwards became the first woman in the history of League football to receive a championship plaque. Grimsby's tally of 88 goals was the highest in the Football League.

The return to the Third Division saw Grimsby, after a poor start which put them in 17th place, pick up with a run of five wins in September which took them through the table to second. Eventually they finished ninth, not at all bad considering that Brentford and Scunthorpe, who had also been promoted, booked an immediate return trip to the basement.

Town under Lawrie McMenemy's managership in 1971-2. Back row (left to right): Graham Rathbone, Mike Czuczman, Stewart Gray, Harry Wainman, Matt Tees, Clive Wigginton. Middle row: Jack Lewis, Stuart Brace, Dave Boylen, Dave Worthington, Lawrie McMenemy (manager), Jimmy Thompson, Alan Woodward. Front row: Ian Park, John Riley, Owen Simpson, Mike Hickman, Alan Campbell.

It had been obvious that Lawrie McMenemy was destined for higher things and the close season saw him move to The Dell to be heir-apparent to Ted Bates. His replacement was Ron Ashman, who had been managing Scunthorpe United. It was somewhat of a shock to both Ashman and the Blundell Park fans when Hereford United, who had won promotion in their first season in the League, went to Grimsby on the opening day of the 1973-4 season and won 3-1 to herald an on-and-off sort of campaign for Town which saw the club go up and down the table before finishing sixth, well behind the promotion hunt. One consolation was a cheque for £6,000 from Watney Mann, presented for the highest-scoring non-promoted team in the division, an award that had been instituted by the brewery to replace the Watney Cup.

The 1974-5 season again opened badly for Grimsby Town. Not only did Blackburn Rovers win at Blundell Park, but the attendance of 7,293 was also over 30% down on that for the previous season's opening day. Grimsby faced another nine months of struggling against relegation and in February, Ron Ashman left the club. Former Newcastle United and Northern Ireland half-back Tom Casey took over the reins and Town finished 16th.

The 1975 close season provided some consolation when the youth team were invited to participate in a tournament in Breda, Holland, and won all five games, scoring 15 goals against five conceded. Amongst the youngsters were Kevin Moore and Bob Cumming, who were to render such sterling service to the club in future years.

It was but brief consolation for the fortunes of Grimsby Town were still on the ebb. Despite a consistency at Blundell Park, where they were undefeated until March, the season saw Grimsby run up one of the worst away records in the history of the club, with only seven out of the 46 available points picked up. The home record, fortunately, preserved Third Division status, albeit only temporarily.

The 1976-7 season saw an innovation, that of the sponsored match. Local estate agents, G.M.Barton, sponsored the first home game against Crystal Palace, a match which Bobby Charlton attended as the guest of Gerry Barton. It did nothing for the club's playing fortunes and Palace took both points with a goal by David Kemp.

Thus, another dismal season got underway and the Blundell Park fans were now becoming accustomed to the gloom. By November, with Town in the bottom four, another manager was clearing his desk, ironically sacked on the day that he was moving into a newly-purchased house. Despite his failure to bring success, Tommy Casey's influence was to be felt several seasons later, when some of the fine youngsters that he had brought to Blundell Park reached footballing maturity.

The new manager was John Newman, who came from Exeter City and who faced an uphill struggle to halt the slide in Town's fortunes. Once again an appalling away record, which yielded only seven points out of a possible 46, helped to make this a dreadful season and 23rd place meant a return to the Fourth Division.

Newman's influence began to be felt more in the next season and it was not until November that Reading became the first club to win at Blundell Park. The Mariners were defeated only three times at home and a slightly more consistent away record might have brought an immediate return to a higher grade. Sixth place, three points behind promoted Brentford, was the best that could be achieved.

To strengthen the coaching side, Newman brought in George Kerr — who had lost the manager's job at Sincil Bank — as his assistant. This partnership laid the foundations for what was to be a meteoric rise in the fortunes of Grimsby Town. Nigel Batch had ousted the long-serving Harry Wainman in goal, Dean Crombie, who had surprsingly been given a free-transfer by Lincoln City, bolstered the central defence and Bobby Mitchell came from Blackburn to add some quality to the midfield.

The 1978-9 season opened inauspiciously, when Reading went to Blundell Park and won 2-1 in front of less than 4,000 spectators, but Town recovered to win their next four games. Varying form throughout the first half of the season promised little more than an above-average conclusion to 1978. The New Year saw a 5-1 defeat of Bradford City and a 7-2 thrashing of Darlington, both at Blundell Park. A 3-1 win against highly-fancied Portsmouth at Fratton Park put the Mariners in the frame for one of the promotion spots. The crowds had begun to return and when promotion rivals, Barnsley, played at Blundell Park on 21 April, an attendance of 15,585 saw the Mariners win 2-0. Three days later, a 2-1 victory at Northampton sealed promotion. Any hopes of the championship faded on 5 May when, despite Town scoring three goals, a hat-trick by ex-Mariner, Jack Lewis, helped Doncaster to win 4-3.

The euphoria at Grimsby was somewhat dampened when John Newman was offered the job of assistant to Colin Addison at Derby. This time Grimsby appointed from within and after a brief spell as 'caretaker' boss, George Kerr was confirmed as the new manager.

In preparation for the 1979-80 Third Division campaign, Kerr imported John Stone from Darlington and in September paid a then club record £60,000 to bring Kevin Kilmore from Scunthorpe. The Mariners scored four goals in each of their first two home games and by Christmas they occupied second place in the table, a point behind Sheffield United. A 2-1 defeat at Colchester on 8 February was to be the last of the season and an unbeaten run of 15 games culminated in a 4-0 defeat of Sheffield United at Blundell Park, thanks to a hat-trick from Kevin

The Mariners arrive for their civic reception after winning the Third Division championship in 1980.

Drinkell. The Third Division championship was Grimsby's and the rise from Fourth to Second Division had been made in successive seasons.

The season was also notable for a fine performance in the League Cup. Wins over Scunthorpe, Huddersfield and Notts County had earned the Mariners a plum draw in the fourth round against Everton, who had finished fourth in Division One and had had seven internationals on their books. The Merseysiders took a large and confident contingent of supporters across the Pennines and they were rewarded when Brian Kidd gave them the lead after 21 minutes. Two minutes later, Mick Brolly put Town back on equal terms and eight minutes later, the same player beat Wood from an impossible angle to give the Mariners a quarter-final home tie against Wolves.

This was the Wolves of old, before the bizarre events of recent years had reduced the club from First to Fourth Division status. Wolves certainly expected an easy ride and Andy Gray had said that this would be 'Grimsby's Cup Final'. After 90 minutes the scoresheet was blank and seven days later, the teams met again at Molineux.

Again the score was even this time at 1-1 after extra-time, thanks to Gray and Palmer (own goal). For the second replay, at Derby, luck deserted the Mariners when a highly debatable penalty from Kenny Hibbitt gave Wolves the lead. John Richards ended all Grimsby's hopes after 57 minutes. Coincidentaly, Merseyside also featured in Town's FA Cup fortunes when the Mariners lost 5-0 at Anfield.

George Kerr was chosen as Bells Whisky Third Division manager of the year and Grimsby Town started their first Division Two season for 17 years with caution. The first 16 games produced only two wins, but only three defeats in the next 20 games provided a change of fortune that gave rise to hopes that a third successive promotion season might be on the cards. These hopes were shattered when eventual champions, West Ham United, visited Blundell Park in April. After an hour, the Hammers were holding on to a 2-1 lead with Town still well in the game. In a bold move, Kerr brought on substitute Ford for Stone, with Bob Cumming dropping back as an overlapping defender. Shortly afterwards, following a tackle from Stewart, the Hammers' right-back, Cumming was carried off. With only ten men and the heart torn out of the defence, the Mariners conceded three goals in the last ten minutes.

Realistically, the Mariners would have had a hard time in the First Division, but seventh place this season was still the peak of their achievements since losing Division One status in 1948.

The following season was to be a grim experience for the supporters. Amidst rumours of a growing rift between Kerr and the board, Town managed only a single home win, against Queen's Park Rangers, before the midway stage. When Mick McGarry, Kerr's strongest ally was ousted as a director, the manager's days were numbered. His fate was probably sealed with the customary statement of support in December and the axe finally fell on 11 January.

Once again, Town promoted from within and Blundell Park veteran Dave Booth was first appointed 'caretaker' and later confirmed as Kerr's successor. Not that any immediate improvement in the fortunes occurred. It was not until 20 March that a second home win, over Derby County, was achieved. Indeed, the Blundell Park crowd were to witness only five home League victories all the season and were lucky to see their team survive in the Second Division, when they finished 17th.

The 1981-2 season was to set a pattern for the 1980s, which has seen, against a constantly simmering background of board room in-fighting, a gradual decline in the fortunes of the Grimsby Town Football Club.

There were hopes at the beginning of 1982-3 that this was to be Town's year when a draw against Leeds on the opening day of the season, followed by six consecutive victories, saw the Mariners in second place in the table at the end of October. There were to be only six more wins for the rest of the season and the

Grimsby Town, 1982-3. Back row (left to right): Phil Crosby, Dean Crombie, Gary Beacock, Kevin Moore, Dave Moore. Middle row: Tony Ford, John Stone, Nigel Batch, Peter Grotier, Neil Cooper, Kevin Kilmore. Front row: John Steeples, Andy O'Dell, Joe Waters, Kevin Drinkell, Trevor Whymark, Bob Cumming.

slide down the table continued. From March onwards, only six points out of a possible 39 were salvaged and once again relegation was avoided by one League position and two points.

The 1983-4 season opened with the news that Irish international centre-back, Chris Nicholl, had been appointed player-assistant manager. With Trevor Whymark as player-coach, this meant three people running a squad of 12 others, an imbalance between 'chiefs' and 'indians'. A good start at Blundell Park produced 13 points from the first five games but was offset by only two gained from the first five away. The influence of Nicholl, however, began to make itself felt. Following a 4-0 defeat at Fratton Park on 5 November, the Mariners strung together an undefeated run of 16 League games to take them into third place. Promotion hopes were jolted when the run was broken and it was Pompey who once again did the damage with a victory at Blundell Park by the odd goal in seven; they were finally dashed when only one point was picked up over Easter. The final League position of fifth was, however, the Mariners' best since their First Division days.

The 1984-5 campaign was notable more for some fierce skirmishes in the continuing boardroom war than for events on the field. In the League, Grimsby led a Jekyll and Hyde existence with some fine wins (5-1 over Wolves and 4-1 against Manchester City) being countered by twice (against Fulham and Brighton) squandering 2-0 leads to lose 4-2. One bright spot was the match against Everton at Goodison Park in the Milk Cup. The Mariners soaked up everything that the Merseysiders could throw at them for 89 minutes and stole the tie when Paul Wilkinson scored from a Phil Bonnyman free-kick on the final whistle. Howard Kendall responded by taking Wilkinson to Goodison for £250,000. In the League, a modest tenth place was

Peter Grotier leads a training session during the 1985-6 season. The other players are (from left) Bob Cumming, Jimmy Gilligan, Tony Ford and Kevin Moore.

Town's playing and training staff at the start of 1985-6. Back row (left to right): Dean Crombie, Richard Dawson, Nigel Batch, Dave Felgate, Jimmy Gilligan. Middle row: John Fraser, Peter Grotier, Paul Emson, Mike Rowbotham, Kevin Moore, Gary Lund, Phil Bonnyman, Tony Ford, Dave Booth. Front row: Neil Robinson, Gary Henshaw, Paul Agnew, Mark Hine, Andy Moore, Bob Cumming, Tony Barratt, Gordon Hobson, Neil Matthews.

achieved. Supporters were not impressed when Kevin Drinkell moved to Norwich for a derisory tribunal fee of £110,000.

As the next season approached, the money raised from the sale of Wilkinson and Drinkell was invested in Jimmy Gilligan from Watford and Andy Peake from Leicester. They cost over £100,000 each and Gordon Hobson, from Lincoln, cost £35,000. The latter proved to be the outstanding buy, but Gilligan had a disastrous season. Dave Booth quit football to go into property management in Tenerife and as Chris Nicholl had already left to manage Southampton, the Grimsby board had to go outside the club in search of a replacement. Opting for a player-manager, they spent several weeks wooing Liverpool captain Phil Neal, and when he eventually declined, they persuaded Sheffield Wednesday centre-back, Mike Lyons, to take the post. Lyons bought in his old Everton colleague, Terry Darracott, as assistant.

It seemed as though the men wished to sweep clean and by March, ten first-team players had been made available for transfer. With the club £500,000 in debt, Lyons options were strictly limited and when Darracott left Blundell Park after a few months, Lyons' world seem to fall apart. It must be said that the last thing Grimsby Town had needed was someone learning the trade and during 1986-7, supporters questioned some of Lyons' team selections. Although an up-and-down season saw the club in eighth place in the middle of March, the last ten matches produced only two points and Town fell to 21st in the table and were relegated to the Third Division.

Many supporters felt that this was not the end of the downward trend and were surprised when the board left it until mid-June before dispensing with the services of Mike Lyons. With obvious discontentment in the squad, most of the experienced players, who were at the end of their contracts, refused new terms and left the club, surprisingly for lower divisions and in three cases for non-League Lincoln City.

When Bobby Roberts was eventually appointed manager in July 1987, he arrived at Blundell Park to find that he had a squad of 12 professionals and no goalkeeper. With limited options in the assembling of a new squad and moulding it into a team, Roberts was on a hiding to nothing and the side struggled at the foot of the table all season.

When veteran Terry Curran added his experience to the squad for a dozen games on temporary contract, things looked better but he was not retained. The struggle continued until the final day of the season, when the last chance of Third Division survival evaporated as Town failed to beat Aldershot. Relegation in two successive seasons signified one of the bleakest periods in the history of the club.

Having been given the customary vote of confidence by the board, only weeks previously, Roberts was on his way out of Blundell Park two days later. His replacement was Alan Buckley, who had enjoyed a successful career, both as player and manager, with Walsall. Only the previous season he had taken GM Vauxhall Conference side, Kettering Town, to the verge of League football.

Morale at Blundell Park was rock-bottom as Buckley rebuilt the squad, virtually from scratch. He assembled a blend of experience and youth, but his plans received a severe blow when key signings, Tom Williams and Steve Stoutt, were injured and missed most of the season.

Forced to blood more youngsters, Buckley struggled to achieve a blend which would have established the Mariners as serious contenders for a return to the Third Division. Instead, they hovered just above the foot of the table as the season gained momentum.

FA Cup victories over high-flying Wolverhampton Wanderers and Rotherham United promised better things, however, and from the half-way stage of the season, Grimsby started to climb up the table and raised hopes of a place in the promotion play-offs. Then the goals dried up and those hopes seemed dead after Town were thrashed 5-0 by Leyton Orient at Brisbane Road on All Fools' Day.

Yet a seven-match undefeated run meant that it was not until the penultimate match of the season, a 3-2 defeat at the home of Tranmere Rovers, a club on the crest of the wave, that Grimsby's aspirations were finally killed off.

It had been a satisfactory season, however. The FA Cup run had continued with a glorious victory at First Division Middlesbrough and a replay win over Reading before Town went down at Wimbledon. No club relishes a visit to Plough Lane these days, but the Mariners' supporters, complete with inflatable 'haddocks', enjoyed seeing their side hold the lead for a while.

As the 1988-9 season drew to a close, the crowds were returning to Blundell Park and hopes were high that the fortunes of Grimsby Town Football Club would take a turn for the better as a new decade dawned.

THE MARINERS' GROUNDS

ALTHOUGH Grimsby Town FC was formed in 1878, it was not until the 1880-81 season that the club acquired a home of its own, early matches having been played on public grounds. Clee Park was situated to the north of Grimsby Road, on the site now covered by parts of Daubney Street and Barcroft Street. This ground was leased at ten shillings per annum.

At first facilities were limited, bathing huts which were not in use during the winter months, were brought from Cleethorpes beach to be used as dressing-rooms.

In about 1883, the first stand was erected — the money being advanced by Alderman Henry Smethurst — by the firm of Henry Marrows. One of the joiners was Jack Taylor, a defender from Spilsby, who was persuaded to sign for the Town. This original stand held about 500 spectators and a season ticket cost five shillings. Another stand was probably added within the next two years.

At the end of the last season at Clee Park, some early attempts at floodlit football took place when matches were played against Rotherham Town on 9 April and a Boston team a week later. The matches were played with the aid of 'Wells Lights'. Eight pylons were placed around the pitch. At the foot of each was a barrel of tar oil, which was pumped under pressure to burners at the top of the pylon where it gasified to produce light. What the quality of the light produced was, is not recorded, but the Town seem to have adapted to the conditions, winning 8-0 and 5-1 respectively.

At the end of the 1888-9 season, the lease on the Clee Park Ground expired, and a short lease on a field in Welholme Road was obtained from Edward Heneage, the MP for Grimsby. This ground was situated on the south side of Welholme Road, between the People's Park and where Farebrother Street now runs.

A match against unknown opponents during the last season at the Abbey Park Ground. The newly-built houses are on the north side of the Welholme Road corner with Legsby Avenue.

The stands were removed from Clee Park, the main stand being erected along the Welholme Road side of the pitch, about where the junction with Legsby Avenue now is. A second stand was situated behind the Cleethorpes End goal and huge banks were built on the Weelsby Road side to provide a 'Kop' for the 'sixpenny subscribers'. The total cost of preparing the ground was between £200 and £300 and was carried out by a Mr C.Simmons of Victoria Street.

The *Eastern Daily Telegraph* (as the *Grimsby Evening Telegraph* was then titled) built their exclusive press-box at the Welholme Road-Farebrother Street corner. A season ticket to the reserved section of the Grandstand cost one guinea. The total ground capacity was about 10,000.

The first match played on this ground was on Saturday, 30 August 1889, when the Town defeated West Bromwich Albion 6-1.

The initial lease on the Abbey Park Ground was for seven years, with no option for renewal as plans for the erection of houses in the area were already in hand. An extension of three years was, however, granted and it was not until the 1899-1900 season that the Town moved to their present ground. Once again the existing stands were dismantled and moved to Blundell Park, being re-erected on the sites of the present Osmond and Findus Stands. It was originally intended that this latter side of the ground be the main one, but, when promotion to Division One came two years later, 150 subscriptions of £10 were raised to build a new stand and dressing-rooms, which now forms the greater portion of the Main Stand. The original Pontoon Stand was built when the move to Blundell Park was made. The first match at Blundell Park was a Second Division game against Luton which finished 3-3.

During the 1925-6 promotion season, a ground committee was formed and over the next year vast improvements took place. Wooden terracing was built in both corners at the Cleethorpes End and one of the old Abbey Park stands was replaced by the former Barrett Stand. In view of the large sums being invested in a ground

An early match at Blundell Park. The stand is the original Pontoon Stand.

which was still on lease, negotiations then opened to purchase Blundell Park and on 13 July 1927 the *Grimsby Telegraph* was able to announce that the club now owned its own ground. It was largely due to the generosity of Alderman Frank Barrett that this purchase was made possible.

In 1931, the Main Stand was extended towards the Cleethorpes End. This extension, can today be distinguished from the original stand as that part without supporting pillars. The last relic of the old Abbey Park Ground lasted until the 1939 close season, when the Osmond Stand replaced the Hazelgrove Stand. This stand saw only two League games before the abandonment of the 1939-40 programme, due to the outbreak of war.

From 1940 to 1944 Town had a temporary home ground at the Old Show Ground, Scunthorpe. After the war, the first major improvement was the installation of floodlights. The concrete pillars can still be seen underneath the present pylons. The first match to be played under these lights was a Midland League game between the Reserves and Gainsborough Trinity on 9 March 1953, a game which attracted a 'gate' of 6,179. The lights were not, however, good enough for League matches and it was not until the present pylons were given by the Supporters Club in 1960 that, on 20 September, Town met Newport County in a floodlit League game.

It was also in 1960 that a scheme was advanced for a new ground to be built in Cambridge Road, near its junction with Littlecoates Road. The site, which is about seven times the area of Blundell Park, was intended to have been used at first as a training ground and to have been developed over a 15-year period, after which the club would have vacated Blundell Park. This plan did not progress any further. During the 1961 close season, the Pontoon Stand, the traditional home of the true Mariners supporter since the opening of the ground, was replaced, due to the generosity of the Supporters Club, by the present stand of that name.

A view of Blundell Park with the Findus Family Stand.

Blundell Park's Findus Family Stand under construction.

In the close season of 1980, the first stage of the recent modernization of Blundell Park began when the Main Stand was given over to all-seating, and new seats installed throughout. One year later the Barrett Stand was condemned as unfit. A projected £1-million replacement for this site had been on the stocks for some time, but more cautious members of the board favoured a more modest construction, similar to that which had recently been built at Cambridge.

Eventually, a compromise was reached, and with the financial support of frozen food giants, Findus, the present Findus Family Stand, incorporating executive boxes, administration block and restaurant was built. Although the small standing area at the front of the stand was used from midway through the 1981-2 season, the Findus Stand came into full use for the opening of the 1982-3 campaign, for the game against Leeds United. Plans for moving the players facilities from the Main Stand to the Findus Stand have been shelved for the moment because of financial constraints.

In 1985-6 came the most controversial move of all. At the behest of the police, who saw it as an aid to crowd control, the club changed the traditional 'home' and 'away' ends. The faithful 'Pontoonites' were unceremoniously uprooted and transported to the Osmond Stand. This move, naturally, upset many a long standing supporter and after a couple of seasons the Grimsby fans were restored to what they have always considered their rightful place.

Town Managers

Haydn Price
July 1920-November 1920

HAYDN Price, who was probably born in Mardy, Glamorgan, in 1885, was an all-round sportsman. As well as being a noted athlete, he played Rugby Union in the Welsh tradition but, in 1900, switched to the Association code, playing for village side Mardy Corinthians. He then played for Cardiff and Aberdare before joining Aston Villa in the 1904-05 season.

Villa had such a depth of reserve strength that Price was unable to command a regular League place, yet he had the remarkable distinction of being selected to play for Wales against Scotland whilst still in Villa's third team.

In 1907, he moved to Second Division Burton United but again failed to win a regular place in the senior squad, making only one League appearance before signing for Wrexham. In 1909-10 he was on the books of Leeds City, where he made eight League appearances, and finished his playing career with Shrewsbury, a club then in membership of the Birmingham & District League. He gained four more Welsh caps, one whilst at Burton and three as a Wrexham player. Throughout his playing career, Price remained a semi-professional, holding a teaching post in Birmingham.

After hanging up his boots, he became secretary of Walsall, the manager-secretary of Mid-Rhondda, from where he accepted the Blundell Park post. Prior to his appointment at Grimsby, the signing of players and team selection had been the prerogative of the directors, but they had to bow to pressure from the supporters who wanted the club to have a manager. In between his appointment and taking up the post, Price transferred four players from his old to his new club, and a fifth followed shortly after his arrival. Strangely, only days before taking up the Grimsby post, he was addressing a public meeting at Tonypandy and stating that his dealing had strengthened the Welsh club and giving the impression that he would continue as manager there.

His appointment at Grimsby was a disaster from the start. Results were poor as the team struggled. The directors blamed Price for his failure to strengthen the squad. Price, for his part, complained of interference in team selection and of not being allowed to go on scouting trips. After only four months in office, he resigned publicly, in a long and aggrieved letter to the *Grimsby Telegraph*. He went back to teaching and in 1921-2 returned to Mid-Rhondda as secretary-manager.

Whatever his faults he appears to have been a fair judge of a player. One of his signings from Mid-Rhondda, Jimmy Carmichael, went on to become one of the greatest forwards in the history of Grimsby Town; another, David Collier, won international honours for Wales.

George Fraser
March 1921-March 1924

FOLLOWING the experience of Haydn Price, the Grimsby Town board were in no hurry to seek a replacement and for four months they reverted to the system whereby control of team affairs was in the hands of the directors. When they did appoint a replacement, it was to neighbours Lincoln City that they turned.

George Fraser was no stranger to Blundell Park. He had joined the Imps from Sunderland in the 1901 close season and played at right-half for Lincoln for over a decade, visiting Grimsby regularly in both the League and Lincolnshire Cup.

After retiring from playing at the outbreak of World War One, Fraser returned to Sincil Bank after hostilities ceased, joining them as secretary early in 1919. It was from this position that he was appointed to the Town managership. After a fairly successful first season, in which the club came third in the Third Division North, there followed two seasons in which nothing better than a mid-table position could be achieved.

It became obvious that the relationship between George Fraser and the board was not a happy one and, shortly before the end of the 1923-4 season, Fraser resigned. It must be said that the board did not allow him a free reign, either in the selection of the team or in the acquisition of players. Many thought that the directors were still not convinced of the necessity for a manager and it caused some surprise when the club advertised immediately for a successor.

Wilf Gillow
June 1924-May 1932

WILF Gillow must rate amongst the top two or three managers in the history of Grimsby Town, for it was upon the foundations laid by him, that the successes of the 1930s were built. When he took over, Town were a moderately-placed Third Division North side. Five seasons later they were in the First Division.

In his own playing days, Gillow had been a skilled ball-player (see *Master Mariners A-Z*) and the basis of his managerial style was the development of these skills in his players. By this means he was able not only to bring success on the field, but also to contribute to the financial stability of the club, as players he had nurtured, such as Robson and Coleman, were sold for substantial fees.

Always firm but fair, he held the respect of his players and Charlie Wilson, who was at Blundell Park during the whole of Gillow's reign, recalled, "He didn't have to be a disciplinarian, he was a good manager and the players knew it."

Despite his success, he found life in the First Division a struggle and early in April 1932, with Town precariously placed, he handed in his resignation. In fact, he remained in office until the end of the season, only to see the club relegated. However, Gillow left behind a good basic squad upon which his successor was able to build.

In March 1934, he returned to First Division management with Middlesbrough, remaining with them for a decade, latterly on a part-time basis until his death on 12 March 1944. He was also a good cricketer who was on Lancashire's staff for a time and played at Minor Counties level for Lincolnshire.

Frank Womack
May 1932-October 1936

FRANK Womack was unquestionably the most successful manager in the history of Grimsby Town Football Club, taking them into the First Division and to within one game of a Wembley FA Cup Final.

Born in Sheffield in 1888, Womack showed no particular interest in the game until the age of 16, when he started playing for Lapham Street, a team in the local Bible Class League. After a further season with Rawmarsh Albion, in the Sheffield Association, he was spotted by Birmingham and moved to St Andrew's, making his League debut on 5 September 1908, at Gainsborough. From Christmas he made the right-back position his own and retained his hold on it for 20 years, over 17 of them as captain. He made 490 League appearances for the Blues — a club record — and 24 FA Cup appearances, but never scored a goal. After leaving St Andrew's, he became player-manager of non-League Worcester and guided them to what was then their best-ever season, when they were Birmingham League champions and reached the first round proper of the FA Cup. In 1929, he moved to Torquay United as manager. The Gulls were in only their third season in the League and were finding life difficult. Faced with a parlous financial situation which forced him to sell any player of above-average ability, he could do little more than lift them to a mid-table position in the Third Division South.

Seeing that opportunities with Torquay were limited, he applied for the vacant Grimsby job and took charge in May 1932. Morale at Blundell Park was low as Town had been relegated after a brief spell in the First Division. Womack struggled to right matters as a second successive relegation loomed. It was March before he achieved his immediate ambition of a balanced side and a run of seven wins and four draws in the last 11 matches took Grimsby to safety. The success continued the next season when the Mariners swept all before them, playing a class of football which made them the biggest draw in the Second Division and gave them away wins at all their nearest promotion rivals.

The following season, the Mariners continued on their glory trail to finish fifth in Division One — and many supporters reckoned that, but for some bad luck and some strange refereeing decisions, they could have been runners-up. The next season saw Womack almost achieve his ambition of taking the club to the FA Cup Final (he narrowly missed going to Wembley as a player) when Grimsby lost to Arsenal by the only goal in the semi-final.

Womack was a 'system' manager who tailored the abilities of his players to fit his conception of the game. Careful analysis of opponents, with each of his players being given specific responsibilities in each match, were the hallmarks of Womack's management. He was a great theorist, working out strategy with his players on the blackboard and testing his ideas in practice games, which he thought were the best form of training. It was a great blow to the club when, in October 1936, he moved to Leicester City. Womack took the Filbert Street club to the Second Division championship in his first season, but their stay was brief and when they were relegated in 1939, he left. He managed Notts County briefly during World War Two and returned to Blundell Park between January and May 1951 to take charge during Charlie Spencer's illness. Frank Womack died at Caistor, Lincolnshire, on 8 October 1968.

Charles Spencer
March 1937-May 1951

CHARLES William Spencer was born in Washington on Tyneside in 1899. He rose through local football to sign for Newcastle United in 1921, where he went on to become one of the first 'stopper' centre-halves in the game. After seven seasons and 175 League games at St James' Park, Spencer moved to Old Trafford for two more seasons, playing another 40 League games for Manchester United. He represented England twice, against Scotland in 1924 and against Wales in 1925.

Spencer became player-manager of Tunbridge Wells in 1930 and was appointed to a similar post at Wigan Athletic on the formation of that club in 1932. It was from Wigan that he joined Grimsby Town, where he was reckoned to be a fortunate man, taking over a fine team and having only to carry on the good work initiated by Womack.

The truth was different. He lost Lewis and Glover, the two leading scorers, at the start of the season. He brought Jackie Coulter, a goalscoring winger from Everton, veteran Scottish international goalscorer Hughie Gallacher from Notts County and John Beattie from Huddersfield.

This reinforcing of the forward line was countered by a string of injuries to key defenders. First Division status looked in danger and was saved only by a late rally when the last three games were won. In Spencer's second season, despite taking the Mariners to the FA Cup semi-final, he achieved little improvement in their League performances. His managerial career interrupted by the war, at one stage he found himself the only staff member at Blundell Park, combining the roles of manager, secretary and groundsman.

On the resumption of League football in 1946, Spencer found himself with an ageing playing staff and a club on the decline. Despite the loss of First Division status, the directors kept faith in him but after two seasons in the Second Division he was taken seriously ill and after a full season's absence, he resigned. On his recovery he managed Hastings United, briefly, before becoming manager of York City. After less than a season at Bootham Crescent, his illness struck again and he died in York on 9 February 1953.

Although he never enjoyed spectacular success as the Mariners' longest serving manager, Charles Spencer is remembered for some of the fine players he brought to the club, notably Tommy Blenkinsopp, Billy Wardle, Billy Cairns and Tommy Briggs.

Bill Shankly
July 1951-January 1954

BILL Shankly was born in Glenbuck, Ayrshire, on 2 September 1913 and played for local side, Cronberry, before joining Carlisle United as a 17-year-old. He made his League debut in 1932-3 and, after 16 appearances that season, Preston North End signed him in July 1933 for £500. During the next 16 seasons, in a career interrupted by the war, he made 300 League appearances for Preston, plus another 87 in wartime football as well as guesting for many other clubs. He was capped five times for Scotland.

In March 1949, Shankly returned to Brunton Park as manager and won the hearts of the Carlisle fans by speaking to them over the public address system at each home match, regarding the progress of the club. He stayed there for two years, establishing the Cumbrian side as one of the best in the Third Division North.

In the spring of 1951, he had been offered the job of coach at Grimsby, under the temporary charge of Frank Womack, but Carlisle had increased his salary to keep him. When Charles Spencer resigned, however, Shankly went to Blundell Park as manager, feeling that there was more chance of success at Grimsby than at Carlisle. He arrived with a reputation as a fitness enthusiast, a disciplinarian and, above all, a football fanatic. He expected the best from all his squad and, once they had given that, he was a players' manager.

Shankly found a depleted and demoralized squad but quickly rebuilt his side with some experienced players. Disaster struck in his second game, against Lincoln City, when first Stan Hayhurst and then Alec McCue were taken off injured. Grimsby's nine men lost 3-2 but, during the rest of the season they handed out some remarkable thrashings, although they could finish only second, three points behind Lincoln.

In his second season, Shankly kept the team in the promotion race until April, but a poor run-in robbed him of Second Division football for the second successive season. By half-way through his third season, he saw that his team of veterans were nearing the end of their careers and he felt funds might not be available to replace them. He moved, surprisingly, to Workington, then struggling for existence, and changed them from a team of 'no-hopers' to a side that just missed out on promotion.

In 1955, Shankly was asked by Andy Beattie to join Huddersfield Town as assistant manager. At the end of the season, the Leeds Road club were relegated and when Beattie was dismissed a few months later, Shankly was promoted to manager. In his three years at Huddersfield, he did not manage to get the club back to the top flight, yet his managerial talents were still apparent.

In 1959, he was approached by Liverpool, then a moderately successful Second Division club living in the shadow of Everton. The rest is history. Liverpool had never won the FA Cup and had lifted the League Championship only once in the previous 40 years (although they had won it four times overall). In five seasons Shankly changed them into the most successful club in the history of the game and one which has dominated English football for a quarter of a century. His Blundell Park days were part of the apprenticeship of one of the greatest managers of all time.

Billy Walsh
February 1954-March 1955

BORN in Dublin on 31 May 1921, Billy Walsh moved with his family to Manchester at the age of seven and joined the Old Trafford groundstaff on leaving school in 1935. In May 1938 he crossed the city to Maine Road as an amateur, signing professional forms a month later. Walsh had to wait until after World War Two to make his League debut, although he appeared for the club in 227 wartime games.

After the war he established himself in City's team, making 109 League appearances over four seasons. He was capped for both Irish sides, as was permissible in the immediate post-war years, playing nine times for the Republic of Ireland and five times for Northern Ireland.

Walsh started his managerial career with Southern League Chelmsford City in April 1951 but left after a few months. He turned down chances to return to the Football League as a player, with both Lincoln and Port Vale, to become player-manager at Canterbury, also in the Southern League, from where he was appointed to Grimsby Town.

His stay was brief, his only full season in charge being one of the worst in the history of the club. Of his signings, only George Higgins and Ray De Gruchy made any lasting impression. In his defence it can be said that he took over a depleted playing staff and at the outset he forecast that the prospects for the season were bleak. They proved too bleak for the directors and, after only 13 months, he was sacked.

Allenby Chilton
March 1955-April 1959

ALLENBY Chilton enjoyed a fine career with Manchester United (see *Master Mariners A-Z*) and had been rested at his own request, following his record appearance run, when the Grimsby board approached United for his services in March 1955. Chilton was granted a free transfer and became Town's player-manager. He arrived to find the club in dire trouble in the Third Division North and with no time before the end of the season to avoid the humiliation of having to apply for re-election.

His first full season in charge started slowly, despite an early 6-1 win over Chester, but with Chilton at the heart of a revamped defence, the club embarked on a 17-match unbeaten run that took them to the top of the table, a position which they kept for most of the season. Thus, Chilton turned Town from a re-election side to a championship-winning team in 12 months.

Despite some team stengthening, notably the signing of Old Trafford colleague Johnny Scott, he failed to establish Grimsby amongst the Second Division's pacemakers; when he retired as a player shortly after the start of the 1956-7 season, his presence in the defence and his on-field generalship were sorely missed. The side struggled on for three seasons, mostly in the lower reaches of the table, and three days before the end of the 1958-9 season, with Grimsby needing to win their last game, at Stoke, to have any chance of avoiding relegation, Chilton resigned, having been informed that his contract was unlikely to be renewed. The reasons for his failure are difficult to quantify. Probably he was just another of the many footballers who have found that a distinguished playing career is not always the grounding for successful management.

Tim Ward
February 1960-June 1962

BORN in Cheltenham in 1917, Tim Ward signed for Derby County in 1937, making 61 League and Cup appearances at wing-half before the outbreak of World War Two. After the war he returned to the Baseball Ground to make another 199 appearances and was capped for England against Belgium in 1948 and Wales in 1949.

In March 1951, Ward moved to Barnsley to replace Danny Blanchflower (who had signed for Aston Villa) and played a further 33 League games before becoming manager at Oakwell in 1953. In his first season the Tykes were relegated to Division Three North but two seasons later Ward steered them back to the Second Division, where they stayed for a further four seasons.

His move to Blundell Park was sudden. He was approached by Grimsby Town at 4.30 in the afternoon and by ten o'clock he had accepted Grimsby's offer, having been preferred to such notable candidates as Raich Carter, his former Derby teammate, and Joe Harvey.

Ward took over a team in sound condition, considering they had been without a manager; in fact some people were surprised when caretaker Bill Lambton was not been given the job permanently. A reserved and diplomatic man, Ward thought the game should be played by the rule book. He would not tolerate foul play, whatever the circumstances, and thought that obscene language had no part in the game.

A good 'public relations' man, Ward was, however, reticent about his own role in the success of the club; even after promotion he allowed his players to have all the limelight. At Blundell Park, he established himself as one of the most respected managers in the game and it was natural, therefore, following the 1961-2 promotion campaign, that his old club, Derby County, should approach him when looking for a successor to ex-Mariner, Harry Storer.

Had he been under contract, Ward might have stayed at Blundell Park, but the offer from the Baseball Ground was too good — and the Rams had always been his first love in football. He kept them in a reasonable Second Division spot without any notable success and his one major contribution was the signing of Kevin Hector from Bradford. His reputation as a 'gentleman' first and foremost went against him in a rapidly changing era and now many thought him lacking the ruthlessness needed to succeed in the modern game. Replaced by Brian Clough in June 1967, Ward managed Carlisle United for a spell before taking up employment outside football. In his 70s he was still playing charity football for an ex-professional team.

Tom Johnston
July 1962-October 1964

BORN in Berwick-on-Tweed in 1918, Tom Johnston started his professional career with Peterborough United, who were then in the Midland League. In 1946 he signed for Nottingham Forest, playing on the left wing and scoring 26 goals in 64 League games before moving across the Trent to Meadow Lane in 1948, to make 268 appearances and score 86 goals for Notts County. Hanging up his boots in 1956, Johnston took up a coaching appointment in Finland and later joined the Birmingham City staff in the same capacity.

He started his management career with Central Alliance club, Heanor Town, before taking over at Rotherham United in 1958. The Millers were then struggling for Second Division survival but Johnston pulled them round and they escaped relegation, ironically at the expense of the Mariners. The following year, Rotherham were serious contenders for promotion to the First Division but fell away towards the end of the season. Johnston also took them to the League Cup Final in 1961.

At Grimsby, he took over a club ill-equipped for their newly-found Second Division status and Town spent the entire season in the lower reaches of the table. Despite some team strengthening, notably the signing of George McLean, Ron Foster and Charlie Wright — all of whom went on to serve the Mariners so well — relegation was only just avoided as Town finished 19th. The reprieve was only temporary and the following season, after gaining only nine wins from 42 games, the club returned to the Third Division. Thereafter, his days as manager were numbered.

Jimmy McGuigan
November 1964-July 1967

GLASGOW born 'Gentleman Jim' McGuigan started his professional career with Hamilton Academical. After a brief spell with Sunderland he moved, in turn, to Stockport, Crewe and Rochdale, playing in a total of 323 League games before returning to Crewe as manager, from where he accepted the Blundell Park post.

McGuigan took over a team which was handily placed in second spot in the Third Division. As Christmas approached they led the table but fell away in the second half of the season to finish tenth. Economies in the close season saw the scrapping of the reserve squad but, on the positive side, Town signed Rod Green from Gillingham to help form the Tees-Green striking partnership, one of the most lethal in Grimsby Town's post-war history. Despite working with limited resources and having to rely on players from the youth side in emergencies, McGuigan maintained the club in a respectable Third Division position without making any serious inroads into the championship.

In March 1966, the Grimsby board sold goalkeeper Charlie Wright to Charlton and nine months later, the partnership of Tees and Green followed, all above the manager's head. Following the departure of the two strikers, the club fell from seventh to 17th in the table and McGuigan's contract was due to expire in November 1967; in July the board announced that 'results did not prompt them to desire to renew his contract.' He found the position untenable and resigned immediately.

McGuigan's talents as a manager were vindicated when he moved immediately to Chesterfield and took them to the Third Division title in 1969-70. In 1973, he joined Rotherham, where he stayed for five years, again managing a promotion side when the Millers attained third place in the 1974-5 Fourth Division table.

Don McEvoy
July 1967-January 1968

DON McEvoy played 350 League games as a centre-half for Huddersfield Town, Sheffield Wednesday, Lincoln City and Barrow. He took up a coaching post with Halifax Town in 1963 and in July 1964 returned to Holker Street as manager, where he remained until accepting the Grimsby job, despite just having taken Barrow to promotion from the Fourth Division.

His stay at Grimsby was brief and he was on a 'loser' from the start as the club's declining fortunes and dwindling attendances meant that no money was made available for him to strengthen his squad. Out of 24 games to the turn of the year, only five were won and after six months he resigned because of 'differences in opinion concerning policy between him and the board'.

Bill Harvey
January 1968-January 1969

BILL Harvey is unique in that he is the only native Grimbarian to manage the club. Born in 1920, he was in the Grimsby Boys team at the age of 12 and was on the Mariners' books, although he never made the senior team. His playing career was interrupted by World War Two and when peace was restored he decided to concentrate on the coaching side of the game.

He was appointed manager of Luton Town in July 1962 but the Hatters were on the decline and were relegated from Division Two at the end of his first season. Their slide continued and in November 1964, with Luton struggling for Third Division survival, he resigned. He then held coaching jobs with Swindon Town and Bristol City and it was from the Robins that he was appointed to the Blundell Park post.

The Mariners were struggling to avoid relegation from the Third Division and Harvey's arrival halted a run of ten games from which only two points had been gained — a 3-0 victory at Scunthorpe being their lone success. The Mariners won four out of their last five games but were relegated by 0.008 of a goal.

During the close season and the early part of 1968-9, many of his best players were sold, notably Graham Taylor and Doug Collins. The board gained £53,000 in transfer fees and spent £18,000 on replacements. Despite a successful run of games from mid-October to the turn of the year, during which time only two out of 13 were lost, Town could not pull clear of the relegation zone, and one year and one day after his arrival, Harvey gave up the struggle and handed in his resignation.

Bobby Kennedy
March 1969-May 1971

FOLLOWING the departure of Bill Harvey, the board opted for a player-manager and turned to Manchester City wing-half, Bobby Kennedy (see *Master Mariners A-Z*). Kennedy accepted the post in mid-February but it was not until a month later, after protracted negotiations as to whether City manager Joe Mercer was willing to release him, that he went to Blundell Park for a £10,000 fee. He arrived too late to steer the club clear of the relegation zone and the Mariners finished next to bottom, with 33 points from 46 games.

The transfer fee and the salary which had been offered to entice Kennedy to Grimsby meant that the club's financial situation was parlous and the options open to the manager to strengthen the playing staff were limited. Completely new to management and with no real access to the network of contacts in the game, he found the task of having to play a full Fourth Division programme and keep both himself and his players fit meant he had little opportunity to develop his talents in the administrative side of management.

For most of his reign, Town struggled in the bottom half of the table and it was not until a lengthy lay-off due to injury late in the 1970-71 season that he was able to concentrate solely on management. Town at last ran into form, avoiding relegation by winning seven and drawing three of the last 11 matches. But the revival came too late, Kennedy's fate had already been sealed and 48 hours after the end of the season he was clearing his desk.

Thereafter, Kennedy served on Bradford City's coaching staff and played in the League of Ireland with Drogheda before returning to Bradford, first as 'honorary' manager of Park Avenue and then as full-time boss of City. He restored the Valley Parade club to Division Three in 1977 but was controversially dismissed in February 1978. Later he was a coach with Blackburn Rovers before leaving the game altogether.

Lawrie McMenemy
May 1971-July 1973

BORN in Gateshead in 1936, Lawrie McMenemy was on the books of Newcastle United in his late teens but a serious leg injury, sustained whilst on National Service with the Coldstream Guards, put an end to any hope of a professional career.

Instead he went into coaching and in 1961 was appointed trainer-coach at Gateshead, a post he filled for three years, twice being acting manager. He then became manager at non-League Bishop Auckland and in two seasons transformed them from a struggling Northern League club into a championship-winning side and into the third round of the FA Cup. His success brought him to the attention of Sheffield Wednesday manager Alan Brown, who added him to the coaching staff at Hillsborough.

In November 1968, McMenemy was appointed manager of Doncaster Rovers and in his first season took them to the Fourth Division title. Rovers lost only two games after his appointment and put together a run of 21 matches without defeat. However, the club did not capitalize upon his success and the Doncaster board sold players; money was not made available for adequate replacements and when Doncaster were relegated after two seasons, McMenemy was sacked. After only two weeks he was appointed manager of Grimsby Town.

McMenemy was a strong disciplinarian, a legacy of his service in the Guards, but he also had the ability to get the very best out of his players. He advocated that the club should be part of the community and insisted that he and his players represented the club at functions of all types; a surprised squad once found themselves assembled at the crack of dawn on the fish pontoon, as he felt that the players should realize what the supporters had to do to earn their money. He also formed a sound relationship with his chairman, Paddy Hamilton, and years later referred to him as the best chairman with whom he had ever worked.

Three weeks before his arrival, Grimsby had finished 19th in the Fourth Division, having scored 46 goals. A year later they were champions with 88 goals to their name. The following season he consolidated the Mariners' position as a Third Division club and they finished ninth.

His talent as a manager had not gone unnoticed and in the summer of 1973 he moved to The Dell as heir-apparent to veteran Southampton manager, Ted Bates; in November of the same year he became manager. It appeared as though the magic touch had left him when Southampton were relegated at the end of that season, but the board backed their judgement in appointing him and he was allowed to rebuild his team, enticing some of the greatest names in the game to The Dell. The side responded by winning the FA Cup in 1976 and regaining Saints' First Division status in 1978.

By 1985, with Southampton firmly established as a First Division club, McMenemy had moved to Roker Park in an attempt to revive the fortunes of the relegated Sunderland club. This time the magic failed to rub off and instead of looking for a quick return to the First Division, the Rokerites were lucky not to be relegated to the Third for the first time in their history. The next season the club fared little better and, with fortunes on the decline and a boardroom battle over McMenemy's alleged financial remuneration, the manager was dismissed. In Grimsby he is still looked upon as a football 'messiah' and whenever the managership at Blundell Park falls vacant, his name is always amongst those bandied about as supporters live in hope of a 'second coming'.

Ron Ashman
July 1973-February 1975

LAWRIE McMenemy was, as they say, a hard act to follow and the appointment of Ron Ashman caused a few raised eyebrows. A one-club man as a player, he had made a record 592 League appearances for Norwich City between 1947 and 1963, captaining them during their FA Cup run of 1958-9 when they just failed to reach Wembley. He then managed the Canaries for three seasons before moving to Scunthorpe, from where he joined Grimsby.

A reserved, cultured man and the very antithesis of the brash, extrovert McMenemy, he always treated his players with respect and consideration and some of them took advantage of him. But it was not because he was let down by his team that he failed. The usual financial situation at Blundell Park left Ashman little scope to strengthen the squad and there were rumours of player dissatisfaction over pay. Whatever the cause of the failure, a run of two months with only one win sealed his fate.

Shortly after leaving Grimsby, he was reappointed to the Old Show Ground managership until replaced by John Duncan in 1981. He then retired from the game and opened a travel agency in Scunthorpe.

Tommy Casey
February 1975-November 1976

IN a playing career that included 332 League appearances as a wing-half, Bangor-born Tommy Casey served five clubs but made most of his appearances with Newcastle United and Bristol City. He also won 12 international caps for Northern Ireland.

After hanging up his boots he held a number of coaching posts, notably at Goodison Park (where one of his young players was another future manager of Grimsby Town, Mick Lyons), and at Coventry from where he was appointed Grimsby boss.

He went to Blundell Park with every confidence, saying that he aimed to be one of the best managers in the game and boasting that he had never been sacked by any club. Perhaps he was unaware that Grimsby was the 13th club with which he had been associated.

Regrettably, resources at Blundell Park were limited and during his 18-month reign he was able to spend money on only three players — Malcolm Partridge, Mike Brolly and Joe Waters, the latter only after intense pressure from the supporters.

The establishment of a sound youth policy was Casey's greatest legacy at Blundell Park, for amongst the talent he brought to the club were Kevin Drinkell, Kevin Moore, Terry Donovan, Tony Ford and Nigel Batch, all of whom were to figure prominently in the good fortune of the early 1980s and were to bring a good deal of revenue to the club in transfer fees.

After two and a half seasons of struggling to avoid relegation, and with the club third from bottom of the Third Division, Casey was sacked, ironically on the day he moved into a newly-purchased house.

John Newman
January 1977-July 1979

FOLLOWING a playing career of 509 League games as a wing-half with Birmingham City, Leicester City, Plymouth Argyle and Exeter City, John Newman was promoted from the St James' Park playing staff to be club manager.

It was from Exeter that he took over struggling Grimsby Town and tried in vain to save them from relegation to the Fourth Division. Quickly rebuilding the team, he almost steered Town to an immediate return, but promotion was just missed and the club finished sixth. In 1978-9, however, assisted by George Kerr, he built the team that was to be such a success in the 1980s and Grimsby returned to the Third Division as runners-up to Reading.

Apart from his ability to get the best out of his players, Newman excelled at public relations, building up a first-class relationship with the Press and always ready to represent Grimsby Town at social functions throughout the district.

When Colin Addison took over as manager at Derby County, he persuaded Newman to join him as his assistant. Newman eventually became manager when Addison was sacked but he inherited a struggling team and the club was just about bankrupt. In different circumstances he might have done as well at Derby as he had at Grimsby but in 1983 he was dismissed from the Baseball Ground. Appointed manager of Hereford United, he remained there for four years until the early part of the 1987-8 season. In July 1988 he was appointed assistant to John Barnwell at Notts County, taking temporary charge when Barnwell was sacked five months later.

George Kerr
August 1979-January 1982

AFTER a playing career of 372 League games as an inside-forward with Barnsley, Bury, Oxford United and Scunthorpe United, George Kerr joined the Lincoln City coaching staff under ex-Mariner, Graham Taylor. When Taylor moved to Watford, Kerr became manager at Sincil Bank but was sacked after only six months, shortly afterwards being recruited by John Newman as trainer at Blundell Park.

Following the 1978-9 promotion season, Newman moved to Derby and Kerr was given the manager's job at Grimsby, steering them to the Third Division championship. Always a player's manager, his forthright manner often found him at odds with his board of directors and some injudicious remarks saw him, at one stage, banned from writing in the club's programme.

Despite a successful first season in the Second Division, Town's fortunes began to slump but it is certain that Kerr's ever-widening rift with the board, as much as the club's lowly League position, caused the axe to fall only weeks after the customary vote of confidence. Since leaving Blundell Park he has managed Rotherham United and had a second spell at Lincoln City. In 1988 he joined Boston United in the GM Vauxhall Conference.

Dave Booth
January 1982-October 1985

DAVE Booth spent almost 14 years at Blundell Park, joining the club as a player from Barnsley in June 1972 and making 199 League appearances for Grimsby as a full-back until an injury ended his career in 1978. He was appointed to the coaching staff and when George Kerr took over as manager from John Newman, Booth became his assistant, taking over as manager when Kerr was sacked.

His period as manager included some of the few successes in recent years. In 1982-3 Grimsby finished fifth in the Second Division — their best League position since leaving the First Division — and the following season saw them beat League leaders Everton in a Milk Cup match at Goodison Park.

Following the break up of the team of the early 1980s, Booth's spending of the revenue from the sale of Wilkinson and Drinkell was questioned, especially in the case of Jimmy Gilligan, who cost £100,000 but never had any success at Blundell Park.

In October 1985, Booth announced that he going into property development in Tenerife but in 1987 he returned to management at Darlington, with a former Mariner Phil Bonnyman as his assistant.

They assembled a squad based largely on ex-Grimsby players but in February 1989, as the Quakers struggled to stay in the League, Booth was sacked, ironically only days before he was due to return to Grimsby as a visiting manager. He is reported to have said that leaving Grimsby in the first place was his biggest mistake.

Mick Lyons
November 1985-June 1987

FOLLOWING the departure of Dave Booth, Mick Lyons was second choice for the post of player-manager, after Grimsby Town had spent several weeks trying to entice Liverpool captain, Phil Neal, to Blundell Park. A Liverpudlian by birth, Lyons went to Grimsby following a career spanning 493 League appearances as a central defender with Everton and Sheffield Wednesday.

It must be said that, in Town's desperate situation, the last thing the club needed was someone with no experience of management, whatever his pedigree as a player. There was no denying Lyons' enthusiasm for the game and his thirst for success for Grimsby Town. Enthusiasm on its own, though, was not enough. When he appointed ex-Goodison colleague, Terry Darracott, from the Everton coaching staff as his assistant, the prospects looked promising but the partnership was brief and, without Darracott's guiding hand, Lyons' world started to fall apart. As Town plunged deeper into trouble, some of his team selections appeared bizarre, owing much to desperation rather than inspiration. There were also reports of strained relationships between the manager and some of his players.

When relegation followed a ten-match run-in that produced only two points and four goals, Lyons' fate seemed sealed. The wonder was that it was mid-June before the axe fell.

Mick Lyons is now back at Goodison on the coaching staff — "I've come home," he said on the day he returned to the club where he had been regarded by supporters as 'Mr Everton'. With a few years' experience, he may yet make a good manager. For Grimsby, he was the wrong choice at that particular time.

Bobby Roberts
July 1987-May 1988

BORN in Edinburgh, Bobby Roberts started his professional career with Motherwell before moving south and making a total of 300 League appearances for Leicester City and Mansfield Town before taking up a coaching appointment at Coventry.

He became manager of Colchester United in succession to Jim Smith and helped them make an immediate return to the Third Division in 1975-6, following relegation the previous season. He remained at Layer Road until 1982, before taking over from Mel Sutton at Wrexham. Dismissed in 1985, Roberts took up a coaching appointment in Kuwait, returning to English football to join the Mariners.

Realistically, Roberts never had a chance at Blundell Park. Appointed late in the close season and faced with a decimated and demoralized squad, following the previous season's relegation, he tried his best, with limited resources, to assemble a squad capable of holding its own in the Third Division.

He nearly made it, too, a lack of goalscoring power being the missing vital ingredient. By the close of the season his fate was sealed when the board announced that, whatever the outcome, he would be retained for a further year. On 7 May, Town were relegated and two days later, Bobby Roberts was sacked. In 1988-9 he joined David Pleat's coaching staff at Leicester.

Alan Buckley
June 1988-

BORN in Mansfield on 20 April 1951, Alan Buckley began his career at Nottingham Forest, joining the City Ground club as an apprentice in 1968. Five seasons and only 16 League games later, it was obvious that there was no future for him at Forest and he moved to Fellows Park for his first spell at Walsall, making 241 League appearances and scoring 125 goals over the next five seasons.

When Dave Mackay vacated the manager's chair at Walsall in 1978, Buckley took over on a caretaker basis but when Alan Ashman was given the job, he moved to Birmingham City as a player, where he remained for less than a season and played 24 League games.

Ashman and then Frank Sibley left Fellows Park in quick succession and Buckley returned to Walsall as player-manager at the start of 1979-80, steering the Saddlers to promotion in his first full season in charge, when they were runners-up in the Fourth Division. In 1981, the much-travelled Neil Martin was brought in as joint manager and, for the 1981-2 season, was given full charge. A season later, Buckley was restored to the manager's chair and remained in control for a further four seasons until his services were dispensed with following the take-over at Fellows Park by millionaire businessman, Terry Ramsden. He had made a further 161 full League appearances for the club.

Moving to Kettering Town, Buckley transformed them in little over a season, from a less-than-average side into one that was in contention for GM Vauxhall Conference championship and a place in the Football League. When Lincoln City — Buckley's brother, Steve, the long-serving Derby full-back was now at Sincil Bank as a player — won that title, Buckley applied for the Blundell Park job and returned to League football as Grimsby Town manager.

He faced an uphill struggle. Following two successive seasons of relegation, morale in both the dressing-room and on the terraces was low. Many of the experienced players, upon whom recovery might have been based, had decided their futures lay elsewhere. Buckley wasted little time and by the start of the season he had installed his own backroom staff and strengthened the squad with players mainly from his familiar Midlands stamping ground.

With boardroom changes having improved the financial position, interest in the club was increased and the expectation of supporters was high as the 1988-9 season dawned. These hopes were soon dashed as injuries sidelined two key signings for most of the season.

Buckley took half the season to mould his players into a squad and, after spending the early days amongst the bottom four, the Mariners slowly climbed the table and entertained brief hopes of reaching the Fourth Division play-offs. In the FA Cup, they reached the fifth round for only the second time since 1945.

As the 1988-9 season came to an end, it appeared that the directors had made a wise choice and that Alan Buckley might ultimately be the man to lead Grimsby Town back to the Second Division.

Master Mariners A-Z

GEORGE AFFLECK

George Affleck was born on 1 July 1888, in Auchendenny, Ireland. His career in Irish football took him to Penicuick in 1908 and he came to England to join Leeds City in the close season of 1909. He arrived at Blundell Park under strange circumstances. In the 1919-20 season, after only eight matches, Leeds City were expelled from the League for allegedly making illegal payments to certain players during World War One. Port Vale took over their fixtures, which meant that Leeds had to offload their players. Town signed two, George Affleck and Arthur Wainwright, the latter only making eight appearances. Affleck was a seasoned performer and was a bargain at £500, while Wainwright cost £200. Affleck was a very strong player, about 5ft 9ins tall, and at 13st he had a weight advantage over most of the opposing players. But he could not prevent Town having to seek re-election in 1920. They failed, but were invited to join the newly-formed Third Division South. A season later they were transferred to the Northern section, so Affleck had the distinction of playing for Town in three different divisions in successive seasons. He left Grimsby Town in July 1925 to take up a coaching appointment in Holland, after making more than 200 League and Cup appearances for the Mariners.

	LEAGUE		*FA CUP*		*TOTAL*	
	App	*Gls*	*App*	*Gls*	*App*	*Gls*
1919-20	18	0	0	0	18	0
1920-21	39	0	3	0	42	0
1921-22	33	0	5	0	38	0
1922-23	37	0	0	0	37	0
1923-24	37	0	4	0	41	0
1924-25	33	0	1	0	34	0
	197	0	13	0	210	0

Born in Lisburn, Northern Ireland, on 15 August 1965, Paul Agnew had trials with Manchester United and Coventry City and was on schoolboy forms with Bolton Wanderers when they started their decline from First to Fourth Division. Despite four Northern Ireland schoolboy and 11 youth caps (five as captain), he was not offered terms and signed as a part-timer with Cliftonville in the Irish League. Whilst with the Northern Ireland squad at Lilleshall, he impressed Grimsby assistant manager Chris Nichol and signed for the Mariners in February 1984. After helping the youth side win the the Northern Intermediate League title, he made his Second Division debut at Oldham on 7 May 1984, but did not become first-choice left-back until Dean Crombie moved to the centre of the defence in 1985-6. The dramatic turnover in playing staff during the club's decline from Second to Fourth Division meant that he was soon their longest-serving professional; when the 1988-9 season started he was the only survivor from the senior squad that had begun the Second Division campaign two seasons previously. Throughout the Mariners' misfortunes, Agnew has remained a loyal club man. A strong-tackling consistent defender who likes to attack. In April 1989 he was selected for the England Under-23 squad but withdrew through injury.

PAUL AGNEW

	LEAGUE		*FA CUP*		*FL CUP*		*TOTAL*	
	App	*Gls*	*App*	*Gls*	*App*	*Gls*	*App*	*Gls*
1983-84	1	0	0	0	0	0	1	0
1984-85	12	0	3	0	2	0	17	0
1985-86	14/2	0	1	0	1	0	16/2	0
1986-87	29	0	3	0	1	0	33	0
1987-88	38	1	2	0	2	0	42	1
1988-89	32/2	0	6	0	2	0	40/2	0
	126/4	1	15	0	8	0	149/4	1

Goalkeeper John 'Jock' Archibald was born at Strathaven, Lanarkshire, in 1895 and started his career in Scotland with Albion Rovers. He joined his first English club, Reading, in 1919. Staying down south, he signed for Chelsea in January 1920. In 1921 he moved back to Scotland to play for Edinburgh St Bernard's but got the wanderlust and returned to England to play for Newcastle United in April 1922, signing for a fee of £200. Town secured his services in May 1923 and he gave them four good seasons, helping the Mariners to the Third Division North championship in 1925-6. Archibald, 6ft tall and weighing 11½st, was very agile and cool under pressure and was reputed to be one of the best goalkeepers of that period. Then things went wrong for him and the team. In January and February 1927, six successive matches were lost with the defence conceding 26 goals. The outcome was that nine players were put on the transfer list, four of whom had played in the championship side the previous season. It seemed, though, that Archibald had shouldered most of the blame. He was banned from the ground and was transferred to Darlington in March 1927, staying with them until 1928.

	LEAGUE		*FA CUP*		*TOTAL*	
	App	*Gls*	*App*	*Gls*	*App*	*Gls*
1923-24	32	0	4	0	36	0
1924-25	27	0	0	0	27	0
1925-26	29	0	4	0	33	0
1926-27	23	0	2	0	25	0
	111	0	10	0	121	0

JOHN ARCHIBALD

TONY ARROWSMITH

When Tony Arrowsmith joined Grimsby Town in May 1910, they had to face a season of non-League football after finishing second from bottom of the Second Division the previous season. They failed to gain re-election and decided to play the first team in the Midland League, hoping for a quick return to League football. The Mariners won the Midland League championship and were readmitted to the Second Division. Tony Arrowsmith had made the maximum appearances (38) and played a major part in a very successful season. Born in North Staveley in 1887, he first played for Anston United, being a miner at Anston Colliery. Grimsby signed him from Worksop Town and this fine, strong defender gave Town great service in his four seasons with them. He struck up a great partnership with right-back, Sid Wheelhouse. Including the Midland League season, they played together as a full-back partnership 153 times. The 1914-15 season was his last with Grimsby and he made no wartime appearances for Town. He was a guest player for Chesterfield Town and then returned to his first job, coal mining. Tony Arrowsmith died in 1950.

	LEAGUE		*FA CUP*		*TOTAL*	
	App	*Gls*	*App*	*Gls*	*App*	*Gls*
1910-11	0	0	3	0	3	0
1911-12	37	0	1	0	38	0
1912-13	36	0	1	0	37	0
1913-14	36	0	1	0	37	0
1914-15	28	0	1	0	29	0
	137	0	7	0	144	0

George Baldry was born in Cleethorpes. After schools and local football he signed for Grimsby in the summer of 1933, but did not get his chance to play in the first team until the end of November 1935, when Grimsby were starting to become an established First Division side. Baldry showed great promise as an outside-right; he could dribble, pass and cross a ball and was also a goalscorer. He played for only one season in Town's first team, but what a fantastic season it was. He made 20 appearances and scored seven goals, retaining his place in the side which took Town to the FA Cup semi-finals for the first time in the club's history. He appeared in all six Cup ties, scoring two goals. He left Grimsby at the end of the 1935-6 season, for Hull City, but did not settle at Hull and left after only five appearances. He went into non-League football with Chelmsford City, teaming up with ex-Mariner, Jack Coulter. Baldry was also a fine musician, playing saxophone in Bob Walker's band, well-known throughout Lincolnshire. He was also in business with his brother on the Grimsby fish docks. There is no doubt that had George concentrated on his football, instead of trying to pursue three careers simultaneously, he could have been amongst the greatest wingers in the club's history. Alas, office-work in the morning, the playing field in the afternoon and the bandstand at night proved too demanding. George Baldry died at Leigh-on-Sea in 1988.

GEORGE BALDRY

	LEAGUE		*FA CUP*		*TOTAL*	
	App	*Gls*	*App*	*Gls*	*App*	*Gls*
1935-36	20	7	6	2	26	9
	20	7	6	2	26	9

ALAN BARNETT

	LEAGUE		*FA CUP*		*FL CUP*		*TOTAL*	
	App	*Gls*	*App*	*Gls*	*App*	*Gls*	*App*	*Gls*
1958-59	20	0	3	0	0	0	23	0
1959-60	42	0	2	0	0	0	44	0
1960-61	6	0	0	0	0	0	6	0
1961-62	42	0	1	0	1	0	44	0
1962-63	6	0	1	0	0	0	7	0
	116	0	7	0	1	0	124	0

Born in Croydon in November 1934, Alan Barnett started his career with local side, Croydon Amateurs, before signing for Portsmouth in September 1955. Irish international 'keeper Norman Uprichard was the first choice at Fratton Park and, after making only 25 League appearances in three and a half seasons, Barnett signed for the Mariners in December 1958, for a fee of £2,500. It proved to be a wise investment by manager Allenby Chilton. When Clarrie Williams was injured at the start of the 1958-9 season, Alex Bell was signed from Exeter City as cover but had to retire after only eight games because of serious back problems. When Williams was out again in December, Barnett was signed and played the remainder of the season. However, his skills were not enough to prevent Town from being relegated to the Third Division. When the Mariners made the return trip three seasons later, he missed only the first four games and made a significant contribution to the promotion campaign. Oddly enough, it was his old club, Portsmouth, who pipped Town for the title. Standing 5ft 10ins and weighing 13st, Barnett was very agile with quick reflexes. In all he was a first-class 'keeper. In July 1963 he was transferred to Exeter City, where he made a further 57 League appearances. His last club was Torquay United, where he moved in June 1966, but he never made the League side at Plainmoor.

NIGEL BATCH

Huddersfield-born goalkeeper Nigel Batch joined Town in July 1976, after Derby had released him, and for two seasons he understudied Harry Wainman, making only 17 appearances. After Wainman broke his arm during pre-season training in 1978, Batch finally established himself and went on to make 185 consecutive appearances, a record for a Grimsby goalkeeper. After missing four matches during 1982-3, he made another 94 consecutive appearances. Batch gave some brilliant performances in helping the Mariners to promotion from Division Four in 1978-9 and to the Third Division championship the following season. He could not, however, prevent the Mariners being relegated in 1986-7. Stading 5ft 10ins tall and weighing 12½st, he commanded his goal-area. He was considered to be the best goalkeeper in the Fourth Division in 1978-9, but no awards came his way, although he was voted Grimsby's 'Player of the Year' in 1980-81. His League appearance tally (348) is the second highest total for a Grimsby 'keeper, beating George Tweedy's figure by just one. In June 1987, Batch declined new terms and joined Lincoln City, helping the Imps to the GM-Vauxhall title and an immediate return to League football. He then found himself out of favour and joined Dave Booth at Darlington, but lost his place there after Booth was dismissed. Batch ended 1988-9 on loan to Stockport.

	LEAGUE		*FA CUP*		*FL CUP*		*TOTAL*	
	App	*Gls*	*App*	*Gls*	*App*	*Gls*	*App*	*Gls*
1976-77	8	0	0	0	0	0	8	0
1977-78	10	0	4	0	0	0	14	0
1978-79	46	0	1	0	3	0	50	0
1979-80	46	0	4	0	9	0	59	0
1980-81	42	0	1	0	2	0	45	0
1981-82	42	0	3	0	2	0	47	0
1982-83	38	0	3	0	2	0	43	0
1983-84	42	0	1	0	4	0	47	0
1984-85	23	0	2	0	6	0	31	0
1985-86	30	0	1	0	1	0	32	0
1986-87	21	0	2	0	4	0	27	0
	348	0	22	0	33	0	403	0

Jackie Bestall was arguably the greatest player to wear a Grimsby Town shirt. Born in Sheffield at the turn of the century, he began with Rotherham United in 1924. In November 1926, he signed for Town for £700 and made his debut on 4 December at Millfields Road, the home of Clapton Orient. Bestall was to dominate the Grimsby midfield for 11 years, a period during which the club experienced its most successful spell with Bestall as captain. Only 5ft 5ins tall, he possessed extraordinary ball-control and his inch-perfect passes 'made' the three great centre-forwards of the decade — Joe Robson, Tim Coleman and Pat Glover — who between them scored 360 goals. At the Grimsby centenary exhibition, Sir Stanley Rous remarked that, had Bestall played for a club like Arsenal, he would have won 40 caps or more. He played for England only once — against Northern Ireland at Goodison Park in February 1935, when he was 34. He made three appearances for the Football League and won a Second Division championship medal in 1933-4. In June 1938 he became coach and chief scout for Birmingham, later managing Doncaster Rovers, Blackburn Rovers and Nelson. He returned to Belle Vue as chief scout and also managed them for another spell. In 1972, aged 71, he retired from full-time football employment after 48 years. His 427 League appearances was a Town record for 30 years and is still exceeded only by Keith Jobling. Jackie Bestall had the unusual honour, for a footballer, of having a street named after him in Grimsby.

JACKIE BESTALL

	LEAGUE		*FA CUP*		*TOTAL*	
	App	*Gls*	*App*	*Gls*	*App*	*Gls*
1926-27	23	7	2	1	25	8
1927-28	41	10	1	0	42	10
1928-29	39	11	2	0	41	11
1929-30	39	10	2	0	41	10
1930-31	42	10	3	2	45	12
1931-32	37	2	3	2	40	4
1932-33	40	5	2	0	42	5
1933-34	42	11	2	0	44	11
1934-35	41	5	1	0	42	5
1935-36	41	2	6	2	47	4
1936-37	31	3	4	0	35	3
1937-38	11	0	2	0	13	0
	427	76	30	7	457	83

Harry Betmead, youngest of the Mariners' famed half-back line of the 1930s, was a local lad who started with Haycroft Rovers in Grimsby League football. He signed professional for Town in October 1930 and established himself in the Midland League side before making his First Division debut on 15 September 1931, in a 2-0 defeat of Bolton. He held his place until the end of the month and then Priestley, Swaby, Alec Hall and William Seddon shared the position with Betmead, as Town were relegated. From 1932-3, Betmead became first-choice centre-half and in 1933-4 was one of seven players who appeared in every game, a consistency that enabled Town to regain their First Division place. For another five seasons Betmead, flanked by Ted Buck and 'Ginger' Hall, frustrated the finest centre-forwards, before his career was interrupted at its peak by the outbreak of war. When peace returned, he played in most of the 1946-7 matches, in Mariners' mostly veteran side, signed for another season but then hung up his boots. Over 6ft tall, he was a fine header of the ball and an uncompromising tackler. He was unfortunate to be around at the same time as Stan Cullis, whose monopoly of the England shirt restricted Betmead to one appearance, against Finland in Helsinki in May 1937. He toured South Africa with the FA in 1939, making two appearances against the national side.

	LEAGUE		*FA CUP*		*TOTAL*	
	App	*Gls*	*App*	*Gls*	*App*	*Gls*
1931-32	17	2	0	0	17	2
1932-33	30	2	2	0	32	2
1933-34	42	0	2	0	44	0
1934-35	26	1	0	0	26	1
1935-36	35	0	5	0	40	0
1936-37	38	1	2	0	40	1
1937-38	38	1	1	0	39	1
1938-39	36	3	7	0	43	3
1946-47	34	0	0	0	34	0
	296	10	19	0	315	10

HARRY BETMEAD

JIMMY BLOOMER (SNR)

Born in Rutherglen, Lanarkshire, Jimmy Bloomer's career began in 1943 at Strathclyde, where he stayed until 1948. Bloomer was in the Army and, during his service days, captained an Army team in India. In February 1948, he signed for Hull City but could not command a regular place and his first-team appearances were limited to four. In June 1949 he signed for Grimsby, as a winger or centre-forward under manager Charlie Spencer, although he would have played anywhere if asked. He was in the side relegated from Division Two in 1950-51. In 1951-2, Bill Shankly had taken over as Town's manager and Jim Bloomer was in the squad that nearly won promotion in Shankly's first season, Town finishing second to Lincoln in the Third Division North. In November 1952, Bloomer had the misfortune to break his leg but he was fit enough to face the 1953-4 season, when he scored four goals in five Cup ties, the most memorable being the last-minute equalizer against Fulham at home to complete his hat-trick in a sensational 5-5 draw. He never seemed to regain his old form after breaking his leg, and, midway through the 1954-5 season, he left to join non-League King's Lynn. He later played for Skegness Town. A likeable and popular man, Jim Bloomer settled in Grimsby, where he became a good club MC and entertainer. He even turned out for a local side called Tartan Forties in the Grimsby and District Sunday League. Every player had to be over 40 to be eligible to play.

	LEAGUE		*FA CUP*		*TOTAL*	
	App	*Gls*	*App*	*Gls*	*App*	*Gls*
1949-50	8	1	0	0	8	1
1950-51	24	10	2	2	26	12
1951-52	31	17	2	1	33	18
1952-53	16	7	1	0	17	7
1953-54	27	6	5	4	32	10
1954-55	3	1	1	0	4	1
	109	42	11	7	120	49

DAVE BOOTH

Born near Barnsley in 1948, Dave Booth went to Oakwell and asked for a trial. They gave him one and he impressed the Colliers enough to gain a regular place in their junior side. Soon he was in the first team. He made 161 League appearances for the Yorkshire club before moving to Grimsby Town in June 1972, for a fee of £5,000. Booth went straight into the first team at Blundell Park and gave some sterling performances, being voted Player of the Year in 1972-3, a just reward for his consistency at left-back. Looking to have a long future with the Mariners, he had averaged over 40 matches per season when misfortune struck. During the second match of the 1976-7 season, an evening game at home to Crystal Palace, he suffered a knee injury which kept him out of the side for half that season. When he returned, he played a further 21 matches, then was out of the team until March 1978. He finished the season (12 matches), then decided to call it a day as a player. With his experience he was too valuable to lose and was taken on to the staff, coaching the juniors before being promoted, to assistant manager under George Kerr. When Kerr left the club in 1982, Dave Booth became manager. He resigned in October 1985 and went to Tenerife to set up a business. In 1987, however, he returned to England and became manager of Darlington. Grimsby Town gave him a testimonial against Derby County in November 1979. A crowd of more than 13,000 paid their tribute to this popular player, a 'gate' boosted by the fact that attendance guaranteed a ticket for the forthcoming League Cup tie against Everton.

	LEAGUE		*FA CUP*		*FL CUP*		*TOTAL*	
	App	*Gls*	*App*	*Gls*	*App*	*Gls*	*App*	*Gls*
1972-73	43	3	5	0	3	0	51	3
1973-74	46	1	4	0	4	0	54	1
1974-75	36	0	3	0	1	0	40	0
1975-76	41	3	1	1	2	0	44	4
1976-77	21/1	0	0	0	2	0	23/1	0
1977-78	12	0	0	0	0	0	12	0
	199/1	7	13	1	12	0	224/1	8

At 5ft 3ins, David Boylen was probably the smallest player that Town had ever had, but that did not deter him from running the midfield for Grimsby for many seasons. Born in Manchester, he signed from Gorton Boys Club in 1964, turning professional in July 1965. Jimmy McGuigan signed Boylen after his club had played a Grimsby XI. He made his League debut at the end of 1966-7 and soon became a great favourite with supporters and his fellow players. He gave the club loyal service under eight different managers. It was rare to see him knocked off the ball and he could often outjump taller opponents. Never shirking a tackle, his work-rate and stamina were remarkable. A member of Lawrie McMenemy's promotion side of 1971-2, he was voted Player of the Year in 1973-4 and was granted a testimonial game in 1975. Older supporters compared him with pre-war star, Jackie Bestall, although Boylen's career was in the Third and Fourth Divisions while Bestall's was in the First and Second. Also, the style of football had changed, with closer marking in Boylen's time. In October 1977, he was transfer-listed and then released to take a job outside football. He moved into non-League football with Skegness and Drewery Sports (Grimsby) and was player-coach at Immingham Town. His last club was Skegness, where he was manager. He also played in the Grimsby Sunday League for Seawave United.

DAVID BOYLEN

	LEAGUE		*FA CUP*		*FL CUP*		*TOTAL*	
	App	*Gls*	*App*	*Gls*	*App*	*Gls*	*App*	*Gls*
1966-67	2	0	0	0	0	0	2	0
1967-68	26	5	0/1	0	1	0	27/1	5
1968-69	32/5	2	1	0	3	0	36/5	2
1969-70	43	2	1	1	1	0	45	3
1970-71	43	7	1	0	1	0	45	7
1971-72	41/3	2	1	0	6	1	48/3	3
1972-73	38/2	1	6	1	1/2	0	45/4	2
1973-74	34/3	6	3	0	0	0	37/3	6
1974-75	44	4	3	0	1	0	48	4
1975-76	33	4	1	0	2	0	36	4
1976-77	32/1	1	3	0	0	0	35/1	1
1977-78	2	0	0	0	2	0	4	0
	370/14	34	20/1	2	18/2	1	408/17	37

A popular player from the 1970s, Stuart Brace was a goalscoring winger. He beat Cyril Lewis's 1936-7 Grimsby record of 18 goals by a winger, netting 25 in 1969-70. Born in Taunton, Brace's career took him to Taunton Town and on to Plymouth Argyle in November 1960. After only nine appearances for Plymouth he was on the move to Watford, where he made 16 appearances. In July 1966 he became a Mansfield Town player, making 55 appearances before a £5,000 fee took him to Peterborough United for 22 appearances. Grimsby were in need of a winger and secured him in October 1968 for £4,000. He settled in well and was soon scoring vital goals. In six seasons at Blundell Park, he made over 200 League and Cup appearances, scoring 81 League goals, by far the most that any winger had ever scored for Town, and was a big success in the 1971-2 championship season. Very fast and direct, he had the happy knack of getting into goalscoring positions. His overall League record of 154 from 412 appearances was proof of this. In October 1973, he moved to Southend United for £6,000, making 106 appearances for them until he left in 1976. For Grimsby he scored a hat-trick in five minutes 55 seconds, against Oldham Athletic on 11 November 1972.

	LEAGUE		*FA CUP*		*FL CUP*		*TOTAL*	
	App	*Gls*	*App*	*Gls*	*App*	*Gls*	*App*	*Gls*
1968-69	30	10	1	0	0	0	31	10
1969-70	46	25	1	0	1	0	48	25
1970-71	43/1	9	1	0	1	0	45/1	9
1971-72	44	19	0/1	0	6	4	50/1	23
1972-73	39	18	6	2	3	0	48	20
1973-74	3	0	0	0	1	1	4	1
	205/1	81	9/1	2	12	5	226/2	88

STUART BRACE

Tommy Briggs was by far the most popular player of the immediate post-war period. Born in Chesterfield and a butcher by trade, he played most of his early football for Doncaster junior sides. Serving in the Royal Navy during the war, he was stationed at Plymouth and guested for Argyle, being recommended to Grimsby by ex-Mariner, Pat Glover, who was living in the area. Briggs signed in May 1947 after a trial. Lacking a little in skill, he was wholehearted and would chase and harry when all seemed lost. His 6ft, 13st frame worried defences and he scored some great goals. Always willing to learn, he would go back to Blundell Park after training to improve his game. In the Second Division he made his mark and was Town's highest scorer for the two seasons before he left. In 1949-50 he was the League's leading goalscorer with 36 goals. Briggs won an England 'B' cap in a 5-0 win over Switzerland at Hillsborough in January 1950, but the tactics did not suit his style and he was never selected again. The same season he scored seven goals in successive games against Luton's England goalkeeper Bernard Streten, three in a League match on 31 January 1949 and all four in an FA Cup tie the following Saturday in Town's 4-3 triumph at Kenilworth Road. In December 1950, he was transferred to Coventry City for £19,550 but did not settle at Highfield Road and, after 11 appearances, went to Birmingham in September 1951. He joined Blackburn in November 1952 for £15,000 and it was here that he had his best days, scoring 140 goals in 194 League appearances; in 1954-5 he was the League's top scorer again with 33 goals. He scored seven goals in succession in a League game for Blackburn against Bristol Rovers, a record equalled by Neil Coleman for Stoke City against Lincoln City in 1957. In 1958, Briggs returned to Grimsby for a small fee. His stay was brief — nine goals in 19 appearances — and in March 1959 he became player-manager of Glentoran, staying with the Irish League club for nearly two seasons, making 36 appearances and scoring 15 goals. He returned to settle in the Grimsby area, where he was a representative for an electrical and television firm. Tom Briggs died suddenly in February 1984 and Town had lost one of their football characters.

TOMMY BRIGGS

	LEAGUE		*FA CUP*		*TOTAL*	
	App	*Gls*	*App*	*Gls*	*App*	*Gls*
1947-48	24	5	1	0	25	5
1948-49	34	26	2	1	36	27
1949-50	41	36	2	4	43	40
1950-51	17	11	0	0	17	11
1957-58	9	5	0	0	9	5
1958-59	10	4	0	0	10	4
	135	87	5	5	140	92

Kilmarnock-born Mike Brolly was capped for Scotland at Schoolboy and Youth level before he joined Chelsea in October 1971. He made only seven appearances for them before his move to Bristol City in June 1974 and could not command a regular place in the newly-promoted First Division side at Ashton Gate. Town secured his signature in September 1976 and he went straight into the first team, but it was a sad season for Town who were relegated to Division Four. A winger or midfield player, Brolly had some memorable games for Town. One unforgettable memory is his two goals which knocked Everton out of the League Cup in October 1979 at Blundell Park. He missed only three League games in the promotion seasons of 1978-9 and 1979-80. More a goalmaker than a goalscorer, he performed in the Second Division as an accurate passer of a ball. He was unselfish, hence his League tally of only 27 goals in 246 appearances. Brolly left the club in August 1982 to join Derby County. He later signed for Scunthorpe United, before drifting into non-League football.

	LEAGUE		*FA CUP*		*FL CUP*		*TOTAL*	
	App	*Gls*	*App*	*Gls*	*App*	*Gls*	*App*	*Gls*
1976-77	41	3	3	0	0	0	44	3
1977-78	45/1	5	5	0	3	0	53/1	5
1978-79	44	8	1	0	0	0	45	8
1979-80	45	4	4	0	9	2	58	6
1980-81	36/4	4	1	0	2	0	39/4	4
1981-82	35/3	3	2	1	2	0	39/3	4
	246/8	27	16	1	16	2	278/8	30

MIKE BROLLY

BILL BROWN

	LEAGUE		*FA CUP*		*TOTAL*	
	App	*Gls*	*App*	*Gls*	*App*	*Gls*
1951-52	46	1	2	0	48	1
1952-53	32	0	2	0	34	0
1953-54	34	0	5	0	39	0
1954-55	36	0	3	0	39	0
1955-56	43	0	4	0	47	0
1956-57	42	0	1	0	43	0
1957-58	32	0	1	0	33	0
	265	1	18	0	283	1

When the full-back partnership of Moody and Fisher came to an end, and with Town relegated to Division Three South, new manager Bill Shankly chose Brown and Galbraith as his new defensive pair. Bill Brown had been appointed player-manager of Elgin City when Shankly persuaded him to go to Blundell Park. Born in 1922, at Larkhall, Lanarkshire, Brown's career had taken him to Larkhall Thistle and Preston North End. It was with Preston that he had teamed up with Shankly, so the manager knew the type of player he was getting. Brown moved from Preston to Queen of the South, but was not there long before his move to Elgin City and Town had to pay Queen of the South a small fee for his services. He was soon installed as captain and in his second match for Grimsby, he went in goal after Hayhurst broke a finger during a game against Lincoln. Alex McCue had been carried off with a suspected broken leg and so Town had their backs against the wall. Brown did well, although he could not prevent the Imps winning 3-2. His career at Blundell Park covered seven seasons and he had several partners at left-back but, because of his astute knowledge of the game, fitted in well with all of them. Well-built, he was always in the thick of things. Dependable and a good captain, Brown sometimes incurred the wrath of opposing fans but he was certainly the man you wanted on your side when the going got tough. He had the disappointment of being in the team that sought re-election in 1954-5 season, after Shankly had left, but was in the 1955-6 championship side under Allenby Chilton. Given a benefit match in April 1956, Bill Brown left Blundell Park to become manager of Barrow, from July 1958 to August 1959, and ended his career as player-manager of the Somerset side Bridgewater Town in the Western League. He died in May 1979, aged 55.

Teddy Buck was born at Dipton, County Durham, the same place as a Town favourite of the 1920s, Tommy Spink. He played for West Stanley before signing for Leeds United in May 1927, but with two international half-backs on their books, his first-team appearances were limited to eight before he signed for Grimsby in December 1929, for £2,000. Buck made his League debut on Christmas Day 1929, in a 4-1 defeat by Leicester, when Harry Barley, Town's outside-right, broke his leg. He was Grimsby's regular left-half until the start of World War Two, making all but seven of his appearances in that position. He was ever present for four seasons and made 32 consecutive appearances in the FA Cup. He also played nearly 200 wartime games and, with County Cup matches, must have made more that 600 appearances for the Mariners. The half-back line of Hall, Betmead and Buck was famous throughout football. They first appeared together in February 1932, and played over 200 League matches. Their last appearance was the first match of the aborted 1939-40 season, although they did play a few wartime matches together. Buck retired towards the end of the war and joined the club's groundstaff. He was groundsman at Town's training ground after wartime service in the fire brigade. A member of the 1933-4 championship side, he also played in both the pre-war FA Cup semi-finals.

TEDDY BUCK

	LEAGUE		*FA CUP*		*TOTAL*	
	App	*Gls*	*App*	*Gls*	*App*	*Gls*
1929-30	23	0	2	0	25	0
1930-31	41	0	3	0	44	0
1931-32	29	1	3	0	32	1
1932-33	30	0	2	0	32	0
1933-34	42	0	2	0	44	0
1934-35	42	1	1	0	43	1
1935-36	42	0	6	1	48	1
1936-37	26	1	4	1	30	2
1937-38	42	1	2	0	44	1
1938-39	37	0	7	0	44	0
	354	4	32	2	386	6

BILLY CAIRNS

	LEAGUE		*FA CUP*		*TOTAL*	
	App	*Gls*	*App*	*Gls*	*App*	*Gls*
1946-47	28	18	3	4	31	22
1947-48	31	16	1	0	32	16
1948-49	26	12	2	1	28	13
1949-50	42	17	2	0	44	17
1950-51	24	16	0	0	24	16
1951-52	43	31	2	4	45	35
1952-53	25	10	0	0	25	10
1953-54	2	0	0	0	2	0
	221	120	10	9	231	129

Billy Cairns was one of those rare 'Peter Pans' of football, still knocking in goals long after his peers had hung up their boots. A native of Newcastle, he joined the St James' Park club for £25, after a spell in local football, and made his League debut on New Year's Day 1935. Before war interrupted his career, he made 91 League appearances and scored 54 goals. Between 1944 and 1946, he was at Gateshead, scoring 42 goals in one season, and was 33 when Charlie Spencer took him to Blundell Park. Some eyebrows were raised as, in addition to his age, he had undergone operations for duodenal ulcers. Spencer's judgement, however, was sound and Cairns became a favourite of the crowd and one of a long line of free-scoring inside-forwards, for which Grimsby has been noted over the years. He made his debut just after his 34th birthday; at 37 he scored his 100th goal; at 38 he netted ten goals in a 25-game run; and in September 1953, a month short of his 41st birthday, he made his final appearance. One of the finest headers of the ball in the game, his skill in front of goal made him a marked man. Although often provoked he never retaliated and never questioned a referee's decision. After retirement he became mine host at a local pub and, such is the affection with which he is remembered, the public bar is still named 'Cairn's Bar' and a photograph of the maestro in action still holds pride of place. Billy Cairns died on 9 January 1988.

Born in Glasgow on 14 December 1894, Jimmy Carmichael spent two seasons with Strathclyde before moving to Wales to play for Mid-Rhondda before World War One. After war service he continued his career with that club. Haydn Price was appointed the first manager of Grimsby in the summer of 1920 and he brought with him four players — Moody, Bache, Collier and Carmichael — in a package deal worth £200. Carmichael outlasted them all and although he made his debut on 28 August 1920, as a centre-half, it was at centre-forward that he gave sterling service to the club and became a legend in the history of Grimsby Town. In 1921-2, he was the League's leading goalscorer with 37 goals. Probably his greatest, if not most spectacular goal, was on 1 May 1926, when he scored the vital goal in Grimsby's 1-0 victory against New Brighton to give Town the Third Division North title. He was given a benefit match with Grimsby on 27 April 1926 but it was badly timed, being only four days before an important game against New Brighton. Town would not risk their first team and the Reserves were easily beaten, 4-0 by Hull City. Carmichael did well, however, and £140 was taken at the turnstiles, plus ticket sales from a benefit dance, a subscription list and the sale of autographed photographs. In 1927, he moved to Worksop Town and Grimsby had lost one of their most prolific goalscorers of all time. After his football career had finished he settled in Grimsby and worked on the docks. Jimmy Carmichael died in August 1967.

JIMMY CARMICHAEL

	LEAGUE		*FA CUP*		*TOTAL*	
	App	*Gls*	*App*	*Gls*	*App*	*Gls*
1920-21	24	2	2	0	26	2
1921-22	37	37	6	1	43	38
1922-23	38	23	0	0	38	23
1923-24	35	20	4	1	39	21
1924-25	38	18	1	1	39	19
1925-26	39	33	3	2	42	35
1926-27	16	4	1	0	17	4
	227	137	17	5	244	142

Although he played only a few matches for Grimsby Town, the club can boast that they once had one of the greatest managers of all time on their books. Born in 1878, at Kiveton, Sheffield, Herbert Chapman was much-travelled as a player and for most of his career he retained amateur status. Before his arrival at Abbey Park (it was to be Grimsby's last season on that ground), he played for Kiveton Park FC, Ashton North End, Stalybridge Rovers and Rochdale. He signed for Town in May 1898 and scored two goals on his debut. After only ten appearances, however, he moved to Swindon Town in 1899, Sheppey United in November 1899 and Worksop in the summer of 1900. In 1901 he turned professional with Northampton Town but reverted to amateur status to play for Sheffield United in May 1902. Chapman then turned professional for the second time, playing for Notts County in 1903, Northampton Town again in the summer of 1904 and Tottenham Hotspur in March 1905, before beginning a third spell with Northampton Town in the summer of 1907, this time as player-manager until 1909, when he retired to concentrate on management. In 1912 he became manager of Leeds City and after World War One gained fame by leading Huddersfield Town towards three successive League championships. He took charge of Arsenal in June 1925 and repeated his feat of setting a club towards a hat-trick of First Division titles. He died in January 1934, best remembered for his contributions as a manager, particularly as the inventor of the 'stopper' centre-half.

HERBERT CHAPMAN

	LEAGUE		*FA CUP*		*TOTAL*	
	App	*Gls*	*App*	*Gls*	*App*	*Gls*
1898-99	10	4	2	0	12	4
	10	4	2	0	12	4

When Billy Walsh left Grimsby Town in March 1955, the club approached Manchester United for the services of centre-half Allenby Chilton as player-manager. Chilton went to Blundell Park on a free transfer but was too late to save the Mariners from having to seek re-election to Division Three North. He was born in South Hylton, County Durham, in 1918, and joined United in 1938, making his League debut on 2 September 1938. The following day war was declared and he had to wait until 31 August 1946 (when United met Grimsby) for his second League appearance. In 1944 he won a War Cup Final (South) winners' medal as a Charlton guest. He had nine successful post-war seasons with United, during which they won the FA Cup (1948), the League Championship (1952) and he won two England caps. He made 178 successive League and Cup appearances for United, playing his last match for them on 23 February 1955. In 1955-6 he led Town to the Third Division North title, when they made history by becoming the first club to seek re-election, then win the championship the following season. Chilton played on until early 1956-7, after which he decided to concentrate on management. He left Town in 1958-9, the season they were relegated, and managed Wigan (then a non-League club). In 1961-2 he scouted for Hartlepools United and was their manager from July 1962 until May 1963. Chilton totalled more than 450 League and Cup appearances with his two League clubs, a remarkable figure considering he lost seven years because of war. He will always be remembered at Grimsby for his leadership and two outstanding signings, Johnny Scott and Jeff Whitefoot.

ALLENBY CHILTON

	LEAGUE		*FA CUP*		*TOTAL*	
	App	*Gls*	*App*	*Gls*	*App*	*Gls*
1954-55	13	0	0	0	13	0
1955-56	42	0	4	0	46	0
1956-57	8	0	0	0	8	0
	63	0	4	0	67	0

Sheffield-born Ron Cockerill embarked on his football career with Huddersfield Town after he had played for Sheffield Schools. A fee of £6,000 took him to Blundell Park in August 1958. Standing well over 6ft and weighing 13½st, he was a centre-half at Huddersfield but at Grimsby played only a few games in that position. He appeared in more than 300 League and Cup games for Town, most of them at left-half or right-half. Because of his powerful kick the fans nicknamed him 'Cannonball'. Testimonies of his shooting power were the two goals he scored against Bert Trautmann in an FA Cup replay against Manchester City at Maine Road — both netted with unstoppable shots. He was a member of the 1961-2 promotion side but, after ten seasons, had to retire because of an injury. A loyal clubman, Cockerill was a hard player to beat, strong in the tackle but fair. He settled in Cleethorpes and his son, Glen, played League soccer for Lincoln, Swindon, Sheffield United and Southampton. His youngest son, John, joined the Mariners from Stafford Rangers at the start of the 1988-9 season.

RON COCKERILL

	LEAGUE		*FA CUP*		*FL CUP*		*TOTAL*	
	App	*Gls*	*App*	*Gls*	*App*	*Gls*	*App*	*Gls*
1958-59	41	4	3	2	0	0	44	6
1959-60	2	0	0	0	0	0	2	0
1960-61	27	4	0	0	0	0	27	4
1961-62	28	2	1	0	1	0	30	2
1962-63	31	1	1	0	0	0	32	1
1963-64	31	2	1	0	1	0	33	2
1964-65	43	7	4	1	2	0	49	8
1965-66	37	3	3	0	2	0	42	3
1966-67	41	2	2	0	5	2	48	4
1967-68	12/1	3	0	0	3	0	15/1	3
	293/1	28	15	3	14	2	322/1	33

Born in Staffordshire, Steve Coglin did the rounds of the junior clubs, playing in turn for Moxley White Star, Darlaston, Lichfield City, Wednesbury Old Athletic and Willenhall until he signed for Sunderland in the summer of 1924. After two and a half seasons at Roker Park, he joined Grimsby Town in February 1927, along with outside-right Jack Prior. Coglin, an inside-left, went straight into the first team. Small, fast and a good ball player, he struck up a fine understanding with left-winger Billy Marshall and was a prominent member of the side promoted to Division One in 1928-9. After only 4 appearances in 1930-31, he moved to Notts County in May 1931 and, after only 13 appearances for County, he drifted out of League football.

	LEAGUE		*FA CUP*		*TOTAL*	
	App	*Gls*	*App*	*Gls*	*App*	*Gls*
1926-27	15	4	0	0	15	4
1927-28	32	11	1	0	33	11
1928-29	35	11	0	0	35	11
1929-30	32	13	2	0	34	13
1930-31	4	0	0	0	4	0
	118	39	3	0	121	39

STEVE COGLIN

ERNEST 'TIM' COLEMAN

	LEAGUE		*FA CUP*		*TOTAL*	
	App	*Gls*	*App*	*Gls*	*App*	*Gls*
1928-29	8	7	0	0	8	7
1929-30	18	2	2	0	20	2
1930-31	38	35	3	1	41	36
1931-32	23	13	2	0	25	13
	87	57	7	1	94	58

In 1928-9, Town were pushing for promotion to Division One when leading goalscorer Joe Robson, who had scored 32 goals in 34 matches, was injured. With 'Pat' Glover thought to be too inexperienced, Town looked to another centre-forward on the books — 'Tim' Coleman, signed from Halifax that February. He did not let his team down, scoring the only goal of his debut match, against Oldham Athletic. When Robson returned for two matches, Coleman kept his place in the side, playing at outside-left, then inside-right. No doubt his appearances at a vital time of the season helped Grimsby to promotion to the First Division. Robson was still first-choice at centre-forward and, although Coleman played 18 games, none of these was at centre-forward. The 1930-31 season was his best, when his 35 goals set a new First Division record for Grimsby, beating Joe Robson's 30 the previous season. In March 1932, Coleman was transferred to Arsenal for £5,000, although there is some doubt over the fee. About that time, Town signed centre-half William Seddon from Arsenal, either in part-exchange or for a straight fee. He was valued at £2,500. Prone to injury, he played only 21 matches for Town, while Coleman won a League Championship medal with Arsenal. From Arsenal he moved to Middlesbrough, where he became a goalmaker instead of a goalscorer, playing with great success at inside-forward. A hard but fair player, his one regret was being sent off while playing for Middlesbrough against Grimsby in the 1936 FA Cup sixth round, after tangling with Harry Betmead, who was also dismissed. Coleman finished his League career with Norwich City just before World War Two. After the war he returned to his native Nottinghamshire to become player-manager of Linby Colliery. In the 1960s he had two spells as team boss at Notts County. Tim Coleman will always be remembered at Grimsby for his goalscoring ability and his teamwork. He died 20 January 1984, aged 76.

One of Tom Johnson's signings in the 1960s, Doug Collins was signed from Johnson's former club, Rotherham United. Yorkshire-born, at Newton, near Doncaster, he was taken on the groundstaff at Rotherham and joined Grimsby as an amateur in March 1963, signing professional forms in June that year. A winger or inside-forward, Collins played in all the forward positions at Blundell Park and as a maker of many goals he seemed to cover every inch of the pitch. Slightly built, he was industrious, a useful player to have in the team. This was proved when Burnley paid £27,000 for him in September 1968 and he went on to win a Second Division championship medal with them in 1972-3, making 37 appearances that season. After 172 League appearances for Burnley, he moved to Plymouth in May 1976, staying there for under a year and making 22 appearances before signing for Sunderland. Collins did not settle at Roker Park and played only four times for the first team before trying his luck in the NASL with Tulsa Roughnecks. Later he worked on Derby County's coaching staff until being appointed player-manager at Rochdale in January 1979. He made six appearances before leaving during the 1979-80 season.

	LEAGUE		*FA CUP*		*FL CUP*		*TOTAL*	
	App	*Gls*	*App*	*Gls*	*App*	*Gls*	*App*	*Gls*
1963-64	3	0	0	0	0	0	3	0
1964-65	5	1	0	0	0	0	5	1
1965-66	26/6	2	6	0	4	0	36/6	2
1966-67	17	3	1	0	0/1	0	18/1	3
1967-68	36/1	3	1	0	2	1	39/1	4
1968-69	9	0	0	0	4	0	13	0
	96/7	9	8	0	10/1	1	114/8	10

DOUG COLLINS

DICK CONNER

Jarrow-born Dick Conner signed for Grimsby Town in August 1952, from South Shields after a spell on Newcastle United's books. He had to wait until 30 January 1954 to make his League debut, this was the period between Bill Shankly's leaving the club and the appointment of Billy Walsh as the new manager. In 1954-5 Conner competed with Reg Scotson and Pat Johnston for one of the wing-half positions. Grimsby finished 23rd and had to seek re-election to Division Three (North). After the departure of Scotson, Conner settled at right-half and in 1955-6, although he missed the first nine matches, he played well enough to retain his place and help Town win promotion to Division Two. He kept his place in the team for two seasons but in 1958-9, which was his last season as a player for Grimsby, he appeared in four different positions in 31 matches as Town were relegated to Division Three. He left Grimsby for Southampton in July 1959 and in two years at The Dell he played in 78 matches for the Saints, helping them to the Third Division title. He moved to Tranmere Rovers in July 1961 and to Aldershot in July 1962, where he retired to become assistant trainer. Conner became Rochdale manager, leaving after three years to take over at Darlington for a year. In 1976-7 he returned to Grimsby Town as trainer-coach under manager Tom Casey and stayed at Blundell Park until 1978-9. In November and December 1976 he was acting manager after Casey left, until the appointment of John Newman. Conner was a hard tackler, speedy and could always be relied on to give his best.

	LEAGUE		*FA CUP*		*TOTAL*	
	App	*Gls*	*App*	*Gls*	*App*	*Gls*
1953-54	2	0	0	0	2	0
1954-55	34	1	3	0	37	1
1955-56	37	0	4	0	41	0
1956-57	41	1	1	1	42	2
1957-58	41	4	1	0	42	4
1958-59	31	2	0	0	31	2
	186	8	9	1	195	9

Charles Buchan, the former Sunderland and England forward and later a noted sports journalist, once wrote that the finest display of inside-forward play he ever saw was given by Joe Cooper of Grimsby Town. It is certain that, had Cooper not combined his playing career with the profession of school teaching, his impact on the game would have been greater. He joined the Mariners from Notts County in 1924 and made his debut on 27 September, against Chesterfield at Blundell Park. He netted his first goal for the club the following Saturday at Accrington. Although primarily a maker of goals, Cooper still averaged a goal every third game, playing alongside the likes of Jimmy Carmichael and Joe Robson, despite his appearances being limited by teaching commitments. The peak of his career was between 1925 and 1929, during which time he won a Third Division North championship medal. On 12 January 1929, he had just scored the equalizer in the Cup tie against West Bromwich and was giving Richardson, the Throstles' centre-half, a hard time, when he was felled by a savage tackle and carried from the pitch. He did not play again for ten months. At the end of the relegation season of 1931-2, Town released Cooper, a decision which baffled the local Press. He joined Lincoln City, scoring a hat-trick in one of his first appearances for the Imps. He retired at the age of 33. Joe Cooper was also a talented cricketer, both with the bat and as a change bowler. He played for the Town Cricket Club, captaining the side for a couple of seasons.

JOE COOPER

	LEAGUE		*FA CUP*		*TOTAL*	
	App	*Gls*	*App*	*Gls*	*App*	*Gls*
1924-25	30	11	1	0	31	11
1925-26	28	11	2	0	30	11
1926-27	28	11	3	0	31	11
1927-28	15	1	0	0	15	1
1928-29	9	5	2	1	11	6
1929-30	8	1	0	0	8	1
1930-31	20	6	2	0	22	6
1931-32	16	1	3	0	19	1
	154	47	13	1	167	48

CHARLIE CRAVEN

	LEAGUE		*FA CUP*		*TOTAL*	
	App	*Gls*	*App*	*Gls*	*App*	*Gls*
1930-31	8	1	0	0	8	1
1931-32	9	1	0	0	9	1
1932-33	31	16	2	1	33	17
1933-34	42	18	2	0	44	18
1934-35	41	18	1	1	42	19
1935-36	42	14	6	2	48	16
1936-37	41	15	4	3	45	18
1937-38	42	12	2	0	44	12
	256	95	17	7	273	102

After weeks of rumours and speculation, Grimsby Town finally got their man when they signed Charlie Craven from Boston United in May 1930. Boston-born Craven had been watched by Grimsby representatives several times and it was felt that he was the man to replace Joe Cooper. Craven was to become a household name with Grimsby in the golden 1930s. He made his debut on 13 September, against Sheffield Wednesday, but Town lost 2-1 and he made only 17 appearances in his first two seasons with Grimsby. On 24 October 1931, the trio of Bestall, Glover and Craven made the first of many appearances together. That was the season Town were relegated, but Craven scored 26 goals for the Reserves, who were Midland League champions. In 1932-3 he commanded a regular place in Town's Division Two side and played a major role in the championship season of 1933-4. That season, Bestall, Glover and Craven played together 39 times and scored 71 goals between them to take the Mariners to Division One. Craven's last season with Grimsby was 1937-8. Although he had played the maximum 42 matches that season, he claimed that a section of the crowd was barracking him. He asked for a transfer and, in June 1938, Manchester United signed him for £6,000. After only 11 appearances and two goals Craven moved to Birmingham in December 1938. He left the League scene in the summer of 1939 to join Tamworth and there followed a long period of wartime football. In the 1951 close season he signed for Sutton Town and, even though he was over 40, still showed his skills. He had a very deceptive swerve which fooled many opponents and, although he never won an England cap, he was selected as reserve against Holland in 1935. Charlie Craven died on 30 March 1972.

Born in August 1957 at Lincoln, Dean Crombie embarked on his football career with his home-town club, playing for the youth team and reserves under ex-Mariner Graham Taylor, then the Imps manager. When he was too old for the youth team, he was released and signed for works side, Ruston-Bucyrus in the Lincolnshire League. The Lincoln management soon recalled him and he joined City as a full professional in February 1977. There was a change of management, Willie Bell taking over from George Kerr, and Crombie did not fit in with the new manager's plans; after 33 games for the Imps, he was released at the end of the 1977-8 season. John Newman signed him for Town in August 1978, arguably the best free transfer in recent years. Other clubs were seeking his services but George Kerr's presence as trainer at Blundell Park probably influenced the player. Making his League debut on 19 August 1978, Crombie went on to appear in the maximum number of League and Cup games in a season in which Town won promotion. The following season he was voted Player of the Year as Grimsby lifted the Third Division championship. He stayed with Grimsby for nine seasons, seven of these in Division Two, but his last season with the Mariners (1986-7) saw them relegated to Division Three. After more than 300 League and Cup matches for Town he was released at the end of that season and joined Bolton Wanderers. Besides being immensely popular with players and supporters alike, this tall, well-built defender did well in any of the positions he filled. He possessed a good shot, although he did not score many goals.

DEAN CROMBIE

	LEAGUE		*FA CUP*		*FL CUP*		*TOTAL*	
	App	*Gls*	*App*	*Gls*	*App*	*Gls*	*App*	*Gls*
1978-79	46	1	1	0	3	0	50	1
1979-80	38/1	0	4	1	5	0	47/1	1
1980-81	33	0	1	0	2	0	36	0
1981-82	38	0	3	0	2	0	43	0
1982-83	30/2	1	3	0	1	0	34/2	1
1983-84	40	0	1	0	4	0	45	0
1984-85	39	0	3	0	6	0	48	0
1985-86	33/1	1	1	0	2	0	36/1	1
1986-87	19	0	0	0	2	0	21	0
	316/4	3	17	1	27	0	360/4	4

MIKE CULLEN

	LEAGUE		*FA CUP*		*FL CUP*		*TOTAL*	
	App	*Gls*	*App*	*Gls*	*App*	*Gls*	*App*	*Gls*
1958-59	35	11	3	1	0	0	38	12
1959-60	41	5	2	0	0	0	43	5
1960-61	44	9	1	0	1	0	46	9
1961-62	42	8	1	0	1	0	44	8
1962-63	16	2	0	0	1	0	17	2
	178	35	7	1	3	0	188	36

Mike made his League debut for Town in the sensational 3-3 draw at Liverpool on the opening day of the 1958-9 season. Cullen, a Glaswegian, started his career with Douglasdale Juniors, going to Luton Town in August 1949. He was a youth international and it was at Luton that he blossomed into a very good player, being capped at 'B' level for Scotland against England in 1956 and gaining a full cap against Austria the same year. He had made 111 appearances for Luton when Town signed him in June 1958, as a replacement for Billy Evans. The fee, between £4,000 and £5,000, was a bargain and Grimsby could now boast that they had three internationals on their books: Cullen, Donovan and Scott. With an average of 35 games per season, Cullen was a real asset and, although he had the misfortune to be in the relegation side in 1958-9, he was rewarded for his efforts by helping Town win promotion in 1961-2. Always cheerful, he was a great favourite with the supporters who saw him play in four forward positions, although most of his 35 goals came from inside-right. A good dribbler, he was often frustrating, but never frightened to have a shot at goal. In November 1962 he joined Tim Ward at Derby County, for about the same fee that Town had paid Luton. After only 24 appearances for Derby he moved to non-League Wellington Town.

Midfield, forward, defender — wherever Bob Cumming was selected to play for the Mariners he always gave 100 per cent, whether for the first team, reserves or even in practice games. Born in Airdrie in December 1955, he made his Scottish League debut with Albion Rovers at the age of 16 in 1971-2. After a spell with Baillieston Juniors, he was invited to Blundell Park by Lawrie McMenemy for trials after winning a Scottish Under-18 cap. He joined Grimsby as an apprentice, turned full professional in March 1974 and made his League debut on 17 August that year. Cumming went on to play over 300 League and Cup games in his 13-season stay with Town. He would have made more but his style of play earned him more than his share of injuries. He never shirked a tackle and was not afraid to take defenders on. Cumming scored over 50 goals, his best season being 1979-80 with 14. He was top scorer in the 1980-81 season with 11 and played a big part in both Town's promotion seasons in the late 1970s. He was also in the relegation teams of 1976-7 and 1986-7. This popular player left Grimsby Town at the end of the 1986-7 season. He joined Lincoln City who were about to embark on their first season in the GM Vauxhall Conference. Grimsby Town gave him a testimonial in 1984. In May 1989, he left for the United States to join Albany Capitals.

	LEAGUE		*FA CUP*		*FL CUP*		*TOTAL*	
	App	*Gls*	*App*	*Gls*	*App*	*Gls*	*App*	*Gls*
1974-75	5	0	0	0	0	0	5	0
1975-76	25/7	2	0	0	1	0	26/7	2
1976-77	41	0	3	0	2	0	46	0
1977-78	25/2	3	5	0	1	0	31/2	3
1978-79	31/3	10	1	0	3	1	35/3	11
1979-80	40	14	3	0	7	4	50	18
1980-81	31/1	11	1	0	2	0	34/1	11
1981-82	23/1	2	1	2	2	0	26/1	4
1982-83	32/1	7	1	0	2/1	0	35/2	7
1983-84	27/3	1	1	0	3/1	0	31/4	1
1984-85	15/5	5	2/1	0	0	0	17/6	5
1985-86	22/2	2	0	0	1	0	23/2	2
1986-87	21/2	1	1	0	2/1	0	24/3	1
	338/27	58	19/1	2	26/3	5	383/31	65

BOB CUMMING

DON DONOVAN

After Bill Brown retired in July 1958, it did not take Grimsby long to find an adequate replacement, when Allenby Chilton signed Don Donovan from Everton for a fee of around £8,000. It proved a shrewd purchase, for Donovan had already played 179 matches for Everton and had been capped five times for the Republic of Ireland. He certainly had the experience that Town needed in defence and he enjoyed a memorable debut, with a quick return to Merseyside to face Liverpool for the opening match of the 1958-9 campaign. Town drew 3-3, despite playing nearly all the second half with ten men after an injury to goalkeeper Clarrie Williams. It proved to be a disappointing season, though, and the Mariners were relegated. Donovan missed only one match that season; indeed, he missed only 26 League games in six seasons and played a major part in Town's promotion from Division Three in 1961-2. An extremely versatile player, he played in both full-back positions, at right-half and left-half and was also team captain for a spell. Strangely, he scored only one goal in more than 250 League and Cup matches for Grimsby. After he left Town he joined ambitious Boston United as player-manager.

	LEAGUE		*FA CUP*		*FL CUP*		*TOTAL*	
	App	*Gls*	*App*	*Gls*	*App*	*Gls*	*App*	*Gls*
1958-59	41	0	2	0	0	0	43	0
1959-60	42	1	2	0	0	0	44	1
1960-61	46	0	1	0	0	0	47	0
1961-62	41	0	1	0	1	0	43	0
1962-63	41	0	1	0	1	0	43	0
1963-64	27	0	1	0	1	0	29	0
1964-65	0	0	4	0	0	0	4	0
	238	1	12	0	3	0	253	1

Don Donovan's son, Terry, also played for Grimsby, but he was a striker who scored 23 goals in his 52 League games for the club. In September 1979, Terry Donovan was transferred to Aston Villa for a fee of £75,000, which was then a Grimsby record. From Villa he went to Oxford (on loan), Burnley and Rotherham United and it was with the last club that he had to retire because of a knee injury. He was a schoolboy international for England and played at Under-21 level for the Republic of Ireland, being eligible for the latter because of his parentage. Both Don and Terry have settled in the Cleethorpes area.

TERRY DONOVAN

	LEAGUE		*FA CUP*		*FL CUP*		*TOTAL*	
	App	*Gls*	*App*	*Gls*	*App*	*Gls*	*App*	*Gls*
1976-77	17/4	6	1	0	0	0	18/4	6
1977-78	31/7	14	4	2	3	2	38/7	18
1978-79	4/1	3	0	0	3	1	7/1	4
	52/12	23	5	2	6	3	63/12	28

'Local boy makes good' is a well-worn cliché but it aptly describes Kevin Drinkell, who joined Grimsby as an apprentice straight from school in 1976. He made his League debut on 11 April 1977, playing in three matches that season, but had to wait another season before he was signed on as a full professional in June 1978. Thereafter he became Town's regular centre-forward and was a member of the promotion side in 1978-9 and leading goalscorer the following season when the Mariners again won promotion. Thus, in four seasons he had gone from club apprentice in Division Four to an accomplished centre-forward in Division Two, scoring most of his goals in that section. The 1980-81 season was a disappointing one for him as far as goalscoring was concerned, but his contribution to the team made up for the lack of goals. In 1984-5 he was joint-top goalscorer with Paul Wilkinson — a good double strike force for Grimsby. His performance had been noted by other clubs but he had his critics and was unsettled at Blundell Park. At the end of 1984-5 he declined a further contract with Grimsby and agreed terms with Norwich City. The clubs could not agree on the transfer fee, the case went to tribunal and the figure was set at £105,000. Norwich City, then a Second Division club, got the bargain of the season; at 24 years of age, Drinkell was a veteran in terms of the number of games he had played. Grimsby, meanwhile, had lost another good centre-forward in their long line of fine players in that position. At Grimsby he was voted Player of the Year in 1982-3 and, had he stayed with the Mariners, he would surely have reached the 100-goal mark in 1985-6. In the summer of 1988, after much speculation that he was on Tottenham Hotspur's shopping list, he was transferred to Glasgow Rangers for £600,000 and in 1988 was scoring regularly in the Premier Division of the Scottish League.

	LEAGUE		*FA CUP*		*FL CUP*		*TOTAL*	
	App	*Gls*	*App*	*Gls*	*App*	*Gls*	*App*	*Gls*
1976-77	3/1	2	0	0	0	0	3/1	2
1977-78	20/6	5	1/3	0	3	1	24/9	6
1978-79	20/10	7	1	0	0	0	21/10	7
1979-80	31/2	16	3/1	1	5/2	0	39/5	17
1980-81	41	7	1	0	2	0	44	7
1981-82	23/5	6	2/1	3	2	0	27/6	9
1982-83	39	17	3	0	4	5	46	22
1983-84	35/1	15	1	1	4	2	40/1	18
1984-85	30/5	14	0	0	0/2	0	30/7	14
	242/30	89	12/5	5	20/4	8	274/39	102

KEVIN DRINKELL

James Middleton Dyson was born in Lancashire in 1907 and signed for Oldham Athletic in 1928 from Northwich Victoria. Joining Grimsby Town in March 1932, he went straight into the first team and soon became a great favourite with the supporters. The diminutive Dyson's spell at Blundell Park spanned seven seasons but, with a surplus of good outside-rights, his appearances were spasmodic and it was not until the 1936-7 season that he managed to make 40 appearances, 32 of these at outside-right. He was a member of the 1933-4 championship team. A very clever ball player, he linked well with his colleagues and had a flair for goals — his total of 38 in 139 appearances was an excellent return for a winger. In 1938-9 he played a few matches for the Reserves before his transfer to Nottingham Forest in February 1939. He was then over 30 years of age and the outbreak of war ended his first-class career.

	LEAGUE		*FA CUP*		*TOTAL*	
	App	*Gls*	*App*	*Gls*	*App*	*Gls*
1931-32	8	8	0	0	8	8
1932-33	22	6	1	1	23	7
1933-34	11	3	0	0	11	3
1934-35	30	8	1	0	31	8
1935-36	15	3	0	0	15	3
1936-37	40	9	4	0	44	9
1937-38	13	1	2	0	15	1
	139	38	8	1	147	39

JIMMY DYSON

JIMMY FELL

A local lad born in Cleethorpes, Jimmy Fell was playing for local side, Waltham FC, when Town signed him on amateur forms. He signed professional terms in 1954 and was gaining valuable experience in the Reserves as he waited for his chance to fill the outside-left spot in the first team, although his football was restricted because of his National Service in the Army; Jimmy Maddison was also playing as well as ever in the number-eleven shirt. At last Fell got his chance, in February 1957, and scored on his debut. From then on he made the position his own for four more seasons until, in March 1961, he was transferred to Everton for a fee in the region of £17,000. After only 27 appearances, he moved to Newcastle United in March 1962, faring a little better with the North East club with 49 appearances. In July 1963, Walsall paid £5,000 for him and after 21 matches for them he moved to his last League club, Lincoln City, in January 1964. He played 63 matches for the Imps before joining non-League Boston United. In his professional career Jimmy Fell made 326 appearances, scoring 69 goals. Tall, direct, with a good turn of speed, he was one of Town's star finds of the 1950s. He had one special claim to fame: on 23 August 1957, the first day of the season, away to Liverpool, he had already scored a goal when Clarrie Williams was injured. Fell went in goal and played a major part in Grimsby's 3-3 draw. For his efforts he earned an 'Andy Capp,' awarded from the *Daily Mirror*, for outstanding performances in matches played the previous Saturday.

	LEAGUE		*FA CUP*		*FL CUP*		*TOTAL*	
	App	*Gls*	*App*	*Gls*	*App*	*Gls*	*App*	*Gls*
1956-57	9	2	0	0	0	0	9	2
1957-58	39	14	1	0	0	0	40	14
1958-59	41	8	3	0	0	0	44	8
1959-60	41	6	2	0	0	0	43	6
1960-61	36	5	1	0	1	0	38	5
	166	35	7	0	1	0	174	35

When Fred Fisher signed for Grimsby in the summer of 1937, he could hardly have imagined that nine years later he would still have made only one League appearance. Fisher, of course, was one of those unlucky players who lost seven seasons of normal League football because of the war. He was born in Wednesbury, Staffordshire, and as a 15-year-old showed great promise with his works team, Falling Heath FC. After Grimsby signed him, Fisher played a few games in the Reserves before making his League debut in February 1939. Military service meant that he managed only two wartime appearances for Grimsby, in 1945-6, the last season before the Football League was resumed. When peacetime football started up again, Grimsby's pre-war full-back partnership of Vincent and Hodgson was coming to an end and four matches into the 1946-7 season, Fred Fisher made his second League appearance for the Mariners. He played in both full-back positions that season and later struck up an understanding with Ken Moody. Both played well in a declining team which went from Division One to Division Three North in four seasons. In June 1951, Fisher moved to Rochdale, where he made only one appearance before going to non-League Boston United in 1952. A good tackler, strong in both full-back positions, Fisher was an asset to any team. When he retired from football he worked for an engineering firm in Cleethorpes and later ran his own driving school.

FRED FISHER

	LEAGUE		*FA CUP*		*TOTAL*	
	App	*Gls*	*App*	*Gls*	*App*	*Gls*
1938-39	1	0	0	0	1	0
1946-47	38	0	3	0	41	0
1947-48	42	0	1	0	43	0
1948-49	37	0	2	0	39	0
1949-50	35	0	2	0	37	0
1950-51	13	0	0	0	13	0
	166	0	8	0	174	0

Although he made only 22 League appearances for the Mariners, Bernard Fleming's contribution to football over a period of 30 years is immense. Born in South Bank, Middlesbrough, on 8 January 1937, he was stationed at RAF Binbrook, near Grimsby, when he came to the notice of Grimsby Town and was signed by Allenby Chilton on his demob in 1957. He was unable to command a first-team spot and in 1961 moved to Workington Town, playing 19 games in his one season there. Finally, he signed for Chester City and spent two seasons there, making 64 League appearances. For nine years he was Town's youth-team manager, during which time such distinguished Mariners as Kevin Drinkell, Kevin Moore, Tony Ford and Bobby Cumming were produced Fleming also managed the Reserves and was assistant to John Fraser in the interregnum between Ron Ashman and Tommy Casey. Some of the lads under his care found the going tough and two notable names, Paul Emson and Gary Lund, left but later returned to Blundell Park as professionals. After leaving Grimsby in 1979, Fleming spent two seasons scouting for Southampton, then managed by ex-Grimsby boss, Lawrie McMenemy. He returned to Blundell Park in a similar capacity in August 1982 and was appointed club secretary two months later. Axed in the economy drive of October 1986, Fleming returned to scouting for Southampton before being appointed secretary of Southend United in February 1987. He left Roots Hall in November of the same year and scouted for Darlington FC, maintaining the Grimsby Town link as ex-Mariner and manager Dave Booth was in charge at Feethams.

BERNARD FLEMING

	LEAGUE		*FA CUP*		*TOTAL*	
	App	*Gls*	*App*	*Gls*	*App*	*Gls*
1957-58	9	0	0	0	9	0
1958-59	8	0	0	0	8	0
1959-60	2	0	0	0	2	0
1960-61	3	0	0	0	3	0
	22	0	0	0	22	0

HARRY FLETCHER

Harry Fletcher, one of three Brummies recruited for the Mariners' first season of League football in 1892, remains, almost a century later, one of the outstanding forwards in the history of the club. He made his debut in the opening League game against Northwich Victoria and quickly established himself as a fast, tricky player with excellent ball control. With Bob Gray on the wing, he and Tommy McCairns forged a deadly partnership that reaped 153 League goals over five seasons, remarkable in view of the fact that the programme comprised only 30 games. At the end of March 1898, Fletcher was transferred to Notts County, who were struggling for First Division survival, and in the four remaining games he made a vital contribution to their achieving safety by only fractions of a goal. After two seasons with Notts, he returned to Grimsby and figured prominently the Second Division championship campaign. In 1903, he left again, this time for Fulham, and moved to Brentford the following season. In October 1905, Fletcher returned for a third spell at Blundell Park. Three years later he was appointed reserve-team manager, although he still made the occasional League appearance, his final game being against Clapton Orient on 22 January 1910. There is no doubt that in today's larger League his record would have been more impressive, but his total of 273 League appearances stood as a club record for 20 years until surpassed by Billy Marshall in September 1930.

	LEAGUE		*FA CUP*		*TOTAL*	
	App	*Gls*	*App*	*Gls*	*App*	*Gls*
1892-93	14	4	4	1	18	5
1893-94	25	14	3	3	28	17
1894-95	30	16	4	1	34	17
1895-96	30	11	7	1	37	12
1896-97	30	17	3	1	33	18
1897-98	25	11	1	0	26	11
1900-01	27	2	1	0	28	2
1901-02	20	4	2	0	22	4
1902-03	32	6	2	1	34	7
1905-06	11	1	1	0	12	1
1906-07	5	3	0	0	5	3
1907-08	21	3	5	0	26	3
1908-09	2	0	0	0	2	0
1909-10	1	0	0	0	1	0
	273	92	33	8	306	100

Tony Ford was another example of a local youngster who played a great part in the history of Grimsby Town Football Club. Born in Grimsby, he showed great promise as a schoolboy footballer. Town took him on as an apprentice in 1975 and he turned fully professional in May 1977. By then he had already made 13 senior appearances. He was the youngest player to make a full appearance for Grimsby when, aged 16 years 164 days, he turned out at Swindon Town on 25 October 1975. In two previous matches he had come on as substitute. A good utility player, Ford could play in defence, midfield or forward positions and his skill and enthusiasm for the game made him a crowd-pleaser. He made over 350 full League and Cup appearances for Grimsby, plus more than 30 appearances as substitute — an impressive record in a span of 11 seasons, during which Town were relegated in 1976-7, Fourth Division runners-up in 1978-9 and Third Division champions in 1979-80. He was voted Young Player of the Year and twice Player of the Year and was leading scorer with 16 goals in 1978-9. When Tony Ford was transferred to Stoke City in 1986, many felt that he could still have done a good job at Blundell Park. On the 1989 transfer deadline, Ford moved to West Brom for £150,000. In May 1989 he was selected for the England 'B' European tour.

TONY FORD

	LEAGUE		*FA CUP*		*FL CUP*		*TOTAL*	
	App	*Gls*	*App*	*Gls*	*App*	*Gls*	*App*	*Gls*
1975-76	11/4	0	0/1	0	0	0	11/5	0
1976-77	2/4	0	0	0	1/1	0	3/5	0
1977-78	31/3	2	1	0	0/1	0	32/4	2
1978-79	43/2	16	1	0	3	0	47/2	16
1979-80	32/5	5	3/1	0	9	4	44/6	9
1980-81	25/3	4	0/1	0	2	0	27/4	4
1981-82	25/10	7	2/1	0	0/1	0	27/12	7
1982-83	36/1	4	3	1	3	0	42/1	5
1983-84	42	8	1	0	4	0	47	8
1984-85	42	6	3	1	6	1	51	8
1985-86	32/2	3	1	0	3	0	36/2	3
	321/34	55	15/4	2	31/3	5	367/41	62

A Londoner born and bred, Ron Foster did the rounds in junior football before signing for Clapton as an amateur. He joined Leyton Orient as a professional in 1957 and helped the O's gain promotion to Division One in 1961-2 when they finished runners-up to Liverpool. In December 1962 he was transferred to Grimsby for £11,500, a fee which was then a record for the Mariners. Foster played in both the inside-forward positions, but favoured the inside-left spot. He was no great goalscorer, but a thoughtful ball player who had the knack of being in the right place at the right time, receiving and dispatching the ball with quick and deadly accuracy. In July 1966, he joined Reading for a fee of £6,000 and seemed to have settled there, but after 44 appearances he took up the challenge of playing soccer in America and in the summer of 1968 signed for Dallas Tornado. After a short spell in the States, Foster came back to play for Brentford, but made only three appearances before he retired.

	LEAGUE		*FA CUP*		*FL CUP*		*TOTAL*	
	App	*Gls*	*App*	*Gls*	*App*	*Gls*	*App*	*Gls*
1962-63	23	4	1	0	0	0	24	4
1963-64	33	4	1	0	1	0	35	4
1964-65	38	10	4	1	2	0	44	11
1965-66	35	6	6	1	5	2	46	9
	129	24	12	2	8	2	149	28

RON FOSTER

HUGHIE GALLACHER

In 1937-8, Charlie Spencer, in his first season as manager of Grimsby Town, found himself with an injury crisis. He signed a goalscoring winger in Irish international Jack Coulter from Everton, then took on the controversial Hughie Gallacher from Notts County. Gallacher's Grimsby career was shortlived, but he instilled confidence into the side and they escaped relegation. Born in Lanarkshire in 1903, he captained his school side which included Alex James and both players turned out to be soccer legends. His scoring achievements took him to Airdrieonians before he became the idol of Tyneside, captaining Newcastle to the League Championship in 1926-7. He scored 142 goals in 174 appearances for United before leaving for Chelsea and such was his popularity on Tyneside that 68,000 packed into St James' Park — with an estimated 10,000 locked out — to see his return. Married at 17 and divorced at 23, when he signed for Derby County in November in 1934, they had to pay off his debts. But he was still a fine footballer and by now had made 19 appearances for Scotland, scoring 22 goals. In September 1936 he signed for Notts County, then for Grimsby in January 1938. Gallacher stood only 5ft 6ins tall, was stockily built and a fine goalscorer. His only weakness was a fiery temper. He had many verbal battles with spectators and his private life hit the headlines as much as footballing achievements. He scored 18 goals in 31 appearances for Gateshead before retiring during World War Two. In June 1957, aged 54, he died under an express train at Dead Man's Crossing, Gateshead, while awaiting trial on a charge of ill-treating his son.

	LEAGUE		*FA CUP*		*TOTAL*	
	App	*Gls*	*App*	*Gls*	*App*	*Gls*
1937-38	12	3	0	0	12	3
	12	3	0	0	12	3

Wilf Gillow was born in Preston on 8 July 1892 and joined Lancaster in the West Lancashire League when he was 15, remaining there until that club disbanded during 1910-11. He was briefly on Preston North End's books, without making a League appearance, and spent a season with Fleetwood before joining Blackpool in 1912. Over two seasons he made 26 League appearances, scoring four goals. In 1914 he returned to Deepdale, making three appearances and scoring one goal before war intervened. Gillow appeared briefly for Preston during the 1918-19 wartime season and on the resumption of League football made another four appearances before moving to Blundell Park as a player in February 1920. Over the next two and a half seasons he made 80 appearances, mostly at right-half, scoring two goals. In 1922 he returned to the re-formed Lancaster club but remained there for only one season before returning to Blundell Park. After a further season as a player he was appointed player-manager, in June 1924, but played his last game on 1 January 1925, having notched up a further 23 League appearances, scoring three goals. He was a skilful player who admired such talents in the players who were later under him as a manager.

WILF GILLOW

	LEAGUE		*FA CUP*		*TOTAL*	
	App	*Gls*	*App*	*Gls*	*App*	*Gls*
1919-20	14	0	0	0	14	0
1920-21	35	0	3	0	38	0
1921-22	31	2	2	0	33	2
1923-24	17	3	0	0	17	3
1924-25	6	0	0	0	6	0
	103	5	5	0	108	5

When older supporters talk about Grimsby's fine centre-forwards, they generally agree that Ernest Matthew 'Pat' Glover was the greatest. Born in Swansea in 1910, he played in Swansea Town's 'A' team before going to Grimsby on trial in 1928. He was homesick but Town talked him out of returning to Wales and signed him in December 1928. Glover soon made his mark as a goalscorer in the Reserves but, with players like Joe Robson and Tim Coleman on the books, he had to wait for regular first-team football. Indeed, he was awarded his first Welsh cap, against Scotland in October 1931, after only 11 League appearances. His 71 goals in 49 games in 1929-30 remains a Midland League record and, once he settled into the League side, the goals continued to flow. For Town he scored five in one match, four on five occasions and six hat-tricks. He was their top scorer for five seasons and his 42 goals in 39 appearances in the 1933-4 Second Division championship season is still a club record. He was also the League's leading scorer that season. His aggregate of 180 goals is also a Grimsby record. Tall and well-built, Glover excelled in the air and his ground control was superb. He combined well with inside-forwards, Bestall and Craven, and many thought that he deserved more than seven full Welsh caps, although they, too, are a record for a Grimsby player. In 1936-7 he scored five goals in three games to help Wales win the Home International Championship. Following the 1939 FA Cup semi-final in which George Moulson had been injured and with George Tweedy ill, the Mariners found themselves without an experienced goalkeeper; on 29 March 1939, Glover kept goal in a First Division match at Charlton which the Mariners lost 3-1. Dogged by a serious knee injury, he left Blundell Park for Plymouth Argyle in May 1939 and retired from football during the war. He became licensee at the King's Arms, in the Devon village of Tamerton Foilot, but illness and near blindness forced him to retire. He died in 1971.

PAT GLOVER

	LEAGUE		*FA CUP*		*TOTAL*	
	App	*Gls*	*App*	*Gls*	*App*	*Gls*
1929-30	1	0	0	0	1	0
1930-31	3	2	1	0	4	2
1931-32	20	12	1	4	21	16
1932-33	32	22	2	2	34	24
1933-34	39	42	2	1	41	43
1934-35	42	34	1	2	43	36
1935-36	34	31	6	4	40	35
1936-37	40	29	4	4	44	33
1937-38	7	4	0	0	7	4
1938-39	9	4	1	0	10	4
	227	180	18	17	245	197

Stewart Gray signed professional forms for his local club, Doncaster Rovers, in September 1968. He joined Grimsby in September 1970, after making 53 appearances for Doncaster, and went straight into the Town defence. He was one of the key figures in the promotion side of 1971-2, being an ever-present that campaign. A consistent performer throughout his seven seasons at Blundell Park, Gray made 299 League and Cup appearances. A good defender, his cool approach got the defence out of many a tricky situation. Never shirking a tackle, his accurate passing of a ball was a feature of his game. He played under five managers and his place was always assured. He was substitute for the first team only once. No-one could criticize his work-rate or his enthusiasm for the game. When he left Grimsby in March 1978, he returned to Doncaster, for whom he made a further six appearances.

STEWART GRAY

	LEAGUE		*FA CUP*		*FL CUP*		*TOTAL*	
	App	*Gls*	*App*	*Gls*	*App*	*Gls*	*App*	*Gls*
1970-71	41	0	1	0	0	0	42	0
1971-72	46	1	1	0	6	1	53	2
1972-73	45	1	6	0	3	0	54	1
1973-74	30	0	4	0	4	0	38	0
1974-75	30/1	0	3	0	1	0	34/1	0
1975-76	40	0	1	0	2	0	43	0
1976-77	31	0	3	1	1	0	35	1
	263/1	2	19	1	17	1	299/1	4

ALEC 'GINGER' HALL

	LEAGUE		*FA CUP*		*TOTAL*	
	App	*Gls*	*App*	*Gls*	*App*	*Gls*
1929-30	6	0	0	0	6	0
1930-31	34	0	1	0	35	0
1931-32	21	1	3	0	24	1
1932-33	32	1	2	0	34	1
1933-34	42	0	2	0	44	0
1934-35	42	0	1	0	43	0
1935-36	42	0	6	0	48	0
1936-37	38	0	4	0	42	0
1937-38	38	1	1	0	39	1
1938-39	42	1	7	0	49	1
1945-46	0	0	1	0	1	0
1946-47	20	0	3	0	23	0
1947-48	1	0	0	0	1	0
	358	4	31	0	389	4

It is remarkable that, despite being a member of Town's great half-back line of the 1930s, Alec 'Ginger' Hall was never a full-time professional. He pursued his trade as a joiner during the day and cycled to the ground for training during the evening. A Grimbarian by birth, he rose through schools football, playing for Grimsby Boys when the town boasted one of the leading junior sides in the country. The Mariners signed him from Cleethorpes Town in the summer of 1929 and after a short 'apprenticeship' in the 'A' team, he made his League debut towards the close of the 1929-30 season, appearing in a 4-2 win at Goodison Park on 12 April. Despite his fiercely competitive style, he missed very few games. Indeed, between 1933 and 1936 he was ever-present for three seasons. Hall succeeded Jackie Bestall as captain, always leading by example, and would have made more appearances had it not been for the war. He made 175 war league appearances and was the club's most consistent player during this period. On the resumption of normal League football, Hall continued for one more season before going to play in Canada, along with his wartime colleague, Joe Rodi, before retiring to his home town. It is surprising that he never appeared for his country, because he was undoubtedly one of the finest half-backs in the game. Had he wished he could have signed for a bigger club, yet was content to pursue his career as a 'chippy' and looked upon his football as a paid hobby.

MIKE HICKMAN

Mike Hickman was a player's player, always giving a 100 per cent plus, which also made him popular with the supporters. Born in Surrey just after World War Two, he went from junior football to Brighton & Hove Albion, where he signed as a professional in 1965. After only 12 appearances for Brighton he was transferred to Grimsby Town, along with full-back John Duncliffe, in June 1968. Both went straight into the first team at the beginning of the 1968-9 campaign but it turned out to be a bad season for Town. They had to seek re-election after their lowest-ever position in the Football League. Hickman, though, recovered from the experience to make 40 appearances in the championship season of 1971-2. A tireless worker, he could play in defence, in midfield and as a striker. He never gave up chasing, which was a testimony to his fitness. In February 1975 he moved to Blackburn Rovers for a fee of £10,000 and helped them to the Third Division championship. He did not settle at Blackburn, however, and only made 23 appearances before he was transferred to Torquay United in October 1975, for £2,000. Hickman stayed with them until 1977 and was later trainer at Plainmoor. Whatever weaknesses Mike Hickman might have possessed in terms of skill were outweighed by his tremendous work-rate and professional approach to the game.

	LEAGUE		*FA CUP*		*FL CUP*		*TOTAL*	
	App	*Gls*	*App*	*Gls*	*App*	*Gls*	*App*	*Gls*
1968-69	38/2	3	1	0	3	2	42/2	5
1969-70	42	13	1	0	0	0	43	13
1970-71	39	4	1	0	1	1	41	5
1971-72	40/2	13	1	0	5	0	46/2	13
1972-73	36	6	6	1	3	0	45	7
1973-74	40	9	3	2	4	0	47	11
1974-75	12/3	0	1	0	1	0	14/3	0
	247/7	48	14	3	17	3	278/7	54

With more than 200 League and Cup appearances for Grimsby, Brian Hill was one of the stars of the 1960s. Born in Mansfield during the war, he was playing for Ollerton Colliery when Town discovered him. Tim Ward signed him as a part-time professional in July 1960 and he turned full professional the following season. With Jimmy Fell, then Freddie Jones holding the outside-left position, Hill's appearances were limited to three in his first two seasons with the Mariners. Once established, however, he retained his place for the next four seasons. Of slim build, he was very fast with good ball control. He was confident and gave plenty of right-backs the runaround, laying on many goals with his accurate centres. He was not a great goalscorer but one memory endures — a hat-trick against neighbours Scunthorpe United, when Town beat them 7-1 at Blundell Park on 7 September 1966. The goalkeeper was future England international Ray Clemence. Rod Green also got a hat-trick in that match, with Matt Tees getting the odd one. Brian Hill's performance that evening impressed several club scouts and after nine more matches in the Town side, he went to Huddersfield, for a fee of £20,000, in November 1966. He played 84 League matches for the Yorkshire club before joining Blackburn Rovers for £30,000 in June 1969. In two seasons at Ewood Park sciatic nerve trouble limited his League appearances to 34 games. In July 1971 he moved to Torquay but after a season at Plainmoor retired from League football. Hill later became player-manager to Market Rasen in the Lincolnshire League, then moved to the Caistor area to play in local soccer. In the late 1980s he was still showing his skills and enjoying his football, not as the dashing winger of the 1960s but in a midfield role.

BRIAN HILL

	LEAGUE		*FA CUP*		*FL CUP*		*TOTAL*	
	App	*Gls*	*App*	*Gls*	*App*	*Gls*	*App*	*Gls*
1960-61	2	1	0	0	0	0	2	1
1961-62	1	0	0	0	0	0	1	0
1962-63	37	3	1	0	1	0	39	3
1963-64	37	5	1	0	0	0	38	5
1964-65	46	4	4	0	2	0	52	4
1965-66	44	7	6	0	5	0	55	7
1966-67	13	6	0	0	5	2	18	8
	180	26	12	0	13	2	205	28

Born at Seaham Harbour, County Durham, just before World War One, Jack Hodgson was playing for Seaham Colliery Welfare when Hartlepool United offered him a trial. Hartlepool did not take him on but Grimsby had no reservations and signed him in January 1932. Standing 6ft 2ins and weighing more than 13st, Hodgson could play at both left and right-back or centre-half. With Hughie Jacobson still first-choice left-back, it was not until 1935-6 that he established himself, playing regularly until the first half of 1947-8. He played in both Town's FA Cup semi-finals, turning out at centre-half against Arsenal in 1936, when Harry Betmead was suspended; in 1939, against Wolves. He went in goal after only 20 minutes when George Moulson was injured and Town eventually lost 5-0. During the war he combined service in the fire brigade with soccer and made more than 200 appearances for the Mariners. With right-back Ned Vincent he forged a fine partnership. Hodgson moved to Doncaster in January 1948 and made 96 appearances for them, winning a Third Division North championship medal before retiring in the 1952 close season. Hodgson proved a good left-back for Grimsby yet, had it not been for the presence of Harry Betmead, he would have been their regular centre-half. He returned to Doncaster for a brief spell in 1958, as manager. His brother, Sam, teamed up with him during the war and in the first two post-war seasons. Jack's son, Brian, made seven appearances for Grimsby in 1956-7. Jack Hodgson died suddenly on 21 June 1970, while playing golf at Louth, Lincolnshire, He was 57.

JACK HODGSON

	LEAGUE		*FA CUP*		*TOTAL*	
	App	*Gls*	*App*	*Gls*	*App*	*Gls*
1932-33	5	0	0	0	5	0
1933-34	0	0	0	0	0	0
1934-35	16	0	1	0	17	0
1935-36	38	0	6	0	44	0
1936-37	37	0	4	0	41	0
1937-38	41	1	2	0	43	1
1938-39	41	1	7	0	48	1
1945-46	0	0	2	0	2	0
1946-47	18	0	0	0	18	0
1947-48	16	0	0	0	16	0
	212	2	22	0	234	2

MAX HOLMES

	LEAGUE		*FA CUP*		*TOTAL*	
	App	*Gls*	*App*	*Gls*	*App*	*Gls*
1931-32	8	7	0	0	8	7
1932-33	9	2	0	0	9	2
1933-34	16	7	2	0	18	7
1934-35	4	1	0	0	4	1
	37	17	2	0	39	17

Max Holmes was born in Pinchbeck, near Spalding, Lincolnshire. From schoolboy football he joined Spalding United before signing for Grimsby during 1931-2. A winger or centre-forward, he also figured at inside-left but never enjoyed an extended run in the first team, despite always giving 100 per cent and scoring some valuable goals. He was a member of the championship side of 1933-4 and of the team which finished fifth in Division One — Town's highest-ever final League position — the following season. His most memorable game was near the end of the 1931-2 season when he scored a hat-trick from centre-forward as Town won 6-5 at West Bromwich Albion. Outside-right Jimmy Dyson got the other three but the win did not prevent Town being relegated to Division Two. Holmes, who was fast and tricky with a strong shot, joined Hull City in May 1935 and went on to Mansfield Town in 1937, where he was converted to a half-back. His last League club was Lincoln, whom he joined in 1938. A teacher by profession, he opened a sports shop just after the war. He was an all-round sportsman, playing Minor Counties cricket for Lincolnshire and Rugby Union for Midland Counties. Now into his 80s, he likes to work in his garden and still enjoys a round of golf.

PHIL HUBBARD

Phil Hubbard gave Grimsby Town excellent service, averaging about 41 appearances for each of his four seasons with the club. He went to Blundell Park as a striker, later moved to midfield and developed into a good utility player. Born at Lincoln, he played for Lincoln Boys. After leaving school he became a trainee pork butcher and played local football. Lincoln City, Scunthorpe United and Grimsby Town began to take notice and Lincoln offered him a trial game in which he scored seven goals; not surprisingly, they immediately signed him as an apprentice professional. Hubbard was in and out of the first team, playing in several different positions before settling at full-back, where he made over 100 consecutive appearances. Then he switched to midfield, began scoring goals and soon the big clubs were watching him. In December 1971, Hubbard signed for Norwich for £22,000, making six appearances for the Canaries in their Second Division championship season. He did not manage a full game for Norwich in the First Division and Town secured his services in October 1972, for £20,000. He stayed with Grimsby until August 1976, when he rejoined Lincoln City and made a further 100 appearances for them. Always a popular player, Hubbard's overall League tally was 400 appearances and 90 goals. He was substitute only 16 times.

	LEAGUE		*FA CUP*		*FL CUP*		*TOTAL*	
	App	*Gls*	*App*	*Gls*	*App*	*Gls*	*App*	*Gls*
1972-73	29/1	10	5	0	0	0	34/1	10
1973-74	41	10	3/1	1	4	0	48/1	11
1974-75	43	11	3	0	1	0	47	11
1975-76	31/1	6	1	0	2	0	34/1	6
	144/2	37	12/1	1	7	0	163/3	38

Hughie Jacobson holds the unique honour of being a member of all three of the Mariners' promotion squads between the two wars. Another of the many Tynesiders to find their way to Blundell Park, he started his career with Blyth Spartans and joined Grimsby in May of 1925, for the token transfer fee of £25, making his debut in the opening game of the 1925-6 season, at home to Doncaster Rovers. Over the next ten seasons he virtually monopolized the left-back position, averaging 36 appearances a season. For eight of them, he was partnered by the redoubtable Charlie Wilson. During their first season together, usually with John Archibald in goal, Town conceded only eight goals in 20 matches at Blundell Park and dropped only one point at home. Thus, despite Town's moderate away performance, Jacobson won his first medal as the club took the Third Division North title. Three seasons later he was ever-present in the side that finished Second Division runners-up and, after they returned to Division Two three years later, he won further honours in 1933-4 when he was again an ever-present, winning another championship medal as the Mariners started the glory days of the mid and late-1930s. It was a great surprise to many when he was released after only one more season in the top flight. He played out his career with Doncaster Rovers, retiring at the close of 1934-5. In 1946 he returned to Blundell Park as reserve-team trainer, a post he held for nine seasons. An uncompromising, clean-kicking full-back, who gave a hard time to many of the game's top wingers, Hughie Jacobson's contribution to Town's rise to the top flight cannot be exaggerated. One of his last visits to Blundell Park was to watch his beloved Mariners meet the club where it all started, Blyth Spartans, in an FA Cup match in November 1973.

HUGHIE JACOBSON

	LEAGUE		*FA CUP*		*TOTAL*	
	App	*Gls*	*App*	*Gls*	*App*	*Gls*
1925-26	34	0	4	0	38	0
1926-27	31	1	3	0	34	1
1927-28	37	0	1	0	38	0
1928-29	42	0	2	0	44	0
1929-30	37	0	2	0	39	0
1930-31	40	0	3	0	43	0
1931-32	40	0	3	0	43	0
1932-33	35	0	2	0	37	0
1933-34	42	0	2	0	44	0
1934-35	22	0	0	0	22	0
	360	1	22	0	382	1

On 14 December 1968, Keith Jobling took his place at left-half in Town's line-up at Saltergate and made his 428th League appearance for the Mariners, beating Jackie Bestall's 427, which Bestall completed in 1937-8. Jobling went on to total 450 League games for the club (not 448 as many record books state). Born in Grimsby in 1934, he went from schools football to play in the local league with New Waltham. He signed amateur forms for the Mariners in 1952 and turned professional in 1953, although it was five seasons before he gained a regular first-team place. Although Jobling did not make an appearance during the 1955-6 Third Division North championship season, he was ever-present when Town finished Third Division runners-up in 1961-2. Standing nearly 6ft tall and weighing over 11st, he played either at wing-half or centre-half. A consistent player and a loyal clubman, Jobling spent his entire League career at Blundell Park before signing for Boston United at the end of 1968-9. His outstanding record seems likely to stand for a long time. Jobling, an upholsterer by trade, went into business in Grimsby.

KEITH JOBLING

	LEAGUE		*FA CUP*		*FL CUP*		*TOTAL*	
	App	*Gls*	*App*	*Gls*	*App*	*Gls*	*App*	*Gls*
1953-54	9	0	0	0	0	0	9	0
1954-55	6	0	1	0	0	0	7	0
1955-56	0	0	0	0	0	0	0	0
1956-57	6	0	0	0	0	0	6	0
1957-58	13	0	0	0	0	0	13	0
1958-59	42	0	3	0	0	0	45	0
1959-60	42	0	2	0	0	0	44	0
1960-61	36	1	1	0	1	0	38	1
1961-62	46	0	1	0	1	0	48	0
1962-63	41	1	1	0	1	0	43	1
1963-64	41	0	1	0	1	0	43	0
1964-65	46	2	4	0	2	0	52	2
1965-66	42	0	6	0	5	0	53	0
1966-67	21	1	2	0	4	0	27	1
1967-68	18	0	1	0	0	0	19	0
1968-69	41	0	1	0	4	0	46	0
	450	5	24	0	19	0	493	5

One of the Mariners' best post-war signings, wing-half Pat Johnston went to Grimsby Town as a replacement for Norman Robinson. In June 1948, Robinson had been transferred from Middlesbrough but was found to have an injury which ended his career. Town approached Middlesbrough for compensation and the Ayresome Park club sold them Johnston for a small fee; he turned out to be a more than adequate replacement. Born in Dublin, Johnston first played for Shelbourne before moving to Middlesbrough in December 1947. At that time, 'Boro had a fine side and Johnston made only three appearances, although he had already represented the League of Ireland against the Irish League and the Football League in 1947. Unfortunately, in the relegation season of 1950-51 he missed a lot of matches for Town through injury. He also missed a few matches in the 1955-6 championship season, when Town returned to Division Two. While with Grimsby, he represented the Football League. Very cool under pressure, Johnston's close marking did not give the opposition much room to perform. He was also a good penalty taker. When he left Grimsby, he signed for Skegness Town. He was married to Brenda Fisher, a famous Channel swimmer who lived in Grimsby. Pat Johnston, who worked for the Ross Group, died suddenly in 1971.

'PAT' JOHNSTON

	LEAGUE		*FA CUP*		*TOTAL*	
	App	*Gls*	*App*	*Gls*	*App*	*Gls*
1948-49	16	0	0	0	16	0
1949-50	42	1	2	0	44	1
1950-51	9	0	0	0	9	0
1951-52	45	8	2	0	47	8
1952-53	40	6	3	2	43	8
1953-54	24	0	1	0	25	0
1954-55	29	0	2	0	31	0
1955-56	18	0	0	0	18	0
1956-57	27	1	1	0	28	1
	250	16	11	2	261	18

Brian Keeble was born in Holbeach just before World War Two and played for Holbeach United before Town took him on amateur forms. He turned full professional in May 1959 and could play in either of the full-back positions, although left-back was the one he favoured during his six seasons with Grimsby Town. A good, reliable defender, he was in the Division Two promotion side in 1961-2, making maximum appearances. Proof of his consistency was the number of his appearances for his two League clubs: — 172 games for Grimsby and 154 for Darlington, whom he joined in July 1965. He stayed at Feethams until 1968, joining non-League Boston United in 1969.

	LEAGUE		*FA CUP*		*FL CUP*		*TOTAL*	
	App	*Gls*	*App*	*Gls*	*App*	*Gls*	*App*	*Gls*
1959-60	34	0	2	0	0	0	36	0
1960-61	43	0	1	0	1	0	45	0
1961-62	46	1	1	0	1	0	48	1
1962-63	24	0	1	0	1	0	26	0
1963-64	10	0	0	0	0	0	10	0
1964-65	15	0	0	0	1	0	16	0
	172	1	5	0	4	0	181	1

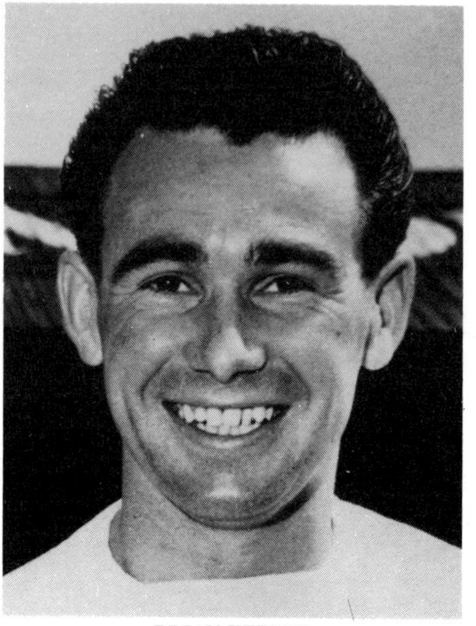

BRIAN KEEBLE

JIM KELLY

	LEAGUE		*FA CUP*		*TOTAL*	
	App	*Gls*	*App*	*Gls*	*App*	*Gls*
1932-33	10	0	0	0	10	0
1933-34	42	3	2	0	44	3
1934-35	33	0	1	0	34	0
1935-36	28	0	6	0	34	0
1936-37	39	0	4	0	33	0
1937-38	8	0	1	0	9	0
	160	3	14	0	174	3

James Kelly was born at Seaham Harbour, County Durham, in 1907. His early footballing days were spent with colliery teams, Dawdon and Murton, before he joined Southport in 1928. Kelly made only seven appearances before moving to Barrow in the close season of 1931 and Town signed him in March 1933, just before the transfer deadline. He went straight into the first team at right-back, playing in the last ten matches that season, in which Town were unbeaten. The following season, 1933-4, he was one of seven Town players who were ever-present and he scored three goals (all penalties), helping Town to the Second Division title. He was in the team that lost 1-0 to Arsenal in the 1936 FA Cup semi-final. Kelly could play on either flank and his full-back partners were Jacobson, Hodgson and Vincent, who all came from the North-East. Stockily built, with a strong kick, he made 14 FA Cup appearances out of a possible 15. The 1937-8 season was his last with Grimsby, when he made only eight first-team appearances and 13 for the Reserves. He moved to Bradford in May 1938, but made only two appearances. During the war he served in the Army Physical Training Corps and guested for Bournemouth and Aldershot. When peace was restored he took a coaching post in Norway, but returned to Barrow and made one Third Division North appearance for them in 1946-7. Kelly spent his summers coaching Freidig Club and Trondheim in Norway, from 1956 to 1967 while he was on the training staff at Oldham. He resumed his Grimsby connections by scouting for them in later years. Jimmy Kelly died at Southport in July 1984.

Bobby Kennedy, who was appointed Grimsby Town player-manager in March 1969, had a fine pedigree as a player. Born in Motherwell, Kennedy started his career with Coltness United and then Kilmarnock, overcoming a serious illness to play in two Scottish Cup Finals, a Scottish League Cup Final and win a Scottish League Championship runners-up medal before moving to Manchester City in 1961. A Scottish Under-23 international, he cost City £45,000 — then a record for a wing-half and also a record for a player moving between Scottish and English clubs — but repaid them with 216 full League appearances during his eight years with the Maine Road club. He was unlucky to play for them at a particularly bad time in their history, although he did help City back to Division One in 1965-6, when he had been converted to full-back, and appeared in European football. When City won the League Championship in 1967-8, Kennedy did not make enough appearances to qualify for a medal but he was still valued by manager Joe Mercer, who thought long and hard before allowing him to go to Grimsby.

	LEAGUE		*FA CUP*		*FL CUP*		*TOTAL*	
	App	*Gls*	*App*	*Gls*	*App*	*Gls*	*App*	*Gls*
1968-69	9	1	0	0	0	0	9	1
1969-70	42	0	1	0	1	0	44	0
1970-71	33	0	1	0	1	0	35	0
	84	1	2	0	2	0	88	1

BOBBY KENNEDY

Utility player, super sub, 'over-age' international — Jack Lewis fitted all three categories. During his eight seasons with Grimsby Town, he played in six different positions, was substitute on 27 occasions and was an over-age player in the Welsh Under-23 side. Although born at Long Eaton, Derbyshire, he was eligible to play for Wales by reason of parentage. He joined the Mariners from Lincoln City in January 1970, for £3,000 after making 47 appearances for the Imps, and at Blundell Park he was a member of the 1971-2 championship side. A loyal clubman, Jack Lewis always gave 100 per cent and his selection for the Welsh Under-23 team was just reward. It was regrettable that he never won a full cap and his other disappointment must have been Town's relegation season of 1976-7, when they went back to Division Four. He left Grimsby Town in August 1977, to join Blackburn Rovers, but after only 24 matches, moved to Doncaster Rovers in August 1978. Lewis made 48 appearances for Rovers, staying with them until 1980. On his first return to Blundell Park, he scored a hat-trick in Doncaster's 4-3 win. This was the last home match of the season but Town were still promoted, whilst Doncaster had to seek re-election. Jack Lewis was only 5ft 8ins tall and weighed 10½st, but was still a successful striker. His overall League tally was 99 goals from 350 appearances. He was substitute on 62 occasions.

	LEAGUE		*FA CUP*		*FL CUP*		*TOTAL*	
	App	*Gls*	*App*	*Gls*	*App*	*Gls*	*App*	*Gls*
1969-70	19	4	0	0	0	0	19	4
1970-71	19/3	7	0	0	1	0	20/3	7
1971-72	24/3	4	1	0	4	1	29/3	5
1972-73	20/14	2	0/3	0	3	0	23/17	2
1973-74	30/6	13	1/1	0	0/3	0	31/10	13
1974-75	41	21	3	1	1	0	45	22
1975-76	44	15	1	0	1	0	46	15
1976-77	34/1	8	2/1	1	2	0	38/2	9
	231/27	74	8/5	2	12/3	1	251/35	77

JACK LEWIS

Stan Lloyd won three England Schoolboy caps in 1937. Born in West Auckland, he went from East Durham schools junior football to Sunderland during World War Two and after the war made 24 appearances for the Wearsiders before signing for Grimsby in August 1948, for £6,000. A utility player, in his first season with Town he played in all the forward positions except centre-forward. Small and light, he was not as fast as some Grimsby wingers, but he was a very thoughtful player, a deceptive dribbler who fed his inside-forward trio with a stream of accurate passes. Not a great goalscorer, he made many for his colleagues. In five seasons with the Mariners, he made 102 of his 148 League appearances on the right wing. In the close season of 1953, he signed for non-League Worksop Town but in July 1954 was tempted back to League football with Scunthorpe United. He was at the Old Show Ground for one season, making only one senior appearance and playing 27 reserve games before leaving the scene.

	LEAGUE		*FA CUP*		*TOTAL*	
	App	*Gls*	*App*	*Gls*	*App*	*Gls*
1948-49	33	8	2	0	35	8
1949-50	32	4	0	0	32	4
1950-51	26	5	2	0	28	5
1951-52	32	3	0	0	32	3
1952-53	25	3	1	0	26	3
	148	23	5	0	153	23

STAN LLOYD

TOMMY McCAIRNS

On 11 April 1896, Tommy McCairns went into Grimsby Town's record books when he scored six goals in the 7-1 home win over Leicester Fosse, in the last League match of the season. The record still stands for a League match for Grimsby. McCairns was a remarkably prolific scorer and in five seasons with the Mariners, he netted 104 goals in 154 League and Cup games. Born at Dinsdale, near Darlington, in 1873, he played for Middlesbrough Ironopolis and Whitby before his move to Grimsby in September 1893. He was very skilful, had a good shot and the knack of being in the right place at the right time. He was selected for the Football League against the Irish League in 1896 — his only honour. McCairns was a much-travelled player and after he left Grimsby he played for eight clubs in six seasons. In the close season of 1898 he went to Bristol Rovers, to Notts County in May 1899 and back to Lincolnshire in November 1899 to play for Lincoln City. Barnsley was his next move in August 1901; Wellingborough in May 1902; Queen's Park Rangers in the summer of 1903; Brighton in December 1903 and Kettering in 1904. Tommy McCairns died in 1932.

	LEAGUE		*FA CUP*		*TOTAL*	
	App	*Gls*	*App*	*Gls*	*App*	*Gls*
1893-94	25	18	5	9	30	27
1894-95	26	18	1	0	27	18
1895-96	28	26	7	8	35	34
1896-97	29	15	3	1	32	16
1897-98	29	9	1	0	30	9
	137	86	17	18	154	104

George Tweedy was Grimsby Town's caretaker manager when he signed Jimmy Maddison from Darlington for a bargain fee of £500. Born in South Shields, Maddison went from junior football to Middlesbrough during World War Two. He was still with Middlesbrough when normal League football was resumed after the war, but had played only one League match for them before moving to nearby Darlington in August 1949. Maddison made 41 appearances there before Tweedy snapped him up in June 1950. He joined Town when they were having a bad spell and it was no fault of his that they were relegated from Division Two at the end of 1950-51. Town had already had three good left-wingers in post-war football: Billy Wardle (1939-48), Billy Pearson (1944-49) and George Hair (1949-51). Wardle and Hair also came from the North-East. Jimmy Maddison became the fourth, once Bill Shankly had taken over, and he made all his 272 League and 19 FA Cup appearances in the number-11 shirt. Slightly built, but with fine ball control, his runs down the left wing and his passes were timed to perfection. A good dribbler, he was more a goal-maker than a goalscorer. Despite some rough treatment from defenders, he never retaliated and was hardly ever spoken to by the referee. He was one of the most popular players Town had in the post-war period but missed a few matches after a cartilage operation in 1951-2. Maddison was a member of the 1954-5 side that had to seek re-election but was also in the history-making team that won the Third Division North title the following season. With the arrival of Jimmy Fell, Maddison's first-team appearances were limited to five in his last two seasons and in March 1959 he joined Chesterfield for £1,500. He made 98 appearances for Chesterfield before moving to non-League Cambridge City in the close season of 1961. A joiner by trade, Maddison settled in Cleethorpes for a while before returning to his native North-East, where he still lives. He had a joint benefit match with Pat Johnston on 3 May 1955, when Town played an All Star XI.

JIMMY MADDISON

	LEAGUE		*FA CUP*		*TOTAL*	
	App	*Gls*	*App*	*Gls*	*App*	*Gls*
1950-51	25	2	2	0	27	2
1951-52	36	9	1	0	37	9
1952-53	44	5	3	0	47	5
1953-54	46	5	5	2	51	7
1954-55	39	4	3	1	42	5
1955-56	44	7	4	1	48	8
1956-57	33	8	1	0	34	8
1957-58	3	0	0	0	3	0
1958-59	2	0	0	0	2	0
	272	40	19	4	291	44

BILLY MARSHALL

When Grimsby Town signed Billy Marshall from Chesterfield in July 1923, they got a quality left-winger who was to grace the Blundell Park scene for nine seasons. His speed and accuracy in crossing a ball were features of his play, giving great service to four Town centre-forwards — Carmichael, Robson and, later, Coleman and Glover. He played a vital part in the 1925-6 Third Division North championship season and also in the team that won promotion to Division Two in 1928-9. He made 326 of his 340 League appearances at outside-left. He left Grimsby for Reading in 1932, then returned to Lincolnshire to play for Boston United. After he had vacated the outside-left position at Grimsby in 1932, Town played 13 different left-wingers from then until 1938-9, which proved what a valuable asset Billy Marshall had been to the club. After his retirement from football, he settled in the Grimsby area. He died in November 1966.

	LEAGUE		*FA CUP*		*TOTAL*	
	App	*Gls*	*App*	*Gls*	*App*	*Gls*
1923-24	38	2	4	0	42	2
1924-25	39	9	1	0	40	9
1925-26	42	9	4	0	46	9
1926-27	42	2	3	1	45	3
1927-28	33	8	1	0	34	8
1928-29	34	5	2	0	36	5
1929-30	38	9	2	0	40	9
1930-31	41	10	3	2	44	12
1931-32	33	6	3	0	36	6
	340	60	23	3	363	63

Ken Moody joined the Mariners in 1943 from local side, Humber United. He managed only a few wartime appearances for Town because he was in the services, but he made guest appearances for Arsenal. A strong, reliable right-back, Moody was with Grimsby for four post-war seasons. The Mariners were going through a lean spell and were relegated twice during his stay, from Division One in 1947-8 and from Division Two in 1950-51. He struck up a good partnership with Freddie Fisher, who had also lost a lot of his League football career because of the war. In the close season of 1951, Moody joined Peterborough, then in the Midland League. He later played for Skegness Town in the Central Alliance. He stood 5ft 8ins, weighing over 12st and was a very reliable full-back with the ability to turn defence into attack with a simple pass or a long ball along the wing. When Moody's footballing days were finished, he settled in the area and was a baker in the family business.

	LEAGUE		*FA CUP*		*TOTAL*	
	App	*Gls*	*App*	*Gls*	*App*	*Gls*
1947-48	10	0	0	0	10	0
1948-49	40	0	2	0	42	0
1949-50	37	0	0	0	37	0
1950-51	27	0	0	0	27	0
	114	0	2	0	116	0

KEN MOODY

Grimsby Town enjoy a record, thought to be unique, of having five members of the same family play League soccer for them. Brothers Norman and Roy Moore made their debuts in 1946 and 1948 respectively, Norman later going on to score 45 goals for Hull City and Roy drifting out of League soccer. It was Roy's three sons, Kevin, Dave and Andy, who established the family name at Blundell Park. Andy Moore is the youngest and signed as an apprentice in 1982. He turned professional in November 1983 and made his League debut in a memorable 1-0 defeat of Sheffield Wednesday on Boxing Day that year, deputizing for Bob Cumming at right-back. He was in and out of the side until the start of 1984-5, when he appeared to have made the centre-back position his own, alongside brother Kevin. The arrival of Mike Lyons as player-manager, however, consigned Andy to the Reserves. After Lyons left, it was surprising that, shortly before the start of 1987-8, Andy joined the mass exodus from Blundell Park and moved to Lincoln City, who had just lost their League place. Many felt that Andy was potentially the best player of the three brothers and deserved a longer run in the first team. Although the Imps won the GM Vauxhall Conference to gain an immediate return to the League, Andy Moore's services were not retained at the end of the season. Released by the Imps on their return to the League, he was unable to fix himself up with an English club and spent the 1988-9 season with Linfield in the Irish League.

	LEAGUE		*FA CUP*		*FL CUP*		*TOTAL*	
	App	*Gls*	*App*	*Gls*	*App*	*Gls*	*App*	*Gls*
1983-84	8/1	0	0	0	0	0	8/1	0
1984-85	13	0	0	0	0	0	13	0
1985-86	31/1	1	0	0	3	0	34/1	1
1986-87	10	0	0	0	1	0	11	0
	62/2	1	0	0	4	0	66/2	1

ANDY MOORE

DAVE MOORE

Dave Moore followed his elder brother, Kevin, to Blundell Park after leaving school, joining the Mariners as an apprentice in 1976 and signing as a full-time professional a year later. He captained the youth side that won the Northern Intermediate League Challenge Cup in 1976-7 and made his Fourth Division debut at Torquay in November 1978, when he replaced the injured Shaun Mawer. He retained his place for the remainder of the season. Moore kept his place for most of the following season, thus participating in two successive promotion campaigns and winning a Third Division championship medal. In the Second Division season of 1980-81, he lost his place to John Stone but recaptured the right-back spot for most of the following season when Stone was injured. Stone never fully recovered and Moore played in that position for most games until his departure to Carlisle in the 1983 close season. His stay at Brunton Park was brief and in December he moved to Blackpool where he stayed for three years, taking part in yet another promotion campaign in 1985-6. In the winter of 1986-7, Mike Lyons took him back to Blundell Park as youth coach and he continued to make the occasional League appearance. A sturdily-built, strong-tackling defender, Dave Moore was not without his critics and often seemed to live in the shadow of his elder brother. His vital contribution in the rapid rise of the Mariners from the Fourth to the Second Division cannot, however, be denied. When Alan Buckley joined the Mariners as manager in June 1988, he chose to bring in his own coaching staff. Moore's links with the club were severed and he joined Dave Booth's growing squad of ex-Mariners at Darlington.

	LEAGUE		*FA CUP*		*FL CUP*		*TOTAL*	
	App	*Gls*	*App*	*Gls*	*App*	*Gls*	*App*	*Gls*
1978-79	30	0	1	0	0	0	31	0
1979-80	29	0	1	0	5	0	35	0
1980-81	5	0	0	0	0	0	5	0
1981-82	34	2	3	0	1	0	38	2
1982-83	38	0	3	0	3	0	44	0
1986-87	3	0	0	0	0	0	3	0
1987-88	0/1	0	1	0	0	0	1/1	0
	139/1	2	9	0	9	0	157/1	2

Schoolboy international Kevin Moore, the eldest of Town's three brothers, joined the club straight from school in 1976, as part of the talented junior squad, built up by Tommy Casey, that was to serve the club so well during the late 1970s and early 1980s. He went straight into the first team, making his senior debut in the League Cup against Sheffield Wednesday and his League debut in the opening match against Bury. He made the left-back spot his own for four seasons before switching to the centre of the defence early in 1980-81. A commanding defender and a useful scorer of goals from set pieces, Moore played a vital part in the side that, in two seasons, was to bounce back to Division Two from the humiliation of relegation to the Fourth Division and that missed the unique record of three successive promotion seasons, only by a lapse in the spring of 1981. Towards the end of the 1986-7 season, with the Mariners' fortunes on the wane, he saw his chance of First Division football declining and moved to Oldham Athletic. When Oldham missed promotion in the end-of-season play-offs, he joined his old Grimsby defensive partner, Chris Nicholl, then manager at The Dell.

KEVIN MOORE

	LEAGUE		*FA CUP*		*FL CUP*		*TOTAL*	
	App	*Gls*	*App*	*Gls*	*App*	*Gls*	*App*	*Gls*
1976-77	27/1	0	3	0	2	0	32/1	0
1977-78	41/1	0	4	0	3	0	48/1	0
1978-79	46	7	1	0	3	0	50	0
1979-80	41	4	3	1	9	0	53	5
1980-81	41	1	1	0	2	0	44	1
1981-82	36	4	3	1	2	1	41	6
1982-83	38	0	3	0	4	1	45	1
1983-84	41	1	1	0	4	0	46	1
1984-85	31	4	3	0	6	1	40	5
1985-86	30/1	2	0	0	3	0	33/1	2
1986-87	25	5	3	1	3	0	31	6
	397/3	28	25	3	41	3	463/3	34

George 'Bodge' Mountain joined Grimsby Town in the 1895-6 season but made only one appearance before leaving to go to sea. Born in Grimsby in 1874, Mountain began his career in 1889 with local side, White Star, a club many considered to be a stepping-stone towards playing for Grimsby Town. After his sojourn at sea he played for Grimsby All Saints but during the 1897-8 season, Town asked him to return. They were short of players because the directors had suspended four men *sine die* for not attending training. Besides 'Bodge', H. Robinson was also invited to play. In 1898-9, the directors made a clean sweep at the club — all the players had to go except George Mountain and John Bell. In 'Bodge' they got a loyal clubman and a solid defender. Only 5ft 6ins tall and weighing 12st, he was fearless and helped Town win the Second Division championship in 1900-01 and promotion to the First Division for the first time in the club's history. He had six good seasons with the Mariners in his second spell and the club thought so highly of him that they granted him a benefit match, although the choice of opponents — Lincoln City — was not very inspiring. The two sides had played each other many times that season and only a small crowd turned up for the match. He left Grimsby in 1903 to join Leicester Fosse but returned in 1904 to play for Grimsby Rangers. Mountain was 'mine host' at the Kings Head, Waltham, for many years, and died in 1936.

GEORGE MOUNTAIN

	LEAGUE		*FA CUP*		*TOTAL*	
	App	*Gls*	*App*	*Gls*	*App*	*Gls*
1895-96	1	0	0	0	1	0
1896-97	0	0	0	0	0	0
1897-98	16	1	1	0	17	1
1898-99	25	0	3	0	28	0
1899-1900	30	1	3	0	33	1
1900-01	26	0	1	0	27	0
1901-02	33	0	2	0	35	0
1902-03	21	2	2	0	23	2
	152	4	12	0	164	4

ALFRED NELMES

Born in Bristol, Alfred 'Happy' Nelmes started his football career in the North-East, playing first for Saltburn, then Middlesbrough (who were then an amateur side). He won two FA Amateur Cup Winners medals with Middlesbrough, in 1895 and 1898. Grimsby saw his potential and secured him on professional forms in August 1898. This was about the time that Town were building their best side since the formation of the club. Nelmes had a distinguished career with Grimsby, making more than 200 League and Cup appearances. After making his League debut at outside-left, he made the left-half position his own, except on one occasion when he played at centre-half. A reliable defender, his passing and heading were his assets. A good clubman, very popular and easy going, he was known as 'Happy'. Even 30 years later, fans were saying that he was the best left-half Town ever had. He was a member of the championship side of 1900-01, missing only two matches, and his one disappointment was being in the relegation team in 1902-03. It was a sad day in May 1906, when he left the club to join Burton United, a Second Division side. After he retired from playing he became trainer with Brighton & Hove Albion from August 1909. In 1915, he was appointed trainer at Manchester United. 'Happy' Nelmes died in February 1940.

	LEAGUE		*FA CUP*		*TOTAL*	
	App	*Gls*	*App*	*Gls*	*App*	*Gls*
1898-99	32	0	5	0	37	0
1899-1900	32	2	4	0	36	2
1900-01	32	6	1	0	33	6
1901-02	27	2	2	0	29	2
1902-03	27	2	0	0	27	2
1903-04	21	1	1	0	22	1
1904-05	21	1	1	0	22	1
1905-06	20	0	0	0	20	0
	212	14	14	0	226	14

Don O'Riordan was born in Dublin on 14 May 1957. He signed for Derby County in 1976, but made only two full first-team appearances. After two games on loan to Doncaster Rovers, he spent the summer of 1978 playing for Tulsa Roughnecks in the NASL. At the start of 1978-9, O'Riordan joined Second Division Preston, staying at Deepdale for five seasons. He made 153 full League appearances (ever-present in 1981-2) and experienced relegation with them in 1981. At the start of 1983-4 he returned to Second Division football with Carlisle United and did not miss a League match for two seasons. In 1985-6 he signed for Middlesbrough and again played in a relegated side when 'Boro dropped into Division Three. Mike Lyons persuaded him to sign for Grimsby and he was given a midfield role and made assistant manager when Terry Darracott returned to Goodison. O'Riordan's performances were one of the few highlights as Grimsby plummeted into Division Three and he then formed, with Dave Burgess, a formidable central defensive pairing. He was voted the *Sunday People's* outstanding Third Division defender, and supporters' Player of the Year with 70 per cent of the votes. Once again his performances were a beacon in another relegation season. He ran training sessions for the unemployed, worked hard in Mike Lyons' 'School of Excellence' and represented the club at functions throughout the town. When Bobby Roberts was sacked, O'Riordan seemed the natural successor but when the board looked outside the club for a manager, he moved to Notts County, the fee being decided by a tribunal.

	LEAGUE		*FA CUP*		*FL CUP*		*TOTAL*	
	App	*Gls*	*App*	*Gls*	*App*	*Gls*	*App*	*Gls*
1986-87	40	6	3	0	4	0	47	6
1987-88	46	8	3	0	2	0	51	8
	86	14	6	0	6	0	98	14

DONAL O'RIORDAN

MALCOLM PARTRIDGE

Signed by new manager Tom Casey, Malcolm Partridge made his debut for Grimsby Town in March 1975. Town looked to be heading for relegation and 'Mally' played in the last 11 matches of the season. Town were only beaten twice and, although he did not score, he made a big contribution to ensure that Grimsby retained their Division Three status. Chesterfield-born, he went to Mansfield Town as an apprentice in 1967, turning full professional in August 1968, on his 18th birthday. After 67 games for Mansfield he was transferred to Leicester City for £50,000, then went on loan to Charlton Athletic, but only played one match for them. He had played only 25 matches (seven in the Second Division championship side of 1970-71), when Town signed him. He settled in well at Blundell Park and was with the Mariners for five seasons before he joined Scunthorpe in July 1979 on a free transfer. He went on to play 91 matches for Scunthorpe before his contract was cancelled in February 1982. His last season with Town was the promotion season of 1978-9. Standing just over 6ft tall, he was equally effective in defence, midfield and attack.

	LEAGUE		*FA CUP*		*FL CUP*		*TOTAL*	
	App	*Gls*	*App*	*Gls*	*App*	*Gls*	*App*	*Gls*
1974-75	11	0	0	0	0	0	11	0
1975-76	33/1	10	1	0	2	0	36/1	10
1976-77	45/1	11	3	2	2	0	50/1	13
1977-78	38/1	4	5	0	3	0	46/1	4
1978-79	7/1	0	0	0	0	0	7/1	0
	134/4	25	9	2	7	0	150/4	27

Gordon 'Gerry' Priestley was one of Grimsby Town's star players of the 1950s. Born in Halifax, he graduated from Army football and was signed by Nottingham Forest in December 1950 but never made a first-team appearance in two and a half years at the City Ground. He was transferred to Exeter City in June 1953, making 42 appearances for the West Country club before Town signed him in June 1955. Going straight into the first team at outside-right, Priestley missed only one League match in the 1955-6 Third Division (North) championship season. A useful winger who could also play in both inside-forward positions, he possessed a good shot and could beat an opponent with speed and supply his other forwards with goalscoring opportunities. In November 1958 he moved south to play for Crystal Palace but did not settle and, after only 28 appearances, returned north to play for his home club, Halifax (a small fee was involved) in July 1960. He stayed at Halifax until 1963 and his 105 appearances for them brought his overall League and Cup appearances to more than 300. Gerry Priestley was no mean performer on the clarinet.

	LEAGUE		*FA CUP*		*TOTAL*	
	App	*Gls*	*App*	*Gls*	*App*	*Gls*
1955-56	45	4	4	1	49	5
1956-57	27	1	1	1	28	2
1957-58	30	6	1	0	31	6
1958-59	8	0	0	0	8	0
	110	11	6	2	116	13

GERRY PRIESTLEY

JOHN PRIESTLEY

Born in Johnstone, Renfrewshire, in 1900, 'Jock' Priestley was a seasoned campaigner when he arrived at Blundell Park, having made around 200 appearances for Chelsea. He signed for Town, who like Chelsea were in Division Two, in the close season of 1928. He could play at centre-half or right-half and it was in the latter position that he made his Grimsby debut on 25 August 1928. At 5ft 8ins and nearly 11st, he took some knocking off the ball and was an ideal wing-half, strong in the tackle and tenacious. He was a member of the 1928-9 promotion side which finished second to Middlesbrough. Unlike his first season with Grimsby, his fourth (and last) was in the other extreme, the club being relegated in 1931-2. In August 1932 he was invited to play on the Continent by a French club but declined and returned to his native Scotland with St Johnstone. In 1933 he joined Cowdenbeath. John Priestley died in 1980.

	LEAGUE		*FA CUP*		*TOTAL*	
	App	*Gls*	*App*	*Gls*	*App*	*Gls*
1928-29	36	1	0	0	36	1
1929-30	41	1	2	0	43	1
1930-31	36	2	2	0	38	2
1931-32	26	3	3	0	29	3
	139	7	7	0	146	7

Born in Northumberland in 1904, Jack Prior played for Blyth Spartans before moving to Sunderland in 1923 for a fee of £250. In February 1927 he moved, with Steve Coglin, to Grimsby Town. Prior was one of the 'old school' of wingers, very speedy and could pass a ball with accuracy. He had six good seasons with the Mariners and was a member of the 1928-9 promotion side. He stayed a season longer than his ex-Sunderland colleague, Coglin, before non-League Ashington paid £350 for his services in September 1932. He was at Ashington for a only a month before returning to League football with Mansfield Town in Division Three North. In the close season of 1933 he went back into non-League football with Stalybridge Celtic. Jack Prior died in 1982.

	LEAGUE		*FA CUP*		*TOTAL*	
	App	*Gls*	*App*	*Gls*	*App*	*Gls*
1926-27	17	5	0	0	17	5
1927-28	29	7	0	0	31	7
1928-29	36	4	2	0	38	4
1929-30	26	3	2	1	28	4
1930-31	30	12	3	1	33	13
1931-32	22	3	1	0	23	3
	160	34	8	2	168	36

JACK PRIOR

JOHN PUGSLEY

John Pugsley had a remarkable career at Blundell Park, staying only two seasons but making 80 League appearances, missing two from each of the 1925-6 and 1926-7 seasons. Born at Grangetown, Cardiff, in 1900, he signed for Cardiff in the summer of 1922. In May 1925 he arrived at Blundell Park and went straight into the first team at left-half for the 1925-6 season, which ended in Town winning the Third Division North championship. Standing 5ft 11ins and weighing 13st, Pugsley was ideally built for a wing-half and Town lost a good player when he moved to Bristol City in May 1927. He signed for Charlton Athletic in May 1928 and it was at The Valley that he enjoyed more success, winning a Third Division South championship medal in 1929. He was capped once for Wales, in a 7-0 defeat in Belfast in 1930. Pugsley retired as a player in the close season of 1934, while still with Charlton. After a short spell in the licensing trade in Cardiff he became Bostall Heath manager in 1938 and assistant trainer at Clapton Orient in July 1939. After the war he was on Cardiff City's training staff. John Pugsley died in August 1976.

	LEAGUE		*FA CUP*		*TOTAL*	
	App	*Gls*	*App*	*Gls*	*App*	*Gls*
1925-26	40	0	4	0	44	0
1926-27	40	6	3	1	43	7
	80	6	7	1	87	7

Ron Rafferty, a native of South Shields, started his professional career at Fratton Park, having been spotted by Portsmouth playing in the Isthmian League for Wycombe Wanderers. His senior appearances were strictly limited and after 18 months he was transferred to Grimsby for £3,500. He made his debut on 12 January 1957, in a 1-1 draw at Leyton Orient, and soon established himself in the long line of fine centre-forwards associated with the club, netting 10 times in 17 appearances that season. With outstanding services from Irish international Johnny Scott on the right wing and Jim Fell on the left, Rafferty's devastating finishing, especially with his head, saw him become Town's leading scorer in four out of the following five seasons. In 1959-60, Ralph Hunt's total of 33 goals was nine better than Rafferty's. In 1961-2, his 34 goals played a vital part in Town's rise from 12th at the end of December to runners-up and promotion, following a run which saw them drop only six points in 21 games from 6 January. Third Division champions were Rafferty's old club, Portsmouth. In July 1963, he joined Hull City for £10,000, but broke an ankle in only his third game for the Tigers. In three seasons he made only 16 first team appearances, scoring six goals. In July 1966 he moved to Aldershot as a centre-half, making a further 79 League appearances and netting ten goals. In July 1969 Rafferty joined Guildford City as player-coach, retiring six months later.

	LEAGUE		*FA CUP*		*FL CUP*		*TOTAL*	
	App	*Gls*	*App*	*Gls*	*App*	*Gls*	*App*	*Gls*
1956-57	17	10	1	1	0	0	18	11
1957-58	40	26	1	0	0	0	41	26
1958-59	39	19	3	0	0	0	42	19
1959-60	46	24	2	1	0	0	48	25
1960-61	45	24	1	0	1	2	47	26
1961-62	46	34	1	1	1	1	48	36
1962-63	31	8	1	0	1	1	33	9
	264	145	10	3	3	4	277	152

RON RAFFERTY

When Grimsby Town signed Graham Rathbone in November 1966, he was no stranger to the hurly-burly of football in the lower divisions, having made 190 League appearances for Newport County. Born in Newport in 1942, he played for junior clubs in the area before signing amateur forms for County, turning professional in March 1961. Rathbone, 6ft tall and weighing over 12 stones, was just the type of player Town were looking for to tighten the centre of the defence. They signed him in November 1966, for £8,000 but he could not prevent the Mariners being relegated in 1967-8. However, he was a member of Lawrie McMenemy's team which won promotion in 1971-2. His career with Grimsby spanned seven seasons and four managers. A favourite with supporters, he was dubbed 'Basil' by them, after the film star Basil Rathbone. Sent off with Don Welbourne (Scunthorpe United) at Blundell Park on 13 September 1969, he was suspended for two months (along with Welbourne) under a 'get tough' policy introduced by the FA. There was an outcry at the severity of the sentences, supporters claiming that the players would have escaped lightly had they been with more fashionable clubs. Whatever, the FA soon forgot their original intentions and lighter sentences were handed out. Graham Rathbone went to Cambridge United on loan in February 1973, signing for them the following month. He left after 35 appearances.

	LEAGUE		*FA CUP*		*FL CUP*		*TOTAL*	
	App	*Gls*	*App*	*Gls*	*App*	*Gls*	*App*	*Gls*
1966-67	30	1	2	0	0	0	32	1
1967-68	40	1	1	0	3	0	44	1
1968-69	40	4	1	0	4	0	45	4
1969-70	36	1	0	0	1	0	37	1
1970-71	44	2	1	0	1	0	46	2
1971-72	26	2	1	0	5	0	32	2
1972-73	16/1	0	0	0	3	0	19/1	0
	232/1	11	6	0	17	0	255/1	11

GRAHAM RATHBONE

Signed in the summer of 1927, Tommy Read had to wait until 21 January 1928 to make his first-team debut. William Cowell was Town's first choice goalkeeper but with 14 goals conceded in three matches, two League and one Cup, he was suddenly out of favour and Read got his big chance. Born in West Bromwich in 1900, he was the ideal build for a goalkeeper, standing just over 6ft and weighing 11¾st. He was agile, had a safe pair of hands and was quick off his line. The Grimsby fans called him 'Rocket'. Read's first-team appearances covered seven seasons and in 1928-9 he only missed one match, the vital last game of the season at Middlesbrough. Both teams were assured of promotion, but if Grimsby won they would be champions. Read was injured, reserve 'keeper Poskett took his place and Town lost 3-0. He was also in the team relegated from Division One in 1931-2. They came back after two seasons, winning the Second Division championship in 1933-4. The following season saw Read in the Reserves, with George Tweedy now first choice. In the summer of 1935, Read signed for Crystal Palace. When he retired from football he settled in the Midlands.

	LEAGUE		*FA CUP*		*TOTAL*	
	App	*Gls*	*App*	*Gls*	*App*	*Gls*
1927-28	18	0	0	0	18	0
1928-29	41	0	2	0	43	0
1929-30	42	0	2	0	44	0
1930-31	41	0	3	0	44	0
1931-32	42	0	3	0	45	0
1932-33	33	0	1	0	34	0
1933-34	30	0	1	0	31	0
	247	0	12	0	259	0

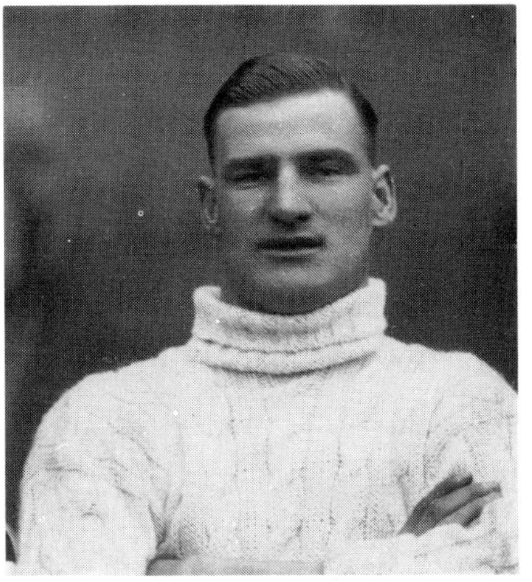

TOMMY READ

TONY REESON

Tony Reeson was born in Rotherham on 24 September 1933. After a spell in local football he joined his home town League club in 1953, as a left winger, but found first-team football hard to come by and made only four League appearances (one goal) in a season and a half at Millmoor. Grimsby player-manager Allenby Chilton, rebuilding his team, after the disastrous 1954-5 season, took Reeson to Blundell Park and converted him to inside-forward. Alongside Jimmy Maddison — the pair's combined weight was under 20st — Reeson helped form a lightweight left flank that proved so effective in the 1955-6 promotion season, during which Reeson missed only two games. The following season his Second Division appearances were limited due to two lengthy spells of injury; he missed a run of eight games in October and November and played in only two of the last 11. When Ron Stockin arrived in the 1957 close season, Reeson lost his place, returning only for a short spell when Stockin was injured. In February 1958, Reeson joined Doncaster Rovers, then managed by ex-Mariner, Jack Hodgson, and in a sixteen-month stay scored six goals in 21 League games. In the summer of 1959, he was transferred to Southport, adding another 42 League games (nine goals) before moving into non-League and ending his playing days with Gainsborough Trinity. A fast player, most effective when running into space, Reeson was a fine creator of chances but was himself sometimes unlucky in front of goal, his shot often being the one that rebounded off the bar or narrowly shaved the post.

	LEAGUE		*FA CUP*		*TOTAL*	
	App	*Gls*	*App*	*Gls*	*App*	*Gls*
1955-56	44	15	4	3	48	18
1956-57	25	4	1	0	26	4
1957-58	7	1	0	0	7	1
	76	20	5	3	81	23

Another product of the North-East, Dave Richardson was born in Billingham, County Durham, in 1932. He played for junior sides in the Middlesbrough area before moving to Leicester City in November 1948. Richardson spent seven years at Filbert Street but made only two League appearances before his move to Blundell Park in June 1955 for a nominal fee. He went straight into Allenby Chilton's team at left-half and in his first season won a Third Division North championship medal. The following season he moved to left-back. He ended his spell with Grimsby on a low note when they were relegated in 1958-9. In June 1960 he moved to Swindon Town but never played in the first team and in July 1961 signed for Barrow, for whom he made 31 appearances before drifting out of League football.

	LEAGUE		*FA CUP*		*TOTAL*	
	App	*Gls*	*App*	*Gls*	*App*	*Gls*
1955-56	37	1	4	0	41	1
1956-57	24	0	1	0	25	0
1957-58	42	0	1	0	43	0
1958-59	35	0	3	0	38	0
1959-60	37	0	2	0	39	0
	175	1	11	0	186	1

DAVE RICHARDSON

Scotsman Dave Riddoch was the first of many forwards who have thrilled Mariners fans over the last 100 years. He joined Grimsby in the Clee Park days, signing in 1887 after spells at Heart of Midlothian, Edinburgh St Bernard and Berwick Rangers. In three seasons of Alliance football, he scored at least 14 goals, for records for 1890-91 are sparse and nine Town goals are unaccounted for. When the Alliance became the Second Division of the Football League in 1892, Riddoch played in the opening match against Northwich Victoria, scoring twice, the first-ever League goals for the Mariners. Bob Lincoln, a founder-member of the club and later a director, says of Riddoch in his *Reminiscences of Sport in Grimsby* : 'He was not only one of the best dribblers of the day but very tricky, a magnificent shot for goal, plucky to a degree and took any amount of stopping, in fact for several seasons he was one of the best forwards in the country.' As Riddoch was already 28 years old when the club attained Second Division status, his career was limited and he retired after only three seasons of League football.

	LEAGUE		*FA CUP*		*TOTAL*	
	App	*Gls*	*App*	*Gls*	*App*	*Gls*
1887-88	0	0	3	0	3	0
1888-89	0	0	8	1	8	1
1889-90	0	0	2	0	2	0
1890-91	0	0	0	0	0	0
1891-92	0	0	2	2	2	2
1892-93	19	7	6	0	25	7
1893-94	21	4	5	4	26	8
1894-95	19	7	3	3	22	10
	59	18	29	10	88	28

DAVE RIDDOCH

THOMAS 'PIP' RIPPON

Thomas Rippon spent nine seasons with Grimsby Town, including four during World War One when League football was suspended. Born at Beighton, near Sheffield, his career took him from Derbyshire junior football to Grimsby Town in the 1910-11 season, although he did not make his League debut until 1911-12, when Grimsby had been voted back. At centre or inside-forward, he possessed a good shot and kept his line moving. Besides his 121 League appearances in peacetime, he made 67 wartime appearances. In the summer of 1920, Rippon moved to Lincoln City, staying for two years before joining Worksop Town. He died in 1950.

	LEAGUE		*FA CUP*		*TOTAL*	
	App	*Gls*	*App*	*Gls*	*App*	*Gls*
1911-12	11	2	0	0	11	2
1912-13	31	13	1	1	32	14
1913-14	27	9	0	0	27	9
1914-15	36	11	1	0	37	11
1919-20	16	2	0	0	16	2
	121	37	2	1	123	38

WILLIS RIPPON

Willis Rippon was two years older than his brother, Thomas, and was also born at Beighton. Also a forward, unlike Thomas he travelled extensively after early days in Sheffield junior football. He played for Kilnhurst Town before beginning his League career at Bristol City in the summer of 1907. He joined Woolwich Arsenal in 1910 and Brentford in October 1911. Rippon then tried his luck in Scotland, Hamilton Academical paying £450 for him in 1913. In October the same year, Grimsby Town paid a similar sum but he stayed for only one season. Slightly taller than his brother, he was two stones heavier at 13st 10lbs. In July 1914, Willis Rippon signed for Rotherham and also assisted them after the war, during which he made 40 guest appearances for Grimsby. The brothers appeared together for Town in 1913-14. Willis Rippon died in 1956.

	LEAGUE		*FA CUP*		*TOTAL*	
	App	*Gls*	*App*	*Gls*	*App*	*Gls*
1913-14	23	12	0	0	23	12
	23	12	0	0	23	12

Grimsby Town in 1914-15. Back row (left to right): Kenny, Holden (trainer), Andrews, Wheelhouse, W.Rippon, Lee, Summers, Martin. Front row: Spink, T.Rippon, Rampton, Mayson, Thompson.

Born in Darlington in 1883, Charlie Roberts played for Darlington St Augustines and Bishop Auckland before his move to Grimsby Town in May 1903. Ideally built for a centre-half, 20-year-old Roberts stood nearly 6ft and weighed 11¾st. Grimsby had unearthed a gem of a player but he stayed for only one season. Other clubs took an interest in the brilliant defender and Manchester United came in with an offer of £700 (some sources state £400). Whichever, it was a record for the Grimsby club and ridiculously low for such a talented player. On 22 April 1904, Charlie Roberts signed for United and it was with them that he had his best years. He had nine successful seasons, becoming the first Manchester United player to be capped for England when he played against Ireland, Scotland and Wales in 1905-06. It was said that at international level Roberts did not seem to be at his best, hence only three caps, but he made nine appearances for the Football League. He captained United's 1909 FA Cup-winning side and played in their League championship teams of 1907-08 and 1910-11, the Second Division runners-up team of 1905-06 and the Charity Shield winning sides of 1907-08 and 1910-11. After more than 300 League and Cup games for United, he moved to Oldham Athletic in August 1913 for £1,750, more than double what United had paid Grimsby. He retired from playing during World War One and was Oldham's manager from July 1921 until December 1922. During his playing career he would return to Grimsby during the close season and sign on for a few trips on a Grimsby trawler to keep himself fit. Sometimes he would be accompanied by Brentford's goalkeeper, Walter Whittaker, also an ex-Grimsby player. He was a founder member of the Players' Union and its chairman for a time. Roberts, who opened a number of newsagents and stationers shops in the Manchester area, died in August 1939.

	LEAGUE		*FA CUP*		*TOTAL*	
	App	*Gls*	*App*	*Gls*	*App*	*Gls*
1903-04	31	4	2	0	33	4
	31	4	2	0	33	4

CHARLIE ROBERTS

NEIL ROBINSON

Born in Walton, Liverpool, on 20 April 1957, full-back Neil Robinson was offered trials by both Merseyside giants but chose Everton, the club he had followed as a schoolboy. He spent five seasons under the successive management of Harry Catterick, Billy Bingham and Gordon Lee, where opportunities were limited. He made only 13 full League appearances, although he did take part in a protracted League Cup Final against Aston Villa and had a brief taste of European football, coming on as substitute against Finn Harps in the UEFA Cup. In 1979, he joined John Toshack at Swansea and made 114 full League appearances in five seasons there, going up to Division One, then down to the Third with the Swans. In 1984, manager Dave Booth signed him for Grimsby and he had the misfortune to put through his own goal with virtually his first touch for the Mariners, against Oxford United. Injuries, then competition from Tony Barratt made life difficult and it was not until he moved to midfield that he established himself. Despite Town's declining fortunes, he was popular with supporters who voted him Player of the Year in the 1986-7 relegation season. However, he suffered loss of form as Grimsby went straight into Division Four and he rejoined Dave Booth, who was expanding his squad of former Mariners at Darlington.

	LEAGUE		*FA CUP*		*FL CUP*		*TOTAL*	
	App	*Gls*	*App*	*Gls*	*App*	*Gls*	*App*	*Gls*
1984-85	17	0	0	0	0	0	17	0
1985-86	22	0	0	0	0	0	22	0
1986-87	30	3	3	0	2	0	35	3
1987-88	40	3	3	0	2	0	45	3
	109	6	6	0	4	0	119	6

After scoring over 200 goals in local football, Gateshead-born Joe Robson joined Grimsby Town in September 1924. He had to wait for three seasons before taking over from Jimmy Carmichael as the regular centre-forward. Thereafter, he proved a great favourite at Blundell Park — 'Give it to Robbie' was the cry — and when Town won promotion in 1928-9, he was top scorer with 32 goals. He maintained his scoring form in Division One, netting four in a game against Everton to send the Merseysiders into Division Two. Apparently he had felt unwell on the way to the ground and did not want to play — until a director chided him by saying, 'Come and sit with me and watch Dixie Dean, a *real* centre-forward'. After only four games in the 1930-31 season, Robson moved to Huddersfield Town for £8,000, another transfer that Town supporters did not want. With Coleman and Glover on the books, however, Grimsby were well off for goalscoring centre-forwards. Robson's best scoring feat for Town was probably his hat-trick in approximately 3½ minutes, in a 6-4 home defeat by Preston. After two seasons at Huddersfield he moved to Bradford, then into non-League football with Gainsborough and Nuneaton. He died at Bradford in 1969, aged 66.

	LEAGUE		*FA CUP*		*TOTAL*	
	App	*Gls*	*App*	*Gls*	*App*	*Gls*
1924-25	8	3	0	0	8	3
1925-26	7	6	1	0	8	6
1926-27	26	24	2	1	28	25
1927-28	39	26	1	0	40	26
1928-29	36	32	2	0	38	32
1929-30	41	30	0	0	41	30
1930-31	4	2	0	0	4	2
	161	123	6	1	167	124

JOE ROBSON

BOBBY ROSS

Born in Edinburgh, Bobby Ross played for Arniston Rangers, East Fife and St Mirren before joining Grimsby Town in June 1965 for a small fee. Town certainly had their money's worth and in six seasons, Ross gave the Mariners excellent service at a time when their fortunes were at a low ebb. A utility player, he was named in seven different positions for the club, although wing-half was undoubtedly his best. Despite playing in a struggling side, Ross enjoyed some outstanding performances. Studious and unruffled, he gave 100 per cent in every one of his 200-plus League appearances for Grimsby Town. In August 1971 he signed for non-League Gainsborough Trinity. Bobby Ross now lives in Cleethorpes.

	LEAGUE		*FA CUP*		*FL CUP*		*TOTAL*	
	App	*Gls*	*App*	*Gls*	*App*	*Gls*	*App*	*Gls*
1965-66	27	4	4	0	3	1	34	5
1966-67	37/1	2	0	0	5	0	42/1	2
1967-68	44	3	2	1	2	0	48	4
1968-69	30	4	0	0	3	0	33	4
1969-70	43	1	1	0	1	0	45	1
1970-71	27/3	4	0	0	1	0	28/3	4
	208/4	18	7	1	15	1	230/4	20

Allenby Chilton returned to his old club, Manchester United, in 1956 to sign John Scott, an outside-right who became probably Town's best ball-player since the 1940s. Born in Belfast in December 1933, he arrived at Old Trafford via Boyland FC (Belfast) and Ormond Star. His appearances for United were limited because of the oustanding form of Johnny Berry, but at Grimsby he was first-choice, from his scoring debut on 25 August 1956 (at home to Notts County) until he left. In his first season he was top scorer. Stockily built, Scott had fine ball-control, speed and an accurate pass. Not afraid to shoot, he scored many great goals. His one weakness was that he could flare up when treated unfairly by opposing defenders. Then the fans saw the 'other' side of the normally mild-mannered, quietly-spoken Irishman. He was in the team that won 7-0 at Eastville in December 1957, when Grimsby wingers Scott and Fell played a big part in victory, and had mixed fortunes with Grimsby, who were relegated to Division Three in 1958-9 and promoted to Division Two in 1961-2. He played centre-forward for Northern Ireland in the 1958 World Cup Finals in Sweden, against France and Czechoslovakia. He was also capped at 'B' level against Rumania. In June 1963, Scott signed for Fourth Division York City and made 21 appearances before moving to non-League Margate in the summer of 1964. Had he stayed with Manchester United, he might have won a regular place after the Munich disaster. Johnny Scott was killed in an accident on a Manchester building site.

JOHNNY SCOTT

	LEAGUE		*FA CUP*		*FL CUP*		*TOTAL*	
	App	*Gls*	*App*	*Gls*	*App*	*Gls*	*App*	*Gls*
1956-57	34	11	0	0	0	0	34	11
1957-58	33	7	1	0	0	0	34	7
1958-59	33	8	3	1	0	0	36	9
1959-60	45	14	2	0	0	0	47	14
1960-61	45	5	0	0	0	0	45	5
1961-62	37	4	1	0	1	1	39	5
1962-63	13	2	1	1	0	0	14	3
	240	51	8	2	1	1	249	54

Walter Scott was one of the first in a long line of fine Grimsby Town goalkeepers. Born in Worksop in 1886, Scott (known as 'Buns') was playing for Worksop when Town signed him in 1907. A big man, 5ft 11ins and 13st, he was very agile, commanded his penalty-area and had great anticipation. At Burnley on 13 February 1909 he saved three of the four penalties that were awarded against the Mariners that day. Those were the days when the goalkeeper could move for a penalty-kick but it was still a fine achievement and remains a Football League record. Scott had two spells with Grimsby, from 1907 to 1910 and again in 1920. In January 1910 he moved to Everton for a fee of £750, to Sunderland in the summer of 1911, then to Shelbourne and later Belfast United, making five appearances for the Irish League. He returned to England during World War One and guested for Brentford and Millwall Athletic. At the end of the war he returned to his first club, Worksop Town, in August 1919. He went back to play for Grimsby in February 1920, but his stay was brief and he moved to his last club, Gainsborough Trinity, in June the same year. Walter Scott died in 1955.

	LEAGUE		*FA CUP*		*TOTAL*	
	App	*Gls*	*App*	*Gls*	*App*	*Gls*
1907-08	21	0	3	0	24	0
1908-09	37	0	1	0	38	0
1909-10	22	0	1	0	23	0
1919-20	19	0	0	0	19	0
	99	0	5	0	104	0

WALTER SCOTT

Born in North Shields in 1880, Martin Spendiff was Grimsby Town's goalkeeper for two spells either side of World War One. He joined them from North Shields Athletic in March 1902 and made his League debut on 27 September that year, at Sunderland where Town lost 5-1. Spendiff could not command a regular place in the side, owing to the brilliance of Whittaker, and his appearances that season were limited. In the next two seasons, however, he made the position his own, missing only nine games. In May 1905, Spendiff moved to Hull City and stayed until 1908, making 104 appearances. From Hull he went to Bradford City, then to Millwall Athletic and returned to Grimsby in the summer of 1913. Spendiff appeared in only four wartime matches for the Mariners but when football returned to normal in 1919-20, he played 21 times in the side that eventually lost Grimsby their Second Division status. Then he retired to run a dairy business in Cleethorpes. He was ideally built, standing nearly 6ft and weighing 12st, and gave Town good service as a fearless 'keeper. Martin Spendiff died on 18 October 1943.

	LEAGUE		*FA CUP*		*TOTAL*	
	App	*Gls*	*App*	*Gls*	*App*	*Gls*
1902-03	7	0	2	0	9	0
1903-04	33	0	2	0	35	0
1904-05	26	0	2	0	28	0
1913-14	35	0	1	0	36	0
1914-15	1	0	0	0	1	0
1919-20	21	0	0	0	21	0
	123	0	7	0	130	0

MARTIN SPENDIFF

JACK SWAIN

Grimsby-born Jack showed great promise as a footballer and cricketer while still at school and joined Town from college in July 1936, turning professional two months later and making his First Division debut in November that year. He could not command a regular place and, in the close season of 1939, moved to Scunthorpe United, then a Midland League side. There was not much football for him at Scunthorpe, either, and he joined the Army for the duration of the war. On his return to civilian life, he became a referee, working his way through the Midland League on to the Football League list. He thus had the unique experience of refereeing teams that he had played against in the First Division before the war. In 1957-8, Grimsby could boast three referees on the League list. Besides Jack Swain, there were Arthur Sparling and Jack Topliss. Add Don Martin of Scunthorpe to the list and Lincolnshire was doing well for referees. Jack Swain is a founder-member of the hospital's broadcasting team which regularly broadcasts football matches from Blundell Park. He writes on cricket and soccer for the local sports paper.

	LEAGUE		*FA CUP*		*TOTAL*	
	App	*Gls*	*App*	*Gls*	*App*	*Gls*
1936-37	6	3	0	0	6	3
1937-38	6	1	0	0	6	1
1938-39	10	2	1	0	11	2
	22	6	1	0	23	6

Graham Taylor made more than 200 League and Cup appearances for Grimsby Town and later became a successful manager. Born at Worksop, he joined Scunthorpe United as an amateur before signing for Grimsby in August 1961, turning professional in July 1962. Taylor did not make the first team until the beginning of 1963-4 but remained with the Mariners until July 1968, when he signed for Lincoln City. He was a good full-back, fair, always calm and a good reader of the game. He struck up a good understanding with his full-back partner, Jimmy Thompson. He left the club the season they were relegated to Division Four, having already experienced relegation with Grimsby to Division Three in 1963-4. He was with Lincoln City until 1977, first as a player (150 matches), then as a manager, when he steered them to the Division Four championship in 1976. He left Lincoln to become manager of Watford and guided Elton John's club to the Fourth Division title in 1977-8, Third Division runners-up in 1978-9 and promotion to Division One in 1981-2. He also took them to an FA Cup Final in 1984. In 1987, he became Villa's boss and took them back to Division One in 1988.

	LEAGUE		*FA CUP*		*FL CUP*		*TOTAL*	
	App	*Gls*	*App*	*Gls*	*App*	*Gls*	*App*	*Gls*
1963-64	27	0	1	0	1	0	29	0
1964-65	32	0	2	0	0	0	34	0
1965-66	40	0	6	0	5	0	51	0
1966-67	46	1	2	0	5	0	53	1
1967-68	44	1	1	0	3	0	48	1
	189	2	12	0	14	0	215	2

GRAHAM TAYLOR

MATT TEES

Matt Tees signed for Town from Airdrie in July 1963, for a fee of £5,000. An inside-forward, he found goals hard to come by and it was not until the arrival of Rodney Green from Gillingham at the start of 1965-6 that he came into his own, forming a partnership that was to produce 57 goals in just over a season and a half. The pair moved to Charlton in February of 1967 for what seems, in retrospect, a derisory combined fee of £25,000. Tees made 88 League appearances for Charlton before moving to Luton in August 1969. There he added a further 13 goals in 33 games. In November 1970, Bobby Kennedy, seeking to revive the flagging fortunes of the Mariners, brought Tees back to Blundell Park. The result was astounding. His return debut against Cambridge United produced an attendance of 7,295, over 3,000 up on the previous game, and Tees celebrated with the first of ten goals that season. A late-season revival was not enough to save Kennedy, and in the summer of 1971 Lawrie McMenemy became manager. He is said to have been unimpressed by Tees' sparse frame but the striker played a vital part in the championship season, netting 27 goals, including five in the two local derbies against Scunthorpe. This was probably his finest season; age and injuries caught up with him and, after the first two months of the following season, his appearances dwindled. He played his final game in the last match of the season against Plymouth Argyle. He ranks high amongst the many class forwards to have played for Grimsby.

	LEAGUE		*FA CUP*		*FL CUP*		*TOTAL*	
	App	*Gls*	*App*	*Gls*	*App*	*Gls*	*App*	*Gls*
1963-64	21	5	0	0	1	0	22	5
1964-65	26	9	2	1	0	0	28	10
1965-66	43	28	6	4	5	4	54	36
1966-67	23	9	2	1	4	2	29	12
1970-71	23	10	1	0	0	0	24	10
1971-72	43	27	1	0	5	2	49	29
1972-73	17	5	2	0	2	2	21	7
	196	93	14	6	17	10	227	109

George Tweedy was arguably the best goalkeeper ever to appear for the Mariners. One of the many Tynesiders who have found their way to Blundell Park, Tweedy joined Grimsby from the Durham club, Willington, as an 18-year-old. Initially part of the Reserve squad, he made his League debut on 19 November 1932, against Bradford City, when regular 'keeper Tommy Read broke a finger. Tweedy lost his place after nine games, when Read regained fitness, but returned to the first team for a brief spell during the 1933-4 season. From 1934-5 until the outbreak of World War Two, he made the first-team spot his own, missing only seven League games over five seasons. On 2 December 1936, Tweedy made his only appearance for England, playing in the 6-2 victory over Hungary at Highbury. There seems little doubt that, but for the presence of Harry Hibbs and Vic Woodley, his international career would have been longer. At the outbreak of war, Tweedy continued to play for Town, making 56 appearances over three seasons. He later guested for both Hibernian and Arsenal, in each case just missing a War Cup Final because of military postings. He returned to League football for the Mariners in 1946-7 and played on until 1950 before retiring to become assistant manager. When Stan Hayhurst broke his finger in the opening home game of the 1951-2 season, manager Bill Shankly persuaded Tweedy to don his jersey again and he made a further 32 League appearances before finally retiring after the Good Friday game against York City in 1953. He was then 40 years of age.

GEORGE TWEEDY

	LEAGUE		*FA CUP*		*TOTAL*	
	App	*Gls*	*App*	*Gls*	*App*	*Gls*
1932-33	9	0	1	0	10	0
1933-34	12	0	1	0	13	0
1934-35	42	0	1	0	43	0
1935-36	41	0	6	0	47	0
1936-37	42	0	4	0	46	0
1937-38	40	0	2	0	42	0
1938-39	38	0	6	0	44	0
1946-47	39	0	3	0	42	0
1947-48	36	0	1	0	37	0
1948-49	15	0	0	0	15	0
1949-50	1	0	0	0	1	0
1951-52	24	0	0	0	24	0
1952-53	8	0	0	0	8	0
	347	0	25	0	372	0

Norman 'Ned' Vincent played in more than 300 matches for Grimsby Town at right-back, 114 in peacetime football and the remainder in wartime. In seven seasons of wartime soccer he missed less then 20 matches. Another loyal clubman, his career covered 13 seasons. Born in Proudhoe, Northumberland, in 1909, Vincent started his football career with Proudhoe United and then went to Stockport County in 1928. Grimsby Town signed him in the summer of 1934 for a fee of £1,200. He was known as 'Chopper' by his followers, not for his unfair play but for the way he broke up the left-wing attacks. He was a strong player, a master of the dead-ball, either from free-kicks or penalties, and he could strike the ball as hard as any footballer playing at that time. He and Jack Hodgson struck up a great partnership during the war. The nearest Vincent came to winning honours was when he appeared in two pre-war FA Cup semi-finals and another two-legged Final in wartime soccer. In the first post-war season of 1946-7, Vincent, now 37 years old, made 15 appearances before leaving the club in the summer of 1947. Norman Vincent died in 1980.

	LEAGUE		*FA CUP*		*TOTAL*	
	App	*Gls*	*App*	*Gls*	*App*	*Gls*
1934-35	17	0	0	0	17	0
1935-36	24	0	1	0	25	0
1936-37	9	0	2	0	11	0
1937-38	37	0	2	0	39	0
1938-39	42	0	7	0	49	0
1945-46	0	0	1	0	1	0
1946-47	15	2	2	0	17	2
	144	2	15	0	159	2

NORMAN VINCENT

Goalkeeper Harry Wainman followed Charlie Wright into the Town side and, although Wright's was a hard act to follow, Wainman went on to forge another link in the chain of great Grimsby 'keepers. Indeed, had he not been forced to retire through an arm injury, he would almost certainly have passed Keith Jobling's club record of 450 League appearances. Born at Hull, Wainman played for Hull Schools and Ainthorpe Old Boys. Hull City signed him as an amateur, but Town took him on the groundstaff in 1963. He turned professional in July 1964 and won an England Youth cap the same year. Wainman played a major part in Lawrie McMenemy's championship side of 1971-2, missing only three matches. He also knew the disappointments of the game, being a member of two relegation sides, in 1967-8 and 1976-7. In October 1972 he went to Rochdale on loan but after nine matches returned to Blundell Park. In August 1978, Wainman suffered the misfortune of breaking his arm. Due to the brilliance of Nigel Batch he never got back into the first team and retired in 1981. He had been Town's Player of the Year in 1971-2 and was one of the few Grimsby players to have two testimonial matches, the first against an All Star XI on 3 March 1973 and the second against Leeds United on 3 February 1981. On 5 November 1977, he joined the select band of Grimsby players to make 400 League appearances. After his retirement he opened a sports shop and is now a Cleethorpes hotelier.

HARRY WAINMAN

	LEAGUE		*FA CUP*		*FL CUP*		*TOTAL*	
	App	*Gls*	*App*	*Gls*	*App*	*Gls*	*App*	*Gls*
1964-65	4	0	0	0	0	0	4	0
1965-66	17	0	0	0	0	0	17	0
1966-67	31	0	2	0	5	0	38	0
1967-68	36	0	2	0	3	0	41	0
1968-69	10	0	0	0	3	0	13	0
1969-70	46	0	1	0	1	0	48	0
1970-71	34	0	1	0	1	0	36	0
1971-72	43	0	1	0	6	0	50	0
1972-73	22	0	5	0	2	0	29	0
1973-74	40	0	4	0	4	0	48	0
1974-75	28	0	0	0	1	0	29	0
1975-76	35	0	0	0	1	0	36	0
1976-77	38	0	3	0	2	0	43	0
1977-78	36	0	1	0	3	0	40	0
	420	0	20	0	32	0	472	0

Joe Waters will go down as one of Town's most popular players as well as one of their greatest. Only 5ft 5ins tall, he was a midfield dynamo who won the hearts of the fans. Born in Limerick, he won Republic of Ireland Schoolboy and Youth caps. Leicester City took him on as an apprentice and he turned full professional in December 1973, but made only 11 League appearances. The highlight of his career with them was in the 1974 FA Cup sixth round at Queens Park Rangers, when he scored two brilliant goals to put Leicester into the semi-final. He went to Grimsby on loan in 1976, and scored on his debut on 26 January, at Millwall in a 1-1 draw. Town were ready to let him return to Filbert Street but such was the outcry from supporters who had taken him to their hearts that Tommy Casey eventually signed him for a fee reported to be between £8,000 and £10,000, with the supporters' club donating about £2,000. He played well but in his first full season, 1976-7, Town were relegated. Under John Newman's managership, he was elected Player of the Year in 1978-9 and captained the side which was promoted to Division Three. George Kerr persuaded him to re-sign just before the 1979-80 season started and Waters proceeded to lead the Mariners to the Third Division title. The PFA selected him in their Fourth Division side and, a year later, for the Third Division side (along with Kevin Moore on both occasions). Waters won his first full cap in 1977, against Turkey and was substitute against Northern Ireland in 1980. Between 2 November 1976 and 31 October 1982 he made 226 consecutive League appearances — a Town record. He left Grimsby in May 1984 and enjoyed success in the American 6's League. In 1987, it was rumoured that he was invited to become Town's manager, before the appointment of Bobby Roberts.

JOE WATERS

	LEAGUE		*FA CUP*		*FL CUP*		*TOTAL*	
	App	*Gls*	*App*	*Gls*	*App*	*Gls*	*App*	*Gls*
1975-76	19	2	0	0	0	0	19	2
1976-77	45	5	3	0	2	0	50	5
1977-78	46	8	5	2	3	3	54	13
1978-79	46	10	1	0	3	1	50	11
1979-80	46	8	4	2	9	0	59	10
1980-81	42	10	1	0	2	1	45	11
1981-82	35/1	7	2	0	2	0	39/1	7
1982-83	40	8	3	1	4	0	47	9
1983-84	37	7	1	0	4	0	42	7
	356/1	65	20	5	29	5	405/1	75

Sid Wheelhouse would be in contention for the right-back position in any 'all-time great' Mariners side, judging by the newspaper reports of the day. Born in Darlington in 1888, he started with Bishop Auckland, then Shildon. Signing for Grimsby in April 1907, the 18-year-old went straight into the first team staying there apart from illness or injury. When Tony Arrowsmith was introduced to the team, they struck up a partnership which was to last until World War One. Wheelhouse had some commendable qualities. He was strong, scrupulously fair, a good captain, a loyal clubman and a gentleman. All his matches were in Division Two except in 1910-11 when he led Grimsby back as Midland League champions. When the war started he enlisted in the Middlesex Regiment, but finished the season with the Mariners. He guested a few times for Clapton Orient and played for the Footballers' Battalion, along with Grimsby teammate Frank Martin. Wounded in action in France (at first it was thought not to be serious) and gassed, he died in military hospital on 18 September 1916. His last match in Town's colours was on 6 May 1916, in a charity match against a combined Army and Navy team.

	LEAGUE		*FA CUP*		*TOTAL*	
	App	*Gls*	*App*	*Gls*	*App*	*Gls*
1907-08	30	0	5	0	35	0
1908-09	38	0	1	0	39	0
1909-10	37	0	1	0	38	0
1910-11	0	0	3	0	3	0
1911-12	32	1	1	0	33	1
1912-13	37	1	1	0	38	1
1913-14	36	0	1	0	37	0
1914-15	24	1	0	0	24	1
	234	3	13	0	247	3

SID WHEELHOUSE

When Grimsby Town were elected to the Football League in 1892, they had little money to spend on players of proven League quality. Instead they signed three Midlands players, Higgins, Fletcher and goalkeeper Jimmy Whitehouse, all of whom gave good service to the club. Whitehouse was with Birmingham St George, who had been in the Football Alliance. He made his debut for Town in their first-ever League match and for the next four seasons did not miss a match. At this time the England team was elected by a committee and Whitehouse was edged out of the reserve goalkeeper's spot by Billy Foulkes. Aston Villa eventually signed him for over £200, an unpopular move with Grimsby followers, but one necessary if they were to buy players for the following season. Whitehouse was a member of the Villa side which did the League and Cup double in 1896-7. He then went into non-League football with Bedminster but returned to Grimsby in May 1899, playing a further 27 matches. Later he played for Newton Heath, Manchester City, Third Lanark, Hull City and Southend, which was probably his last club. His main assets were his handling and his quick clearances to get his forward line moving. Jimmy Whitehouse died on 7 February 1934.

	LEAGUE		*FA CUP*		*TOTAL*	
	App	*Gls*	*App*	*Gls*	*App*	*Gls*
1892-93	22	0	5	0	27	0
1893-94	28	0	5	0	33	0
1894-95	30	0	3	0	33	0
1895-96	30	0	7	0	37	0
1899-1900	27	0	4	0	31	0
	137	0	24	0	161	0

JIMMY WHITEHOUSE

Charlie Wilson was born in Cleethorpes in 1904 and, although he went to school there, he captained Grimsby Boys. He played for Cleethorpes Town and was signed for Grimsby Town by George Fraser in May 1923. His first 67 appearances were at right-half but, once settled at right-back, he made that position his own. He was a good wing-half but a better full-back and struck up a good partnership with Hughie Jacobson. He played a major part in the 1925-6 championship season, missing only four matches, and was a member of the team when Town again won promotion in 1928-9. He was also in the relegation team of 1931-2. Wilson was granted a joint testimonial with Billy Marshall, against Oldham Athletic on 30 March 1929 when Town won 1-0 before a crowd of 13,915. In August 1933 he signed for Bournemouth, a move which did not go down too well with supporters. A year later, Wilson returned to Lincolnshire and joined Grantham, later playing for Peterborough United. When he retired from football he settled in Cleethorpes and in 1989 was probably the oldest living Mariner, still enjoying his garden and a visit to the local.

CHARLIE WILSON

	LEAGUE		*FA CUP*		*TOTAL*	
	App	*Gls*	*App*	*Gls*	*App*	*Gls*
1923-24	26	1	4	0	30	1
1924-25	27	0	1	0	28	0
1925-26	38	0	4	0	42	0
1926-27	21	1	0	0	21	1
1927-28	16	0	1	0	17	0
1928-29	21	0	2	0	23	0
1929-30	42	0	2	0	44	0
1930-31	40	0	2	0	42	0
1931-32	35	0	3	0	38	0
1932-33	7	0	0	0	7	0
	273	2	19	0	292	2

DAVE WORTHINGTON

Born in Halifax, Dave Worthington turned professional in April 1962 with Halifax Town and made 37 appearances for them before moving to Barrow in July 1964, making 60 appearances for them before Town signed him on a free transfer in June 1966. He made his debut at centre-forward, then played at outside-right and inside-right before moving to right-back, his best position. He missed only one match when Town were relegated in 1967-8 but it was hardly a new experience for him: he had been relegated with Halifax and was with Barrow when they had to seek re-election. His 224 consecutive appearances for the Mariners was a club record until Joe Waters beat it a decade later. Worthington captained the championship side of 1971-2, proving popular with players and supporters alike. He went on loan to Halifax in October 1973, making five appearances before being transferred from Town to Southend United in November 1973. He stayed with them until 1975, making 92 League appearances to take his League tally to 486. He is now on the advisory board at Halifax. Two younger brothers also played League football. Frank, an England international, was much travelled but played mainly for Huddersfield Town (166 appearances) and Leicester City (209). Bob was a consistent performer with Notts County (230 games). Between them they notched up more than 1,200 League games.

	LEAGUE		*FA CUP*		*FL CUP*		*TOTAL*	
	App	*Gls*	*App*	*Gls*	*App*	*Gls*	*App*	*Gls*
1966-67	29	4	1	0	5	3	35	7
1967-68	45	3	2	1	3	1	50	5
1968-69	46	2	1	0	4	0	51	2
1969-70	46	2	1	0	1	0	48	2
1970-71	46	0	1	0	1	0	48	0
1971-72	46	1	1	0	6	0	53	1
1972-73	34/1	2	5	0	3	0	42/1	2
	292/1	14	12	1	23	4	327/1	19

Charlie Wright was born in Glasgow just before World War Two. He showed great promise as a schoolboy goalkeeper and played for East Kilbride YMCA and Glentyan Thistle before signing for Glasgow Rangers in 1956. In 1958 he joined Workington Town and when Grimsby were looking for an experienced goalkeeper, they signed Wright in February 1963 for £6,500. Standing over 6ft tall and weighing 13st, he was alert, quick and possessed great powers of concentration. His inspiration helped Town avoid relegation in his first season at Blundell Park but, although he was ever-present the following season, he could not prevent Town dropping to Division Three by .045 of a goal. In March 1966 he joined Second Division Charlton Athletic for around £10,000 and went on to make more than 200 League and Cup appearances for them. In June 1971 he signed for Bolton but, after 88 appearances, had to retire through an injury in April 1974, becoming club coach at Burnden Park. He was a member of Bolton's Third Division championship side of 1973. From November 1977 until 1980 he managed York City, later returning to Bolton as chief coach before being appointed manager in February 1985. Wright, who made a total of 535 League appearances, is the brother-in-law of Matt Tees, another Town favourite of the 1960s and '70s.

	LEAGUE		*FA CUP*		*FL CUP*		*TOTAL*	
	App	*Gls*	*App*	*Gls*	*App*	*Gls*	*App*	*Gls*
1962-63	16	0	0	0	0	0	16	0
1963-64	42	0	1	0	1	0	44	0
1964-65	42	0	4	0	2	0	48	0
1965-66	29	0	6	0	5	0	40	0
	129	0	11	0	8	0	148	0

CHARLIE WRIGHT

Charlie Wright in action at Blundell Park.

Match to Remember 1 — 25 November 1882

Grimsby Town 1 Phoenix Bessemer 9

WHEN Grimsby Town first entered the FA Cup, they faced the prospect of a baptism of fire. There was great excitement in the town when the leading Glasgow club, Queen's Park, were drawn to play at Clee Park, in what was then known as the English Cup competition, but the Scots withdrew and Grimsby moved into the second round to entertain Phoenix Bessemer, a Rotherham works side.

Having lost the toss, Town had to play into a strong wind that was blowing straight down the pitch. With a formation of six forwards and two half-backs, it soon became obvious that, although the home side possessed a lot of effort and enthusiasm, they did not possess as much skill as the Yorkshire team.

Some doughty defending, especially by Evans in goal, kept the score-sheet blank for half an hour before Willey headed home in a goalmouth mêlée to put the visitors ahead. Two minutes later, after some clever approach work, Thomas added a second. This double set-back disheartened the home defence and Thomas soon scored a third following a corner before Willey, again with his head, made it 4-0. Shortly before half-time, one of Grimsby's rare good moves saw Monument pull a goal back.

Any hopes that Town's fortunes would improve when they got the wind behind them were quickly dashed five minutes into the second half, when a rare mistake by Evans let in Marples for number five.

With the home side now floundering, Emmett scored a hat-trick, and Marples got his second to make it nine. In the last half-hour, Grimsby moved Flowers into the attack in an effort to salvage just a little respectability, but a knock he had received earlier in the game rendered his finishing somewhat erratic. Thus, Grimsby Town's first venture into the FA Cup resulted in complete humiliation. Fortunately it remains their worst-ever performance in the competition.

Grimsby Town: Evans; Rev Flowers, Jenkinson, Warner, Hall, Noble, Tonge, Chapman, France, Monument, Ousey.
Phoenix Bessemer: Platts; Bone, Rawlin, C.E.Thomas, Cutts, Bennett, Emmett, Marples, Douglas, Willey, F.W.Thomas.

Referee: R.Flowers (Brigg) *Attendance: Unrecorded*

Three members of the Grimsby Town side which played in the club's first-ever FA Cup match. From left to right, Noble, Monument and France. Harry Monument scored the Mariners' first Cup goal but his side were still thrashed by a record score.

The Grimsby Town team which lost to Preston in a controversial Cup game. Standing: Holtby. Seated (left to right): J.H.Taylor, Reid, Lundie, Smith, Doyle. Front: Sutherland, J.Taylor, Riddoch, McBeth, Hunt.

Match to Remember 2 — 16 February 1889

Grimsby Town 0 Preston North End 2

CONTROVERSIAL refereeing decisions and the subsequent castigation of the unfortunate official by the Press has been with us as long as the professional game, a fact illustrated by an incident during Preston's historic League and Cup double during the first season of League football.

Grimsby Town had come through seven Cup matches, including three replays, for the honour of entertaining the game's outstanding club and the tie had drawn spectators from a wide area.

On a cold, cheerless afternoon Grimsby won the toss and opted to play with the wind behind them. Preston kicked off and immediately went into the attack but the home defence, with Dan Doyle in especially good form at left-back, withstood the onslaught. Preston did not have it all their own way but their experienced defence soaked up all that the Town could offer, although Riddoch might have scored, had he not shot too hastily. A fiercely contested first half ended goalless.

As the second half progressed, the visitors' superiority began to show and Holtby, assisted by Doyle, had to work hard to keep them at bay. In a rare breakaway, Sutherland should have scored for Town but, like Riddoch, was over-eager and shot wide.

Preston did get the ball over the line but the goal was disallowed for offside. Then came the controversial decision. Holmes cleared over the touchline for Preston. McBeth took the throw-in for Town, Hunt picked up his throw and passed to Jack Taylor, whose shot was helped in by Riddoch. The home crowd's jubilation was quickly stilled as Mr Clegg indicated 'no-goal', and the cheers turned to loud catcalls. Grimsby were now a disheartened team and 15 minutes from time, Goodall gave Preston the lead. Ross soon added the second.

The *Grimsby News* correspondent could not decide upon the reason for the disallowed goal but favoured hands as the only possible reason. As the only handling was at McBeth's throw-in, the *News* commented sarcastically: 'Mac should learn to throw-in without using his hands.' This was only part of a strong attack on the referee.

It is part of footballing history that Preston did the double without losing a game and without conceding a Cup goal — a record that is due in part to a hotly-disputed refereeing decision.

Grimsby Town: Holtby; Lundie, Doyle, J.H.Taylor, Smith, Reid, J.Taylor, Sutherland, Riddoch, McBeth, Hunt.
Preston North End: Mills-Roberts; Howarth, Holmes, Drummond, Russell, Graham, Thompson, Dewhurst, Goodall, Ross, Gordon.

Referee: J.Clegg (Sheffield) — *Attendance: 8,000*

Match to Remember 3 — 3 September 1892

Grimsby Town 2 Northwich Victoria 1

IT was a sunny afternoon as the players ran out at the Abbey Park Ground for the Mariners' first match as a Football League club. Having won the toss, the visitors elected to kick towards the railway end, leaving Grimsby Town to face the sun and the slight wind that prevailed.

For most of the first half, play was fairly even. Early shots from Riddoch for the home side and Hayes for the visitors came to nothing and, despite several free-kicks and corners to each side, the first half remained goalless.

On the resumption, the Mariners immediately took the initiative and after only 90 seconds pressure, the ball was passed via Sandy Higgins and John Ackroyd to Dave Riddoch, who netted the Mariners' first-ever League goal. Almost from the restart the home side pressed again and forced a corner. Geordie Murrell floated the ball into the penalty-area and once again Riddoch was on hand to crash the ball home. By now the game was all Grimsby and it was not long before dangerman Riddoch once more got the ball over the line. After protests from Victoria, referee Mr Fox ruled the effort offside, thus robbing Riddoch of an historic hat-trick. In one of the visitors' rare attacks, Adam Ogilvie fouled a Northwich forward, leaving Scanlon to convert from the penalty spot to give the visitors a scoreline which their performance scarcely merited.

Grimsby Town: Whitehouse; Lundie, Frith, Murrell, Walker, Ogilvie, Higgins, Henderson, Brayshaw, Ackroyd, Riddoch.
Northwich Victoria: Gow; Nesbitt, Scanlon, Stanley, Ross, Ramsey, Hayes, McCombie, Finnerhan, Hayes, McBeth.

Referee: Mr Fox (Sheffield) — *Attendance: 2,000*

The first season of the Second Division saw Grimsby Town finish in fourth place, 13 points behind champions Small Heath, who later became Birmingham City. Town's matches against the title-winners produced contrasting results. At home, the Mariners scored a 3-2 win, with Higgins netting all their goals. But at St Andrew's, Small Heath won 8-3, helped by a hat-trick from Billy Walton.

Town were involved in some high-scoring defeats that season, losing 5-3 at Northwich, 6-1 at Darwen and 5-1 at Burton Swifts.

Match to Remember 4 11 April 1896

Grimsby Town 7 Leicester Fosse 1

AS the Grimsby public was expecting a one-sided affair, less than 3,000 spectators had gathered when the teams ran out on a fine but windy afternoon for this Second Division match.

The Midlands side won the toss and opted to play with the wind behind them but less than two minutes had elapsed before the fears of the absentee spectators began to be realized. Fletcher gathered the ball and passed to McCairns, who put it into the penalty-area, expecting Pratt or Bell to get in a shot. Instead, Thraves rushed out of his goal to clear, missed the ball completely, and it rolled slowly over the line.

For a while, play became bogged down in midfield, with Leicester trying to take advantage of the high wind. They broke down the right wing and MacArthur sent in a high shot which Whitehouse momentarily lost in the sun, but eventually gathered.

Play switched to the other end, and with both Bailey and Baird being unable to clear the ball effectively, Bell got in a couple of good shots which Thraves saved. In a rare Leicester attack, MacArthur again got in a long, dropping shot which struck the crossbar.

A long period of Grimsby pressure eventually paid off. McCairns put in a weak shot, which the 'keeper should have saved, and scored his second goal, adding a third some minutes later after the Leicester defence failed to clear a shot from Bell. Following another midfield spell, during which Fletcher lost several teeth in an incident with Graham, Sandy Higgins added Grimsby's fourth goal.

From the restart Dorrell sprinted up the field before crossing to Brown, who passed to Manson. With Whitehouse once again losing the ball in the sun, Fosse reduced the arrears with a shot from the latter. In the second half the game was all the Mariners and for much of the time was most notable for some inconsistent refereeing. In the closing stages, with the Grimsby defence in complete control, the forwards indulged in some fancy ball play, during which Tommy McCairns scored a second-half hat-trick. His six goals in a League game remains a club record.

Grimsby Town: Whitehouse; Lindsay, Davis, Munn, Higgins, Graham, Bell, Pratt, McCairns, Fletcher, Gray.
Leicester Fosse: Thraves; Bailey, Baird, Lord, Walker, MacArthur, Trainer, Dorrell, Manson, Gallacher, Brown.

Grimsby Town, 1895-6. Back row (left to right): J.Shephard (secretary), R.C.Hall, C.White (vice president), F.B.Coulson (president), M.Jennison, W.H.Bellamy (treasurer), W.Allan (trainer). Middle row: T.Blair, Munn, Higgins, Graham, Lindsay, Whitehouse, Frith, Hudson, Davis. Front row: Bailey, Bell, Pratt, McCairns, Fletcher.

Match to Remember 5 — 15 April 1899

Grimsby Town 9 Darwen United 2

FEW of the sparse crowd that attended the last League match to be staged at the Abbey Park ground came in anticipation of a real contest. In their 16 away matches that season, the Lancashire side had scored only four times, whilst the defence had conceded exactly one hundred goals.

In anticipation of an easy run, the Mariners rested three of the first team and, despite losing the toss, took the initiative from the kick-off, McIver saving well from both Jenkinson and Bell in the opening minutes. After only five minutes it was Bell who sent the ball through the legs of a Darwen defender and it rolled over the line.

The Town forwards were teasing the Darwen defence, Jenkinson, Bell and Richards indulging in a spell of passing that denied the opposition any touch of the ball and Richards eventually netting Grimsby's second goal with a long-distance shot. With McIver doing wonders in the visitors' goal, the Mariners were denied again and again until a cross from Jenkinson was met by the head of Chatburn for the third.

The home team were now taking it easy, yet it needed little effort to rain in shot after shot and Jenkinson got the fourth and Cockshutt the fifth. Between these, Darwen's only shot of the half gave Bagshaw little trouble.

The second half was notable mainly for the outstanding display by McIver, who kept the Grimsby forwards at bay time and time again but could do little to stop Cockshutt (twice) and Jenkinson (twice) adding to the total.

Between the eighth and ninth goals, Bagshaw, evidently feeling sorry for the beleagured Lancastrians, made no effort to prevent weak shots from Bleasdale and Holding entering the net, these being the only threat of the half from the visitors. Thus, Grimsby's Abbey Park swan-song became their record League win. Darwen, of course, ceased to be a League team after that season.

Grimsby Town: Bagshaw; Lockie, Nidd, Griffiths, Bell, Nelmes, Jenkinson, Richards, Cockshutt, Robinson, Chatburn.
Darwen United: McIver; Wolfall, Cawthorne, Moore, Livesey, Wilson, Fish, Bleasdale, Bibly, Holding, Collinson.

Referee: Mr. Quorn (Lincoln) — *Attendance: 2,500*

Grimsby Town's nine-goal defeat of struggling Darwen was not the Mariners' only big win that season. They scored six goals each against Blackpool and Lincoln City and five against Luton Town. On the other side of the coin, Grimsby opened the season with a 7-2 defeat at Hyde Road, where Billy Meredith and Billy Gillespie both scored hat-tricks for Manchester City. Town also lost their last game of the season, 5-1 against Gainsborough Trinity in a game played at Sincil Bank, Lincoln.

Match to Remember 6 2 September 1899

Grimsby Town 3 Luton Town 3

WHEN the *Grimsby News* reporter arrived at Blundell Park for the christening of the new ground, his main impression was of the lack of a press-box.

The Grimsby Town team contained only two 'new' faces: goalkeeper Jimmy Whitehouse, who had left for Aston Villa three seasons previously, returned to the club; and Beveridge had arrived from Burnley. Luton, however, fielded a virtually new side. From the kick-off, the home side dominated and after only seven minutes a shot from Cockshutt squeezed between the legs of several players and into the net.

From the restart the Mariners again attacked but eventually Luton managed to break clear, only for Whitehouse to collect the long ball and throw out to the defence. The ball was not cleared but Brock, with an open goal, shot wide. Although it was obvious that Luton would be no pushovers, Grimsby had the upper hand. The second goal was somewhat of a surprise when a long, dropping shot from Nidd, who was almost on the halfway line, curled over the head of Daw and into the net. Despite the occasional Luton attack, Grimsby now dominated, the only fault being Richards' inclination to hold on to the ball too long. Eventually, in a goalmouth scrimmage, the ball went over the line. After consulting with his linesman, the referee awarded the third goal with Ratcliffe claiming the honours. The rest of the half was played amidst thunder and lightning, storm clouds which were to be reflected in Grimsby's second-half performance.

The storm was still raging when the teams ran out for the restart, but the referee failed to appear until the weather improved. From the kick-off, Brock set off down the field, slipped past the defence and beat Whitehouse with an easy shot. With the players having difficulty in mastering both the greasy ball and the sodden pitch, Beveridge was finding it hard to clear his defence, although play remained evenly balanced.

After a clearance from a Jenkinson shot found Brock, a mistake by Griffiths let the Luton forward in for his second goal, despite a brave attempt by Whitehouse. This gave the visitors new heart and they dominated the rest of the game, despite some doughty defending from Ratcliffe A few minutes before time McInnes shot through in a goalmouth scrimmage and the points were shared.

Grimsby Town: Whitehouse; Beveridge, Nidd, Griffiths, Gray, Nelmes, Jenkinson, Richards, Cockshutt, Ratcliffe, Greenwood.
Luton Town: Daw; Dow, McCurdy, Morrison, Stewart, Williams, Inglis, Brock, Fairgreave, McInnes, Eckford.

Referee: Mr. Hines (Nottingham) *Attendance: 4,000*

Blundell Park saw plenty of goals in its first season — Town beat Barnsley 8-1, Burton Swifts 6-0 and Leicester Fosse 6-1— but the darkest moment was when Newton Heath (later Manchester United) won 7-0 there on Boxing Day.

The Mariners' playing staff at the start of 1900-01, the season they won promotion to Division One. Back row (left to right): C. White, H.N. Hickson, C. Withers, Mr Page, Bellingham, Tennant, Craddock. Third row: Brocklesby, Nelmes, Mountain, Hemmingfield, Gray, Blyth, Fletcher, Griffiths, Unknown, Unknown. Second row: Mellor, Watkins, Harris, Hall, Harper, McConnell, Long, Appleyard. Front row: Ronaldson, Leigh, Lakey, McAvoy.

Match to Remember 7 — 27 April 1901

Middlesbrough 0 Grimsby Town 0

THE Mariners travelled to Middlesbrough for the last game of the 1900-01 season, already assured of promotion to the First Division. They were second in the table, level on 48 points with Small Heath but with a vastly inferior goal average.

Depending on how Small Heath fared at Burnley, the championship was still possible and to give the team every chance the Grimsby directors had agreed to an overnight stay in Saltburn.

On a fine but cold afternoon, Middlesbrough had most of the running in the early stages, with the visitors getting forward only rarely. Mellor missed a good chance when he shot over the bar after some clever approach work by himself and Watkins.

Middlesbrough received a set-back when Cochrane was taken off after receiving a kick in the eye but they continued to dominate the game, only some fine work in the Grimsby defence, especially from Leiper, denying them the opportunity to turn this domination into goals.

Grimsby were getting the occasional break and following a fine save by McFarlane from Wardrope, play moved swiftly up to the home end. Frail had to tip an awkward bouncing over the crossbar.

Shortly before half-time, Cochrane returned to the field and was quickly in action, breaking up a move by Hall and Fletcher. This pair soon set up another nice move from which Leigh headed over the bar. Middlesbrough had the upper hand but the first half closed goalless.

When the match resumed, Cochrane failed to reappear and Middlesbrough played with one full-back. The Mariners, however, were unable to take advantage of having an extra man and Middlesbrough continued to enjoy the run of play. When Grimsby did get forward, they often fell foul of the home side's offside tactics. Neither side managed to break the deadlock and the game ended with the score-sheet still blank.

Without the advantage of modern communications, both players and supporters had to wait for some time for the news that Small Heath had gone down by the only goal of the match at Burnley, which meant that Grimsby Town were Second Division champions.

Middlesbrough: Frail; Dow, Cochrane, Smith, Higgins, Davidson, Moran, Brearley, Robertson, McCowie, Wardrope.
Grimsby Town: McFarlane; Mountain, Leiper, Hemingfield, Gray, Nelmes, Fletcher, Hall, Leigh, Mellor, Watkins.

Referee: A.J. Barker (Hanley) — *Attendance: 8,000*

Match to Remember 8 — 3 September 1901

Grimsby Town 1 Derby County 1

IT was a fine afternoon as the players came out at a vastly refurbished Blundell Park for the Mariners' first match as a First Division club. It was no easy initiation, for included in the Rams team were some of the finest players of the day, notably Steve Bloomer, the England international forward. A greatly remodelled Grimsby side included only five players who had concluded the Second Division campaign the previous May.

The game was barely a minute old when the Mariners scored their first-ever First Division goal. Nelmes took a throw-in on the left, Bellingham gathered the ball and put it forward into the box where Leigh headed home.

Although Fryer in the Rams goal was perhaps guilty of an error, it was fitting that, as Leigh's goal had virtually ensured promotion the previous season, he should have the honour of opening the First Division account.

Derby immediately put on the pressure in trying to pull the goal back, but it was the Town who again went near when a terrific shot from Dean grazed the upright. Both sides were able to get in some good attacks but defences stood firm and the score remained unaltered until shortly before half-time, when Fulton beat Mountain on the left to level the scores. Minutes later, only a good tackle on Bloomer by Hemingfield prevented the visitors taking the lead.

The second half was evenly contested with both sides continuing to have chances, from which Dean for Grimsby and Crawford for the visitors might have done better. The Rams class was starting to show, but the Grimsby defence, with 'Bodge' Mountain having a particularly good game, held firm.

The Derby forwards were not helped by a particularly strong wind which carried several attempts at goal over the bar. The game continued to swing from end to end but neither side was able to improve on the scoreline.

Thus, the Mariners induction into First Division football ended in a draw, a not unsatisfactory result in view of the quality of the opposition.

Grimsby Town: Tennant; Mountain, Leiper, Hemingfield, Bellingham, Nelmes, Dean, Harper, Ronaldson, Leigh, Gardner.
Derby County: Fryer; Methven, Morris, May, Leckie, Warren, Crawford, Bloomer, Wombwell, Fulton, Haslam.

Referee: R.Horrocks (Bolton) — *Attendance: 7,000*

Left-back Joe Leiper joined Grimsby Town from Derby County in July 1900 and, just over a year later, turned out against his former club in Town's first match as a First Division club. Leiper, who played in an FA Cup Final for the Rams and also won a League Championship runners-up medal with them, made 46 League appearances for the Mariners before signing for Chesterfield in the close season of 1903. He later served Partick Thistle (his club before joining Derby), Hull City and Aberdare Athletic. He was known as 'Fossil' to the Derby players but one newspaper described him as a 'dashing and fearless back'.

Grimsby outside-right Prior beats a Middlesbrough defender.

Match to Remember 9

4 May 1929

Middlesbrough 3 Grimsby Town 0

IT seems fitting that Grimsby Town's golden jubilee season should have seen one of the most exciting finishes in the history of the club. Town travelled to Ayresome Park for the last day of the season, with both sides already assured of promotion. Both had 53 points but Middlesbrough led the table with a superior goal-average. The winners, therefore, would be assured of the Second Division championship — indeed a draw would suffice for Middlesbrough.

The heavy rain which had fallen throughout the morning had cleared to leave a fine afternoon. Town had already suffered a blow when goalkeeper 'Rocket' Read, who had not missed a match all season, was declared unfit and gave way to Thomas Poskett.

From the kick-off it was evident that a football treat was in store, with both teams opting for attack, and as the game progressed the Mariners had the slight edge in a keenly contested game. Indeed, they nearly took the lead when Coleman blasted a Prior centre inches wide.

It was Middlesbrough, though, who went in front after 20 minuutes when right winger Emmerson took the ball down his line and centred to Camsell, who evaded Charlie Wilson's tackle to beat Poskett.

Town were undaunted and their swift and accurate passing was causing the home defence some problems. Although they were at this stage by far the better side, Grimsby seemed fated not to score. Mathieson fisted out a Priestley shot; a Bestall effort hit the upright; Bestall then hit the underside of the bar and saw the ball rebound out to Mathieson, who was robbed by Coleman. The ball was loose in the box for some seconds before being cleared.

In the second half the home side were on more equal terms and, despite an attacking game which moved from goalmouth to goalmouth, only one goal separated the sides. Then, four minutes from the end, Middlesbrough put the issue beyond doubt. Poskett came out to gather a cross from the right but the ball evaded him and Camsell found himself with an empty net to shoot home. Although the Mariners pressed desperately during the closing minutes, Middlesbrough added a third with the last kick of the game when Williams deceived Poskett with a long shot.

The golden jubilee season did not, therefore, bring a trophy to Blundell Park but the prospect of First Division football more than made up for it. The national Press agreed that the scoreline flattered Middlesbrough, but that both teams merited Division One status.

Middlesbrough: Mathieson; Freeman, Smith, Miller, Ferguson, Peacock, Emmerson, Carr, Camsell, Bruce, Williams.
Grimsby Town: Poskett; Wilson, Jacobson, Priestley, Wrack, Calderwood, Prior, Bestall, Coleman, Coglin, Wright.

Referee: W.P.Harper (Stourbridge) *Attendance: 36,503*

Match to Remember 10 — 12 April 1930

Everton 2 Grimsby Town 4

ON a fine spring afternoon the Mariners ran out at Goodison Park to meet a side that only two seasons earlier had carried off the League Championship but now, despite some expensive team strengthening, were struggling alongside Grimsby to avoid the drop to Division Two.

Several changes in the Grimsby side included the introduction of young right-half Alec 'Ginger' Hall for his first League game. From the whistle, the Mariners took the initiative and an early shot from Robson was deflected for a corner. The same player forced a second corner only minutes later, but Everton gradually came more into the game and only a magnificent save by Read from Griffiths prevented them from taking the lead. Town had another let-off when Dixie Dean, perfectly placed, chose to pass to Martin instead of shooting.

It was Grimsby who took the lead after 20 minutes. Bestall found Prior on the right wing and his return ball to the centre found Robson, who beat Coggins, playing his first League match for Everton. The home side responded, attacking fiercely, and a highly competitive game moved quickly from end to end. After 33 minutes it was Jackie Bestall, again, who initiated the move which led to Town's second goal. Instead of the expected pass to Prior, he slipped the ball into the box where Robson eluded the defence to net his second goal.

It took only two more minutes for the Grimsby centre-forward to complete his hat-trick when, fouled well outside the penalty-area, he took the free-kick himself and hit an unstoppable ball into the top corner of the goal. Everton were now in a desperate mood and threw everything into the attack but some fine work from Read kept them out until the interval.

They came out determined to get back into the game but all too often were making the extra pass inside the box when a shot might have proved more effective. Read, who was having a fine game, did some good work in cutting out several threatening balls into the box.

Everton forced a number of corners and after 75 minutes Martin converted one through a ruck of players. Five minutes later the Merseysiders went further back into the game. Critchley took the ball down the right wing and his centre found Johnson who shot home from close range. The Mariners' defence had to work hard as Everton pressed for a share of the points but, three minutes from time, it was Bestall and Robson who again combined to give the latter his fourth goal and make the game safe.

By winning four of their remaining five games, Grimsby preserved their First Division status. Everton were not so lucky and dropped to the Second Division.

Everton: Coggins; Creswell, O'Donnell, McPherson, Griffiths, Thompson, Critchley, Martin, Dean, Johnson, Rigby.
Grimsby Town: Read; Wilson, Jacobson, Hall, Priestley, Buck, Prior, Bestall, Robson, Cooper, Marshall.

Referee: H.N.Mee (Mansfield) — *Attendance: 47,407*

FOOTBALL AT THE HAWTHORNS

J.O.C. PELHAM SHIELD FINAL
METROPOLITAN WELFARE v. BROOKFIELDS
On Monday, May 2nd. Kick-off 6-30 p.m.
Admission 3d. Wing Stand only.

W. W. HACKETT CHARITY CUP FINAL
ROWLEY SCHOOLBOYS v. WEST BROMWICH SCHOOLBOYS
On Tuesday, May 3rd. Kick-off 6 p.m.
Ground, Boys 2d., Adults 4d. Reserves extra.

BIRMINGHAM AND DISTRICT WORKS AMATEUR FOOTBALL ASSOCIATION

ALBION SHIELD FINAL
BIRMINGHAM RAILWAY CARRIAGE WORKS v. RATCLIFFS (GT. BRIDGE)
On Wednesday, May 4th. Kick-off 6-30 p.m.
Admission 6d. Wing Stand only.

PALETHORPE'S CHALLENGE BALL FINAL
BRADES STEEL WORKS v. KINGSBURY COLLIERY
On Thursday, May 5th. Kick-off 6-30 p.m.
Admission 6d. Wing Stand only.

Central League Championship Match No. 51 **LEEDS UNITED** **On Saturday, May 7th Kick-off 3-15 p.m. Usual Prices**

WEST BROMWICH ALBION

Colours.—Blue and White Striped Shirts, White Knickers.

Right PEARSON (1) Left

SHAW (2) TRENTHAM (3)

MURPHY (4) RICHARDSON, W. (5) EDWARDS (6)

GLIDDEN (7) CARTER (8) RICHARDSON, W. G. (9) SANDFORD (10) WOOD (11)

DODDS (12) MORALEE (13) HOLMES (14) BESTALL (15) DYSON (16)

WILSON, C. (17) SEDDON (18) BETMEAD (19)

JACOBSON (20) WILSON, C. H. (21)

Left READ (22) Right

GRIMSBY TOWN

Colours.—White Shirts, Black Knickers.

Referee : Mr. S. BOARDMAN (Hale).

Linesmen : Messrs. D. G. KIRBY (Red) and P. GUEST (Blue).

Match to Remember 11 — 30 April 1932

West Bromwich Albion 5 Grimsby Town 6

ONE of the most extraordinary League games in the history of Grimsby Town took place in the penultimate match of the 1931-2 season. The fact that the Mariners were bottom of the table and the Throstles, although comfortably placed, had nothing left to play for, was reflected in the sparse attendance, not helped by heavy rain which fell shortly before the kick-off.

Town received an early shock when, after good work by Glidden and Carter, centre-forward Richardson scored from a cross after only three minutes. Grimsby soon regained their composure and for some time the game was even, with both sides having chances. Then an error by Shaw in the Albion defence allowed Dyson to gain possession and pass to Holmes to level the scores 20 minutes from the start.

In the 26th minute, Read failed to gather a cross which found Wood on the left. The ball was returned to Sanford who headed into an empty goal. Only two minutes elapsed before Bestall's through-ball found Holmes to make the scores level again.

As the half drew to a close, the Mariners began to take the upper hand and Bestall missed a good chance to put them ahead. On 37 minutes, however, Dyson headed home a Marshall corner to give the Mariners the lead for the first time. It was short-lived and only a minute had elapsed before Carter made it 3-3.

Only a minute after the restart, Albion were awarded a penalty after Sanford was upended. Read managed to parry Edwards' spot-kick but as both players went for the loose ball, Edwards restored Albion's lead, leaving the Grimsby 'keeper motionless on the pitch. It was evident that Read could not continue and Bateman donned the blue jersey. Albion were quick to take advantage, Glidden making it 5-3 three minutes later.

Grimsby did not give up and were back with a chance when Dyson headed home a Marshall cross. Before the game was restarted Read returned to the fray, his face swathed in bandages. Albion now had a fight on their hands and only minutes later Shaw attempted to upend Holmes as the Grimsby centre-forward went clear in the box. With the referee on the point of giving a penalty, Holmes recovered and beat Pearson to put the scores level.

At 75 minutes, Town were awarded an indirect free-kick inside the box when Pearson was penalized for taking too many steps with the ball. Bestall slipped the ball sideways to Dyson and the Mariners once again had the lead. This disheartened the Midlanders, who now looked like a beaten side. Indeed, Town were unfortunate not to increase their lead.

Despite this magnificent battle, Grimsby remained anchored at the foot of the table and, although winning again the following week, were relegated.

West Bromwich Albion: Pearson; Shaw, Trentham, Murphy, W.Richardson, Edwards, Glidden, Carter, W.G.Richardson, Sanford, Wood.
Grimsby Town: Read; Bateman, Jacobson, Hall, Seddon, C.Wilson, Dyson, Bestall, Holmes, Moralee, Marshall.

Referee: S.Boardman (Hale) *Attendance: 13,101*

Match to Remember 12 — 7 April 1934

Hull City 0 Grimsby Town 1

WITH Grimsby Town already assured of First Division football, and virtually certain of the Second Division championship, the team made the short journey across the Humber to the Anlaby Road ground to wrap up the formalities.

Leading scorer Pat Glover was out with an injury, his place being taken by Ponting. The cross-Humber ferries had been packed to the gunwales and a large contingent of supporters greeted the Mariners as they followed Hull out on a fine afternoon.

It took only eight minutes for Town to take the lead. Jennings picked up the ball from a throw-in and found Craven on the wing. His centre found stand-in centre-forward Ponting unmarked in the box and, with the entire goal to aim at, he had no trouble in steering the ball out of the reach of Maddison.

Two minutes later Craven nearly made it two when latching on to a Dyson ball which the Hull 'keeper could only fist clear. The same Grimsby player also wasted a second chance to increase the lead.

The second half belonged almost entirely to Hull. Harry Betmead twice cleared off the line when Read was beaten and the big centre-half caused Grimsby hearts to flutter when, in attempting to head away a corner, he nearly put the ball through his own goal.

With only the occasional foray forward, the Mariners were continually forced back into defence and there were some dangerous moments when Read had to recover after dropping a bobbling ball and McNaughton blasted a fierce shot only inches over the bar. Twice in the closing minutes, Craven had chances to wrap up the game and with four minutes to go Maddison saved well from Ponting.

So, with four matches still to play, the Mariners had sealed the Second Division championship in what was statistically their best season ever.

Hull City: Maddison; Goldsmith, Woodhead, Allan, Melville, Speed, Hubbard, McNaughton, Jordan, Longden, Bullock.
Grimsby Town: Read; Kelly, Jacobson, Hall, Betmead, Buck, Dyson, Bestall, Ponting, Craven, Jennings.

Referee: N.Natrass (New Seaham) — *Attendance: 20,077*

Town group pictured in 1933-34, including nine of the side which beat Hull City to seal the Second Division title. Back row (left to right): Hall, Kelly, Betmead, Read, Jacobson, Buck. Front row: Lewis, Bestall, Glover, Craven, Jennings.

Pat Glover shoots wide of the Arsenal goal during the 1936 FA Cup semi-final.

Match to Remember 13 — 21 March 1936

Arsenal 1 Grimsby Town 0

A LEEDS Road semi-final against an Arsenal side that included nine internationals, and before a crowd of 63,210, was the closest that the Mariners ever came to a Wembley appearance.

Grimsby's case was not helped by the absence of Betmead, who was suspended following a clash with former Mariner Tim Coleman in the previous round against Middlesbrough. Left-back Jack Hodgson moved to centre-half and the left-back position was filled by Jimmy Kelly, who normally played right-back.

Grimsby were up against it from the start. With wing-halves Hall and Buck pressed into assisting the beleagured defence, and Craven not having one of his better days, Pat Glover received little service and close policing by Roberts rendered him ineffective for most of the match. Jackie Bestall had come in for some harsh treatment from Wilf Copping early in the game, from which he never fully recovered, so little was seen of the Mariners' attack.

Indeed, it was only by some gallant defending that the Arsenal were kept at bay for 38 minutes. Then Bowden slipped Hodgson and the unmarked centre-forward took a pass from his left-half. With Bastin up with him and only Hodgson left in defence, it was a two-to-one situation. Hodgson made his tackle but Bowden slipped the ball to Bastin who placed it past the advancing George Tweedy and into the net.

That was to prove the only goal of the match. An exceptional show from the Grimsby defence and four world-class saves from Tweedy kept Arsenal at bay in the second half. Indeed, the Mariners' left winger, Smailes, did manage to get the ball into the Arsenal net but the referee ruled that he had controlled it with his hand.

Arsenal: Wilson; Male, Hapgood, Crayston, Roberts, Copping, Hulme, Bastin, Bowden, James, Beasley.
Grimsby Town: Tweedy; Vincent, Kelly, Hall, Hodgson, Buck, Baldry, Bestall, Glover, Craven, Smailes.

Referee: T.J.Botham (Walsall) — *Attendance: 63,210*

Cyril Lewis entertains at the piano before the 1939 semi-final.

Dennis Westcott scores the second of his four goals, beating stand-in 'keeper Jack Hodgson.

The players leave the field after Town's semi-final defeat.

Match to Remember 14 — 25 March 1939

Wolverhampton Wanderers 5 Grimsby Town 0

WHEN the Mariners reached the FA Cup semi-finals for the second time in four seasons, an interesting game looked in prospect. Wolves were chasing a League and Cup double and were especially strong in attack. The Mariners, in a comfortable mid-table position and very strong in the half and full-back lines, entertained strong hopes of reaching Wembley for the first time.

From the kick-off in front of a record attendance at Old Trafford, it was the Mariners who took the early initiative with Jones drawing a save from Scott and Crack shooting wide. It was not until the sixth minute that George Moulson, deputizing in the Grimsby goal for the injured George Tweedy, got a touch of the ball and that was from a back-pass by Hodgson. Although Wolves gradually crept into the game, they were meting out some harsh treatment to the Town but, despite being awarded several free-kicks, the Mariners could not get ahead.

In the 20th minute tragedy struck. A through-ball from Wolves eluded both Betmead and Hodgson. As Westcott shot, Moulson came out and parried the ball. Dicky Dorsett, following up for Wolves, collided heavily with the Grimsby 'keeper and both players lay motionless on the grass.

Eventually stretchers were called and both men were carried off. Jack Hodgson went into goal, with Hall dropping back into the right-back position and Crack reverting to half-back.

The depleted Mariners briefly looked capable of overcoming their adversity and Scott was quickly off his line after a good move involving Beattie and Howe.

After 32 minutes, McIntosh latched on to a loose pass from Hall and, combining with Mullen, brought the ball forward. Despite appeals for offside from the Grimsby defence, the ball came through to Westcott who put the Wolves ahead against the run of play. Nine minutes later it was Westcott, again, who beat Teddy Buck and gave Hodgson no chance with his second goal. Wolves were by now back to full strength, Dorsett having returned with a bandaged leg.

After half-time Town appeared with only nine men. Moulson had been diagnosed to be suffering from concussion and would take no further part in the game. Boyd was still receiving treatment for a cut eye, but re-appeared before play commenced.

The fates continued to treat the Mariners harshly. It was Westcott again who beat Betmead. In trying to recover the ball, the Grimsby centre-half felled his opponent and a penalty was awarded, which Galley converted. The second half was less than three minutes old.

The Mariners' depleted attack, although they never gave up, could make no impression on Wolves' defence and in the dying minutes Westcott compounded the Mariners' misery with a further two goals in as many minutes.

Some players left the pitch prematurely and there was a minor incursion of Wolves fans when a whistle from the referee was mistaken for the final one. The pitch had to be cleared and the players recalled before the Town were finally put out of their misery.

Grimsby Town: Moulson; Vincent, J.V.Hodgson, Hall, Betmead, Buck, Boyd, Beattie, Howe, Jones, Crack.
Wolverhampton Wanderers: Scott; Morris, Taylor, Galley, Cullis, Gardiner, Maguire, McIntosh, Westcott, Dorsett, Mullen.

Referee: F.W.Wort (Hale) — *Attendance: 76,962*

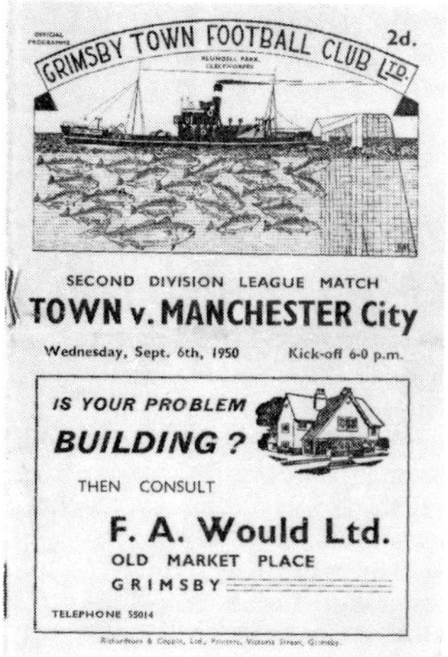

Match to Remember 15 — 6 September 1950

Grimsby Town 4 Manchester City 4

IN a club where honours have been few and far between, it is outstanding performances in run-of-the-mill League matches that are best remembered. One such performance took place on a cold, wet evening at Blundell Park, at the start of the 1950-51 season, in a Second Division encounter. Manchester City were already heading the table and Town were struggling, having scraped only three points from their first five games.

It was City who opened the scoring in the 17th minute when Oakes was allowed to advance to the by-line. Chisholm went to narrow the angle but the ball was cut back to Westcott, the man who had destroyed Town for Wolves in the 1939 FA Cup semi-final and he drove it home. Seven minutes later, Cairns was brought down on the edge of the box. He took the kick himself and, despite Trautmann's dive to his right, the scores were level. Encouraged, the Mariners took the initiative and when Shearer put Westwood under pressure, the defender's back-pass caught out Trautmann and Grimsby were ahead. Minutes later Briggs squandered a 'sitter'. With Town looking on top, the balance suddenly changed as Clarke beat both Moody and McMillan before crossing to Oakes, who should have scored. The loose ball came back to Clarke who put City on terms again.

The second half was only minutes old when Trautmann and Jock Shearer were involved in a violent collision and the Grimsby forward was carried off with a fractured leg. Despite a valiant fight by the Mariners, City took control and increased their lead through Spurdle and Westcott.

Two goals down and reduced to ten men, all looked lost, but with five minutes to go, a Grimsby cross was only partly parried by Trautmann. McMillan, who had advanced unnoticed to assist the attack, rammed home the loose ball. Two minutes after that, Mackenzie gathered the ball and passed to Cairns in the centre-circle. The veteran striker set off goalwards, with a City defender in pursuit. Roared on by the crowd, Cairns found an unmarked Briggs, who steered the ball past the advancing Trautmann. The ball rolled agonizingly slowly goalwards before crossing the line to the delight of both crowd and Grimsby players. It was one of the few moments of joy in a season which saw Town finish at the bottom of the table. It was a full year before Jock Shearer returned to first team football.

Grimsby Town: Chisholm; Moody, Fisher, Johnston, McMillan, Mackenzie, Lloyd, Shearer, Briggs, Cairns, Hair.
Manchester City: Trautmann; Phillips, Westwood, Paul, Rigby, Spurdle, Oakes, Hart, Westcott, Smith, Clarke.

Referee: A. Holland (Barnsley) *Attendance: 18,529*

Match to Remember 16 — 25 April 1956

Grimsby Town 2 Southport 0

AS more than 23,000 eager fans packed Blundell Park it presented a marked contrast to the scenes a year before. It had taken the Mariners a bare eight seasons to descend from being a First Division club to the humiliation of having to apply for re-election at the end of the 1954-5 season.

In an attempt to restore the flagging fortunes of the club, the board had appointed Manchester United and England centre-half, Allenby Chilton, to the post of player-manager just too late to avoid that re-election. But in the close season, with little money to spend, Chilton had rebuilt the team with some shrewd buys. He purchased five virtual rejects for a total of £2,000 and found that he had five stars.

The Mariners had started the season slowly, but on 13th September, began a run of 13 games without defeat which took them to the top of the Third Division North. A mid-season hiccup, however, gave the chasing clubs the opportunity to catch up and by February, Town had dropped to fourth place. Magnificent away wins at promotion rivals Accrington and Derby put them back in the race and as they ran out against Southport, they knew that a win would clinch the championship.

The visitors were in no mood to give the Mariners an easy ride and, although their forwards were rarely seen in the Grimsby penalty area, the solidly-packed yellow shirts seemed impregnable in defence. By half-time the score-sheet was still blank, but soon after the restart came the breakthrough. Inside-right Bill Evans latched on to a loose ball well outside the box. Ray Minshull in the Southport goal got a hand to the ball but could not prevent it from thundering into the back of his net. The delight of the crowd who packed the stands and the touchline was further fuelled when a cross from Jimmy Maddison on the left was met by the head of Bob Crosbie and promotion was safe.

Thus, Grimsby created a record by being the first team to go from re-election to championship in one season, a season in which Crosbie, who had cost less than £1,500, notched 35 goals in 42 League games, and the defence was beaten only 29 times in 46 games.

Grimsby Town: Williams; Brown, De Gruchy, Conner, Chilton, Johnston, Priestley, Evans, Crosbie, Reeson, Maddison.
Southport: Minshull; Parkinson, Hitchen, Gryba, Barratt, Charlton, Lawrenson, Beadnell, Bromilow, McIlvenny, McDermott.

Referee: L. Tirebuck (Halifax) — *Attendance: 23,056*

Grimsby Town in 1956. Back row (left to right): Bill Lambton (trainer), Dick Conner, Bill Brown, Jimmy Maddison, Clarrie Williams, Ray De Gruchy, Paddy Johnston. Front row: Gerry Priestley, Tony Reeson, Allenby Chilton, Bob Crosbie, Bill Evans.

Match to Remember 17 — 14 December 1957

Bristol Rovers 0 Grimsby Town 7

FROM the first whistle no Rovers supporter could be aware what a shock was in store for them in this Second Division game. It was the home side who went straight into attack as Biggs set off down the right wing before crossing to the unmarked Hooper who blasted the ball yards wide. Almost immediately Biggs featured again as he latched on to a bad back-pass but finished weakly.

Rovers, however, were in for a quick double shock. After six minutes, following a foul on Fell, Scott headed Richardson's free-kick goalwards. Nicholls only partly cleared and Stockin stabbed home the loose ball. Two minutes later Nicholls again failed to clear properly and this time Priestley was on hand to punish the error. With the Mariners' defence foiling Bristol's close game, the home side were creating few chances, whilst Town, dominant in midfield, were providing plenty of service to Johnny Scott and Jim Fell on the wings.

Although Rovers twice came close, through Biggs and Petherbridge, the score remained unchanged until a minute before the interval, when Priestley managed to get the ball back into the box from the by-line. Scott's attempt was cleared but he hit home the rebound and the Mariners went in for half-time well on top.

Rovers seemed to have gained little from any half-time pep talk and a combination of hesitant play and appalling passing gave Grimsby's defence little trouble as the visitors continued to dominate the game. After 70 minutes Sampson was adjudged to have fouled Priestley and, despite protests from City, a penalty was awarded which Rafferty converted. Seven minutes later, Fell set off on a solo run from the centre circle, outwitted a couple of demoralized Rovers defenders and became the fifth forward to get on the score-sheet.

Minutes later another lone run from Fell was treated with less ceremony and he finished up a heap in the penalty-box. This time, however, Rafferty blasted the ball high over the bar.

The Mariners were not finished, however, and with four minutes remaining, Scott, after cutting through from the left wing, scored his second. With two minutes to go Stockin made it seven. It was a black day indeed for Bristol football, as City were beaten 5-1 at Swansea.

Bristol Rovers: Nicholls; Bamford, Watling, Fitt, Hale, Sampson, Petherbridge, Biggs, Sykes, Ward, Hooper.
Grimsby Town: Williams; Brown, Richardson, Conner, Player, Whitefoot, Scott, Priestley, Rafferty, Stockin, Fell.

Referee: P.J.Smyth (London) *Attendance: 14,577*

Match to Remember 18 — 1 May 1962

Brentford 0 Grimsby Town 2

WITH the last full Saturday programme complete and Portsmouth assured of the Third Division championship, the second promotion place had still to be decided. If Queen's Park Rangers could win at Lincoln on the Monday and at Halifax on Thursday, and Town lost at Brentford on Tuesday, then QPR, not Town, would go up.

A large number of Mariners supporters travelled to Sincil Bank but their encouragement could not save the Imps from a 5-0 thrashing. So Grimsby ran out at Griffin Park the following evening before a large and chiefly hostile crowd, mostly QPR supporters, knowing that a point at least was necessary to ensure promotion.

The Bees, who were fighting to avoid relegation, went straight on to the attack but, despite much activity in the Grimsby penalty area, Barnett was rarely troubled. Although the Mariners settled, Brentford were still dominant in the attack and just after the half-hour, Donovan and then Keeble headed off the line to keep out Summers and Francis respectively.

After the interval it was Brentford who again went into the attack but in the 51st minute Rafferty was felled. Scott's free-kick rebounded off the defensive wall and Cliff Portwood put Town into the lead by scoring from an oblique angle. The Mariners now took control of the game and their fast and accurate passing had the home defence floundering.

After 80 minutes a Grimsby cross came in from the right. Coote should have cleared but was beaten to the ball by Rafferty, who put it past an advancing Cakebread to ensure Second Division football for the Mariners the following season. Condemned to a further season of Third Division football, QPR could manage only a 1-1 draw at Halifax two days later.

Brentford: Cakebread; Coote, Gitsham, Gelson, Dargie, Higginson, Summers, Brooks, Francis, McLeod, Black.
Grimsby Town: Barnett; Donovan, Keeble, Cockerill, Jobling, Knights, Scott, Cullen, Portwood, Rafferty, Jones.

Referee: W.D.Smith (Gloucester) — *Attendance: 19,080*

MIDDLESEX CHRONICLE
FOR ALL SPORTS
FRIDAY — 3d.
136, High Street, Hounslow—0016

ALL-ENGLAND CLEANING CO. LTD.
Hersham Trading Estate, Walton-on-Thames, Surrey
TELEPHONE: WALTON-ON-THAMES 20571 P.B.X
DAILY OFFICE CLEANING AND GENERAL CLEANING CONTRACTS

HEAVY DUTY — PART EXCHANGE
SPEEDWELL BATTERIES (LONDON) LTD.
Business Hours: 8.30 a.m. to 5.30 p.m. (early closing Thurs. 1 p.m.)
Head Office: 3a MARDALE STREET, LONDON, W.12
Telephone: SHE 4224

For Full Reports of ALL Brentford Matches — and the Inside News and Gossip
YOU WANT THE
"BRENTFORD & CHISWICK TIMES"
(On sale Fridays, 3d.)

Tel.: ISLeworth 3839
H. F. Davis (Brentford) Ltd.
BUILDERS AND CONTRACTORS
Reg. Office:
CLIFDEN CORNER
BOSTON MANOR ROAD
BRENTFORD, MIDDX.
Works:
POTTERY ROAD, BRENTFORD

BRENTFORD PRINTING AND PUBLISHING CO. LTD.
Day and Night
Commercial
and Colour Printers
Albany Works, Brentford
Phone: ISLeworth 7216 (3 lines)

RIGHT WING — BRENTFORD — LEFT WING
Colours—RED AND WHITE STRIPES
CAKEBREAD
2—COOTE 3—GITSHAM
4—GELSON 5—DARGIE 6—HIGGINSON
8—BROOKS 10—McLEOD
7—SUMMERS 9—FRANCIS 11—BLOCK

Referee:
Mr. D. W. SMITH
(Glos.)

Linesmen:
Messrs.
M. R. Nester (Red Flag)
R. A. Pipe (Yellow Flag)

11—JONES 9—PORTWOOD 7—SCOTT
10—RAFFERTY 8—CULLEN
6—KNIGHTS 5—JOBLING 4—COCKERILL
3—KEEBLE 2—DONOVAN
BARNETT
GRIMSBY TOWN
Colours—WHITE AND BLACK
LEFT WING — RIGHT WING

THERE ARE NO
CRISPS
LIKE
SMITH'S

BRENTFORD F.C. BIRMINGHAM F.C.
JACK GOODWIN
SPORTS SPECIALIST
near NORTHFIELDS STATION
Suppliers to the England Team
EALING 7577

BRENTFORD TIMBER CO. LTD.
ISLeworth 3028
MEDINA WHARF, KEW BRIDGE RD., BRENTFORD, MIDDLESEX
HOURS: MON.—FRI. 8—5.30 SAT. 9—12
Wholesale and Retail

Brentford's Premier Hire Service
G. DAVIS & SON
EALING ROAD GARAGE
EALING ROAD, BRENTFORD
Phone: ISLeworth 1718 and 5471

S. J. WILSON & SON
Phone: ISL 6465 Prop.: L. R. WINTER
Albany Dairy,
34 & 35, Albany Road, Brentford

Telephone: ISLeworth 7158
H. R. BOHEE & SON LTD.
Colour and Commercial
Printers
58 and 59, HIGH STREET
BRENTFORD — Middlesex

four — five

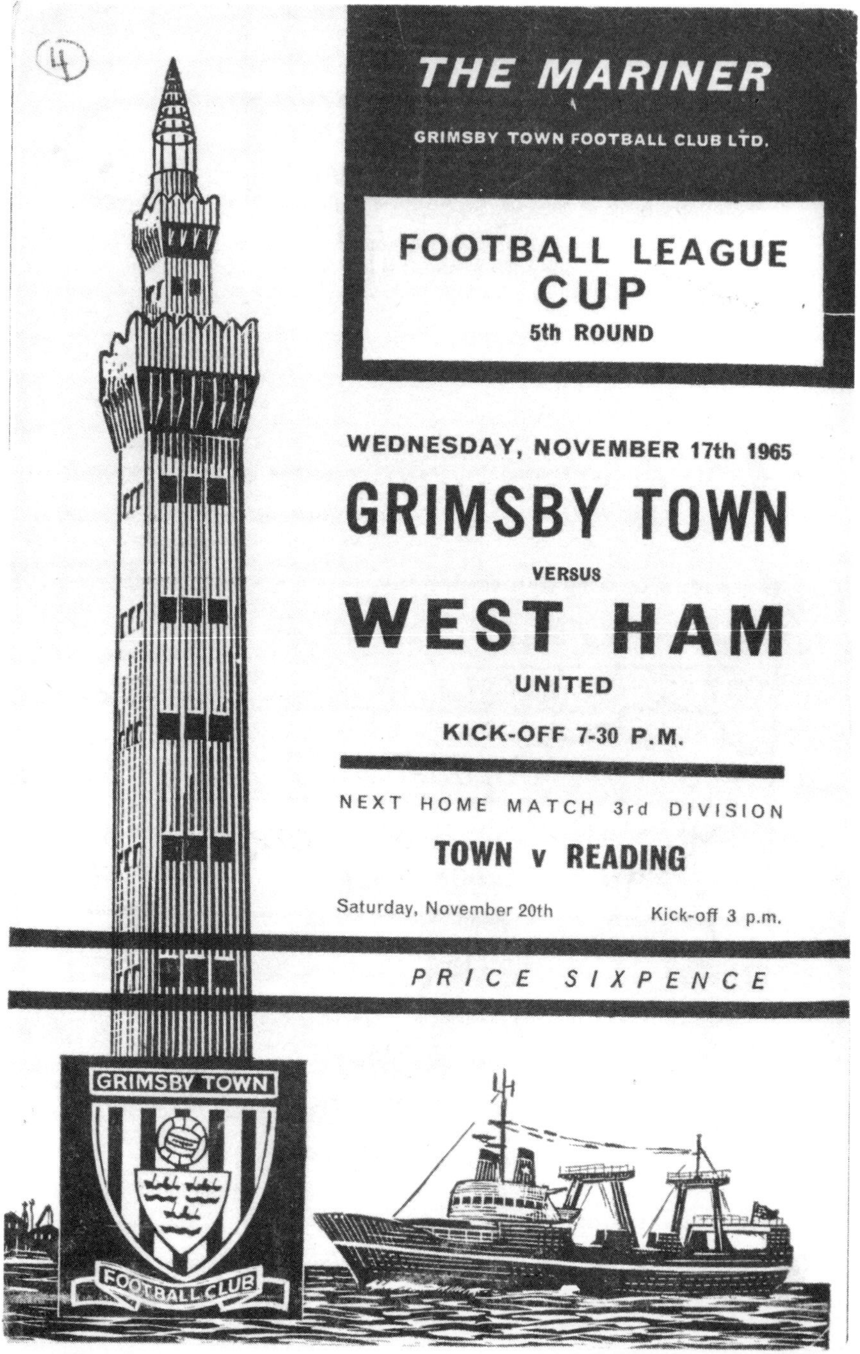

THE MARINER

GRIMSBY TOWN FOOTBALL CLUB LTD.

FOOTBALL LEAGUE
CUP
5th ROUND

WEDNESDAY, NOVEMBER 17th 1965

GRIMSBY TOWN
VERSUS
WEST HAM
UNITED

KICK-OFF 7-30 P.M.

NEXT HOME MATCH 3rd DIVISION

TOWN v READING

Saturday, November 20th Kick-off 3 p.m.

PRICE SIXPENCE

Match to Remember 19 — 17 November 1965

Grimsby Town 2 West Ham United 2

IT was a crowd eager with anticipation that packed the terraces at Blundell Park, their enthusiasm not dampened by the persistent rain that had fallen throughout the day and that had at one stage put the match in jeopardy.

The Mariners, comfortably placed in the Third Division, were enjoying a good run in the League Cup, having disposed of Second Division opposition in the three previous rounds.

The reward for the Blundell Park faithful was a tie against the redoubtable Hammers for a place in the semi-finals. This was West Ham at their peak, holders of the European Cup-winners' Cup and fielding three players who were to form a vital part of Alf Ramsey's England World Cup winning team the following summer, Geoff Hurst, Martin Peters and skipper Bobby Moore.

The Mariners suffered a blow when half-back Bobby Ross reported unfit. Seventeen-year-old Angus Davidson came in to make his senior debut for Grimsby. Despite the appalling state of the pitch, following the non-stop rain, the crowd was to witness a classic with the Mariners taking West Ham on at their own game, with a display of cultured football.

It took only 11 minutes for Town to snatch the lead. Debutant Davidson sent a perfect cross to Doug Collins on the right flank and Collins made room for himself before floating an equally perfect cross for Matt Tees to head the ball over the head of the advancing Jim Standen.

Despite the Hammers' ability to move the ball from defence to attack, the home defence seemed impregnable. It was a freak goal which put the match level in the 32nd minute, when left-back John Charles took the ball up the wing and lifted it goalwards. Caught by the wind, the ball completely deceived Wright and entered the net. Encouraged by this stroke of fortune, West Ham launched attack after attack but the defence stood firm and at half-time the scores were still level.

After the restart it was Grimsby who again drew first blood, when Rod Green chased a Brian Hill pass, caught it near the by-line and drove the ball into the net from an almost impossible angle. At this stage the Mariners probably thought that a place in the semi-final was theirs, for the Hammers' attack was foundering again and again on a rock-like Grimsby defence. After 70 minutes, however, a rare defensive error let in Geoff Hurst and the sides were level again.

In the following night's *Grimsby Evening Telegraph*, the referee was quoted as saying, "It was the best game I have seen in years — I would have paid to referee it."

A month later, at Upton Park, it took the Hammers 80 minutes to breach the Mariners' defence, when a goal by Geoff Hurst decided the tie.

Grimsby Town: Wright; Thompson, Taylor, Davidson, Jobling, Clifton, Collins, Tees, Green, Foster, Hill.
West Ham United: Standen; Kirkup, Charles, Bovington, Brown, Moore, Brabrook, Peters, Britt, Hurst, Sissons.

Referee: P.Rhodes (York) — *Attendance: 16,281*

Match to Remember 20 — 7 September 1966

Grimsby Town 7 Scunthorpe United 1

TO be on the wrong end of a 7-1 thrashing could put a young goalkeeper off the game for life. Luckily for football, such an experience did not deter 18-year-old Ray Clemence after he conceded seven at Blundell Park.

Clemence was part of a Scunthorpe defence that included four teenagers in the Iron's youngest-ever squad. They were unfortunate enough to meet the Mariners on one of those nights when everything goes right and the combined experience of Barry Horstead and Bob Smith was not able to stem the avalanche of goals to come.

It took eight minutes for the cracks to appear. Graham Taylor foiled a Scunthorpe attack and fed Hill on the left wing. The winger, beating Barker for speed, centred the ball to Tees, who blasted it past Clemence. Four minutes later it was right-back Thompson who provided the cross which Clemence might have gathered, but he was slow off his line and Green headed home. After 24 Horsted failed to clear cleanly and the loose ball went to Hill, who provided the pass for Green to take his second. Fifteen minutes later the left winger added his own name to the score-sheet when, eluding the attention of three defenders, he cut into the box and shot into the top corner. Hill got his second four minutes from the interval when he latched on to a clearance from his own free-kick.

In the first 15 minutes of the second half, both Green and Hill completed their hat-tricks. It was the left winger who provided the corner for an unmarked Green to head home number six and Hill got the seventh when a wild Clemence clearance landed at his feet, leaving him to shoot into an empty net.

For the last half-hour, the Mariners coasted and six minutes from time Bedford scored a consolation goal for the Iron. The fact that Ray Clemence recovered from the experience to serve both Liverpool, Spurs and England with such distinction is part of football history.

The superiority of the Mariners on the night was not reflected over the season, as they finished 17th, just one place above the Iron and with one more point.

Grimsby Town: Wainman; Thompson, G.Taylor, Ross, Jobling, Cockerill, Worthington, Tees, Green, Rudd, Hill.
Scunthorpe United: Clemence; Barker, S.Taylor, Smith, Horsted, Welbourne, Bramley, Bedford, Thomas, Ash, Colquhoun.

Referee: H.P.Hackney (Barnsley) *Attendance: 8,044*

Ron Cockerill, one of the unsung heroes of Town's victory over Scunthorpe. The tough-tackling wing-half did not get his name on the scoresheet but dealt competently with what few threats the visitors posed.

Evening Telegraph 11th Aug 1971

Hands across the sea — Grimsby Town captain Dave Worthington exchanges pennants with Japanese skipper Ogi before the start of last night's game. Referee Ray Tinkler, of Boston, looks on.

A feast for the fans

GRIMSBY TOWN 7, JAPAN 2. Attendance: 3,353.

NINE great goals, including two from 17-years-old Durham City trialist Geoff Hart, and a hat-trick from Mike Hickman, provided 90 minutes of action-packed, entertaining football when Grimsby Town met the Japanese national side at Blundell Park last night.

by Vince McDonagh

Blundell Park will see nothing like it for a long time to come. A game almost devoid of fouls, it had the 3,300 crowd in a standing ovation for both teams at the end.

Inside right Yosh...

...runner from Durham, came on as substitute 25 minutes from the end and soon showed that he has plenty of potential.

Five minutes after his appearance he scored with a simple close - range header ... completed his hat...

Match to Remember 21 — 10 August 1971

Grimsby Town 7 Japan 2

AN unusual pre-season friendly occurred when Japan's national side visited Blundell Park. The Japanese, whose soccer history went back only to the 1964 Tokyo Olympics, were on a European tour to gain experience and had, the previous week, suffered heavy defeats at Hull and Southampton.

It was clear from the kick-off that, although the visitors possessed skill as individuals, they were completely ineffective as a team. It took only three minutes for Town to take the lead with a shot from Lewis. With Grimsby in the ascendancy and the Japanese relying on quick breaks, Town were unlucky not to go further ahead as shots from Brace, Boylen and Woodward cannoned off the perplexed Oriental defence.

In the 41st minute the Japanese were on level terms, however, when a cross from Yoshimura found the head of Kamamoto. Two minutes later, Tees restored Grimsby's lead after latching on to the ball as Yokoyama punched out a Woodward cross.

During the second half the Mariners were completely in control and two goals from Mike Hickman put them 4-1 ahead. Twenty minutes into the half, the Grimsby defence were caught napping and Kamamoto pulled a goal back.

At this stage Town brought on Geoff Hart, a trialist from Durham, for Jack Lewis, and after five minutes he got on the score sheet after the heading the ball home. Mike Hickman completed a second-half hat-trick in the 78th minute and Hart headed his second in the dying minutes of the game. Despite of his brace of goals, Hart was not offered terms.

Grimsby Town: Wainman; Worthington, Campbell (Simpson), Thomson, Rathbone (Wigginton), Gray, Brace (Park), Lewis (Hart), Tees, Boylen, Woodward (Hickman).
Japan: Yokoyama; Katayama, Ogi, Kawakami, Yamaguchi, Mori, Ashigaka, Yoshimura, Kamamoto, Sugiyama.

Referee: R.Tinkler (Boston) — *Attendance: 3,353*

Match to Remember 22 — 3 May 1980

Grimsby Town 4 Sheffield United 0

AS the teams ran out for the final game of the season, the Mariners were already assured of Second Division football. Three points would send them up as champions and a draw meant that Blackburn would have to win 5-0 to overtake them. United headed the table half-way through the season, but had fallen out of the reckoning.

The Mariners went straight into attack and only a brave save by Richardson from Waters prevented them taking the lead in the first minute.

Town, however, were dominating the game and after 18 minutes an inswinging corner from Mike Brolly found Kevin Drinkell unmarked by the far post and Grimsby were ahead. Two minutes later, Cumming again got the ball into the net but the referee had spotted an infringement and the goal was disallowed.

On 38 minutes, Joe Waters gathered the ball on the right, waltzed around three United defenders and made it 2-0. Two minutes later a ball from Bobby Mitchell found Drinkell again unmarked and the half-time whistle came with Town 3-0 in the lead.

In the second half, although the Mariners were dominating the match, they could only add one more, after Kevin Moore took a free-kick from the half-way line. After a mêlée in the penalty-box, the loose ball found Drinkell, who completed his hat-trick and put the championship beyond any doubt.

Grimsby Town: Batch; D.Moore, K.Moore, Waters, Wigginton, Crombie, Brolly, Ford, Drinkell, Mitchell (Stone), Cumming.
Sheffield United: Richardson; Cutbush, Tibbott, Kenworthy, A.Moore, Matthews, De Goey (Charles), Speight, Brown, Sabella, Wiggan.

Referee: R.W.Toseland — *Attendance: 19,276*

Grimsby Town players salute the Blundell Park crowd after beating Sheffield United 4-0 to clinch the Third Division championship.

Trevor Whymark (left) squandered a chance to give Grimsby the lead but Paul Emson (right) was on target for the second goal.

Match to Remember 23 — 17 December 1983

Chelsea 2 Grimsby Town 3

DURING the 1983-4 season, the Fiat motor company sponsored an award whereby the week's outstanding performance by a League club won £250 and a new strip for a local boys' club nominated by the winners. The Mariners gained this award for the 1st Cleethorpes Boys Brigade with this win at Stamford Bridge.

Although Chelsea were amongst the clubs fancied for a return to the First Division, the Mariners went to London with a positive attitude. Whymark and Wilkinson squandered chances to take the lead. In the 27th minute, however, an offence by Kevin Moore earned the home side a penalty, which Kerry Dixon converted. Twelve minutes into the second half, John Bumstead added a second to make the points look safe for Chelsea.

The Mariners had other ideas, however. On 66 minutes, Joe Waters, whose midfield play was the inspiration of the revival, beat Niedzwiecki with a 30-yard chipped shot. Eight minutes later, Paul Emson jinked round the home defence and the Chelsea 'keeper could only get a finger-tip to the ball as it entered the net.

By now the Blues were in some disarray and it was no surprise when, three minutes later, it was again Emson who sent an inch-perfect cross for Tony Ford, who made it three to stun the occupants of the Shed into unaccustomed silence. In between these last goals, referee D.J. Axcell had to be stretchered off the field, to be replaced by his linesman, D.H. Nevin.

Chelsea: Niedzwiecki; Hollins, Jones, Pates, McLaughlin, Bumstead, Nevin, Spackman, Dixon, Speedie (Lee), Canoville.
Grimsby Town: Batch; Cumming, Crombie, Waters, Nicholl, Moore, Ford, Wilkinson, Whymark, Bonnyman, Emson.

Referee: D.J.Axcell (Southend) *Attendance: 13,151*

Match to Remember 24 — 20 November 1984

Everton 0 Grimsby Town 1

WHEN the Mariners were drawn to play at Goodison Park in the fourth round of the Milk Cup, supporters' memories went back five years to when the Toffees had fallen 2-1 at Blundell Park in the same competition, then called simply the League Cup.

This time the task looked more formidable. Everton headed the First Division, were unbeaten at Goodison since the first day of the season and had won their last ten matches. For the 3,000 Mariners fans who made the trip up the M62, it proved to be a heart-stopping 90 minutes, with all 11 players manning the defences and only a long shot from Steve Foley in the eighth minute calling Neville Southall into action.

For the remainder of the match it was constant attack from Everton. Mastered by a superb midfield display from Peter Reid, they probed and harried for the vital breakthrough. As the match progressed, despite the continuous onslaught, the beleagured Grimsby defence stood firm, with Kevin Moore, Chris Nicholl and Chris Seagraves all making goal-line clearances when Batch was well beaten.

Batch kept the Mariners in the game by turning aside a goal-bound drive from Paul Bracewell. When an injured Steve Foley was taken off in favour of Kevin Drinkell in the 50th minute, the Everton midfield became even more dominant and it is indicative of their superiority that with Southall a spectator they forced 19 corners to the Mariners none.

With a replay at Blundell Park looking a certainty, Town were in no hurry to take the free-kick when Gary Lund was brought down by Peter Reid in one of their rare attacks. With Bonnyman, Crombie and Ford surrounding the ball, it was Phil Bonnyman who elected to take the kick. He lobbed the ball over the Everton defence and on to the head of the advancing Paul Wilkinson. Southall was beaten and a stunned Goodison crowd saw the ball nestling in the back of the net.

That, however, was the end of the fairy-story and in the next round Norwich City went to Blundell Park and won by the only goal. Howard Kendall's reaction was to take Wilkinson on to Everton's books for £250,000, towards the end of the season.

Everton: Southall; Stevens, Van den Hauwe, Ratcliffe, Mountfield, Reid, Steven, Heath, Sharp, Bracewell (Gray), Sheedy.
Grimsby Town: Batch; Seagraves, Crombie, Foley (Drinkell), Nicholl, K.Moore, Ford, Wilkinson, Lund, Bonnyman, Emson.

Referee: T.J.Holbrook (Wolverhampton) — *Attendance: 26,298*

Chris Nicholl made a goal-line clearance after Nigel Batch was beaten.

Paul Wilkinson's last-minute header beats Neville Southall to give Grimsby a famous Milk Cup victory.

Paul Bonnyman, whose free-kick was headed home by Wilkinson.

Wilkinson salutes the Mariners' supporters as the ball is in the Everton net.

Match to Remember 25 7 January 1989

Middlesbrough 1 Grimsby Town 2

MOST of the 2,000 Mariners' fans who made the trip from the Humber to the Tees did so more in hope than anticipation. Despite beating Wolves and Rotherham, respective leaders of the Third and Fourth Divisions, in the previous two rounds, Grimsby were struggling at the wrong end of the lower division. The 'Boro were comfortably placed amongst the middle clubs in the First Division and were firm favourites for this third-round FA Cup tie.

Having been ousted from the Littlewoods Cup by Tranmere Rovers, another Fourth Division club, the home side would be anxious to avoid another humiliation.

The expected early onslaught from Middlesbrough failed to materialize, with Grimsby more than holding their own. The play swung from end to end and it was 20 minutes before the first clear-cut shot at goal came, when Paul Reece saved well from Peter Davenport.

Five minutes later, Shaun Cunnington latched on to a through-ball from John McDermott, but after a solo run of almost half the length of the pitch, he was foiled by 'Boro goalkeeper Pears.

The match remained even until the 40th minute. A ball from Hamilton, on the home side's left flank, was helped on by Ripley for leading scorer Bernie Slaven to put Middlesbrough ahead at half-time.

After half-time the Mariners came more and more into the game but were failing to convert their chances. Pears saved well from O'Kelly in the 54th minute; in the 65th, Alexander shot over when well placed. With 20 minutes remaining, manager Buckley brought on substitute Marc North for O'Kelly.

The substitution was made during a break for a Grimsby throw-in. Jobling's throw reached Alexander, who beat England's Gary Pallister to pass to North, who turned sharply in the box and drove the ball past Pears with his first touch of the game.

With both sides out for the deciding goal, it was an exciting last 20 minutes and, with Reece beaten, Gary Pallister headed on to the bar.

With three minutes remaining, a Blundell Park replay looked inevitable. Then Jobling and Alexander combined and got the ball to North, whose diving header put Grimsby Town into the fourth round.

Middlesbrough: Pears; Burke, Cooper, Mowbray, Hamilton, Pallister, Slaven(Mohan), Brennan, Glover, Davenport, Ripley.

Grimsby Town: Reece; McDermot, Agnew, Tillson, Lever, Cunnington, Jobling, Saunders, O'Kelly(North), Cockerill, Alexander.

Referee: A.Seville (Birmingham) *Attendance: 19,190*

Substitute Marc North was Grimsby's hero. Top: North puts Town level with his first kick of the game. Bottom: North's diving header gives the Mariners a place in the fourth round.

OFFICE
SYSTEMS

FAX

Grimsby in the Football League 1892-93 to 1988-89

		HOME					*AWAY*						
	P	W	D	L	F	A	W	D	L	F	A	Pts	Pos
					DIVISION TWO								
1892-93	22	8	1	2	25	7	3	0	8	17	34	23	4th
1893-94	28	11	1	2	47	16	4	1	9	24	42	32	5th
1894-95	30	14	0	1	51	16	4	1	10	28	36	37	9th
1895-96	30	14	1	0	51	9	6	1	8	31	29	42	3rd
1896-97	30	12	2	1	44	15	5	2	8	22	30	38	3rd
1897-98	30	9	1	5	44	24	1	3	11	8	38	24	12th
1898-99	34	10	3	4	39	17	5	2	10	32	43	35	10th
1899-1900	34	10	3	4	46	24	7	3	7	21	22	40	6th
1900-01	34	14	3	0	46	11	6	6	5	14	22	49	1st
					DIVISION ONE								
1901-02	34	11	3	3	33	16	2	3	12	11	44	32	15th
1902-03	34	6	5	6	28	22	2	4	17	15	40	25	17th
					DIVISION TWO								
1903-04	34	12	5	0	39	12	2	3	12	11	37	36	6th
1904-05	34	9	3	5	22	14	2	5	10	11	32	30	13th
1905-06	38	11	7	1	33	13	4	3	12	13	33	40	8th
1906-07	38	13	2	4	34	16	3	1	15	23	46	35	15th
1907-08	38	8	5	6	27	24	3	3	13	16	47	30	18th
1908-09	38	9	5	5	23	14	5	2	12	18	40	35	13th
1909-10	38	8	3	8	31	19	1	3	15	19	58	24	19th
1910-11	Not re-elected. Played in Midland League												
1911-12	38	9	6	4	24	18	6	3	10	24	37	39	9th
1912-13	38	10	8	1	32	11	5	2	12	19	39	40	7th
1913-14	38	10	4	5	24	15	3	4	12	18	43	34	15th
1914-15	38	10	4	5	36	24	1	5	13	12	52	31	17th
1919-20	42	8	4	9	23	24	2	1	18	11	51	25	22nd
					DIVISION THREE								
1920-21	42	12	5	4	32	16	3	4	14	17	43	39	13th
					DIVISION THREE NORTH								
1921-22	38	15	4	0	54	15	6	4	9	18	32	50	3rd
1922-23	38	10	3	6	35	18	4	2	13	20	34	33	14th
1923-24	42	11	9	1	30	7	3	4	14	19	40	41	11th
1924-25	42	10	6	5	38	21	5	3	13	22	39	39	12th
1925-26	42	20	1	0	61	8	6	8	7	30	32	61	1st
					DIVISION TWO								
1926-27	42	6	7	8	39	39	5	5	11	35	52	34	17th
1927-28	42	8	6	7	41	41	6	6	9	28	42	40	11th
1928-29	42	16	2	3	49	24	8	3	10	33	37	53	2nd
					DIVISION ONE								
1929-30	42	8	6	7	39	39	7	1	13	34	50	37	18th
1930-31	42	13	2	6	55	31	4	3	14	27	56	39	13th
1931-32	42	11	4	6	39	28	2	2	17	28	70	32	21st
					DIVISION TWO								
1932-33	42	8	10	3	49	34	6	3	12	30	50	41	13th
1933-34	42	15	3	3	62	28	12	2	7	41	31	59	1st
					DIVISION ONE								
1934-35	42	13	6	2	49	25	4	5	12	29	35	45	5th
1935-36	42	13	4	4	44	20	4	1	16	21	53	39	17th
1936-37	42	13	3	5	60	32	4	4	13	26	49	41	11th
1937-38	42	11	5	5	29	23	2	7	12	22	45	38	20th

	P	W	D	L	F	A	W	D	L	F	A	Pts	Pos
		HOME					*AWAY*						
DIVISION ONE													
1938-39	42	11	6	4	38	26	5	5	11	23	43	43	16th
1946-47	42	9	6	6	37	35	4	6	11	24	47	38	16th
1947-48	42	5	5	11	20	35	3	1	17	25	76	22	22nd
DIVISION TWO													
1948-49	42	10	5	6	44	28	5	5	11	28	48	40	11th
1949-50	42	13	5	3	53	25	3	3	15	21	48	40	11th
1950-51	42	6	8	7	37	38	2	4	15	24	57	28	22nd
DIVISION THREE NORTH													
1951-52	46	19	2	2	59	14	10	6	7	37	31	66	2nd
1952-53	46	15	5	3	47	19	6	5	12	28	40	52	5th
1953-54	46	14	5	4	31	15	2	4	17	20	62	41	17th
1954-55	46	10	4	9	28	32	3	4	16	19	46	34	23rd
1955-56	46	20	1	2	54	10	11	5	7	22	19	68	1st
DIVISION TWO													
1956-57	42	12	4	5	41	26	5	1	15	20	36	39	16th
1957-58	42	13	4	4	54	30	4	2	15	32	53	40	13th
1958-59	42	7	7	7	41	36	2	3	16	21	54	28	21st
DIVISION THREE													
1959-60	46	12	7	4	48	27	6	9	8	39	43	52	4th
1960-61	46	14	4	5	48	32	6	6	11	29	37	50	6th
1961-62	46	18	3	2	49	18	10	3	10	31	38	62	2nd
DIVISION TWO													
1962-63	42	8	6	7	34	26	3	7	11	21	40	35	19th
1963-64	42	6	7	8	28	34	3	7	11	19	41	32	21st
DIVISION THREE													
1964-65	46	11	10	2	37	21	5	7	11	31	46	49	10th
1965-66	46	15	6	2	47	25	2	7	14	21	37	47	11th
1966-67	46	13	5	5	46	23	4	4	15	15	45	43	17th
1967-68	46	10	7	6	33	21	4	2	17	19	48	37	22nd
DIVISION FOUR													
1968-69	46	5	7	11	25	31	4	8	11	22	38	33	23rd
1969-70	46	9	9	5	33	24	5	6	12	21	34	43	16th
1970-71	46	13	4	6	37	26	5	3	15	20	45	43	19th
1971-72	46	18	3	2	61	26	10	4	9	27	30	63	1st
DIVISION THREE													
1972-73	46	16	2	5	45	18	4	6	13	22	43	48	9th
1973-74	46	14	6	3	48	21	4	9	10	19	29	51	6th
1974-75	46	12	8	3	35	19	3	5	15	20	45	43	16th
1975-76	46	13	7	3	39	21	2	3	18	23	53	40	18th
1976-77	46	10	6	7	29	22	2	3	18	16	47	33	23rd
DIVISION FOUR													
1977-78	46	14	6	3	30	15	7	5	11	27	36	53	6th
1978-79	46	15	5	3	51	23	11	4	8	31	26	61	2nd
DIVISION THREE													
1979-80	46	18	2	3	46	16	8	8	7	27	26	62	1st
DIVISION TWO													
1980-81	42	10	8	3	21	10	5	7	9	23	32	45	7th
1981-82	42	5	8	8	29	30	6	5	10	24	35	46	17th
1982-83	42	9	7	5	32	26	3	4	14	13	44	47	19th
1983-84	42	13	6	2	36	15	6	7	8	24	32	70	5th
1984-85	42	13	1	7	47	32	5	7	9	25	32	62	10th
1985-86	42	11	4	6	35	24	3	6	12	23	28	52	15th
1986-87	42	5	8	8	18	21	5	6	10	21	38	44	21st
DIVISION THREE													
1987-88	46	6	7	10	25	29	6	7	10	23	29	50	22nd
DIVISION FOUR													
1988-89	46	11	9	3	33	18	6	6	11	32	41	66	9th

The Combination 1888-89

1	Sep	1	(h)	Long Eaton R	L	1-3	Mudie	1,200
2	Dec	8	(h)	Gainsborough T	W	4-2	Reid, McBeth, Doyle, Unknown	
3		22	(h)	Derby Midland	W	1-0	Gilbert (og)	1,500
4		24	(h)	Northwich V	D	2-2	McBeth, Hunt	1,500
5		25	(h)	Port Vale	W	6-2	Doyle 4, McBeth, Hunt	1,500
6		26	(h)	Halliwell	D	1-1	Doyle	1,500
7	Mar	9	(h)	Nottingham F	W	4-0	Doyle, Hunt, Sutherland, Unknown	
8	Apr	1	(a)	Gainsborough T	W	7-1	J.H.Taylor 2, J.Taylor, Sutherland, Hunt, Unknown, opp og	4,000
9		6	(a)	Port Vale	L	1-2	Unknown	
10		20	(h)	Crewe A	W	3-1	J.H.Taylor, Sanderson, Unknown	1,500
11		27	(a)	Bootle	L	1-2	Riddoch	
12	May	4	(h)	Newton Heath	W	3-0	? Taylor, Riddoch, McBeth	1,000
13		11	(h)	Bootle	W	7-1	? Taylor 2, Sutherland 2, Riddoch 2, Hughes (og)	800
								Appearances
								Goals

FA Cup

P1	Oct	6	(h)	Lincoln C	D	1-1
R		13	(a)	Lincoln C	D	1-1
2R		24	(n*)	Lincoln C	W	3-1
P2		27	(a)	Newark	D	4-4
R	Nov	3	(h)	Newark	W	9-0
P3		17	(h)	Cleethorpes T	W	5-0
1	Dec	15	(h)	Sunderland Albion	W	3-1
2	Feb	16	(h)	Preston NE	L	0-2

*Played at Bramall Lane, Sheffield.

Note: The identity of the Taylor who scored for Grimsby in the final two games of this season has never been established.

In season 1888-89, a number of Midlands and Lancashire clubs joined together in an organization named the Combination to draw up a formal programme of matches.

With no administrative back-up, the fixture list soon fell into disarray and clubs failed to meet their obligations.

In April, the Combination was dissolved, although some clubs continued to play arranged matches.

Whether these matches have any official standing is doubtful, but details of other members of the Combination are given as a matter of record.

Holtby	Lundie	Taylor H	Taylor JH	Smith	Ogilivie	Mudie	Hunt	Riddoch	Lee	Pearce	Doyle	Hopewell	Reid	Sutherland	McBeth	Plumtree	Taylor J (Jnr)	Sanderson	Thickett	Hall	Croft	Beckett	Twyman	
1	2	3	4	5	6	7	8	9	10	11														1
1	2		4	5			11	9			3	6	7	8	10									2
1	2		4	5			11	9			3	6	7	8	10									3
1	2		7	5			11		8		3	6	4	9	10									4
1	2		4	5			11	8			9	6	3	7	10									5
1	2		4	5			11	9			7		3	8	10	6								6
1	2		4	5			11	9			3		6	8	10		7							7
1	2		4	5			10	9			3		6	8			7	11						8
	2		1	5			10	9					3	8			7	11	4	6				9
1	2		4	5	6								3			9	7	11			8	10		10
1	2		4	5	6		11	9					3	8	10		7							11
1	2		4	5	6		11	9					3	8	10		7							12
	2		4	5	6		11	9					3	8	10		7						1	13
11	13	1	13	13	5	1	12	11	2	1	7	4	12	11	9	2	7	3	1	1	1	1	1	
			3			1	4	4			7		1	4	4		1	1						

3 own-goals, 5 unknown, Taylor ? 3

Football Alliance 1889-90

1	Sep	14	(h)	Long Eaton R	W	4-1	Riddoch, Black, McKnight, McDill	2,500
2		21	(h)	Nottingham F	W	4-0	McBeth, Sutherland 2, Black	
3		28	(a)	Walsall	D	2-2	McKnight, McDill	
4	Oct	5	(a)	Nottingham F	W	2-1	McBeth, Southward (og)	2,000
5		19	(a)	Birmingham St G	D	3-3	McBeth 2, A.Rose	
6	Nov	2	(h)	Sunderland A	L	1-2	McKnight	4,000
7		9	(a)	Crewe A	L	0-6		
8		23	(a)	Small Heath	L	1-3	McKnight	
9		30	(h)	Walsall	W	4-0	McBeth, McKnight, Ross, Riddoch	
10	Dec	7	(h)	Sheffield W	L	0-4		
11		21	(h)	Darwen	W	7-3	McKnight 3, Reid 2, Black, J.H.Taylor	1,500
12		26	(h)	Small Heath	W	4-0	McBeth 2, Riddoch, A.Rose	
13	Jan	25	(a)	Darwen	L	0-3		
14	Feb	8	(h)	Newton Heath	W	7-0	H.Rose 2, McBeth 2, Black, Riddoch, McKnight	2,400
15		22	(a)	Bootle	L	1-2	Reid	
16	Mar	1	(a)	Sunderland A	L	0-4		
17		22	(a)	Sheffield W	L	3-4	Black, Hughes, Reid	6,500
18	Apr	4	(h)	Birmingham St G	W	5-4	McBeth 3, Reid, May	2,500
19		5	(h)	Crewe A	W	3-1	McBeth, Reid, May	
20		12	(h)	Bootle	W	3-2	Reid 2, Black	
21		14	(a)	Newton Heath	W	1-0	McBeth	
22		19	(a)	Long Eaton R	W	3-2	McBeth 2, McKnight	
	FINAL LEAGUE POSITION: 4th in Football Alliance							Appearances
								Goals

FA Cup

1	Jan	18	(h)	Newcastle U	W	2-1
2	Feb	1	(a)	Blackburn R	L	0-3

Turnbull	Lundie	Reid	Taylor JH	Smith H	Ogilive	McDill	Riddoch	McKnight	McBeth	Black	Stovin	Langley	Ross	Findley	Sutherland	Rose A	Walker	Rose H	Hughes	Haines	May	Mundahl	
1	2	3	4	5	6	7	8	9	10	11													1
1	2	3	4	5	6	7		9	10	11					8								2
1	2	3	4	5	6	7	10	9		11					8								3
1	2	3	4	5			10	9	8	11					6	7							4
1	2	3	4	5			10	9	8	11					6	7							5
	2	3	4	5			10	9	8	11	1				6	7							6
	2	3	4	5			8	9		11	1				6		7					10	7
1	2	3	4	5			8	9	10	11					6	7							8
1	2	3	4	5			8	9	10	11			7		6								9
1	2	3		5	4		8	9	10	11			7		6								10
1	2	3	4	5			8	9	10	11			7		6								11
1	2	3	4				8	9	10	11			5		6	7							12
	2	3	4	5	1		10	11					8	9	6	7							13
	2		4	3	1		8	9	10	11				5	6			7					14
	2	3	4	5	1		8	7	10	11				9	6								15
	2	3	4		1		8	9	10	11				5	6	7							16
	2	7	4	5	1				10	11		3			6				8		9		17
	2	7	4	5	1		8		10	11		3			6						9		18
	2	7	4	5	1		8		10	11		3			6						9		19
	2	7	4	5	1			9	10	11		3			6					8			20
	2	7	4	5	1			9	10	11		3			6						8		21
	2	7	4	5	1			9	10	11		3			6			8					22
10	22	21	21	20	14	3	17	19	19	21	2	6	5	4	21	7	1	2	1	1	4	1	
		8	1			2	4	10	16	6			1		2	2		2	1		2		

1 own-goal

Football Alliance 1890-91

1	Sep	13	(h)	Newton Heath	W 3-1	Cosgrove 3	2,000
2		20	(a)	Stoke C	L 1-2	Walker	
3		27	(h)	Small Heath	W 3-1	Cosgrove 2, 1 unknown	2,500
4	Oct	4	(h)	Stoke C	D 1-1	Cosgrove	3,000
5		18	(a)	Newton Heath	L 1-3	Unknown	4,000
6		25	(h)	Bootle	W 1-0	Unknown	500
7	Nov	1	(a)	Darwen	D 1-1	Cosgrove or Black	4,000
8		15	(a)	Sheffield W	L 1-2	H.Rose	8,000
9		22	(a)	Bootle	D 0-0		
10	Dec	6	(a)	Birmingham St G	L 0-2		
11		13	(a)	Sunderland A	L 1-2	Unknown	
12		27	(a)	Nottingham F	D 1-1	Cosgrove	1,500
13	Jan	3	(a)	Crewe A	L 3-4	Cosgrove 2, Mack (og)	2,000
14	Feb	21	(a)	Small Heath	W 2-1	Hughes, Riddoch	
15		28	(h)	Walsall	W 3-0	H.Rose, Langley, Black	1,500
16	Mar	7	(h)	Sheffield W	W 3-0	H.Rose, Riddoch, Black	2,000
17		14	(h)	Darwen	W 4-1	Black 3, Haines	2,500
18		21	(a)	Walsall	W 1-0	Unknown	
19		27	(h)	Birmingham St G	W 5-3	Black 2, Haines 2, Riddoch	4,000
20		28	(h)	Crewe A	D 3-3	H.Rose, H.Reid, Riddoch	
21	Apr	4	(h)	Sunderland A	W 2-0	Rose, H.Walker	1,500
22		9	(h)	Nottingham F	W 3-0	Riddoch, Haines, Unknown	4,000
	FINAL LEAGUE POSITION: 3rd in Football Alliance						Appearances
							Goals

FA Cup

1	Oct	11	(a)	Ecclesfield	L 2-8	

As a protest, because they had to play in the qualifying rounds of the FA Cup, Grimsby sent the Reserve side to play Ecclesfield.

Ogilvie	Lundie	Langley	Reid	Smith H	Sutherland	McNichol	Rose H	Walker	Cosgrove	Black	Taylor JH	Rose A	Riddoch	Haines	Mundahl	Frith C	Shaw	Arnold	Hughes	Murrell	
1	2	3	4	5	6	7	8	9	10	11											1
1	2	3	4	5	6	7	8	9	10	11											2
1	2	3		5		7	8	9	11		4				6				10		3
1	2	3	6	5		7	8	9	10	11	4										4
1	2		3	5	6		7	9	10	11	4		8								5
1	2	4	3	5			8	9	10	11		7								6	6
1	2	3	5				7	9	10	11	4		8			6					7
1	2	3	4		6		7	9	10	11			8				5				8
1	2	3	5				7	9	10	11	4		8			6					9
1	2	3	6				7	9	10	11	4		8				5				10
1	2	3	6				7	9	10	11	4						5	8			11
1	2	3	5		6		7	9	10	11	4		8								12
1	2	3	5		6		7	9	10	11	4		8								13
1	2	3	5				7	9		11			10		6	4			8		14
1	2	3		5			8			11	4	7	9	10		6					15
1	2	3	6	5			8			11		7	9	10	4						16
1	2		3	5			8	4		11		7	9	10		6					17
1	2		3	5			7	9		11	4		8	10		6					18
1	2	3	6	5			8	4		11		7	9	10							19
1	2	3	6	5			8	4		11		7	9	10							20
1	2	3	6	5			8	4		11		7	9	10							21
1	2	3	6	5			8	4		11		7	9	10							22
22	22	19	20	14	6	4	22	20	13	21	11	8	16	8	3	6	3	1	2	1	
		1	1				5	2	8	6			5	4					1		

9 unknown, 1 own-goal

Football Alliance 1891-92

1	Sep	19	(a)	Sheffield W	L	2-4	H.Rose, Riddoch	10,000
2	Oct	10	(h)	Bootle	W	4-1	Unknown 4	500
3		17	(h)	Newton Heath	D	2-2	Ackroyd, Unknown	3,000
4		31	(a)	Walsall	L	0-2		
5	Nov	21	(a)	Nottingham F	D	3-3	H.Rose 2, A.Rose	
6		28	(h)	Burton S	L	0-1		
7	Dec	12	(a)	Lincoln C	L	2-3	Ackroyd, Unknown	
8		19	(h)	Small Heath	L	1-2	Ackroyd	
9		25	(a)	Ardwick	L	1-3	Ackroyd	
10		26	(h)	Crewe A	D	1-1	Unknown	
11	Jan	2	(a)	Burton S	L	1-2	Unknown	
12		30	(h)	Ardwick	W	4-0	Smalley 3, H.Rose	
13	Feb	13	(a)	Crewe A	L	0-1		
14		20	(a)	Birmingham St G	D	0-0		
15	Mar	5	(h)	Lincoln C	W	6-1	Ackroyd 4, Riddoch, H.Rose	2,000
16		12	(a)	Bootle	L	1-6	Ackroyd	
17		19	(h)	Sheffield W	W	1-0	Elliman	
18		26	(a)	Newton Heath	D	3-3	Ackroyd, Riddoch 2 (1 pen)	6,000
19	Apr	2	(a)	Small Heath	L	0-3		
20	'	15	(h)	Birmingham St G	W	5-0	Ackroyd, Devlin, Elliman 3	
21		16	(h)	Walsall	W	2-0	Ackroyd, Riddoch	
22		28	(h)	Nottingham F	D	1-1	Ackroyd	

FINAL LEAGUE POSITION: 10th in Football Alliance

(Grimsby had two points deducted for fielding an ineligible player.)

Appearances

Goals

FA Cup

Q1	Oct	3	(h)	Long Eaton R	W	2-1
Q2		24	(h)	Boston	W	1-0
Q3	Nov	14	(h)	Sheffield U	L	1-2

Ogilvie	Lundie	Gray	Walker	Reid	Murrell	Devlin	Rose H	Riddoch	Ackroyd	MacBeth	Frith T	Haines	Rose A	Elliman	Frith C	Hopewell	Bellamy	Smalley	Blythe	Dore	Smith H	McUrich	Taylor JH	
1	2	3	4	5	6	7	8	9	10	11														1
1	2	3	4	5	6	7	8	9	10			11												2
1	2	3	4	5	6		8	9	10			11	7											3
1	2	3	4	5	6	7	8	9	10			11												4
1	2	3	4	5			8	9	10			11	7		6									5
1	2	3			4		8	9	10			11	7		6						5			6
1	2	3	5		6		8	9	10		4	11	7											7
1	2	3	4	5	6		8	9	10			11	7											8
1	2	3	4	5	6		8	9	10			11	7											9
1		3	4	5	6			9			2	11	7							10		8		10
1			4	5	6			9			2	11			7	8	10						3	11
1	2		4	5	6	11	8	9	10		3							7						12
1	2		4	5	6		8	9	10		3						11	7						13
1	2		9	5	4	7	8	10	11		3					6								14
1	2		5	6	4	7	8	9	10		3			11										15
1	2	4		6	5	7	8	9	10		3			11										16
1	2		4	5	6	7	8	9	10		3			11										17
1	2		5		4		8	9	10		3			11		6			7					18
1	2		5	6	4		8	9	10		3			11			7							19
1	2		5	6	4	7	8	9	10		3			11										20
1	2				4	7	8	9	10		3			11	5	6								21
1	2		5		4	7	8	9	10		3			11	6									22
22	20	11	19	17	21	11	20	22	20	1	14	10	7	8	5	4	3	2	1	1	1	1	1	
						1	5	5	13				1	4				3						

8 unknown goalscorers

1892-93

1	Sep	3	(h)	Northwich V	W 2-1	Riddoch 2	
2		10	(a)	Crewe A	L 0-1		2,000
3		17	(h)	Darwen	L 0-1		3,000
4		26	(a)	Sheffield U	L 0-2		5,000
5	Oct	1	(h)	Small Heath	W 3-2	Higgins 3	
6		8	(h)	Bootle	W 3-0	Ackroyd 2, Higgins	
7		22	(a)	Walsall	L 1-3	Ackroyd (pen)	2,000
8	Nov	5	(h)	Ardwick	W 2-0	Mullen, Higgins	3,000
9	Dec	3	(h)	Burton S	W 4-0	Ackroyd 2, Riddoch, Mullen	
10		17	(a)	Bootle	L 1-3	Riddoch	
11		24	(h)	Crewe A	W 4-0	Mullen, Ackroyd, Fletcher, Riddoch	
12	Jan	7	(a)	Northwich V	L 3-5	Mullen, Unknown 2	
13		14	(h)	Port Vale	W 2-0	Higgins, Unknown	500
14		30	(a)	Ardwick	W 3-0	Riddoch, Fletcher 2	2,000
15	Feb	11	(a)	Port Vale	W 1-0	Ackroyd	
16		18	(h)	Lincoln C	D 2-2	Ackroyd, Murrell	2,000
17		25	(a)	Small Heath	L 3-8	Ackroyd 2, Mullen	3,000
18	Mar	4	(a)	Lincoln C	W 3-1	Riddoch, Fletcher, Mullen	5,000
19		18	(a)	Darwen	L 1-6	W.Smith	
20		31	(h)	Sheffield U	L 0-1		4,000
21	Apr	1	(h)	Walsall	W 3-0	Ackroyd, Higgins 2	
22		8	(a)	Burton S	L 1-5	Ackroyd	

FINAL LEAGUE POSITION: 4th in Division Two

Appearances

Goals

FA Cup

Q1	Oct	15	(a)	Attercliffe	W 2-0
Q2	Nov	10	(a)	Doncaster R	W 2-1
Q3		19	(h)	Gainsborough T	W 1-0
Q4	Dec	10	(h)	Lincoln C	W 5-0
1	Jan	21	(h)	Stockton	W 5-0
2	Feb	3	(a)	Darwen	L 0-2

Whitehouse	Lundie	Frith T	Murrell A	Walker	Ogilvie	Higgins	Henderson	Brayshaw	Ackroyd	Riddoch	Reid	McHardy	Fairley	Rose H	Smith W	Mullen	Fletcher	Linton	
1	2	3	4	5	6	7	8	9	10	11									1
1	2	3	4	5	6	8	9		10	11				7					2
1	2	3	4	5	6	7	8		10	11	9								3
1	2	3	4	5	6	11	8		10				9		7				4
1	2		4	5	6	7	8		10	11	3		9						5
1	2		4	5	6	7	8		10	11	3		9						6
1	2	3		5	6	7	8		10	11	4					9			7
1	2	3	4	5	6	7	8			11						9	10		8
1	2		4	5	3	8			7	11			6			9	10		9
1	2		4	5	3	8			7	11			6			9	10		10
1			4	5	3		8	2	7	11			6			9	10		11
1			4	5	3	7	8			11	2		6			9	10		12
1	2		4		5	8			7	11	3		6			9	10		13
1	2		4		5	8			7	11	3		6			9	10		14
1	2		4		5		8		7	11	3		6			9	10		15
1	2		4		5	10	8		7	11	3		6			9			16
1	2		4		5	8			7	11	3		6			9	10		17
1	2	3	4		5	8			7	11			6			9	10		18
1	2	3	4	5		8			11				6		7	9	10		19
1	2		4		3	8			7			5	6			9	10	11	20
1	2		4		3	8			7	11		5	6			9	10		21
1	2		4		3	8			7	11		5	6			9	10		22
22	20	8	21	13	21	20	12	2	20	19	10	3	17	1	2	16	14	1	
			1			8			12	7					1	6	4		

3 unknown goalscorers

1893-94

1	Sep	2	(h)	Northwich V	W	7-0	Russell 3, Fletcher 2, Ackroyd, Crawford	
2		9	(a)	Rotherham T	L	3-4	Crawford 2, Jones	
3		16	(h)	Burton S	W	2-1	Fletcher 2	5,000
4		23	(a)	Lincoln C	W	2-1	Crawford 2	6,000
5		25	(a)	W Arsenal	L	1-3	C.Frith	2,000
6		30	(h)	Walsall	W	5-2	McCairns 2, Jones, Higgins, Crawford	2,500
7	Oct	5	(a)	Notts C	L	0-3		
8		7	(a)	Small Heath	L	2-5	Fletcher, Higgins	
9		21	(h)	Notts C	W	5-2	McCairns 2, Higgins, Fletcher, Ackroyd	4,000
10		28	(h)	Lincoln C	L	2-4	McCairns 2	4,000
11	Nov	11	(a)	Middlesbrough I	W	6-2	McCairns 2, Fletcher, Ackroyd, Jones, (og)	
12	Dec	2	(h)	Port Vale	W	4-0	McCairns, Jones, Ackroyd, Riddoch	2,000
13		4	(a)	Port Vale	L	1-6	McCairns	
14		9	(a)	Ardwick	L	1-4	McCairns	3,000
15		26	(h)	W Arsenal	W	3-1	McCairns 2, Jones	3,000
16		30	(a)	Liverpool	L	0-2		2,000
17	Jan	13	(h)	Ardwick	W	5-0	McCairns 2, Fletcher 2, H.Robinson	
18		20	(a)	Crewe A	D	3-3	Riddoch, Fletcher, Russell	2,000
19	Feb	3	(h)	Middlesbrough I	W	2-1	Riddoch, Ackroyd	
20		10	(h)	Rotherham T	W	7-1	Robinson 3, Fletcher, McCairns, Opp own-goal, Unknown 1	1,500
21		17	(a)	Northwich V	W	1-0	McCairns	
22		24	(a)	Newcastle U	L	1-4	H.Rose	
23	Mar	3	(h)	Small Heath	W	2-1	H.Rose, McCairns	3,000
24		10	(h)	Crewe A	W	3-2	Fletcher 3	1,500
25		24	(a)	Walsall	L	0-5		
26		31	(h)	Liverpool	L	0-1		
27	Apr	7	(a)	Burton S	W	3-0	H.Rose, Jones, Riddoch	
28		14	(h)	Newcastle U	D	0-0		2,000

FINAL LEAGUE POSITION: 5th in Division Two

Appearances

Goals

FA Cup

Q1	Oct	14	(h)	Kilnhurst	W	5-1
Q2	Nov	4	(a)	Lincoln C	W	5-2
Q3		25	(a)	Grantham R	W	2-1
Q4	Dec	16	(h)	Gainsborough T	W	6-1
1	Jan	27	(a)	Liverpool	L	0-3

Whitehouse	Lundie	Frith T	Murrell A	Graham	Riddoch	Ackroyd	Crawford	Russell	Fletcher	Jones	Higgins	Gregory	Frith C	Rose H	McCairns	Robinson H	
1	2	3	4	5	6	7	8	9	10	11							1
1	2	3	4	5	6	7	10	9		11	8						2
1	2	3	4		6	7	8	9	10	11			5				3
1	2	3	4	5	10	7	8			11			6		9		4
1	2	3	4	5		7	8		10	11			6		9		5
1	2	3	4	5	6		8		10	11	7				9		6
1	2	3	4	5	10	7	8	6		11					9		7
1	2	3	4			7		6	10	11	8		5		9		8
1	2	3	4	5		7		6	10	11	8				9		9
1	2	3	4	5		7		6	10	11	8				9		10
1	2		4	5	8	7		6	10	11	3				9		11
1	2			5	8	7		6	10	11	3		4		9		12
1	2			5	8	7		6	10	11	3		4		9		13
1	2			5	8			6	10	11	7	3	4		9		14
1	2	3		5	8	7		6	10	11	4				9		15
1	2	3		5	8	7		6	10	11	4				9		16
1	2	3		5		7		6	8	11	4				9	10	17
1	2	3		5	10	7		6	8	11	4				9		18
1	2	3		5	10	7		6	8	11	4				9		19
1	2	3		5				6	8	11	7		4		9	10	20
1	2	3		5	10			6	8	11	4			7	9		21
1	2	3		5	10			6	8	11	4			7	9		22
1	2	3		5	10			6	8	11	4			7	9		23
1	2	3		5	10			6	8	11	4			7	9		24
1	2	3		5	10			6	8	11	4			7	9		25
1	2	3		5	8			6	10	11	4			7	9		26
1	2	3		5	8			6	10	11	4			7	9		27
1	2	3				8		6	10	11	4		5	7	9		28
28	28	24	11	25	21	18	7	25	25	28	23	1	9	8	25	2	
					4	5	6	4	14	6	3		1	3	18	4	

1 unknown, 2 own-goals

1894-95

1	Sep	1	(h)	Leicester F	W	4-3	McCairns, Fletcher 2, Bailey (og)	5,000
2		8	(a)	Walsall	L	3-4	McCairns, Eccleston 2	
3		10	(a)	W Arsenal	W	3-1	Fletcher 2, Eccleston	
4		15	(h)	Newcastle U	W	3-0	McCairns, Eccleston 2	4,000
5		19	(a)	Burton S	L	1-2	McCairns	4,000
6		22	(a)	Manchester C	W	5-2	McCairns, Eccleston, Fletcher 2, H.Rose	5,000
7		29	(h)	Burton W	W	7-2	McCairns 2, Eccleston 2, Fletcher, Stott, Riddoch	4,000
8	Oct	4	(a)	Notts C	L	2-3	Eccleston, Fletcher	
9		6	(a)	Bury	L	1-5	H.Rose	5,000
10		20	(a)	Lincoln C	W	5-1	Riddoch, Higgins, Frost, H.Rose, Neill (og)	3,000
11		27	(h)	Rotherham U	W	4-1	Riddoch, H.Rose, Fletcher, Frost	3,000
12	Nov	10	(h)	Lincoln C	W	3-0	Fairburn, Frost, Irvine (og)	4,000
13		17	(h)	Newton Heath	W	2-1	Fairburn, Stott	3,000
14	Dec	1	(a)	Newcastle U	W	4-1	McCairns, Riddoch, Fletcher, Higgins	2,000
15		8	(h)	Crewe A	W	5-0	McCairns 2 (1 pen), Fletcher, Eccleston 2	2,000
16		26	(h)	W Arsenal	W	4-2	McCairns 2, Riddoch, Stott	5,000
17	Jan	5	(h)	Bury	W	3-2	McCairns, Riddoch, Fletcher	5,000
18		7	(a)	Rotherham T	L	2-3	McCairns, Higgins	
19		12	(a)	Darwen	L	1-4	McCairns	
20		26	(h)	Port Vale	W	4-1	Higgins 3, Fletcher	
21	Feb	5	(h)	Notts C	L	0-1		4,000
22		9	(a)	Crewe A	L	1-2	McCairns	
23	Mar	9	(h)	Burton S	W	7-1	McCairns, Fletcher 2, Eccleston 2, Stott, Frost	2,000
24		16	(h)	Walsall	W	1-0	McCairns	3,000
25		23	(a)	Newton Heath	L	0-2		9,000
26		30	(h)	Darwen	W	2-1	Frost, Riddoch	4,000
27	Apr	6	(a)	Port Vale	L	0-5		500
28		13	(a)	Burton W	D	0-0		
29		15	(a)	Leicester F	L	0-1		
30		20	(h)	Manchester C	W	2-1	Fletcher, Higgins	2,000

FINAL LEAGUE POSITION: 9th in Division Two

Appearances
Goals

FA Cup

1	Oct	13	(a)	Lincoln C	W	3-0
2	Nov	3	(h)	Attercliffe	D	2-2
R		5	(h)	Attercliffe	W	8-0
3		24	(h)	Worksop T	L	0-1

Whitehouse	Lindsay	Frith T	Higgins	Stott	Waterson	Rose H	Eccleston	McCairns	Fletcher	Frost	Lundie	Graham	Murrell A	Murray	Riddoch	Fairburn	Cooper	
1	2	3	4	5	6	7	8	9	10	11								1
1	2	3	4	5	6	7	8	9	10								11	2
1	2	3	4	5	6	7	8	9	10						11			3
1	2	3		5	6	7	8	9	10			4			11			4
1	2	3	4	5		7	8	9	10			6			11			5
1	2	3	4	5	6	7	8	9	10						11			6
1	2	3	4	5	6	7	8	9	10						11			7
1	2	3	4	5	6	7	8	9	10						11			8
1	2	3		5	6	7	8	9	10	11		4						9
1	2	3	4	5	6	7	8		10	11					9			10
1	2	3	4	5	6	7	8		10	11					9			11
1	2	3	4	5	6	7	8		10	11						9		12
1	2		4	5		7	8		10	11	3	6				9		13
1	2	3	7	5	6		8	9	10			4			11			14
1	2		3	5	6	7	8	9	10			4			11			15
1	2		3	5	6	7	8	9	10			4			11			16
1	2		3	5	6	7	8	9	10			4			11			17
1	2	3	7	5	4	11	8	9	10			6						18
1	2		3	5	6	7	8	9	10			4			11			19
1	2	3	7	5	6		8	9	10			4			11			20
1	2	3	7	5	6		8	9	10			4			11			21
1	2		3	5	6		8	9	10			4		7	11			22
1	2	3	4	5		7	8	9	11	10		6						23
1	2	3	4	5			8	9	11	10		6		7				24
1	2	3	4	5		7	8	9	11	10		6						25
1	2	3	4				7	9	8	11		6	5		10			26
1	2	3		5			7	9	8	11		6	4		10			27
1	2	3	5	10		7		9	8	11		6	4					28
1	2	3	5	6			7	9	8	11		4					10	29
1	2	3	5	6		7	4	9	8	11					10			30
30	30	24	27	29	20	22	29	26	30	14	1	20	3	2	19	2	2	
			7	4		4	13	18	16	5					7	2		

3 own-goals

1895-96

1	Sep	2	(a)	W Arsenal	L	1-3	McCairns	8,000
2		7	(h)	Lincoln C	W	4-2	McCairns 4	4,000
3		14	(a)	Darwen	D	3-3	Bell 2, Gray	3,000
4		21	(h)	Manchester C	W	5-0	Fletcher 2, Gray 2, Pratt	5,000
5		28	(a)	Lincoln C	W	5-2	McCairns, Higgins, Fletcher, Gray, Pratt	5,000
6	Oct	3	(a)	Notts C	L	3-5	Pratt, Fletcher, Unknown 1	
7		5	(a)	Burton W	L	1-2	Gray	4,000
8		19	(h)	Liverpool	W	1-0	Gray	
9		26	(a)	Manchester C	L	1-2	Bell	14,000
10	Nov	9	(a)	Burton S	L	1-2	Unknown	
11		16	(a)	Port Vale	W	4-1	McCairns 2, Gray, Pratt	300
12		30	(h)	Loughborough T	W	2-0	Pratt 2	
13	Dec	21	(a)	Loughborough T	W	1-0	McCairns	
14		26	(h)	Newcastle U	W	2-1	Pratt 2	
15		28	(h)	Burton S	W	3-0	Bell 2, Higgins	
16	Jan	1	(a)	Newton Heath	L	2-3	McCairns, Fletcher	3,000
17		4	(h)	Port Vale	W	6-1	Fletcher 2, McCairns 2, Pratt, Davis	2,000
18		11	(a)	Newcastle U	W	5-1	McCairns, Fletcher, Higgins 2, Pratt	
19		25	(h)	Darwen	W	5-0	McCairns, Fletcher, Robinson 2, Pratt	4,000
20	Feb	8	(a)	Rotherham T	L	0-1		2,000
21		22	(a)	Liverpool	L	1-3	Gray	10,000
22		29	(h)	Crewe A	W	2-0	Robinson, Higgins	
23	Mar	3	(h)	Rotherham T	W	4-0	Pratt 2, Fletcher, Porteus (og)	
24		7	(a)	Crewe A	W	1-0	McCairns	
25		14	(h)	Newton Heath	W	4-2	McCairns, Pratt 2, Graham	
26		21	(h)	Notts C	W	3-0	McCairns 2, Bell	
27		28	(h)	Burton W	W	2-1	McCairns, Fletcher	
28	Apr	4	(h)	W Arsenal	D	1-1	Higgins	6,000
29		6	(a)	Leicester F	W	2-1	McCairns, Gray	
30		11	(h)	Leicester F	W	7-1	McCairns 6, Higgins	

FINAL LEAGUE POSITION: 3rd in Division Two

Appearances
Goals

FA Cup

Q1	Oct	12	(a)	Staveley	W	5-0
Q2	Nov	2	(a)	Kilnhurst	W	4-1
Q3		23	(a)	Lincoln C	W	4-2
Q4	Dec	14	(h)	Rotherham T	W	4-0
1	Feb	1	(a)	Darwen	W	2-0
2		15	(h)	West Brom A	D	1-1
R		20	(a)	West Brom A	L	0-3

Whitehouse	Lindsay	Davis	Higgins	Blair	Graham J	Bell J	Pratt	McCairns	Fletcher	Gray	Hudson	Frith T	Munn	Bailey	Robinson H	Rose H	Mountain	
1	2	3	4	5	6	7	8	9	10	11								1
1	2		4		6	7		9	10	11		3	5	8				2
1	2		5		6	7	8	9	10	11	4	3						3
1	2		5		6	7	8	9	10	11		3	4					4
1	2		5		6	7	8	9	10	11		3	4					5
1	2	3	5		6	7	8	9	10	11			4					6
1	2		5		6	7	8	9	10	11	3		4					7
1	2		5		6	7	8	9	10	11		3	4					8
1	2		5		6	7	8	9	10			3	4				11	9
1	2		5		6	9	8		10	11		3	4	7				10
1	2		5		6	7	8	9	10	11		3	4					11
1			5		6	7	8	9	10	11	2	3	4					12
1	2		5		6	7	8	9	10	11		3	4					13
1	2		5		6	7	8	9	10	11		3	4					14
1	2		5		6	7	8	9	10	11		3	4					15
1	2		5		6	7	8	9	10	11		3	4					16
1	2	11	5		6	7	8	9	10			3	4					17
1	2		5		6	7	8	9	10	11		3	4					18
1	2	3	5		6	7	8	9	11				4		10			19
1	2	3			6	7	5	9	10	11			4		8			20
1	2	3	5		6	7	8	9	10	11			4					21
1	2	7	5		6		8	9	11		3		4		10			22
1	2	3	5		6	9	8		11				4		10	7		23
1	2	3	5		6	10	8	9	11				4			7		24
1	2	3	5		6	7	8	9	11				4		10			25
1	2	3			6	7	8	9	11		5		4			10		26
1	2	3	5		6	7	8	9	10	11			4					27
1	2	3	5		6	7	8	9	10	11			4					28
1	2	3	5		6	7	8	9	10	11			4					29
1	2	3	5		6	7	8	9	10	11			4					30
30	29	15	28	1	30	29	29	28	30	22	5	15	28	2	5	3	1	
		1	7		1	6	15	26	11	9					3			

2 unknown, 1 own-goal

1896-97

1	Sep	2	(a)	Loughborough T	W 4-1	Fletcher 2, McCairns, Thompson (og)	2,000
2		5	(h)	Gainsborough T	D 1-1	Gray	
3		12	(a)	Burton W	L 1-5	Rogers	
4		19	(h)	Newton Heath	W 2-0	Rogers, Fletcher	3,000
5		26	(h)	Lincoln C	W 3-1	Rogers, Fletcher, Lindsay	5,000
6	Oct	1	(a)	Notts C	W 3-1	Rogers 2, Gray	10,000
7		3	(a)	Gainsborough T	D 1-1	McCairns	4,000
8		10	(a)	Newcastle U	L 0-3		4,000
9		17	(h)	Loughborough T	W 8-1	McCairns 3, Higgins 2, Fletcher, Rogers, Bell	3,000
10		24	(h)	Manchester C	W 3-1	McCairns, Fletcher 2	4,000
11		31	(a)	Small Heath	W 1-0	Rogers	7,000
12	Nov	7	(a)	Newton Heath	L 2-4	Rogers, Fletcher	5,000
13		21	(h)	Notts C	W 3-1	McCairns, Fletcher, Bell	7,000
14		28	(a)	W Arsenal	L 2-4	McCairns, Fletcher	8,000
15	Dec	5	(a)	Leicester F	L 2-4	Gray, Fletcher	8,000
16		12	(h)	Small Heath	W 2-1	Gray, Bell	3,500
17		19	(a)	Manchester C	L 1-3	Gray	10,000
18		26	(h)	Newcastle U	W 3-2	McCairns, Rogers 2	10,000
19	Jan	1	(a)	Blackpool	L 0-1		5,000
20		2	(h)	Burton W	W 3-0	Rogers, Bell, Fletcher	2,000
21		9	(a)	Lincoln C	W 3-0	McCairns, Rogers, Morris	2,000
22		16	(a)	Burton S	D 0-0		
23		23	(h)	Leicester F	W 4-1	McCairns, Gray 2, Fletcher	3,000
24	Feb	20	(h)	Blackpool	D 2-2	Fletcher, Bell	5,000
25		27	(a)	Walsall	W 1-0	McCairns	6,000
26	Mar	6	(h)	Darwen	W 4-2	McCairns 3, Fletcher	5,000
27		13	(h)	Walsall	L 0-1		5,000
28		20	(a)	Darwen	L 1-3	Leach (og)	1,000
29	Apr	3	(h)	Burton S	W 3-0	Fletcher 2, Graham	3,000
30		8	(h)	W Arsenal	W 3-1	Gray 2, Rogers	10,000

FINAL LEAGUE POSITION: 3rd in Division Two

Appearances
Goals

FA Cup

1	Jan	28	(h)	Bolton W	D 0-0
R	Feb	3	(a)	Bolton W	D 2-2
2R		11	(a*)	Bolton W	L 2-3

*Played at Bramall Lane, Sheffield.

Cain	Lindsay	Frith T	Higgins	Chapman T	Graham	Bell	Morris H	McCairns	Fletcher	Gray	Wallace	Daw	Hardie	Davis	Rogers	Munn	Hogan	
1	2	3	4	5	6	7	8	9	10	11								1
1	2	3	4	5	6	7	8	9	10	11								2
	2			5	6		8	9	10		1			3	7	4	11	3
	2		5		6		8	9	10	11	1			3	7	4		4
	2		5	6			8	9	10	11	1			3	7	4		5
	2		5	6			8	9	10	11	1			3	7	4		6
	2		5	6			8	9	10	11	1			3	7	4		7
	2		5	6		7	8		10	11	1			3	9	4		8
	2		5	6		8	11	9	10		1			3	7	4		9
	2		5	6		8	11	9	10		1			3	7	4		10
	2		5	6		8	11	9	10		1			3	7	4		11
	2			6	5	8	11	9	10		1			3	7	4		12
	2		5	6		8		9	10	11	1			3	7	4		13
	2		5	6		8	11	9	10		1			3	7	4		14
	2	3	5		6	8	7	9	10	11		1				4		15
	2	3	5		6	8		9	10	11	1				7	4		16
	2	3	5	6			8	9	10	11	1				7	4		17
	2	3	5	6			8	9	10	11	1				7	4		18
	2	3	5	6			8	9	10	11	1				7	4		19
	2	3	5	6		8	11	9	10		1				7	4		20
	2	3	5	6			8	9	10	11	1				7	4		21
	2	3	5	6			8	9	10	11	1				7	4		22
	2	3	5	6			8	9	10	11	1				7	4		23
		3	5	6		8		9	10	11		1		2	7	4		24
		3	5	6		7	8	9	10	11			1		2	4		25
		3	5	6		8	7	9	10	11			1		2	4		26
	2	3	5	6		8		9	10	11			1		7	4		27
	2	3	5	6		8		9	10	11			1	7		4		28
		3	2	6	5	8		9	10	11			1		7	4		29
		3	2	6	5	8		9	10	11			1		7	4		30
2	25	18	28	27	9	19	23	29	30	23	20	2	6	14	26	28	1	
	1		2		1	5	1	15	17	9					13			

2 own-goals

1897-98

1	Sep	1	(a)	W Arsenal	L	1-4	Fletcher	6,000
2		4	(h)	Gainsborough T	W	4-2	Fletcher, Rogers 2, Pumfrey (og)	5,000
3		11	(h)	Darwen	W	5-0	Robinson 2, Rogers 2, Goldie	4,000
4		18	(h)	Leicester F	D	0-0		3,000
5		25	(a)	Gainsborough T	L	0-2		4,000
6	Oct	2	(h)	Lincoln C	W	4-2	Gray 3, Goldie	5,000
7		9	(a)	Manchester C	L	0-3		12,000
8		16	(a)	Darwen	L	0-1		3,000
9		23	(h)	Burnley	W	2-1	Rogers, Goldie	4,000
10	Nov	6	(h)	Newcastle U	W	2-0	McCairns, Fletcher	4,000
11		13	(h)	Small Heath	W	3-1	Fletcher 2, Mountain	2,000
12		20	(a)	Walsall	D	1-1	Peers (og)	
13		27	(a)	Newton Heath	L	1-2	Rogers	3,000
14	Dec	1	(a)	Burton U	L	0-4		
15		4	(h)	Loughborough T	W	7-0	Fletcher 4, Goldie, Rogers, Barton	700
16		11	(a)	Burnley	L	0-6		4,000
17		18	(h)	Manchester C	L	3-4	McCairns 2, Gray	5,000
18		25	(a)	Lincoln C	D	1-1	McLean	5,000
19		27	(a)	Luton T	L	0-6		
20	Jan	22	(h)	Luton T	L	1-3	Gray	5,000
21	Feb	5	(h)	Burton U	W	7-2	McCairns 4, Gray 2, Rogers	2,000
22		12	(h)	W Arsenal	L	1-4	Rogers	4,000
23	Mar	5	(h)	Walsall	L	1-2	Goldie	2,000
24		12	(a)	Small Heath	W	2-0	McCairns, Fletcher	2,500
25		19	(h)	Blackpool	W	3-0	McCairns, Fletcher, Rogers	2,500
26		26	(a)	Newcastle U	L	0-4		4,000
27	Apr	2	(h)	Newton Heath	L	1-3	Blyth	3,000
28		9	(a)	Loughborough T	L	1-2	McLean	1,500
29		11	(a)	Leicester F	L	0-1		
30		16	(a)	Blackpool	D	1-1	Ball	1,000

FINAL LEAGUE POSITION: 12th in Division Two — Appearances / Goals

FA Cup

1	Jan	29	(a)	Nottingham F	L	0-4

Whittaker	Lindsay	Frith	Munn	McLean	Chapman	Rogers	Richardson W	McCairns	Fletcher	Gray	Leaning	Parker	Mountain	Brocklesby	Mount	Bell	Johnston	Hyde	Chatburn	Taylor F	Goldie	Robinson H	Frost	Blythe T	Barton	
1	2	3	4	5	6	7	8	9	10	11																1
1	2	3	4	5	6	7		9	10	11											8					2
1	2	3		5		7			10				4		6			11			8	9				3
1	2	3		5		7		9	10				4		6			11			8					4
1	2	3	4	6	5	7		9	10	11											8					5
1	2	3	4	6	5	7		9	10	11											8					6
1	2	3	4	6	5	7		9	10	11			8													7
	2	3	4	6	5			9	10	8	1		7												11	8
1	2	3	4	6	5	7		9	10												8				11	9
1	2	3		4	5	7		9	10	11							6				8					10
	2	3		4	5			9	10	11	1		7				6				8					11
1	2	3		4	5	7		9	10								6	11			8					12
1	2	3		4	5	7		9	10	11							6				8					13
1	2	3		4	5	7		9	10	11							6				8					14
1	2			4	5	7		9	10						3		6				8				11	15
1	2	3		4	5	7		9	10	11							6				8					16
1	2			4	5	7		9	10	11					3		6				8					17
1	2	3		6	5	7		9	10	11			4								8					18
1	2	3		5		7		9	10	11			4					6			8					19
1	2	3		4				9	10	11						5			6		7	8				20
1	2	3		6		7		9	10	11			4			5					8					21
1	2	3		6		7		9	10	11			4			5					8					22
1		3		6	5	7		9	10	11		2	4								8					23
1		3		4	6	7		9	8	11			2			5					10					24
1		3		4	6	7		9	8	11			2			5							10			25
1		3		4	6	7		9		11			2			5					8		10			26
1		3		4	6	7		9		11			2			5					8			10		27
1		3		4	6	7		9		11				2		5					8			10		28
1		3		4	6	7		9		11			10	2		5					8					29
1		3		4		7		9					10	2		5				6	8			11		30
28	22	28	7	30	23	27	1	29	25	24	2	1	16	3	4	10	8	4	1	1	26	2	2	3	3	
				2		10		9	11	7			1			1				2	5	2		1	1	

2 own-goals

1898-99

1	Sep	3	(a)	Manchester C	L 2-7	Chapman 2	10,000
2		10	(h)	Glossop NE	D 1-1	Jenkinson	2,500
3		17	(a)	Walsall	L 1-4	Cockshutt	5,000
4		24	(h)	Burton S	L 1-3	Chapman	3,000
5	Oct	1	(a)	Port Vale	L 0-2		
6		8	(h)	Small Heath	W 2-0	Greenwood, Cockshutt	4,000
7		22	(h)	Blackpool	W 2-1	Greenwood 2	4,000
8	Nov	5	(a)	Newton Heath	L 2-3	Jenkinson, Ratcliffe	5,000
9		12	(h)	New Brighton	D 2-2	Greenwood, Cockshutt	4,500
10		26	(h)	W Arsenal	W 1-0	Gray	
11	Dec	3	(a)	Luton T	L 1-3	Griffiths	
12		17	(a)	Darwen	W 2-0	Chapman, Edmondson (og)	300
13		24	(h)	Gainsborough T	L 0-2		3,500
14		26	(h)	Barnsley	L 0-1		4,500
15	Jan	7	(a)	Glossop NE	L 2-4	Greenwood 2	
16		14	(h)	Walsall	W 2-1	Greenwood, Griffiths	4,000
17		21	(a)	Burton S	W 2-1	Ratcliffe, Richards	
18	Feb	4	(a)	Small Heath	L 1-2	Cockshutt (pen)	2,000
19		11	(h)	Loughborough T	W 5-0	Richards 3, Jenkinson, Greenwood	3,500
20		18	(a)	Blackpool	W 6-3	Greenwood 2, Jenkinson 2, Cockshutt (pen), Richards	2,000
21		21	(h)	Port Vale	W 3-1	Jenkinson, Cockshutt, Richards	2,500
22		25	(a)	Barnsley	D 2-2	Cockshutt, Richards	2,000
23	Mar	4	(h)	Newton Heath	W 3-0	Cockshutt 3	4,000
24		11	(a)	New Brighton	L 0-2		6,000
25		18	(h)	Lincoln C	D 1-1	Cockshutt	5,000
26		25	(a)	W Arsenal	D 1-1	Richards	4,000
27		31	(h)	Leicester F	W 1-0	Jenkinson	5,000
28	Apr	1	(h)	Luton T	W 5-0	Ratcliffe 2, Richards, Cockshutt, Bell	5,000
29		3	(a)	Leicester F	L 0-2		6,000
30		8	(a)	Lincoln C	W 6-1	Ratcliffe 3, Richards, Bissett (og), Greenwood	
31		11	(h)	Manchester C	L 1-2	Richards	
32		15	(h)	Darwen	W 9-2	Jenkinson 3, Cockshutt 3, Chatburn, Richards, Bell	2,500
33		17	(a)	Loughborough T	W 3-1	Jenkinson 2, Richards	
34		22	(a*)	Gainsborough T	L 1-5	Cockshutt	

FINAL LEAGUE POSITION: 10th in Division Two

*Played at Sincil Bank, Lincoln.

Appearances

Goals

FA Cup

Q1	Oct	29	(h)	Mexborough	W 5-0
Q2	Nov	19	(h)	Lincoln C	W 2-1
Q3	Dec	10	(a)	Barnsley	D 0-0
R		14	(h)	Barnsley	W 1-0
1	Jan	28	(a)	Preston NE	L 0-7

Bagshaw	Pennington	Frith T	Cherry	Gray P	Griffiths	Greenwood	Chapman H	Cockshutt	Ratcliffe	Nelmes	Mountain	Stewart	Nidd	Lockie	Lowe	Bell	Jenkinson	Richards	Blythe	Pangbourne	Richardson	Robinson H	Chatburn	
1	2	3	4	5	6	7	8	9	10	11														1
1		3			6		8	9	10		2				4	5	7			11				2
1				5	6	7	8	9			2				3	4	11			10				3
1		3		5	4	7	9		8	6	2						11			10				4
1					5	9	8		10	6	11	2	3			4	7							5
1				5	11	8		9	10	6	2		3			4	7							6
1				5	11	8		9	10	6	2		3			4	7							7
1				5	11	8		9	10	6	2		3			4	7							8
1				5	11	8		9	10	6	2		3			4	7							9
1				5	11	8		9	10	6	2		3			4	7							10
1			4	5	11	8		9	10	6	2		3				7							11
1		3	4	5	11	8	10	9		6			2				7							12
1		3	7	5	11	8	10	9		6			2			4								13
1		3	4	5	11		8	10		6			2				7		9					14
1		3	4		5	11	10	9		6			2				7	8						15
1		3	4	5	11	7	8		10	6			2					9						16
1				5	4	11		9	10	6	2		3				7	8						17
1				5		11		9	10	6	2		3			4	7	8						18
1				5	4	11		9		6	2		3				7	8			10			19
1				5	4	11		9	10	6	2		3				7	8						20
1				5	4	11		9	10	6	2		3				7	8						21
1				5	4	11		9	10	6	2		3				7	8						22
1				5	4	11		9	10	6	2		3				7	8						23
1				5	4	11		9	10	6	7		3	2				8						24
1				5		11		9	10	6	7		3	2		4		8						25
1				5	4	11		9	10	6	2		3				7	8						26
1					4	11		9	10	6	2		3			5	7	8						27
1					4	11		9	10	6			3	2		5	7	8						28
1					4	11		9	10	6	2		3			5	7	8						29
1					4	11		9	10	6	2		3			5	7	8						30
1					4	11		9	10	6	2		3			5	7	8						31
1					4			9		6			3	2		5	7	8				10	11	32
1				5		11		9	10	6			3	2		4	7	8						33
1				5	4	11		9	10	6	3			2			7	8						34
34	1	8	7	25	31	31	10	31	27	32	25	1	29	6	2	18	29	20	1	3	1	1	1	
				1	2	11	4	16	7							2	12	13					1	

2 own-goals

1899-1900

1	Sep	2	(h)	Luton T	D	3-3	Cockshutt, Nidd, Ratcliffe	4,000
2		9	(a)	Port Vale	W	3-2	Jenkinson 2, Richards	3,000
3		16	(h)	Walsall	W	4-2	Richards 2, Jenkinson, Ratcliffe	4,500
4		23	(a)	Middlesbrough	L	0-1		4,000
5	Oct	7	(a)	Gainsborough T	W	3-2	Beveridge 2, Ratcliffe	2,500
6		14	(h)	Bolton W	D	0-0		5,000
7		21	(a)	Loughborough T	D	0-0		2,000
8	Nov	11	(h)	Lincoln C	W	5-2	Mountain, Jenkinson, Nelmes, Richards 2 (2 pens)	5,000
9		25	(h)	New Brighton	L	1-2	Richards	4,500
10	Dec	2	(a)	Burton S	W	2-1	Jenkinson, Ratcliffe	
11		16	(h)	Barnsley	W	8-1	Jenkinson 2, Ratcliffe 2, Cockshutt 2, Richards, Hemingfield	2,500
12		23	(a)	Leicester F	L	0-3		
13		25	(h)	Chesterfield	L	0-3		6,000
14		26	(h)	Newton Heath	L	0-7		4,500
15		30	(a)	Luton T	W	4-0	Richards 3, Ratcliffe	
16	Jan	2	(a)	Sheffield W	L	1-2	Richards	
17		6	(h)	Port Vale	D	1-1	Greenwood	
18		13	(a)	Walsall	D	1-1	Tennant (og)	2,000
19		20	(h)	Middlesbrough	W	2-0	Richards, Hughes (og)	3,500
20	Feb	3	(a)	Chesterfield	L	1-3	Lakey	
21		10	(h)	Gainsborough T	W	3-0	Cockshutt, Richards 2	2,000
22		12	(a)	Small Heath	W	1-0	Ratcliffe	
23		17	(a)	Bolton W	W	2-1	Ratcliffe, McAteer (og)	3,000
24		24	(h)	Loughborough T	W	3-0	Ratcliffe, Richards, Griffiths	2,500
25	Mar	3	(a)	Newton Heath	L	0-1		8,000
26		24	(h)	Small Heath	W	2-0	Greenwood, Hemingfield	3,000
27		31	(a)	New Brighton	L	1-2	Nelmes	
28	Apr	7	(h)	Burton S	W	6-0	Richards 3, Jenkinson, Cockshutt, Kirkland	2,000
29		13	(h)	Sheffield W	L	1-2	Richards	7,000
30		14	(h)	W Arsenal	W	1-0	Richards	
31		16	(a)	W Arsenal	L	0-2		3,000
32		21	(a)	Barnsley	W	1-0	Jenkinson	
33		27	(a)	Lincoln C	D	1-1	Lakey	3,000
34		28	(h)	Leicester F	W	6-1	Hemingfield 2, Ratcliffe 2, Lakey, Jenkinson	3,000

FINAL LEAGUE POSITION: 6th in Division Two

Appearances

Goals

FA Cup

Q3	Oct	28	(h)	Doncaster R	W	3-1
Q4	Nov	21	(h)	Barnsley	W	3-2
Q5	Dec	9	(h)	Chesterfield	W	3-2
1	Jan	27	(a)	Nottingham F	L	0-3

Whitehouse	Beveridge	Nidd	Griffiths	Gray	Nelmes	Jenkinson	Richards	Cockshutt	Ratcliffe	Greenwood	Mountain	Finlayson	McAvoy	Hemingfield	Lakey	Robinson S	
1	2	3	4	5	6	7	8	9	10	11							1
1	2		4	5	6	7	8	9	10			3			11		2
1		3	4	5	6	7	8	9	10	11	2						3
1		3	4	5	6		8	9	10	11	2			7			4
1	7	3	4	5	6		8	9	10	11	2						5
1	7	3	4	5	6		8	9	10	11	2						6
1	7	3	4	5	6		8	9	10	11	2						7
1		3		5	6	7	8	9	11	4	2			10			8
1		3		5	6	7	8		10	4	2			9	11		9
1		3	4	5	6	7	8	9	10			2		11			10
1		3	4	5	6	7	8	9	10		2			11			11
1				5	6	7	8	9	10	4	2	3		11			12
1				5	6	7	8	9	10	4	2	3		11			13
1			8	5	6	7		9	10	4		2			11	3	14
1			3	5	6	7	8	9	10	11	2			4			15
1			3	5	6	7	8	9	10	11	2			4			16
1		3	5		6	7	8	9	10	11	4		2				17
1			4	5	6	7	8	9		11	2		3		10		18
1			4	5	6	7	8	9		10	2		3	11			19
		1	4		6	7	8	9	10		2		3	5	11		20
1			4		6	7	8	9	10		2		3	5	11		21
1		7	4		6			9	10	8	2		3	5	11		22
1		3	4	5		7	10	9	8	11	2			6			23
1		3	4	5		7	10	9	8	11	2			6			24
1			4		6	7	8	9	10	11	2		3	5			25
1			4	5	6	7	8	9		11	2		3	10			26
1			4	5	6	7	8	9		11	2		3	10			27
1				5	6	7	8	9	10	11	2		3	4			28
		1	4	5	6	7	8	9	10	11	2		3				29
		1	4	5	6	7	8	9	10	11	2		3				30
		1	3	5	6	7	8	9	10	11	2				4		31
		1	4	5	6	7	8		10		2		3	9	11		32
		1	4	5	6	7	8		10		2		3	9	11		33
		1	4	5	6	7	8		10		2		3	9	11		34
27	5	21	29	29	32	29	32	30	30	26	30	5	15	22	11	1	
	2	1	1		2	10	20	5	12	2	1			4	3		

4 own-goals

1900-01

1	Sep	1	(a)	Burnley	L	0-3		
2		8	(h)	Port Vale	W	6-1	Lakey 2, Leigh 2, Hemingfield 2	4,000
3		15	(a)	Leicester F	L	0-4		
4		22	(h)	New Brighton	W	5-2	Richards 2, Jenkinson, Nelmes, Arridge (og)	4,500
5		29	(a)	Gainsborough T	W	1-0	Jenkinson	5,000
6	Oct	6	(h)	Walsall	D	0-0		
7		13	(a)	Burton S	W	2-1	Nelmes, Lakey	
8		20	(h)	Barnsley	W	1-0	Hemingfield	
9		27	(a)	W Arsenal	D	1-1	Richards	8,000
10	Nov	3	(a)	Port Vale	D	0-0		3,000
11		10	(h)	Stockport C	W	5-1	Richards 2 (1 pen), Mellor, Hemingfield, Gray	5,000
12		17	(h)	Small Heath	D	1-1	Griffiths	5,000
13		24	(h)	Chesterfield	W	5-2	Lakey, Leigh, Griffiths, Mellor, Holleworth (og)	6,000
14	Dec	1	(h)	Lincoln C	W	4-0	Richards, Leigh 3	7,000
15		8	(h)	Newton Heath	W	2-0	Richards, Lakey	6,000
16		15	(a)	Glossop NE	D	0-0		1,500
17		22	(h)	Middlesbrough	W	2-0	Lakey, Nelmes	5,000
18		25	(a)	Lincoln C	W	1-0	Lakey	7,000
19		29	(h)	Burnley	W	2-1	Lakey, Lockhart (og)	7,000
20	Jan	12	(h)	Leicester F	W	4-1	Mellor 2, Lakey, Hall	5,000
21		19	(a)	New Brighton	L	0-5		
22		26	(h)	Blackpool	W	2-0	Leigh, Berchall (og)	
23	Feb	9	(a)	Walsall	D	0-0		
24		16	(h)	Burton S	W	5-2	Watkins 2, Brumley, Nelmes, Fletcher	3,000
25		23	(a)	Barnsley	W	3-2	Richards, Hall, Brumley	2,000
26	Mar	2	(h)	W Arsenal	W	1-0	Nelmes	4,000
27		9	(a)	Blackpool	W	1-0	Richards	2,000
28		16	(a)	Stockport C	W	1-0	Watkins	5,000
29		30	(a)	Chesterfield	D	3-3	Watkins, Fletcher, Nelmes	
30	Apr	1	(a)	Small Heath	L	1-2	Watkins	
31		5	(h)	Gainsborough T	D	0-0		8,000
32		13	(a)	Newton Heath	L	0-1		
33		20	(h)	Glossop NE	W	1-0	Leigh	6,000
34		27	(a)	Middlesbrough	D	0-0		8,000

FINAL LEAGUE POSITION: 1st in Division Two

Appearances

Goals

FA Cup

Sup	Jan	5	(h)	Middlesbrough	L	0-1

Harris	Mountain	Leiper	Griffiths	Gray	Nelmes	Jenkinson	Richards	Leigh	Mellor	Hemingfield	Leaning	McFarlane	McAvoy	Brumley	Watkins	Fletcher	Hall	Lakey	
1	2	3	4	5	6	7	8	9	10	11									1
1	2	3	4	5	6		8	9	10	7								11	2
1	2	3	4	5		7	8	9	10	6								11	3
1		3	4	5	6	7	8	9	10				2					11	4
1		3	4	5	6	7	8	9	10				2					11	5
1	2	3	4	5	6	7	8	9	10									11	6
1		3	4	5	6	7	8	9	10				2					11	7
		3	4	5	6	7	8			9	1		2			10		11	8
1		3	4	5	6		8	9	10	11			2			7			9
1		3	4	5	6		8	9	10	11			2			7			10
1		3	4	5	6		8	9	10	11			2			7			11
1		3	4	5	6	7	8		10				2			9		11	12
	2	3	4	5	6		8	9	10		1					7		11	13
	2	3	4	5	6		8	9	10		1					7		11	14
1	2		4	5	6		8	9	10				3			7		11	15
	2	3	4	5	6		8	9	10			1				7		11	16
	2	3	4	5	6		8	9	10			1				7		11	17
	2	3	4	5	6		8	9	10			1				7		11	18
	2		4		6		8	9	10	5		1	3			7		11	19
	2		4		6			9	10	5		1	3			7	8	11	20
	2	3	4		6		8	9	10	5		1				7		11	21
	2	3	4	5	6		8	9	10			1				7		11	22
	2	3	4		6		8	9	10	5		1				7	11		23
	2	3			6			9	10	4		1		5	11	7	8		24
	2	3			6		8		10	4		1		5	11	7	9		25
	2	3		5	6		8	9	10	4		1			11	7			26
	2	3		5			8	9	10	4		1			6	7		11	27
	2	3		5	6		8	9	10	4		1			11	7			28
	2	3		5	6		8	9	10	4		1			11	7			29
	2	3		5	6			9	10	4		1			11	7	8		30
1	2	3		5	6			9	10	4					11	7	8		31
	2	3	4	5	6			9	10	8		1			11	7			32
	2	3		5	6		8	9	10	4		1			11	7			33
	2	3		5	6			9	10	4		1			11	7	8		34
13	26	31	24	28	32	8	28	31	33	22	3	18	11	2	11	27	7	19	
			2	1	6	2	9	8	4	4				2	5	2	2	9	

4 own-goals

1901-02

1	Sep	3	(h)	Derby C	D 1-1	Leigh	7,000
2		7	(a)	Sheffield W	L 1-3	Dean	
3		14	(h)	Nottingham F	W 1-0	Ronaldson	8,000
4		21	(a)	Notts C	L 0-3		
5		28	(h)	Bury	W 2-0	Ronaldson, Leigh	7,000
6	Oct	5	(a)	Bolton W	L 0-4		5,000
7		12	(h)	Blackburn R	W 2-0	Leigh 2	
8		19	(a)	Manchester C	L 0-3		20,000
9		26	(h)	Stoke	L 1-2	Stevenson	6,000
10	Nov	2	(a)	Wolves	L 0-2		
11		9	(h)	Everton	L 0-2		5,000
12		23	(h)	Sunderland	D 3-3	Harper 2, Hemingfield	
13		30	(a)	Newcastle U	L 1-5	Gray	
14	Dec	7	(h)	Small Heath	W 1-0	Harper	4,500
15		14	(a)	Aston Villa	L 1-4	Gardner	12,000
16		25	(a)	Blackburn R	L 0-2		
17		28	(h)	Sheffield U	L 0-1		4,000
18	Jan	1	(a)	Bury	D 1-1	Ronaldson	
19		4	(h)	Sheffield W	W 3-1	Ronaldson, Appleyard, Fletcher	
20		11	(a)	Nottingham F	W 1-0	Gardner	8,000
21		18	(h)	Notts C	W 1-0	Fletcher	7,000
22	Feb	1	(h)	Bolton W	W 4-1	Ronaldson 2, Appleyard, Nelmes	
23		11	(a)	Sheffield U	D 2-2	Long, Fletcher	
24		15	(h)	Manchester C	W 3-2	Appleyard 2, Fletcher	4,500
25		22	(a)	Small Heath	L 0-6		10,000
26	Mar	1	(h)	Wolves	W 3-0	Appleyard 2, Ronaldson	5,000
27		8	(a)	Everton	W 1-0	Nelmes	10,000
28		15	(h)	Liverpool	D 1-1	Gardner	6,000
29		22	(a)	Sunderland	L 1-3	Ronaldson	10,000
30		28	(h)	Newcastle U	W 3-0	Gardner, Ronaldson, Long	7,000
31	Apr	1	(a)	Derby C	L 0-2		4,000
32		12	(h)	Aston Villa	W 4-1	Appleyard 3 (1 pen), Ronaldson	6,000
33		14	(a)	Stoke	L 0-2		
34		21	(a)	Liverpool	D 2-2	Long, Gray	

FINAL LEAGUE POSITION: 15th in Division One

Appearances
Goals

FA Cup

1	Jan	25	(a)	Portsmouth	D 1-1	
R		29	(h)	Portsmouth	L 0-2	

Tennant	Mountain	Leiper	Hemingfield	Bellingham	Nelmes	Dean	Harper	Ronaldson	Leigh	Gardner	Clutterbuck	Whittaker	McConnell	Hall	Griffiths	Gray	Brumley	Skinner	Fletcher	Stevenson	Appleyard	Long	
1	2	3	4	5	6	7	8	9	10	11													1
1		3	4	5	6	7	8	9	10	11			2										2
1	2	3	4		6	7		9	8	11						5			10				3
1	2	3	4		6	7	10	9	8	11						5							4
1	2	3	4		6			9	8	11						5			7	10			5
1	2	3	4		6	7		9	8	11						5				10			6
1	2	3	4		6	7		9	8	11						5				10			7
1	2	3	4	6		7		8	9	11						5				10			8
1	2	3	6			10		9	11						4	5			7	8			9
1	2		4		6	7	10	9	11				3			5				8			10
1	2		4		6	7	10	9	11				3			5				8			11
	2	3	4		6	7	10	8	9	11	1					5							12
1	2		4			7	10		9	11			3			5		6		8			13
1	2	3	4		6	7	10	8	9	11						5							14
	2	3	4		6	7	10	8	9	11		1				5							15
	2	3	4		6	7		8	10	11		1				5					9		16
	2	3	4	5	6	7	10	8		11		1									9		17
	2		4		6		10	8		11		1	3			5			7		9		18
	2		4		6		10	8		11		1	3			5			7		9		19
	2		4		6		10	8		11		1	3			5			7		9		20
	2		4		6		10	8		11		1	3			5			7		9		21
	2		4		6			8	10	11		1	3			5			7		9		22
	2		4		6			8		11		1	3			5			7		9	11	23
	2				6			8		11		1	3	4		5			7		9	11	24
	2					6		8		11		1	3	4		5			7		9	11	25
	2				6			8		11		1	3	4		5			7		9	11	26
	2				6			8		11		1	3	4			5		7		9	11	27
	2		4		6			8		11		1	3			5			7		9	11	28
	2		4		6			8		11		1	3			5			7		9	11	29
	2		4		6			8		11		1	3			5			7		9	11	30
	2	3	4		6			8		11		1				5			7		9	11	31
	2		4					8		11		1	6	3		5			7		9	11	32
	2		4					8		11		1	6	3		5			7		9	11	33
	2		4					8		11		1	3	6		5			7		9	11	34
13	33	15	30	4	27	17	14	33	17	31	1	20	20	7	1	30	1	1	20	8	19	12	
			1		2	1	3	10	4	4						2			4	1	9	3	

1902-03

1	Sep	9	(h)	Nottingham F	L	0-1		5,000
2		13	(a)	Bury	L	1-2	Appleyard	5,000
3		20	(h)	Blackburn R	W	4-1	Appleyard 2 (1 pen), Fletcher, Singleton	6,000
4		27	(a)	Sunderland	L	1-5	Singleton	
5	Oct	4	(h)	Stoke	D	2-2	Ronaldson, Gray	4,000
6		11	(a)	Everton	L	2-4	Long, Nelmes	14,000
7		18	(h)	Sheffield W	L	0-1		
8		25	(a)	West Brom A	L	0-1		15,000
9	Nov	1	(h)	Notts C	D	1-1	Nelmes	
10		8	(h)	Bolton W	D	1-1	Fletcher	3,000
11		15	(h)	Middlesbrough	D	2-2	Appleyard 2	
12		22	(a)	Newcastle U	L	0-1		8,000
13		29	(h)	Wolves	L	1-2	Ronaldson	4,000
14	Dec	6	(a)	Liverpool	L	2-9	Appleyard, Hogg	10,000
15		13	(h)	Sheffield U	L	1-2	Ronaldson	4,000
16		20	(h)	Derby C	W	4-1	Appleyard 2, McLatchie, Fletcher	4,000
17		25	(h)	Everton	D	0-0		6,000
18		27	(a)	Aston Villa	D	2-2	Fletcher, Mountain	20,000
19	Jan	2	(a)	Bolton W	W	1-0	Mountain	16,000
20		3	(a)	Nottingham F	L	1-2	Ronaldson	
21		10	(h)	Bury	W	2-1	Glen, Ronaldson	6,000
22		17	(a)	Blackburn R	L	0-2		10,000
23		24	(h)	Sunderland	L	2-4	Appleyard 2 (1 pen)	
24		31	(a)	Stoke	D	1-1	Hall	6,000
25	Feb	14	(a)	Sheffield W	D	1-1	Fletcher	9,000
26		28	(a)	Notts C	W	1-0	Fletcher	8,000
27	Mar	14	(a)	Middlesbrough	L	0-2		12,000
28		21	(h)	Newcastle U	W	1-0	Hall	4,000
29		28	(a)	Wolves	L	0-3		3,000
30	Apr	4	(h)	Liverpool	W	3-1	Ronaldson 2, Rouse	2,500
31		10	(h)	West Brom A	W	4-0	Ronaldson 2, Rouse, Long	6,000
32		11	(a)	Sheffield U	L	0-3		
33		22	(a)	Derby C	D	2-2	Long 2	
34		25	(h)	Aston Villa	L	0-2		1,500

FINAL LEAGUE POSITION: 17th in Division One

Appearances
Goals

FA Cup

1	Feb	7	(h)	Newcastle U	W	2-1
2		21	(h)	Notts C	L	0-2

Whittaker	Gardner	McConnell A	Hemingfield	Gray	Nelmes	Fletcher	Ronaldson	Appleyard	Long	Glen	Spendiff	Mountain	Dunn	Hall	Morgan	Brumley	Atherton	Harper	Hogg	Rouse	Paterson	Singleton	McLatchie	
1	2	3	4	5	6	7	8	9	10	11														1
1	2	3	4	5	6	7	8	9	10													11		2
1		3	4	5	6	7	8	9	10			2										11		3
	3		5		6	7	8	9			1	2		4				10				11		4
1	3			5	6	7	8	9				2		4				10				11		5
	3		4	5	6	7		9	10		1	2						8				11		6
1	3		4	5	6	7	10	9				2		11				8						7
1	3		4	5	6		11	9				2					7	8			10			8
1	3		4		6	7	11	9				2		10	5			8						9
1	3		4	5	6	7	9					2		10			11	8						10
1	3		4	5	6	7	8	9				2									10	11		11
1		3	4		6	7	8	9	10			2		5								11		12
1		3	4		6	7	8	9	10			2		5								11		13
1		3	4		6	10	7	9					2	5					8				11	14
1	3	2			6	7	8	9	10				4	5									11	15
1	3	2				7	8	9	10			4	6	5									11	16
1	3	2	4			7	8	9	10				6	5									11	17
1	2	3	4			7	9			10		8	6	5									11	18
1	3	2			6	7	9			10		8	4	5									11	19
1	3	2			6	7	9			10		8	4	5									11	20
1	3	2			6	7	8	9		10			4	5									11	21
1	3	2			6	7	8	9		10			4	5									11	22
1	3	2			6	7	8	9		10			4	5								11		23
	3		4				7	9		10	1	2	6	5					8			11		24
	3		4			7	8	9		10	1	2	6	5								11		25
	3	2	4			7		9	11	10	1	8	6	5										26
	3	2	4			7		9		11	1		6	5					10	8				27
1	3				6	7	8	9		10		2	4	5								11		28
1		3			6	7	10	9				2	4	5						8		11		29
1	3	2			6	7	9		10				4	5						8		11		30
1	3	2			6	7	9		10				4	5						8		11		31
1		3	4		6	7	9		10			2	5							8		11		32
1	3	2			6	7	9		10				4			5				8		11		33
	3	2			6	7	9		10	8	1		4			5						11		34
27	28	23	20	9	27	32	31	25	15	13	7	21	21	25	1	2	2	7	3	6	2	18	9	
				1	2	6	9	10	4	1		2		2					1	2		2	1	

1903-04

1	Sep	1	(h)	Bradford C	W	2-0	Dunn, Rouse	4,000
2		5	(a)	Lincoln C	L	1-2	Lappin	6,000
3		12	(h)	Stockport C	W	2-1	Nichol 2	4,000
4		19	(a)	Chesterfield	W	1-0	Rouse	3,000
5		26	(h)	Bolton W	D	0-0		5,000
6	Oct	3	(a)	Burnley	L	0-2		5,000
7		10	(h)	Preston NE	D	1-1	Speight	4,000
8		17	(h)	Port Vale	W	3-1	Long, Rouse, Roberts (pen)	3,000
9		24	(a)	Leicester F	D	1-1	Roberts	5,000
10		31	(a)	Preston NE	L	0-2		10,000
11	Nov	21	(a)	Bristol C	L	0-4		8,000
12	Dec	5	(a)	Glossop NE	D	1-1	Hodgkinson	1,000
13		19	(a)	W Arsenal	L	1-5	Rouse	12,000
14		26	(h)	Barnsley	W	5-1	Hodgkinson 2, Long, Lappin, Wilkinson	4,000
15	Jan	2	(h)	Lincoln C	D	1-1	Rouse	5,000
16		9	(a)	Stockport C	D	1-1	Rouse	3,000
17		16	(h)	Chesterfield	W	1-0	Williams	
18		23	(a)	Bolton W	L	0-4		6,000
19		30	(h)	Burnley	D	0-0		4,000
20	Feb	13	(a)	Port Vale	W	2-1	Rouse, Elkins (pen)	
21		20	(h)	Leicester F	W	4-3	Lappin, Nelmes, Elkins, Roberts	4,000
22		27	(a)	Blackpool	L	0-3		2,000
23	Mar	5	(h)	Gainsborough T	W	3-1	Lappin, Nichol, Hodgkinson	
24		12	(a)	Burton U	L	0-1		
25		19	(h)	Bristol C	W	2-0	Rouse, Elkins	
26		26	(a)	Manchester U	L	0-2		10,000
27	Apr	1	(h)	Burton U	W	4-0	Rouse 3, Roberts	
28		2	(h)	Glossop NE	W	2-0	Rouse, Baker	4,000
29		4	(h)	Blackpool	W	4-0	Long 2, Elkins, Roberts	4,500
30		6	(a)	Gainsborough T	L	2-4	Elkins 2 (1 pen)	
31		9	(a)	Bradford C	L	0-1		8,000
32		12	(h)	Manchester U	W	3-1	Rouse 2, Long	3,000
33		16	(h)	W Arsenal	D	2-2	Phillips, Long	
34		23	(a)	Barnsley	L	1-3	Phillips	

FINAL LEAGUE POSITION: 6th in Division Two

Appearances
Goals

FA Cup

Sup	Dec	12	(h)	Barnsley	W	2-0	
1	Feb	6	(a)	Preston NE	L	0-1	

Spendiff	McConnell A	Gardner	Dunn	Roberts	Nelmes	Nichol	Rouse	Miller	Long	Lappin	Harmsworth	McDairmond	Hodgkinson	Phillips	Grant	Baker	Elkins	Wilkinson	Speight	Williams	McConnell J	Horner	
1	2	3	4	5	6	7	8	9	10	11													1
1	2	3	4	5	6	7	8	9		11								10					2
1	2	3	4	5	6	7	8	9		11								10					3
1	2	3	4	5		7	8		9	11		6						10					4
1	2	3	4	5		7	8	9		11		6						10					5
1	2	3	4	5		7	8		9	11		6							10				6
1	2	3	4	5	6	7	8		9	11									10				7
1	2	3	4	5	6	7	8		9	11									10				8
1	2	3	4	5		7	8		9	11		6							10				9
1	2	3	4	5		7	8		9	11		6							10				10
1	2	3	4	5		7	8		9			6	11						10				11
1	2	3	4	5			9		7			6	8					10		11			12
1	2	3	4	5			9		7			6	8					10		11			13
1	2	3	4		6		9		7	11		5	8					10					14
1	2	3	4	5			9		7	11		6	8					10					15
1	2	3	4	5			9		7	11		6	8					10					16
1	2		4	5			9		7			6	8					10		11	3		17
1	2	3		5	6		9		7	8		4	11				10						18
1	2			5	6	7	9		8		3	4	11					10					19
1	2		3	5	6	7	8		10	11		4					9						20
1	2		3	5	6	7	8		10	11		4					9						21
1	2	3		5	6		8		10	11		4	7				9						22
1	2	3	4	5		7			10	11		6	8				9						23
1	2	3		5		7			10	11	4	6			8		9						24
1	2	3	4		6		8		7		5		11				9	10					25
1	2	3		5	6		8		7		4		11				9	10					26
1	2	3		5	6		8		7		4		11	9		10							27
1	2		3	5	6		10		7	11		4				8	9						28
1	2			5	6		10		7			4	11			8	9				3		29
1	2		3	5	6		10		7			4	11	9			8						30
1	2			5	6		10					4		7		8	9			11	3		31
1	2			5	6		10		7			4		9		8		11			3		32
1	2			5	6		10		7			4		9		8		11			3		33
	2		5		6				7			4		9		8	10	11			3	1	34
33	34	23	24	31	21	16	31	4	30	20	5	26	16	6	1	7	13	16	6	4	6	1	
			1	4	1	3	13		6	4			4	2		1	7	2	1	1			

1904-05

1	Sep	3	(h)	Barnsley	D 0-0		4,500
2		10	(a)	West Brom A	W 2-0	Ross, Morley	10,000
3		17	(h)	Burnley	W 1-0	Ross	5,000
4		24	(a)	Bolton W	L 1-4	Ross	12,000
5	Oct	1	(a)	Blackpool	D 1-1	Ross	2,000
6		8	(h)	Doncaster R	W 2-1	Ross, Baker	
7		15	(a)	Gainsborough T	L 1-2	Phillips	6,000
8		22	(h)	Burton U	W 1-0	Baker	
9		29	(a)	Liverpool	L 0-5		14,000
10	Nov	5	(h)	Port Vale	L 0-3		
11		12	(a)	Bristol C	L 0-5		10,000
12		19	(h)	Manchester U	L 0-1		3,000
13	Dec	3	(h)	Chesterfield	W 3-1	Higgins 2, Phillips	2,000
14		17	(h)	Lincoln C	W 1-0	Phillips	4,000
15		24	(a)	Leicester F	L 1-5	Higgins	
16		26	(a)	Burnley	L 0-1		
17		27	(a)	Bradford C	D 0-0		15,000
18		31	(a)	Barnsley	D 2-2	Ross, Hunter	3,000
19	Jan	7	(h)	West Brom A	L 1-3	Higgins	4,000
20		21	(h)	Bolton W	D 2-2	McDairmid, Baker	
21		28	(h)	Blackpool	W 2-0	Ross, Baker	3,000
22	Feb	11	(h)	Gainsborough T	D 0-0		
23		18	(a)	Burton U	L 0-1		3,000
24		25	(h)	Liverpool	L 0-1		
25	Mar	4	(a)	Port Vale	L 0-2		2,000
26		11	(h)	Bristol C	W 4-0	Butler 2, Reynolds, Baker	
27		18	(a)	Manchester U	L 1-2	Butler	14,000
28		25	(h)	Glossop NE	W 3-0	Phillips 2, Reynolds (pen)	
29	Apr	1	(a)	Chesterfield	D 0-0		
30		8	(h)	Bradford C	L 0-2		6,000
31		15	(a)	Lincoln C	D 0-0		5,000
32		22	(h)	Leicester F	W 2-0	Padley 2	2,500
33		24	(a)	Doncaster R	W 2-0	Reynolds, Phillips	
34		29	(a)	Glossop NE	L 0-2		

FINAL LEAGUE POSITION: 13th in Division Two

Appearances
Goals

FA Cup

Prel	Jan	14	(h)	Gainsborough T	W 2-0
1	Feb	14	(a)	Stoke	L 0-2

Spendiff	McConnell A	McConnell J	McDairmid	Coles	Nelmes	Reynolds J	Baker	Morley	Turner	Ross	Cartledge	McGregor	Ayre	Mochan	Higgins	Hunter	Phillips	Elkins	Butler	Padley	Oakes	Thompson AJ	
1	2	3	4	5	6	7	8	9	10	11													1
1	2	3	4	5	6	7	8	9	10	11													2
1	2	3	4	5	6	7	8	9	10	11													3
1	2	3	4	5	6	7		9	10	11					8								4
1	2		4	5	6	7		9	10	11			3		8								5
1	2		4	5	6	7	8	9		11			3		10								6
1		3	4	5	6	7	8	2		11					10		9						7
1	2		4	5	6	7	8	3	10	11					9								8
1			5	2	6	7	8	3	10	11					4		9						9
1			4	5	6		7	2	10	11			3		8			9					10
1			4	5	6	7		3	10	11		2			8			9					11
			8	5	6	7		2		11	1	4		3	10			9					12
1			8	5	6	7		2		11		4		3	10		9						13
1			8	5	6			2		11		4		3	10	7	9						14
			6	5		7	8	2		11	1	4		3	10		9						15
			6	5		7	8	2		11	1	4		3	10		9						16
		3	6	5		7		2	8	11	1	4			10		9						17
		3	6	5				2	8	11	1	4			10	7	9						18
		3	6		5		8	2		11	1	4			10	7	9						19
1			5		6	7	8	2		11		4		3		10	9						20
			9	5	6	7	8	2		11	1	4		3		10							21
1			5		6		8	2	10	11		4		3		7		9					22
1			5		6	7	8	2	10	11		4		3				9					23
1			5		6	7	9	2	10	11		4		3	8								24
1			5			7	9	2		10		4		3	6		8				11		25
1		3	5		6	7	8	2		11		4			10				9				26
1		3	5		6	7	8	2		11		4			10				9				27
1		3	5		6	7	8	2				4			10		11		9				28
1		3	5		6	7	8	2				4				10			9			11	29
			5		6	7	8	2		9	1	4		3		10						11	30
1		3	8	5	6	7	10	2		11		4							9				31
1		3	4	5	6	7	8	2		11							10			9			32
1		3	4	5	6	7	8	2		11							10			9			33
1		3	6	5		7	8	2		11		4					10			9			34
26	7	16	34	23	28	29	26	34	14	32	8	22	3	12	21	8	15	5	5	3	1	2	
			1			3	5	1		7					4	1	7		2	2			

1905-06

1	Sep	2	(a)	Chesterfield	W 4-1	Swarbrick, Grant, Baker, Morley	
2		9	(h)	Manchester U	L 0-1		6,000
3		16	(a)	Port Vale	D 2-2	Burnett, Nelmes	2,000
4		23	(h)	Glossop NE	D 1-1	Burnett	4,000
5		30	(a)	Barnsley	L 0-2		
6	Oct	7	(h)	Stockport C	W 2-0	Baker 2	3,000
7		14	(a)	Clapton O	W 2-1	Baker, Swarbrick	
8		21	(h)	Blackpool	D 1-1	Baker	
9		28	(a)	Burnley	D 0-0		4,000
10	Nov	4	(h)	Bradford C	W 1-0	Burnett	4,000
11		11	(a)	Leeds C	L 0-3		7,000
12		25	(a)	Burton U	L 0-1		
13	Dec	2	(h)	Leicester F	D 1-1	Padley	3,000
14		9	(a)	Chelsea	L 0-2		3,000
15		16	(a)	Hull C	W 1-0	Johnson	
16		23	(h)	Gainsborough T	W 2-0	Burnett 2	
17		25	(a)	Lincoln C	L 1-3	Johnson	
18		27	(h)	Bristol C	D 1-1	Fletcher	4,000
19		30	(h)	Chesterfield	W 2-0	Swarbrick, Baker	
20	Jan	6	(a)	Manchester U	L 0-5		15,000
21		20	(h)	Port Vale	W 5-0	Padley 2, Baker 2 (1 pen), McGregor	3,000
22		27	(a)	Glossop NE	L 0-2		
23	Feb	3	(h)	West Brom A	W 3-2	Hooper, Padley, Baker (pen)	
24		10	(a)	Stockport C	D 2-2	Baker (pen), McGregor	1,000
25		17	(h)	Clapton O	W 4-1	Robinson 2, Swarbrick, Hooper	
26		24	(a)	Leicester F	L 0-2		
27	Mar	3	(h)	Burnley	W 2-0	Young 2 (1 pen)	4,000
28		7	(a)	Blackpool	L 0-2		
29		17	(h)	Leeds C	D 1-1	Milnes	3,000
30		24	(a)	West Brom A	L 0-2		
31		31	(h)	Burton U	W 1-0	Grant	
32	Apr	5	(h)	Barnsley	W 2-1	Hooper, Robinson	
33		7	(a)	Bradford C	W 1-0	Johnson	
34		13	(h)	Lincoln C	D 2-2	Burnett, Robinson	6,000
35		14	(h)	Chelsea	D 1-1	Robinson	
36		17	(a)	Bristol C	L 0-2		6,000
37		21	(h)	Hull C	W 1-0	Robinson	
38		28	(a)	Gainsborough T	L 0-1		

FINAL LEAGUE POSITION: 8th in Division Two

Appearances
Goals

FA Cup

1	Jan	16	(h*)	Newcastle U	L 0-6	

*Played at St James' Park, Newcastle.

Cartledge	Morley	McConnell J	McGregor	McDairmid	Nelmes	Swarbrick	Baker	Burnett	Grant	Johnson J	Horner	Butler	Coles	Openshaw	Milnes	Higgins	Hooper	Bisby	Fletcher	Robinson F	Pynegar	Padley	Young	Reynolds	No.
1	2	3	4	5	6	7	8	9	10	11															1
1	2		4	5	6	7	8	9	10	11			3												2
1	2	3	4	5	6	7	8	9	10	11															3
1	2	3	4	5	6	7	8	9	10	11															4
1	2		4		6			10	8	11			5	3			7					9			5
1	2		4			10	8	9		11			5	3		6	7								6
1	2		4			10	8	9		11			5	3		6	7								7
1	2		4		6	10	8	9		11			5	3			7								8
1	2	3	4		6	10	8	9		11			5				7								9
1	2	3	4			10	8	9		11			6		5		7								10
1	2	3	4			10	8	9		11		5	6				7								11
1	2	3	4			11		10					6			5	7		8		9				12
1	2	3	4			11		10					6			5	7		8			9			13
1	2	3	4					10		11			5			6	7		8			9			14
1	2	3	4				9	10		11			5			6		7		8					15
1	2	3	4		6		9	10		11			5					7		8					16
1		3	4				9	10		11		2	5			6		7		8					17
1	2	3	4			10		9		11					5	6			7	8					18
1	2	3	4			11	8								5	6			7			9		10	19
1	2	3	4			11	8	9		7					5	6								10	20
1	2	3	4			11	8	10							5	6			7			9			21
1	2	3	4			11	8	5								6			7	10		9			22
1	2		4			11	8					3			5	6	7			10		9			23
	2		4			11	8				1	3			5	6	7			10		9			24
	2		4			11	8				1	3			5	6	7			10		9			25
	2		4			11	8	9			1	3			5	6	7			10					26
	2		4		6	11					1	3			5				7	10	8		9		27
	2		4		6	11		8			1	3			5				7	10			9		28
	2	3	4		6	11	8				1				5				7				9	10	29
1	2	3	4		6	11		9	8						5				7					10	30
1	2	3	4		6	11			8						5		7					9		10	31
1		3	4		6	11			8			2			5		7					9		10	32
1	2	3	4		6	10		9		11					5		7			8					33
1		3	4		6	10		9		11		2			5		7			8					34
1	2	3	4		6	11	8	9							5		7			10					35
1	2	3	4		6	11	8	9							5		7			10					36
1	2	3	4		6	10	8								5		7	11		9					37
1		3	4		6	10	8					2			5		7	11		9					38
32	34	27	38	4	20	33	26	28	8	19	6	11	14	4	21	16	22	5	11	17	2	11	3	6	
	1		2		1	4	10	6	2	3					1		3		1	6		4	2		

1906-07

1	Sep	1	(h)	Nottingham F	W 3-1	Robinson, R.Morris, Swarbrick (pen)	7,000
2		3	(a)	Leicester F	L 0-2		
3		8	(a)	Lincoln C	L 1-2	F.Bisby	5,000
4		15	(h)	Burton U	D 1-1	Swarbrick	5,000
5		22	(a)	Chesterfield	W 3-1	Hakin, R.Morris, Rodger	4,000
6		29	(a)	Port Vale	L 2-3	Fletcher, Hakin	
7	Oct	6	(h)	Burnley	W 1-0	McGregor (pen)	4,000
8		13	(a)	Leeds C	L 3-4	Morris, Rodger, Hakin	10,000
9		20	(h)	Barnsley	W 1-0	Rodger	
10		27	(a)	Chelsea	L 0-2		15,000
11	Nov	3	(h)	Wolves	W 2-1	Hakin, Swarbrick	
12		10	(a)	Clapton O	L 0-1		5,000
13		17	(a)	Gainsborough T	L 1-2	Morley	
14		24	(a)	Stockport C	L 0-3		4,000
15	Dec	1	(h)	Hull C	L 1-3	Hakin	7,000
16		15	(h)	Blackpool	D 0-0		
17		22	(a)	Bradford C	L 0-1		10,000
18		25	(a)	West Brom A	L 1-6	Robinson	19,047
19		26	(h)	Gainsborough T	W 2-0	R.Morris, Rodger	
20		29	(a)	Nottingham F	W 3-0	Rodger 2, Hooper	
21	Jan	5	(h)	Lincoln C	W 4-0	Swarbrick, Roger, Burnett, R.Morris	
22		19	(a)	Burton U	W 3-2	Rodger, Burnett, R.Morris	
23		26	(h)	Chesterfield	W 3-1	Rodger, Higgins, Burnett	
24	Feb	9	(a)	Burnley	L 0-2		
25		12	(a)	Glossop NE	L 0-1		
26		16	(h)	Leeds C	W 4-0	R.Morris, Rodger, Hooper, Burnett	4,000
27	Mar	2	(h)	Chelsea	W 2-1	Swarbrick (pen), Burnett	
28		9	(a)	Wolves	L 0-5		
29		16	(h)	Clapton O	L 1-2	Swarbrick (pen)	
30		21	(h)	Port Vale	W 2-0	Fletcher 2	
31		29	(h)	West Brom A	W 2-1	Hakin, Burnett	
32		30	(h)	Stockport C	W 3-1	Rodger 3	
33	Apr	1	(h)	Leicester F	L 0-1		
34		6	(a)	Hull C	L 2-4	Swarbrick (pen), Hakin	
35		11	(a)	Barnsley	D 1-1	Hakin	
36		13	(h)	Glossop NE	W 2-1	J.C.Bisby, Swarbrick	
37		20	(a)	Blackpool	L 3-4	Burnett, Barr, Hakin	
38		27	(h)	Bradford C	L 0-2		

FINAL LEAGUE POSITION: 15th in Division Two

Appearances
Goals

FA Cup

1	Jan	12	(h)	W Arsenal	D 1-1	
R		16	(a)	W Arsenal	L 0-3	

Carledge	Morley	MacDonald	McGregor	Milnes	Higgins	Rodger T	Robinson F	Hakin	Morris R	Swarbrick	Horner	Carmichael	Butler	Coles	Openshaw	Lee	Fleet	Bisby	Hooper	Chantry	Cook	Barr	Fletcher	Burnett	Bisby F	Morris T	
1	2	3	4	5	6	7	8	9	10	11																	1
1	2		4	5	6	7	8	9	10	11																3	2
1			4	5	6	7	8	9	10				2												11	3	3
1	2	3	4			7	8	9	10	11				5			6										4
1	2	3	4	5		7	8	9	10	11							6										5
1		3	4	5		7		9	10	11							6						8			2	6
1		3	4	5		7	10	9		11							6						8			2	7
1	2	3	4	5	6	7	8	9	10	11																	8
	3		4	5	6	7	8	9	10	11	1		2														9
1	3		4	5	6	7		9	10				2											8	11		10
1	3		4		6	7		9	10	11			2											8		5	11
	3				6	7		9	10	11	1		2			4								8		5	12
1	3	2		5	6		10	9		11						4			7	8							13
1	3				4	8		10		11			2	5				6	7	9							14
	3		4	5	6	7	10	9	8	11	1		2														15
	2		4		6	8		10		11	1		3							7				9		5	16
	2		4		6	8			10	11	1		3							7				9		5	17
	2		4		6		10	9			1		3						7				8		11	5	18
	2		4		6	8			10	11		1	3						7					9		5	19
	2		4		6	8			10	11		1	3						7					9		5	20
	2		4		6	8			10	11		1	3						7					9		5	21
	2	3	4		6	8			10	11		1							7					9		5	22
	2		4		6	8			10	11		1	3						7					9		5	23
	2		4		6	8			10	11		1	3						7					9		5	24
		2	4		6	8			10	11	1		3						7					9		5	25
		2	4		6	8			10	11		1	3						7					9		5	26
	2		4	6		8			10	11		1	3								7			9		5	27
	2		4	6		7			8			1	3	5				10						9	11		28
	2		4	6		7	10		8	11		1			3									9		5	29
	2		4		6	7		10		11		1	3										8	9		5	30
		2	4		6	8		10		11		1	3								7			9		5	31
		2	4		6	8		10		11		1	3									7		9		5	32
		2	4		6	8		10		11		1	3								7			9		5	33
		2	4		6	7	8	10		11		1	3											9		5	34
							8	10		11		1	3	2		4		6			7			9		5	35
					10		8	9		11		1	3	2		4		6			7					5	36
		2	4		6	8		10		11		1	3									7		9		5	37
		2	4		6	7	9	10		11		1	3										8			5	38
12	25	16	33	14	30	34	16	26	24	34	7	19	28	5	1	4	4	4	11	4	5	2	5	23	4	28	
	1		1		1	13	2	9	7	8								1	2			1	3	7	1		

1907-08

1	Sep	3	(h)	Gainsborough T	L	1-4	Kilbourne	
2		7	(a)	Lincoln C	L	0-1		
3		9	(a)	Stockport C	L	0-3		
4		14	(h)	Stockport C	W	2-1	Hakin, Pattinson	5,000
5		21	(a)	Fulham	W	1-0	Pattinson	24,000
6		28	(h)	Glossop NE	W	4-0	Fletcher 3, Hakin	5,000
7	Oct	5	(a)	Barnsley	L	1-2	Hakin	4,500
8		12	(h)	Leicester F	D	1-1	Jewel	4,500
9		19	(a)	Chesterfield	D	0-0		
10		26	(h)	Blackpool	D	2-2	Blanthorne 2	4,500
11	Nov	2	(a)	Burnley	L	1-5	Blanthorne	4,000
12		9	(h)	Stoke	W	1-0	Jewel	
13		16	(a)	Oldham A	L	0-2		8,000
14		23	(h)	West Brom A	D	2-2	Blanthorne 2	4,000
15		30	(a)	Clapton O	L	1-2	Blanthorne	5,000
16	Dec	7	(h)	Bradford C	L	0-1		4,000
17		14	(a)	Leeds C	L	1-4	Kilbourne	6,000
18		21	(a)	Hull C	L	2-4	Blanthorne 2	5,000
19		25	(a)	Derby C	L	0-4		12,000
20		26	(a)	Gainsborough T	L	2-3	Blanthorne, Hakin	4,000
21		28	(a)	Wolves	L	1-5	Kilbourne	
22	Jan	4	(h)	Lincoln C	L	0-2		3,000
23		18	(h)	Fulham	L	0-4		5,000
24		25	(a)	Glossop NE	W	2-1	Blanthorne, Kilbourne	1,500
25	Feb	8	(a)	Leicester F	D	1-1	Hakin	
26		29	(h)	Burnley	L	0-1		3,000
27	Mar	14	(h)	Oldham A	W	2-0	Stokes, Hakin	6,000
28		19	(a)	Stoke	L	0-5		
29		21	(a)	West Brom A	W	2-1	Kilbourne, Bush	10,000
30		28	(h)	Clapton O	D	0-0		
31	Apr	1	(a)	Blackpool	L	0-3		
32		4	(a)	Bradford C	D	1-1	Blanthorne	17,000
33		9	(h)	Barnsley	W	4-1	Blanthorne, Kilbourne, Hakin, Bush	
34		11	(h)	Leeds C	W	2-0	Kilbourne, Higgins (pen)	4,000
35		17	(h)	Wolves	L	0-1		
36		18	(h)	Hull C	D	1-1	Higgins	6,000
37		20	(h)	Derby C	W	1-0	Blanthorne	
38		29	(h)	Chesterfield	W	4-3	Blanthorne, Kilbourne, Higgins, Bradley	

FINAL LEAGUE POSITION: 18th in Division Two

Appearances
Goals

FA Cup

1	Jan	11	(a)	Bristol C	D	0-0
R		15	(h)	Bristol C	W	2-1
2	Feb	1	(h)	Carlisle U	W	6-2
3		22	(h)	Crystal P	W	1-0
4	Mar	7	(a)	Newcastle U	L	1-5

Carmichael	Wheelhouse	Crapper	Lee	Bowden	Higgins	Pattinson	Kilbourne	Jack	Hakin	Jewel	Scott	Blanchard	McConnell J	Vincent	McDairmid	Hatton	Cook	Fletcher	Stokes	Bradley	Bisby F	Bush	Blanthorne	Coles	Bisby JC	Young	
1	2	3	4	5	6	7	8	9	10	11																	1
1	2	3	4	5		7	8		9	11						6			10								2
1	2	3	4			7	9		10	11						6									5		3
1	2		4		5	7	8		9	11				3		6		10									4
1	2		4		5	7	8		9	11				3		6		10									5
1	2		4		5	7	8		9	11				3		6		10									6
1	2		4	5		7	8		9	11				3		6		10									7
1	2		4	5		7	8		9	11				3		6		10									8
1	2		4	5	6	7	8			11				3					10							9	9
1	2		4	5	6	7	8			11				3					10				9				10
1	2		4		6	7	8							3	10						11		9	5			11
1	2		4			7	10			11				3	5	6		8					9				12
	2		4			7	8		10	11	1			3	5	6							9				13
	2		4	5		7	8		10	11	1			3		6							9				14
	2		4	5			8		10	11	1			3		6	7						9				15
	2				5	7	4		8		1			3		6					11		9				16
	2		4		5		8		10		1		3			6		7			11		9				17
	2		4		5		8		10	11	1		3			6		7					9				18
1	2		4		5		8		10	11				3		6		7					9				19
1	2		4		5		8		10	11					3	6		7					9				20
1	2				5		8		10	11				3	4	6		7					9				21
	2				6	7			10	11	1	5		3	4								9			8	22
	2		4		5		8		10		1			3		6		11	7				9				23
	2		4	5			8		10		1			3		6	7	11					9				24
1	2			5	4		8		10					3			7	11					9		6		25
1			4	5			8		10			2		3		6		11	7								26
	2		4		5		8		10		1			3		6			7			11	9				27
	2				4	7	8		10		1			3	5	6						11	9				28
	2			5	4	7	8		10		1			3		6						11	9				29
	2			5	4	7	8		10		1			3		6						11	9				30
	2		4	5	6		8		10		1			3				7				11	9				31
			4	5	10				8		1		2	3				7				11	9		6		32
			4	5	6		10		8		1		2	3				7				11	9				33
			4	5	6		10		8		1		2	3				7				11	9				34
			4	5	6		10		8		1			3				7				11	9				35
			4	5	6		8				1			3		7				10		11	9	2			36
			4		5		7		10		1	2		3		6				8		11	9				37
			4		5		10				1		2	3		6		7		8		11	9				38
17	30	3	31	19	28	19	36	1	32	19	21	3	6	32	7	27	3	21	6	3	3	12	28	2	3	2	
					3	2	8		7	2								3	1	1		2	14				

Coulbeck played number 8 in Match 3; Glennon played number 10 in Match 16; Burkinshaw played number 9 in Match 26; Rudd played number 2 in Match 35.

1908-09

1	Sep	1	(h)	Stockport C	W	3-0	Coxon, Owen, Springthorpe	5,000
2		5	(h)	West Brom A	D	1-1	Bradley	
3		12	(a)	Birmingham	L	1-3	Kilbourne	15,000
4		19	(h)	Gainsborough T	L	1-2	Springthorpe	
5		26	(a)	Bolton W	L	0-2		
6	Oct	3	(a)	Fulham	L	2-5	Owens 2	
7		10	(h)	Burnley	L	0-1		
8		17	(a)	Bradford	W	2-0	Burkinshaw, Coxon	9,000
9		24	(h)	Wolves	W	3-0	Burkinshaw, Bradley 2	
10		31	(a)	Oldham A	L	0-4		15,000
11	Nov	7	(h)	Clapton O	W	1-0	Burkinshaw	
12		14	(a)	Leeds C	L	1-4	Stokes	3,000
13		21	(h)	Barnsley	D	0-0		6,500
14		28	(a)	Tottenham H	L	0-2		14,000
15	Dec	5	(h)	Hull C	D	0-0		
16		12	(a)	Derby C	L	1-2	Bradley (pen)	5,000
17		19	(h)	Blackpool	W	2-1	Appleyard (pen), Springthorpe	
18		26	(h)	Chesterfield	W	1-0	Satterthwaite	
19	Jan	1	(a)	Stockport C	W	1-0	Beadling	
20		2	(a)	West Brom A	L	0-7		5,177
21		9	(h)	Birmingham	L	0-3		
22		23	(a)	Gainsborough T	W	3-0	Coxon, Leonard 2	5,000
23		30	(h)	Bolton W	W	1-0	Leonard	4,000
24	Feb	6	(a)	Chesterfield	W	2-1	Leonard, Bradley	
25		13	(a)	Burnley	L	0-2		
26		20	(h)	Bradford	D	1-1	Satterthwaite	6,000
27		27	(a)	Wolves	D	0-0		8,000
28	Mar	13	(a)	Clapton O	L	1-2	Appleyard (pen)	
29		16	(a)	Glossop NE	L	0-1		
30		20	(h)	Leeds C	L	0-1		5,500
31		25	(h)	Fulham	D	2-2	Beadling, Coxon	
32		27	(a)	Barnsley	L	1-3	Little (og)	
33	Apr	3	(h)	Tottenham H	L	1-2	Coxon	
34		10	(a)	Hull C	W	1-0	Kilbourne	
35		12	(h)	Glossop NE	W	2-0	Beadling 2	
36		17	(h)	Derby C	W	2-0	Kilbourne, Leonard	5,000
37		20	(h)	Oldham A	W	2-0	Beadling, Leonard	
38		24	(a)	Blackpool	D	2-2	Kelly, Coxon	

FINAL LEAGUE POSITION: 13th in Division Two

Appearances
Goals

FA Cup

1	Jan	20	(h)	Stockport C	L	0-2

Scott	Wheelhouse	Bidmead	Lee	Davidson	Forster	Bradley M	Owens	Springthorpe	Kilbourne	Coxon	Lonsdale	Henderson CG	Glennon	Hargreaves	Kelly	Hatton	Leonard	Stokes	Bacon	Beadling	Satterthwaite	Burkinshaw	Appleyard	Fletcher	
1	2	3	4	5	6	7	8	9	10	11															1
1	2		4	5	6	7	9	10	7	11		3													2
1	2		4	5	6	8	10		7	11		3					9								3
1	2		4	5	6	10		9	8	11		3					7								4
1	2		4	5		8	9			11		3				6	10	7							5
1	2		4	5		8	9			11		3				6	10	7							6
1	2		4	5		8	9	10		11		3				6		7							7
1	2			5	4	8				11		3		6			10	7				9			8
1	2		4	5		8				11		3		6			10	7				9			9
1	2		4	5		8				11		3		6			10	7				9			10
1	2		4	5		8				11		3		6			10	7				9			11
1	2		4	5		9				11		3		6			10	7			8				12
1	2		4	5						11		3		6			10			7	8		9		13
1	2		4	5				10				3		6						7	8		9	11	14
	2		4	5		8		10			1	3				6				7			9	11	15
1	2		4	5		8				11		3				6	9			7	10				16
1	2			5				8		11		3	4			6				7	10		9		17
1	2			5						11		3	4			6	8			7	10		9		18
1	2		4	5						11		3				6	8			7	10		9		19
1	2		4	5						11		3				6	8			7	10		9		20
1	2		4	5				8		11		3				6				7	10		9		21
1	2		4	5		8				11		3				6	9			7	10				22
1	2		4	5		8				11		3				6	9			7	10				23
1	2		4	5		8				11		3				6	9			7	10				24
1	2		4	5		8				11		3				6	9			7	10				25
1	2			5		8				11		3	4			6	9			7	10				26
1	2			5						11		3	4			6	8			7	10		9		27
1	2			5						11		3	4			6	8			7	10		9		28
1	2			5						11		3	4			6	8			7	10		9		29
1	2			5					8	11		3	4			6				7	10		9		30
1	2			5		8			10	11		3	4			6	9			7					31
1	2					8			10	11		3	4	5		6	9			7					32
1	2					8			10	11		3		4	5	6			7				9		33
1	2		4			8			10	11		3			5	6	9			7					34
1	2		4			8			10	11		3			5	6	9			7					35
1	2		4			8			10	11		3			5	6	9			7					36
1	2		4						10	11		3			5	6	9			7	8				37
1	2		4						10	11		3			5	6	9			7	8				38
37	38	1	27	31	5	25	6	8	13	36	1	37	9	9	6	27	29	8	1	25	20	4	13	2	
						5	3	3	3	6					1		6	1		5	2	3	2		

1 own-goal

1909-10

1	Sep	1	(h)	Bradford	L	0-1		
2		4	(a)	Lincoln C	D	0-0		6,000
3		11	(h)	Clapton O	W	2-0	Leonard, Kilbourne	5,000
4		18	(a)	Blackpool	L	0-1		4,000
5		25	(h)	Hull C	L	2-3	Leonard, Bell	10,000
6	Oct	2	(a)	Derby C	L	0-6		5,000
7		9	(h)	Stockport C	L	0-1		4,000
8		16	(a)	Glossop NE	L	0-3		4,000
9		23	(h)	Birmingham	L	0-2		5,000
10		30	(a)	West Brom A	L	3-4	Coulbeck, Leonard 2	8,000
11	Nov	6	(h)	Oldham A	D	0-0		5,000
12		13	(a)	Barnsley	L	1-2	Kelly (pen)	
13		20	(h)	Fulham	L	0-2		4,000
14		27	(a)	Burnley	L	1-3	Springthorpe	
15	Dec	4	(h)	Leeds C	W	3-1	Kilbourne, Springthorpe, Gates	
16		11	(a)	Wolves	L	1-8	Hargreaves	
17		18	(h)	Gainsborough T	W	2-1	Kilbourne 2	3,000
18		25	(a)	Leicester F	L	1-3	Bell	10,000
19		27	(a)	Manchester C	L	0-2		
20	Jan	1	(a)	Hull C	L	1-5	Bell	7,000
21		8	(h)	Lincoln C	L	1-2	Rowston	4,000
22		22	(a)	Clapton O	D	0-0		
23	Feb	8	(a)	Bradford	L	1-6	Brooks	
24		12	(h)	Derby C	D	1-1	Gates	
25		15	(h)	Blackpool	L	0-1		
26		19	(a)	Stockport C	L	1-2	Bell	
27		26	(h)	Glossop NE	W	4-0	Kilbourne, Leonard 3	
28	Mar	5	(a)	Birmingham	W	4-2	Bell 3, Leonard	
29		12	(h)	West Brom A	W	3-0	Leonard 2, Hatton	
30		19	(a)	Oldham A	L	1-4	Leonard	
31		25	(h)	Manchester C	L	0-1		10,000
32		26	(h)	Leicester F	D	0-0		
33	Apr	2	(a)	Fulham	L	2-3	Leonard, Coulbeck	
34		9	(h)	Burnley	W	5-3	Leonard 3 (1 pen), Coulbeck, Bamford (og)	
35		16	(a)	Leeds C	L	1-3	Leonard	
36		23	(h)	Wolves	W	1-0	Leonard	
37		26	(h)	Barnsley	W	7-0	Bell 2, Coulbeck 2, Kelly (pen), Little (og), Brooks	
38		30	(a)	Gainsborough T	D	1-1	Hatton	

FINAL LEAGUE POSITION: 19th in Division Two

Appearances
Goals

FA Cup

1	Jan	15	(h)	Bristol R	L	0-2

Grimsby finished second from bottom and were not re-elected. They played the first team in the Midland League the following season and won the championship.

Scott	Wheelhouse	Henderson	Lee	Porter	Hatton	Blackburn	Gildea	Warren	Bell TD	Coxon	Davidson	Leonard	Gates	Kelly	Kilbourne	Lonsdale	Rowston	Springthorpe	Beadling	Coulbeck	Bacon	Brooks	Hargreaves	Ramsden	Shaw J	Dart	Leafe	Ainsworth	Blanchard	Fletcher	Gordon	Robinson	Huxford	
1	2	3	4	5	6	7	8	9	10	11																								1
1	2	3	4		6	7	8		10	11		9		5																				2
1	2	3	5		6				10	11		9			8		7									4								3
1	2	3	5			7			10	11		9	4		8											6								4
1	2	3	5		6				10	11		9	5		8		7																	5
1	2	3					8		10	11		9	5		6		7									4								6
1	2	3							10	11		9	4		4		7						6				8							7
1	2	3							9		5						7	10		8			6					11						8
1	2	3	4						11		6			5			7	10		8					9									9
1	2	3	4						11		6	9	10	5			7	10		8														10
1	2	3	4						11		6	9		5			7			8														11
1	2	3	4						10	11	6	9		5				8		7														12
1	2	3	4			7			10	11	6	9		5						8														13
1	2	3	4			7				11	6		9	5	10			8							9									14
1	2	3	4			7				11	6		9	5	10			8																15
1		3	4								5		9		10			8	7				6					11	2					16
1	2		4								5				10			8	7				6	3				11						17
1	2		4						10	11	5				8				7				6	3	9									18
1	2		4						10	11	5				8				7				6	3	9									19
1	2		4						10	11	5				8				7				6	3	9									20
1	2		4							11		10		5			7	8					6	3	9									21
1	2		4						10		5	9	3				7	8					6							11				22
1	2		4		6				10		5		3		8	1			7		11	9												23
	2	3	4		6				10		5		9			1		8	7		11													24
	2	3	4		6					11	5		9			1	7				10	8												25
	2	3	4		6				10		5	7	9			1					11	8												26
	2	3	4		6				10	11		9			8	1					7										5			27
	2	3			6				10	11	5	9		4	8	1					7													28
	2	3			6				10	11	5	9		4		1		8			7													29
	2	3			6				10	11	5	9		4		1		8			7													30
	2	3			6				10	11	5	9		4		1		8			7													31
	2	3			6				10	11		9		4	8	1			7												5			32
	2	3			6						5	9		4	10	1	11			8												7		33
	2	3			6				10		5	9		4		1	11			8												7		34
	2	3			6				10	11	5	9		4		1	7			8														35
	2				6				10	11	5	9	3	4		1	7			8														36
	2				6				10	11	5		3	4		1			7	8		9												37
	2				6				10		5	9	3	4		1			7	8													11	38
22	37	28	24	1	20	6	3	1	31	25	28	24	17	20	17	16	15	14	10	12	9	4	9	5	6	3	1	3	1	1	2	2	1	
					2				9			17	2	2	5		1	3		4		2	1											

2 own-goals

Dart played number 4 in Matches 3 & 6 and number 6 in Match 4; Leafe played number 7 in Match 8; Ainsworth played number 11 in Matches 8, 16 & 17; Blanchard played number 2 in Match 16; Fletcher played number 11 in Match 22; Gordon played number 5 in Matches 26 & 27; Robinson played number 7 in Matches 33 & 34; Huxford played number 11 in Match 38.

1910-11

1	Sep	1	(a)	Nottingham F Res	W	1-0	Leonard	
2		3	(h)	Barnsley Res	D	1-1	Kelly	3,000
3		10	(a)	Castleford	L	0-2		
4		17	(h)	Leicester F Res	W	8-1	Leonard 5, Jackson, Worth, Springthorpe	
5		24	(h)	Denaby U	W	4-0	Leonard 2, Hobson, Worth	3,000
6	Oct	1	(h)	Sheffield U Res	W	4-2	Leonard, Hobson, Springthorpe 2	
7		13	(a)	Hull C Res	L	0-1		
8		15	(h)	Leeds C Res	W	4-0	Leonard 2, Jackson, Kelly	
9		22	(a)	Sheffield U Res	D	0-0		
10		29	(a)	Lincoln C Res	D	1-1	Leonard (pen)	2,500
11	Nov	5	(a)	Leicester F Res	W	2-1	Gordon, Worth	
12		12	(h)	Mexborough	W	6-0	Hubbard 2, Worth 2, Springthorpe, Leonard	3,000
13		19	(h)	Gainsborough T Res	W	3-1	Hubbard, Worth 2	
14		26	(h)	Worksop	W	7-0	Bell 4, Leonard 2, Worth	
15	Dec	10	(h)	Lincoln C Res	W	4-1	Henderson 2, Hubbard, Leonard	2,000
16		24	(h)	Chesterfield	W	2-1	Leonard	
17		26	(h)	Hull C Res	D	2-2	Leonard, Hubbard	7,000
18		27	(a)	Barnsley Res	L	1-2	Leonard	
19		31	(h)	Notts C Res	W	4-2	Leonard 2, Huxford 2	
20	Jan	2	(a)	Chesterfield	L	0-1		
21		7	(h)	Rotherham T	W	3-2	Springthorpe, Hubbard 2 (1 pen)	3,000
22		21	(h)	Castleford	W	4-2	Leonard, Springthorpe, Hubbard, Worth	
23		28	(a)	Huddersfield T	W	1-0	Leonard	
24	Feb	11	(a)	Rotherham C	D	0-0		
25		18	(a)	Leeds C Res	W	3-0	Young 2, Springthorpe	
26	Mar	4	(h)	Huddersfield T	W	3-1	Huxford 2, Hobson	
27		11	(a)	Sheffield W Res	L	1-2	Springthorpe	
28		18	(a)	Doncaster R Res	W	3-0	Gordon 2, Hubbard	
29		25	(a)	Gainsborough T Res	D	0-0		
30		29	(a)	Notts C Res	L	1-2	Huxford	
31	Apr	1	(a)	Mexborough	W	1-0	Bell	
32		8	(a)	Denaby U	W	3-1	Gordon, Hobson, Huxford	
33		14	(h)	Sheffield W Res	W	2-0	Hobson, Young	7,000
34		15	(h)	Doncaster R Res	W	3-2	Hubbard, Worth 2	
35		17	(h)	Nottingham F Res	W	2-0	Bell, Gordon	
36		18	(a)	Rotherham T	D	0-0		
37		22	(a)	Worksop	W	6-1	Hubbard 3, Gordon 2, Hubbard	
38		27	(h)	Rotherham C	W	4-0	Huxford, Young 3	

FINAL LEAGUE POSITION: 1st in Midland League

Appearances

Goals

FA Cup

1	Jan	26	(h)	Croydon Com*	W	8-1
2	Feb	4	(a)	Crewe A	W	5-1
3		25	(a)	Bradford C	L	0-1

*Replay of match declared void on 14 January.

Lonsdale	Wheelhouse	Arrowsmith	Kelly	Gordon	Henderson WP	Hobson	Jackson	Leonard	Bell	Worth	Bradley	Lee	Norton	Bacon	Hubbard	Springthorpe	Young	Huxford	
1	2	3	4	5	6	7	8	9	10	11									1
1	2	3	4	5	6	7	8	9	10	11									2
1	2	3	4	5	6	7	8	9	10	11									3
1	2	3		5	6	7	8	9		11		4				10			4
1	2	3		5	6	7	8	9		11		4				10			5
1	2	3	4	5	6	7	8	9		11						10			6
1	2	3	6	5	10	7	8	9		11		4							7
	2	3	4	5	6	7	8	9	10	11	1								8
	2	3	6	5		7	8	9	10	11	1	4							9
	2	3	6	5		7		9	10	11	1	4		8					10
	2	3	9	5	6	7		8	10	11	1	4							11
	2	3	6	5		7		9		11	1	4			8	10			12
	2	3	6	5		7		9		11	1	4			8	10			13
	2	3	4	5	6	7		9	10	11	1				8				14
	2	3	4	5	6	7		9	10	11	1				8				15
	2	3	4	5	6	7		9	10	11	1				8				16
	2	3	4	5		7		9	10	11	1	6			8				17
	2	3	6	5		7		9	10	11	1	4			8				18
	2	3	6	5		7		9		11	1	4			8			10	19
1	2	3	6	5		7		9		11		4			8			10	20
1	2	3	4	5	6	7			10	11					9	8			21
1	2	3	6	5		7		9		11		4			8	10			22
1	2	3		5	6	7		9	10	11		4			8				23
1	2	3	6	5		7			10	11		4			8		9		24
1	2	3	6	5		7				11		4			8	10	9		25
1	2	3	6	5		7				11		4			8		9	10	26
1	2	3	6	5		7		9		11		4			8	10			27
1	2	3	6	5	4	7		9		11					8	10			28
1	2	3	6	5		7		9		11		4			8	10			29
1	2	3	6	5		7		9		11		4			8			10	30
1	2	3	6	9	5	7			10			4			8			11	31
1	2	3	6	9	5	7			10			4			8			11	32
1	2	3		5	6	7			10	11		4			8		9		33
1	2	3		5	6	7			10	11		4			8		9		34
1	2	3		5	6	7			10	11		4			8		9		35
1	2	3		9	6	7			10	11		4	5		8				36
	2	3	6	9	5	7				11	1	4			8			10	37
	2	3	6	8	5	7				11	1	4					9	10	38
24	38	38	31	38	23	38	9	26	21	36	14	28	1	1	26	11	7	8	
			2	7	2	5	2	24	6	11					13	8	6	8	

1911-12

1	Sep	2	(h)	Wolves	D 0-0		6,000
2		9	(a)	Leicester F	W 2-0	Rampton, Hubbard (pen)	
3		16	(h)	Gainsborough T	D 3-3	Hubbard 2 (1 pen), Staniforth	
4		23	(a)	Burnley	D 1-1	Hodgkinson	
5		26	(h)	Barnsley	D 0-0		5,000
6		30	(a)	Nottingham F	L 0-1		
7	Oct	7	(h)	Chelsea	W 2-1	Huxford, Staniforth	7,000
8		14	(a)	Clapton O	L 0-1		13,000
9		21	(h)	Bristol C	W 3-0	Gordon, Hubbard 2 (1 pen)	6,000
10		28	(a)	Birmingham	D 2-2	Gordon, Hubbard	15,000
11	Nov	4	(h)	Huddersfield T	L 1-2	Hubbard	
12		11	(a)	Blackpool	W 2-1	Mayson 2	3,000
13		25	(a)	Hull C	L 0-1		15,000
14	Dec	2	(h)	Bradford	D 0-0		
15		4	(a)	Leeds C	W 2-1	Hodgkinson 2	3,000
16		9	(a)	Bradford	L 1-4	Wheelhouse (pen)	5,000
17		16	(h)	Fulham	W 1-0	Rampton	
18		23	(h)	Derby C	L 0-3		
19		25	(a)	Derby C	L 1-2	Mayson	
20		26	(h)	Stockport C	D 2-2	Hubbard, Staniforth	8,000
21		30	(a)	Wolves	W 2-1	Mounteney, Hubbard	6,000
22	Jan	6	(h)	Leicester F	W 4-0	Gordon, Staniforth, Mounteney, Martin	3,000
23		20	(a)	Gainsborough T	W 3-2	Hubbard 2, Mounteney	
24		23	(h)	Leeds C	L 1-2	Hubbard	3,000
25		27	(h)	Burnley	W 1-0	T.Rippon	
26	Feb	10	(a)	Chelsea	L 1-4	Mounteney (pen)	25,000
27		17	(h)	Clapton O	W 2-1	Mounteney (pen), Staniforth	
28		24	(a)	Bristol C	L 0-3		
29	Mar	2	(h)	Birmingham	W 1-0	Worth	
30		9	(a)	Huddersfield T	L 0-2		
31		16	(h)	Blackpool	W 1-0	Mounteney	4,000
32		20	(h)	Nottingham F	L 1-4	Mounteney	3,000
33		23	(a)	Glossop NE	L 2-5	Mounteney (pen), T.Rippon	
34		30	(h)	Hull C	W 1-0	Worth	6,000
35	Apr	5	(a)	Stockport C	L 0-3		7,000
36		6	(a)	Barnsley	D 2-2	Mounteney, Hubbard	
37		8	(h)	Glossop NE	D 0-0		
38		20	(a)	Fulham	W 3-1	Mounteney 3	

FINAL LEAGUE POSITION: 9th in Division Two

Appearances
Goals

FA Cup

Prel	Nov	18	(a)	Lincoln C	L 2-3	

Lonsdale	Wheelhouse	Arrowsmith	Seeburg	Gordon	Martin	Staniforth	Hubbard	Mountney	Springthorpe	Worth	Bradley	Blanchard	Bacon	Henderson W	Speak	Browell	Fuljames	Higgins	Hodgkinson	Rippon T	Rampton	Mayson	Bell	Huxford	Ashton	
1	2	3	4	5	6	7	8	9	10	11																1
1	2	3	4	5	6	7	8			11									9		10					2
1	2	3	4	5	6	7	8			11									9		10					3
1	2	3	4	5	6	7	8			11				9					10							4
1	2	3	4	5	6	7	8			11				9					10							5
1	2	3	4	5	6	7	8												9		10			11		6
1	2	3	4	5	6	7	8	9											10					11		7
1	2	3	4	5	6	7	8	9											10					11		8
1	2	3	4	5	6	7	8	9														10		11		9
1	2	3	4	5	6	7	8	9														10		11		10
1	2	3	4	5		7	8	9										6				10		11		11
	2	3	4	5	6	7	8	9		11	1											10				12
	2	3	4	5	6	7	8	9		11	1											10				13
1	2	3	4	5	6	7		9		11									8			10				14
1	2	3		5	6	7		9		11						4			8			10				15
1	2	3		5	6	7		9		11						4			8			10				16
1	2	3		5	6	7		8								4					9	10		11		17
1	2	3		5	6	7		8								4					9	10		11		18
1	2	3		5	6	7	9	8								4						10		11		19
1	2	3		5	6	7	9	8								4						10		11		20
1	2	3	9	5	6	7	10	8								4						11				21
1	2	3	9	5	6	7	10	8								4						11				22
1	2	3	9	5	6	7	10	8								4						11				23
1	2	3		5	6	7	10	8								4			9			11				24
1	2	3		5	6	7	10	8								4				9		11				25
1	2	3	9	5	6	7	10	8								4						11				26
1		2	9	5	6	7		8							3	4				10		11				27
1	2	3			6	7		8		11						4	5			9		10				28
1		3		5	6	7		8		11		2				4						9	10			29
1		2		5	6	7	9			11					3	4				8		10				30
1	2	3		5	6	7	9	8		11						4						10				31
1		3		5	6	7		8	10	11			2			4				9						32
1	2		4	5	6	7		8		11					3				10	9						33
1	2	3		5	6	7		8		11						4				9		10				34
1	2	3		5	6	7	10	8		11						4				9						35
1		3		5	6	7	10	8		11				2		4				9						36
1		3		5	6	7		8		11				2		4				9					10	37
1	2	3		5	6	7		8								4				9		10		11		38
36	32	37	20	37	37	38	25	32	2	20	2	1	1	4	3	23	1	1	12	11	5	25	1	11	1	
	1			3	1	5	13	12		2									3	2	2	3		1		

1912-13

1	Sep	3	(h)	Blackpool	D	1-1	Mounteney	
2		7	(a)	Bury	L	2-4	Birch, T.Rippon	7,000
3		9	(a)	Blackpool	L	1-2	Mounteney	
4		14	(h)	Fulham	W	2-1	Mounteney (pen), T.Rippon	6,000
5		21	(a)	Barnsley	L	0-3		
6		28	(h)	Bradford	W	3-0	Staniforth 2, Mayson	4,000
7	Oct	5	(a)	Wolves	L	0-3		12,000
8		12	(h)	Leicester F	W	2-0	T.Rippon, Staniforth	
9		19	(a)	Stockport C	D	1-1	Mayson	4,000
10		26	(h)	Preston NE	D	0-0		
11	Nov	2	(a)	Burnley	L	2-3	Mounteney (pen), Mayson	12,000
12		9	(h)	Hull C	W	2-0	Mounteney, Gordon	8,000
13		16	(a)	Glossop NE	L	0-2		
14		23	(h)	Clapton O	L	1-2	Mayson	
15	Dec	7	(h)	Nottingham F	D	0-0		
16		14	(a)	Bristol C	D	2-2	Mayson, T.Rippon	4,000
17		21	(h)	Birmingham	D	2-2	Rampton, Crossthwaite (og)	
18		25	(a)	Leeds C	W	2-1	Armstrong, Gordon	16,000
19		26	(a)	Huddersfield T	W	2-0	T.Rippon 2	
20		28	(h)	Bury	W	4-0	Mayson 2, T.Rippon, Wheelhouse (pen)	
21	Jan	4	(a)	Fulham	W	1-0	Mayson	
22		18	(h)	Barnsley	D	1-1	Rampton	
23		25	(a)	Bradford	L	0-3		
24	Feb	1	(a)	Lincoln C	L	0-3		13,000
25		8	(h)	Wolves	W	2-1	Rippon, Mayson	
26		15	(a)	Leicester F	L	0-1		
27		22	(h)	Stockport C	W	4-1	Mayson 3 (1 pen), T.Rippon (pen)	
28	Mar	1	(a)	Preston NE	L	0-2		10,000
29		11	(h)	Burnley	W	2-0	Rampton, Mayson	
30		15	(a)	Hull C	L	0-5		
31		21	(h)	Leeds C	W	3-2	Mayson, T.Rippon 2	8,000
32		22	(h)	Glossop NE	D	0-0		
33		24	(h)	Huddersfield T	D	0-0		
34		29	(a)	Clapton O	W	3-1	Rampton, Mayson, T.Rippon	
35	Apr	5	(h)	Lincoln C	D	0-0		
36		12	(a)	Nottingham F	W	2-1	Rampton 2	7,000
37		19	(h)	Bristol C	W	3-0	Rippon, Quin, Nicholson (og)	
38		26	(a)	Birmingham	L	1-2	Quin	

FINAL LEAGUE POSITION: 7th in Division Two

Appearances
Goals

FA Cup

1	Jan	18	(a)	Sheffield W	L	1-5	

Bradley P	Wheelhouse	Arrowsmith	Andrews	Gordon	Martin	Staniforth	Mounteney	Quin	Mayson	Birch	Lonsdale	Speak	Blanchard	Rushby	Whitchurch	Rippon T	Rampton	Armstrong	Johnson N	Pickering	Springthorpe	Ashton	Duncan	Cassidy	
1	2	3	4	5	6	7	8	9	10	11															1
1	2	3	4	5	6	7		9	10	11						8									2
1	2	3	4	5	6	7	8		10							9						11			3
	2	3	4	5	6	7	8		10		1					9						11			4
	2	3	4	5	6	7	8				1					9		10				11			5
	2	3	4	5	6	7	8	9	10		1											11			6
	2	3	4	5	6	7	8	9	10		1											11			7
	2	3	4	5	6	7	8		10		1					9						11			8
	2	3	4	5	6	7	8		10	11	1					9									9
	2	3	4	5	6	7	8				1					9					10	11			10
	2	3	4	5	6	7	8	9	10	11	1														11
	2	3	4	5	6	7	8	9	10	11	1														12
	2	3	4	5	6	7	8	9	10	11	1														13
	2	3	4	5	6	7	8	9	10	11	1														14
	2	3	4	5	6	7		9	10	11	1					8									15
	2	3	4	5	6	7		9	10	11	1					8									16
	2	3	4	5	6	7			10	11	1					8	9								17
	2	3	4	5	6	7			10	11	1					8		9							18
	2	3	4	5	6	7			10	11	1					8		9							19
	2	3	4	5	6	7			10	11	1					8	9								20
	2	3	4	5	6	7			10	11	1					8	9								21
	2	3		5	6	7			10	11	1			4		8	9								22
	2	3	4	5	6	7			10	11	1					8	9								23
1	2	3	4	5	6	7			10	11						8			9						24
	2	3	4	5	6	7			10	11	1					8				9					25
	2	3		5	6			7	10	11	1			4		8				9					26
		2	4	5				7	10		1	3			6	8	9						11		27
	2	3	4	5				7	10		1				6	8		9					11		28
	2	3	4	5	6			7	10	11	1					8	9								29
	2	3		5	6			7	10	11	1				4	8	9								30
	2	3	4	5	6			7	10	11	1					8	9								31
	2	3	4	5	6			7	10	11	1					8	9								32
	2		4	5	6			7	10	11	1		3			8	9								33
	2		4	5	6			7	10	11	1		3			8	9								34
	2	3	4	5	6	7			10	11	1					8	9								35
	2	3	4	5	6	7			10	11	1					8	9								36
	2	3		5	6	7		9		11	1			4		8	10								37
	2	3		5	6	7		9		11				4		8	10							1	38
4	37	36	33	38	36	29	13	21	34	29	33	1	2	4	3	31	16	4	1	2	1	7	2	1	
	1			2		3	5	2	15	1						13	6	1							

2 own-goals

1913-14

1	Sep	6	(h)	Notts C	D 0-0		5,000
2		10	(a)	Bradford	L 0-3		8,000
3		13	(a)	Leicester F	L 0-2		17,000
4		20	(h)	Wolves	W 1-0	Miller	7,000
5		27	(a)	Hull C	L 1-2	Gregson	14,000
6	Oct	14	(h)	Barnsley	D 1-1	Gregson	8,000
7		11	(a)	Bury	L 1-3	Gregson	12,000
8		18	(h)	Huddersfield T	W 2-1	Gregson, T.Rippon	6,000
9		25	(a)	Lincoln C	W 3-1	Gregson, T.Rippon, Gordon	12,000
10	Nov	1	(h)	Blackpool	W 2-0	W.Rippon, Jones (og)	8,000
11		8	(a)	Nottingham F	L 1-4	T.Rippon	
12		15	(h)	W Arsenal	D 1-1	W.Rippon	8,000
13		22	(a)	Fulham	D 2-2	W.Rippon, Rampton	16,000
14		29	(a)	Birmingham	W 2-1	W.Rippon 2	20,000
15	Dec	6	(h)	Bristol C	W 1-0	Rampton	6,000
16		13	(a)	Leeds C	L 1-4	Quin	
17		20	(h)	Clapton O	W 2-0	Gregson 2	
18		25	(h)	Stockport C	W 2-0	Fagan (og), W.Rippon	10,000
19		26	(a)	Stockport C	D 2-2	Gregson 2	
20		27	(a)	Notts C	L 0-4		
21	Jan	3	(h)	Leicester F	W 3-0	W.Rippon 2, Gregson	
22		17	(a)	Wolves	L 1-4	W.Rippon	8,000
23		24	(h)	Hull C	L 1-3	Mayson	12,000
24	Feb	7	(a)	Barnsley	L 1-3	T.Rippon	
25		14	(h)	Bury	W 1-0	W.Rippon	
26		21	(a)	Huddersfield T	W 2-1	T.Rippon 2	3,500
27		24	(h)	Bradford	D 0-0		
28		28	(h)	Lincoln C	L 1-3	W.Rippon (pen)	
29	Mar	7	(a)	Blackpool	D 1-1	W.Rippon	4,000
30		14	(h)	Nottingham F	W 3-0	T.Rippon 2, Gregson	8,000
31		28	(h)	Fulham	L 0-3		8,000
32	Apr	4	(h)	Birmingham	L 0-2		
33		10	(a)	Glossop NE	L 0-3		
34		11	(a)	Bristol C	L 0-1		
35		13	(h)	Glossop NE	W 3-0	Rampton 2, T.Rippon	
36		18	(h)	Leeds C	L 0-1		
37		23	(a)	W Arsenal	L 0-2		
38		25	(a)	Clapton O	D 0-0		10,000

FINAL LEAGUE POSITION: 15th in Division Two — Appearances / Goals

FA Cup

1	Jan	10	(a)	West Brom A	L 0-2	

Spendiff	Wheelhouse	Lee J A	Andrews	Gordon	Martin	Miller J	Rippon T	Kenny	Rampton	Birch	Lonsdale	Arrowsmith	Gregson	Quin	Rippon W	Scott	Mayson	McKenna	Whitchurch	Gimblett	Chalmers	Blanchard	Hodgson	Rushby	Thompson	Whelpton	
	2	3	4	5	6	7	8	9	10	11	1																1
1	2		4	5	6	7	8	9	10	11		3															2
1	2		4	5		7	10					3	8	9		11								6			3
1	2		4	5	6	7	10					3	8	9		11											4
1	2		4	5	6	7	10					3	8	9		11											5
1	2		4	5	6	7	8		9			3	10			11											6
1	2		4	5	6		8		9			3	10	7		11											7
1	2		4	5	6		8	9				3	10	7		11											8
1	2		4	5	6		8					3	10	7	9	11											9
1	2		4	5	6		8					3	10	7	9	11											10
1	2		4	5	6		8			11		3	10	7	9												11
1	2		4	5	6							3	8	7	9	11	10										12
1	2			5	6				10			3	8	7	9	11			4								13
1	2		4	5	6				10			3	8	7	9	11											14
1	2		4	5	6				10			3	8	7	9	11											15
1	2			5	6				10			3	8	9		11		4		7							16
1	2			5	6				10			3	8	7	9	11		4									17
1	2			5	6				10			3	8	7	9	11		4									18
1	2		4	5								3	8	7	9	11	10	6									19
1	2		10	5	6							3		7	9	11	8	4									20
1		2	4	5	6		8					3	10		9	11				7							21
1		2	4	5	6				10	11		3	8		9					7							22
1	2		4	5	6					11		3	8		9		10			7							23
1	2		4	5	6		8					3	10	7	9	11											24
1	2		4	5	6		8					3	10	7	9	11											25
1	2		4		6		8	5				3	10	7	9	11											26
1	2		4		6		8	5				3	10	7	9	11											27
1	2		4	5			8		10			3		7	9		11	6									28
1	2	3	4	5			8						10	7	9	11			6								29
1	2		4	5			8					3	10	7	9	11			6								30
1	2		4	5	7		8					3	10		9	11			6								31
	2		4	5	6		8					3	7				10				9				11	1	32
1	2		4	5	6		8					3	10	7	9	11											33
1	2		4	5	6		8		9			3	10	7		11											34
1	2		4	5	6		8		9			3	10	7		11											35
1	2		4	5	6		8		9			3	10	7		11											36
1	2		4	5	6		8		9			3	10	7		11											37
	2		4	5	6		8					3	10	7							9	1	11				38
35	36	4	34	36	33	6	27	5	16	5	1	36	34	30	23	30	6	6	4	4	2	1	1	1	1	1	
				1		1	9		4				11	1	12		1										

2 own-goals

1914-15

1	Sep	1	(h)	Preston NE	D	2-2	T.Rippon, Gordon	
2		5	(a)	Nottingham F	L	2-4	Mayson 2	
3		7	(a)	Preston NE	L	0-3		
4		12	(h)	Leicester F	W	1-0	Rampton	
5		19	(a)	Barnsley	D	0-0		
6		26	(h)	Glossop NE	W	1-0	Rampton	5,000
7	Oct	3	(a)	Wolves	W	1-0	T.Rippon	8,000
8		10	(h)	Fulham	D	1-1	Quin	
9		17	(a)	Stockport C	D	1-1	Rampton	
10		24	(h)	Hull C	D	1-1	Quin	9,000
11		31	(a)	Leeds C	L	0-5		
12	Nov	7	(h)	Clapton O	W	2-1	T.Rippon, Rampton	
13		14	(a)	W Arsenal	L	0-6		
14		21	(h)	Derby C	L	1-2	Rampton	
15		28	(a)	Lincoln C	L	1-2	Rampton	
16	Dec	5	(h)	Birmingham	W	1-0	Rippon	
17		12	(h)	Blackpool	W	2-0	Rampton 2	
18		19	(a)	Huddersfield T	L	1-3	Scott	
19		25	(h)	Bristol C	L	2-3	T.Rippon 2 (1 pen)	11,000
20		26	(a)	Bristol C	L	0-7		
21	Jan	2	(h)	Nottingham F	W	4-0	Mayson, Rampton, Rippon, Andrews	
22		16	(a)	Leicester F	L	0-2		
23		23	(h)	Barnsley	L	2-3	Padley, Gregson	
24		30	(a)	Glossop NE	D	0-0		
25	Feb	6	(h)	Wolves	L	1-4	Padley	
26		13	(a)	Fulham	L	1-2	T.Rippon	
27		20	(h)	Stockport C	W	6-1	Rampton 3, Mayson 2, Andrews	
28	Mar	6	(h)	Leeds C	L	2-5	Mayson, T.Rippon	
29		13	(a)	Clapton O	L	1-2	Mayson	
30		20	(h)	W Arsenal	W	1-0	Rampton	
31		27	(a)	Derby C	D	1-1	Mayson	
32	Apr	2	(a)	Bury	D	2-2	Rampton, Wheelhouse (pen)	4,000
33		3	(h)	Lincoln C	W	5-1	Rampton 3, Mayson, T.Rippon	
34		5	(h)	Bury	W	1-0	T.Rippon	7,000
35		10	(a)	Birmingham	L	0-3		
36		17	(a)	Blackpool	L	0-5		4,000
37		24	(h)	Huddersfield T	D	0-0		
38		29	(a)	Hull C	L	1-4	Rampton	

FINAL LEAGUE POSITION: 17th in Division Two

Appearances
Goals

FA Cup

1	Jan	9	(h)	Northampton T	L	0-3

Summers	Wheelhouse	Arrowsmith	Andrews	Gordon	Martin	Spink	Rippon T	Chalmers	Mayson	Scott	Blanchard	Spendiff	Atkin	McKenna	Lee	Kenny	Whitchurch	Quin	Gregson	Rampton	Padley	Thompson	Huxford	
1	2	3	4	5	6	7	8	9	10	11														1
1	2	3	4	5	6	7	8	9	10	11														2
1	2	3	4	5	6	7	8	9	10											11				3
1	2	3	4	5	6		8		10	11								7		9				4
1	2	3	4	5	6	7	8			11									10	9				5
1		3	4	5		7	8			11			2				6		10	9				6
1		3	4	5		7	8			11			2				6		10	9				7
1		3	4	5		7	8			11			2				6	9		10				8
1		3	4	5		7	8						2				6	9	10	11				9
1	5	3	4		6	7	8						2					9	10	11				10
1		3	4		6	7	8						2			5		9	10	11				11
1	2	3	4	5	6	7	8		10											9		11		12
1	2	3	4	5	6	7	8		10											9		11		13
1	2	3	4	5		7	8		11								6	9		10				14
1	2	3	4			7	9			11						5	6		8	10				15
1	2	3	4			7	8			11						5	6		10	9				16
1	2	3	4			7	8			11						5	6		10	9				17
1	2	3	4			7	8			11						5	6		10	9				18
1	2	3	4			7	8			11						5	6		10	9				19
1	2	3	4			7	8			11						5	6		10	9				20
1			4	5	6	7	8		10	11			2		3					9				21
1		3	4		5	7	8						2				6	9	10	11				22
1		3	4			7							2	6		5		9	8	11	10			23
		3	4			7				11	1		2	6		5			8	9	10			24
		3	4			7	8			11	1		2	6		5				9	10			25
		3	4			7	8			11	1		2	6		5				9	10			26
1	2	3	4			7	8		10					6		5				9			11	27
1	2	3	4			7	8		10					6		5				9			11	28
1	2		4			7	8		10					6	3	5				9			11	29
1	2		4			7	8		10					6	3	5				9		11		30
1	2		4		6	7	8		10						3	5				9		11		31
1	2		4		6	7	8		10						3	5				9		11		32
1	2		4		6		8		10						3	5		7		9		11		33
1	2		4		6		8		10						3	5		7		9		11		34
1	2		4		6	7	8		10						3	5				9		11		35
1		2	4		6	7	8		10						3	5				9		11		36
			4		6	7	8		10			1		2	3	5				9		11		37
1			4		6	7	8		10					2	3	5				9		11		38
34	24	28	38	13	19	35	36	3	20	17	3	1	12	10	11	23	12	10	15	36	4	11	3	
	1		2	1			11		9	1								2	1	18	2			

1915-16

1	Sep	4	(h)	Nottingham F	D	1-1	Young	4,000
2		11	(a)	Barnsley	L	2-3	Woulds, T.Rippon	
3		18	(h)	Leicester F	D	0-0		3,000
4		25	(a)	Sheffield U	L	1-6	T.Rippon	6,000
5	Oct	2	(h)	Bradford C	W	3-1	Young 2, Coulbeck	4,000
6		9	(a)	Huddersfield T	L	1-4	Young	3,000
7		16	(a)	Lincoln C	L	0-1		
8		23	(h)	Notts C	D	2-2	T.Rippon, Young	
9		30	(a)	Derby C	L	2-3	Coulbeck, Young	2,000
10	Nov	6	(h)	Sheffield W	W	2-1	Young 2	3,000
11		13	(a)	Bradford	L	0-2		
12		20	(h)	Leeds U	D	0-0		3,000
13		27	(a)	Hull C	L	1-4	Young	3,000
14	Dec	4	(a)	Nottingham F	L	0-2		1,000
15		11	(h)	Barnsley	W	4-1	Huxford, Young, T.Rippon, McGuire (pen)	
16		18	(a)	Leicester F	L	0-2		3,000
17		25	(h)	Sheffield U	W	2-1	Hooper, Rampton	1,000
18	Jan	1	(a)	Bradford C	D	0-0	*	1,000
19		8	(h)	Huddersfield T	L	0-1		1,000
20		15	(h)	Lincoln C	W	1-0	McGuire (pen)	2,000
21		22	(a)	Notts C	W	2-1	Young, T.Rippon	
22		29	(h)	Derby C	W	2-1	Huxford, Coulbeck	
23	Feb	5	(a)	Sheffield W	L	1-2	T.Rippon	
24		12	(h)	Bradford	D	1-1	Young	
25		19	(a)	Leeds C	L	1-3	Young	
26		26	(h)	Hull C	L	2-3	McGuire 2 (1 pen)	

FINAL LEAGUE POSITION: 13th in Midland Section Principle Competition — Appearances

*Abandoned after 65 minutes, result stood. — Goals

27	Mar	4	(a)	Rotherham C	L	2-3	Young 2
28		11	(h)	Sheffield W	D	0-0	
29		18	(a)	Hull C	W	5-2	Young 2, McGuire 2, W.Rippon
30		25	(h)	Sheffield U	L	0-1	
31	Apr	1	(a)	Lincoln C	W	2-1	Young, T.Rippon
32		8	(h)	Rotherham C	W	7-1	Young 5, W.Rippon, Huxford
33		15	(a)	Sheffield W	L	1-2	Young (pen)
34		22	(h)	Hull C	W	5-0	Young 3, W.Rippon, Huxford
35		24	(h)	Lincoln C	W	3-0	Young, W.Rippon, T.Rippon
36		29	(a)	Sheffield U	D	0-0	

FINAL LEAGUE POSITION: 1st in Midland Section Subsidiary Competition — Appearances

Goals

Sewell	Wheelhouse	McGuire	Hatton	Johnson N	Whitchurch	Walsh	Rippon T	Young	Coulbeck	Rippon W	Hooper	Huxford	Lee	Ormiston	Rushby	Webster	Rampton	Birch	McIver	Spink	Woulds	Butler R	Graham	Helsetine	Green	Martin	Pattison	Spendiff	Marshall	Cooper	Heath	Mayson	Sparham	Robinson					
1	2	3	4	5	6	7	8	9	10	11																													1
1		3		5	6	7	8		10									11			9			4	2														2
1		3		5	6		8	9	10		7					2		11						4															3
1		3		5	4		8	9	10		7					2		11					6																4
1		3		5	6		8	9	10		7	11			4	2																							5
1		3			6		8	9	10		7	11		5	4	2																							6
1					6		8	9	10		7	11	3	5		2										4													7
1	2				6		8	9	10		7	11	3	5	4																								8
1					6		8	9	10			11	3	5	4												2						7						9
1					6	7	8	9	10			11	3	5	4	2																							10
1				2	6	7	8	9	10			11		5	4								3																11
1		3			6		8	9	10		7	11		5	4	2																							12
1		3			6		7	9	10			11		5	4	2					8																		13
1		3			6		7		10			11		5	4	2	9				8																		14
1		3			6		7	9	10			11	2	5	4		8																						15
1		3			6		7		10			11	2	5	4		9				8																		16
		3			6		8	9			7	11	2	5	4		10											1											17
1		3		5	6		7		10			11	2		4		9				8																		18
1		3			6		7		10			11	2	5	4		8					9																	19
1		3			6		8	9	10		7	11		5	4	2																							20
1		3			6		8	9	10			11	2	5	4				7																				21
1		3		5	6		8	9	10			11	2		4				7																				22
1		3		5	6		8	9	10			11	2		4					7																			23
1		3		5	6		8	9	10		7				4	2		11																					24
1		3		5	6		8	9	10			11	2		4					7																			25
1		3			6		8	9	10			11	2	5						7									4										26
25	2	21	1	11	26	4	26	21	25	1	10	21	14	16	20	11	6	4	2	3	5	1	2	2	1	1	1	1	1				1						
		4					6	13	3		1	2					1				1																		

Sewell	Wheelhouse	McGuire	Hatton	Johnson N	Whitchurch	Walsh	Rippon T	Young	Coulbeck	Rippon W	Hooper	Huxford	Lee	Ormiston	Rushby	Webster	Rampton	Birch	McIver	Spink	Woulds	Butler R	Graham	Helsetine	Green	Martin	Pattison	Spendiff	Marshall	Cooper	Heath	Mayson	Sparham	Robinson					
		3		5	6		8	9		10		11	2		4					7										1									27
		3			6		8	9				11		5	4	2						10						1						7					28
		3			6		8	9		10		11		5	4	2				7											1								29
1		3			6		8	9				11		5	4	2						10												7					30
1		3			6		8	9		10		11		5	4	2				7																			31
1		3			6		8	9		10		11		5	4	2				7																			32
1		3			6		8	9		10		11		5	4	2				7																			33
1		3			6		8	9		10		11		5	4	2				7																			34
1		3			6		8	9		10		11		5	4	2				7																			35
1		3		5	6		8			9		11			4	2				7												10							36
7		10		2	10		10	9		8		10	1	8	10	9				8		2						1		1	1	1		2					
		2					2	15		4		2																											

1916-17

1	Sep	2	(a)	Barnsley	D	2-2	T.Rippon 2	1,000
2		9	(h)	Leeds C	L	1-6	Young	4,000
3		16	(a)	Sheffield U	L	3-5	W.Rippon, T.Rippon, Charles	8,000
4		23	(h)	Bradford C	L	1-3	W.Rippon (pen)	
5		30	(a)	Leicester F	D	0-0		
6	Oct	7	(h)	Chesterfield	L	1-3	Bratley	
7		14	(h)	Notts C	D	3-3	T.Rippon 3	
8		21	(a)	Rotherham C	L	0-3		
9		28	(h)	Huddersfield T	W	2-1	W.Rippon, Young	
10	Nov	4	(a)	Lincoln C	D	1-1	W.Rippon	
11		11	(h)	Sheffield W	W	1-0	Young	
12		18	(a)	Bradford	L	0-9		
13		25	(h)	Birmingham	W	3-0	T.Rippon 2, Young	
14	Dec	2	(a)	Hull C	L	0-2		
15		9	(h)	Barnsley	D	2-2	Huxford, Whitchurch	
16		16	(a)	Leeds C	L	0-1		
17		23	(h)	Sheffield U	W	2-0	Colebrook, Benfield	
18		25	(a)	Nottingham F	L	1-5	Huxford	
19		26	(h)	Nottingham F	D	1-1	T.Rippon	3,000
20		30	(a)	Bradford C	L	0-3		
21	Jan	6	(h)	Leicester F	L	1-3	T.Rippon	
22		13	(a)	Chesterfield	W	5-4	T.Rippon, Hadley (og), Colebrook 2, Allott	
23		20	(a)	Notts C	W	3-2	Pickering, W.Rippon, Langley	
24		27	(h)	Rotherham C	W	1-0	Young	
25	Feb	3	(a)	Huddersfield T	L	0-1		2,000
26		10	(h)	Lincoln C	W	1-0	Young	
27		17	(a)	Sheffield W	L	1-3	Colebrook	
28		24	(h)	Bradford	L	0-2		
29	Mar	3	(a)	Birmingham	L	0-3		10,000
30		10	(h)	Hull C	L	2-3	Colebrook, Young	

FINAL LEAGUE POSITION: 14th in Midland Section Principal Competition

Appearances
Goals

31	Mar	17	(h)	Lincoln C	D	1-1	Isherwood	
32		31	(h)	Chesterfield	L	2-3	Benfield 2	
33	Apr	6	(h)	Hull C	W	2-1	Benfield, Colebrook	
34		7	(a)	Lincoln C	W	3-1	T.Rippon, W.Rippon, Huxford	
35		9	(a)	Hull C	D	2-2	T.Rippon, Johnson	
36		21	(a)	Chesterfield	L	2-3	Ashling, W.Rippon	1,000

FINAL LEAGUE POSITION: 8th in Midland Section Subsidiary Competition

Appearances
Goals

During 1916-17, brothers W. and T.Rippon, and W.Butler and J.Butler (father and son respectively) played together in five games.

Sewell	Webster	Lee	Rushby	Johnson	Whitchurch	Smith	Rippon T	Rippon W	Bratley	Huxford	Butler J	Butler W	Colebrook	Ormiston	Spink J	Spink T	Sutcliffe	Pickering	Hall	Benfield	Ashling	McQuillen	Nevins	Allott	Young	Charles	Coulbeck	Cooney	Holden	Fearnley	Wild	Langley	Wilkinson	Halley	Raybould	Lyons	Booth	Crutchley	Whittaker	
1	2	3	4	5	6	7	8	9	10	11																														1
1	2	3	4		6	7	8	10		11				5											9															2
1	2	3			6	7	8	9	4	11				5												10														3
1	2	3	7		6		8	9	4	11				5													10													4
1	2		4		6		8	10	3	11				5		7			9																					5
1	2	3	4		6		8	10	9	11				5														7												6
1	2		4		6		8	10	3	11				5		7									9															7
1	2				6		8		3	10				5	4	7									9			11												8
1	2			5	6		8	10	3	11					4	7									9															9
1	2				6		8	10		11	3			5	4	7									9															10
1	2				6		8	10		11				5	4	7							3		9															11
	2				6		8	10		11				5	4	7							3		9				1											12
1	3				6		8			11	2			5	4	7				10					9															13
	3				6		8	10		11	2			5	4	7	1								9															14
	3			5	6		8	10		11	2				4	7	1								9															15
	3				6		8	9	10		2			5	4	7	1											11												16
	3			6						11	2		10	5	4	7	1			8					9															17
					6		8	10		11	2			5	4	7	1				9	3																		18
	2				6		8	10		11				5	4	7	1					3			9															19
	2				6		7	10			5		11				1				9	3								8	4									20
	2		4	5	6		8	10		11			7				1					3			9															21
	3			5	6		8	10			2	4	11				1	9						7																22
	3				6		8	10			2	4	11				1	9						7								5								23
	3			5	6		8	10			2	4	11				1							7	9															24
	3				6		8	10		11	2	4					1	9	5					7																25
	3			4	6		8	10			2		11				1		5						9								7							26
	3				6			10			2	4	11				1	9						7										5	8					27
	3			4	6			10			2		11				1			8	9												7	5						28
											3						1																			2	4	5	6	29
	3			4			8	10		11	2		7				1		5						9															30
12	28	5	7	10	27	3	26	26	9	21	17	5	10	16	12	14	17	4	4	3	3	4	2	5	16	1	1	3	1	1	1	1	2	2	1	1	1	1	1	
					1		11	5	1	2			5					1		1				1	7	1						1								

1 own-goal

				4				9		11	2	3					1		5	8																				31
	3			5				10			2	4	11				1	9		7																				32
	3			6			8	10		11	2	4	7				1		5	9																				33
	2			5			8	10		11		4	7				1	9																						34
				5			8	3		11			7				1	9																						35
	2			5				10				4	11				1	9			8																			36
	4			6			3	6		4	3	5	5				6	4	2	3	1																			
				1			2	2		1			1							3	1																			

Taylor played number 7 in Match 29; Nash played number 8 in Match 29; Rampton played number 9 in Match 29; Peplow played number 11 in Match 29; Humphrey played number 10 in Match 29; Cheetham played number 6 in Match 30; Graham played number 6 in Match 31; Warren played number 7 in Match 31; Isherwood played number 10 in Match 31, scoring once; Graham played number 6 in Match 32; Stainsby played number 8 in Match 32; Atkinson played number 3 in Match 34; Graham played number 6 in Match 34; Walsh played number 4 in Match 35; Page played number 10 in Match 35; Atkinson played number 2 in Match 35; Graham played number 6 in Match 35; Atkinson played number 3 in Match 36; Clerk played number 6 in Match 36; Gladwin played number 7 in Match 36.

1917-18

1	Sep	15	(h)	Barnsley	L	1-3	Bounds (og)
2		22	(a)	Barnsley	L	0-4	
3		29	(h)	Bradford	L	1-2	Benfield (pen)
4	Oct	6	(a)	Bradford	L	1-4	W.Butler
5		13	(a)	Sheffield U	L	0-5	
6		20	(h)	Sheffield U	D	0-0	
7		27	(a)	Leeds C	D	2-2	Goodfellow, Hollins
8	Nov	3	(h)	Leeds C	L	0-4	
9		10	(a)	Nottingham F	L	0-5	
10		17	(h)	Nottingham F	D	1-1	Johnson
11		24	(a)	Leicester F	L	1-6	Knighton
12	Dec	1	(h)	Leicester F	D	1-1	Fenny
13		8	(a)	Birmingham	W	1-0	Brooks
14		15	(h)	Birmingham	D	2-2	Hendrie 2
15		22	(a)	Notts C	L	0-8	2,000
16		26	(a)	Hull C	L	1-7	Hendrie
17		29	(h)	Notts C	W	2-0	Johnson, Knighton
18	Jan	5	(a)	Huddersfield T	L	0-2	
19		12	(h)	Huddersfield T	W	1-0	Martin
20		26	(h)	Sheffield W	D	0-0	
21	Feb	2	(h)	Rotherham C	D	2-2	Huxford 2
22		9	(a)	Rotherham C	D	1-1	Wild (og)
23		16	(h)	Lincoln C	W	4-1	Pickering 2, Huxford, Stainsby
24		23	(a)	Lincoln C	L	0-1	
25	Mar	2	(a)	Bradford C	W	1-0	Stainsby
26		9	(h)	Bradford C	D	0-0	
27	Apr	13	(h)	Hull C	D	0-0	
28		27	(a)	Sheffield W	D	1-1	Sankey

FINAL LEAGUE POSITION: 12th in Midland Section Principal Competition

Appearances
Goals

29	Mar	16	(h)	Gainsborough T	W	4-0	Ward 2, Stainsby 2
30		23	(a)	Gainsborough T	W	3-0	Pickering, Stainsby, Clark
31		29	(h)	Hull C	W	2-0	Williams, Stainsby
32		30	(a)	Lincoln C	L	0-1	
33	Apr	1	(a)	Hull C	D	2-2	Pickering, Stainsby
34		6	(h)	Lincoln C	W	2-0	Cooper, Martin

FINAL LEAGUE POSITION: 1st in Midland Section Subsidiary Competition

Appearances
Goals

Sutcliffe	Webster	Ward	Marshall	Johnson	Martin	Wilkinson	Knighton	Ashling	Benfield	Spotiswood	Branston	Clarke	Huxford	Hendrie	Pickering	Sankey	Stainsby	Harris	Hobson	Fearnley	Cordall	Isherwood	Rawlinson	Butler W	Goodfellow	Cooper	Wilson	Bryant	Wightman	Raybould	White	Barraclough	Allott	Hollins	Walker	Andrews	Ritchie	Lee	Codd	
1	2	3	4	5	6	7	8	9	10	11																														1
1	2		4					9		7									10								3	5	6	8	11									2
1	2	3	4	5	6		8	9	7	11			10																											3
1	2	3	4		5														10	8		11		9								6	7							4
1	2	3		5	6			9										7	10	8		11		4																5
1	2	3		5	6			9										7	10			11		4										8						6
1	2	3		4										5				7	10			11			9									8	6					7
1	2	3		4	6									5				7							9		11							8		10				8
1	2	3		4	6													7							9									8			5	10	11	9
1	2	3		4	6								11	5					10			7			9															10
1	2	3			6		8	9																														10		11
	2	3		4	6			8						5			10	7				11																		12
		3			6																		1																	13
	2	3		4	6								11	9			8				5		1																	14
	2				6										10			7		9	5		1														3	11		15
				2									11	9			8				5				7															16
	2			4	6		8		7				11	9							5		1																	17
	2			4			8		7			6		9							5		1																	18
	2			4	6			9					11				8				5																			19
	2	3		5	4						1		11				8			10																				20
	2	3		4	6								11	9			8			10	5						7													21
	2	3				4						6			9	10								5		1														22
	2	3			5	4					1	6	11		9		8			10																				23
	2	3			5	4					1	6				10				9																				24
	2	3				4					1	6			9	10	8							5																25
	2	3			5	4					1	6	11	9			8			10																				26
	2				5	4					1	6	11		9	10	8									7														27
					5	4					1	6			9	10	8									7														28
11	25	20	4	16	22	8	5	8	4	3	7	8	11	10	6	5	11	7	6	8	7	6	5	5	5	3	3	1	1	1	1	1	1	4	1	1	2	3	1	
				2	1		2		1				3	3	2	1	2							1	1									1						

2 own-goals

	2	11			5	4					1	6		9		10	8									3														29
		3			5	4					1	6			9	10			2							7														30
	2	3			5						1	6			9	10	8																							31
	2	3			5	4					1	6			9	10	8																							32
				2	5	4					1	6	11	7	9	10	8										3													33
	2	3		4	5						1	6	11		9	10	8									7														34
	4	5		2	6	4					6	6	2	2	5	6	5		1							3	1													
		2			1							1			2		5									1														

Osmond played number 8 in Match 10; Dawson played number 4 in Match 11; Hall played number 5 in Match 11; Burton played number 7 in Match 11; Winship played number 11 in Match 11; Hinton played number 1 in Match 12; Fenny played number 9 in Match 12, scoring once; Pennington played number 2 in Match 13; Ducat played number 4 in Match 13; Kenny played number 5 in Match 13; Harrold played number 7 in Match 13; Price played number 8 in Match 13; Battersby played number 9 in Match 13; Bell played number 10 in Match 13; Brooks played number 11 in Match 13, scoring once; Forman played number 7 in Match 14; McDermott played number 10 in Match 14; Hawley played number 4 in Match 15; Pykett played number 8 in Match 15; Smith played number 1 in Match 16; Patterson played number 3 in Match 16; Elvin played number 4 in Match 16; Pace played number 6 in Match 16; Slide played number 10 in Match 16; Gaskell played number 3 in Match 17; McDermott played number 10 in Match 17; Atkinson played number 3 in Match 18; Walsh played number 11 in Match 18; McDermott played number 10 in Match 18; Robinson played number 1 in Match 19; Atkinson played number 3 in Match 19; Black played number 7 in Match 19; McDermott played number 10 in Match 19; Graham played number 6 in Match 20; Walsh played number 7 in Match 20; Richards played number 9 in Match 20; Spendiff played number 1 in Match 21; W.Rippon played number 7 in Match 22; Smith played number 8 in Match 22; Summers played number 11 in Match 22; Forman played number 7 in Match 23; Cavanagh played number 3 in Match 24; Forman played number 7 in Match 24; Howarth played number 11 in Match 24; McKenzie played number 7 in Match 25; W.Rippon played number 11 in Match 25; Forman played number 7 in Match 26; Cookson played number 3 in Match 27; Thorpe played number 2 in Match 28; Binks played number 3 in Match 28; Towlan played number 11 in Match 28; Forman played number 7 in Match 29; Danesborough played number 8 in Match 30; Scott played number 11 in Match 30; Graham played number 4 in Match 31; Richmond played number 7 in Match 31; Williams played number 11 in Match 31, scoring once; Brown played number 7 in Match 32; Blevins played number 11 in Match 32.

1918-19

1	Sep	7	(a)	Coventry C	L	4-7	Sankey, Hooper, Sandlin, Ballance
2		14	(h)	Coventry C	D	1-1	Sankey
3		21	(a)	Barnsley	W	4-2	Hooper 2, Ballance, Birkenshaw
4		28	(h)	Barnsley	D	0-0	
5	Oct	5	(a)	Leicester F	L	3-5	Wilkinson, Knighton, Sankey
6		12	(h)	Leicester F	W	4-1	Kitchen, Sankey 2, Stainsby
7		19	(h)	Nottingham F	L	0-2	
8		26	(a)	Nottingham F	L	1-6	Bertie
9	Nov	2	(h)	Leeds C	L	0-2	
10		9	(a)	Leeds C	L	1-3	Thompson
11		16	(h)	Sheffield U	D	2-2	Martin 2 (2 pens)
12		23	(a)	Sheffield U	L	1-3	Knighton
13		30	(h)	Bradford	W	4-0	Thompson 3, Stainsby
14	Dec	7	(a)	Bradford	L	0-5	
15		14	(h)	Huddersfield T	D	1-1	Knighton
16		21	(a)	Huddersfield T	L	0-1	
17		25	(h)	Hull C	D	1-1	Sankey
18		26	(a)	Hull C	L	0-2	
19		28	(h)	Sheffield W	L	0-2	
20	Jan	11	(a)	Bradford C	W	3-1	Battiste, Sankey, Newton
21		18	(h)	Bradford C	W	3-2	Huxford, Knighton 2
22		25	(a)	Lincoln C	W	1-0	Ward
23	Feb	1	(h)	Lincoln C	L	1-2	Battiste
24		8	(h)	Rotherham C	W	1-0	Huxford
25		15	(a)	Rotherham C	L	0-2	
26		22	(h)	Birmingham	L	1-4	Ball (og)
27	Mar	1	(a)	Birmingham	L	0-4	
28		8	(h)	Notts C	D	0-0	
29		15	(a)	Notts C	L	1-3	Storer
30	Apr	22	(a)	Sheffield W	L	2-5	Battiste, Kenny

FINAL LEAGUE POSITION: 15th in Midland Section Principal Competition

Appearances
Goals

31	Mar	22	(h)	Coventry C	D	1-1	Clarke
32		29	(a)	Coventry C	L	1-2	Gregson
33	Apr	5	(h)	Lincoln C	W	2-1	Spink, Battiste
34		12	(a)	Lincoln C	W	2-1	Battiste 2
35		19	(h)	Hull C	L	1-2	Martin (pen)
36		26	(a)	Hull C	L	1-3	Storer

FINAL LEAGUE POSITION: 3rd in Midland Section Subsidiary Competition

Appearances
Goals

Branston	Gray G	Webster	Wilkinson	Martin F	Crane	Rampton	Sandlin	Ballance	Sankey	Hooper	Clarke	Dawson S	Huxford	Kenny	Battiste	Stainsby	Thompson	Cooke	Hill	Wilson	Holt	Johnson	Knighton	McKenzie	Storer	Spink	Cookson	Birkenshaw	Kitchen	Willetts	Bertie	Dawson F	Rudd	Waine	Laws	Nicholson	Whitchurch	Pickering	Dunn	Match
1	2	3	4	5	6	7	8	9	10	11																														1
1		2	4	5				9	10	7	6		11			8											3													2
1		2	4					9	10	7	6	3						11				5						8												3
1		2	4					9	10	7	6	3	11			8						5																		4
1		2	4	5			7		10		6	3				8		11					9																	5
1			4	5				9	10			3	11			8				6		2							7											6
1			4	5				8	9			3	11					7		6		2								10										7
1	2		4	5				8	10		6	3						11					9								7									8
1				5							6	3				8						2										4	7	9	10	11				9
1	2		4	5							6	3					7		8																		10	9	11	10
1		2		5					10		6	3																									8		11	11
1	2		4	5					10			3							7				8																	12
1	2		4	5					10		6	3				9	8		7																					13
1	2		4	6					10			3		5		9	8																							14
1	2		4	5					10		6		11			9							8			7														15
1	2			6					10		11	3		5			9																							16
1	2			4					10		6	3	11	5			8																							17
1				4					10		6	3	11	5		9	8																							18
1	2			5					10		6	3	11			9	8																							19
1	2			5					10		6	3			4		8							7															20
1	2		4						10		6	3	11		6		8						9	7															21
1	2		4						10		6	3			6		8						9																22
1		2	4	5					10		6	3	11		9	8																								23
1	2			4							6	3	11	5	9		8				7			10															24
1	2			4							6	3		5	10		8								9														25
	2			4							6	3	11	5	7		10								9														26
1	2			6					10		11	3		5	4		8				7				9														27
1	2								10		6	3	11	5	4		8				7				9														28
	2										6	3		5	4						7		10		9														29
1				6							4			5	8						3						7													30
28	19	7	16	24	1	1	2	7	23	4	25	26	13	11	11	11	15	4	3	3	4	5	7	3	5	2	1	1	1	1	1	1	1	1	1	1	2	1	2	
			1	2			1	2	7	3			2	1	3	2	4						5		1			1	1		1									

1 own-goal

1	2										6	3		5	10						7				9														31
1	2			6		9					11	3		5	7																								32
1	2			6							4	3		5	8										9	7														33
1				6							4			5	9		8																							34
1	2			6							4			5	10		8									7														35
				6							11			5	8						3					9	7														36
5	4			5		1					6	3		6	6		2			1	1				3	3													
				1							1				3										1	1													

Rushby played number 4 in Match 11; Finneran played number 7 in Match 11; Henderson played number 9 in Match 11; Beach played number 6 in Match 12; Talbot played number 9 in Match 12; Dodds played number 11 in Match 12; Kirkham played number 11 in Match 13; Kirkham played number 11 in Match 14; Williams played number 7 in Match 14; Ward played number 3 in Match 15; Beswick played number 7 in Match 16; Andrews played number 4 in Match 16; Sagar played number 8 in Match 16; Whitworth played number 7 in Match 17; Young played number 9 in Match 17; Lee played number 2 in Match 18; Whitworth played number 7 in Match 18; Day played number 4 in Match 19; Newton played number 7 in Match 19; Newton played number 7 in Match 20; Newton played number 9 in Match 20, scoring once; Farrah played number 11 in Match 20; Smith played number 7 in Match 22; Ward played number 11 in Match 22, scoring once; Scrimshaw played number 7 in Match 23; T.Rippon played number 7 in Match 25; Booth played number 11 in Match 25; Lawrence played number 1 in Match 26; T.Rippon played number 8 in Match 26; Summers played number 1 in Match 29; Horton played number 8 in Match 29; Scott played number 11 in Match 29; Thorpe played number 2 in Match 30; Broom played number 9 in Match 30; Gregson played number 10 in Match 30; A.Gray played number 11 in Match 30; Bailey played number 4 in Match 31; Davis played number 8 in Match 31; J.Gray played number 11 in Match 31; Searson played number 4 in Match 32; Davis played number 8 in Match 32; Gregson played number 10 in Match 32, scoring once; Gregson played number 10 in Match 33; R.Gray played number 11 in Match 33; Murray played number 2 in Match 34; Thorpe played number 3 in Match 34; Minney played number 7 in Match 34; A.Gray played number 10 in Match 34; J.Martin played number 11 in Match 34; Brelsford played number 3 in Match 35; A.Gray played number 11 in Match 35; Broom played number 9 in Match 35; Spendiff played number 1 in Match 36; Thorpe played number 2 in Match 36; Murray played number 4 in Match 36; A.Gray played number 10 in Match 36.

1919-20

1	Aug	30	(h)	Stockport C	L	0-3		
2	Sep	1	(a)	Wolves	L	1-6	Storer	12,000
3		6	(a)	Stockport C	W	2-1	Storer 2	
4		8	(h)	Wolves	L	0-1		
5		13	(h)	Huddersfield T	W	1-0	Smith	
6		20	(a)	Huddersfield T	L	0-3		
7		27	(h)	Blackpool	D	1-1	Storer	
8	Oct	4	(a)	Blackpool	L	0-2		
9		11	(h)	West Ham U	L	0-1		
10		18	(a)	West Ham U	L	0-1		
11		25	(h)	Hull C	W	2-1	Storer, T.Rippon	10,000
12	Nov	1	(a)	Hull C	L	1-4	Wainwright	
13		8	(h)	Rotherham C	L	0-1		
14		15	(a)	Rotherham C	L	1-3	Wainwright	
15		22	(a)	Stoke	L	0-3		
16		29	(h)	Stoke	W	2-0	Smith, T.Rippon	
17	Dec	6	(a)	Bristol C	L	1-3	Storer	
18		13	(h)	Bristol C	D	2-2	Smith, Broom	
19		20	(h)	Birmingham	L	0-3		
20		25	(a)	Fulham	L	1-2	Storer	
21		27	(a)	Birmingham	L	0-4		20,000
22	Jan	1	(h)	Coventry C	L	0-1		
23		3	(h)	Leicester C	L	1-2	Broom (pen)	
24		17	(a)	Leicester C	L	0-2		
25		24	(h)	Barnsley	D	1-1	Storer	
26	Feb	7	(h)	Nottingham F	W	1-0	Clark	
27		9	(a)	Barnsley	W	1-0	Huxford	
28		14	(a)	Nottingham F	L	0-2		
29		21	(h)	Lincoln C	D	2-2	Clark, Kemp	
30		28	(a)	Lincoln C	L	0-2		
31	Mar	6	(a)	Bury	D	1-1	Clark	
32		13	(h)	Bury	L	1-2	Smith	
33		20	(a)	Port Vale	L	1-2	Storer	
34		27	(h)	Port Vale	W	2-0	Storer, Spink	
35	Apr	2	(h)	Fulham	L	0-2		
36		3	(a)	Clapton O	L	0-3		10,000
37		6	(a)	Coventry C	L	0-2		
38		10	(h)	Clapton O	W	2-0	Smith (pen), Spink	
39		17	(a)	Tottenham H	L	1-3	Storer	35,000
40		24	(h)	Tottenham H	W	2-0	Storer, Bird	
41		26	(a)	South Shields	L	0-2		
42	May	1	(h)	South Shields	W	3-1	Thompson, Bird, Cresswell (og)	

FINAL LEAGUE POSITION: 22nd in Division Two

Appearances

Goals

FA Cup

1	Jan	10	(h)	Bristol C	L	1-2

Spendiff	Dawson	McEachran	Battiste	Kenny	Whitchurch	Spink	Clark	Storer	Golightly	Smith Albert	Jennings	Scott	Martin	Affleck	Welsh	Gillow	Burton	Duke	Brooks	Rippon	Thompson A	Kemp	Bird	Broom	Wainwright	Huxford	Abbot	Gray	
1	2	3	4	5	6	7	8	9	10	11																			1
1	2	3	4	5	6	7	8	9	10	11																			2
1	2	3	4	5	6	7	8	9	10	11																			3
1	2	3	4	5	6	7	8	9	10	11																			4
1	2	3	4	5	6	7	8	9	10	11																			5
1	2	3	4	5	6		8	9	10	11									7										6
1		3	4	5	6	7	8	9	10	11			2																7
1	2	3	4	5	6	7				11										8				9		10			8
1	2	3		5	6	7		9		11					4					8								10	9
1	2	3		5	6	7		9	10	11					4					8									10
1	2	3		5		7	10	9		11			6		4					8									11
1	2			5		7		9		11			6	3	4					8					10				12
1	2		4	5		7		9		11			6	3						8					10				13
1	2		4	5	6	7		9		11				3						8					10				14
1	2		4	5		7		9		11			6	3						8					10				15
1	2	3	4	5		7		9		11			6							8					10				16
1	2	3	4	5				9		11			6						7	8					10				17
1	2	3	4	5		7		9		11			6							8				10					18
1	2	3	8					10		11			6		4		5		7		9								19
1	2	3		5		7		10		11			4				6			8					9				20
1	2	3	7	5				10		11			4				6			8					9				21
	10	3	7	5				9		11	1		4	2			6			8									22
	2	3	7	5				9		11	1		4				6			8				10					23
	2	3	4	5		7	9	10		11		1	6								8								24
	2	3	4	5		7	8	10		11		1	6									9							25
	2	3		5		7	9			11		1	6			4				8		10							26
	2	3	8	5		7	9	10				1	6			4										11			27
		3	4	5		7	9	10				1	6	2								8				11			28
	2	3	4	5		7	9	10		11		1	6									8							29
	2			5		7	9			11		1	6	3		4						10	8						30
	2		7				9			11		1	5	3		4	6					10	8						31
	2		10			7	9			11		1	5	3		4	6						8						32
	2					7	9	10		11		1	5	3		4	6					8							33
	2		8			7		9		11		1	5	3		4	6										10		34
	2		8	5		7		9		11		1		3		4	6					10							35
	2		8			7		9	10	11		1	5	3		4	6												36
		3	8			7		9		11		1	5	2		4	6					10							37
		3	8			7		9		11		1	6	2		4		5									10		38
	2					7		9		11		1	6	3		4		5					8				10		39
	2	3				7		9		11		1	6			4		5					8				10		40
	2					7		9		11		1	6	3		4		5					8				10		41
	2		10			7				11		1	4	3			6	5			9		8						42
21	38	28	31	30	11	35	18	36	9	40	2	19	31	18	5	14	13	5	3	16	3	9	7	3	8	3	5	1	
						2	3	12		5										2	1	1	2	2	2	1			

1 own-goal

1920-21

1	Aug	28	(h)	Northampton T	W	2-0	Macauley 2	
2		30	(h)	Southend U	W	1-0	Bache	
3	Sep	4	(a)	Northampton T	L	1-4	Storer	
4		6	(a)	Southend U	L	1-3	Collier	7,000
5		11	(a)	Bristol R	L	0-2		20,000
6		18	(h)	Bristol R	W	3-1	Morrall, Clark 2	
7		25	(a)	Reading	L	1-4	Clark	
8		29	(a)	Brighton & HA	W	3-1	Clark 2, Collier	8,000
9	Oct	2	(h)	Reading	W	2-0	Collier 2	
10		9	(a)	Luton T	L	1-3	Storer	
11		16	(h)	Luton T	L	0-1		
12		23	(a)	Merthyr T	L	1-3	Morrall	15,000
13		30	(h)	Merthyr T	D	1-1	Clark	
14	Nov	6	(a)	Swansea T	L	1-3	Storer	15,000
15		13	(h)	Swansea T	L	0-2		
16		20	(h)	Queen's Park R	W	2-1	Macauley, Smith (pen)	
17		27	(a)	Queen's Park R	L	0-2		
18	Dec	4	(a)	Southampton	W	1-0	Collier	
19		11	(h)	Southampton	W	3-0	Macauley, Collier, Smith	
20		25	(h)	Norwich C	D	1-1	Collier	
21		27	(a)	Norwich C	D	0-0		
22	Jan	1	(h)	Brighton & HA	D	2-2	Carmichael, Smith	
23		15	(a)	Plymouth A	D	0-0		
24		22	(h)	Plymouth A	D	1-1	Storer	
25	Feb	5	(h)	Crystal P	W	1-0	Talks	
26		9	(a)	Crystal P	L	0-2		
27		12	(a)	Exeter C	D	1-1	Clark	
28		19	(h)	Exeter C	W	2-0	Storer, Morrall	
29		26	(a)	Millwall	W	1-0	Storer	
30	Mar	5	(h)	Millwall	L	0-2		
31		12	(a)	Newport C	L	1-2	Clark	8,000
32		19	(h)	Newport C	D	1-1	Smith (pen)	
33		25	(h)	Brentford	W	2-0	Collier, Elliott (og)	
34		26	(h)	Gillingham	W	2-0	Deacey, Smith (pen)	
35		28	(a)	Brentford	L	0-5		
36	Apr	2	(a)	Gillingham	L	1-2	Talks	
37		9	(h)	Swindon T	W	3-0	Clark, Smith 2	
38		16	(a)	Swindon T	D	0-0		
39		23	(h)	Portsmouth	L	0-3		
40		30	(a)	Portsmouth	L	1-2	Collier	12,000
41	May	2	(h)	Watford	W	3-0	Carmichael, Morrall, Smith (pen)	
42		7	(a)	Watford	L	2-4	Collier, Morrall	

FINAL LEAGUE POSITION: 13th in Division Three

Appearances
Goals

FA Cup

6	Dec	18	(a)	Kettering T	W	4-2
1	Jan	8	(h)	Norwich C	W	1-0
2		29	(h)	Southampton	L	1-3

Whalley	Dawson	Affleck	Gillow	Carmichael	Broom	Spink	Collier	Storer	Macauley	Bache	Moody	Smith Joe	Irvine	McEachran	Smith A	Bradford	Duke	Deacey	Martin	Blake	Sykes	Clarke	Morrall	Bell	Johnston	Sankey	Talks	Kent	
1	2	3	4	5	6	7	8	9	10	11																			1
1	2	3	4	5	6	7	8	9		10					11														2
1	2	3	4	5	6	7	8	9		10					11														3
		3	4	5		7	8	9		10	1	2							6	11									4
		2	4	9		7	8	10			1			3			5		6	11									5
1	2	3	4		5	7	8			11						6						9	10						6
1	2	3		5	4	7	8									6						9	10				10	11	7
1	2	3		5		7	8	11								4				6		9	10						8
1	2	3		5		7	9	6								4				11		8	10						9
1	2	3		5		7	8	6								4				11		9	10						10
1	2	3	4	5		7	8	6												11		9	10						11
1		3	4	5		7		6	10				2							11		9	8						12
1		2		5				7	8					3	11	4			6			9	10						13
		2	4	5	6			9	8		1			3	11						7		10						14
		2	4	5			7	9			1			3	11	6						8	10						15
1		2	4	5			7	9	10					3	11	6							8						16
1		2	4	5		7		9	10					3	11	6							8						17
1		2	4	5			7	6	10					3	11								8			9			18
1		2	4	5			7	6	10					3	11								8			9			19
1		2	4	5			7	6	10					3	11								8			9			20
1		2	4	9			7	6	10					3	11			5					8						21
1		2	4	9			7	6	10					3	11			5					8						22
1		2					7	6						3	11	4		5				9	8			10			23
1		2					7	6	10					3	11	4		5				9	8						24
		2	4			7	8	6			1			3	11			5					10				9		25
		2	4			7	8	6			1			3	11			5					10				9		26
		2	4			7		6			1			3	11			5				8	10				9		27
	2		4			7	8	6			1			3	11			5					10				9		28
			4				8	6			1		2	3	11			5				7	10				9		29
			4				8	6			1		2	3	11			5				7	10				9		30
		2	4				7		8		1			3	11	6		5				9	10						31
		2	4		6	7					1			3	11			5				9	10	8					32
		2	4			7	8				1			3	11	6		5				9	10						33
		2	4			7	8				1			3	11	6		5					10	9					34
		2	4				7				1			3	11	6		5				9	10	8					35
		2	4				7		10		1			3	11	6		5							8		9		36
1		2	4				7		10					3	11	6		5				9	8						37
1		2	4				7		10					3	11	6		5				9	8						38
1		2	4			7	8							3	11	6		5				9	10						39
		2	4	7			8				1			3	11	6		5					10				9		40
		2	4	8			7				1			3	11	6		5					10				9		41
		2	4	8			7				1			3	11	6		5					10				9		42
23	10	39	35	24	7	21	36	28	16	5	19	1	3	31	32	22	1	22	3	7	1	21	36	3	1	4	10	1	
				2			10	6	4	1					8			1				9	5				2		

1 own-goal

1921-22

1	Aug	27	(a)	Ashington	L	0-1	
2	Sep	3	(h)	Ashington	W	6-1	J.Miller 3, Deacey, Gillow, Carmichael
3		6	(h)	Walsall	W	3-1	Carmichael, Deacey, Gillow
4		10	(a)	Stalybridge C	L	0-3	
5		17	(h)	Stalybridge C	D	1-1	Collier
6		24	(a)	Wigan B	D	1-1	Carmichael
7	Oct	1	(h)	Wigan B	D	1-1	Carmichael
8		8	(h)	Hartlepools U	W	2-0	Talks, Smith (pen)
9		15	(a)	Hartlepools U	D	0-0	
10		22	(a)	Southport	L	1-7	Talks
11		29	(h)	Southport	D	0-0	
12	Nov	5	(a)	Stockport C	W	1-0	Carmichael
13		12	(h)	Stockport C	W	2-1	Carmichael, J.Miller
14		19	(a)	Rochdale	W	2-0	Smith, Carmichael
15		26	(h)	Rochdale	W	3-0	Carmichael, J.Miller 2
16	Dec	10	(a)	Walsall	L	1-2	Raby
17		24	(h)	Halifax T	W	4-1	Carmichael 4 (inc 1 pen)
18		26	(h)	Chesterfield	D	2-2	Collier 2
19		27	(a)	Chesterfield	L	1-4	Carmichael
20		31	(a)	Tranmere R	D	2-2	Carmichael, Morrall
21	Jan	14	(h)	Tranmere R	W	5-1	Laws 2, Carmichael 2, J.Miller
22		16	(a)	Halifax T	L	0-2	
23		21	(a)	Barrow	D	2-2	Carmichael 2
24		28	(h)	Barrow	W	4-0	Carmichael 4
25	Feb	4	(a)	Durham C	W	2-1	Carmichael 2
26		11	(h)	Durham C	W	5-2	Carmichael, J.Miller 3, Morrall
27		18	(a)	Wrexham	W	1-0	Carmichael
28		25	(h)	Wrexham	W	2-0	Carmichael, J.Miller
29	Mar	4	(a)	Nelson	L	0-3	
30		11	(h)	Nelson	W	3-1	Casson, Carmichael 2 (1 pen)
31	Apr	1	(h)	Crewe A	W	3-0	Carmichael 2 (1 pen), Laws
32		8	(a)	Crewe A	W	2-1	Laws 2
33		14	(h)	Lincoln C	W	3-1	J.Miller, Carmichael, Morrall
34		15	(h)	Accrington S	W	2-1	Carmichael, Spink
35		17	(a)	Lincoln C	W	2-0	Carmichael 2 (1 pen)
36		22	(a)	Accrington S	L	0-1	
37		29	(h)	Darlington	W	3-1	J.Miller, Carmichael 2
38	May	6	(a)	Darlington	L	0-2	

FINAL LEAGUE POSITION: 3rd in Division Three North

Appearances
Goals

FA Cup

Q5	Dec	3	(h)	Kettering T	D	1-1
R		8	(a)	Kettering T	W	2-0
Q6		17	(h)	Tufnell Park	D	1-1
R		22	(a)	Tufnell Park	W	2-1
1	Jan	7	(h)	Notts C	D	1-1
R		12	(a)	Notts C	L	0-3

Moody	Affleck	McEachran	Gillow	Deacey	Bradford	Spink	Carmichael	Miller J	Morrall	Smith Albert	Jones	Harrison	Hughes	Stevenson	Felton	Millar H	Coupland	Smith Joe	Robinson R	Collier	Casson	Barrass	Talks	Raby	Laws	
1	2	3	4	5	6	7	8	9	10	11																1
1	2	3	4	5	6	7	8	9	10	11																2
1	2	3	4	5	6	7	8	9	10	11																3
1	2	3	4	5	6	7	8	9	10	11																4
	2	3	4	5			10	9		11	1						6		7	8						5
1			4	5	6	7	8	9	10	11				2	3											6
1			4	5	6	7	8		10	11				2	3							9				7
1			4	5		7	8			11				2	3			6				10	9			8
1			4	5		7	8			11				2	3			6				10	9			9
1			4	5		7	8			11				2	3			6				10	9			10
1	2	3	6	5		7											4			8			9	10	11	11
1	2		6	5		7	8			10					3		4						9		11	12
1	2		6	5		7	8	9		10					3		4								11	13
1	2			5	6	7	8	9	10	11					3		4									14
1	2			5	6	7	8	9	10	11					3		4									15
	2			5	6	7	8	9		11	1					3	4							10		16
	2			5	6	7	9		10			1				3	4			8					11	17
	2			5	6	7	9		10			1				3	4			8					11	18
	2			5	4	7	9		10			1				3		6		8					11	19
	2			5	6		9	10	8	11	1					3	4			7						20
	2		4	5	6		9	10	8				1		3					7					11	21
	2		4	5	6		9	10	8				1		3					7					11	22
	2		4	5	6		9	10	8				1		3				7						11	23
	2		4	5	6		9	10	8				1		3				7						11	24
	2		4	5	6		9	10	8				1		3				7						11	25
	2		4	5	6		9	10	8				1		3				7						11	26
	2		4	5	6		9	10	8				1		3				7						11	27
	2		4	5	6		9	10	8				1		3				7						11	28
	2		4	5	6		9	10	8				1		3				7						11	29
	2		4	5	6		9	10					1		3				7		8				11	30
	2		4	5	6		9	10	8	7			1		3										11	31
	2		4	5	6	7	9	10	8				1		3										11	32
	2		4	5	6	7	9	10	8				1		3										11	33
	2		4	5	6	7	9	10	8				1		3										11	34
	2	3	4	5		7	9	10	8				1				6								11	35
	2		4	5		7	9	10	8				1		3		6								11	36
	2		4	5		7	9	10	8			1			3		6								11	37
	2		4	5		7	9	10	8			1			3		6								11	38
14	33	7	31	38	27	25	37	29	29	17	3	5	16	5	26	5	14	4	9	8	1	4	5	2	24	
			2	2		1	37	13	3	2										3	1		2	1	5	

1922-23

1	Aug	26	(h)	Wrexham	W 4-0	Carmichael 2 (1 pen), J.Miller 2
2	Sep	2	(a)	Wrexham	D 1-1	Graver
3		9	(a)	Durham C	W 3-0	Coupland 2, J.Miller
4		16	(h)	Durham C	W 1-0	J.Miller
5		23	(h)	Wigan B	D 0-0	
6		30	(a)	Wigan B	L 0-1	
7	Oct	7	(h)	Chesterfield	W 3-1	Carmichael, Kirsopp 2
8		14	(a)	Chesterfield	L 2-3	Carmichael, Ritchie
9		21	(h)	Rochdale	D 1-1	Carmichael
10		28	(a)	Rochdale	W 1-0	Casson
11	Nov	4	(h)	Crewe A	L 2-3	Casson, Deacey
12		11	(a)	Crewe A	L 0-3	
13		18	(h)	Walsall	L 1-2	Carmichael
14		25	(a)	Walsall	L 0-1	
15	Dec	23	(h)	Halifax T	L 0-1	
16		25	(h)	Accrington S	W 7-1	McKenna 3 (1 pen), Carmichael 2, Ritchie, J.Miller
17		30	(h)	Bradford	L 0-1	
18	Jan	1	(a)	Accrington	L 0-4	
19		6	(a)	Bradford	L 1-2	J.Miller
20		20	(h)	Tranmere R	D 0-0	
21		22	(a)	Halifax T	L 0-1	
22		27	(a)	Tranmere R	L 2-3	Casson, Carmichael
23	Feb	3	(h)	Barrow	W 2-0	
24		10	(a)	Barrow	L 0-2	
25		17	(a)	Ashington	L 1-2	J.Miller (pen)
26		24	(h)	Ashington	W 7-4	Carmichael 4, J.Miller 2 (1 pen), Kettle
27	Mar	3	(h)	Southport	W 2-1	Carmichael 2
28		10	(a)	Southport	L 1-3	Kettle
29		17	(a)	Stalybridge C	L 2-3	Carmichael, J.Miller
30		24	(h)	Stalybridge C	W 3-0	Carmichael, J.Miller, McKenna
31		30	(h)	Darlington	L 0-1	
32		31	(a)	Nelson	D 1-1	Ritchie
33	Apr	2	(a)	Darlington	W 3-1	Carmichael 2 (1 pen), Kettle
34		7	(h)	Nelson	L 0-2	
35		14	(a)	Lincoln C	W 2-1	Carmichael 2
36		21	(h)	Lincoln C	W 1-0	McKenna
37		28	(a)	Hartlepools U	L 0-2	
38	May	5	(h)	Hartlepools U	W 1-0	Carmichael

FINAL LEAGUE POSITION: 14th in Division Three North

Appearances
Goals

FA Cup

Q5	Dec	22	(h)	Worksop T	L 0-2

Hughes	Affleck	Felton	Coupland	Deacey	Bradford	Cumming	Graver	Carmichael	Miller J	Laws	Harrison	Smith WE	Atter	Millar H	Stevenson	Binks	Crozier	Hilton	Cook	Ritchie	Kettle	Kirsopp	McKenna	Casson	
1	2	3	4	5	6	7	8	9	10	11															1
1	2	3	4	5	6	7	8	9	10	11															2
1	2	3	4	5	6	7	8	9	10	11															3
1	2	3	4	5	6	7	8	9	10	11															4
1	2	3	4	5	6	7	8	9	10	11															5
1	2	3	4	5	6	7		9	10	11												8			6
1	2	3	4	5	6			9	10	11										7		8			7
1	2	3	4	5	6			9	10	11										7		8			8
1	2	3	4	5				9	10	11							6			7		8			9
1	2	3	4	5				8	10	11							6			7				9	10
1	2	3	4	5				8	10	11							6			7				9	11
1	2	3		5	6			9	10	11							4				7			8	12
1	2	3		5	6			9	10	11							4			7				8	13
		3	4	5			8	9		11	1			2			6					7	10		14
	2	3	4	5				9	10	11	1						6			7			8		15
	2	3	4	5				9	10	11	1						6			7			8		16
1	2	3	4	5				9	10	11							6			7			8		17
1	2		4	5				9	10	11				3			6			7			8		18
	2		4	5				9	10	11		1		3			6			7			8		19
	2		4	5	6			9	10	11		1		3						7		8			20
	2		4	5	6			8	10	11		1		3						7				9	21
	2		4	5	6			8	10	11		1		3						7				9	22
	2		4	5	6			8	10	11		1				3				7				9	23
	2		4	5	6			9	10			1				3				7	11			8	24
	2		4	5	6			9	10			1				3				7	11			8	25
	3		4		6			9	8	11		1			2			5			7		10		26
	3				6			9	8	11		1			2		4	5			7		10		27
	3		4		6			9	8	11		1			2			5			7		10		28
	3		4		6			9	10	11			1	2				5		8	7				29
	3				6			9	10	11			1	2			4	5			7		8		30
	3							9	10	11			1	2			4	5	6		7		8		31
	3				4			9	10				1	2				5	6	7	11		8		32
	3			5	4			9	10				1	2					6	7	11		8		33
	3			5	4			9	10				1	2					6	7	11		8		34
	3			5	4			9	10				1	2					6	7	11		8		35
	3		6	5	4			9	10				1	2						7	11		8		36
	3		6	5	4			9	10				1	2						7	11		8		37
	3		6		4			9	10				1	2				5		7	11			8	38
15	37	17	29	30	28	6	6	38	37	29	3	10	10	16	3	3	14	8	5	25	16	6	17	10	
			2	1			1	23	11											4	3	2	5	3	

1923-24

1	Aug	25	(a)	Tranmere R	L	1-2	Carmichael
2		27	(h)	Bradford	W	2-0	J.Miller 2
3	Sep	1	(h)	Tranmere R	D	0-0	
4		3	(a)	Bradford	L	1-2	Carmichael
5		8	(a)	Halifax T	W	3-1	Carmichael, J.Miller 2
6		15	(h)	Halifax T	D	1-1	J.Miller
7		22	(a)	Lincoln C	W	3-1	Carmichael 3
8		29	(h)	Lincoln C	D	2-2	J.Miller, Honeyman
9	Oct	6	(a)	Hartlepools U	D	1-1	J.Miller
10		13	(h)	Hartlepools U	L	0-1	
11		20	(a)	New Brighton	D	0-0	
12		27	(h)	New Brighton	D	0-0	
13	Nov	3	(a)	Wolves	L	1-4	Carmichael
14		10	(h)	Wolves	W	2-0	Carmichael, Marshall
15		17	(h)	Walsall	W	1-0	Carmichael
16		24	(a)	Walsall	L	0-2	
17	Dec	8	(a)	Ashington	L	0-1	
18		22	(a)	Wigan B	L	0-4	
19		25	(h)	Crewe A	W	2-0	Carmichael 2
20		26	(a)	Crewe A	D	0-0	
21		29	(h)	Durham C	W	1-0	Carmichael
22	Jan	1	(a)	Accrington S	L	0-2	
23		5	(a)	Durham C	W	1-0	Thomson
24		19	(a)	Chesterfield	L	2-4	Thomson, McKenna
25		26	(h)	Chesterfield	D	0-0	
26	Feb	2	(a)	Rotherham C	L	1-2	Wilson
27		9	(h)	Rotherham C	D	1-1	Marshall
28		16	(a)	Wrexham	D	1-1	J.Miller
29		23	(h)	Wrexham	D	0-0	
30	Mar	1	(a)	Doncaster R	L	1-2	Dent
31		8	(h)	Doncaster R	D	1-1	McKenna
32		15	(h)	Rochdale	W	1-0	Carmichael
33		22	(a)	Rochdale	L	2-4	Carmichael, Dent
34		27	(h)	Wigan B	D	1-1	Thomson
35		29	(h)	Southport	W	1-0	Dent
36	Apr	5	(a)	Southport	L	0-3	
37		8	(h)	Ashington	W	4-0	Carmichael 3, Dent
38		12	(h)	Darlington	W	3-0	Carmichael, Gillow 2
39		18	(h)	Accrington S	W	2-0	Carmichael, Davies
40		19	(a)	Darlington	L	0-1	
41		26	(h)	Barrow	W	5-0	Gillow, Dent 3, Carmichael
42	May	3	(a)	Barrow	L	1-3	Casson

FINAL LEAGUE POSITION: 11th in Division Three North

Appearances
Goals

FA Cup

Q5	Dec	1	(a)	Hinckley	W	3-0
Q6		15	(a)	Chesterfield	D	0-0
R		18	(h)	Chesterfield	W	2-0
1	Jan	12	(a)	Exeter C	L	0-1

Atter	Ackroyd	Affleck	Gillow	Leddy	Bradford	McKenna	Thomson D	Carmichael	Miller J	Flanaghan	Archibald	Arch	McClennon	Millar H	Davies	Wilson CH	Hilton	Dixon	Honeyman	Boylen	Shaw A	Kitching	Dent	Casson	Marshall	
1	2	3	4	5	6	7	8	9	10	11																1
1	2	3	4	5	6	7	8	9	10	11																2
1	2	3	4	5	6	7	8	9	10	11																3
1	2	3	4		6		8	9	10								5		7						11	4
1	2	3	4		6		8	9	10								5		7						11	5
1	2	3	4		6		8	9	10								5		7						11	6
1		3	4	5	6			9	10			2							7			8			11	7
1		3	4	5	6			9	10			2							7			8			11	8
1		3			6	7			10			2			4		5		8					9	11	9
1		3			6	7		9	10			2			4		5		8						11	10
		3	4		6			9	10		1	2					5		7			8			11	11
		3	4		6			9	10		1	2					5		7			8			11	12
		3	4		6		8	9	10		1	2					5		7						11	13
		3			6		8	9			1	2				4	5		7				10		11	14
		3			6		8	9			1	2				4	5		7				10		11	15
		3			6		8	9			1	2				4	5		7				10		11	16
		3			6	7	8	9	10		1	2				4	5								11	17
		3			6	7	8	9	10		1	2				4	5								11	18
					6		8	9	10		1	2		3		4	5		7						11	19
					6		8	9	10		1	2		3		4	5		7						11	20
					6		8	9	10		1	2		3		4	5		7						11	21
					6	10	8	9			1	2		3		4	5		7						11	22
		3			6	10	8	7			1	2				4	5							9	11	23
		3			6	10	8				1	2				4	5			7				9	11	24
		3	4		6	10	8				1	2					5			7				9	11	25
		3			6	10	8		9		1	2				4	5			7					11	26
		3			6	8		9	10		1	2				4	5			7					11	27
		3		4	6	7	8	9	10		1	2					5								11	28
		3		4	6	7	8		10		1	2					5							9	11	29
		3			6				10		1	2				4	5		7				8	9	11	30
		3		6		10					1	2				4	5		7				8	9	11	31
		3		5	6	10		9			1	2				4			7				8		11	32
		3		6		10		9			1	2				4	5		7				8		11	33
		3		6		7	8	9			1	2				4	5						10		11	34
		3		6		8		9			1	2		7		4	5						10		11	35
		3		6		10		9			1		2			4	5				7	8	11			36
			8					9			1	3	2		6	4	5				7		10		11	37
		3	8					9			1	2			6	4	5				7		10		11	38
		3	8					9			1	2			6	4	5				7		10		11	39
		3	8					9			1		2		6	4	5				7		10		11	40
		3	8				7	9			1	2				4	5	6					10		11	41
		3					7	9			1	2				4	5	6					10	8	11	42
10	6	37	17	13	31	21	25	35	23	3	32	34	3	5	6	26	36	2	21	4	5	5	16	8	38	
			3			2	3	20	8						1	1			1				7	1	2	

1924-25

1	Aug	30	(h)	Darlington	L 0-2		
2	Sep	1	(h)	Hartlepools U	W 2-1	Thain, Carmichael	
3		6	(a)	Bradford	W 1-0	Thain	12,000
4		10	(a)	Hartlepools U	L 1-2	Marshall	4,200
5		13	(h)	Wrexham	L 0-1		
6		20	(a)	Rotherham C	L 0-3		
7		27	(h)	Chesterfield	D 0-0		
8	Oct	4	(a)	Accrington S	W 3-0	Cooper, Dent 2	
9		11	(h)	Halifax T	D 1-1	Dent	
10		18	(a)	New Brighton	L 2-3	Dent, Gray	
11		25	(a)	Lincoln C	D 0-0		
12	Nov	1	(h)	Barrow	W 2-1	Robson, Carmichael (pen)	
13		8	(a)	Nelson	L 0-1		
14		15	(h)	Rochdale	D 1-1	Cooper	
15		22	(a)	Southport	L 1-3	Dent	
16	Dec	6	(a)	Durham C	L 1-6	Marshall	
17		13	(h)	Crewe A	D 0-0		
18		20	(a)	Wigan B	L 1-3	Carmichael	
19		25	(h)	Walsall	W 2-1	Kitching, Thain	
20		26	(a)	Walsall	L 0-2		
21		27	(a)	Darlington	D 0-0		
22	Jan	1	(h)	Doncaster R	D 1-1	Marshall	
23		3	(h)	Bradford	W 2-0	Robson, Cooper	
24		10	(h)	Ashington	L 1-3	Robson	
25		17	(h)	Wrexham	W 2-1	Carmichael, Marshall	4,000
26		24	(h)	Rotherham C	W 3-1	Carmichael, Marshall, Cooper	
27	Feb	7	(h)	Accrington S	W 4-0	Cooper, Carmichael 2, McKenna	
28		14	(a)	Halifax T	L 0-1		2,000
29		21	(h)	New Brighton	L 2-3	Carmichael 2	
30		28	(a)	Lincoln C	L 1-2	Carmichael	
31	Mar	7	(a)	Barrow	L 2-3	McKenna, Carmichael	
32		14	(h)	Nelson	W 2-0	Cooper, McKenna	
33		21	(a)	Ashington	W 2-0	McKenna, Marshall	
34		28	(h)	Southport	W 3-1	Cooper, Carmichael, Marshall	
35	Apr	4	(a)	Doncaster R	D 2-2	Marshall, Thain	
36		10	(a)	Tranmere R	W 3-2	Marshall, Cooper, McKenna	
37		11	(h)	Durham C	D 1-1	Cooper	
38		13	(h)	Tranmere R	W 6-1	Coverdale, Carmichael 2, Cooper 2, McKenna	
39		14	(a)	Chesterfield	L 0-2		
40		18	(a)	Crewe A	L 1-3	Carmichael	5,000
41		25	(h)	Wigan B	W 4-0	Carmichael 3, McKenna	
42	May	2	(a)	Rochdale	L 0-2		

FINAL LEAGUE POSITION: 12th in Division Three North

Appearances
Goals

FA Cup

5	Nov	29	(h)	Chesterfield	L 1-2	

Archibald	Arch	Affleck	Wilson CH	Hilton	Davies	Thain	Burley	Carmichael	Dent	Marshall	Atter	Pearson	McClennon	Coverdale	Field	Dixon	Thompson	Oakton	Kitching	Cooper	Gillow	Robson	McKenna	Gray RE	Reay	
1	2	3	4	5	6	7	8	9	10	11																1
1	2	3	4	5		7	8	9		11					6								10			2
1	2	3	4	5		7	8	9		11					6								10			3
1	2	3	4	5		7	8	9		11					6								10			4
1	2	3	4	5		7		8	10	11					6							9				5
1	2	3	4	5			8	9		11					6		7						10			6
	2	3	4	5				9	10	11	1				6		7			8						7
	2	3	4	5				9	10	11	1			6			7			8						8
	2	3	4	5		7		9	10	11	1			6							8					9
	2	3		5					10		1			4		6	7			8		9		11		10
	2	3		5				7		11	1			4		6				8		9		10		11
	2	3		5				7		11	1			4		6				8		9		10		12
	2	3		5				7			1			4		6				8		9	10	11		13
	2	3		5		7		9		11	1			4	6					8	10					14
	2	3	4	5				9	10	11	1					6	7			8						15
	2		4	5	6	7		9		11	1	3								8			10			16
1	2		4	5	6			9		11			3				7			8			10			17
1	2			5	6			9					3	8	4		7						10		11	18
1	2			5	6	7		9		11			3		4				8		10					19
1	2	3		5	6	7		9		11					4				8		10					20
1	2	3		5		7		9		11				6	4					8	10					21
1	2	3		5		7		9		11				6	4				8		10					22
1	2	3		5		7				11				6	4				8	10		9				23
1	2	3		5		7				11				6	4				8	10		9				24
1				5		7		9		11		2	3	6	4					8			10			25
1				5		7		9		11		2	3	6	4					8			10			26
1	2			5		7		9		11			3	6	4					8			10			27
1	2		4			7		9		11			3	6	5					8			10			28
1	2		4			7		9		11			3	6	5					8			10			29
1	2	3	4			7		9		11				6	5					8			10			30
1	2	3	4			7		9		11				6	5					8			10			31
1	2	3	4					9		11				6	5			7		8			10			32
1	2	3	4			7		9		11				6	5					8			10			33
1	2	3	4					9		11				6	5			7		8			10			34
1		3	4			7				11		2		6	5					8		9	10			35
1	2	3	4					9		11				6	5				7	8			10			36
1	2	3	4					9		11				6	5				7	8			10			37
	2	3	4					9		11	1			6	5				7	8			10			38
	2	3	4			7		9		11	1			6	5					8			10			39
	2	3	4			7		9		11	1			6	5					8			10			40
	2	3	4					9		11	1			6	5				7	8			10			41
	2	3	4			7		9	8	11	1			6	5								10			42
27	39	33	27	27	6	26	5	38	8	39	15	4	8	30	32	5	7	2	9	30	6	8	26	4	1	
						4		18	5	9				1					1	11		3	7	1		

1925-26

1	Aug	29	(h)	Doncaster R	W 3-0	Carmichael 2, McKenna	9,012
2		31	(h)	Walsall	W 5-1	McKenna 3, Marshall, Carmichael	8,225
3	Sep	5	(a)	Rotherham U	L 1-2	Carmichael	5,388
4		7	(a)	Walsall	D 2-2	Carmichael 2	3,605
5		12	(h)	Halifax T	W 1-0	Carmichael	7,722
6		14	(h)	Tranmere R	W 8-0	Carmichael, Cooper 3, McKenna 2, Devan, Marshall	7,109
7		19	(a)	Accrington S	L 0-1		2,981
8		26	(h)	Durham C	W 3-1	Cooper, Carmichael, McKenna	6,817
9	Oct	1	(a)	Tranmere R	D 0-0		4,604
10		3	(a)	Hartlepools U	D 1-1	Carmichael (pen)	6,096
11		10	(h)	Rochdale	W 3-0	Carmichael 2, Cooper	11,602
12		17	(h)	Southport	W 3-2	McKenna, Marshall, Tyler (og)	7,339
13		24	(a)	Lincoln C	L 1-4	Carmichael	13,078
14		31	(h)	Coventry C	W 2-0	Carmichael 2 (1 pen)	9,318
15	Nov	7	(a)	Wrexham	L 1-4	Carmichael	5,774
16		14	(h)	Wigan B	D 1-1	Foster	7,763
17		21	(a)	Ashington	L 2-4	Carmichael, Gardner	4,537
18	Dec	5	(a)	Nelson	D 1-1	Cooper	5,675
19		19	(a)	New Brighton	W 4-1	Robson 3, Mehaffy (og)	4,101
20		25	(h)	Bradford	W 3-0	Robson 3	13,230
21		26	(a)	Bradford	W 1-0	Devan	18,599
22	Jan	16	(h)	Rotherham U	W 3-0	Carmichael, Hardy, Devan	7,059
23		23	(a)	Halifax T	W 2-0	Hardy, Devan	7,896
24		30	(h)	Accrington S	W 5-2	Carmichael 3, McKenna, Cooper	8,573
25	Feb	6	(a)	Durham C	D 0-0		2,869
26		13	(h)	Hartlepools U	W 2-0	Marshall, Hardy	7,859
27		20	(a)	Rochdale	L 2-5	Marshall, McKenna	7,544
28		25	(h)	Barrow	W 4-0	Marshall, McKenna, Devan, Cooper	5,350
28		27	(a)	Southport	W 1-0	Cooper	4,099
30	Mar	6	(h)	Lincoln C	W 4-0	Carmichael 2, McKenna, Devan	12,575
31		13	(a)	Coventry C	D 1-1	Devan	11,695
32		20	(h)	Wrexham	W 1-0	Carmichael	9,319
33		25	(h)	Crewe A	W 2-0	Carmichael, Cooper	8,355
34		27	(a)	Wigan B	D 2-2	Carmichael, McKenna	6,689
35	Apr	2	(h)	Chesterfield	W 1-0	Marshall	16,086
36		3	(h)	Ashington	W 3-1	Carmichael 2, Cooper	10,284
37		5	(a)	Chesterfield	L 0-2		11,867
38		10	(a)	Barrow	W 3-0	Carmichael 2, McKenna	1,910
39		17	(h)	Nelson	W 3-0	Carmichael, Gardner, Marshall	9,641
40		22	(a)	Doncaster R	W 4-1	Carmichael, Marshall, Devan, Gardner	9,711
41		24	(a)	Crewe A	D 1-1	Devan	5,571
42	May	1	(h)	New Brighton	W 1-0	Carmichael	14,548

FINAL LEAGUE POSITION: 1st in Division Three North

Appearances
Goals

FA Cup

1	Nov	18	(a)	Walsall	W 1-0
2	Dec	12	(a)	Kettering T	D 1-1
R		15	(h)	Kettering T	W 3-1
3	Jan	9	(a)	Birmingham	L 0-2

Atter	Arch	Jacobson	Wilson CH	Hardy	Pugsley	Foster	Cooper	Carmichael	McKenna	Marshall	Archibald	Pearson	Jackson	Evans	McLachlan	Wrack	Dixon	Devan	Kitching	Gardner	Robson	
1	2	3	4	5	6	7	8	9	10	11												1
1	2	3	4		6	7	8	9	10	11						5						2
1	2	3	4	5	6	7	8	9	10	11												3
1	2	3	4	5	6	7		9	10	11									8			4
1	2	3	4	5	6	7	8	9	10	11												5
1	2	3	4	5	6		8	9	10	11								7				6
1	2	3	4		6			9	10	11						5		7	8			7
1	2	3			6		8	9	10	11				4		5		7				8
1	2	3			6			8	10	11				4		5		7			9	9
1	2	3			6		8	9	10	11				4		5		7				10
1	2	3	4		6		8	9	10	11						5		7				11
1	2	3	4		6		8	9	10	11						5		7				12
1	2	3	4		6	7	8	9	10	11						5						13
	2	3	4			7	8	9		11	1					5	6			10		14
	2	3	4			7	8	9		11	1					5	6			10		15
	2	3		5	6	7	8	9	10	11	1			4								16
	2	3	4	5	6	7		9	10	11	1									8		17
		3	4	5	6		8	9	10	11	1	2						7				18
			2	5	6				10	11	1		3		4			7		8	9	19
		3	2	5	6				10	11	1				4			7		8	9	20
		3	2	5	6				10	11	1				4			7		8	9	21
		3	2	5	6		8	9	10	11	1				4			7				22
		3	2	5	6			8	10	11	1				4			7			9	23
		3	2	5	6		8	9	10	11	1				4			7				24
		3	2	5	6		8	9	10	11	1				4			7				25
		3	2	5	6			9	10	11	1				4			7		8		26
		3	2		6		8	9	10	11	1				4	5		7				27
			2		6		8	9	10	11	1		3		4	5		7				28
			2		6		8	5	10	11	1		3		4			7			9	29
			2	5	6		8	9	10	11	1		3		4			7				30
			2	5	6		8	9	10	11	1		3		4			7				31
			2	5	6		8	9	10	11	1		3		4			7				32
		3	2	5	6		8	4	10	11	1							7			9	33
	2	3	4	5	6			9	10	11	1			8				7				34
		3	2	5	6		8	9	10	11	1				4			7				35
		3	2	5	6		8	9	10	11	1				4			7				36
		3	2	5	6		8	9	10	11	1				4			7				37
			2	5	6			9	10	11	1		3		4			7		8		38
			2	5	6			9	10	11	1		3		4			7		8		39
		3	2	5	6			9	10	11	1				4			7		8		40
		3	2	5	6			9	10	11	1				4			7		8		41
		3	2	5	6		8	9	10	11	1				4			7				42
13	18	34	38	29	40	10	28	39	40	42	29	1	8	5	22	12	2	32	2	11	7	
				3		1	11	33	14	9								8		3	6	

3 own-goals

1926-27

1	Aug	28	(a)	Barnsley	L 1-2	Hardy	7,004
2		30	(h)	Swansea T	L 0-1		14,926
3	Sep	4	(h)	Manchester C	D 2-2	Devan, Carmichael	16,559
4		6	(a)	Nottingham F	D 1-1	Devan	4,659
5		11	(a)	Darlington	W 3-2	Cooper 2, Carmichael	7,982
6		13	(a)	Swansea T	D 1-1	Carmichael	14,229
7		18	(h)	Portsmouth	D 0-0		14,503
8		25	(a)	Oldham A	L 1-3	Cooper	9,384
9	Oct	2	(h)	Fulham	W 2-0	Cooper, McKenna	12,162
10		9	(a)	Preston NE	L 2-3	McKenna, Carmichael	12,529
11		16	(h)	Hull C	L 0-1		16,023
12		23	(a)	South Shields	L 2-3	McKenna, Devan	4,871
13		30	(h)	Chelsea	D 0-0		12,423
14	Nov	6	(a)	Bradford C	D 2-2	Cooper, Gardner	5,786
15		13	(h)	Southampton	L 0-1		9,196
16		20	(a)	Port Vale	L 1-6	Pugsley (pen)	5,327
17	Dec	4	(a)	Clapton O	W 4-2	Marshall, Cooper 2, Bestall	11,859
18		18	(a)	Wolves	W 4-3	Robson, Pugsley (pen), Cooper 2	9,869
19		25	(h)	Blackpool	W 2-1	Cooper, Bestall	15,492
20		27	(a)	Blackpool	L 2-6	Robson 2	13,980
21	Jan	1	(h)	Nottingham F	D 1-1	Bestall	13,406
22		15	(h)	Barnsley	L 1-3	Robson	10,596
23		22	(a)	Manchester C	L 0-2		21,212
24		29	(h)	Notts C	L 1-4	Marshall	9,347
25	Feb	5	(a)	Portsmouth	L 2-5	Devan, Robson	13,969
26		8	(h)	Middlesbrough	L 4-7	Robson 3, Pugsley (pen)	10,288
27		12	(h)	Oldham A	L 2-5	Pugsley (pen), Robson	11,313
28		19	(a)	Fulham	W 5-0	Bestall, Coglin, Robson 3	6,617
29		26	(h)	Preston NE	W 5-2	Coglin 2, Prior, Robson 2	15,183
30	Mar	5	(a)	Hull C	W 3-2	Jacobson, Robson, Bestall	22,274
31		12	(h)	South Shields	D 1-1	Robson	15,190
32		19	(a)	Chelsea	L 0-2		35,239
33		26	(h)	Bradford C	W 4-2	Robson, Bestall, Coglin, Prior	9,940
34		29	(h)	Darlington	W 2-1	Bestall, Robson	11,161
35	Apr	2	(a)	Southampton	D 0-0		5,713
36		9	(h)	Port Vale	D 4-4	Prior, Robson 2, C.H.Wilson	8,717
37		15	(h)	Reading	L 0-1		18,040
38		16	(a)	Middlesbrough	L 0-3		22,503
39		18	(a)	Reading	D 1-1	Pugsley	16,378
40		23	(h)	Clapton O	D 2-2	Pugsley, Cooper	10,003
41		30	(a)	Notts C	L 0-3		9,196
42	May	7	(h)	Wolves	W 6-0	Robson 4 (1 pen), Prior 2 (1 pen)	9,218

FINAL LEAGUE POSITION: 17th in Division Two

Appearances
Goals

FA Cup

1	Nov	17	(h)	Halifax T	W 3-2
2	Dec	11	(h)	York C	W 2-1
3	Jan	9	(a)	Burnley	L 1-3

Archibald	Wilson CH	Jacobson	McLachlan	Hardy	Pugsley	Devan	Cooper	Carmichael	McKenna	Marshall	Prout	Cowell	Jackson	Harris	Newton	Wrack	Hunter	Swaby	Parry	Ferguson	Bestall	Prior	Gardner	Robson	Williamson	Coglin	Gray	
1	2	3	4	5	6	7	8	9	10	11																		1
1		3	4	5	6	7	8	9		11				2											10			2
1		3	4	5		7	10	9		11				2	6								8					3
1		3	4	5		7	10	9		11				2	6								8					4
1		3	4	5	6	7	10	9		11				2									8					5
1		3	4	5	6	7		9		10				2									8				11	6
1		3	4	5	6	7	10	9		11				2									8					7
1		3	4	5	6	7	10	9		11				2									8					8
1		3	4	5	6	7	8	9	10	11				2														9
1		3	4	5	6	7	8	9	10	11				2														10
1		3	4	5	6		8	9	10	11				2					7									11
1		3	4	5	6	7		9	10	11				2									8					12
1		3	4	5	6	7	10	8		11			2											9				13
1		3		5	6		8	9		11			2		4					7			10					14
1		3		5	6		8	9		11			2		4					7			10					15
1		3	4	5	6	7	8		10	11			2											9				16
1		3	4		6	7	10			11			2			5					8			9				17
		3			6		10		7	11	1		2		4	5					8			9				18
		3			6		10		7	11	1		2		4	5					8			9				19
		3			6		10		7	11	1		2		4	5					8			9				20
		3			6		10			11	1		2		4	5				7	8			9				21
1		3		5	6	7			10	11			2		4						8			9				22
1	2	3			6	7	10			11					4	5					8			9				23
1	2				6	7	10	9		11			3		4		5				8							24
1	2	3	4		6	7	10			11							5				8			9				25
1	2	3	4		6					11							5				8	7		9		10		26
1	2	3			6					11					4		5				8	7		9		10		27
	2	3	4		6					11		1					5				8	7		9		10		28
	2	3	4		6					11		1				5					8	7		9		10		29
	2	3	4		6					11		1				5					8	7		9		10		30
	2	3	4		6					11		1				5					8	7		9		10		31
	2	3	4		6					11		1				5					8	7		9		10		32
	2		4		6					11		1	3			5					8	7		9		10		33
	2		4		6					11		1		3		5					8	7		9		10		34
	2		4		6					11		1		3		5					8	7		9		10		35
	2		4		6		8			11		1		3		5						7		9		10		36
	2				6					11		1		3	4	5					8	7		9		10		37
	2				6		10			11		1		3	4	5					8	7		9				38
	2		4		6		8			11		1		3		5					7	9				10		39
	2		4		6		8			11		1		3		5						7		9		10		40
	2		4		6		10			11		1		3				5			8	7		9				41
	2		4		6		8			11		1		3		5						7		9		10		42
23	21	31	30	17	40	18	28	16	10	42	4	15	12	20	14	19	5	1	1	3	23	17	9	26	1	15	1	
	1	1		1	6	4	11	4	3	2											7	5	1	24		4		

1927-28

1	Aug	27	(h)	Clapton O	D	2-2	Marshall, Robson	15,051
2		30	(h)	Reading	D	3-3	Coglin 3	13,431
3	Sep	3	(a)	West Brom A	L	1-3	Prior	16,525
4		10	(h)	Bristol C	L	1-4	Robson	13,006
5		14	(a)	Reading	D	2-2	Prior 2	6,295
6		17	(a)	Stoke C	D	0-0		15,216
7		24	(h)	Southampton	D	2-2	Prior, Robson	11,298
8	Oct	1	(a)	Notts C	L	2-3	Robson 2	7,174
9		8	(h)	Oldham A	L	1-2	Bestall	10,400
10		15	(a)	Hull C	W	1-0	Bestall	18,862
11		22	(h)	Leeds U	W	3-2	Coglin, Meikle, Robson	11,909
12		29	(a)	Nottingham F	L	2-5	Coglin (pen), Meikle	14,546
13	Nov	5	(h)	Manchester C	W	4-1	Marshall, Robson 2, Bestall	12,522
14		12	(a)	South Shields	W	2-1	Coglin, Marshall	6,430
15		19	(h)	Port Vale	W	3-0	Bestall, Marshall, Harris	10,119
16		26	(a)	Fulham	D	2-2	Robson, Coglin	6,395
17	Dec	3	(h)	Barnsley	W	3-1	Coglin, Robson, Marshall	10,241
18		10	(a)	Wolves	W	1-0	Marshall	7,431
19		17	(h)	Swansea T	L	1-2	Robson	9,581
20		24	(a)	Preston NE	L	0-3		12,706
21		26	(h)	Chelsea	D	1-1	Coglin (pen)	18,630
22		31	(a)	Clapton O	W	2-1	Coglin, Marshall	8,738
23	Jan	2	(a)	Blackpool	W	5-4	Bestall 4, Twell	10,347
24		7	(h)	West Brom A	L	0-6		12,242
25		21	(a)	Bristol C	D	0-0		11,690
26	Feb	4	(a)	Southampton	L	0-5		7,180
27		11	(h)	Notts C	W	1-0	Prior	7,666
28		18	(a)	Oldham A	L	0-1		15,701
29		25	(h)	Hull C	D	1-1	Coglin	15,986
30	Mar	3	(a)	Leeds U	D	0-0		23,567
31		6	(h)	Stoke C	L	1-2	Wrack	8,279
32		10	(h)	Nottingham F	W	2-1	Robson 2	7,466
33		14	(a)	Chelsea	L	0-4		14,278
34		17	(a)	Manchester C	L	0-2		49,185
35		24	(h)	South Shields	W	4-1	Robson 2, Prior, Wright	7,868
36		31	(a)	Port Vale	D	2-2	Robson, Bestall	9,125
37	Apr	6	(h)	Blackpool	D	3-3	Prior, Robson, Cooper	15,097
38		7	(h)	Fulham	W	1-0	Robson	9,005
39		14	(a)	Barnsley	W	4-1	Robson 3, Marshall	4,516
40		21	(h)	Wolves	L	0-1		7,248
41		28	(a)	Swansea T	L	2-3	Robson 2	9,208
42	May	5	(h)	Preston NE	L	4-6	Robson 3, Bestall	8,747

FINAL LEAGUE POSITION: 11th in Division Two

Appearances
Goals

FA Cup

3	Jan	14	(a)	Reading	L	0-4

Cowell	Wilson CH	Jacobson	Cowper	Hunter	Powell	Prior	Cooper	Robson	Coglin	Marshall	Read	Harris	Calderwood	Coupland	Tyler	Wrack	Meikle	Bestall	Twell	Wright N	
1	2	3	4	5	6	7	8	9	10	11											1
1	2	3	4		6	7		9	10	11						5		8			2
1	2	3	4		6	7		9	10	11						5		8			3
1	2	3	4		6	7		9	10	11						5		8			4
1					6	7		9	10	11		2	3	4		5		8			5
1					6	7		9	10	11		2	3	4		5		8			6
1					6	7		9	10	11		2	3	4		5		8			7
1					6	7		9	10	11		2	3	4		5		8			8
1					6			9	10	11		2	3	4		5	7	8			9
1		3			6			9	10	11			2	4		5	7	8			10
1	2	3			6			9	10	11				4		5	7	8			11
1	2	3						9	10	11			6	4		5	7	8			12
1		3						9	10	11		2	6	4		5	7	8			13
1		3						9	10	11		2	6	4		5	7	8			14
1		3			6			9	10	11		2	4			5	7	8			15
1		3			6			9	10	11		2	4			5	7	8			16
1		3			6			9	10	11		2	4			5	7	8			17
1		3			6			9	10	11		2	4			5	7	8			18
1		3			6			9	10	11		2	4			5	7	8			19
1		3			6			9	10	11		2	4			5	7	8			20
1		3			6			9	10	11		2	4			5	7	8			21
1		3			6	7			10	11			2	4		5		8	9		22
1		3			6	7			10	11			2	4		5		8	9		23
1		3			6	7			10	11			2	4		5		8	9		24
	4	3			6	7	10	9		11	1	2				5		8			25
	4	3			6	7	10	9	11		1	2				5		8			26
	4	3			6	7	10	9	11		1		2			5		8			27
	4	3			6	7	10	9		11	1		2			5		8			28
	4	3			6	7		9	10	11	1		2			5		8			29
	4	3			6	7		9	10	11	1		2			5		8			30
		3			6	7	10	9	11		1		2		4	5		8			31
		3			6	7		9	10		1	2	4			5		8		11	32
		3			6	7		9	10		1	2	4			5		8		11	33
		3			6	7	10	9			1	2	4			5		8		11	34
		3			6	7	10	9			1	2	4			5		8		11	35
		3			6	7	10	9			1	2	4			5		8		11	36
		3			6	7	10	9			1	2	4			5		8		11	37
	4	3				7	10	9		11	1	2	6			5		8			38
	4	3				7	10	9		11	1	2	6			5		8			39
	4	3				7	10	9		11	1	2	6			5		8			40
		3				7	4	9	10	11	1	2	6			5		8			41
	4	3			6	7	10	9		11	1	2				5		8			42
24	16	37	4	1	35	29	15	39	32	33	18	27	34	13	1	41	13	41	3	6	
						7	1	26	11	8		1				1	2	10	1	1	

1928-29

1	Aug	25	(a)	Bristol C	D 2-2	Robson 2	16,083
2		27	(h)	Barnsley	W 2-1	Robson, Bestall	12,967
3	Sep	1	(h)	Nottingham F	D 2-2	Priestley, Robson	12,330
4		8	(a)	West Brom A	L 0-1		13,888
5		15	(h)	Clapton O	W 6-1	Coglin 4, Robson 2	10,280
6		22	(a)	Stoke C	W 2-1	Robson, Prior	15,538
7		29	(h)	Hull C	L 0-1		17,048
8	Oct	6	(h)	Bradford	W 4-2	Robson 3, Cooper	11,360
9		13	(a)	Swansea T	L 1-2	Cooper	10,443
10		20	(a)	Tottenham H	L 1-2	Marshall	22,218
11		27	(h)	Reading	W 4-0	Bestall, Robson, Prior, Cooper	6,293
12	Nov	3	(a)	Preston NE	L 2-5	Bestall, Cooper	18,819
13		10	(h)	Port Vale	W 3-1	Robson 3	9,017
14		17	(a)	Oldham A	W 3-0	Coglin, Robson 2	9,396
15		24	(h)	Southampton	W 2-1	Robson, Hair	9,663
16	Dec	1	(a)	Wolves	D 2-2	Marshall, Bestall	12,545
17		8	(h)	Notts C	D 2-2	Robson 2	12,381
18		15	(a)	Millwall	L 1-4	Hair	12,576
19		22	(h)	Middlesbrough	L 1-4	Bestall	10,984
20		25	(h)	Blackpool	L 1-4	Robson	15,457
21		26	(a)	Blackpool	D 1-1	Powell (pen)	15,337
22		29	(h)	Bristol C	W 3-2	Robson 2, Prior	8,018
23	Jan	1	(a)	Barnsley	W 2-0	Cooper, Marshall	9,049
24		5	(a)	Nottingham F	W 1-0	Robson	7,361
25		19	(h)	West Brom A	W 3-1	Robson, Swaby, Coglin (pen)	9,276
26	Feb	2	(h)	Stoke C	W 2-1	Coglin 2	9,706
27		9	(a)	Hull C	W 3-2	Bestall, Robson, Marshall	10,453
28		23	(h)	Swansea T	W 4-1	Marshall, Robson 2, Coglin	9,422
29	Mar	2	(h)	Tottenham H	W 2-0	Robson 2	13,850
30		4	(a)	Clapton O	L 1-3	Robson	5,209
31		9	(a)	Reading	W 3-1	Bestall 2, Prior	9,620
32		16	(h)	Preston NE	W 1-0	Robson	13,268
33		23	(a)	Port Vale	W 3-0	Robson, Bestall, Coglin	13,085
34		29	(h)	Chelsea	W 1-0	Bestall	23,644
35		30	(h)	Oldham A	W 1-0	Coleman	13,915
36	Apr	1	(a)	Chelsea	L 2-3	Coleman, Wrack	25,079
37		6	(a)	Southampton	L 1-3	Coleman	17,057
38		13	(h)	Wolves	W 2-0	Bestall, Coglin	12,699
39		20	(a)	Notts C	W 2-1	Coleman 2	28,139
40		27	(h)	Millwall	W 3-0	Coleman 2, Wright	16,658
41		29	(a)	Bradford	L 0-1		12,143
42	May	4	(a)	Middlesbrough	L 0-3		36,503

FINAL LEAGUE POSITION: 2nd in Division Two

Appearances

Goals

FA Cup

3	Jan	12	(h)	West Brom A	D 1-1
R		16	(a)	West Brom A	L 0-2

Read	Calderwood	Jacobson	Priestley	Wrack	Powell	Prior	Bestall	Robson	Coglin	Marshall	Wilson CH	Swaby	Hair W	Cooper	Coleman	Wright N	Poskett	
1	2	3	4	5	6	7	8	9	10	11								1
1	2	3	4	5	6	7	8	9	10	11								2
1	2	3	4	5	6	7	8	9	10	11								3
1	2	3	4	5	6	7	8	9	10	11								4
1	2	3	4	5	6	7	8	9	10	11								5
1	2	3	4	5	6	7	8	9	10	11								6
1	2	3	4	5	6	7	8	9	10	11								7
1	2	3	4	5	6	7		9	10	11				8				8
1	2	3	4	5	6	7		9	10	11				8				9
1	2	3	4	5	6	7	8	9		11				10				10
1	2	3	4	5	6	7	8	9		11				10				11
1	2	3	4	5	6	7	8	9		11				10				12
1	2	3	4	5	6		8	9	10	11			7					13
1	2	3	4	5	6		8	9	10	11			7					14
1	2	3	4	5	6		8	9	10	11			7					15
1	2	3	4	5	6		8	9	10	11			7					16
1	2	3	4	5	6		8	9	10	11			7					17
1	2	3	4	5	6		8	9	10	11			7					18
1	2	3	4	5	6	7	8	9	10	11								19
1	2	3	4	5	6	7	8	9	10	11								20
1	2	3			6	7	8	9		11	4	5		10				21
1	2	3			6	7	8	9		11	4	5		10				22
1	2	3			6	7	8	9		11	4	5		10				23
1	2	3			6	7	8	9		11	4	5		10				24
1	2	3		5		7	8	9	10	11	4	6						25
1		3	4	5		7	8	9	10	6	2					11		26
1		3	4	5		7	8	9	10	11	2	6						27
1		3	4	5	6	7	8	9	10	11	2							28
1		3	4	5	6	7	8	9	10	11	2							29
1		3	4	5	6	7	8	9	10	11	2							30
1	2	3		5	6	7	8	9	10	11	4							31
1		3	4	5	6	7	8	9	10	11	2							32
1	6	3	4	5		7	8	9	10	11	2							33
1	6	3	4	5		7	8	9	10	11	2							34
1		3	4	5	6	7	8		10		2				9	11		35
1		3	4	5	6	7	8		10		2				9	11		36
1		3	4	5	6	7	8		10		2				9	11		37
1	2	3	4	5	6	7	8	9	10						11			38
1		3	4	5	6	7	8		10		2				9	11		39
1		3	4	5	6	7	8		10		2				9	11		40
1	6	3	4	5		7		9	10		2				8	11		41
	6	3	4	5		7	8		10		2				9	11	1	42
41	31	42	36	38	35	36	39	36	35	34	21	6	6	9	8	8	1	
			1	1	1	4	11	32	11	5		1	2	5	7	1		

1929-30

1	Aug	31	(a)	Sheffield U	W 3-2	Marshall, Bestall 2	22,683
2	Sep	4	(h)	Portsmouth	D 1-1	Robson	19,329
3		7	(h)	Newcastle U	W 4-0	Robson, Coglin (pen), Priestley, Swaby	22,390
4		11	(a)	Portsmouth	D 1-1	Robson	12,211
5		14	(a)	Blackburn R	L 1-4	Robson	18,187
6		21	(h)	Middlesbrough	L 0-3		15,863
7		24	(h)	Middlesbrough	W 4-2	Robson 2, Bestall, Marshall	14,989
8		28	(a)	Liverpool	L 0-2		41,960
9	Oct	5	(h)	West Ham U	D 2-2	Bestall, Coglin	15,542
10		12	(a)	Manchester U	W 5-2	Robson 2, Coglin, Bestall, Coleman	21,494
11		19	(a)	Arsenal	L 1-4	Robson	43,794
12		26	(h)	Aston Villa	L 0-2		20,225
13	Nov	2	(a)	Leeds U	L 0-6		24,013
14		9	(h)	Manchester C	D 2-2	Robson, Prior	14,311
15		16	(a)	Burnley	L 1-3	Marshall	11,660
16		23	(h)	Sunderland	L 0-1		10,640
17		30	(a)	Bolton W	W 3-2	Marshall 2, Robson	8,506
18	Dec	7	(h)	Everton	L 0-3		9,503
19		14	(a)	Derby C	L 4-5	Bestall, Carr (og), Wright, Robson	13,880
20		25	(h)	Leicester C	L 1-4	Barley	16,173
21		26	(a)	Leicester C	L 0-1		35,644
22		28	(h)	Sheffield U	W 4-1	Coglin 2 (2 pens), Robson 2	13,267
23	Jan	4	(a)	Newcastle U	L 1-3	Coleman	31,803
24		18	(h)	Blackburn R	W 5-3	Bestall, Prior, Coglin, Robson 2	11,773
25	Feb	1	(h)	Liverpool	W 3-2	Coglin 3	11,184
26		5	(h)	Sheffield W	L 0-5		12,514
27		8	(a)	West Ham U	L 0-2		15,034
28		15	(h)	Manchester U	D 2-2	Robson, Prior	9,337
29		22	(h)	Arsenal	D 1-1	Robson	17,151
30	Mar	5	(a)	Middlesbrough	W 5-1	Robson 2, Marshall, Coglin, Bestall	8,880
31		8	(h)	Leeds U	L 1-2	Coglin (pen)	16,951
32		15	(a)	Manchester C	L 1-3	Robson	26,462
33		22	(h)	Burnley	W 4-0	Coglin 2, Robson, Marshall	11,262
34		29	(a)	Sunderland	L 0-2		23,842
35	Apr	2	(a)	Aston Villa	L 1-4	Bestall	8,965
36		5	(h)	Bolton W	D 1-1	Robson	12,081
37		12	(a)	Everton	W 4-2	Robson 4	47,407
38		18	(h)	Birmingham	W 2-1	Cooper, Robson	19,884
39		19	(h)	Derby C	W 2-1	Robson, Marshall	14,829
40		22	(a)	Birmingham	W 2-0	Marshall, Robson	18,482
41		26	(a)	Sheffield W	L 0-1		22,524
42	May	3	(a)	Huddersfield T	W 1-0	Bestall	14,525

FINAL LEAGUE POSITION: 18th in Division One

Appearances

Goals

FA Cup

3	Jan	11	(a)	Brighton & HA	D 1-1	
R		14	(h)	Brighton & HA	L 0-1	

Read	Wilson CH	Jacobson	Priestley	Wrack	Powell	Prior	Bestall	Robson	Coglin	Marshall	Bateman	Calderwood	Hall	Swaby	Buck	Coleman	Barley	Cooper	Glover	Wright N	
1	2	3	4	5	6	7	8	9	10	11											1
1	2	3	4	5	6	7	8	9	10	11											2
1	2	3	4				8	9	10	11		6		5		7					3
1	2	3	4				8	9	10	11		6		5		7					4
1	2	3	4				8	9	10	11		6		5		7					5
1	2	3	4		6		8	9	10	11				5		7					6
1	2	3	4		6		8	9	10	11				5		7					7
1	2	3	4		6	7	8	9	10	11				5							8
1	2	3	4		6	7	8	9	10	11				5							9
1	2	3			6		8	9	10	11		4		5		7					10
1	2	3	4		6		8	9	10	11				5		7					11
1	2	3	4	5			8	9	10	11				6		7					12
1	2	3	4			7	8	9	10	11	6			5							13
1	2	3	4			7		9	10	11		6		5		8					14
1	2	3	4			7	8	9		11		6		5		10					15
1	2	3	4			7	8	9	10	11		6		5							16
1	2	3	4					9	10	11		6		5			7	8			17
1	2	3	4					9	10			6		5			7	8		11	18
1	2	3	4	6			8	9						5		10	7			11	19
1	2	3	4				8	9						5	6	10	7			11	20
1	2	3	4	5			8	9	10	11					6	7					21
1	2	3	4	5			8	9	10	11					6	7					22
1	2	3	4	5			8	9	10	11					6	7					23
1	2	3	4	5		7	8	9	10	11					6						24
1	2	3	4	5		7	8	9	10	11					6						25
1	2	3	4	5		7	8	9	10	11					6						26
1	2	3	4			7	8		10	11				5	6				9		27
1	2	3	4	5		7	8	9	10						6	11					28
1	2	3	4			7	8	9		11				5	6	10					29
1	2	3	4			7	8	9	10	11				5	6						30
1	2	3	4			7	8	9	10	11				5	6						31
1	2		4	5		7	8	9	10	11	3				6						32
1	2		4			7	8	9	10	11	3			5	6						33
1	2		4			7	8	9	10	11	3			5	6						34
1	2		4	5			8	9	10	11	3				6	7					35
1	2		4	5		7	8	9	10	11	3				6						36
1	2	3	5			7	8	9		11			4		6			10			37
1	2	3	5			7	8	9		11			4		6			10			38
1	2	3	5			7	8	9		11			4		6			10			39
1	2	3	5			7	8	9		11			4		6			10			40
1	2	3	5			7	8	9		11			4		6			10			41
1	2	3	5			7	8	9		11			4		6			10			42
42	42	37	41	14	8	26	39	41	32	38	6	9	6	24	23	18	4	8	1	3	
			1			3	10	30	13	9				1		2	1	1		1	

1 own-goal

1930-31

1	Aug	30	(h)	Chelsea	L 0-1		20,294
2	Sep	1	(a)	Huddersfield T	D 2-2	Marshall 2	11,690
3		6	(a)	Newcastle U	W 2-1	Robson 2	27,155
4		9	(h)	Aston Villa	L 1-2	Bestall	19,224
5		13	(h)	Sheffield W	L 2-3	Prior 2	17,310
6		15	(a)	Aston Villa	L 0-2		22,301
7		20	(a)	Derby C	L 0-1		13,207
8		27	(a)	Manchester U	W 2-0	Coleman, Fielding	14,695
9	Oct	4	(h)	West Ham U	W 4-0	Marshall, Coleman 2, Cooper	14,423
10		11	(a)	Bolton W	L 2-4	Coleman 2	14,979
11		18	(h)	Portsmouth	L 0-3		13,095
12		25	(a)	Manchester C	L 0-1		24,770
13	Nov	1	(h)	Leicester C	W 8-2	Coleman 4, Prior 2, Priestley, Fielding	9,868
14		8	(a)	Sunderland	L 2-3	Coleman 2	21,225
15		15	(h)	Blackburn R	W 2-0	Marshall, Bestall	9,715
16		22	(a)	Birmingham	L 1-4	Coleman	13,639
17		29	(h)	Leeds U	W 2-0	Bestall, Prior	6,783
18	Dec	13	(h)	Sheffield U	W 2-1	Bestall, Coleman	11,735
19		20	(a)	Blackpool	L 1-3	Priestley	11,427
20		25	(h)	Liverpool	D 0-0		18,564
21		26	(a)	Liverpool	D 1-1	Coleman	38,203
22		27	(a)	Chelsea	L 0-5		23,467
23	Jan	1	(a)	Middlesbrough	L 1-2	Glover	23,845
24		3	(h)	Newcastle U	D 2-2	Bestall (pen), Prior	10,565
25		17	(a)	Sheffield W	L 1-4	Glover	19,729
26		28	(a)	Arsenal	L 1-9	Prior	15,751
27		31	(h)	Manchester U	W 2-1	Bestall, Cooper	9,305
28	Feb	3	(h)	Derby C	W 5-3	Bestall, Coleman 2, Marshall, Prior	8,308
29		7	(a)	West Ham U	W 4-3	Coleman 3, Marshall	15,559
30		17	(h)	Bolton W	W 4-1	Coleman 2, Cooper, Prior	5,741
31		21	(a)	Portsmouth	L 3-4	Cooper, Marshall, Coleman (pen)	12,522
32		28	(h)	Manchester C	L 3-5	Coleman, Marshall, Bestall	12,611
33	Mar	7	(a)	Leicester C	W 1-0	Coleman	12,163
34		21	(a)	Blackburn R	L 2-5	Coleman 2	8,890
35		24	(h)	Sunderland	W 2-1	Marshall, Coleman	9,396
36		28	(h)	Birmingham	W 4-1	Coleman 3, Prior	10,994
37	Apr	3	(h)	Middlesbrough	W 4-1	Cooper, Coleman 2, Prior	19,821
38		4	(a)	Leeds U	D 0-0		14,951
39		11	(h)	Arsenal	L 0-1		22,394
40		18	(a)	Sheffield U	L 1-2	Cooper	9,103
41		25	(h)	Blackpool	W 6-2	Coleman 3, Craven, Prior, Marshall	8,042
42	May	2	(h)	Huddersfield T	W 2-1	Bestall 2	16,583

FINAL LEAGUE POSITION: 13th in Division One

Appearances

Goals

FA Cup

3	Jan	10	(a)	Scarborough	W 2-1
4		24	(h)	Manchester U	W 1-0
5	Feb	14	(a)	Everton	L 3-5

Read	Wilson CH	Jacobson	Hall	Priestley	Buck	Prior	Bestall	Robson	Cooper	Marshall	Poskett	Bell WT	Bateman	Wrack	Swaby	Coleman	Fielding	Craven	Ponting	Barley	Glover	Coglin	
1	2	3	4	5	6	7	8	9	10	11													1
1	2	3	4	5	6		8	9		11						7						10	2
1	2	3	4	5	6		8	9		11						7						10	3
1	2	3	4	5	6		8	9		11						7						10	4
1	2	3	4	5	6	7	8			11						9		10					5
1	2		4		6	7	8			11			3	5		9		10					6
1	2	3	4	5	6	7	8			11						9		10					7
1	2	3	4	5	6		8		10	11						9	7						8
1	2	3	4	5	6		8		10	11						9	7						9
1	2	3	4	5	6		8		10	11						9	7						10
1	2	3	4	5	6		8		10	11						9	7						11
1	2	3	4	5	6	7	8			10						9	11						12
1	2	3	4	5	6	7	8			10						9	11						13
1	2	3	4	5	6	7	8			10						9	11						14
1	2	3	4	5	6	7	8			10						9	11						15
1	2	3	4	5	6	7	8			10						9	11						16
1	2	3		4	6	7	8			10					5	9	11						17
1	2	3		4	6		8			10					5	9	11	7					18
1	2	3		4	6		8			10					5	9	11	7					19
1	2	3		4	6	7	8			10					5	9	11						20
1	2	3	4		6		8			10					5	9	11		7				21
1	2	3	4		6		8		10	9					5		11		7				22
	4	3			6		8			10	1	2			5		11			7	9		23
1	4	3			6	7	8		10			2			5		11				9		24
1	4	3			6	7	8			11		2			5	10					9		25
1				4	6	7	8			11		2	3		5	9						10	26
1	2	3	4	5	6	7	8		10	11						9							27
1	2	3	4	5	6	7	8		10	11						9							28
1	2	3	4	5	6	7	8		10	11						9							29
1	2	3	4	5	6	7	8		10	11						9							30
1	2	3	4	5	6	7	8		10	11						9							31
1	2	3	4	5	6	7	8		10	11						9							32
1	2	3	4	5	6	7	8		10	11						9							33
1	2	3	4	5	6	7	8			11						9		10					34
1		3	4	5	6	7	8		10	11		2				9							35
1	2	3	4	5	6	7	8		10	11						9							36
1	2	3	4	5	6	7	8		10	11						9							37
1	2	3	4	5	6	7	8		10	11						9							38
1	2	3	4	5	6	7	8		10	11						9							39
1	2	3	4	5	6	7	8		10	11						9							40
1	2	3	4	5		7	8			11					6	9		10					41
1	2	3	4	5	6	7	8			11						9		10					42
41	40	40	34	36	41	30	42	4	20	41	1	5	2	1	11	38	17	8	2	1	3	4	
				2		12	10	2	6	10						35	2	1			2		

1931-32

1	Aug	29	(a)	Huddersfield T	D	1-1	Coleman	13,668
2		31	(a)	Sheffield W	L	1-4	Chalmers	16,734
3	Sep	5	(h)	Newcastle U	L	1-2	Fairhurst (og)	12,248
4		9	(a)	Bolton W	L	3-5	Marshall, Coleman 2	9,700
5		12	(a)	Aston Villa	L	0-7		18,753
6		15	(h)	Bolton W	W	2-0	Glover, Piror	10,857
7		19	(h)	Leicester C	W	3-0	Glover 2, Marshall	13,156
8		26	(a)	Liverpool	L	0-4		26,153
9	Oct	3	(h)	Arsenal	W	3-1	Marshall, Glover 2	17,840
10		10	(h)	Chelsea	L	1-2	Glover	16,050
11		17	(a)	Birmingham	L	1-2	Glover	16,313
12		24	(h)	Sheffield U	L	0-2		9,063
13		31	(a)	Blackburn R	L	2-3	Coleman 2	8,102
14	Nov	7	(h)	Portsmouth	W	3-1	Prior, Fielding, Coleman	7,247
15		14	(a)	Manchester C	L	1-4	Fielding	20,352
16		21	(h)	Everton	L	1-2	Prior	16,508
17		28	(a)	Blackpool	L	3-4	Priestley (pen), Coleman, Glover	12,700
18	Dec	5	(h)	Sunderland	L	1-3	Priestley (pen)	8,962
19		12	(a)	Derby C	D	3-3	Fielding 3	10,695
20		19	(h)	West Brom A	D	0-0		9,225
21		25	(h)	West Ham U	W	2-1	Bestall, Glover	15,132
22		26	(a)	West Ham U	L	1-3	Glover	23,859
23	Jan	2	(h)	Huddersfield T	L	1-4	Coleman	7,921
24		16	(a)	Newcastle U	L	0-2		27,837
25		30	(a)	Leicester C	W	2-1	Marshall, Coleman	13,907
26	Feb	2	(h)	Aston Villa	D	2-2	Bestall, Coleman	11,132
27		6	(h)	Liverpool	W	5-1	Buck, Coleman 3, Priestley (pen)	13,124
28		17	(a)	Arsenal	L	0-4		20,980
29		20	(a)	Chelsea	L	1-4	Betmead	24,422
30		27	(h)	Birmingham	D	1-1	Cooper	9,454
31	Mar	5	(a)	Sheffield U	L	1-2	Betmead	19,284
32		12	(h)	Blackburn R	W	4-3	Holmes, Marshall, Hall, Glover	10,531
33		19	(a)	Portsmouth	L	0-2		13,961
34		25	(h)	Middlesbrough	W	2-0	Holmes, Dyson	19,005
35		26	(h)	Manchester C	W	2-1	Marshall, Glover	11,481
36		28	(a)	Middlesbrough	L	0-4		8,373
37	Apr	2	(a)	Everton	L	2-4	Craven, Dyson	28,456
38		9	(h)	Blackpool	D	0-0		8,651
39		16	(a)	Sunderland	L	0-2		17,614
40		23	(h)	Derby C	W	2-1	Dyson 2	7,386
41		30	(a)	West Brom A	W	6-5	Holmes 3, Dyson 3	13,101
42	May	7	(h)	Sheffield W	W	3-1	Holmes 2, Dyson	16,049

FINAL LEAGUE POSITION: 21st in Division One

Appearances

Goals

FA Cup

3	Jan	9	(h)	Exeter C	W	4-1
4		23	(h)	Birmingham	W	2-1
5	Feb	13	(a)	Liverpool	L	0-1

Read	Wilson CH	Jacobson	Hall	Priestley	Buck	Prior	Bestall	Chalmers	Coleman	Marshall	Bell	Bateman	Dow	Gardner T	Betmead	Seddon	Donaldson	Craven	Fielding	Dyson	Ponting	Glover	Holmes	Cooper	Wilson C	Moralee	Dodds	Swaby	
1	2	3	4	5	6	7	8	10	9	11																			1
1	2	3	4	5	6	7	8	10	9	11																			2
1	2	3	4		6	7	8	10	9	11																		5	3
1	2	3			6			10	9	11			4				7	8										5	4
1	2	3	5		6		8	10	9	11			4					7											5
1	2	3			6	7	8			11				4	5							9		10					6
1	2	3			6	7	8			11				4	5							9		10					7
1	2	3			6	7	8			11				4	5							9		10					8
1	2	3		5	6	7	8			11				4								9		10					9
1		3		5	6	7	8			11	2			4								9		10					10
1	2	3		5	6	7			8	11				4								9		10					11
1	2	3	4	5	6		8		7	11								10				9							12
1	2	3	6	5		7	8		9					4				10	11										13
1	2	3	6	5		7			9					4				8	11					10					14
1	2	3	6	5		7	8		9					4					11					10					15
1	2	3		4	6	7	8		9						5				11					10					16
1	2	3		4	6	7			9	10					5				11			8							17
1	2	3		4	6	7			9	10					5				11			8							18
1	2	3			6	7	8		9	10				4	5				11										19
1	2	3			6	7	8		9	10				4	5				11										20
1	2	3			6	7	8			10				4	5				11			9							21
1	2	3		4	6		8			11					5				7			9		10					22
1	2	3				7	8		10	6				4	5				11			9							23
1	2	3	4	5	6	7	8		9	11														10					24
1			4	5	6		8		9	11	2	3							7					10					25
1			4	5	6		8		9	11	2	3							7					10					26
1	2	3	4	5	6		8		9	11									7					10					27
1		3	4	5	6		8		9	11	2							10	7										28
1	2	3	4		6		8		9	11					5			10	7										29
1	2	3	4	5	6		8		9	11									7					10					30
1		3		4	6	7	8				2				5				11			9		10					31
1		3	4	5			8			11	2								7			9	10		6				32
1	2	3		4	6		8			11					5					7			9		10				33
1	2	3		4			8			11					5					7		9	10		6				34
1	2	3	4	5			8			11										7		9	10		6				35
1	2	3		5	4		8			11										7		9	10		6				36
1	2	3	4				10									5		8		7		9			6		11		37
1	2	3	4	5		7	10											8				9			6		11		38
1	2	3					8	10							4	5					7	9			6		11		39
1	2	3					8								4	5				7			9		6	10	11		40
1		3	4				8			11		2				5				7			9		6	10			41
1	2	3	4				8			11						5				7			9		6	10			42
42	35	40	21	26	29	22	37	6	23	33	6	3	2	13	17	5	1	9	19	8	1	20	8	16	11	3	4	2	
			1	3	1	3	2	1	13	6					2			1	5	8		12	7	1					

1 own-goal

1932-33

1	Aug	27	(h)	Nottingham F	D	1-1	Holmes	13,423
2		31	(a)	Plymouth A	L	0-4		22,760
3	Sep	3	(a)	Charlton A	W	3-2	Craven, Holmes, Dyson (pen)	8,416
4		6	(h)	Plymouth A	L	2-3	Craven, Dyson	9,140
5		10	(h)	Stoke C	L	0-1		9,173
6		17	(a)	Manchester U	D	1-1	Fielding	17,662
7		24	(h)	Tottenham H	W	3-2	Dyson, Glover 2	9,597
8	Oct	1	(a)	Lincoln C	L	3-6	Glover, Wilson, Dodsworth	14,102
9		8	(a)	Oldham A	W	1-0	Glover	4,208
10		15	(h)	Preston NE	D	5-5	Glover 4, Dyson	8,166
11		22	(h)	Bury	W	1-0	Glover	8,187
12		29	(a)	Southampton	L	0-3		10,081
13	Nov	5	(h)	Millwall	D	1-1	Craven	7,996
14		12	(a)	West Ham U	L	2-5	Dyson, Wilson (pen)	11,481
15		19	(h)	Bradford C	D	1-1	Fielding	6,594
16		26	(a)	Swansea T	L	0-1		9,304
17	Dec	3	(h)	Notts C	D	1-1	Jennings	6,065
18		10	(a)	Chesterfield	W	2-1	Jennings, Fielding	8,138
19		17	(h)	Fulham	W	1-0	Jennings	6,006
20		24	(a)	Port Vale	L	2-4	Armitage (og), Bestall	8,342
21		26	(h)	Burnley	L	1-2	Bestall	11,186
22		27	(a)	Burnley	L	0-2		13,602
23		31	(a)	Nottingham F	L	2-3	Glover, Craven	9,641
24	Jan	7	(h)	Charlton A	D	5-5	Glover 2, Craven, Fielding, Dyson	5,697
25		21	(a)	Stoke C	L	0-2		8,724
26		31	(h)	Manchester U	D	1-1	Jennings	4,020
27	Feb	4	(a)	Tottenham H	L	3-4	Craven, Glover, Jennings	33,395
28		11	(h)	Lincoln C	D	3-3	Jennings 3	11,088
29		18	(h)	Oldham A	W	5-1	Craven 3, Bestall, Jennings	5,026
30	Mar	2	(a)	Preston NE	L	2-4	Craven, Jennings (pen)	7,449
31		4	(a)	Bury	L	1-4	Robinson (og)	9,039
32		11	(h)	Southampton	D	2-2	Craven, Seddon	7,257
33		18	(a)	Millwall	W	1-0	Glover	17,355
34		25	(h)	West Ham U	W	2-1	Glover 2	8,546
35	Apr	1	(a)	Bradford C	D	2-2	Glover, Jennings	10,272
36		8	(h)	Swansea	W	2-1	Bestall, Jennings	7,809
37		14	(h)	Bradford	W	5-1	Craven 2, Jennings, Betmead, Glover	16,836
38		15	(a)	Notts C	W	3-1	Bestall, Craven, Jennings (pen)	9,230
39		17	(a)	Bradford	D	1-1	Glover	8,961
40		22	(h)	Chesterfield	D	1-1	Craven	7,351
41		29	(a)	Fulham	W	1-0	Glover	17,467
42	May	6	(h)	Port Vale	W	6-1	Glover 2, Craven, Fielding, Betmead, Hall	6,349

FINAL LEAGUE POSITION: 13th in Division Two

Appearances
Goals

FA Cup

3	Jan	14	(h)	Portsmouth	W	3-2
4		28	(a)	Bolton W	L	1-2

Read	Bateman	Jacobson	Hall	Seddon	Wilson C	Dyson	Bestall	Holmes	Moralee	Fielding	Tweedy	Wilson CH	Wright J	Kelly	Annables	Betmead	Hodgson	Buck	Wattam	Jennings	Craven	Ponting	Dodds	Dodsworth	Glover	
1	2	3	4	5	6	7	8	9	10	11																1
1	2	3		5	6	7	8	9	10	11							4									2
1	2	3		5	6	7	8	9		11							4				10					3
1	2	3		5	6	7	8									4					10	9	11			4
1		3			6	7	8					2				5					10	9	11	4		5
1		3			10	7	8			11		2				5		6						4	9	6
1		3			10	7	8			11		2				5		6						4	9	7
1	2	3		5	10	7	8											6		11				4	9	8
1		3		4	10	7	8					2				5		6		11					9	9
1		3		4	10	7	8					2				5		6		11					9	10
1		3	4			7	8	10					2			5		6		11					9	11
1		3	4			7	8	10					2			5		6		11					9	12
1		3	4			7	10						2			5		6		11	8				9	13
1		3	4	5	10	7				11			2					6			8				9	14
		3	4		10	7		9		11	1		2				5	6			8					15
		3	4	6			8			11	1		2				5			7	10				9	16
		3	4	5			8			11	1		2					6		7	10				9	17
		3	4	5			8			11	1		2					6		7	10				9	18
		3	4	5			8			11	1		2					6		7	10				9	19
		3	4		10		8	9		11	1		2				5	6		7						20
		3	4		5		8	9		11	1		2					6		7	10					21
		3	4			7	8			11	1		2			5			6		10				9	22
		3	4			7	8				1		2			5		6		11	10				9	23
1		3	4			7	8			11			2			5		6			10				9	24
1		3	4			7	8			11			2			5		6			10				9	25
1		3	4				8			11			2			5		6		7	10				9	26
1		3	4	6			8			11			2			5				7	10				9	27
1		3	4	6			8			11			2			5				7	10				9	28
1		3	4				8			11			2			5			6	7	10				9	29
1	3		4				8			11			2			5			6	7	10				9	30
1	3		4		10		8	9		11			2			5		6		7						31
1				4	3	7	8			6			2			5				11	10	9				32
1		3	4				8			11				2		5		6		7	10				9	33
1		3	4				8			11				2		5		6		7	10				9	34
1		3	4				8			11				2		5		6		7	10				9	35
1		3	4				8			11				2		5		6		7	10				9	36
1		3	4				8			11				2		5		6		7	10				9	37
1		3	4				8			11				2		5		6		7	10				9	38
1			4				8			11				2	3	5		6		7	10				9	39
1			4				8			11				2	3	5		6		7	10				9	40
1			4			7	8			11		2		3		5		6			10				9	41
1			4			7	8			11		2		3		5		6			10				9	42
33	7	35	32	15	16	22	40	9	2	33	9	7	22	10	2	30	5	30	3	28	31	3	2	4	32	
			1	1	2	6	5	2		5						2				14	16			1	22	

2 own-goals

1933-34

1	Aug	24	(h)	Burnley	W 1-0	Jennings	10,501
2		29	(h)	Bolton W	L 2-3	Glover, Jennings	9,961
3	Sep	2	(a)	Oldham A	W 5-1	Glover 3, Bestall, Craven	7,449
4		4	(a)	Bolton W	W 4-0	Glover, Jennings, Bestall, Dodds	9,370
5		9	(h)	Preston NE	W 3-0	Glover 2, Bestall	13,025
6		16	(a)	Bradford	L 1-2	Glover	15,672
7		23	(h)	Port Vale	L 1-2	Craven	10,503
8		30	(h)	Nottingham F	W 2-1	Dyson, Glover	9,103
9	Oct	7	(a)	West Ham U	L 1-3	Glover	23,481
10		14	(h)	Plymouth A	W 5-1	Glover 2, Jennings, Dyson, Bestall	8,394
11		21	(a)	Notts C	W 2-1	Glover 2	16,890
12		28	(h)	Swansea T	W 3-1	Jennings, Bestall, Craven	6,378
13	Nov	4	(a)	Millwall	W 1-0	Ponting	10,931
14		11	(h)	Lincoln C	W 3-0	Glover, Craven 2	11,791
15		18	(a)	Bury	W 3-1	Glover 2, Jennings	8,693
16		25	(h)	Hull C	W 4-1	Glover 2, Craven, Holmes	16,631
17	Dec	2	(a)	Fulham	L 0-1		14,650
18		9	(h)	Southampton	W 3-1	Glover, Bestall, Jennings	8,604
19		16	(a)	Blackpool	W 4-3	Jennings, Holmes, Bestall 2	15,332
20		23	(h)	Bradford C	L 1-4	Glover	10,353
21		25	(a)	Manchester U	W 3-1	Glover 3	29,443
22		26	(h)	Manchester U	W 7-3	Holmes, Glover 2, Jennings, Bestall 2, Craven	15,801
23		30	(a)	Burnley	L 0-2		9,598
24	Jan	6	(h)	Oldham A	W 2-1	Glover, Craven	9,071
25		20	(a)	Preston NE	W 2-1	Glover 2	24,312
26		30	(h)	Bradford	W 3-2	Glover 2, Craven	7,486
27	Feb	5	(a)	Port Vale	W 1-0	Craven	12,662
28		10	(a)	Nottingham F	L 2-4	Holmes, Glover	12,230
29		17	(h)	West Ham U	D 1-1	Glover	10,627
30		24	(a)	Plymouth A	W 2-0	Glover, Craven	18,301
31	Mar	3	(h)	Notts C	D 2-2	Jennings, Kelly (pen)	10,918
32		10	(a)	Swansea T	D 1-1	Bestall	10,029
33		17	(h)	Millwall	W 5-2	Craven, Glover 3, Kelly (pen)	8,101
34		24	(a)	Lincoln C	D 3-3	Craven 2, Kelly (pen)	8,723
35		30	(h)	Brentford	D 2-2	Craven, Glover	23,233
36		31	(h)	Bury	W 2-0	Dyson, Glover	10,975
37	Apr	2	(a)	Brentford	W 2-1	Moralee, Glover	26,934
38		7	(a)	Hull C	W 1-0	Ponting	20,077
39		14	(h)	Fulham	W 3-1	Craven, Glover, Lewis	9,340
40		21	(a)	Southampton	L 2-4	Jennings 2	8,843
41		28	(h)	Blackpool	W 7-0	Holmes 3, Craven 2, Moralee, Jennings	7,090
42	May	5	(a)	Bradford C	L 1-2	Glover	8,571

FINAL LEAGUE POSITION: 1st in Division Two

Appearances
Goals

FA Cup

3	Jan	13	(h)	Clapton O	W 1-0
4		27	(a)	Portsmouth	L 0-2

Read	Kelly	Jacobson	Hall	Betmead	Buck	Jennings	Bestall	Glover	Craven	Dodds	Tweedy	Waring	Dyson	Lewis	Ponting	Holmes	Moralee	
1	2	3	4	5	6	7	8	9	10	11								1
1	2	3	4	5	6	7	8	9	10	11								2
1	2	3	4	5	6	7	8	9	10	11								3
1	2	3	4	5	6	7	8	9	10	11								4
1	2	3	4	5	6	7	8	9	10	11								5
1	2	3	4	5	6	7	8	9	10	11								6
1	2	3	4	5	6	7	8	9	10	11								7
1	2	3	4	5	6	11	8	9	10				7					8
1	2	3	4	5	6	11	8	9	10				7					9
1	2	3	4	5	6	11	8	9	10				7					10
1	2	3	4	5	6	11	8	9	10				7					11
1	2	3	4	5	6	11	8	9	10				7					12
	2	3	4	5	6	11	8		10		1		7		9			13
	2	3	4	5	6	11	8	9	10	7	1							14
	2	3	4	5	6	7	8	9	10		1					11		15
	2	3	4	5	6	7	8	9	10		1					11		16
	2	3	4	5	6	7	8	9	10		1					11		17
	2	3	4	5	6	7	8	9	10		1					11		18
	2	3	4	5	6	7	8	9	10		1					11		19
	2	3	4	5	6	7	8	9	10		1					11		20
	2	3	4	5	6	7	8	9	10		1					11		21
	2	3	4	5	6	7	8	9	10		1					11		22
	2	3	4	5	6	7	8	9	10		1					11		23
	2	3	4	5	6	7	8	9	10		1					11		24
1	2	3	4	5	6	7	8	9	10							11		25
1	2	3	4	5	6	7	8	9	10							11		26
1	2	3	4	5	6	7	8	9	10							11		27
1	2	3	4	5	6	7	8	9	10							11		28
1	2	3	4	5	6	7	8	9	10							11		29
1	2	3	4	5	6	11	8	9	10				7					30
1	2	3	4	5	6	11	8	9	10				7					31
1	2	3	4	5	6	11	8	9	10			7						32
1	2	3	4	5	6	11	8	9	10			7						33
1	2	3	4	5	6	11	8	9	10					7				34
1	2	3	4	5	6	11	8	9	10					7				35
1	2	3	4	5	6	11	8	9	10				7					36
1	2	3	4	5	6		8	9	10				7				11	37
1	2	3	4	5	6	11	8		10				7		9			38
1	2	3	4	5	6	11	8	9	10					7				39
1	2	3	4	5	6	11	8	9	10					7				40
1	2	3	4	5	6	7	8		10							9	11	41
1	2	3	4	5	6	11	8	9	10					7				42
30	42	42	42	42	42	41	42	39	42	8	12	2	11	5	2	16	2	
	3					13	11	42	18	1			3	1	2	7	2	

1934-35

1	Aug	25	(a)	Preston NE	L 0-1		26,805
2		28	(h)	Sunderland	D 0-0		15,604
3	Sep	1	(h)	Portsmouth	W 3-0	Glover 2, Bestall	14,552
4		5	(a)	Sunderland	L 0-3		27,753
5		8	(h)	Everton	D 0-0		16,343
6		15	(a)	Huddersfield T	W 5-1	Jennings, Glover 4	10,011
7		22	(h)	Wolves	W 2-1	Burley, Bestall	9,594
8		29	(a)	Chelsea	L 0-2		25,373
9	Oct	6	(h)	Aston Villa	W 5-1	Craven 3, Burley, Glover	17,732
10		13	(a)	Derby C	W 4-1	Bestall, Glover 3	21,139
11		20	(a)	Liverpool	D 1-1	Dyson	28,047
12		27	(h)	Leeds U	W 3-2	Glover 2, Craven	10,940
13	Nov	3	(a)	Blackburn R	D 2-2	Glover, Craven	13,308
14		10	(h)	Arsenal	D 2-2	Glover (pen), Burley	26,288
15		17	(a)	Birmingham	L 2-3	Craven 2	18,604
16		24	(h)	Stoke C	W 3-1	Glover 2, Dyson	14,656
17	Dec	1	(a)	Manchester C	L 0-1		31,642
18		8	(h)	Middlesbrough	D 2-2	Dyson, Betmead	12,174
19		15	(a)	West Brom A	L 2-4	Glover 2	17,262
20		22	(h)	Sheffield W	W 3-1	Craven, Dyson, Glover	10,438
21		25	(h)	Tottenham H	W 3-0	Craven, Buck, Glover	19,706
22		26	(a)	Tottenham H	L 1-2	Glover	45,512
23		29	(h)	Preston NE	W 3-1	Jennings, Moralee, Glover	10,007
24	Jan	5	(a)	Portsmouth	L 0-1		18,821
25		19	(a)	Everton	L 1-3	Craven	24,493
26	Feb	2	(a)	Wolves	W 3-0	Burley, Craven, Glover	21,383
27		9	(h)	Chelsea	W 3-1	Bestall, Holmes, Glover (pen)	12,442
28		16	(a)	Aston Villa	L 2-3	Glover 2	32,020
29		23	(h)	Derby C	L 1-3	Dyson	12,742
30	Mar	2	(h)	Liverpool	W 3-2	Burley, Glover 2	10,691
31		9	(a)	Leeds U	L 1-3	Glover (pen)	15,458
32		16	(h)	Blackburn R	L 1-2	Glover	10,778
33		23	(a)	Arsenal	D 1-1	Glover	33,591
34		30	(h)	Birmingham	W 4-3	Glover 2, Dyson 2	9,837
35	Apr	2	(h)	Huddersfield T	D 1-1	Glover	8,073
36		6	(a)	Stoke C	D 0-0		13,442
37		13	(h)	Manchester C	D 1-1	Moralee	13,394
38		19	(h)	Leicester C	W 3-1	Craven 2, Dyson	19,531
39		20	(a)	Middlesbrough	W 2-0	Lewis, Craven	12,124
40		22	(a)	Leicester C	D 2-2	Craven 2	25,195
41	May	1	(h)	West Brom A	W 3-0	Craven 2, Bestall	12,304
42		4	(a)	Sheffield W	L 1-0		21,046

FINAL LEAGUE POSITION: 5th in Division One

Appearances

Goals

FA Cup

3	Jan	12	(a)	Everton	L 3-6	

Tweedy	Kelly	Jacobson	Hall	Betmead	Buck	Lewis	Bestall	Glover	Craven	Jennings	Vincent	Wright J	Hodgson	Dyson	Moralee	Burley Ben	Holmes	Annables	
1	2	3	4	5	6	7	8	9	10	11									1
1	2	3	4		6	7	8	9	10	11			5						2
1	2	3	4		6		8	9	10	7			5			11			3
1	2	3	4		6		8	9	10	7			5			11			4
1	2	3	4	5	6		8	9	10	7						11			5
1	2	3	4	5	6		8	9	10	7						11			6
1	2	3	4	5	6		8	9	10	7						11			7
1	2	3	4	5	6		8	9	10	7						11			8
1	2	3	4	5	6		8	9	10					7		11			9
1	2	3	4	5	6		8	9	10					7		11			10
1	2	3	4	5	6		8	9	10					7		11			11
1	2	3	4	5	6		8	9	10					7		11			12
1	2	3	4	5	6		8	9	10					7		11			13
1	2	3	4	5	6		8	9	10					7		11			14
1	2	3	4	5	6		8	9	10					7		11			15
1	2	3	4	5	6		8	9	10					7		11			16
1	2	3	4	5	6		8	9	10					7		11			17
1	2	3	4	5	6		8	9	10	11				7					18
1	2	3	4	5	6		8	9	10					7		11			19
1	2		4	5	6		8	9	10			3		7		11			20
1	2		4	5	6		8	9	10			3		7		11			21
1	2		4	5	6		8	9	10	11		3		7					22
1	2		4		6		8	9		11		3	5	7	10				23
1	2		4		6		8	9	10	11		3	5	7					24
1	3		4	5	6		8	9	10	11	2			7					25
1	3		4	5	6			9	8		2			7	10	11			26
1	3		4	5	6		8	9	10		2			7			11		27
1	3		4	5	6		8	9	10		2			7			11		28
1	3		4	5	6		8	9	10		2			7	11				29
1	3		4	5	6		8	9	10		2			7		11			30
1	3		4		6		8	9	10		2		5	7		11			31
1	3		4	5	6		8	9	10		2			7		11			32
1	3		4		6		8	9	10	11	2		5	7					33
1			4		6		8	9	10	3	2		5	7			11		34
1			4		6		8	9	10	3	2		5	7			11		35
1			4		6		8	9	10		2		5	7	11			3	36
1			4		6		8	9	10		2		5	7	11			3	37
1			4		6		8	9	10		2		5	7	11			3	38
1			4		6	7	8	9	10		2		5		11			3	39
1		2	4		6	7	8	9	10	3			5		11				40
1		3	4		6	7	8	9	10		2		5		11				41
1		3	4		6	7	8	9	10		2		5		11				42
42	33	22	42	26	42	6	41	42	41	17	17	5	16	30	10	22	4	4	
				1	1	1	5	34	18	2				8	2	5	1		

1935-36

1	Aug	31	(a)	Blackburn R	L 0-1		14,035
2	Sep	3	(h)	Arsenal	W 1-0	Craven	25,978
3		7	(h)	Chelsea	L 1-3	Moralee	14,917
4		11	(a)	Arsenal	L 0-6		33,633
5		14	(a)	Liverpool	L 2-7	Craven, Dyson	24,180
6		21	(h)	Bolton W	W 3-1	Glover 2 (1 pen), Craven	12,768
7		28	(h)	Leeds U	L 0-1		11,236
8	Oct	5	(a)	West Brom A	L 1-4	Ponting	20,821
9		12	(h)	Sunderland	W 4-0	Glover 3, Craven	11,751
10		19	(a)	Huddersfield T	L 0-1		10,687
11		26	(h)	Middlesbrough	L 0-1		12,108
12	Nov	2	(a)	Aston Villa	W 6-2	Glover 4, Dyson, Craven	35,311
13		9	(h)	Wolves	W 2-1	Dyson, Glover	10,207
14		16	(a)	Sheffield W	L 0-3		19,376
15		23	(h)	Everton	L 0-4		10,247
16		30	(a)	Preston NE	L 0-1		17,103
17	Dec	7	(h)	Brentford	W 6-1	Glover 3 (1 pen), Baldry, Craven 2	5,276
18		14	(a)	Derby C	L 0-2		17,113
19		21	(h)	Portsmouth	L 1-2	Glover	7,772
20		25	(h)	Birmingham	W 1-0	Baldry	11,810
21		26	(a)	Birmingham	D 1-1	Baldry	28,978
22		28	(h)	Blackburn R	D 1-1	Lewis	8,068
23	Jan	1	(a)	Manchester C	W 3-0	Craven 2, Lewis	32,470
24		4	(a)	Chelsea	W 2-0	Lewis, Baldry	30,381
25		18	(h)	Liverpool	D 0-0		9,289
26		29	(a)	Bolton W	L 0-4		10,068
27	Feb	1	(a)	Leeds U	W 2-1	Glover, Baldry	24,212
28		8	(h)	West Brom A	W 4-2	Lewis, Baldry, Glover 2	11,122
29		19	(a)	Sunderland	L 1-3	Glover (pen)	12,108
30		22	(h)	Huddersfield T	D 1-1	Glover (pen)	10,994
31	Mar	4	(a)	Wolves	L 0-1		8,633
32		7	(h)	Preston NE	D 0-0		9,172
33		14	(a)	Middlesbrough	L 1-5	Tomlinson	14,174
34		24	(h)	Sheffield W	W 4-0	Bestall, Craven 2, Glover	7,887
35		28	(a)	Everton	L 0-4		24,720
36	Apr	4	(h)	Aston Villa	W 4-1	Callaghan (og), Glover 2 (1 pen), Baldry	10,413
37		10	(h)	Stoke C	W 3-0	Glover 2, Craven	19,575
38		11	(a)	Brentford	L 0-3		24,830
39		13	(a)	Stoke C	L 0-1		22,882
40		18	(h)	Derby C	W 4-1	Glover 3, Bestall	11,860
41		25	(a)	Portsmouth	L 2-3	Glover, Craven	8,918
42	May	2	(h)	Manchester C	W 3-1	Craven, Glover 2 (1 pen)	8,974

FINAL LEAGUE POSITION: 17th in Division One

Appearances
Goals

FA Cup

3	Jan	11	(a)	Hartlepools U	D 0-0
R		14	(h)	Hartlepools U	W 4-1
4		25	(a)	Port Vale	W 4-0
5	Feb	15	(h)	Manchester C	W 3-2
6		29	(h)	Middlesbrough	W 3-1
SF	Mar	21	(a*)	Arsenal	L 0-1

*Played at Leeds Road, Huddersfield.

Tweedy	Vincent	Kelly	Hall	Hodgson	Buck	Dyson	Bestall	Glover	Craven	Moralee	Betmead	Jennings	Baldry	Lewis	Ponting	Smailes	Tomlinson	Robertson A	Theaker	Crack	
1	2	3	4	5	6	7	8	9	10	11											1
1	2	3	4	5	6	7	8	9	10	11											2
1	2	3	4	5	6	7	8	9	10	11											3
1	2	3	4		6	7	8		10	11	5				9						4
1	2	3	4	5	6	7	8		10			11			9						5
1	2	3	4		6		8	9	10		5	7				11					6
1	2	3	4		6		8	9	10		5	7				11					7
1	2	3	4		6		8	9	10		5	7				11					8
1	2		4	3	6		8	9	10		5	7				11					9
1	2		4	3	6		8	9	10		5	7				11					10
1	2		4	3	6	8	11	9	10		5	7									11
1	2		4	3	6	7	8	9	10		5	11									12
1	2		4	3	6	7	8	9	10		5	11									13
1	2		4	3	6	7	8	9	10		5	11									14
1	2		4	3	6	7		9	8	10	5	11									15
1	2		4	3	6		11	9	8	10	5		7								16
1	2		4	3	6		8	9	10		5		7	11							17
1	2		4	3	6		8	9	10		5		7	11							18
1	2		4	3	6		8	9	10		5		7	11							19
1	2		4	3	6		8	9	10		5		7	11							20
1	2		4	3	6		8		10		5		7	11	9						21
1	2		4	3	6		8		10		5	9	7	11							22
1		2	4	3	6		8		10		5	7		11	9						23
1		2	4	3	6		8	9	10		5		7	11							24
1		2	4	3	6		8	9	10		5		7	11							25
1		2	4	3	6		8	9	10		5		7	11							26
1		2	4	3	6		8	9	10		5		7	11							27
1		2	4	3	6		8	9	10		5		7	11							28
1		2	4	3	6		8	9	10				7			11		5			29
1		2	4	3	6		8	9	10		5		7			11					30
1		2	4	3	6		8		10		5		7			11	9				31
		2	4	3	6		8		10		5		7			11	9		1		32
1		2	4	3	6		8		10		5		7			11	9				33
1	2	3	4	5	6	7	8	9	10	11											34
1	2	3	4	5	6	7	8	9	10	11											35
1		2	4	3	6		8	9	10		5		7	11							36
1		2	4	3	6		8	9	10	11	5		7								37
1		2	4	3	6		8	9	10	11	5		7								38
1		2	4	3	6	7	8	9	10		5			11							39
1		2	4	3	6	7	8	9	10		5			11							40
1		2	4	3	6	7	8	9	10		5			11							41
1		2	4	3	6		8	9	10		5			7						11	42
41	24	28	42	38	42	15	41	34	42	10	35	13	20	17	4	10	3	1	1	1	
						3	2	31	14	1			7	4	1		1				

1 own-goal

1936-37

1	Aug	29	(h)	Charlton A	L 0-1		12,696
2	Sep	3	(a)	Chelsea	L 2-3	Lewis, Glover	25,671
3		5	(a)	Bolton W	W 2-1	Craven, Glover	21,207
4		8	(h)	Chelsea	W 3-0	Craven, Lewis, Dyson	12,667
5		12	(a)	Liverpool	L 1-7	Craven	20,972
6		14	(a)	Stoke C	L 0-2		18,332
7		19	(h)	Leeds U	W 4-1	Lewis, Dyson, Glover 2	11,217
8		26	(a)	Birmingham	W 3-2	Lewis, Craven, Glover (pen)	21,985
9	Oct	3	(h)	Middlesbrough	W 5-1	Dyson, Glover 4	13,073
10		10	(a)	West Brom A	L 2-4	Lewis 2	24,447
11		17	(h)	Brentford	W 2-0	Lewis, Craven	11,858
12		24	(a)	Arsenal	D 0-0		51,202
13		31	(h)	Preston NE	W 6-4	Lewis 4, Dyson, Craven	12,341
14	Nov	7	(a)	Sheffield W	L 0-2		19,636
15		14	(h)	Manchester U	W 6-2	Lewis 3, Bestall, Glover, Craven	9,844
16		21	(a)	Derby C	L 1-3	Dyson	17,504
17		28	(h)	Wolves	D 1-1	Lewis	10,776
18	Dec	5	(a)	Sunderland	L 1-5	Glover	25,040
19		12	(h)	Huddersfield T	D 2-2	Glover (pen), Craven	8,580
20		19	(a)	Everton	L 0-3		21,616
21		25	(h)	Manchester C	W 5-3	Lewis 2, Glover 2, Craven	17,921
22		26	(a)	Charlton A	L 0-1		30,733
23		28	(a)	Manchester C	D 1-1	Lewis	16,146
24	Jan	2	(h)	Bolton W	W 3-1	Bestall, Dyson, Glover	9,719
25		9	(h)	Liverpool	W 2-1	Glover, Hobson (og)	10,015
26		23	(a)	Leeds U	L 0-2		11,752
27	Feb	2	(h)	Birmingham	D 1-1	Lewis	6,773
28		6	(a)	Middlesbrough	D 0-0		20,457
29		13	(h)	West Brom A	L 2-3	Glover, Swain	9,898
30		27	(h)	Arsenal	L 1-3	Craven	18,216
31	Mar	3	(a)	Brentford	W 3-2	Betmead, Glover 2	14,103
32		10	(a)	Preston NE	L 2-3	Glover, Buck	9,557
33		13	(h)	Sheffield W	W 5-1	Bestall, Craven, Glover, Crack 2	9,978
34		20	(a)	Manchester U	D 1-1	Crack	26,636
35		26	(h)	Portsmouth	W 1-0	Craven	18,141
36		27	(h)	Derby C	L 3-4	Craven 2, Crack	13,418
37		29	(a)	Portsmouth	L 1-2	Dyson	21,219
38	Apr	3	(a)	Wolves	L 2-5	Dyson, Hinchcliffe	16,413
39		12	(h)	Sunderland	W 6-0	Glover 5, Swain	8,306
40		17	(a)	Huddersfield T	W 3-0	Glover 2, Craven	6,189
41		24	(h)	Everton	W 1-0	Glover	9,773
42	May	1	(h)	Stoke C	L 1-3	Swain	6,585

FINAL LEAGUE POSITION: 11th in Division One

Appearances

Goals

FA Cup

3	Jan	16	(a)	Cardiff C	W 3-1
4		30	(h)	Walsall	W 5-1
5	Feb	20	(h)	Wolves	D 1-1
R		24	(a)	Wolves	L 2-6

Tweedy	Kelly	Hodgson	Hall	Betmead	Buck	Dyson	Bestall	Glover	Craven	Lewis	Robertson	Vincent	Wattam	Quigley	Hinchcliffe	Tomlinson	Swain	Crack	Robinson	
1	2	3	4	5	6	7	8	9	10	11										1
1	2	3	4	5		7	8	9	10	11			6							2
1	2	3	4	5		7	8	9	10	11			6							3
1	2	3	4	5		7	8	9	10	11			6							4
1	2	3	4	5		7	8	9	10	11			6							5
1		3	4	5		7	8	9	10	11	2		6							6
1	2	3	4	5		7	8	9	10	11			6							7
1	2	3	4	5		7	8	9	10	11			6							8
1	2	3	4	5		7	8	9	10	11			6							9
1	2	3	4	5		7	8	9	10	11			6							10
1	2	3	4	5		7	8		10	11			6			9				11
1	2	3	4	5		7	8	9	10	11			6							12
1	2	3	4	5		7	8	9	10	11			6							13
1	2	3	4	5		7	8	9					6		10		11			14
1	2	3	4	5		7	8	9	10	11			6							15
1	2	3	4	5		7	8	9	10	11			6							16
1	2	3	4	5		7	8	9	10	11			6							17
1	2	3		5	4	7	8	9	10	11			6							18
1	2	3		5	4	7		9	10	11			6		8					19
1	3	5			6	7	8	9	10	11		2	4							20
1	3		4	5	6	7	8	9	10	11		2								21
1	3	5	4	9	6	7	8		10	11		2								22
1	3		4	5	6	7	8	9	10	11		2								23
1	3		4	5	6	7	8	9	10	11		2								24
1	3		4	5	6	7	8	9	10	11		2								25
1	2	5	4		6	7	8	9	10	11									3	26
1	3	5	4		6	7		9	8	11		2			10					27
1	2	5	4		6	7	8	9	10	11									3	28
1	2		4	5	6	7	8	9	10								11		3	29
1	2	3	4	5	6	7	8	9	10	11										30
1	2	3	4	5	6	8		9	10					7				11		31
1	2	3	4	5	6	8		9	10					7				11		32
1		3	4	5	6		8	9	10			2		7				11		33
1		3	4	5	6		8	9	10			2		7				11		34
1	2	3	4	5	6	8		9	10					7				11		35
1	2	3		5	6	4	8	9	10	7								11		36
1	2	3	4	5	6	7		9	10	11					8					37
1	2	3	4	5	6	7		9	10						8			11		38
1	2	3	4	5	6	8		9	10					7			11			39
1	2	3	4	5	6	8		9	10					7			11			40
1	2	3	4	5	6	8		9	10					7			11			41
1	2	3	4	5	6	8		9	10					7			11			42
42	39	37	38	38	26	40	31	40	41	30	1	9	19	9	5	1	6	7	3	
				1	1	9	3	29	15	19					1		3	4		

1 own-goal

1937-38

1	Aug	28	(a)	Preston NE	L 1-4	Swain	22,098
2		31	(h)	Charlton A	D 1-1	Buck	13,347
3	Sep	4	(h)	Bolton W	L 0-1		10,642
4		6	(a)	Charlton A	D 0-0		16,471
5		11	(h)	Leeds U	D 1-1	Craven	9,328
6		15	(a)	Chelsea	L 0-1		15,617
7		18	(a)	Liverpool	L 1-2	Hinchcliffe	26,350
8		25	(h)	West Brom A	L 1-4	Quigley	9,410
9	Oct	2	(a)	Birmingham	D 2-2	Craven 2	25,644
10		9	(h)	Middlesbrough	W 2-1	Hinchcliffe, Craven	10,569
11		16	(a)	Huddersfield T	W 2-1	Craven, Coulter	15,408
12		23	(h)	Everton	W 2-1	Craven, Coulter	10,308
13		30	(a)	Wolves	D 1-1	Craven	28,032
14	Nov	6	(h)	Arsenal	W 2-1	Hinchcliffe, Coulter	20,244
15		13	(a)	Sunderland	D 2-2	Dyson, Coulter	23,171
16		20	(h)	Brentford	L 0-1		13,206
17		27	(a)	Manchester C	L 1-3	Coulter	27,526
18	Dec	4	(h)	Leicester C	W 2-1	Tomlinson, Lewis	8,246
19		11	(a)	Blackpool	D 2-2	Coulter, Craven	12,880
20		18	(h)	Derby C	D 0-0		8,649
21		25	(h)	Stoke C	L 1-5	Coulter	17,673
22		27	(a)	Stoke C	D 1-1	Craven	34,114
23	Jan	1	(h)	Preston NE	D 1-1	Lewis	9,427
24		15	(a)	Bolton W	L 1-3	Hinchcliffe	14,342
25		26	(a)	Leeds U	D 1-1	Craven	10,512
26		29	(h)	Liverpool	D 0-0		9,750
27	Feb	5	(a)	West Brom A	L 1-2	Hall	20,067
28		12	(h)	Birmingham	W 4-0	Coulter, H.Shaw, Beattie, Betmead	9,256
29		19	(a)	Middlesbrough	L 0-1		20,156
30		26	(h)	Huddersfield T	W 4-2	Craven, H.Shaw, Gallacher 2	12,085
31	Mar	5	(a)	Everton	L 2-3	Coulter, Gallacher	35,637
32		12	(h)	Wolves	W 1-0	Coulter	17,259
33		19	(a)	Arsenal	L 1-5	Coulter	40,701
34		29	(h)	Sunderland	L 0-2		11,393
35	Apr	2	(a)	Brentford	L 1-6	Craven	17,994
36		9	(h)	Manchester C	W 3-1	Glover 2, Quigley	11,413
37		15	(h)	Portsmouth	W 1-0	Glover	21,197
38		16	(a)	Leicester C	L 0-1		16,733
39		18	(a)	Portsmouth	L 0-3		30,616
40		23	(h)	Blackpool	W 1-0	Lewis	10,042
41		30	(a)	Derby C	W 2-1	Hodgson, Lewis	8,035
42	May	7	(h)	Chelsea	W 2-0	Beattie, Glover	14,601

FINAL LEAGUE POSITION: 20th in Division One

Appearances
Goals

FA Cup

3	Jan	12	(h)	Swindon T	D 1-1
R		16	(a)	Swindon T	L 1-2

Tweedy	Kelly	Hodgson	Hall	Betmead	Buck	Quigley	Hinchcliffe	Glover	Craven	Swain	Vincent	Dyson	Shaw J	Robertson AC	Theaker	Lewis	Bestall	Beattie	Tomlinson	Lumby	Gallacher	Coulter	Crack	Shaw H	
1	2	3	4	5	6	7	8	9	10	11															1
1	2	3	4	5	6	7			10	11		8							9						2
1		3	4	5	6				10	11	2	7					8		9						3
1	5	3	4		6		10		9		2	7					8						11		4
1	5	3	4	9	6		10		8		2	7											11		5
1		3	4	5	6		10		9		2	7					8						11		6
1		3	4	5	6		10		7	11	2						8		9						7
1		3	4	5	6	7	10		8	11	2								9						8
1		3	4	5	6		8		10		2	7					11		9						9
1	2	3	4	5	6		8		10			7					11		9						10
1		3	4	5	6		8		10		2	7							9			11			11
1		3	4	5	6		8		10		2					7			9			11			12
1		3	4	5	6		8		10		2					7			9			11			13
1		3	4	5	6		8		10		2	7							9			11			14
1		3	4	5	6		8		10		2	7							9			11			15
1		3	4	5	6		8		10		2	7							9			11			16
1		3	4	5	6		8		10		2					7			9			11			17
1		3	4	5	6		8		10		2					7			9			11			18
1		3	4	5	6		8		10		2						7		9			11			19
1		3	4	5	6		8		10		2						7		9			11			20
1		3	4	5	6		8		10		2						7			9		11			21
1	2			5	6	7			8	10	3	4								9		11			22
1		3		5	6	7			8		2	4				11				9		10			23
1		3	4	5	6	7	9		10		2						8					11			24
1		3		5	6		8		10		2		4								9	11		7	25
1		3		5	6		8		10		2		4								9	11		7	26
		3	8	5	6				10		2		4		1						9	11		7	27
		3	4	5	6				10		2				1			8			9	11		7	28
1		3	4	5	6				10		2							8			9	11		7	29
1	2	3	4	5	6				10									8			9	11		7	30
1	2	3	4	5	6				10									8			9	11		7	31
1		3	4	5	6				10		2							8			9	11		7	32
1		3	4	5	6				10		2							8			9	11		7	33
1		3	4	5	6				10		2							8			9	11		7	34
1		3	4	5	6				10		2							8			9	11		7	35
1		3	4	5	6	7		9	10		2							8					11		36
1		3	4	5	6	7		9	10		2							8					11		37
1		3	4		6	7		9	10		2			5		11	8								38
1		3	4		6				10		2			5		7		8			9		11		39
1		3	4		6	7		9	10		2			5		11		8							40
1		3	4	5	6	7		9	10		2					11		8							41
1		3	4	5	6	7		9	10		2					11		8							42
40	8	41	38	38	42	12	22	7	42	6	37	13	3	3	2	10	11	14	16	3	12	25	6	11	
		1	1	1	1	2	4	4	12	1		1				4		2	1		3	11		2	

1938-39

1	Aug	27	(h)	Aston Villa	L 1-2	Jones	19,177
2		31	(a)	Everton	L 0-3		25,017
3	Sep	3	(a)	Sunderland	D 1-1	H.Shaw	23,318
4		6	(h)	Portsmouth	W 2-1	Beattie, Boyd	11,289
5		10	(h)	Manchester U	W 1-0	Betmead	14,077
6		17	(h)	Derby C	D 1-1	Swain	12,451
7		24	(a)	Blackpool	L 1-3	Beattie	27,349
8	Oct	1	(h)	Brentford	D 0-0		12,106
9		8	(a)	Arsenal	L 0-2		39,174
10		15	(a)	Middlesbrough	L 2-3	Beattie, Bartholomew	21,720
11		22	(h)	Birmingham	W 1-0	Bartholomew	11,022
12		27	(a)	Stoke C	W 2-1	Howe, Boyd	19,990
13	Nov	5	(h)	Chelsea	W 2-1	Howe, Beattie	11,461
14		12	(a)	Preston NE	D 1-1	Beattie	15,506
15		19	(h)	Charlton A	W 1-0	Bartholomew	11,691
16		26	(a)	Bolton W	D 1-1	Howe	16,229
17	Dec	3	(h)	Leeds U	W 3-2	Howe, Boyd, Beattie	11,202
18		10	(a)	Liverpool	D 2-2	Boyd, Betmead	26,343
19		17	(h)	Leicester C	W 6-1	Boyd, Howe 4, Beattie	9,389
20		24	(a)	Aston Villa	W 2-0	Lewis 2	25,195
21		26	(h)	Wolves	L 2-4	Howe, Beattie	18,655
22		27	(a)	Wolves	L 0-5		44,131
23		31	(h)	Sunderland	L 1-3	Howe	11,565
24	Jan	14	(a)	Manchester U	L 1-3	Hodgson	25,654
25		28	(h)	Blackpool	W 2-0	Glover, Swain	12,126
26	Feb	1	(a)	Derby C	L 1-4	Jones	11,165
27		4	(a)	Brentford	W 2-1	Jones, Bartholomew	17,380
28		18	(h)	Middlesbrough	L 0-2		11,717
29		21	(h)	Arsenal	W 2-1	Howe, Boyd	10,845
30		25	(a)	Birmingham	D 1-1	Beattie	23,231
31	Mar	7	(h)	Stoke C	W 3-1	Howe 2, Crack	9,452
32		11	(a)	Chelsea	L 1-5	Boyd	17,102
33		18	(h)	Preston NE	D 1-1	Howe	10,600
34		29	(a)	Charlton A	L 1-3	Boyd	8,469
35	Apr	1	(h)	Bolton W	D 1-1	Jones	8,558
36		7	(h)	Huddersfield T	D 3-3	Beattie, Betmead, Hall	18,835
37		8	(a)	Leeds U	W 1-0	Glover	19,700
38		11	(a)	Huddersfield T	L 0-2		21,747
39		16	(h)	Liverpool	W 2-1	Howe, Jones	6,164
40		19	(a)	Portsmouth	L 1-2	Beattie	16,514
41		22	(a)	Leicester C	W 2-0	Crack 2	17,326
42	May	6	(h)	Everton	W 3-0	Glover 2, Boyd	11,016
	FINAL LEAGUE POSITION: 10th in Division One						Appearances
							Goals

FA Cup

3	Jan	10	(h)	Tranmere R	W 6-0
4		21	(a)	Millwall	D 2-2
R		24	(h)	Millwall	W 3-2
5	Feb	11	(a)	Sheffield U	D 0-0
R		14	(h)	Sheffield U	W 1-0
6	Mar	4	(a)	Chelsea	W 1-0
SF		15	(a*)	Wolves	L 0-5

*Played at Old Trafford, Manchester.

Tweedy	Vincent	Hodgson	Hall	Betmead	Buck	Boyd	Temple	Beattie	Jones	Bartholomew	Theaker	Glover	Anderson	Fisher	Taylor RE	Charlesworth	Shaw J	Wattam	Kurz	Howe	Swain	Crack	Lewis	Shaw H	Quigley	
1	2	3	4	5	6	7	8	9	10	11																1
1	2	3	4	5	6	7	8	9	10	11																2
1	2	3	4	5	6	8		9	10													11		7		3
1	2	3	4	5	6	8		9	10												11			7		4
1	2	3	4	5	6	8		9	10												11			7		5
1	2	3	4	5	6			8	10										9		11		7			6
1	2	3	4	5	6	7		8	10										9		11					7
	2	3	4	5	6	7		8	10		1								9		11					8
	2	3	4	5	6	7		8	10		1									9	11					9
1	2	3	4	5	6	7		8	10	11										9						10
1	2	3	4		6	7		8	10	11					5					9						11
1	2	3	4	5	6	7		8		11										9	10					12
1	2	3	4	5	6	7		8		11										9	10					13
1	2	3	4	5	6	7		8	10	11										9						14
1	2	3	4	5	6	7		8	10	11										9						15
1	2	3	4	5	6	7		8	10	11										9						16
1	2	3	4	5	6	7		8	10	11										9						17
1	2	3	4	5	6	7		8	10	11										9						18
1	2	3	4	5	6	7		8	10											9			11			19
1	2	3	4	5	6	7		8	10											9			11			20
1	2	3	4	5	6			8	10											9			11	7		21
1	2	3	4	5	6			8	10											9		7	11			22
1	2	3	4	5	6	7		8	10											9			11			23
1	2	3	4	5	6	7		8	10											9			11			24
1	2	3	4	5	6	7		8	10			9									11					25
1	2	3	4		5	7		8	10			9					6				11					26
1	2		4		5	7		8	10	11		9		3			6									27
1	2	3	4	5	6			8	10			9										11			7	28
1	2	3	4	5		7		8	10								6			9		11				29
1	2	3	4	5				8	10								6			9		11			7	30
1	2	3	4		5	7		8	10									6		9		11				31
1	2	3	4		5	7		8	10									6		9		11				32
1	2	3	4	5	6	7		8	10											9		11				33
	2	3	4	5	6	7		8	10			1								9		11				34
	2	3	4	5	6	7		8	10				1							9		11				35
1	2	3	4	5		7		8	10			9						6		11						36
1	2	3	4	5		7		8	10			9						6		11						37
1	2	3	4	5		7		8	10			9						6		11						38
1	2	3	4	5	6	7		8	10											9		11				39
1	2	3	4		6	7		8	10							5				9		11				40
1	2	3	4	5	6	7		8	10											9		11				41
1	2	3	4	5	6	7		8	10			9										11				42
38	42	41	42	36	37	37	2	42	40	12	2	9	1	1	1	1	4	5	3	29	10	14	7	4	2	
		1	1	3		9		11	5	4		4								15	2	3	2	1		

1939-40

1	Aug	26	(a)	Manchester U	L 0-4		22,357
2		29	(h)	Wolves	D 0-0		12,192
3	Sep	2	(h)	Preston NE	W 2-0	Howe 2	6,932

FINAL LEAGUE POSITION: 14th in Division One (League abandoned)

Appearances

Goals

Regional League East Midland Division

1	Oct	21	(h)	Mansfield T	W 2-1	Roberts, Kurz	22,357
2	Nov	4	(h)	Sheffield W	W 3-2	Holmes, Hall, J.W.Johnson	12,192
3		11	(h)	Lincoln C	W 7-3	K.Reeve 3, Moralee, Bartholomew, Vincent, J.W.Johnson	6,936
4		18	(a)	Rotherham U	L 1-2	Buck	5,000
5	Dec	2	(a)	Notts C	W 2-1	Bartholomew 2	7,000
6		9	(h)	Chesterfield	W 1-0	Betmead	3,000
7		23	(a)	Barnsley	L 1-4	Howe	2,000
8	Jan	6	(a)	Doncaster R	L 0-2		2,215
9	Mar	9	(a)	Lincoln C	L 1-4	Vincent	2,000
10		16	(h)	Rotherham U	W 3-1	Vincent (pen), Dodd, Hall	2,000
11		22	(h)	Sheffield U	W 2-0	Ponting, Dodd	3,000
12		23	(a)	Sheffield W	L 1-2	Hall	4,000
13		30	(h)	Notts C	W 3-2	Dodd, Crack 2	2,000
14	Apr	6	(a)	Chesterfield	L 0-5		6,000
15		13	(h)	Barnsley	D 0-0		3,000
16	May	4	(a)	Mansfield T	L 1-4	Beattie	1,000
17		13	(a)	Nottingham F	D 1-1	Beattie	2,255
18		18	(a)	Sheffield U	L 0-3		
19	Jun	1	(h)	Doncaster R	W 7-4	Lumby, Howe 3, Hall 2, Moralee	
20		8	(h)	Nottingham F	W 4-3	Pearson 2, Lumby, Hall	

FINAL LEAGUE POSITION: 4th in Regional League East Midland Division

Appearances

Goals

League Cup

1	Apr	20	(a)	Middlesbrough	L 1-4
1		27	(h)	Middlesbrough	W 3-1

Grimsby Town lost 5-4 on aggregate

Tweedy	Vincent	Hodgson	Hall	Betmead	Buck	Boyd	Beattie	Howe	Jones	Crack	Reeve	Johnson	Wardle	
1	2	3	4	5	6	7	8	9	10	11				1
1	2	3		5	6		8	9	10		4	7	11	2
1	2	3		5	6		8	9	10		4	7	11	3
3	3	3	1	3	3	1	3	3	3	1	2	2	2	
								2						

Tweedy	Vincent	Hodgson JV	Buck	Betmead	Wattam	Johnson JW	Roberts	Kurz	Jones	Crack	Hall	Charlesworth	Lumby	Reeve K	Ponting	Bartholomew	Dodd	Howe	Holmes	Moralee	Pridmore	Taylor	Beattie	Pearson	Ward	Bestall	Wardle	Hillard	Little	Collins	Burton	Neish	Robinson	
1	2	3	4	5	6	7	8	9	10	11																								1
1	2	3	6	5		7	8				4			9		11			10															2
1	2	3	6	5		7	8				4			9		11				10														3
1	2	3	10	5	6	7	8				4			9		11																		4
1	2	3			6	7					4	5			9	11			10						8									5
1	2	3		5	6	7					4				9			10							8		11							6
1	2	3	6	5		7					4					11		9	10						8									7
1	2	3			6	7					4	5	8	9		11			10															8
	2	3			6						4	5	8	9					10		11	1						7						9
	2	3			6						8	5	4		9		10				7	1							11					10
1	2	3			6	7					8	5	4		9		10												11					11
1	2	3			6	7					8	5	4		9		10		11															12
1	2	3	5		6					11	4		7		9		10									8								13
1	2	3	6								4	5	7		10					11						8				9				14
1	2	3	6								4	5					11	9		10			8								7			15
	2		3		6						4	5		10							11	1	8					7		9				16
	2	3	10		6						4	5	7	9							11	1	8											17
1	2	3	4		6							5	7							8	11			9								10		18
1	2	3	6	5							4		7					9		8				10									11	19
1	2	3	4	5	6						8		7					9						10								11		20
16	20	19	13	8	14	10	4	1	1	2	18	11	11	7	7	6	5	5	6	5	5	4	3	3	3	2	1	2	2	2	1	2	1	
	3		1	1		2	1	1		2	6		2	3	1	3	3	4	1	2			2	2										

1940-41

1	Aug	31	(a)	Lincoln C	D	2-2	Annables, Scrimshaw	2,500
2	Sep	7	(h)	Lincoln C	W	2-1	J.W.Johnson, Hall	1,000
3		14	(a)	Rotherham U	L	0-1		2,000
4		21	(a)	Sheffield U	L	1-6	Scrimshaw	3,000
5		28	(h)	Middlesbrough	L	1-3	Reeve	1,000
6	Oct	12	(h)	Sheffield U	W	3-1	Reeve, Betmead, Jennings	2,000
7		19	(h)	Doncaster R	W	3-2	Syred 2, Jennings	2,000
8		26	(a)	Rotherham U	L	2-3	Betmead, Reeve	1,800
9	Nov	9	(h)	Bradford C	W	3-2	Gorman, Jennings, Betmead (pen)	600
10		16	(a)	Newcastle U	L	1-3	Reeve	5,000
11		23	(a)	Doncaster R	L	0-6		2,500
12		30	(h)	Chesterfield	L	4-5	H.Johnson, Wattam, Hall, Reeve	3,490
13	Dec	7	(a)	Chesterfield	W	3-0	Flowers 2, H.Johnson	2,500
14		14	(a)	Middlesbrough	L	1-2	H.Johnson	2,000
15		25	(h)	Hull C	D	1-1	H.Johnson	4,500
16		28	(a)	Newcastle U	L	2-5	H.Johnson, Flowers	4,000
17	Jan	4	(h)	Sheffield U	W	3-2	H.Johnson, Nightingale, Jennings	2,000
18		11	(h)	Newcastle U	W	4-0	H.Johnson 3, Witcomb	3,500
19		18	(h)	Sheffield W	W	2-1	H.Johnson, Jennings	1,500
20	Feb	1	(h)	Bradford	L	0-3		2,000
21	Mar	22	(a)	Hull C	W	8-2	Reeve 3, Flowers, Johnson 2, Jennings, Buck	1,000
22		29	(h)	Hull C	L	0-1		1,200
23	Apr	5	(a)	Bradford C	W	4-2	H.Johnson, Jennings, Crack, Reeve	1,000
24		12	(a)	York C	L	2-3	H.Johnson, Jennings	3,000
25		19	(h)	Rotherham U	W	5-3	Rudkin 3, H.Johnson, Flowers	1,000
26		26	(h)	York C	W	2-0	Jennings, H.Johnson	1,100
27	May	10	(a)	Mansfield T	L	1-3	Flowers	600

FINAL LEAGUE POSITION: 21st in North Regional League

League table decided on goal average. Match number 27 was an inter-league game.

Appearances

Goals

War Cup

1	Feb	15	(h)	Doncaster R	W	1-0
1	Mar	1	(a)	Doncaster R	D	0-0
2		8	(a)	Barnsley	D	1-1
2		15	(h)	Barnsley	D	2-2*

*After extra-time, score at normal time was 1-1. This tie was abandoned after 161 minutes play when the referee had to return to RAF duties. The tie was awarded to Barnsley because of their superior league record.

Tweedy	Vincent	Hodgson	Hall	Betmead	Buck	Logie	Scrimshaw	Annables	Holland	Holmes	Reeve K	Jennings	Johnson H	Allen	Flowers	Fields	Maw	Witcomb	Wattam	Crack	Frost	Gorman	Nightingale	Syred	Ward	Millington	Joyce	Howshall	Chadwick	Wilkin	Gott	Moulson	Bainbridge	Middleton	Swinburne	Charlesworth	Kurz	Rudkin	
1	2	3	4	5	6	7	8	9	10	11																													1
	2	3	4	5	6	8	10			11						1											9												2
1	2	3	4		5	8	10			11	9								6									7											3
	2	3	4	5	6		8			11	9								10										7	1									4
1	2	3	4	5	6	7	8			11	9						10																						5
1	2	3	4	9	5		10				7	8					11		6																				6
1	2	3	4		5					11	7	8					10		6					9															7
1	2	3	4	9	5		11				7							4	6					10															8
1	2	3	4	5	6		10			11		8										9									7								9
1	2	3	4	5	6		10			11	7	8										9																	10
1	2	3	9	5	6		8		10	11	7							4																					11
	2	3	4		6		10				7	8	9			1			11							5													12
	2	3	4		6						7	8	9	11	10											5						1							13
	2	3			6		4				7	8	9	11	10						1					5													14
	2	3	4		6		8				7		9	11	10	1										5													15
	2	3	4		6							8	9		10					11	1					5							7						16
1	2	3	7		6							8	9	11				4					10			5													17
1	2	3	7		6		10					8	9	11				4								5													18
1	2	3	4		6		10					8	9	11				7								5													19
1	2	3	4		6	10						8	9	11				7								5													20
1	2	3	4		6						7	8	9	11	10											5													21
	2	3	4		6						7	8	9	11	10											5								1					22
1	2	3	4								7	8	9		10			6		11						5													23
	2	3	4								7	8	10		11			6																	1	5	9		24
1	2	3	4		6						7		9		10								8			5												10	25
1	2	3	4		6						7	8	9	11											10	5													26
1	2	3	4		6						7		9	11	10										8	5													27
18	27	27	26	9	25	5	15	1	2	9	19	17	16	11	10	3	3	8	6	2	2	2	2	2	2	15	1	1	1	1	1	1	1	1	1	1	1	1	
			2	3	1		2	1			9	9	16		6			1	1	1		1	1	2														3	

J.W.Johnson played number 7 in Match 2, scoring once.

1941-42

League North (First Competition)

1	Aug	30	(a)	Barnsley	L 1-2	Stocks	3,000
2	Sep	6	(h)	Barnsley	D 1-1	Rudkin	2,500
3		13	(h)	Sheffield W	D 1-1	Vincent (pen)	2,000
4		20	(a)	Sheffield W	W 2-0	Rudkin, H.Johnson	3,000
5		27	(a)	Rotherham U	W 3-2	H.Johnson 2, Davies	2,800
6	Oct	4	(h)	Rotherham U	W 6-2	Rudkin, Thomas 3, Flowers 2	2,000
7		11	(a)	Huddersfield T	L 1-5	Rudkin	2,268
8		18	(h)	Huddersfield T	D 2-2	Thomas 2	2,000
9		25	(h)	Lincoln C	L 1-3	Thomas	4,000
10	Nov	1	(a)	Lincoln C	D 1-1	Hullett	5,500
11		8	(a)	Doncaster R	W 3-1	Rudkin, Ferrier, Thomas (pen)	2,515
12		15	(h)	Doncaster R	W 2-0	Buck, Rudkin	3,400
13		22	(h)	Sheffield U	W 7-1	Rudkin 3, Ferrier 3, Doherty	2,000
14		29	(a)	Sheffield U	D 0-0		3,500
15	Dec	6	(a)	Mansfield T	W 3-1	Ferrier, Doherty 2 (1 pen)	500
16		13	(h)	Mansfield T	L 4-5	Hodgson, Doherty, Ferrier 2	1,500
17		20	(a)	Chesterfield	D 1-1	Marsh	1,000
18		25	(h)	Chesterfield	L 2-3	H.Johnson 2	2,237

FINAL LEAGUE POSITION: 13th in League North (First Competition)

Appearances
Goals

League North (Second Competition)

19	Dec	27	(h)	York C	D 0-0		2,000
20	Jan	3	(a)	York C	L 2-3	Doherty 2	4,500
21		10	(a)	Barnsley	D 0-0		3,000
22		17	(h)	Barnsley	W 2-0	Nightingale, Davies	1,500
23		24	(a)	Lincoln C	W 2-1	Ferrier 2	3,000
24	Feb	21	(a)	Doncaster R	W 2-1	Thomas, Hall	871
25		28	(a)	Halifax T	D 2-2	H.Johnson, Doherty	3,000
26	Mar	14	(h)	Huddersfield T	L 1-2	Ferrier	1,500
27		21	(h)	Halifax T	L 1-3	Davies	2,000
28		28	(h)	Lincoln C	W 4-2	Doherty 2, Ferrier 2	1,500

FINAL LEAGUE POSITION: 11th in League North (Second Competition). Some matches counted towards the League War Cup.

Appearances
Goals

League War Cup

1	Apr	4	(a)	Barnsley	W 2-1
1		6	(h)	Barnsley	D 1-1
2		11	(h)	Nottingham F	W 3-1
2		18	(a)	Nottingham F	W 5-1
3		25	(a)	Norwich C	L 0-1
3	May	2	(h)	Norwich C	W 2-0
SF		9	(a)	Sunderland	D 0-0
SF		16	(h)	Sunderland	L 2-3

Tweedy	Vincent	Hodgson JV	Hall	Millington	Buck	Stocks	Jennings	Johnson H	Flowers	Rudkin	Thomas	Davies	Ferrier	Doherty	Robertson	Dodds LS	Moore N	Johnston JW	Middleton	Nightingale	Wilson	Butler	Crack	Fleetwood	Harris	Hullett	Jones W	Moore R	Kurz	Murphy	Marsh	Moody K	Wardle	Lumby	Pridmore	Platts	Iggleden	
1	2	3	4	5	6	7	8	9	10	11																												1
1	2		3	5	6	7	8	9		11														10	4													2
1	2		4	5	6	7	8	9		11		10															3											3
1	2	3	4	5	6		8	9		11	10	7																										4
	2	3	4	5	6			9	10		8	7											11					1										5
1	2	3	4	5	6		8		10	11	9	7																1										6
1	2	3	4	5	6		8	9		11	10	7																										7
1	2	3	4	5	6		8	9		11	10										7																	8
1	2	3	4	5	6		7	9	10	11	8																											9
1	2	3	4	5	6			7	10	11	8															9												10
1	2	3	4	5	6				10	11	8		7																9									11
1	2	3	4	5	6		8			11	10		9		7																							12
1	2	3	4	5	6					11	8		9	10	7																							13
1	2	3	4	5	6		8			11	10		9		7																							14
1	2	3	4	5	6			7					9	10	8		11																					15
1	2	3	4	5	6					11	8		9	10																7								16
1	2	3	4	5	6			7			8		9	10																	11							17
1		3	2	5	6			7			10	11	9		8						4																	18
17	17	16	18	18	18	3	10	12	6	14	14	6	8	4	5		1				2		1	1	1	1	1	1	1	1	1							
	1	1		1	1	1		5	2	9	7	1	7	4												1					1							

Tweedy	Vincent	Hodgson JV	Hall	Millington	Buck	Stocks	Jennings	Johnson H	Flowers	Rudkin	Thomas	Davies	Ferrier	Doherty	Robertson	Dodds LS	Moore N	Johnston JW	Middleton	Nightingale	Wilson	Butler	Crack	Fleetwood	Harris	Hullett	Jones W	Moore R	Kurz	Murphy	Marsh	Moody K	Wardle	Lumby	Pridmore	Platts	Iggleden	
1		3	4	5	6			9			8	11	10		7																	2						19
1	2	3	4	5	6						8		9	10								7											11					20
1	2	3	4	5	6						8	11	9	10																				7				21
1	2	3	4	5	6						10	7	9			11				8																		22
1	2	3	4	5	6						8	7	9	10																					11			23
	2	3	4	5	6			9			8	7	10			11		1																				24
	2	3		5	6			7			8		9	10		11	4	1																				25
	2	3	4	5				10				7	9			11				6																1	8	26
	2	3	4	5	6			10				7	9			11	8		1																			27
	2	3	4	5	6						8	7	9	10		11			1																			28
5	9	10	9	10	9			5			8	8	10	5	1	6	2	2	2	2		1										1	1	1	1	1	1	
			1					1			1	2	5	5						1																		

1942-43

Football League North (First Competition)

1	Aug	29	(a)	Chesterfield	L	0-2		2,500
2	Sep	5	(h)	Chesterfield	W	3-1	Butler, Doherty 2	1,250
3		12	(h)	Lincoln C	W	5-2	Kurz, Davies, Clewlow, Ranshaw 2	2,150
4		19	(a)	Lincoln C	D	2-2	Ranshaw, Doherty	3,639
5		26	(a)	Barnsley	W	3-1	Vincent, Davies, Ranshaw	4,482
6	Oct	3	(h)	Barnsley	D	1-1	Doherty (pen)	2,750
7		10	(h)	Sheffield W	W	2-0	Kippax, Doherty	2,370
8		17	(a)	Sheffield W	L	0-2		6,000
9		24	(a)	York C	L	2-5	Black, Crack	5,000
10		31	(h)	York C	L	0-1		2,000
11	Nov	7	(h)	Lincoln C	D	2-2	Davies, Moralee	2,500
12		14	(a)	Lincoln C	D	2-2	Doherty, Moralee	5,000
13		21	(a)	Sheffield U	D	3-3	Ranshaw 2, Moralee	7,000
14		28	(h)	Sheffield U	W	4-3	Moralee, Eastham, Ranshaw, Vincent	2,000
15	Dec	5	(a)	Rotherham U	W	6-1	Allard, Ranshaw 4, Black	2,000
16		12	(h)	Rotherham U	W	4-1	Moore 2, Ranshaw, Moralee	1,711
17		19	(h)	Doncaster R	W	3-2	Eastham, Vincent (pen), Hall	1,400

FINAL LEAGUE POSITION: 16th in Football League North (First Competition)

Appearances
Goals

Football League North (Second Competition) first ten games were Cup qualifying matches.

18	Dec	26	(h)	Sheffield U	D	3-3	Johnson 3 (2 pens)	3,326
19	Jan	2	(a)	Sheffield U	L	3-5	Doherty (pen), Moralee, Nightingale (og)	6,000
20		9	(a)	Rotherham U	W	3-1	Kurz 2, Black	1,000
21		16	(h)	Rotherham U	D	3-3	Black 3	1,200
22		23	(h)	Doncaster R	W	5-2	Moralee 5	2,000
23		30	(a)	Doncaster R	L	0-1		3,074
24	Feb	6	(a)	Lincoln C	D	1-1	Doherty	5,500
25		13	(h)	Lincoln C	W	1-0	Doherty	2,000
26		20	(a)	Sheffield W	D	2-2	Davies, Kurz	10,000
27		27	(h)	Sheffield W	L	1-2	N.Moore	4,000
28	Mar	27	(a)	Doncaster R	L	2-3	Moralee, Clewlow	2,000
29	Apr	3	(h)	Doncaster R	W	2-0	Browning 2	700
30		26	(a)	Nottingham F	W	4-3	Ranshaw, Browning, Moralee 2	2,876

FINAL LEAGUE POSITION: Grimsby Town failed to qualify in the Cup Competition.

Appearances
Goals

Smith	Vincent	Hodgson JV	Hall	Millington	Buck	Davies	Ely	Chamberlain	Doherty	Archer	Blenkinsopp	Ranshaw	Moralee	Eastham	Black	Kippax SP	Kurz	McKenzie	Moody	Moore N	Bradley	Johnson H	Lilley	Browning N	Butler	Crack	Moulson	Clewlow	Marsh	Sackett	Platts	Raynor	Squires	Reeve K	Greenfield	Sears	Brain	Allard	Fields	
1	2	3		5	6	7	8	9	10	11	4																													1
1	2	3	4	5	6	7			10			11					8								9															2
1	2	3	4	5	6	7						11					9			10								8												3
1		3	4	5	6	7			10			11							2			9							8											4
1	2	3	4	5	6	7						11		8		9														10										5
	2	3	4	5	6	7			10			11		8		9															1									6
	2	3	4	5	6	7			10			11			8	9															1									7
1	2	3	4	5	6							11	10	8		9										7														8
1	2	3	4	5	6							11	9		8											7						10								9
1		3	4	5	6	7						11	10						2													8	9							10
1	2	3	4	5	6	7						11	9	10	8																									11
1	2	3		5	6				10			11	8	7											4									9						12
	2	3	4	5	6	7						11	10	8				1																	9					13
	2	3	4	5	6	7						11	9	8																						1	10			14
	2	3	4	5	6	7						11	10		8			1																				9		15
	2	3	4	5	6	7						11	10		8			1		9																				16
1	2	3	4	5	6	10						11	9	8									7																	17
11	15	17	15	17	17	14	1	1	6	1	1	16	10	8	5	4	2	3	2	2		1	1		2	2		1	1	1	2	2	1	1	1	1	1	1		
	3		1			3			6			12	5	2	2	1	1			2					1	1		1										1		

Smith	Vincent	Hodgson JV	Hall	Millington	Buck	Davies	Ely	Chamberlain	Doherty	Archer	Blenkinsopp	Ranshaw	Moralee	Eastham	Black	Kippax SP	Kurz	McKenzie	Moody	Moore N	Bradley	Johnson H	Lilley	Browning N	Butler	Crack	Moulson	Clewlow	Marsh	Sackett	Platts	Raynor	Squires	Reeve K	Greenfield	Sears	Brain	Allard	Fields	
	2	3	4	5	6	7						11	10	8				1				9																		18
	2	3	4	5	6	7			8			11	10																										1	19
	2	3	4	5	6	7						11	10		8		9																							20
	2	3	4		6	7	5					11	10		8						1	9																		21
	2	3	4	5	6							11	9		8						1	7																		22
	2	3	4	5	6				10			11			8						1		7																	23
	2	3		5	6				10			11	8						4			7			9		1													24
	2	3	4	5	6				10			11	8	7											9		1													25
1	2	3	4	5	6	7			10			11	8				9																							26
1	2	3	4	5	6	7			10			11	9							8																				27
		3	4	5	6								9						2									8												28
1	2	3	4	5	6	7							10	8										9																29
1	2	3	4	5	6							11	10	8									7	9																30
4	12	13	12	12	13	7	1		6			11	12	4	4		2	1	2	1	3	4	2	2	2		2	1											1	
						1			3			1	9		4		3			1		3		3				1												

1 own-goal

Ferrier played number 9 in Match 19; White played number 1 in Match 20; Miller played number 10 in Match 22 & number 9 in Match 23; Frost played number 1 in Match 28; Pridmore played number 7 in Match 28 & number 11 in Match 29; Gilchrist played number 10 in Match 28; Pearson played number 11 in Match 28.

1943-44

Football League North (First Competition)

1	Aug	28	(h)	York C	W	3-1	Rudkin 2, Dunderdale	1,100
2	Sep	4	(a)	York C	L	0-2		4,182
3		11	(h)	Chesterfield	D	0-0		1,500
4		18	(a)	Chesterfield	W	2-1	Vincent (pen), Dunderdale	
5		25	(h)	Barnsley	W	1-0	Pridmore	2,300
6	Oct	2	(a)	Barnsley	L	0-3		4,162
7		9	(a)	Lincoln C	D	2-2	Ranshaw, Baines	3,000
8		16	(h)	Lincoln C	W	3-2	Eastham, Ranshaw, Vincent (pen)	2,000
9		23	(a)	Sheffield W	W	3-2	Dunderdale 3	10,000
10		30	(h)	Sheffield W	L	1-3	Johnson	2,500
11	Nov	6	(a)	Lincoln C	L	0-4		4,000
12		13	(h)	Lincoln C	W	3-2	Ranshaw, Johnson, Sears	2,500
13		20	(h)	Sheffield U	W	4-2	Hall, Sears 2, Dorsett	2,500
15		27	(a)	Sheffield U	D	1-1	Dorsett	7,000
15	Dec	4	(h)	Rotherham U	W	4-1	Ranshaw, Dorsett, Brain, Forsyth	2,500
16		11	(a)	Rotherham U	L	3-4	Dorsett, Vinson 2	2,000
17		18	(a)	Doncaster R	L	1-2	Dorsett	2,914
18		25	(h)	Doncaster R	L	1-3	Forsyth	3,000

FINAL LEAGUE POSITION: 21st in Football League North (First Competition)

Appearances
Goals

Football League North (Second Competition) first ten games were Cup qualifying matches.

19	Dec	27	(a)	Doncaster R	L	0-1		
20	Jan	1	(h)	Doncaster R	D	1-1	Dorsett	5,000
21		8	(h)	Sheffield U	W	2-0	Hall, Rook	5,000
22		15	(a)	Sheffield U	L	1-3	Ranshaw	10,000
23		22	(a)	Lincoln C	W	3-1	Rook, Ranshaw, Forsyth	3,000
24		29	(h)	Lincoln C	W	3-0	Ranshaw, Johnson, Vincent	6,000
25	Feb	5	(h)	Rotherham U	W	2-1	Rook, Brain	5,000
26		12	(a)	Rotherham U	L	1-6	Brain	7,000
27		19	(a)	Chesterfield	L	1-5	Pearson	1,500
28		26	(h)	Chesterfield	W	4-1	Dorsett 2, Vincent (pen), Ranshaw	4,000
29	Apr	10	(a)	Lincoln C	W	1-0	Dunderdale	5,000

FINAL LEAGUE POSITION: 42nd in Football League North (Second Competition). Grimsby Town qualified for the Cup Competition.

Appearances
Goals

Football League North Cup

1	Mar	4	(a)	Rotherham U	D	2-2
1		11	(h)	Rotherham U	W	2-1
2		18	(a)	Sheffield U	L	0-4
2		25	(h)	Sheffield U	L	0-1

Grimsby Town played their home matches at Blundell Park from 1 Jan 1944.

Moulson GB	Vincent	Hodgson JV	Hall	Millington	Buck	Rudkin	Eastham	Dunderdale	Glaister	Ranshaw	Rook	Dorsett	Brain	Forsyth	Baines	Johnson H	Pearson	Sears	Pridmore	Bytheway	Ewing	Gibson	Hodgson S	Kurz	Moody	Moore N	Courtier	Browning	Ferrier	Vinson	Moulson C	Roberts	Canning	Major	Arthur	
1	2	3	4	5	6	7	8	9	10	11																										1
1	2	3	4	5	6	7		9						8	10		11																			2
1	2	3	4	5	6			9		11				7	10												8									3
1	2	3	4	5	6	7		9		11					10													8								4
1	2	3	4	5	6			9		11					10				7									8								5
1	2	3	4	5	6			9		11				10					7									8								6
1	2	3	4	5	6		8	9		11				7	10																					7
1	2	3	4	5	6		8			11					10			7											9							8
1	2	3	4	5	6			9		11	7				10										8											9
1	2	3	4	5	6			9		11				8	10	7																				10
1	2	3	4	5	6	7		9		11				10				8																		11
1	2	3	10	5	6			9		11						7		8					4													12
1	2	3	9	5	6					11		10				7		8					4													13
1	2	3		5	6					11	7	10		9				8					4													14
1	2	3	4	5	6					11	7	10	8	9																						15
1	2	3	4	5	6					11	7	10		8																9						16
1	2	3	4	5	6					11		10	8	9						7																17
1	2	3		5	6					11	7	10	8	9												4										18
18	18	18	16	18	18	4	3	11	1	17	5	6	3	11	8	3	1	5	2	1			3		1	1	1	3	1	1						
	2		1			2	1	5		4		5	1	2	1	2		3	1											2						

1	2	3		5	6					11	7	10	8	9												4										19
1	2	3	4	5	6					11	7	9	8		10																					20
1	2	3	4	5	6					11	7	10	8											9												21
1	2			5	6					11	7		10	3						8											4	9				22
1	2	3		5	6					11	7			10		9					4												8			23
1	2	3		5	6					11	7		8	10		9						4														24
1	2	3		5						11	7		8	10		9					6	4														25
1		3	4	5						11	7	10	8	9								6			2											26
1	2	3	4	5	6					11			8	10		9	7																			27
1	2	3	4	5	6					11		10	8				7							9												28
1	2	3		5	6			9		11	7		8																					4	10	29
11	10	10	5	11	9			1		11	9	5	10	7	1	4	2			1	2	3		2	1	1					1	1	1	1	1	
	2		1							4	3	3	2	1		1	1																			

1944-45

Football League North (First Competition)

1	Aug	26	(h)	Mansfield T	W	5-1	Reeve 2, Hall, Pearson, Lewis	6,000
2	Sep	2	(a)	Mansfield T	D	1-1	Reeve	3,000
3		9	(a)	Doncaster R	W	3-1	Hall, Vincent, Pearson	6,000
4		16	(h)	Doncaster R	W	2-1	Kurz 2	2,000
5		23	(h)	Rotherham U	D	1-1	Kurz	5,000
6		30	(a)	Rotherham U	L	0-2		10,000
7	Oct	7	(a)	Derby C	L	2-3	Dunderdale, Lamb	10,000
8		14	(h)	Derby C	W	3-1	Lamb 2, Green	5,000
9		21	(h)	Lincoln C	W	4-0	Dunderdale (pen), Wallbanks, Lamb, Hall	4,000
10		28	(a)	Lincoln C	L	2-5	Bean (og), Johnston (og)	4,000
11	Nov	4	(a)	Sheffield U	L	1-3	Ranshaw	10,000
12		11	(h)	Sheffield U	W	1-0	Dunderdale	5,000
13		18	(h)	Sheffield W	L	1-2	Dunderdale	5,000
14		25	(a*)	Sheffield W	W	3-2	Lamb, Lewis 2	4,000
15	Dec	2	(a)	Hull C	L	3-4	Symons (og), Lamb, Huxford	5,000
16		9	(h)	Hull C	D	0-0		4,000
17		16	(h)	Nottingham F	W	3-1	Hall, Dunderdale, Huxford	2,000
18		23	(a)	Nottingham F	W	2-1	Lamb 2	6,000

FINAL LEAGUE POSITION: 17th in Football League North (First Competition) — Appearances

*Played at Belle Vue, Doncaster. — Goals

Football League North (Second Competition) first ten games were Cup qualifying matches.

19	Dec	25	(h)	Lincoln C	D	2-2	Huxford, Moore	5,000
20		30	(a)	Lincoln C	W	2-0	Dunderdale 2	4,000
21	Jan	6	(h)	Sheffield W	W	4-1	Vincent, Lamb, Bateman, Dunderdale	3,000
22		13	(a)	Sheffield W	D	2-2	Hodgson, Beattie	6,000
23		20	(h)	Doncaster R	L	1-2	Ranshaw	4,000
24		27	(a)	Doncaster R	L	1-5	Ranshaw	5,272
25	Feb	3	(a)	Sheffield U	D	2-2	Ranshaw 2	13,500
26		10	(h)	Sheffield U	L	1-2	Beattie	7,000
27		17	(h)	Rotherham U	W	5-0	Ranshaw, Vincent (pen), Huxford 3	5,000
28		24	(a)	Rotherham U	L	0-3		8,000
29	Mar	3	(a)	Hull C	L	1-3	Johnson	4,000
30		10	(h)	Bradford C	W	3-2	Hall, Rodi 2	3,000
31		17	(h)	Hull C	W	4-0	Hall 2, Vincent (pen), Rodi	3,000
32		24	(a)	Leeds U	D	1-1	Rodi	7,000
33		31	(h)	Lincoln C	W	4-2	Rodi, Ranshaw, Johnson, Hall	3,000
34	Apr	2	(a)	Lincoln C	D	3-3	Ranshaw, Johnson, Bainbridge	5,000
35		7	(h)	Leeds U	W	3-0	Rodi 2, Glass	6,000
36		14	(h)	Lincoln C	W	4-3	Hall (pen), Ranshaw, Rodi, Hodgson	4,000
37		21	(a)	Lincoln C	D	2-2	Foulston, Rodi	3,000
38	May	5	(h)	Notts C	W	3-1	Rodi 3	4,000
39		12	(a)	Notts C	W	3-1	Rodi, Chadwick, Vincent	2,000

FINAL LEAGUE POSITION: 19th in Football League North (Second Competition). — Appearances

Grimsby Town failed to qualify in the Cup Competition. — Goals

Moulson GB	Vincent	Hodgson JV	Gray	Millington	Buck	Rook	Hall	Reeve K	Lewis	Pearson	Ranshaw	Dunderdale	Rodi	Lamb	Glass	Green	Huxford	Bateman	Beattie	Wallbanks	Grogan	Chadwick	Kurz	Williams	Wood	Pridmore	Frazer	Matthewson	Rudkin	Darley	Jones	Tallant	Taylor	D'Arcey	Birch	Blenkinsopp	Moore R	Johnson J	Corbett	
1	2	3	4	5	6	7	8	9	10	11																														1
1	2	3	4	5			6	9	10	11														8		7														2
1	2	3	4	5	6		9			11						10								7			8													3
1	2	3	4		6					11						8				7			9					5	10											4
1	2	3		4	6					11						10	7						9	8				5												5
1	2	3	4	5	6		8			11		9				10				7																				6
1	2	3	4	5			6			11		9		8		10				7																				7
1	2	3		5	6		4				11			8		10				7										9										8
1		3	2		6		4		10		11	9		8						7											5									9
1	2	3		5	6		4		7		11	9		8		10																								10
1	2	5			6		4		10		11	9		8																		7	3							11
1	2	3		5	6		4				11	9		8																		7		10						12
1	2	3		5	6		4				11	9		8									7												10					13
1	2	3		5	6		4		10		11	9		8			7																							14
1	2	3		5	6		4		10		11	9		8			7																							15
1	2	3		5	6		4		10		11			8																9		7								16
1	2	3		5	6		8		10		11	9			4		7																							17
1	2	3			6				10		11	9		7					8		4															5				18
18	17	18	7	14	16	1	15	2	10	7	11	11		11	1	7	4		1	5	1		3	3		1	1	2	1	2	1	3	1	1	1	1				
	1						4	3	3	2	1	5		8		1	2			1			3																	

3 own-goals

1	2	3		5	6		9		10		11			8			7																				4			19
1	2	3		5			8				11	9		7	4			10			6																			20
1	2	3		5			8				11	9		7	4			10			6																			21
1	2	3		5			8				11			7	4			10	9		6																			22
1	2	3		5			8				11			7	4			10			6																			23
1	2	3		5	6		4				11			7				10																					8	24
1	2	3		5	6		4				11	9		7					8																					25
1	2	3		5	6		4				11	9		10					8				7																	26
1	2	3		5	6		8				11				4		9												10											27
1	2	3		5	6		8				11		10		4		9																							28
	2	3		5											4																							9		29
	2	3		5			8				7		9		4										6															30
1	2	3		5			8				11		9	7	4										6															31
1	2	3		5	6		4						10	7																								9		32
1	2	3			6		4				11		10	7					8																		5	9		33
1	2	3		5							11				4				10						6													9		34
1	2	3			5		6				11		9	10	4							7																		35
1		3		8			6				11		9		4			10				7																		36
1	2	3		5	6		8				11		9		4																									37
1	2	3			6		10				11		9		4							7																		38
1	2	3		5	6		10				11		9	8								7																		39
19	20	21		18	12		19		1		19	4	10	13	14		3	6	5		4	4	1		3				1								2	4	1	
	4	2					5				8	3	13	1	1		4	1	2			1															1	3		

R.Johnson played number 9 in Match 23; Stevenson played number 9 in Match 24; Atkinson played number 10 in Match 25; Brown played number 7 in Matches 27 & 28; Bellamy played number 1 in Matches 29 & 30; Blewitt played number 6 in Match 29; Robertson played number 7 in Match 29; Robertson played number 8 in Match 32; Dolan played number 8 in Matches 29 & 34; Hurley played number 10 in Matches 29 & 31; Pashley played number 11 in Matches 29 & 32; Moody played number 10 in Match 30; Sampson played number 11 in Match 30; Bainbridge played number 7 in Match 34, scoring once; Browning played number 8 in Match 35; Minto played number 2 in Match 36; Horden played number 5 in Match 36; Harvey played number 7 in Match 37; Foulston played number 10 in Match 37, scoring once; Charlesworth played number 5 in Match 38; N.Moore played number 8 in Match 38; Bellas played number 4 in Match 39.

1945-46

1	Aug	25	(a)	Blackburn R	L 2-3	Chadwick, Lamb	18,000
2	Sep	1	(h)	Blackburn R	W 2-0	Betmead, Chadwick	6,000
3		8	(h)	Bradford	W 2-1	Kurz, Chadwick	8,950
4		15	(a)	Bradford	W 3-2	Hepworth (og), Rodi, Kurz	10,669
5		22	(a)	Manchester C	W 2-0	Wardle, Lamb	20,000
6		29	(h)	Manchester C	L 0-2		12,620
7	Oct	6	(h)	Newcastle U	L 0-2		13,000
8		13	(a)	Newcastle U	L 2-6	Blenkinsopp, Davies	45,000
9		20	(a)	Sheffield W	L 1-4	Rodi	18,000
10		27	(h)	Sheffield W	L 1-2	Davies	10,083
11	Nov	3	(h)	Huddersfield T	W 5-3	Rodi, J.Johnson, Chadwick 2, Davies	10,275
12		10	(a)	Huddersfield T	L 2-3	N.Moore, Rodi	10,774
13		17	(a)	Chesterfield	W 2-0	N.Moore, Rodi	15,000
14		24	(h)	Chesterfield	D 3-3	Rodi, Hodgson, Buck	12,000
15	Dec	1	(h)	Barnsley	D 0-0		11,000
16		8	(a)	Barnsley	L 0-2		11,000
17		15	(a)	Everton	L 1-2	Pearson	25,000
18		22	(h)	Everton	L 1-2	N.Moore	11,000
19		25	(h)	Bolton W	L 0-2		10,000
20		29	(a)	Preston NE	W 2-1	Rodi, Buck	9,000
21	Jan	1	(a)	Bolton W	D 0-0		20,000
22		12	(a)	Manchester U	L 0-5		20,789
23		19	(h)	Manchester U	W 1-0	Charlesworth	9,000
24		26	(h)	Leeds U	W 3-2	N.Moore 2, Howe	9,750
25	Feb	2	(a)	Sunderland	L 0-2		18,000
26		9	(a)	Sheffield U	L 1-7	Buck	20,000
27		16	(h)	Sheffield U	L 1-6	Howe	11,000
28		23	(h)	Middlesbrough	D 1-1	Vincent (pen)	9,000
29	Mar	2	(a)	Middlesbrough	L 1-3	Baines	11,000
30		9	(a)	Leeds U	D 2-2	Wardle, Vincent	8,000
31		16	(h)	Stoke C	L 0-2		15,000
32		23	(h)	Burnley	D 1-1	N.Moore	9,000
33		26	(h)	Sunderland	W 4-1	Baines 2, Clifton, Vincent (pen)	
34		30	(a)	Burnley	W 2-1	Baines, Clifton	15,000
35	Apr	6	(h)	Blackpool	W 4-2	Jones 2, Clifton 2	12,000
36		13	(a)	Blackpool	L 3-5	Jones 2, Clifton	10,000
37		15	(a)	Stoke C	L 2-4	Vincent (pen), Lewis	
38		19	(a)	Liverpool	L 0-2		45,000
39		20	(h)	Bury	D 1-1	Temple	12,000
40		22	(h)	Liverpool	D 1-1	J.Johnson	14,000
41		27	(a)	Bury	D 1-1	J.Johnson	4,000
42	May	4	(h)	Preston NE	W 1-0	Beattie, Roger (og)	11,000

FINAL LEAGUE POSITION: 17th in Football League North

Appearances

Goals

FA Cup

3	Jan	5	(h)	Sunderland	L 1-3
		9	(a)	Sunderland	L 1-2

Moulson	Vincent	Hodgson JV	Hall	Betmead	Buck	Chadwick	Lamb	Rodi	Bell	Davies	Charlesworth	Hodgson S	Wardle	Johnson J	Jones	Pearson	Clifton	Harris	Howe	Moore N	Tweedy	Lewis	Blenkinsopp	Baines	Moody	Baird	Kurz	Candice	Harvey	Vinson	Rudkin	Bateman	Rook	Mouncer	Browning	Glass	Robertson	Crack	
1	2	3	4	5	6	7	8	9	10	11																													1
1	2	3	10	5	6	7	8	9		11								4																					2
1	2	3	4	5	6	7		10								11				8							9												3
1	2	3	4		6	7	8	10		11	5																9												4
1	2	3		5	6		8	10		7			11			9		4																					5
1	2	3	4	5	6	7		8					11			9										10													6
	2	3	4	5	6	7	8	9	10	11											1																		7
1	2	3		5	6	7		8		11								4					9			10													8
1	2	3		5	6			9	7	11								4								10		8											9
1		3		5	6		8	9		11								4							2	10			7										10
1		3		5	6	7		10		11				9				4		8					2														11
1		3		5	6	7		10		11				9				4		8					2														12
1		3		5	6	7		10						9				4		8					2					11									13
1		3			6			10						9		11		4		8			5		2		7												14
1	2	3			6	7		10			5			9		11		4		8																			15
1	2	3			6	7		10			5	4		9		11				8																			16
1	2	3			6	7					5	4		9	10	11				8																			17
1	2	3			6	7					5	4		9	10					8											11								18
1	2	3			6	7		9			5							4		8										11		10							19
1	2	3			6			10			5	4				11				8													7		9				20
1		3			6			10			5				11			4											7					2	9	8			21
1	2	3									5	4	11	7	10	9				8																6			22
1	2	3			6			10			5	4			11	9				8																	7		23
1	2	3			6	7		10			5	4				11			9	8																			24
1	2	3			6						5	4		7	11		8		9	10																			25
	2	3		5	6							4				11	8		9	7	1																10		26
1		3		5	6	7		10									8		11	9														2		4			27
1	2	3		6		7					5	4	11				8			9				10															28
1	2	3				7					5	4	11				8			9			6	10															29
1	2	3		6		7					5	4	11		10				9	8																			30
1	2	3			6						5	4	11		10				9	8																		7	31
1	2	3	4		6						5		11		10					9				8														7	32
1	2	3	4		6						5		11				8					7	9	10															33
1		3			6						5		11				10		9	4		7		8															34
1	2	3			6						5		11		10		8		9	4		7																	35
1	2	3			6						5		11		10		8		9	4		7																	36
	2	3			6						5	4	11		10		8		9		1	7																	37
	2	3									5	4	11		10		8		9		1		6																38
		3		5	6							4	11							8	1	7		10															39
	2	3	6	5								4	11	9	10						1	7		8															40
	2	3	6	5								4	11	9	10		8				1	7																	41
	2	3	4	5									11	9			8			6	1	10																	42
34	33	42	11	20	34	20	6	22	3	10	23	18	18	13	15	12	13	12	11	27	8	9	5	7	5	4	3	1	2	2	1	1	1	2	2	3	2	2	
	4	1		1	3	5	2	7		3	1		2	3	4	1	5		2	6		1	1	4			2												

2 own-goals

Fisher played number 2 in Matches 34 & 39; Temple played number 9 in Match 39, scoring once; J.W.Johnson played number 7 in Match 42.

1946-47

1	Aug	31	(a)	Manchester U	L 1-2	McGowan	41,025
2	Sep	3	(h)	Wolves	D 0-0		18,327
3		7	(h)	Preston NE	L 2-3	Jones 2	18,571
4		14	(a)	Sheffield U	D 1-1	Vincent	31,777
5		21	(h)	Chelsea	W 2-1	Jones, N.Moore	21,932
6		23	(a)	Wolves	L 0-2		30,357
7		28	(a)	Bolton W	W 2-1	Clifton 2	30,547
8	Oct	5	(h)	Liverpool	L 1-6	Wardle (pen)	20,189
9		12	(a)	Leeds U	L 0-1		28,877
10		19	(a)	Sunderland	W 2-1	Blenkinsopp 2	42,763
11		26	(h)	Portsmouth	W 3-2	Clifton, Cairns, Blenkinsopp	16,885
12	Nov	2	(a)	Everton	D 3-3	Blenkinsopp 2, Whitfield	48,817
13		9	(h)	Huddersfield T	W 1-0	Blenkinsopp	14,815
14		16	(a)	Blackpool	W 3.2	Wardle, Cairns 2	17,511
15		23	(h)	Brentford	D 2-2	Blenkinsopp, Wallbanks	16,570
16		30	(a)	Blackburn R	D 1-1	Cairns	22,677
17	Dec	7	(h)	Aston Villa	L 0-3		18,257
18		14	(a)	Derby C	L 1-4	Wardle	18,809
19		21	(h)	Arsenal	D 0-0		13,308
20		25	(h)	Charlton A	W 3-1	Clifton 2, Cairns	17,841
21		26	(a)	Charlton A	D 0-0		30,804
22		28	(h)	Manchester U	D 0-0		17,183
23	Jan	1	(a)	Middlesbrough	L 0-3		39,947
24		4	(a)	Preston NE	L 0-3		27,262
25		18	(h)	Sheffield U	W 2-1	J.Johnson, Vincent	17,691
26	Feb	1	(h)	Bolton W	D 2-2	Clifton 2	11,467
27		8	(a)	Chelsea	D 0-0		17,896
28		12	(a)	Liverpool	L 0-5		20,648
29	Mar	1	(a)	Portsmouth	L 1-4	Wardle (pen)	27,099
30		8	(h)	Everton	D 2-2	Keeble, Cairns	11,277
31		15	(a)	Huddersfield T	L 2-3	Cairns 2	17,201
32		22	(h)	Blackpool	L 2-3	Cairns, Wardle (pen)	13,452
33		29	(a)	Brentford	W 1-0	Cairns	19,778
34	Apr	4	(h)	Stoke C	L 2-5	Clifton, Wardle (pen)	26,537
35		5	(h)	Blackburn R	W 2-1	Cairns, K.Reeve	12,975
36		7	(a)	Stoke C	L 0-3		34,386
37		12	(a)	Aston Villa	D 3-3	J.Johnson, Clifton 2	37,741
38		19	(h)	Derby C	W 2-0	Clifton, Cairns	16,200
39		26	(a)	Arsenal	L 3-5	Cairns, K.Reeve, Clifton	42,100
40	May	3	(h)	Middlesbrough	W 4-0	Cairns 2, Whitfield, K.Reeve	13,376
41		10	(h)	Sunderland	L 1-2	K.Reeve	12,777
42		17	(h)	Leeds U	W 4-1	Cairns 3, Wardle (pen)	10,795

FINAL LEAGUE POSITION: 16th in Division One

Appearances
Goals

FA Cup

3	Jan	11	(h)	Reading	D 2-2
R		14	(a)	Reading	W 3-1
4		25	(a)	Liverpool	L 0-2

Tweedy	Vincent	Hodgson JV	Hodgson S	Charlesworth	Reeve FW	Johnson Jack	Clifton	Johnson Jim	McGowan	Wardle	Moulson	Chisholm	Mouncer	Fisher	Blenkinsopp	Hall	Taylor RE	Penrose	Whitfield	Betmead	Pearson	Wallbanks	Jones	Hansen	Moore N	Cairns	Reeve K	Keeble	
1	2	3	4	5	6	7	8	9	10	11																			1
1	2	3	4			7		9	10	11					6					5			8						2
1	2	3	4			7		9	10	11					6					5			8						3
1	2	3	4			7	8								6					5	11		10		9				4
1	2		4				8			11				3	6					5	7		10		9				5
1			4			7	8			11			2	3	6					5			10		9				6
1	2		4				8			11				3	6		5				7		10		9				7
1	2		4				8			11				3	6					5	7		10		9				8
1		3			6	7	8			11				2	4					5					9			10 ·	9
1		3			6	7	10			11				2	9	4			8	5									10
1		3			6	7	8			11				2	9	4				5						10			11
1		3	4		6					11				2	9				8	5		7				10			12
1		3	4				8			11				2	9		6			5		7				10			13
1		3			6		8			11				2	9		4			5		7				10			14
1		3			6		8			11				2	9		4			5		7				10			15
1		3			6		8			11				2	9	4				5		7				10			16
1		3			6		8			11				2	9		4			5		7				10			17
1		3			6	7	8			11				2	9			4		5						10			18
1		3				7	8	9		11				2	6	4				5						10			19
1		3			6	7	8			11				2	9	4				5						10			20
1	2				6	7								3	9				4	5	11			8		10			21
1	2				6	7	8			11				3	9	4				5						10			22
1	2				6	7	10			11				3	9	4			8	5									23
1	2	5			6	7				11				3	9	4							8			10			24
1	2				6		8	9		11				3		4	5					7						10	25
1	2				6		10			11				3	9	4	5					7			8				26
1						7	8						2	3	6	4	5				11					9		10	27
1						7	8						2	3	6	4	5				11						9	10	28
1	2					7	8			11				3	6	4	5									9		10	29
1	2					7	8			11				3	6	4				5						9		10	30
1						7	8			11			2	3	6	4				5						9		10	31
1		3				7	8		10	11				2	6	4				5						9			32
1					6	7	8			11			2	3	10		4			5						9			33
					6		8			11	1		2	3	10		4			5		7				9			34
					6		8			11		1	2	3		4				5	7					10	9		35
					6	7	8			11		1	2	3		4				5						10	9		36
1			4		6	7	8			11			2	3						5						10	9		37
1			4		6	7	8			11			2	3						5						10	9		38
1			4		6	7	8			11			2	3						5						10	9		39
1					6	7				11			2	3		4			8	5						10	9		40
1					6	7	8			11			2	3		4				5						10	9		41
1					6	7	8			11			2	3	9				4	5						10			42
39	15	18	13	1	27	29	36	5	4	38	1	2	14	38	33	20	12	1	6	34	8	9	8	1	7	28	8	7	
	2					1	12	1	1	7					7				2		1	1	3		1	18	4		

1947-48

1	Aug	23	(h)	Aston Villa	W 3-0	Cairns 2, J.Johnson	20,532
2		27	(a)	Wolves	L 1-8	Cairns	43,289
3		30	(a)	Sunderland	L 2-4	Cairns, Clifton	35,937
4	Sep	3	(h)	Wolves	L 0-4		21,173
5		6	(h)	Sheffield U	L 0-3		18,103
6		10	(a)	Huddersfield T	L 1-5	Briggs	20,145
7		13	(h)	Manchester C	W 1-0	Clifton	16,766
8		17	(h)	Huddersfield T	W 3-0	Clifton, Cairns 2	17,658
9		20	(a)	Blackburn R	L 0-4		24,254
10		27	(h)	Blackpool	L 0-1		25,576
11	Oct	4	(a)	Derby C	L 1-4	Cairns	24,274
12		11	(a)	Manchester U	W 4-3	Cairns 3, Blenkinsopp	41,202
13		18	(h)	Preston NE	D 1-1	Wilson	17,915
14		25	(a)	Stoke C	L 1-2	Cairns	29,980
15	Nov	1	(h)	Burnley	L 1-2	Cairns	17,697
16		8	(a)	Liverpool	L 1-3	K.Reeve	36,796
17		15	(h)	Middlesbrough	L 0-5		14,812
18		22	(a)	Portsmouth	L 0-4		23,459
19		29	(h)	Bolton W	L 0-2		11,901
20	Dec	6	(a)	Charlton A	W 3-2	Wardle 2, Cairns	14,667
21		13	(h)	Arsenal	L 0-4		18,700
22		20	(a)	Aston Villa	D 2-2	Wardle, Briggs	31,577
23		25	(h)	Chelsea	D 0-0		19,666
24		27	(a)	Chelsea	W 3-2	Wardle, Briggs, Whitfield	34,068
25	Jan	3	(h)	Sunderland	L 1-2	Whitfield	15,882
26		17	(a)	Sheffield U	L 0-4		27,930
27		31	(a)	Manchester C	L 1-3	Whitfield	36,971
28	Feb	7	(h)	Blackburn R	D 2-2	Cairns 2	14,231
29		14	(a)	Blackpool	L 1-3	Pearson	21,612
30		21	(h)	Derby C	L 2-3	Armitage, Cairns	11,607
31	Mar	6	(a)	Preston NE	L 1-2	Armitage	25,534
32		13	(h)	Stoke C	D 0-0		9,631
33		17	(h)	Manchester U	D 1-1	McGowan	12,284
34		20	(a)	Burnley	L 1-4	Pearson	19,522
35		26	(h)	Everton	W 3-0	Blenkinsopp, Pearson 2	18,279
36		27	(h)	Liverpool	L 0-2		15,781
37		29	(a)	Everton	L 1-3	Blenkinsopp	37,926
38	Apr	3	(a)	Middlesbrough	L 1-4	Clifton	24,130
39		10	(h)	Portsmouth	W 1-0	Briggs	10,400
40		17	(a)	Bolton W	L 0-2		23,378
41		24	(h)	Charlton A	L 1-3	Briggs	8,655
42	May	1	(a)	Arsenal	L 0-8		34,644

FINAL LEAGUE POSITION: 22nd in Division One

Appearances
Goals

FA Cup

3	Jan	10	(h)	Everton	L 1-4

Tweedy	Fisher	Hodgson JV	Blenkinsopp	Taylor RE	Reeve FW	Johnson Jack	Clifton	Briggs	Cairns	Wardle	Chisholm	Mouncer	Moody	Sibley	Hall	Penrose	Hodgson S	Galley	Whitfield	Wilson	Burnett	Armitage	McGowan	Reeve K	Boulton	Pearson	
1	2	3	4	5	6	7	8	9	10	11																	1
1	2	3	4	5	6	7	8	9	10	11																	2
1	3		4	5	6	7	8		10	11		2												9			3
1	3		4	5	6				10	11		2							8	7				9			4
1	3		4	5	6				10	11		2							8	7				9			5
1	2	3	6	5		7	8	9	10	11					4												6
1	2	3	6	5			8	9	10	11						4				7							7
1	2	3	6	5			8	9	10	11						4				7							8
	2	3	6	5			8	9	10	11	1					4				7							9
	2	3	6	5			8	9	10	11	1					4				7							10
	2	3	6	5				9	10	11	1					4				7			8				11
1	2	3	9	5	6				10	11						4				7			8				12
1	2	3	9	5	6				10	11						4				7			8				13
1	2	3	9	5	6				10	11						4				7			8				14
1	2	3	9	5	6				10	11							4			7			8				15
1	2	3	6	5				9	10	11							4			7				8			16
1	2	3	6	5		7	8		10	11							4							9			17
	2	3	5		6				10	11	1							4	8	7				9			18
	3		5		6				10	11	1	2					4			7	8			9			19
1	3		5		6	7			10	11				2				4			8			9			20
1	3		5		6	7		9	10	11				2				4			8						21
1	3		5		6			9	10	11				2				4			8					7	22
1	2	3	5		6	7		9	10	11							4				8						23
1	3		5		6			9	10	11				2			4		8		7						24
1	3		5		6			9	10	11				2				4	8		7						25
1	3			5	6	7			10	11				2				4	8			9					26
1	3		5		6				10	11				2				4	8		7	9					27
1	3		6	5					9	10				2				4	8			7				11	28
1	3		6	5					9	10		2					4					7		8		11	29
1	3		6	5					9	10		2						4				7		8		11	30
1	3		6						10	11		2						5	4	7		9		8			31
1	3		6			7				11				2				5	4			9		8		10	32
1	3		6					8					2					5	4	7		9	10			11	33
1	3		6	5				8					2						4	7			10	9		11	34
1	3		6			7		9					2					5	4				10	8		11	35
1	3		6			7		9					2					5	4				10	8		11	36
1	3		6			7	8	9					2					5	4					10		11	37
	3		6	5		7	8	9		11	1		2						4				10				38
1	3		6				8	9		11			2					5	4				10			7	39
1	3		6				8	9					2					5	4		7		10			11	40
1	3		6				8	9					2					5	4		7				10	11	41
1	3		6			7		9		10			2				4	5					8			11	42
36	42	16	41	23	19	15	14	24	31	35	6	7	10	9	1	8	8	19	19	17	10	8	13	16	1	14	
			3			1	4	5	16	4									3	1		2	1	1		4	

1948-49

1	Aug	21	(h)	Fulham	L 2-3	Clifton, Cairns	19,271
2		24	(h)	Nottingham F	L 1-2	Cairns	18,298
3		28	(a)	Plymouth A	W 2-0	Briggs, Pearson	24,618
4	Sep	1	(a)	Nottingham F	D 0-0		21,897
5		4	(h)	Blackburn R	L 1-2	McStay (pen)	15,671
6		8	(a)	Chesterfield	W 3-0	Cairns, McKenna, Pearson	11,846
7		11	(a)	Cardiff C	L 0-3		32,156
8		14	(h)	Chesterfield	D 3-3	Clifton 2, McGowan	14,838
9		18	(h)	Queen's Park R	W 4-1	McGowan, Pearson, Cairns, Forrest	15,141
10		25	(a)	Luton T	D 1-1	Clifton	18,173
11	Oct	2	(h)	Bradford	L 0-3		15,931
12		9	(h)	Lincoln C	D 2-2	Briggs, McKenna	22,169
13		16	(a)	Sheffield W	L 1-4	Briggs	34,095
14		23	(h)	Coventry C	W 4-1	Briggs 3, Clifton	13,334
15		30	(a)	Leeds U	L 3-6	Lloyd (pen), Galley, Briggs	33,581
16	Nov	6	(h)	Leicester C	W 1-0	Galley	14,774
17		13	(a)	Brentford	L 0-2		24,992
18		20	(h)	Tottenham H	D 1-1	Lloyd	15,863
19	Dec	4	(h)	Bury	L 2-3	Lloyd 2 (2 pens)	13,523
20		11	(a)	West Brom A	L 2-5	Briggs, Pearson	22,664
21		18	(a)	Fulham	L 1-3	Lloyd	19,996
22		25	(h)	Barnsley	W 3-0	Briggs, Cairns, Clifton	18,369
23		27	(a)	Barnsley	L 1-2	Clifton	19,848
24	Jan	1	(h)	Plymouth A	D 2-2	Briggs, Cairns	12,175
25		15	(a)	Blackburn R	D 3-3	Whitfield, Cairns, Lloyd	13,418
26		22	(h)	Cardiff C	D 2-2	Whitfield, Cairns	15,210
27	Feb	5	(a)	Queen's Park R	W 2-1	Briggs 2	19,813
28		12	(a)	West Ham U	L 0-1		20,795
29		26	(a)	Bradford	W 1-0	Briggs	15,139
30	Mar	5	(a)	Lincoln C	W 3-2	Briggs 3	23,146
31		12	(h)	Sheffield W	W 2-0	Briggs, Shearer	18,425
32		19	(a)	Coventry C	L 1-4	Lloyd	22,278
33		26	(h)	Leeds U	W 5-1	Briggs 2, Shearer, Cairns, Lloyd	15,848
34	Apr	2	(a)	Leicester C	D 1-1	Briggs	35,847
35		9	(h)	Brentford	W 3-0	Briggs, McStay, Cairns	15,695
36		15	(h)	Southampton	L 0-1		25,931
37		16	(a)	Tottenham H	L 2-5	Cairns, Hair	25,808
38		18	(a)	Southampton	D 0-0		26,064
39		23	(h)	West Ham U	W 3-0	Briggs 2, Shearer	15,803
40		30	(a)	Bury	L 1-5	Briggs	9,036
41	May	3	(h)	Luton T	W 2-1	Briggs, Cairns	13,809
42		7	(h)	West Brom A	W 1-0	Briggs	18,564

FINAL LEAGUE POSITION: 11th in Division Two

Appearances

Goals

FA Cup

3	Jan	18	(h)	Exeter C	W 2-1
4		29	(h)	Hull C	L 2-3

Tweedy	Moody	Sibley	McKenna	Galley	Forrest	McStay	Clifton	Cairns	Lloyd	Pearson	Chisholm	Fisher	Johnston	Robinson N	Moore R	McMillan	Boulton	Whitfield	Shearer	Duthie	Briggs	McGowan	Lynn	Hair	Mouncer	
1	2	3	4	5	6	7	8	9	10	11																1
1	2	3	4		6	7	8	10		11				5							9					2
1	2	3	4		6	7			8	11				5							9	10				3
1	2	3	4		6	7			8	11				5							9	10				4
1	2	3	4	5	6	7			8	11											9	10				5
1	2		4	5	6	7	10	9	8	11		3														6
1	2		4	5		7	6	9	8	11		3										10				7
1	2		4	5	6	7	8	9		11		3										10				8
1	2		4		6	7	8	9		11		3		5								10				9
1	2		4		6		8	9	7			3		5								10	11			10
1	2		4	5	6		8	9	7			3										10	11			11
1	2		4	5	6		8		7	11		3									9	10				12
1	2		4	5	6				7	11		3						8			9	10				13
1	2		4	5	6	7	8		11			3									9	10				14
1	2		4	5	6	7	8		11			3									9	10				15
	2		4	5	6	7	8		11		1	3									9	10				16
	2		4	5	6	7	8		11		1	3									9	10				17
	2		4	5	6	7			11		1	3						8			9	10				18
	2		4		6	7	8		11		1	3			5						9	10				19
	2		4		6	7			8	11	1	3			5						9	10				20
	2	5	4		6	7		9	8	11	1	3					10									21
	2	5	4		6	7	8	10	11		1	3									9					22
	2	5	4		6	7	8	10	11		1	3									9					23
	2	5	4		6	7	8	10	11		1	3									9					24
	2	5	4		6	7		10	11		1	3						8			9					25
	2	5	4		6	7		10	11		1	3						8			9					26
	2	5	4		6	7			8		1	3	10								9			11		27
	2		4		5	7	10		8		1	3	6								9			11		28
	2		4		5	7		10			1	3	6						8		9			11		29
	2		4		5	7		10			1	3	6						8		9			11		30
	2		4		5	7			10		1	3	6						8		9			11		31
	2		4		5	7			10		1	3	6						8		9			11		32
	2		4		5			10	7		1	3	6						8		9			11		33
	2		4		5			10	7		1	3	6						8		9			11		34
	2		4			7		10			1	3	6			5			8		9			11		35
	2		4			7		10			1	3	6			5			8		9			11		36
	2		4			7	8	10			1	3	6			5					9			11		37
	2	6	8					10			1	3	4			5	7				9			11		38
		2	4					10	7		1	3	6			5			8		9			11		39
			4					10	7		1	3	6			5				8	9			11	2	40
	2		4			7		10	8		1	3	6			5					9			11		41
	2		4			7		10	8		1	3	6			5					9			11		42
15	40	14	42	13	33	33	19	26	33	13	27	37	16	5	2	8	2	4	9	1	34	17	2	16	1	
			2	2	1	2	7	12	8	4								2	3		26	2		1		

1949-50

1	Aug	20	(a)	Southampton	W 2-1	Briggs 2	26,222
2		24	(a)	Preston NE	L 0-2		30,935
3		27	(h)	Coventry C	W 3-2	Briggs 3	18,635
4		31	(h)	Preston NE	L 1-3	Briggs	24,190
5	Sep	3	(a)	Luton T	D 0-0		16,717
6		7	(h)	Swansea T	W 2-1	Briggs 2	19,465
7		10	(h)	Barnsley	D 2-2	Briggs, Hair	19,071
8		17	(a)	West Ham U	L 3-4	Briggs 2, Shearer	28,194
9		24	(h)	Sheffield U	W 4-0	Lloyd (pen), Cairns 2, Briggs	18,348
10	Oct	1	(a)	Hull C	D 2-2	Shearer, Briggs	46,282
11		8	(h)	Sheffield W	W 4-1	Lloyd 3 (2 pens), Cairns	24,822
12		15	(a)	Plymouth A	L 2-4	Briggs 2	24,276
13		22	(h)	Chesterfield	W 5-2	MacKenzie, Briggs 2, Cairns 2	17,055
14		29	(a)	Bradford	L 1-4	Briggs	15,474
15	Nov	5	(h)	Leicester C	W 2-1	Cairns, Briggs	14,114
16		12	(a)	Bury	L 1-3	Cairns	10,287
17		19	(h)	Tottenham H	L 2-3	Hair, Briggs	22,580
18		26	(a)	Cardiff C	L 0-1		22,664
19	Dec	3	(h)	Blackburn R	L 1-2	Briggs	15,005
20		10	(a)	Brentford	L 0-1		16,273
21		17	(h)	Southampton	D 1-1	Cairns	12,818
22		24	(a)	Coventry C	D 1-1	Briggs	24,058
23		26	(h)	Queen's Park R	D 1-1	Briggs	22,336
24		27	(a)	Queen's Park R	W 2-1	Shearer, Briggs	22,884
25		31	(h)	Luton T	W 6-1	Briggs 3, Hair, Cairns, Shearer	16,932
26	Jan	14	(a)	Barnsley	L 2-7	Cairns, Shearer	18,519
27		21	(h)	West Ham U	W 2-0	Briggs 2	17,046
28	Feb	4	(a)	Sheffield U	L 1-3	Cairns	33,108
29		18	(h)	Hull C	W 1-0	Cairns	26,476
30	Mar	4	(h)	Plymouth A	D 2-2	Briggs, Johnston	15,551
31		11	(a)	Chesterfield	L 1-2	Bloomer	11,703
32		18	(h)	Bradford	W 4-0	Hair 2, Cairns, Briggs	15,346
33		25	(a)	Leicester C	L 0-1		31,635
34	Apr	1	(h)	Cardiff C	D 0-0		14,922
35		7	(h)	Leeds U	W 2-0	MacKenzie (pen), Charles (og)	21,469
36		8	(a)	Blackburn R	L 0-3		15,363
37		10	(a)	Leeds U	L 0-1		17,991
38		15	(h)	Bury	W 4-2	Shearer, Cairns 2, Briggs	14,232
39		22	(a)	Tottenham H	W 2-1	Cairns, Briggs	46,423
40		26	(a)	Sheffield W	L 0-4		40,862
41		29	(h)	Brentford	W 4-1	Briggs 2, Cairns, Hair	12,585
42	May	6	(a)	Swansea T	L 1-2	Briggs	18,723

FINAL LEAGUE POSITION: 11th in Division Two

Appearances
Goals

FA Cup

3	Jan	7	(a)	Luton T	W 4-3
4		28	(a)	Portsmouth	L 0-5

Chisholm	Moody	Fisher	McKenna	McMillan	Johnston	McStay	Lloyd	Briggs	Cairns	Hair	Bircham	Tweedy	Harnby	Taylor	Moore R	Duthie	MacKenzie	Bloomer	Mulholland	Rankin	Barney	Shearer	Johnson Jim	
1	2	3	4	5	6	7	8	9	10	11														1
1	2	3	4	5	6	7	8	9	10	11														2
1	2	3	4	5	6	7	8	9	10	11														3
1	2	3	4	5	6	7	8	9	10	11														4
1	2	3	4	5	6		7	9	10	11											8			5
1	2	3	4	5	6		7	9	10	11											8			6
1	2	3	4	5	6		7	9	10	11											8			7
1	2	3	4	5	6		7	9	10	11												8		8
1	2	3		5	4		7	9	10	11							6					8		9
1	2	3		5	4		7	9	10	11							6					8		10
1	2	3		5	4		7	9	10	11							6					8		11
1	2	3		5	4		7	9	10	11							6					8		12
1	2	3		5	4		7	9	10	11							6					8		13
1	2	3		5	4		7	9	10	11							6					8		14
1	2	3		5	4		7	9	10	11							6					8		15
1	2	3			4		7	9	10	11					5		6				8			16
1	2	3		5	4		7	9	10	11							6				8			17
1	2	3		5	4	7		9	10	11							6				8			18
1	2	3		5	4			9	10	11							6	7				8		19
	2				4			9	10	11	1		3			5	6		7			8		20
	2			5	4		7	9	10	11	1		3			6						8		21
	2			5	4	11	7	9	10		1		3			6						8		22
	2			5	4	11	7	9	10		1		3			6						8		23
		2		5	4	11	7	9	10		1		3			6						8		24
		2		5	4	7		9	10	11	1		3			6						8		25
		2		5	4	7		9	10	11	1		3			6						8		26
		2		5	4	7		9	10	11	1		3			6						8		27
1		2		5	4		7	9	10	11			3				6				8			28
1	2			5	4		7	9	10	11				3			6					8		29
1	2			5	4	7		9	10	11				3			6					8		30
1	2			5	4	7			10	11				3			6	8					9	31
1	2	3		5	4		7	9	10	11							6	8						32
1	2	3		5	4		7	9	10	11							6	8						33
1	2	3		5	4		7	9	10	11							6	8						34
1	2	3		5	4		7	9	10	11							6	8						35
1	2	3		5	4		7	9	10	11							6	8						36
1	2	3		5	4	11		9	10								6	8		7				37
1	2	3		5	4		7	9	10	11							6					8		38
1	2	3		5	4		7	9	10	11							6					8		39
1	2	3		5	4		7	9	10	11							6					8		40
	2	3		5	4	7		9	10	11		1					6					8		41
1	2	3		5	4		7	9	10	11							6					8		42
33	37	35	8	40	42	15	32	41	42	38	8	1	9	3	1	8	27	8	1	1	7	24	1	
					1		4	36	17	6							2	1				6		

1 own-goal

1950-51

1	Aug	19	(h)	Cardiff C	D 0-0		20,083
2		21	(a)	Chesterfield	D 2-2	Briggs, Hair	15,910
3		26	(a)	Birmingham C	D 1-1	Briggs	33,017
4		30	(h)	Chesterfield	L 1-2	MacKenzie (pen)	18,268
5	Sep	2	(a)	Hull C	L 1-2	Briggs	38,332
6		6	(h)	Manchester C	D 4-4	Cairns, Westwood (og), McMillan, Briggs	18,529
7		9	(h)	Notts C	L 1-4	Cairns	21,432
8		16	(a)	Preston NE	L 0-2		24,461
9		23	(h)	Bury	W 2-1	Squires, Cairns	14,956
10		30	(a)	Queen's Park R	L 1-7	Briggs	16,331
11	Oct	7	(a)	Barnsley	L 1-3	Briggs	18,417
12		14	(h)	Sheffield U	D 2-2	Cairns 2	12,643
13		21	(a)	Blackburn R	L 0-2		23,235
14		28	(h)	Southampton	W 4-1	Bloomer 4	13,383
15	Nov	4	(a)	Doncaster R	L 1-3	MacKenzie	23,197
16		11	(h)	Brentford	W 7-2	MacKenzie, Bloomer 3, Squires, Rankin	14,985
17		18	(a)	Luton T	L 0-4		12,144
18		25	(h)	Leeds U	D 2-2	MacKenzie 2 (1 pen)	15,561
19	Dec	2	(a)	West Ham U	L 1-2	Cairns	18,518
20		9	(h)	Swansea T	W 4-2	Briggs 2, Lloyd, MacKenzie	13,754
21		16	(a)	Cardiff C	L 2-5	Briggs 2	15,364
22		23	(h)	Birmingham C	D 1-1	Briggs	13,141
23		25	(h)	Leicester C	L 0-2		17,565
24		26	(a)	Leicester C	D 0-0		28,296
25		30	(h)	Hull C	D 1-1	Maddison	20,268
26	Jan	13	(a)	Notts C	L 2-3	Cairns, Maddison	24,849
27		20	(h)	Preston NE	L 0-4		16,836
28	Feb	3	(a)	Bury	W 3-2	Cairns 2, Lloyd	12,775
29		17	(h)	Queen's Park R	D 2-2	Cairns, Lloyd	14,005
30		24	(h)	Barnsley	W 3-1	Cairns, MacKenzie (pen), Lloyd	14,862
31	Mar	3	(a)	Sheffield U	L 2-4	Cairns, MacKenzie (pen)	23,558
32		10	(h)	Blackburn R	D 1-1	Cairns	13,216
33		17	(a)	Southampton	L 1-5	Cairns	14,598
34		23	(h)	Coventry C	L 1-2	Cairns	18,841
35		24	(h)	Doncaster R	W 1-0	Bloomer	18,754
36		27	(a)	Coventry C	L 0-1		26,441
37		31	(a)	Brentford	L 1-5	Cairns	15,777
38	Apr	7	(h)	Luton T	L 0-2		12,435
39		14	(a)	Leeds U	L 0-1		15,524
40		21	(h)	West Ham U	L 0-1		10,674
41		28	(a)	Swansea T	W 3-1	Wood 2, Bloomer	14,485
42	May	5	(a)	Manchester C	D 2-2	Bloomer, Lloyd	20,293

FINAL LEAGUE POSITION: 22nd in Division Two

Appearances

Goals

FA Cup

3	Jan	6	(h)	Exeter C	D 3-3
R		10	(a)	Exeter C	L 2-4

Chisholm	Moody	Fisher	Johnston	McMillan	MacKenzie	Bloomer	Squires	Briggs	Cairns	Hair	Turnbull	Hayhurst	Harnby	Taylor	Greetham	Gray G	Barratt A	Scotson	Duthie	Walker	McStay	Lloyd	Mulholland	Rankin	Jenkins	Shearer	Maddison	Wood	
1	2	3	4	5	6	7	8	9	10	11																			1
1	2	3	4	5	6		8	9	10	11											7								2
1	2	3	4	5	6		8	9	10	11											7								3
1	2	3	4	5	6		8	9	10	11											7								4
1	2	3	4	5	6		8	9	10	11											7								5
1	2	3	4	5	6			9	10	11												7				8			6
1	2	3	4	5	6	8		9	10	11												7							7
1	2			5	4		8	9	10	11			3						6				7						8
1	2	3		5	4		8	9	10	11									6		7								9
1	2	3	4	5			8	9	10	11									6			7							10
1	2			5		7	8	9	10				3			4			6								11		11
1	2			5		7	8	9	10				3			4			6								11		12
1	2			5	10	7	8	9					3			4			6								11		13
1	2			5	10	9	8						3				4		6		7						11		14
1	2			5	10	9	8						3				4		6		7						11		15
1	2			5	10	9	8							3			4		6					7			11		16
1	2			5	10	9	8							3			4		6					7			11		17
1	2			5	10	9	8							3			4		6					7			11		18
1	4	2			10		8		9					3			6		5					7			11		19
1	2				10		8	9						3			6	4	5			7					11		20
1	2	3			10		8	9									6	4	5			7					11		21
1	2				10		8	9						3			6	4	5			7					11		22
1	2		4		10		8	9						3			6		5			7					11		23
		2				9	8		10	11	1			3			6	4	5			7							24
		2			10	9	8				1			3			6	4	5			7					11		25
1					10		8		9				2	3			6	4	5			7					11		26
						9	8		10			1	2	3			6	4	5			7					11		27
						9	8		10			1	2	3			6	4	5			7					11		28
					10		8		9			1	2	3			6	4	5			11			7				29
					10	9			8			1	2	3			6	4	5			11			7				30
					10		8		9			1	2	3			6	4	5			11			7				31
						9	8		10			1	2	3			6	4	5			7					11		32
						9	8		10			1	3	2			6	4	5			7					11		33
				5			8		9			1	3	2			4		6		7	10					11		34
	2			5	4	9	8					1	3						6		7	10					11		35
	2			5	4	9	8					1	3						6		7	10					11		36
	2			5	6				8			1	3					4	9		7	10					11		37
	2				6	9	8					1	3					4	5		7	10					11		38
				5	8	9						1	3		2			4		6	7	10					11		39
				5	8	9				11		1	3		2			4		6		10			7				40
				5		9	8			11		1	3		2		4			6		7						10	41
				5		9	8			11		1	3		2		4			6		7						10	42
24	27	13	9	26	31	24	36	17	24	14	2	16	23	18	4	3	23	17	31	4	13	26	1	4	4	1	25	2	
				1	9	10	2	11	16	1												5		1			2	2	

1 own-goal

1951-52

1	Aug	19	(a)	Chesterfield	L 1-3	Cairns	10,625
2		22	(h)	Lincoln C	L 2-3	Cairns 2	21,479
3		25	(h)	Bradford	W 3-0	Marlow, Cairns 2	14,476
4		29	(a)	Lincoln C	W 2-0	Hernon, Marlow	19,522
5	Sep	1	(a)	Halifax T	L 0-3		9,879
6		5	(h)	Barrow	W 1-0	Cairns	16,250
7		8	(h)	Mansfield T	D 1-1	Marlow	17,574
8		13	(a)	Barrow	L 1-3	Marlow	7,821
9		15	(a)	Rochdale	D 0-0		6,181
10		22	(h)	Accrington S	W 2-1	Marlow, Cairns	13,095
11		29	(a)	Carlisle U	W 2-1	Marlow, Jenkins	14,114
12	Oct	6	(h)	Tranmere R	W 1-0	McDonald (og)	14,500
13		13	(a)	Southport	L 0-2		7,015
14		20	(h)	Crewe A	L 0-1		12,772
15		27	(a)	Gateshead	D 1-1	Hernon	11,398
16	Nov	3	(h)	Darlington	W 3-0	McCue, Hernon, Bloomer	12,803
17		10	(a)	Oldham A	D 1-1	Cairns	21,502
18		17	(h)	Hartlepools U	W 2-0	Cairns 2	12,296
19	Dec	1	(h)	York C	D 0-0		12,398
20		8	(a)	Chester	W 3-0	Cairns 2, Hernon	4,935
21		22	(a)	Bradford	L 2-3	Cairns, Bloomer	12,169
22		25	(h)	Scunthorpe U	W 3-2	Cairns, Bloomer, Maddison	19,351
23		26	(a)	Scunthorpe U	W 3-1	Cairns, Bloomer 2	15,734
24		29	(h)	Halifax T	W 8-1	Johnston 2 (2 pens), Hernon 2, Cairns 2, Maddison, Bloomer	13,548
25	Jan	5	(a)	Mansfield T	D 2-2	Bloomer 2	9,471
26		12	(a)	Wrexham	L 0-2		9,755
27		19	(h)	Rochdale	W 4-0	Bloomer 2, Maddison, Johnston	12,780
28		26	(a)	Accrington S	W 3-0	Bloomer, Cairns, Maddison	4,210
29	Feb	2	(h)	Wrexham	W 1-0	Hernon	14,162
30		9	(h)	Carlisle U	W 4-1	Bloomer 2, Hernon, Johnston (pen)	16,148
31		16	(a)	Tranmere R	W 3-2	Johnston (pen), Bloomer, Hernon	9,160
32		23	(a)	Workington	W 4-2	Cairns 2, Hernon, Lloyd	6,736
33	Mar	1	(h)	Southport	W 4-1	Cairns 3, Lloyd	15,639
34		8	(a)	Crewe A	W 2-1	Bloomer, Maddison	6,959
35		15	(h)	Gateshead	W 2-0	Hernon, Cairns	16,306
36		22	(a)	Darlington	W 2-0	Bloomer, Cairns	6,707
37		29	(h)	Oldham A	W 3-1	Cairns, Hernon, Maddison	12,402
38	Apr	5	(a)	Hartlepools U	L 1-2	Carins	9,063
39		11	(h)	Stockport C	W 4-0	Johnston (pen), Maddison, Lloyd, Bloomer	26,605
40		12	(h)	Bradford C	W 2-1	Maddison, Cairns	16,892
41		14	(a)	Stockport C	D 1-1	Hernon	16,300
42		19	(a)	York C	D 1-1	Hernon	11,335
42		23	(a)	Bradford C	W 2-0	Johnston (pen), Cairns	8,961
44		26	(h)	Chester	W 2-1	Hernon, McCue	12,434
45		30	(h)	Chesterfield	W 2-0	Johnston (pen), Maddison	10,162
46	May	3	(h)	Workington	W 5-0	Cairns 2, Hernon, Brown, Jenkin	7,591

FINAL LEAGUE POSITION: 2nd in Division Three North

Appearances
Goals

FA Cup

1	Nov	24	(h)	Darlington	W 4-0	
2	Dec	15	(a)	Lincoln C	L 1-3	

Hayhurst	Brown W	Harnby	Scotson	Bellas	Wheatley	Lloyd	McKenzie Don	Cairns	Johnston	McCue	Tweedy	Daley	Galbraith	Freeburn	McMillan	Wood	Bloomer	Jenkin	Campbell	Marlow	Hernon	Goodwin	Green K	Maddison	Walker	
1	2	3	4	5	6	7	8	9	10	11																1
1	2	3	4			7	8	9	6	11					5						10					2
	2		4		6	7		9	3		1				5					8	10			11		3
	2		4		6	7		9	3			1			5					8	10			11		4
	2		4		6	7		9				1	3		5					8	10			11		5
	2		4					9	6			1	3		5		7			8	10			11		6
	2		4		6			9	3			1			5		7			8	10			11		7
	2		4			10			6			1	3		5		9	7		8				11		8
	2		4			10		9	6			1	3		5			7		8				11		9
	2		4					9	6			1	3		5			7		8	10			11		10
	2			5		11		9	6		1		3		4			7		8	10					11
	2			5		11		9	6		1		3		4			7		8	10					12
	2			5				9	6		1		3		4			7		8	10			11		13
	2			5		11		10	6		1		3		4		9	7			8					14
1	2		4					10	6	11			3		5		9		7		8					15
1	2		4					9	6	11			3		5		8		7		10					16
1	2		4					9	6	11			3		5		8		7		10					17
1	2		4					9	5	11			3			6	8		7		10					18
1	2		4					9	6	11			3		5		8		7		10					19
1	2		4					9	6				3		5		8		7		10			11		20
1	2		4			7		9	6				3		5		8				10			11		21
1	2		4			7		9	6				3		5		8				10			11		22
1	2		4			7		9	6				3		5		8				10			11		23
1	2		4			7		9	6				3		5		8				10			11		24
1	2		4			7		9	6				3		5		8				10			11		25
	2		4			7			6		1		3		5		8				10	9		11		26
	2		4			7		9	6		1		3		5		8				10			11		27
	2		4			7		9	6		1		3		5		8				10			11		28
	2		4			7			6		1		3		5		8				10		9	11		29
	2		4			7		9	6		1		3		5		8				10			11		30
	2		4			7		9	6		1		3		5		8				10			11		31
	2		4			7		9	6		1		3		5		8				10			11		32
	2		4			7		9	6		1		3		5		8				10			11		33
	2		4			7		9	6		1		3		5		8				10			11		34
	2		4			7		9	6		1		3		5		8				10			11		35
	2		4			7		9	6		1		3		5		8				10			11		36
	2		4			7		9	6		1		3		5		8				10			11		37
	2		4			7		9	6		1		3		5		8				10			11		38
	2		4			7		9	6		1		3		5		8				10			11		39
	2		4			7		9	6		1			3	5					8	10			11		40
	2		4			7		9	6		1		3		5		8				10			11		41
	2		4					9	6	7	1		3		5		8				10			11		42
	2		4				8	9	6	7	1		3		5						10			11		43
	2		4				8	9	6	7	1		3		5						10			11		44
1	2		4			8		9	5	7			3								10			11	6	45
1	2		4					9	6	8			3		5			7			10			11		46
15	46	2	42	5	5	32	4	43	45	12	24	7	40	1	43	1	31	8	6	12	43	1	1	36	1	
	1					3		31	8	2							17	2		6	16			9		

1 own-goal

1952-53

1	Aug	23	(h)	Wrexham	W	2-0	Cairns, Bloomer	16,676
2		28	(a)	Scunthorpe U	W	1-0	Johnston (pen)	18,794
3		30	(a)	Bradford	W	3-0	Cairns 2, Bloomer	16,998
4	Sep	3	(h)	Scunthorpe U	W	1-0	Bloomer	22,213
5		6	(h)	Oldham A	W	1-0	Bloomer	20,013
6		8	(a)	Barrow	D	1-1	Lloyd	6,275
7		13	(a)	Mansfield T	D	1-1	Bloomer	12,980
8		17	(h)	Barrow	W	2-1	F.Smith 2	16,990
9		20	(h)	Halifax T	W	2-0	F.Smith, Bloomer	17,862
10		25	(a)	Carlisle U	L	0-3		9,528
11		27	(a)	Accrington S	W	2-1	Cairns, F.Smith	5,774
12	Oct	1	(h)	Tranmere R	W	3-1	Cairns 2, F.Smith	14,398
13		4	(h)	Workington T	W	2-0	F.Smith, Maddison	16,223
14		11	(a)	Stockport C	D	2-2	Cairns, Scotson	13,260
15		18	(h)	Bradford C	D	0-0		16,043
16		25	(a)	Rochdale	W	2-0	McCue 2	12,291
17	Nov	1	(h)	Darlington	W	2-0	Bloomer, Johnston (pen)	14,618
18		8	(a)	Gateshead	L	0-2		11,451
19		15	(h)	Hartlepools U	W	7-0	F.Smith 4, Hernon, Millar, Johnston (pen)	13,096
20		29	(h)	Southport	W	1-0	McCue	12,312
21	Dec	13	(h)	Port Vale	D	1-1	McMillan	13,801
22		20	(a)	Wrexham	L	1-3	Maddison	9,420
23		25	(h)	Chesterfield	D	0-0		18,848
24		27	(a)	Chesterfield	L	2-3	Hart, Maddison	15,519
25	Jan	1	(a)	Tranmere R	L	1-2	McCue	8,769
26		3	(h)	Bradford	L	2-3	Grant, Rayner	12,201
27		13	(h)	Chester	W	5-4	McCue 2, Hernon, F.Smith, Johnston (pen)	6,204
28		17	(a)	Oldham A	D	1-1	Johnston (pen)	26,840
29		24	(h)	Mansfield T	W	5-1	McCue 2, Hart 2, Hernon	13,890
30		31	(a)	Chester	W	2-0	Maddison, McCue	4,005
31	Feb	7	(a)	Halifax T	L	2-3	Maddison, Lloyd	9,038
32		14	(h)	Accrington S	W	3-0	Jenkin, Hernon, McCue	11,118
33		21	(a)	Workington T	L	1-3	McCue	10,454
34		28	(h)	Stockport C	L	0-1		13,148
35	Mar	7	(a)	Bradford C	L	0-1		13,651
36		14	(h)	Rochdale	W	3-2	McCue 2,Scotson	10,578
37		21	(a)	Darlington	D	1-1	Hernon	6,613
38		28	(h)	Gateshead	D	0-0		10,445
39	Apr	3	(h)	York C	W	2-1	Grant, Lloyd	18,551
40		4	(a)	Hartlepools U	L	0-2		8,714
41		6	(a)	York C	L	0-2		12,356
42		11	(h)	Carlisle U	L	2-3	Lord, Jenkin	10,260
43		18	(a)	Southport	L	3-4	Cairns 2, Millar	6,687
44		25	(h)	Crewe A	W	1-0	Cairns	8,187
45		29	(a)	Crewe A	W	2-1	F.Smith, Johnston	4,162
46		30	(a)	Port Vale	L	0-4		7,964

FINAL LEAGUE POSITION: 5th in Division Three North

Appearances
Goals

FA Cup

1	Nov	22	(a)	Darlington	W	3-2
2	Dec	6	(h)	Bath C	W	1-0
3	Jan	10	(h)	Bury	L	1-3

Tweedy	Brown	Galbraith	Scotson	McMillan	Johnston	Lloyd	Bloomer	Cairns	Hernon	Maddison	Hayhurst	Daley	Freeburn	Robson	Player	Grant	Walker	Jenkin	McCue	Millar	Hart	Lord	Smith F	Rayner	Williams C	Smith D	Cadden	
1	2	3	4	5	6	7	8	9	10	11																		1
1	2	3	4	5	6	7	8	9	10	11																		2
1	2	3	4	5	6	7	8	9	10	11																		3
1	2	3	4	5	6	7	8	9	10	11																		4
1	2	3	4	5	6	7	8	9	10	11																		5
1	2	3	4	5	6	7	8	9	10	11																		6
1	2	3	4	5	6	7	8	9	10	11																		7
	2	3	4	5	6	7	8		10	11	1												9					8
	2	3	4	5	6	7	8		10	11	1												9					9
	2	3	4	5	6	7	8		10	11	1												9					10
	2	3	4	5	6		8	10		11	1							7					9					11
	2	3	4	5	6		7	8	10	11	1												9					12
	2		4	5	6		7	8	10	11	1			3									9					13
	2		4	5		7		8	10	11	1			3			6						9					14
	2	3	4	5				8	10	11	1						6	7					9					15
	2	3	4	5	6		8		10	11	1								7				9					16
	2	3	4	5	6		8		10	11	1								7				9					17
	2	3	4	5	6		8	9	10	11	1								7									18
	2	3	4	5	6				10	11	1								7	8			9					19
	2	3	4	5	6	8				11	1								7	10			9					20
	2	3	4	5	6	7			10	11	1								8				9					21
	2	3	4	5	6			8	10	11	1								7					9				22
	2	3	4	5	6			9	10	11	1								7		8							23
	2	3	4	5	6				10	11	1								7		8			9				24
			4	5	6					11	1		2	3		8			7		10		9					25
			4	5	6					11	1		2	3		8			7		10			9				26
		3	4	5	6	7			10	11	1		2						8				9					27
	2	3	4	5	6	7			10	11	1								8		9							28
	2	3	4	5	6	7			10	11	1								8		9							29
	2	3	4	5	6	7			10	11	1								8		9							30
	2	3	4	5	6	7			10	11	1								8		9							31
	2	3	4	5	6				10	11	1							7	8		9							32
	2	3	4		6				10	11	1							7	8		9						5	33
	2	3	4	5	6				10	11	1							7	8		9							34
	2	3	4	5	6			8	10	11	1								7		9							35
		3	4	5	6	7		9		11	1		2						8		10							36
		3	4	5	6	7		9	10	11	1		2						8									37
		3	4	5	6	7		9	10	11	1		2						8									38
1		3	4	5	10	7		9					2			8	6		11									39
		3		5	4	7		9	10			1	2			8	6		11									40
		3		5				9		11		1	2		4	8	6	7		10								41
				5				9		11		1	2	3	4	6		7		10		8						42
				5				9		11		1	2	3	6	4		7		10		8						43
				5				10		11		1	2	3	6	4		7				8	9					44
				5	10	7				11			2	3		4	6					8	9		1			45
				5	10	7				11		1		3		4	6					8	9			2		46
8	32	37	39	45	40	25	16	25	34	44	31	6	13	9	4	10	7	9	25	5	13	5	18	3	1	1	1	
			2	1	6	3	7	10	5	5						2		2	13	2	3	1	12	1				

1953-54

1	Aug	19	(h)	York C	W 3-0	Maddison 2, F.Smith	16,320
2		22	(h)	Scunthorpe U	L 0-1		18,246
3		26	(h)	Carlisle U	W 3-2	F.Smith 2, Hernon	14,516
4		29	(a)	Stockport C	L 2-3	F.Smith, Stroud	8,698
5	Sep	1	(a)	Carlisle U	D 3-3	Jenkins 2, Maddison	10,267
6		5	(h)	Rochdale	W 3-2	Wright 2, F.Smith	12,305
7		9	(h)	Accrington S	W 2-0	Bloomer, Dubois	11,357
8		12	(a)	Wrexham	L 0-4		13,748
9		16	(a)	Accrington	L 1-3	Wright	7,591
10		19	(h)	Mansfield T	L 0-2		9,929
11		23	(h)	Halifax T	W 2-1	Grant 2	7,752
12		26	(a)	Barrow	L 0-4		8,006
13		28	(a)	Halifax T	L 0-2		3,710
14	Oct	3	(h)	Bradford C	W 1-0	F.Smith	8,677
15		10	(h)	Gateshead	W 2-0	F.Smith, Stroud	9,166
16		17	(a)	Hartlepools U	L 0-3		9,039
17		24	(h)	Darlington	W 1-0	Robson	8,907
18		31	(a)	Barnsley	D 0-0		8,438
19	Nov	7	(h)	Bradford	D 0-0		8,551
20		14	(a)	Port Vale	L 0-2		14,889
21		21	(a)	Chester	D 1-1	Bloomer	5,327
22	Dec	5	(h)	Southport	L 1-2	Bloomer	7,469
23		19	(a)	Scunthorpe U	L 1-2	Bloomer	9,985
24		25	(h)	Tranmere R	W 1-0	Bloomer	12,054
25		26	(a)	Tranmere R	W 4-2	N.Wright 2, Stroud, Bloomer	8,662
26	Jan	2	(h)	Stockport C	W 1-0	Wright	8,683
27		16	(a)	Rochdale	L 1-4	F.Smith	4,934
28		23	(h)	Wrexham	D 0-0		7,744
29		30	(h)	Workington T	W 1-0	Stroud	5,590
30	Feb	6	(a)	Mansfield T	L 1-5	Maddison	6,513
31		13	(h)	Barrow	W 1-0	Wright	6,882
32		20	(a)	Bradford C	L 0-3		11,996
33		27	(a)	Gateshead	L 1-7	Wright	4,922
34	Mar	6	(h)	Hartlepools U	W 3-0	F.Smith 2, Robson	5,628
35		13	(a)	Darlington	L 0-3		4,652
36		17	(a)	Workington T	L 0-2		7,458
37		20	(h)	Barnsley	L 0-1		6,616
38		27	(a)	Bradford	L 1-4	Grant	5,302
39	Apr	3	(h)	Port Vale	D 2-2	F.Smith, Hernon	9,952
40		10	(a)	Crewe A	D 1-1	Rayner	3,415
41		12	(a)	York C	W 2-1	Rayner, Maddison	3,826
42		16	(h)	Chesterfield	D 1-1	F.Smith (pen)	11,913
43		17	(h)	Chester	D 0-0		7,330
44		19	(a)	Chesterfield	L 0-1		7,475
45		24	(a)	Southport	L 1-2	Sowerby	2,887
46		28	(h)	Crewe A	W 3-1	Scotson, Wright, Stroud	4,963

FINAL LEAGUE POSITION: 17th in Division Three North

Appearances
Goals

FA Cup

1	Nov	21	(h)	Rochdale	W 2-0
2	Dec	12	(a)	Witton A	D 1-1
R		15	(h)	Witton A	W 6-1
3	Jan	9	(h)	Fulham	D 5-5
R		13	(a)	Fulham*	D 0-0
R		18	(a)	Fulham	L 1-3

*Abandoned at half-time, ground waterlogged.

Williamson C	Brown	Robson	Scotson	McMillan	Johnston	Bloomer	Wright	Smith F	Hernon	Maddison	Nicholson	Freeburn	Smith D	Jobling	Tucker	Grant	Walker	Williams D	Stroud	Jenkins	Dubois	Newton	Cairns	Lord	Conner	Rayner	Sowerby	Player	
1	2	3	4	5	6	7	8	9	10	11																			1
1	2	3	4	5	6	7	8		10	11													9						2
1	2	3	4	5	6	7	8	9	10	11																			3
1	2	3	4	5	6	8	10	9		11									7										4
1	2	3	4	5	6	8	10	9		11										7									5
1	2	3	4	5	6	8	10	9		11										7									6
1		3	4	5	6	8	10	9		11		2									7								7
1		3	4	5	6	8	10	9		11		2									7								8
		3	4		5		10	9		11	1	2					6				7		8						9
		3	4		5	8	10	9		11	1	2					6				7								10
1	2	3	4		5		10	9		11						8	6				7								11
1	2	3	4		5	7	10	9		11						8	6												12
1	2	3	4		5		10	9		11						8	6		7										13
1	2	3	4		5	8	10	9		11							6					7							14
1	2	3	4		5		10	9		11							6		7			8							15
1	2	3	4		5		10	9		11							6		7			8							16
1	2	10	4		5		8	9		11			3				6		7										17
1	2	3	4		5	9	10			11							6		7					8					18
1	2	3	4		5	9	10			11						8	6		7										19
1	2	3	4		5	9	10			11							6		7							8			20
1	2	3	4	5		8	10	9		11							6		7										21
1	2	3	4	5		8	10	9		11							6		7										22
1	2	3	4	5		8	10			11							6		7							9			23
1	2	3	4	5		8	10			11							6		7							9			24
1	2	3	4	5		8	10			11							6		7							9			25
1	2	3	4	5		8	10			11							6		7							9			26
1	2	3	4	5		9	10	8		11							6		7										27
1	2	3	4	5	8	9	10			11							6				7								28
1	2	3	4	5	6	9	10			11									7						8				29
1	2	3	4	5	6	9	10			11									7						8				30
1		3	4		6	9	8			11		2		5					7								10		31
		3	4			9	8			11	1	2		5				6	7								10		32
		3	4				8	9		11	1	2		5				6	7								10		33
		3	4			7	8	9		11	1	2		5				6									10		34
		3	4				8	9		11	1	2		5				6	7								10		35
		3	4				8	9	10	11	1	2		5				6	7										36
		3	4				8	9	10	11	1	2		5			6		7										37
		3	5				7	9	10	11	1	2		4		6			8										38
	2	3	4					8	10	11	1			5			6		7							9			39
	2	3	4	5				8	10	11	1						6		7							9			40
	2	3	4	5				8	10	11	1						6		7							9			41
	2	3	4	5				8	10	11	1						6		7							9			42
	2		4	5				8	10	11	1		3				6		7								9		43
	2		4						10	11	1		3		5		6		7					8			9		44
	2	3	6					8	10	11	1				5				7								9	4	45
	2	3	6				8	9	10	11	1				5				7									4	46
29	34	44	46	22	24	27	39	32	14	46	17	12	3	9	3	5	27	5	32	2	6	3	2	2	2	9	8	2	
		2	1			6	9	12	2	5						3			5	2	1					2	1		

1954-55

1	Aug	21	(a)	Rochdale	W 3-0	Hughes 2, DeGruchy	6,915
2		24	(h)	Scunthorpe U	L 1-4	Harrison	19,736
3		28	(h)	Tranmere R	D 2-2	Hughes 2 (1 pen)	10,669
4	Sep	2	(a)	Scunthorpe U	L 0-1		15,547
5		4	(a)	Stockport C	D 0-0		10,400
6		8	(h)	Chester	W 3-1	Stroud, Lowry, Harrison	10,117
7		11	(h)	Hartlepools U	W 1-0	Stroud	10,117
8		15	(a)	Chester	L 0-1		5,133
9		18	(a)	Gateshead	L 0-1		6,698
10		22	(h)	Crewe A	W 2-1	Harbertson, Hughes (pen)	8,134
11		25	(h)	Darlington	L 0-2		8,727
12		27	(a)	Crewe A	L 0-2		4,519
13	Oct	2	(a)	Chesterfield	L 0-1		11,125
14		9	(h)	Wrexham	L 1-3	Harbertson	8,291
15		16	(a)	Accrington S	L 0-3		8,416
16		23	(h)	Mansfield T	W 3-2	Hughes 2 (1 pen), Stroud	7,359
17		30	(a)	Workington T	D 2-2	Hughes 2	9,430
18	Nov	6	(h)	Barrow	W 1-0	Stroud	6,192
19		13	(a)	Southport	D 2-2	Maddison 2	3,026
20		27	(a)	Halifax T	L 2-3	Conner, Stroud	8,589
21	Dec	4	(h)	Oldham A	D 1-1	Bloomer	5,950
22		18	(h)	Rochdale	D 1-1	Hughes	7,853
23		25	(h)	Barnsley	L 1-3	Harbertson	10,400
24		27	(a)	Barnsley	W 3-1	Stokes, Stroud, Maddison	16,887
25	Jan	1	(a)	Tranmere R	L 0-2		4,806
26		15	(h)	Stockport C	W 1-0	Harrison	5,611
27		29	(a)	Carlisle U	L 1-3	Harbertson	5,082
28	Feb	5	(h)	Gateshead	D 1-1	Stokes	6,982
29		12	(a)	Darlington	W 3-1	Harrison 2, Maddison	4,588
30		19	(h)	Chesterfield	L 1-2	Harrison	5,513
31	Mar	5	(h)	Accrington S	W 2-1	Harrison, Stokes	6,672
32		8	(h)	Carlisle U	W 2-0	Faulkner, Hill (og)	3,690
33		12	(a)	Mansfield T	L 0-3		6,250
34		19	(h)	Workington T	L 0-1		10,519
35		23	(a)	Hartlepools U	L 2-3	Philips, Harbertson (pen)	4,134
36		26	(a)	Barrow	L 0-2		2,825
37	Apr	2	(h)	Southport	L 0-1		7,088
38		8	(h)	Bradford	W 1-0	Hughes	11,610
39		9	(a)	York C	D 0-0		12,436
40		11	(a)	Bradford	L 1-2	Harbertson	5,850
41		16	(h)	Halifax T	L 0-1		5,916
42		20	(a)	Bradford C	L 0-4		5,937
43		23	(a)	Oldham A	L 0-4		4,296
44		27	(h)	York C	W 2-1	Stroud, Scotson	7,184
45		30	(h)	Bradford C	L 1-4	DeGruchy	6,879
46	May	4	(a)	Wrexham	L 0-5		2,927

FINAL LEAGUE POSITION: 23rd in Division Three North

Appearances
Goals

FA Cup

1	Nov	30	(h)	Halifax T	W 2-1
2	Dec	11	(h)	Southampton	W 4-1
3	Jan	8	(h)	Wolves	L 2-5

Archer	Brown	Higgins	Scotson	McMillan	Conner	Stroud	Pringle	Harrison	Hughes	DeGruchy	Williams	Maddison	Freeburn	Johnston	Robson	Jobling	Player	Redding	Chilton	Sowerby	Walker	Lowry	Harbertson	Faulkner	Bloomer	Slater	Phillips	Weatherall	Tinsley	Stokes	
1	2	3	4	5	6	7	8	9	10	11																					1
1	2	3	4	5		7	8	9	10	11										6											2
1	2	3	4	5	6	8		9	10	11												7									3
1	2	3	4		6	8		9	10			11					5					7									4
1	2	3	4		6			9	10			11					5			8		7									5
1	2	3	4		6	8		9	10			11					5					7									6
	2	3	4		6	8		9	10		1	11					5					7									7
	2	3	4		6	8		9	10		1	11					5					7									8
	2	3			4	10		9	6		1	11					5					7	8								9
	2	3			4	10		9	6		1				11		5					7	8								10
	2	3			4	10		9	6		1				11		5					7	8								11
		2		5	4	10		9	6		1			3	11							7	8								12
		2			6	8		9	10		1	11			3	4	5						7								13
1	2	3				7		10	6			11				4	5					8	9								14
1	2	3	8		6	7			10			11				4	5						9								15
1	2	3	8		6	7		9	10			11				4	5														16
1	2	3	8		6	7		9	10			11				4	5														17
	2	3	8		4	7			10		1	11		6			5						9								18
	2	3			4	7		9	10		1	11		6			5								8						19
	2	3			4	7		9			1	11		10		6	5								8						20
	2	3			4	7		9	10		1	11		6			5								8						21
	2	3			4	7		8	10		1	11		6			5						9								22
	2	3			4	7		9	10		1	11		6			5						8								23
	2	3			4	7					1	11						5			6		8			10				9	24
	2	3			4	7					1	11		6				5					8			10				9	25
	2				4	7		10			1	11		5	3						6		8							9	26
	2	3			4	7		10			1	11		5				6					8							9	27
	2	3			4	7		10			1	11		5							6		8							9	28
	2	3			4			10			1	11		5							6		7			8				9	29
		3			4			10			1	11	2	5							6		7			8				9	30
		3			4			10			1	11	2	5							6		8	7						9	31
		3			4			10			1	11	2	5							6		8	7			9				32
		3			4			10			1	11	2	5							6		8	7						9	33
		3			4			10			1	11	2	6					5				8	7						9	34
		3			4	7		10			1	11	2	6					5				8				9				35
		3			4	7		10			1	11	2	6					5				8				9				36
		3				7		10			1	11	2	4					5		6		8				9				37
	2	3	4			7			8			11		6					5	10								9	1		38
	2	3	4			7			10			11		6					5	8								9	1		39
	2	3	4			7			10			11		6					5				8					9	1		40
	2	3	4			7		10				11		6					5				8				9		1		41
	2	3	4			7		9				11		10			6		5								8		1		42
	2	3	4			7				10		11		6					5									8	1	9	43
	2	3	4			7		9		10		11		6					5									8	1		44
	2	3	4			7		9		10		11		6					5									8	1		45
	2	3				7		9		10				6			5		4					11				8	1		46
10	36	45	20	4	34	39	2	38	25	7	27	39	8	29	5	6	21	3	13	4	9	11	26	5	3	4	6	7	9	11	
			1		1	7		7	11	2		4										1	6	1	1		1			3	

1 own-goal

1955-56

1	Aug	20	(h)	Rochdale	D 1-1	Evans	11,694
2		23	(h)	Chester	W 6-1	Crosbie 4, Reeson 2	10,573
3		27	(a)	Chesterfield	L 0-1		8,881
4		31	(a)	Chester	L 0-2		6,193
5	Sep	3	(h)	Tranmere R	W 1-0	Richardson	9,852
6		6	(h)	Carlisle U	W 1-0	Weatherall	12,194
7		10	(a)	Southport	L 0-2		3,650
8		13	(a)	Carlisle U	W 2-1	Evans, Reeson	12,294
9		17	(h)	Gateshead	W 3-1	Maddison, Reeson, Crosbie (pen)	11,266
10		21	(a)	Bradford C	W 2-0	Priestley, Crosbie	11,547
11		24	(a)	Darlington	W 1-0	Evans	9,270
12		27	(h)	Barrow	W 3-0	Crosbie 2, Reeson	19,874
13	Oct	1	(h)	Accrington S	W 3-0	Maddison, Reeson, Crosbie	19,069
14		8	(a)	Oldham A	D 1-1	Crosbie	10,300
15		15	(h)	Halifax T	W 4-0	Evans, Crosbie, Maddison, Reeson	13,092
16		22	(a)	York C	W 4-3	Reeson 3, Evans	14,566
17		29	(h)	Derby C	W 2-1	Maddison, Crosbie	19,874
18	Nov	5	(a)	Crewe A	D 0-0		6.165
19		12	(h)	Hartlepools U	W 1-0	Crosbie	14,481
20		26	(h)	Mansfield T	W 2-0	Crosbie, Priestley	12,572
21	Dec	3	(a)	Wrexham	L 0-1		7,654
22		17	(a)	Rochdale	L 0-2		4,547
23		24	(h)	Chesterfield	W 3-0	Crosbie 3	13,304
24		26	(h)	Bradford	W 2-0	Crosbie (pen), Maddison	17,908
25		27	(a)	Bradford	L 1-2	Crosbie	12,102
26		31	(a)	Tranmere R	W 1-0	Maddison	9,005
27	Jan	2	(a)	Barrow	D 0-0		11,329
28		21	(a)	Gateshead	L 0-2		4,247
29		28	(h)	Workington T	L 1-2	Crosbie	10,772
30	Feb	11	(a)	Accrington S	W 1-0	Evans	13,305
31		15	(a)	Stockport C	D 0-0		4,000
32		18	(h)	Oldham A	W 5-1	Reeson, Pell, Crosbie 3	10,070
33	Mar	3	(h)	York C	W 2-1	Reeson, Crosbie	14,529
34		10	(a)	Derby C	W 3-1	Upton (og), Crosbie, Priestley	33,330
35		17	(h)	Stockport C	W 3-0	Reeson, Crosbie, Evans	13,958
36		24	(a)	Hartlepools U	W 2-1	Evans, Crosbie	10,360
37		30	(h)	Scunthorpe U	L 0-1		23,399
38		31	(h)	Crewe A	W 5-1	Crosbie 4, Reeson	12,615
39	Apr	2	(a)	Scunthorpe U	W 1-0	Evans	19,067
40		7	(a)	Mansfield T	W 2-0	Priestley, Reeson	15,562
41		14	(h)	Wrexham	W 1-0	Crosbie	14,560
42		17	(h)	Darlington	W 1-0	Crosbie	16,803
43		21	(a)	Workington T	D 0-0		8,605
44		25	(h)	Southport	W 2-0	Evans, Crosbie	23,056
45		28	(h)	Bradford C	W 2-0	Evans, Maddison	15,733
46		30	(a)	Halifax T	W 1-0	Crosbie	4,315

FINAL LEAGUE POSITION: 1st in Division Three North

Appearances

Goals

FA Cup

1	Nov	19	(a)	Netherfield	W 5-1
2	Dec	10	(a)	Southport	D 0-0
R		14	(h)	Southport	W 3-2
3	Jan	7	(a)	Portsmouth	L 1-3

	Williams	Brown	DeGruchy	Johnston	Chilton	Richardson	Priestley	Evans	Crosbie	Reeson	Maddison	Conner	Pell	Anderson	Stokes	Weatherall	Player	Higgins	Lowry
1	1	2	3	4	5	6	7	8	9	10	11								
2	1	2	3	4	5	6	7	8	9	10	11								
3	1	2	3	4	5	6	7	8	9	10	11								
4	1	2	3	4	5	6	7	8	9	10	11								
5	1	2	3	4	5	6	7	8		10	11					9			
6	1	2	3	4	5	6	7	8		10	11					9			
7	1	2	3	4		6	7	8		10	11					9	5		
8	1	2	3	4	5	6	7	8	9	10	11								
9	1	2	3	4	5	6	7	8	9	10	11								
10	1	2	3		5	6	7	8	9	10	11	4							
11	1	2	3		5	6	7	8	9	10	11	4							
12	1	2	3		5	6	7	8	9	10	11	4							
13	1	2	3		5	6	7	8	9	10	11	4							
14	1	2	3		5	6	7	8	9	10	11	4							
15	1		3		5	6		8	9	10	11	4		2					7
16	1		3		5	6	7	8	9	10	11	4		2					
17	1		3		5	6	7	8	9	10	11	4		2					
18	1	2	3		5	6	7	8	9	10	11	4							
19	1	2	3		5	6	7	8	9	10	11	4							
20	1	2	3		5	6	7	8	9	10	11	4							
21	1	2	3		5	6	7	8		10	11	4			9				
22	1	2	3		5	6	7	8	9	10	11	4							
23	1	2	3		5	6	7	8	9	10	11	4							
24	1	2	3		5	6	7	8	9	10	11	4							
25	1	2			5	6	7	8	9	10	11	4						3	
26	1	2	3		5	6	7	8	9	10	11	4							
27	1	2	3		5	6	7	8	9	10	11	4							
28	1	2	3		5	6	7	8	9	10	11	4							
29	1	2	3		5	6	7	8	9	10	11	4							
30	1	2	3		5	6	7	8	9		11	4			10				
31	1	2	3		5	6	7	8	9		11	4			10				
32	1	2	3		5	6	7	8	9	11		4	10						
33	1	2	3		5	6	7	8	9	10		4	11						
34	1	2	3		5	6	7	8	9	10	11	4							
35	1	2	3		5	6	7	8	9	10	11	4							
36	1	2	3		5	6	7	8	9	10	11	4							
37	1	2	3		5	6	7	8	9	10	11	4							
38	1	2	3	6			7	8	9	10	11	4					5		
39	1	2	3	6			7	8	9	10	11	4					5		
40	1	2	3	6	5		7	8	9	10	11	4							
41	1	2	3	6	5		7	8	9	10	11	4							
42	1	2	3	6	5		7	8	9	10	11	4							
43	1	2	3	6	5		7	8	9	10	11	4							
44	1	2	3	6	5		7	8	9	10	11	4							
45	1	2	3	6	5		7	8	9	10	11	4							
46	1	2	3	6			7	8	9	10	11	4					5		
	46	43	45	18	42	37	45	46	42	44	44	37	2	3	3	3	4	1	1
						1	4	11	35	15	7		1			1			

1 own-goal

1956-57

1	Aug	18	(a)	Bristol R	D	0-0		27,818
2		20	(a)	Stoke C	L	0-1		20,921
3		25	(h)	Notts C	W	2-1	Reeson, Scott	18,241
4		28	(h)	Stoke C	W	4-1	Evans 2, Scott, Crobie	17,922
5	Sep	1	(a)	Liverpool	L	2-3	Crosbie 2	43,222
6		4	(h)	Middlesbrough	W	3-2	Crosbie, Evans, Maddison	20,296
7		8	(h)	Leyton O	D	0-0		18,251
8		12	(a)	Middlesbrough	L	1-2	Crosbie	15,999
9		15	(a)	Huddersfield T	L	1-2	Maddison	18,312
10		22	(h)	Bury	L	0-1		15,698
11		29	(a)	Lincoln C	L	0-1		18,973
12	Oct	6	(h)	Swansea T	W	5-0	Crosbie 2, Evans 2, Johnston (pen)	13,295
13		13	(a)	Fulham	L	1-3	Scott	31,727
14		20	(h)	Port Vale	W	1-0	Scott	13,879
15		27	(a)	West Ham U	W	1-0	Hodgson	24,236
16	Nov	3	(h)	Blackburn R	L	1-3	Maddison	16,616
17		10	(a)	Bristol C	W	2-0	Scott, Maddison	18,976
18		17	(h)	Sheffield U	L	1-2	Evans	15,601
19		24	(a)	Barnsley	L	0-2		11,281
20	Dec	1	(h)	Nottingham F	D	0-0		13,814
21		8	(a)	Rotherham U	L	1-2	Maddison	10,642
22		15	(h)	Bristol R	W	3-2	Priestley, Evans, Crosbie	10,460
23		22	(a)	Notts C	W	1-0	Reeson	4,869
24		25	(h)	Leicester C	D	2-2	Maddison 2 (1 pen)	16,381
25		29	(h)	Liverpool	D	0-0		15,504
26	Jan	12	(a)	Leyton O	D	1-1	Maddison	16,400
27		19	(h)	Huddersfield T	L	1-2	Reeson	14,929
28		26	(a)	Leicester C	L	3-4	Rafferty 2, Ogilvie (og)	34,773
29	Feb	2	(a)	Bury	W	3-2	Scott, Rafferty 2	12,623
30		9	(h)	Lincoln C	W	2-0	Emery (og), Rafferty	18,523
31		16	(a)	Swansea T	L	1-3	Scott	17,569
32		23	(h)	Fulham	W	3-1	Fell, Crosbie, Scott	13,060
33	Mar	2	(a)	Port Vale	L	0-3		15,293
34		9	(h)	West Ham U	W	2-1	Fell, Crosbie	13,996
35		16	(a)	Blackburn R	L	0-2		23,195
36		23	(h)	Bristol C	L	0-3		12,692
37		30	(a)	Sheffield U	L	0-2		18,380
38	Apr	6	(h)	Barnsley	W	4-1	Reeson, Rafferty, Evans 2	10,307
39		13	(a)	Nottingham F	L	1-2	Rafferty	21,316
40		19	(h)	Doncaster R	W	4-2	Rafferty 2, Evans, Scott	15,393
41		20	(h)	Rotherham U	W	3-2	Rafferty, Scott 2	13,474
42		22	(a)	Doncaster R	W	1-0	Conner	8,981

FINAL LEAGUE POSITION: 16th in Division Two

Appearances

Goals

FA Cup

3	Jan	7	(a)	West Ham U	L	3-5

Williams C	Brown	DeGruchy	Conner	Chilton	Johnston	Priestley	Evans	Crosbie	Reeson	Maddison	Richardson	Tucker	Scott	Player	Walker	Jobling	Pell	Hodgson D	Stokes	Rafferty	Fell	Daley	Redding	Williams D	Higgins	
1	2	3	4	5	6	7	8	9	10	11																1
1	2	3	4	5	6	7	8	9	10	11																2
1	2	3	4	5	6		8	9	10	11			7													3
1	2	3	4	5	6		8	9	10	11			7													4
1	2	3	4	5	6		8	9	10	11			7													5
1	2	3	4	5	6		8	9	10	11			7													6
1	2	3	4	5	6		8	9	10	11			7													7
1	2	3	4		6		8	9	10	11			7	5												8
1	2	3	4		6	8	10	9		11			7	5												9
1	2	3	4	5	6	9	8		10	11			7													10
1	2	3	4		6	8		9	10	11			7	5												11
1	2	3	4		6	10	8	9		11			7	5												12
1	2	3	4		6	10	8	9		11			7	5												13
1	2	3	4		6	10	8	9		11			7	5												14
1	2	3	4		6	10	8			11			7	5				9								15
1	2	3	4		6	10	8			11			7	5				9								16
1	2	3	4		5	10	8			11	6		7					9								17
1	2	3	4		5	10	8			11	6		7					9								18
1	2	3	4		5	10	8			11	6		7					9								19
1	2		4		6				10	11	3	5	7				8		9							20
1	2		4		6		8	9	10	11		5	7										3			21
1	2		4		6	7	8	9	10	11	3	5														22
1	2		4		6	7	8	9	10	11	3	5														23
1	2		4			7	8	9	10	11	3	5			6											24
1	2		4			7	8	9	10	11	3	5			6											25
1	2		4		6		8		10	11	3	5								9				7		26
	2		4		6		8		10	11	3	5								9		1		7		27
1	2					8			10	11	3	5	7		6					9					4	28
1	2		4			8			10	11	3	5	7		6					9						29
1	2		4			8			10	11	3	5	7		6					9						30
1	2		4			8			10	11	3	5	7		6					9						31
1	2		4		6	8		9			3	5	7							10	11					32
1	2		4		6	8					3	5	7						9	10	11					33
1	2		4			8		9			3	5	7			6				10	11					34
1	2		4			8		9			3	5	7			6				10	11					35
1	2	3	4			8		9		11		5	7			6				10						36
1	2		4			8		9		11	3	5	7			6				10						37
1	2		4				8		10		3	5	7			6				9	11					38
1	2		4				8		10		3	5	7			6				9	11					39
1	2		4				8				3	5	7		6			10		9	11					40
1	2		4				8				3	5	7		6			10		9	11					41
1	2		4				8		10		3	5	7		6					9	11					42
41	42	20	41	8	27	27	30	23	25	33	24	23	34	8	9	6	1	7	2	17	9	1	1	2	1	
			1		1	1	10	10	4	8			11					1		10	2					

2 own-goals

1957-58

1	Aug	24	(h)	Leyton O	W	7-2	Fell, Evans, Rafferty, Stockin, Conner, Priestley 2	14,274
2		27	(h)	Cardiff C	D	1-1	Evans	18,014
3		31	(a)	Charlton A	L	0-2		19,969
4	Sep	4	(a)	Cardiff C	W	3-1	Rafferty, Fell, Evans	13,433
5		7	(h)	Doncaster R	W	3-1	Stockin 2, Rafferty	16,575
6		10	(a)	Bristol C	D	2-2	Rafferty, Stockin	19,887
7		17	(h)	Bristol C	D	1-1	Priestley	12,004
8		21	(h)	Huddersfield T	W	4-1	Scott, Evans, Rafferty 2	14,380
9		28	(a)	Lincoln C	W	4-1	Rafferty, Fell 2, Reeson	17,221
10	Oct	5	(a)	Stoke C	L	1-4	Conner	18,540
11		12	(h)	Notts C	W	2-0	Rafferty, Fell	14,055
12		19	(a)	Ipswich T	L	2-3	Rafferty 2	18,577
13		26	(h)	Blackburn R	L	3-4	Conner, Rafferty 2	14,761
14	Nov	2	(a)	Sheffield U	L	1-3	Fell	19,675
15		9	(h)	West Ham U	L	1-2	Evans	11,878
16		16	(a)	Barnsley	D	3-3	Stockin, Rafferty 2	16,091
17		23	(h)	Fulham	W	3-1	Stockin, Rafferty 2	15,102
18		30	(a)	Swansea T	W	2-0	Whitefoot, Fell	12,573
19	Dec	7	(h)	Derby C	W	3-2	Scott, Rafferty, Fell	12,246
20		14	(a)	Bristol R	W	7-0	Stockin 2, Scott 2, Fell, Rafferty (pen), Priestley	14,577
21		21	(a)	Leyton O	L	1-5	Whitefoot	13,274
22		25	(h)	Liverpool	W	3-1	Scott, Whitefoot, Fell	17,705
23		26	(a)	Liverpool	L	2-3	Priestley, Rafferty	47,776
24		28	(h)	Charlton A	W	4-2	Rafferty 2, Whitefoot (pen), Fell	17,537
25	Jan	11	(a)	Doncaster R	D	3-3	Fell 2, Scott	10,817
26		18	(h)	Rotherham U	W	3-1	Rafferty, Fell, Whitefoot	12,278
27	Feb	1	(a)	Huddersfield T	L	0-1		14,333
28		8	(h)	Lincoln C	W	4-0	Priestley, Evans 2, Rafferty	13,464
29		15	(a)	Rotherham U	L	0-2		9,864
30		22	(a)	Fulham	L	0-6		21,316
31	Mar	1	(h)	Ipswich T	L	0-2		13,263
32		8	(a)	Blackburn R	L	0-3		27,923
33		15	(h)	Sheffield U	L	1-3	Briggs	16,701
34		22	(a)	West Ham U	L	0-2		25,900
35		29	(h)	Barnsley	W	2-1	Rafferty, Briggs	9,622
36	Apr	4	(h)	Middlesbrough	W	4-1	Briggs 3, Rafferty	17,233
37		5	(a)	Notts C	L	0-2		11,555
38		7	(a)	Middlesbrough	L	1-5	Stockin	22,204
39		12	(h)	Swansea T	D	2-2	Stockin, Scott	11,275
40		19	(a)	Derby C	L	0-1		13,549
41		22	(h)	Stoke C	D	0-0		10,841
42		26	(h)	Bristol R	W	3-2	Sinclair, Conner, Rafferty	10,030

FINAL LEAGUE POSITION: 13th in Division Two

Appearances
Goals

FA Cup

3	Jan	4	(a)	Sheffield U	L	1-5		

Williams	Brown	Richardson	Conner	Tucker	Walker	Priestley	Evans	Rafferty	Stockin	Fell	Fleming	Player	Jobling	Whitefoot	Scott	Briggs	Reeson	Welbourne	DeGruchy	Sinclair	Laverick	Maddison	Tinsley	
1	2	3	4	5	6	7	8	9	10	11														1
	2	3	4	5	6	7	8	9	10	11													1	2
	2	3	4	5	6	7	8	9	10	11													1	3
		3	4	5	6	7	8	9	10	11	2												1	4
		3	4	5	6	7	8	9	10	11	2												1	5
		3	4	5	6	7	8	9	10	11	2												1	6
	2	3	4	5	6	7	8	9	10	11													1	7
	2	3	4	5			8	9	10	11					7			6					1	8
	2	3	4	5			8	9		11					7		10	6					1	9
	2	3	4	5			8	9		11					7		10	6					1	10
	2	3	4	5			8	9		11					7		10	6					1	11
	2	3	4	5			8	9							7		10	6				11	1	12
	2	3	4	5			8	9		11					7		10	6					1	13
	2	3	4	5	6	8		9		11					7		10						1	14
	2	6	4			7	8	9		11		5					10		3				1	15
1		3	4			8		9	10	11		5		6	7				2					16
1	2	3	4			8		9	10	11		5		6	7									17
1	2	3	4			8		9	10	11		5		6	7									18
1	2	3	4			8		9	10	11		5		6	7									19
1	2	3	4			8		9	10	11		5		6	7									20
1	2	3	4			8		9	10	11		5		6	7									21
1	2	3	4			8		9	10	11		5		6	7									22
1	2	3	4			8	10	9		11		5		6	7									23
1	2	3	4			8	10	9		11		5		6	7									24
1	2	3	4			8	10	9		11		5		6	7									25
1	2	3	4			8	10	9		11			5	6	7									26
1	2	3	4			8	10	9		11			5	6	7									27
1	2	3	4			8	10	9		11			5	6	7									28
1	2	3	4			8	10	9		11			5	6	7									29
1	2	3	4			8	10	9		11			5	6	7									30
1		3				8		9		11	2		5	6	7			4			10			31
1	2	3	4			8		9	10			5		6	7							11		32
1	2	3	4			7		8	10	11		5		6		9								33
1	2	3	4			8		10		11		5		6	7	9								34
1	2	3	4			8		10		11		5		6	7	9								35
1	2	3	4					10	8	11			5	6	7	9								36
1	2	3	4					10	8	11			5	6	7	9								37
		3	4				8		10	11	2		5	6	7	9							1	38
1		3	4				8		10		2		5	6	7	9						11		39
1		3	4			8		10		11	2		5	6	7	9								40
1		3	4				8	10		11	2		5	6	7	9								41
1		3	4				8	10		11	2		5		7			6		9				42
27	32	42	41	14	8	30	26	40	21	39	9	15	13	26	33	9	7	8	2	1	1	3	15	
			4			6	7	26	10	14				5	7	5	1			1				

1958-59

1	Aug	23	(a)	Liverpool	D 3-3	Fell, Scott, Rafferty	47,502
2		26	(h)	Lincoln C	W 4-2	Cullen 2, Scott 2	22,261
3		30	(h)	Middlesbrough	W 3-2	Cullen 2, Rafferty	21,004
4	Sep	3	(a)	Lincoln C	D 4-4	Rafferty 4	19,759
5		6	(a)	Charlton A	L 1-2	Fell	18,609
6		10	(a)	Brighton & HA	L 0-2		20,880
7		13	(h)	Bristol C	W 2-0	Cockerill, Fell	15,298
8		16	(h)	Brighton & HA	D 1-1	Briggs	15,349
9		20	(a)	Cardiff C	L 1-4	Cullen	22,007
10		27	(h)	Huddersfield T	W 2-1	Cullen 2	14,401
11	Oct	4	(a)	Barnsley	L 1-3	Scott	10,157
12		11	(h)	Fulham	D 2-2	Cockerill, Fell	16,644
13		18	(a)	Sheffield W	L 0-6		29,866
14		25	(h)	Scunthorpe U	D 1-1	Briggs	16,753
15	Nov	1	(a)	Sunderland	L 0-1		23,045
16		8	(h)	Derby C	W 3-0	Upton (og), Briggs, Fell	11,044
17		15	(a)	Bristol R	L 3-7	Briggs, Cullen, Rafferty	15,733
18		22	(h)	Ipswich T	L 2-3	Rafferty 2	9,499
19		29	(a)	Swansea T	D 1-1	Cullen	14,244
20	Dec	6	(h)	Stoke C	D 2-2	Cockerill, Rafferty	9,255
21		13	(a)	Leyton O	W 1-0	Scott (pen)	7,632
22		20	(h)	Liverpool	L 2-3	Rafferty, Cullen	10,402
23		25	(h)	Sheffield U	L 1-2	Scott (pen)	13,946
24		27	(a)	Sheffield U	L 1-2	Rafferty	27,555
25	Feb	7	(h)	Cardiff C	W 5-1	Scott (pen), Fell, Cockerill, Rafferty 2	9,662
26		14	(a)	Huddersfield T	L 0-2		11,389
27		21	(h)	Barnsley	D 3-3	Scott (pen), Cullen, Welbourne	8,130
28		24	(a)	Bristol C	L 0-1		15,138
29		28	(a)	Derby C	L 0-3		22,293
30	Mar	7	(h)	Sheffield W	L 0-2		13,109
31		11	(a)	Middlesbrough	L 0-1		11,799
32		14	(a)	Scunthorpe U	W 3-1	Conner, Stockin, Rafferty	13,539
33		21	(h)	Sunderland	D 1-1	Stockin	10,193
34		27	(h)	Rotherham U	D 1-1	Rafferty	14,797
35		28	(a)	Fulham	L 0-3		25,517
36		30	(a)	Rotherham U	L 1-2	Stockin	8,815
37	Apr	4	(h)	Bristol R	L 1-2	Rafferty	9,217
38		11	(a)	Ipswich T	L 1-2	Fell	12,202
39		14	(h)	Charlton A	L 1-5	Fell	11,009
40		18	(h)	Swansea T	L 0-1		8,818
41		21	(h)	Leyton O	W 4-1	Conner, Rafferty 2, Stockin	7,754
42		25	(a)	Stoke C	L 0-4		6,855
FINAL LEAGUE POSITION: 21st in Division Two							Appearances
							Goals

FA Cup

3	Jan	10	(h)	Manchester C	D 2-2
R		24	(a)	Manchester C	W 2-1
4		28	(a)	Nottingham F	L 1-4

Williams C	Donovan	Richardson	Conner	Jobling	Cockerill	Scott	Cullen	Rafferty	Priestley	Fell	Barnett A	Bell	White	Bratley	Fleming	Burnett J	Welbourne	Player	Paul	Williams D	Briggs	Pearce	Barratt R	Stockin	Ritchie	Maddison	Bemrose	
1	2	3	4	5	6	7	8	9	10	11																		1
	2	3	4	5	6	7	8	9	10	11		1																2
	2	3	4	5	6	7	8	9	10	11		1																3
	2	3	4	5	6	7	8	9		11		1												10				4
	2	3	4	5	6	7	8	9		11		1												10				5
	2	3	4	5	6	7	8	9	10	11		1																6
	2	3	4	5	6	7	10	9		11		1									8							7
	2	3	4	5	6	7	10	9		11		1									8							8
	2	3	4	5	6	7	8	9		11		1													10			9
1	2	3	4	5	6	7	8	9		10																11		10
1		3	4	5	6	7	8	9		10				2												11		11
1	2	3	4	6	10	7	8	9		11								5										12
	2	3	4	6	10		8	9	7	11			1					5										13
1	2		4	6			8	10		11						3		5	7		9							14
1	2	3	4	6	5		8	10	7	11											9							15
1	2	3	4	6	5		8	10	7	11											9							16
1	2	3	4	6	5		8	10	7	11											9							17
1	2	3	4	6	5	7	8	10		11											9							18
1	2	3	6	5	10		7	8		11							4				9							19
1	2	3	6	5	10		7	8		11							4				9							20
1	2	3	6	5	10	7	8	9		11							4											21
1	2	3	6	5	10	7	8	9		11							4											22
	2	3	6	5	10	7	8	9		11	1						4											23
	2	3		5	6	7	8	9		11	1						4							10				24
	2	3		5	6	7	8	9		11	1						4							10				25
	2	3		5	6	7	8			11	1						4				9			10				26
	2	3		5	6	10	8	9		11	1						4			7								27
	2			5	6	10	8			11	1				3		4			7			9					28
	2			5	6	8	10			11	1				3		4			7			9					29
	2			5	6	7	8	10		11	1				3		4						9					30
	2		8	5	6	7		9		11	1				3		4							10				31
	2	3	8	5	6	7		9		11	1						4							10				32
	2	3	8	5	6			9		11	1						4			7				10				33
	2		8	5	6	7		9		11	1				3		4							10				34
	2	3		5	6		8	9			1						4			7				10			11	35
	3		4	5	6	7		9		11	1			2								8		10				36
	2	3		5	6	7	8	9		11	1						4							10				37
	2	3		5	6	7	8	9		11	1						4							10				38
	2	3		5	6	7	8	9		11	1						4							10				39
	4	3	10	5	6	7	8	9		11	1				2													40
	4	3	8	5	6	7		9		11	1				2									10				41
	4	3	8	5	6	7		9		11	1				2									10				42
13	41	35	31	42	41	33	35	39	8	41	20	8	1	2	8	1	20	3	1	5	10	1	3	16	1	2	1	
			2		4	8	11	19		8							1				4			4				

1 own-goal

1959-60

1	Aug	22	(h)	Chesterfield	W 5-1	Hunt 2, Rafferty 2, Cullen	11,794
2		24	(a)	Colchester U	D 2-2	Rafferty, Hunt	9,683
3		29	(a)	Newport C	W 2-0	Hunt, Scott (pen)	9,511
4	Sep	1	(h)	Colchester U	W 4-1	Scott, Hunt 3	14,455
5		5	(h)	Accrington S	W 4-0	Rafferty, Hunt, Sneddon (og), Scott (pen)	14,528
6		9	(a)	Swindon T	L 2-3	Hunt, Rafferty	22,678
7		12	(a)	Bournemouth	L 2-4	Hunt, Scott	12,292
8		15	(h)	Swindon T	W 3-0	Hunt, Scott 2 (1 pen)	11,608
9		19	(h)	Tranmere R	D 1-1	Hunt	13,227
10		21	(a)	York C	D 3-3	Rafferty, Hunt 2	11,500
11		26	(a)	Wrexham	L 1-2	Cullen	10,184
12		29	(h)	York C	D 2-2	Scott, Hunt	11,500
13	Oct	3	(h)	Brentford	L 1-3	Hunt	11,209
14		5	(a)	Queen's Park R	D 0-0		15,257
15		10	(a)	Southend U	L 0-3		10,462
16		13	(h)	Queen's Park R	W 3-1	Rafferty 2, Duff	6,024
17		17	(h)	Mansfield T	W 2-1	Rafferty 2	11,207
18		24	(a)	Halifax T	W 2-1	Lonsdale (og), Fell	6,147
19		31	(h)	Norwich C	D 1-1	Cullen	15,018
20	Nov	7	(a)	Barnsley	D 3-3	Cullen, Rafferty, Fell	6,521
21		21	(a)	Reading	W 2-1	Rafferty, Donovan	11,987
22		28	(h)	Shrewsbury T	W 2-1	Fell, Scott (pen)	10,958
23	Dec	12	(h)	Bury	D 2-2	Scott (pen), Hunt	9,899
24		19	(a)	Chesterfield	D 2-2	Hunt 2	3,863
25		26	(a)	Bradford C	L 1-3	Hunt	14,207
26		28	(h)	Bradford C	D 2-2	Hunt, Rafferty	18,033
27	Jan	2	(h)	Newport C	L 0-1		9,188
28		16	(a)	Accrington S	W 4-2	Rafferty, Scott, Hunt, Fell	4,243
29		23	(h)	Bournemouth	D 1-1	Rafferty	7,779
30	Feb	10	(a)	Port Vale	L 1-2	Hunt	22,987
31		13	(h)	Wrexham	W 3-1	Hunt, Rafferty, Scott	7,002
32		20	(a)	Brentford	W 2-0	Scott 2	10,900
33		22	(a)	Tranmere R	L 0-2		8,909
34		27	(h)	Southend U	D 1-1	Rafferty	8,860
35	Mar	5	(a)	Mansfield T	L 2-3	Fell, Rafferty	9,111
36		12	(h)	Halifax T	W 3-2	Hunt 2, Rafferty	7,116
37		19	(a)	Shrewsbury T	L 2-5	Hunt 2	6,107
38		26	(h)	Barnsley	W 2-0	Hunt 2	4,621
39	Apr	2	(a)	Southampton	D 1-1	Rafferty	20,367
40		9	(h)	Reading	L 0-1		7,389
41		15	(h)	Coventry C	W 3-0	Rafferty, Fell, Cullen	11,819
42		16	(a)	Norwich C	D 1-1	Hunt	33,720
43		19	(a)	Coventry C	W 2-0	Kearns (og), Rafferty	16,737
44		23	(h)	Port Vale	D 1-1	Hunt	8,186
45		26	(h)	Southampton	W 3-2	Rafferty 2, Hunt	11,550
46		30	(a)	Bury	D 1-1	Scott (pen)	4,430

FINAL LEAGUE POSITION: 4th in Division Three

Appearances
Goals

FA Cup

1	Nov	14	(a)	Rhyl	W 2-1
2	Dec	5	(h)	Wrexham	L 2-3

Barnett	Donovan	Richardson	Welbourne	Jobling	Birbeck	Scott	Cullen	Rafferty	Hunt	Fell	Keeble	Williams C	Fleming	Stockin	Pearce	Carrington	Cockerill	Knights	Williams D	Sinclair	Laverick	Duff	
1	2	3	4	5	6	7	8	9	10	11													1
1	2	3	4	5	6	7	8	9	10	11													2
1	2	3	4	5	6	7	8	9	10	11													3
	2	3	4	5	6	7	8	9	10	11		1											4
1	2	3	4	5	6	7	8	9	10	11													5
1	2	3	4	5	6	7	8	9	10	11													6
	2	3		5	6	7	8	9	10	11		1		4									7
	2	3		5	6	7	8	9	10	11		1		4									8
	2	3		5	6	7	8	9	10	11		1		4									9
1	2	3	4	5	6	7	8	9	10	11													10
1	2	3	4	5	6	7	8	9	10	11													11
1	2	3	4		6	7	8	9	10	11	5												12
1	2	3	4	5	6	11	8	9	10										7				13
1	2	6	4	5			7	10			3			8						9	11		14
1	2	6	4	5		7	8	10			3									9	11		15
1	2	6	4	5		7	8	9			3			10								11	16
1		3	4	5		7	8	9			2			10			6					11	17
1		3	4	5		7	8	10		11	2						6			9			18
1	4	6		5		7	8	9		11	2		3	10									19
1	4	6		5		7	8	9		11	2		3	10									20
1	4	3		5	6	7	8	9	10	11	2												21
1	4	3		5	6	7	8	9	10	11	2												22
1	4	3		5		7		8	9	11	2			10				6					23
1	4	3		5	6	7		8	9	11	2			10									24
1	4	3		5	6	7		8	9	11	2			10									25
1	6	3	4			7	10	8	9	11	2					5							26
1		3	4		6	7		8	9	11	2			10		5							27
1	6	3	4			7		8	9	10	2					5						11	28
1	6	3	4	5		7	8	9	10	11	2												29
1	6	3	4	5		7	8	9	10	11	2												30
1	6	3	4	5		7	8	9	10	11	2												31
1	6	3	4	5		7	8	9	10	11	2												32
1	6	3	4	5		7	8	9	10	11	2												33
1	6	3	4	5		7	8	9	10	11	2												34
1	6	3	4	5		7	8	9	10	11	2												35
1	6	3	4	5		7	8	9	10	11	2												36
1		3	4	5		7	8	9	10	11	2							6					37
1	2		4	5		7	8	9	10	11	3							6					38
1	2		4	5		7	9	8	10	11	3							6					39
1	2		4	5		7	9	8	10	11	3							6					40
1	2		4	5		7	9	8	10	11	3							6					41
1	2			5		7	9	8	10	11	3				4			6					42
1	2			5		7	9	8	10	11	3				4			6					43
1	2			5		7	9	8	10	11	3				4			6					44
1	2			5		7	9	8	10	11	3				4			6					45
1	2			5		7	9	8	10	11	3				4			6					46
42	42	37	31	42	18	45	41	46	39	41	34	4	2	12	5	3	2	11	1	3	2	3	
	1					14	5	24	33	6												1	

3 own-goals

1960-61

1	Aug	20	(h)	Chesterfield	D 0-0		11,282
2		22	(a)	Colchester U	D 1-1	Parker (og)	7,194
3		27	(a)	Hull C	W 3-2	Hunt, Rafferty, Davidson (og)	14,252
4		30	(h)	Colchester U	W 2-1	Cullen, Rafferty	16,122
5	Sep	3	(h)	Reading	W 3-1	Rafferty, Cullen, Scott	10,846
6		6	(h)	Bradford C	W 1-0	Cullen	10,811
7		10	(a)	Coventry C	D 0-0		13,906
8		13	(a)	Bradford C	W 3-1	Rafferty, Scott, Williams	7,546
9		17	(h)	Bristol C	W 5-2	Rafferty 2, Scott, Williams, Fell	11,839
10		20	(h)	Newport C	W 2-1	Williams, Cullen	12,500
11		24	(a)	Queen's Park R	L 0-2		11,042
12		26	(a)	Newport C	D 1-1	Rafferty	9,233
13	Oct	1	(h)	Notts C	D 1-1	Rafferty	12,448
14		5	(a)	Bournemouth	L 1-2	Rafferty	5,987
15		8	(h)	Walsall	W 3-1	Rafferty, Williams, Jobling	10,068
16		15	(a)	Shrewsbury T	L 1-2	Skeetch (og)	7,184
17		22	(h)	Halifax T	W 6-1	Williams 2, Rafferty 2, Cullen, Scott (pen)	10,423
18		29	(a)	Tranmere R	W 6-3	Williams 4, Marklew, Fell (pen)	8,991
19	Nov	12	(a)	Brentford	W 1-0	Fell	8,120
20		28	(h)	Swindon T	W 3-2	Williams 2, Fell	7,234
21	Dec	3	(h)	Port Vale	L 0-5		8,843
22		10	(a)	Southend U	D 1-1	Fell	5,952
23		17	(a)	Chesterfield	W 3-2	Williams, Cullen, Rafferty	4,451
24		20	(h)	Barnsley	W 3-2	Rafferty 3	5,915
25		26	(a)	Barnsley	L 2-3	Cockerill 2	10,725
26		31	(h)	Hull C	W 2-0	Cockerill, Williams	12,712
27	Jan	14	(a)	Reading	L 1-3	Rafferty	7,304
28		28	(h)	Watford	L 1-3	Scott	6,692
29	Feb	4	(a)	Bristol C	L 1-2	Cullen	11,141
30		6	(a)	Torquay U	D 0-0		5,328
31		11	(h)	Queen's Park R	W 3-1	Hunt, Cullen, Rafferty	10,599
32		18	(a)	Notts C	W 1-0	Welbourne	22,292
33		25	(a)	Port Vale	L 2-3	Rafferty 2	9,367
34	Mar	4	(h)	Shrewsbury T	L 0-2		9,388
35		11	(a)	Halifax T	D 0-0		4,089
36		18	(h)	Tranmere R	W 4-1	Rafferty 3, Williams	6,117
37		25	(a)	Watford	L 0-2		10,384
38		31	(h)	Bury	D 2-2	Cockerill, Williams	14,779
39	Apr	1	(h)	Brentford	D 0-0		14,779
40		4	(a)	Bury	L 0-2		13,306
41		8	(a)	Swindon T	L 0-3		10,117
42		15	(h)	Torquay U	W 4-2	Hunt 3, Hill	5,437
43		18	(h)	Coventry C	L 2-3	Cullen, Hunt	5,694
44		22	(a)	Walsall	L 1-2	Rafferty	16,446
45		25	(h)	Bournemouth	L 0-1		4,679
46		29	(h)	Southend U	L 1-0	Williams	3,852

FINAL LEAGUE POSITION: 6th in Division Three

Appearances
Goals

FA Cup

1	Nov	15	(a)	Darlington	L 0-2

League Cup

1				Bye	
2	Oct	26	(a)	Bolton W	L 2-6

White	Donovan	Keeble	Pearce	Jobling	Knights	Scott	Rafferty	Cullen	Hunt	Fell	Barnett	Fleming	Welbourne	Cockerill	Williams	Marklew	Carrington	Mills	Brader	Bemrose	Sinclair	Laverick	Hill	
1	2	3	4	5	6	7	8	9	10	11														1
1	2	3	4	5	6	7	8	9	10	11														2
1	2	3	4	5	6	7	8	9	10	11														3
1	2	3	4	5		7	8	9		11				6								10		4
1	2	3	4	5		7	8	9		11				6							10			5
1	2	3	4	5	6	7	8	9		11									10					6
1	2	3	4	5	6	7	8	9		11											10			7
1	2	3	4	5		7	8	9		11			6		10									8
1	2	3	4	5		7	8	9		11			6		10									9
1	2	3	4	5		7	8	9		11			6		10									10
1	2	3	4	5		7	8	9		11			6		10									11
1	2	3	4	5		7	8	9		11			6		10									12
1	2	3	4	5		7	8	9		11			6		10									13
1	2	3	4			7	8	9		11			6		10		5							14
1	2	3	4	5		7	8	9		11			6		10									15
1	2	3	4			7	8	9		11			6	5	10									16
1	2	3	4	5		7	8	9		11			6		10									17
1	2	3	4	5			8	9		11			6		10	7								18
1	2	3	4	5		7	8	9		11			6		10									19
1	2	3	4	5		7	8	9		11			6		10									20
1	2	3	4	5		7	8	9		11			6		10									21
	2	3		5		7	8	9		11	1		4	6	10									22
	2	3		5		7	8	9		11	1		4	6	10									23
	2	3		5		7	8	9		11	1		4	6	10									24
	2	3		5		7	8	9		11	1		4	6	10									25
	2			5		7	8	9		11	1	3	4	6	10									26
	2			5		7	8	9		11	1	3	4	6	10									27
1	2		6			7	8	9		11		3	4	5	10									28
1	2	3	6			7	8	9		11			4	5	10									29
1	2	3	6			7	8	9	10	11			4	5										30
1	2	3	6			7	9	8	10	11			4	5										31
1	2	3	6			7	9	8	10	11			4	5										32
1	2	3	6			7	9	8	10	11			4	5										33
1	2	3	6			7		8	10	11			4	5	9									34
1	2	3	6			7	9	10		11			4	5	8									35
1	2	3		5		7	9	10		11			4	6	8									36
1	2	3		5		7	9	10					4	6	8	11								37
1	2	3		5		7	10	9					4	6	8	11								38
1	2	3		5		7	10	9					4	6	8	11								39
1	2	3		5		7	9		10				4	6	8	11								40
1	2	3		5		11	8	9	10				4	6	7									41
1	2	3	6	5		7	9	8	10				4										11	42
1	2	3		5		7	9	8	10				4	6									11	43
1	2	3		5		7	9	8	10					6	11			4						44
1	2	3		5		7	9	8	10					6				4		11				45
1	2	3		5		7	9						4	6	10	11			8					46
40	46	43	30	36	5	45	45	44	14	36	6	3	37	27	32	6	1	2	2	1	2	1	2	
				1		5	24	9	6	5			1	4	17	1							1	

3 own-goals

1961-62

1	Aug	19	(a)	Newport C	W	2-0	Cullen 2	11,018
2		22	(h)	Torquay U	L	2-3	Cullen, Scott	10,995
3		26	(h)	Southend U	W	3-1	Rafferty, Cullen, Jones	8,834
4		30	(a)	Torquay U	W	2-1	Rafferty, Portwood	7,637
5	Sep	2	(a)	Notts C	L	0-2		9,289
6		5	(h)	Brentford	W	1-0	Portwood	8,800
7		9	(h)	Shrewsbury T	W	2-1	Portwood, Cockerill	7,650
8		16	(a)	Peterborough U	L	1-2	Cullen	14,804
9		20	(a)	Reading	W	2-1	Williams 2	17,265
10		23	(h)	Port Vale	D	1-1	Cullen	8,715
11		26	(h)	Reading	W	4-0	Rafferty 3, Welbourne	9,846
12		29	(a)	Bristol C	L	0-3		10,976
13	Oct	3	(a)	Swindon T	D	0-0		11,308
14		7	(h)	Lincoln C	W	4-1	Portwood 3, Cullen	8,820
15		10	(h)	Swindon T	L	0-1		8,930
16		14	(a)	Northampton T	L	0-7		11,201
17		21	(h)	Queen's Park R	D	1-1	Rafferty	6,420
18		28	(a)	Halifax T	D	3-3	Rafferty, Fidler 2	4,776
19	Nov	11	(a)	Crystal P	L	1-4	Rafferty	13,661
20		18	(h)	Portsmouth	W	1-0	Rafferty	6,889
21	Dec	2	(h)	Hull C	W	1-0	Rafferty	6,647
22		9	(a)	Watford	L	1-2	Fidler	8,910
23		16	(h)	Newport C	W	1-0	Jones	4,575
24		23	(a)	Southend U	L	0-2		4,365
25		26	(a)	Coventry C	L	0-2		11,199
26	Jan	6	(h)	Bournemouth	W	3-0	Purvis, Rafferty, Jones	5,367
27		13	(h)	Notts C	W	2-1	Rafferty 2	5,773
28		20	(a)	Shrewsbury T	W	2-1	Purvis, Rafferty	7,576
29		27	(a)	Barnsley	W	3-0	Rafferty 2, Portwood	8,086
30	Feb	3	(h)	Peterborough U	W	2-1	Rafferty 2	11,465
31		10	(a)	Port Vale	W	2-0	Rafferty 2	10,071
32		17	(h)	Bristol C	W	1-0	Rafferty	11,662
33		23	(a)	Lincoln C	D	1-1	Rafferty	13,795
34	Mar	3	(h)	Northampton T	W	3-2	Rafferty, Keeble, Portwood	9,086
35		10	(a)	Queen's Park R	L	2-3	Rafferty 2	8,374
36		17	(h)	Halifax T	W	3-0	Portwood 2, Jones	8,000
37		**24**	**(a)**	**Bournemouth**	**W**	**3-2**	**Rafferty 2, Portwood**	**12,620**
38		30	(h)	Crystal P	D	0-0		12,611
39	Apr	7	(a)	Portsmouth	W	2-0	Rafferty, Cockerill (pen)	19,285
40		10	(h)	Coventry C	W	2-0	Rafferty, Portwood	12,760
41		14	(h)	Barnsley	W	4-0	Jones 2, Rafferty, Waite	11,022
42		21	(a)	Hull C	L	1-2	Portwood	11,404
43		23	(h)	Bradford	W	3-2	Cullen, Jones, Scott (pen)	14,170
44		24	(a)	Bradford	W	1-0	Rafferty	11,783
45		28	(h)	Watford	W	5-3	Rafferty 2, Scott 2, Jones	14,229
46	May	1	(a)	Brentford	W	2-0	Portwood, Rafferty	19,080

FINAL LEAGUE POSITION: 2nd in Division Three

Appearances
Goals

FA Cup

1	Nov	4	(a)	Mansfield T	L	2-3

League Cup

1	Sep	13	(a)	Doncaster R	L	2-3

White	Donovan	Keeble	Welbourne	Jobling	Cockerill	Scott	Portwood	Rafferty	Cullen	Jones F	Barnett	Wealthall	Pearce	Knights	Waite	Fidler	Purvis	Williams	Hill	
1	2	3	4	5	6	7	8	9	10	11										1
1	2	3	4	5	6	7	8	9	10	11										2
1	2	3	4	5	6	7	8	9	10	11										3
1		3	4	5	6	7	8	9	10	11		2								4
		3	4	5	6	7	8	9	10	11	1	2								5
		3	4	5	6	7	8	9	10	11	1	2								6
		3	4	5	6	7	8	9	10	11	1	2								7
		3	4	5	6	7	8	9	10	11	1	2								8
	2	3	4	5	6	7		9	10	11	1							8		9
	2	3	4	5	6	7		9	10	11	1							8		10
	2	3	4	5	6	7		9	10	11	1							8		11
	2	3	4	5	6	7		9	10	11	1							8		12
	2	3	4	5	6	7	8	9	10	11	1									13
	2	3	4	5	6	7	8	9	10	11	1									14
	2	3	4	5	6	7	8	9	10	11	1									15
	2	3	4	5	6	7	8	9	10		1					11				16
	2	3	4	5	6	7	8	9	10		1					11				17
	2	3	4	5	6	7	8	9	10		1					11				18
	2	3	4	5	6	7	8	9	10		1					11				19
	2	3	4	5	6	7	8	9		11	1					10				20
	2	3	4	5	6		8	9		11	1				7	10				21
	2	3	4	5			8	9		11	1			6	7	10				22
	2	3	4	5		7	8	9		11	1			6		10				23
	2	3	4	5				10	8	11	1			6		7	9			24
	2	3	4	5		7		10	8		1			6			9		11	25
	2	3		5		7		10	8	11	1		4	6			9			26
	2	3		5		7		10	8	11	1		4	6			9			27
	2	3		5		7		10	8	11	1		4	6			9			28
	2	3		5		7	9	10	8	11	1		4	6						29
	2	3		5		7	9	10	8	11	1		4	6						30
	2	3		5		7	9	10	8	11	1		4	6						31
	2	3		5		7	9	10	8	11	1		4	6						32
	2	3		5			9	10	8	11	1		4	6			7			33
	2	3		5		7	9	10	8	11	1		4	6						34
	2	3		5		7	9	10	8	11	1		4	6						35
	2	3	4	5		7	9	10	8	11	1			6						36
	2	3	4	5		7	9	10	8	11	1			6						37
	2	3		5	4		9	10	8	11	1			6	7					38
	2	3		5	4		9	10	8	11	1			6	7					39
	2	3		5	4		9	10	8	11	1			6	7					40
	2	3		5	4		9	10	8	11	1			6	7					41
	2	3		5	4		9	10	8	11	1			6	7					42
	2	3		5		7	9	10	8	11	1		4	6						43
	2	3		5		7	9	10	8	11	1		4	6						44
	2	3		5	4	7	9	10	8	11	1			6						45
	2	3		5	4	7	9	10	8	11	1			6						46
4	41	46	27	46	28	37	37	46	42	41	42	5	12	25	7	9	6	4	1	
		1	1		2	4	14	34	8	8					1	3	2	2		

1962-63

1	Aug	18	(a)	Plymouth A	L 0-2		17,090
2		21	(h)	Portsmouth	D 1-1	Scott (pen)	14,778
3		25	(h)	Scunthorpe U	W 3-0	Cullen, Portwood, Scott (pen)	16,533
4		29	(a)	Portsmouth	L 1-2	Rafferty	19,087
5	Sep	1	(h)	Norwich C	L 0-2		12,873
6		8	(a)	Walsall	L 1-4	Portwood	10,691
7		12	(a)	Cardiff C	L 3-5	Portwood 2, Knights	14,426
8		15	(h)	Newcastle U	L 0-1		12,721
9		18	(h)	Cardiff C	L 1-2	Hill	10,962
10		22	(a)	Derby C	W 4-2	Young 3, Jones	12,807
11		29	(h)	Middlesbrough	L 3-4	Rafferty 2, Cullen	11,853
12	Oct	6	(a)	Bury	L 0-2		9,962
13		13	(h)	Rotherham U	L 1-2	McLean	10,255
14		20	(a)	Charlton A	W 3-0	McLean 2, Jobling	14,028
15		27	(h)	Stoke C	D 1-1	Rafferty	14,656
16	Nov	3	(a)	Sunderland	L 2-6	McLean, Portwood	43,087
17		10	(h)	Leeds U	D 1-1	Cockerill	9,329
18		17	(a)	Swansea T	L 0-1		5,606
19		24	(h)	Chelsea	L 0-3		10,823
20	Dec	1	(a)	Luton T	D 2-2	Portwood, McLean	7,202
21		8	(h)	Southampton	W 4-1	Hill 2, Portwood, McLean	7,188
22		15	(h)	Plymouth A	D 1-1	Fincham (og)	8,833
23		21	(a)	Scunthorpe U	D 1-1	McLean	12,698
24		29	(h)	Huddersfield T	D 1-1	Portwood	9,814
25	Feb	16	(a)	Middlesbrough	W 1-0	Clifton	17,804
26	Mar	9	(h)	Charlton A	W 2-1	McLean, Portwood (pen)	7,623
27		16	(a)	Stoke C	L 1-4	Portwood	24,950
28		23	(h)	Sunderland	L 1-2	Foster	12,332
29		27	(a)	Newcastle U	D 0-0		27,884
30		30	(a)	Leeds U	L 0-3		13,938
31	Apr	6	(h)	Swansea T	W 1-0	Rafferty	8,670
32		12	(h)	Preston NE	W 2-0	Rafferty, McLean	14,115
33		13	(a)	Chelsea	L 1-2	McLean	21,768
34		15	(a)	Preston NE	D 0-0		11,487
35		20	(h)	Luton T	W 3-1	McLean, Pennington, Rafferty	9,504
36		24	(a)	Huddersfield T	D 0-0		14,281
37		30	(h)	Walsall	W 3-1	Foster, Rafferty, McPherson (og)	12,502
38	May	4	(h)	Derby C	D 0-0		12,141
39		7	(a)	Rotherham U	D 0-0		7,765
40		11	(a)	Norwich C	D 0-0		10,295
41		13	(a)	Southampton	L 1-4	Foster	9,220
42		18	(h)	Bury	W 5-1	McLean 4, Foster	8,080

FINAL LEAGUE POSITION: 19th in Division Two

Appearances

Goals

FA Cup

3	Jan	8	(h)	Leicester C	L 1-3

League Cup

2	Sep	25	(a)	Barnsley	L 2-3

Barnett	Donovan	Keeble	Cockerill	Jobling	Knights	Scott	Cullen	Portwood	Rafferty	Jones	White	Wright	Thompson J	Wealthall	Welbourne	Wheaton	Clifton B	Waite	Catley	Pennington	Foster	Young	McLean	Purvis	Hill	
1	2	3	4	5	6	7	8	9	10	11																1
1	2		4	5	6	7	8	9	10	11				3												2
1	2		4	5	6	7	8	9	10	11				3												3
1	2		4	5	6	7	8	9	10	11				3												4
1	2	3	4	5	6	7	8	9	10																11	5
1	2	3	4	5	6	8		10										7				9			11	6
	2	3	4	5	6		10	8		7	1											9			11	7
	2	3	4	5	6		8	10		7	1												9		11	8
	2	3	4	5	6		8	10		7	1												9		11	9
	2	3	4	5	6		8		10	7	1											9			11	10
	2	3	4	5	6		10		8	7	1											9			11	11
	2	3	4	5	6		10		8	7	1											9			11	12
	2	3	6	4		7		8		11	1					5							9	10		13
	2	3		4	6	7	8	10			1					5							9		11	14
	2	3		4	6	7			8		1					5	10						9		11	15
	2			4	6		8	7	10		1			3		5							9		11	16
	2	3	6	4		7	8		10		1					5							9		11	17
	2	3	6		4	7	10	8			1					5							9		11	18
	2	3	6	4		7	8		10		1					5							9		11	19
	2	3	6	5				8	4	7	1										10		9		11	20
	2	3	6	5				8	4	7	1										10		9		11	21
	2	3	6	5				8	4	7	1										10		9		11	22
	2	3	6	5				8	4	7	1										10		9		11	23
	2	3		5				8	4	7	1				6						10		9		11	24
	2	3		5				8	4			1					6		7		10		9		11	25
	2	3		5				8	4			1					6		7		10		9		11	26
	2	3		5		7		8	4			1					6				10		9		11	27
	3			5				7	8			1	2		4		6				10		9		11	28
	3			5	9			7	8			1	2		4		6				10				11	29
	3			5				7	8			1	2		4		6				10		9		11	30
	3		4	5					10			1	2				6			7	8		9		11	31
	3		4	5					10			1	2				6			7	8		9		11	32
		3	4	5				10		7		1	2				6				8		9		11	33
	3		4	5					10			1	2				6			7	8		9		11	34
	3		4	5					10			1	2				6			7	8		9		11	35
	3			5	4				10			1	2				6			7	8		9		11	36
	3		4	5					10			1	2				6			7	8		9		11	37
	3		4	5					10			1	2				6			7	8		9		11	38
	3		4	5					10			1	2				6			7	8		9		11	39
	3		4	5				10				1	2				6			7	8		9		11	40
	3		4	5	6						1		2				10			7	8		9		11	41
	3		4	5				10			1		2				6			7	8		9		11	42
6	41	24	31	41	19	13	16	27	31	17	20	16	15	4	4	7	19	1	2	11	23	5	31	1	37	
			1	1	1	2	2	10	8	1							1			1	4	3	15		3	

2 own-goals

1963-64

1	Aug	24	(a)	Swansea T	D	1-1	Tees	10,740
2		27	(h)	Swindon T	L	1-2	McLean	15,085
3		31	(h)	Southampton	D	2-2	Clifton (pen), Tees	11,526
4	Sep	3	(a)	Swindon T	L	1-2	Hill	22,059
5		7	(a)	Middlesbrough	L	0-6		21,458
6		10	(h)	Charlton A	L	0-2		11,619
7		14	(h)	Newcastle U	W	2-1	Young, Foster	10,106
8		17	(a)	Charlton A	L	1-2	Portwood	13,326
9		21	(a)	Huddersfield T	W	2-1	Portwood, Tees	14,258
10		28	(h)	Derby C	L	1-3	Portwood	9,061
11	Oct	2	(a)	Cardiff C	D	0-0		10,903
12		5	(a)	Plymouth A	L	2-3	Hill, Portwood	9,729
13		12	(h)	Manchester C	D	1-1	Portwood	9,754
14		19	(a)	Bury	D	1-1	Young	6,878
15		26	(h)	Norwich C	W	3-1	Young, Pennington, Walker (pen)	8,981
16	Nov	2	(a)	Sunderland	L	0-3		29,044
17		9	(h)	Leeds U	L	0-2		12,369
18		16	(a)	Rotherham U	L	0-1		7,601
19		23	(h)	Portsmouth	L	0-3		7,979
20		30	(a)	Scunthorpe U	D	2-2	Mclean, Pennington	8,403
21	Dec	7	(h)	Northampton T	W	4-1	McLean 2, Cockerill 2 (1 pen)	6,305
22		13	(h)	Swansea T	D	1-1	Foster	6,762
23		21	(a)	Southampton	L	0-6		19,242
24		26	(h)	Leyton O	D	1-1	McLean	8,834
25		28	(a)	Leyton O	D	0-0		9,589
26	Jan	11	(h)	Middlesbrough	W	3-1	Young 2, Foster	6,681
27		18	(a)	Newcastle U	L	0-4		23,681
28	Feb	1	(h)	Huddersfield T	D	2-2	Hill, Foster	7,266
29		8	(a)	Derby C	D	0-0		10,229
30		15	(h)	Plymouth A	D	1-1	McLean	6,774
31		22	(a)	Manchester C	W	4-0	Portwood 2, Hill, Tees	11,411
32		29	(h)	Rotherham U	L	1-3	Porwood	7,623
33	Mar	7	(a)	Norwich C	L	0-2		11,461
34		21	(a)	Leeds U	L	1-3	Ham	23,351
35		27	(h)	Preston NE	L	0-3		12,138
36		28	(h)	Bury	W	1-0	Portwood	4,949
37		30	(a)	Preston NE	L	0-1		24,125
38	Apr	4	(a)	Portsmouth	D	2-2	Young, Portwood	8,207
39		11	(h)	Scunthorpe U	W	2-0	Young, Tees	10,656
40		15	(h)	Cardiff C	L	0-2		8,914
41		18	(a)	Northampton T	W	2-1	McLean, Young	10,285
42		25	(h)	Sunderland	D	2-2	Portwood, Hill	16,442

FINAL LEAGUE POSITION: 21st in Division Two

Appearances
Goals

FA Cup

3	Jan	24	(a)	Blackburn R	L	0-4	

League Cup

1	Sep	25	(h)	Rotherham U	L	1-3	

Wright	Donovan	Thompson	Cockerill	Jobling	Clifton	Pennington	Foster	McLean	Tees	Hill	Taylor Graham	Keeble	Welbourne	Walker	Howells	Knights	Portwood	Young	Ham	Collins	Bogie	
1	2	3	4	5	6	7	8	9	10	11												1
1	3	2	4	5	6	7	8	9	10	11												2
1	3	2		5	6	7	8	9	10	11			4									3
1	3	2		5	6	7	8	9	10	11			4									4
1	2	3		5	6	7	8	9	10	11			4									5
1	3	2		5	6	7	10	9		11				4			8					6
1		2		5	6	7	10			11	3			4			8	9				7
1		2	6	5		7	8	9	10		3			4			11					8
1		2	6	5		7	8		10		3			4			11	9				9
1		2	6	5		7	8	9			3			4			10				11	10
1		2	6	5		7	10				3			4			8	9		11		11
1		2	6	5		7	8			11		3		4			10	9				12
1		2	6	5		7	10			11	3			4			8	9				13
1	2	3		4	8	7			10	11				6	5			9				14
1		2		4		7			10	11	3			6	5		8	9				15
1	2			4		7			10	11	3			6	5		8	9				16
1	2			4		7	10			11	3			6	5		8	9				17
1	2			4		7	10	9		11	3			6	5		8					18
1	2			6		7	8		10	11	3			4	5			9				19
1	2		6	5		7	10	9		11	3			4			8					20
1	2		4	5		7	10	9		11	3					6	8					21
1	2		4	5		7	10	9		11	3					6	8					22
1	2		4	5		7	10	9		11	3					6	8					23
1	2		4	5		7	10	9		11	3					6	8					24
1	2		4	5		7	10	9		11	3					6	8					25
1	2		4	5		7	10	9		11	3					6		8				26
1	2		4	5		7	10	9		11	3					6		8				27
1	2		4	5		7	8	9		11	3					6				10		28
1	2		4	5		7	10	9		11	3					6		8				29
1	2		4	5		7		9		11	3					6		8		10		30
1	2		4	5		7		9	8	11	3					6	10					31
1	2		4	5		7		9	8	11	3					6	10					32
1	2		4	5		7		9	8	11	3					6	10					33
1	2		4	5		7	10	9		11	3	6							8			34
1	2		4	5		7	10	9		11	3	6							8			35
1		2	4	5			8		10	11		3				6	7	9				36
1		2	4	6	5	11	10		8			3					7	9				37
1		2	4	5	6		10		8	11		3					7	9				38
1		2	4	5	6		10		8	11		3					7	9				39
1		2	4	5	6		10		8	11		3					7	9				40
1		2	4		5			10	8	11		3				6	7	9				41
1		2	4	6	5			9	10	11		3					7	8				42
42	27	22	31	41	14	36	33	27	21	37	27	10	3	15	6	15	28	21	2	3	1	
			2		1	2	4	7	5	5				1			11	8	1			

1964-65

1	Aug	22	(a)	Oldham A	W	5-1	McLean 4, Tees	11,420
2		25	(h)	Bristol R	D	1-1	Foster	11,302
3		29	(h)	Exeter C	W	2-1	Anderson (og), Jobling	7,958
4	Sep	1	(a)	Bristol R	L	3-5	Hill, Tees, Pennington	15,542
5		5	(a)	Bournemouth	W	2-1	Pennington 2	8,872
6		9	(h)	Brentford	W	2-1	Tees, McLean	9,629
7		12	(h)	Peterborough U	W	2-0	Tees, Hill	10,912
8		15	(a)	Brentford	L	0-2		12,759
9		19	(h)	Barnsley	W	3-2	Foster, McLean 2	7,613
10		26	(a)	Mansfield T	D	2-2	McLean, Cockerill	10,620
11		30	(h)	Colchester U	W	2-0	McLean 2	8,686
12	Oct	3	(h)	Luton T	D	2-2	Foster, Young	8,410
13		5	(a)	Colchester U	W	1-0	Foster	3,837
14		10	(a)	Walsall	L	0-1		5,157
15		17	(h)	Walsall	W	1-0	Tees	7,116
16		21	(h)	Carlisle U	D	1-1	Young	5,345
17		24	(a)	Workington T	D	2-2	Hill, Barratt	6,434
18		28	(h)	Southend U	W	1-0	Jobling	5,729
19		31	(h)	Hull C	W	3-0	McLean 2, Pennington	9,650
20	Nov	7	(a)	Gillingham	D	0-0		11,087
21		21	(a)	Queen's Park R	D	1-1	Foster	6,213
22		28	(h)	Shrewsbury T	D	2-2	McLean, Tees	7,006
23	Dec	12	(h)	Oldham A	W	3-1	Foster, Haydock 2	6,158
24		19	(a)	Exeter C	L	1-4	Tees	5,438
25		26	(a)	Scunthorpe U	L	1-2	Foster	10,867
26	Jan	2	(h)	Bournemouth	D	2-2	McLean 2	7,228
27		9	(a)	Carlisle U	L	1-3	Foster	7,144
28		16	(a)	Peterborough U	L	1-3	McLean	13,343
29	Feb	6	(h)	Mansfield T	D	1-1	Hill	6,546
30		13	(a)	Luton T	D	1-1	Cockerill	5,160
31		20	(h)	Walsall	D	2-2	Cockerill, McLean	5,064
32		27	(a)	Watford	D	1-1	Foster	6,931
33	Mar	6	(h)	Reading	D	1-1	Allen	4,955
34		9	(h)	Bristol C	L	0-2		5,973
35		13	(a)	Hull C	D	3-3	Clifton, McLean, Cockerill	26,564
36		20	(h)	Gillingham	D	1-1	McLean	4,191
37		24	(a)	Reading	L	0-2		6,326
38		26	(a)	Bristol C	L	0-4		11,464
39		30	(a)	Barnsley	L	0-1		2,633
40	Apr	3	(h)	Queen's Park R	D	0-0		4,207
41		6	(h)	Scunthorpe U	W	3-0	Tees, Foster, Cockerill	6,756
42		10	(a)	Shrewsbury T	W	3-1	Pennington, Clifton, Haydock	3,868
43		16	(h)	Port Vale	W	2-0	Cockerill 2 (1 pen)	8,325
44		17	(h)	Workington T	L	0-1		5,542
45		20	(a)	Port Vale	W	3-2	Tees, Collins, Haycock	3,569
46		24	(a)	Southend U	L	0-4		6,550

FINAL LEAGUE POSITION: 10th in Division Three

Appearances
Goals

FA Cup

1	Nov	14	(a)	Barrow	D	1-1
R		17	(h)	Barrow	D	2-2*
2R		23	(a†)	Barrow	W	2-0
2	Dec	5	(a)	Stockport C‡	D	0-0
2		7	(a)	Stockport C	L	0-1

*After extra-time. †Played at Old Trafford, Manchester. ‡Abandoned after 50 minutes.

League Cup

1	Sep	23	(h)	Oldham A	W	3-1
2	Oct	19	(h)	Leicester C	L	0-5

Wright	Thompson J	Keeble	Cockerill	Jobling	Clifton	Pennington	Tees	McLean	Foster	Hill	Taylor G	Haydock	Lancaster	Young	Barratt L	Allen K	Beckers	Collins	Wainman	
1	2	3	4	5	6	7	8	9	10	11										1
1	2	3	4	6	5	7	8	9	10	11										2
1	2	3	4	6	5	7	8	9	10	11										3
1	2	3	4	5		7	8	9	10	11	6									4
1	2	3	4	6	5	7	8	9	10	11										5
1	2	3	4	6	5	7	8	9	10	11										6
1	2	3	4	6	5	7	8	9	10	11										7
1	2	3	4	6	5	7	8	9	10	11										8
1	2	3	4	6	5	7	8	9	10	11										9
1	2	3	4	6	5	7	8	9	10	11										10
1	2	3	4	6	5	7	8	9	10	11										11
1	2	3	4	6	5	7		9	8	11				10						12
1	2	3	4	6	5	7		9	10	11				8						13
1	2	3	4	6	5	7		9	10	11				8						14
1	2	3	4	6	5	7	9		10	11				8						15
1	2		4	6	5	7		9	10	11	3			8						16
1	2		4	6	5	7		9		11	3			8	10					17
1	2		4	6	5	7		9	10	11	3			8						18
1	2		4	6	5	7		9	10	11	3				8					19
1	2		4	6	5	7		9	10	11	3				8					20
1	2		4	6	5	7	9		10	11	3				8					21
1	2		4	6	5	7	8	9	10	11	3									22
1	2		4	5		7	9		10	11	3	8	6							23
1	2		4	5		7	9		10	11	3	8	6							24
1	2		4	5		7	9		10	11	3	8	6							25
1	2			6	5	7		9	10	11	3	8	4							26
1	2			6	5		8	9	10	11	3	7	4							27
	2			6	5	7		9	10	11	3	8	4						1	28
	2		4	6	5	7		9	10	11	3	8							1	29
	2		4	6	5	7			10	11	3	8	9						1	30
	2		4	6	5	7		9	10	11	3	8							1	31
1	2		4	6	5	7		9	10	11	3	8								32
1	2		4	6	5	7		9		11	3	10				8				33
1	2		4	5	6	7		9	10	11	3					8				34
1	2		4	5	6	7		9	10	11	3					8				35
1	2		4	5	6	7		9	10	11	3					8				36
1	2		4	5	6			9	10	11	3	7				8				37
1	2		4	5	6			9	10	11	3	7				8				38
1	2		4	5	6		8	9	10	11	3	7								39
1	2		4	5	6	7	9			11	3	8						10		40
1	2		4	5	6	7	9		10	11	3	8								41
1	2		4	5	6	7	9			10	3	8						11		42
1	2		4	5	6	7	9			10	3	8						11		43
1	2		4	5	6	7	9			10	3	8						11		44
1	2		4	5	6	7	9			10	3	8						11		45
1	2		4	5	6	7	9			10	3	8					11			46
42	46	15	43	46	42	42	26	33	38	46	32	21	7	7	4	6	1	5	4	
			7	2	2	5	9	19	10	4		4		2	1	1		1		

1 own-goal

1965-66

1	Aug	21	(h)	Bristol R	D	1-1	Tees	5,606
2		24	(h)	Brentford	W	3-2	Tees, Cockerill (pen), Green	5,238
3		27	(a)	York C	D	1-1	Green	8,764
4	Sep	4	(h)	Oxford U	D	1-1	Foster	5,720
5		11	(a)	Swansea T	L	0-1		7,620
6		15	(h)	Brighton & HA	W	3-1	Tees, Foster, Ross	5,374
7		18	(h)	Walsall	W	3-0	Tees 2, Hill	5,292
8		25	(a)	Workington T	L	0-1		2,328
9	Oct	2	(h)	Bournemouth	W	2-0	Tees, Clifton	5,780
10		5	(a)	Brighton & HA	W	2-1	Tees 2	14,070
11		9	(h)	Watford	W	2-1	Cockerill, Tees	7,195
12		16	(a)	Oldham A	W	4-1	Tees 2, Green 2	6,445
13		23	(h)	Gillingham	W	3-1	Tees 2, Foster	8,176
14		30	(a)	Millwall	L	1-2	Hill	17,299
15	Nov	6	(h)	Peterborough U	W	3-0	Tees, Green, Ross	9,982
16		20	(h)	Reading	D	3-3	Tees, Green, Foster	7,715
17		24	(a)	Brentford	L	2-3	Hill, Green	5,180
18		27	(a)	Hull C	D	1-1	Tees	20,681
19	Dec	11	(a)	Queen's Park R	L	0-3		6,671
20		18	(h)	Oldham A	W	3-1	Hill 2, Tees	6,242
21		27	(h)	Swindon T	D	2-2	Hill, Fielding	13,518
22	Jan	1	(a)	Watford	D	1-1	Foster	7,022
23		8	(h)	Exeter C	D	1-1	Ross	7,737
24		29	(a)	Bristol R	L	1-2	Ross	8,303
25	Feb	5	(h)	York C	W	3-1	Tees 2, Foster	7,549
26		19	(a)	Oxford U	L	0-2		7,661
27		26	(h)	Swansea T	D	2-2	Tees 2	6,867
28	Mar	5	(a)	Gillingham	L	2-3	Green, Fielding	7,915
29		12	(a)	Walsall	L	0-1		9,228
30		19	(h)	Workington T	W	1-0	Tees	5,691
31		26	(a)	Bournemouth	L	0-1		6,703
32	Apr	2	(a)	Peterborough U	D	1-1	Tees	5,601
33		8	(h)	Scunthorpe U	L	1-3	Fielding	10,960
34		9	(h)	Mansfield T	L	0-1		4,228
35		12	(a)	Scunthorpe U	D	2-2	Tees 2	7,783
36		23	(h)	Hull C	W	1-0	Fielding	18,018
37		25	(a)	Southend U	L	1-3	Hill	7,526
38		30	(a)	Mansfield T	L	1-2	Thompson	4,961
39	May	2	(a)	Shrewsbury T	L	1-3	Fielding	3,012
40		4	(h)	Shrewsbury T	W	2-1	Cockerill (pen), Fielding	3,417
41		7	(h)	Queen's Park R	W	4-2	Collins 2, Fielding, Tees	5,586
42		10	(a)	Swindon T	D	0-0		8,226
43		17	(h)	Southend U	W	1-0	Roberts (og)	4,554
44		21	(a)	Exeter C	L	0-2		3,770
45		23	(a)	Reading	D	0-0		5,432
46		28	(h)	Millwall	W	2-0	Tees 2	6,008

FINAL LEAGUE POSITION: 11th in Division Three

Appearances
Sub Appearances
Goals

FA Cup

1	Nov	13	(a)	Barrow	W	2-1
2	Dec	4	(a)	Barnsley	D	1-1
R		8	(h)	Barnsley	W	2-0
3	Jan	22	(h)	Portsmouth	D	0-0
R		26	(a)	Portsmouth	W	3-1
4	Feb	12	(a)	Manchester C	L	0-2

League Cup

2	Sep	22	(a)	Crystal P	W	1-0
3	Oct	13	(h)	Bolton W	W	4-2
4	Nov	13	(h)	Preston NE	W	4-0
5		17	(h)	West Ham U	D	2-2
R	Dec	15	(a)	West Ham U	L	0-1

Wright	Thompson J	Taylor Graham	Cockerill	Jobling	Clifton	Ross	Tees	Green	Foster	Hill	Collins	Wainman	Bloomer	Lancaster	Davidson	Wilkinson	Fielding	Garland	Taylor George	Kerry	
1	2	3	4	5	6	7	8	9	10	11											1
1	2	3	4	5	6	7	8	9	10	11											2
1	2	3	4	5	6	7	8*	9	10	11				12							3
1	2	3	4	5	6	7	8	9	10	11											4
1	2	3		5	6	7	8	9	10	11				4							5
1	2	3	6	5		7	8	9	10	11				4							6
1	2	3	6	5		7	8	9	10	11	12			4*							7
1	2	3	6	5	4	7	8	9	10	11											8
1	2	3	6	5	4	7	8	9	10	11											9
1	2	3*	6	5		4	8	9	10	7	11								12		10
1	2		6	5		4	8	9	10	7	11					3					11
1	2	3	6	5		4	8	9	10	7	11										12
1	2	3	6	5		4	8	9	10	7	11										13
1	2	3	6	5		4	8	9	10	7	11										14
1	2	3		5	6	4	8	9	10	11	7										15
1	2	3		5	6		8	9	10	11	7				4						16
1	2	3		5	6	4*	8	9	10	11	7				12						17
1	2	3		5	6		8	9	10	11	7				4						18
1	2	3		5	6	4	8	9	10	11	7										19
1	2	3		5	6		8	9*	10	11	7				4					12	20
1	2	3		5	6	9	8*		10	11	12				4		7				21
1	2	3		5	6	9			10	11	7				4		8				22
1	2	3	4	5	6	9	8		10	11							7				23
1	2	3	4	5		6	8	9	10	11	7										24
1	2	3	6	5		4	8	9	10	11	7										25
1	2	3	6		5	7		9	10	11				4			8				26
1	2	3	6		5	4	8	9	10	11							7				27
1	2	3	6		5	4*	8	9	10	11	12						7				28
1	2	3	6		5		8	9*	10	11	12			4			7				29
	2	3	6	5	4		8	9		10	11	1					7				30
	2	3	6	5	4		8	10		11		1					7	9			31
	2	3	6	5	4		8	9		10	11	1					7				32
	2	3*	6	5	4		8	9		10	11	1		12			7				33
			6	5	4		8	10			11	1	2			3	7	9			34
	4		6	5	10		8	9			11	1	2			3	7				35
	2		6	5	4		8*	9	10	11	12	1				3	7				36
	2		6	5	4			9	10	8	11	1				3	7				37
	2	3	6	5	4*		8	9	10	11	12	1					7				38
		3	6	5		4*	8	9		10	11	1	2			12	7				39
	4	3	6	5			8	9		10	11	1	2				7				40
	4	3	6	5			8	9		10	11	1	2				7				41
	4		6	5			8		9	10	11	1	2			3	7				42
	2	3	6	5		4	8	9		10	11	1					7				43
	4	3	6	5			8	9		10	11	1	2				7				44
	4	3	6	5			8	9	10	11		1	2				7				45
	4	3	6	5			8	9	10	11		1	2				7				46
29	44	40	37	42	29	27	43	42	35	44	26	17	9	5	5	6	24	2			
											6			2	1	1			1	1	
	1		3		1	4	28	8	6	7	2						7				

1 own-goal

1966-67

1	Aug	20	(a)	Workington T	L 1-2	Thompson	2,645
2		27	(h)	Walsall	W 3-1	Worthington, Fielding, Hill	5,864
3	Sep	3	(a)	Peterborough U	L 1-2	Ross	6,958
4		7	(h)	Scunthorpe U	W 7-1	Tees, Green 3, Hill 3	8,255
5		10	(h)	Torquay U	W 1-0	Tees	6,861
6		17	(a)	Brighton & HA	W 2-0	Tees 2	9,762
7		24	(h)	Darlington	W 4-1	Hill 2, Worthington, Taylor	6,558
8		27	(a)	Scunthorpe U	D 0-0		11,373
9	Oct	1	(a)	Queen's Park R	L 1-5	Green	9,097
10		8	(h)	Oldham A	W 1-0	Green	8,321
11		15	(a)	Oxford U	L 1-3	Collins	6,707
12		19	(h)	Reading	W 2-0	Tees, Green	6,140
13		22	(h)	Bristol R	D 0-0		7,271
14		29	(a)	Colchester U	L 0-4		6,330
15	Nov	5	(h)	Shrewsbury T	D 1-1	Worthington	5,309
16		12	(a)	Middlesbrough	W 1-0	Tees	14,162
17		16	(a)	Reading	L 0-6		4,355
18		19	(h)	Swansea T	W 2-1	Cockerill (pen), Martin	4,475
19	Dec	3	(h)	Leyton O	L 1-2	Rudd	3,744
20		10	(a)	Gillingham	L 0-2		5,327
21		17	(h)	Workington T	W 4-1	Rudd, Green 2, Martin	2,936
22		23	(a)	Doncaster R	L 2-3	Green (pen), Tees	9,185
23		26	(h)	Doncaster R	W 4-1	Tees, Green 2, Jobling	9,182
24		31	(a)	Walsall	L 0-1		8,812
25	Jan	14	(a)	Torquay U	L 1-3	Tees	8,872
26		21	(h)	Brighton & HA	L 2-3	Worthington, Green	5,094
27	Feb	4	(a)	Darlington	L 0-1		5,258
28		11	(h)	Queen's Park R	D 1-1	Rudd	7,157
29		24	(a)	Oldham A	W 1-0	Rudd	9,411
30		28	(a)	Swindon T	L 1-3	Cockerill (pen)	11,620
31	Mar	4	(h)	Oxford U	W 1-0	Moore	6,033
32		18	(a)	Bristol R	D 0-0		9,474
33		24	(h)	Mansfield T	L 1-2	Rudd	10,017
34		25	(h)	Colchester U	D 0-0		4,682
35		28	(a)	Mansfield T	L 0-4		11,734
36	Apr	1	(a)	Shrewsbury T	W 1-0	Rathbone	4,035
37		5	(h)	Swindon T	L 3-4	Wilson, Moore, Rudd	4,948
38		8	(h)	Middlesbrough	W 2-1	Collins, Moore	5,106
39		12	(h)	Watford	L 0-2		4,662
40		15	(a)	Swansea T	L 0-2		4,821
41		22	(h)	Bournemouth	W 1-0	Wilson	3,668
42		25	(a)	Watford	L 1-3	Wilson	8,902
43		29	(a)	Leyton O	D 1-1	Wilson	6,459
44	May	2	(h)	Peterborough U	D 1-1	Ross	3,661
45		6	(h)	Gillingham	W 4-0	Collins, Wilson 3	3,658
46		13	(a)	Bournemouth	D 0-0		3,411

FINAL LEAGUE POSITION: 17th in Division Three

Appearances
Sub Appearances
Goals

FA Cup

1	Nov	26	(a)	Crewe A	D 1-1
R		30	(h)	Crewe A	L 0-1

League Cup

1	Aug	24	(a)	Barnsley	W 2-1
2	Sep	14	(a)	Bradford	D 0-0
R		21	(h)	Bradford	W 3-1
3	Oct	5	(h)	Workington T	W 3-0
4		26	(h)	Birmingham C	L 2-4

Wainman	Bloomer	Taylor Graham	Thompson	Jobling	Cockerill	Fielding	Ross	Green	Rudd	Hill	Oakley	Worthington	Smith	Lancaster	Rathbone	Collins	Housley	Tees	Moore G	Wilson	Martin	Boylen	
1	2	3	4	5	6	7	8	9	10	11													1
1	2	3	4	5	6	7	8		10	11		9											2
1	2	3	4	5	6	7	8		10	11		9											3
1		3	2	5	6		4	9	10	11		7						8					4
1		3	2	5	6		4	9	10	11		7						8					5
1		3	2		6		4	9	10	11		7		5				8					6
1		3	2		6		4	9	10	11		7		5				8					7
1		3	2		6		4	9	10	11		7		5				8					8
1		3	2*		6	12	4	9	10	11		7		5				8					9
1	2	3		5	6		4	9	10	11		7						8					10
1	2	3		5	6		4		10	11		9				7		8					11
1		3	2	5	6		4	9	10	7						11		8					12
1		3	2	5	6		4	9	10			7				11		8					13
1		3	2	5	6		4	9	10	7						11		8					14
1		3	2	5	6		4	9	10			7						8			11		15
1		3	2	5	6		4	9	10			7						8			11		16
1		3	2		6		4	9	10			7			5			8			11		17
1		3	2	4	6			9	10			7			5			8			11		18
1		3	2	4	6		7	9	10						5			8			11		19
		3	2	4	6		7	9	10		1				5			8			11		20
		3	2	6			4	9	10		1				5	7		8			11		21
		3	2	6			4	9	10		1				5	7		8			11		22
		3	2	6			4	9	10		1	7			5			8			11		23
		3	2	6			4	9	10		1	7			5			8			11		24
		3	2		6			9	10		1	7	4		5			8			11		25
1		3	2	6				9	10			7	4		5			8			11		26
1		3	2		6	7	9		10			8	4		5						11		27
1		3	2	4	6	7	9		10				8		5						11		28
1		3	2		6		9		10			8	4		5		7				11		29
1		3	2		6				10			8	4		5		7		9		11		30
1		3	2		6				10				4		5		7		8	9	11		31
1	2	3			6		7		10				4		5				9	8	11		32
1	2	3			6		7		10				4		5				9	8	11		33
1	2	3			6		7		10				4		5				9	8	11		34
1	2	3			6		7		10				4		5				9	8	11		35
1	2	3			6				10				4		5	7			9	8	11		36
1	2	3			6				10				4		5	7			9	8	11		37
	2	3			6				10		1		4		5	7			9	8	11		38
	2	3			6		12		10		1		4		5	7			9*	8	11		39
		3			6		8		10		1	2	4		5	11	7			9			40
		3			6		10		8		1	2	4		5	7				9	11		41
		3			6		10		7		1	2	4		5	11			8	9			42
		3			6		10				1	2	4		5	8	7			9	11		43
		3			6		10				1	2	4		5	8	7			9	11		44
		3			6		8				1	2	4		5	7				9	11	10	45
		3			6		8				1	2	4		5	7				9	11	10	46
31	13	46	29	21	41	5	37	23	42	13	15	29	22	4	30	17	6	23	11	16	30	2	
						1	1																
		1	1	1	2	1	2	12	6	6		4			1	3		9	3	7	2		

1967-68

1	Aug	19	(h)	Leyton O	D 0-0		6,233
2		26	(a)	Northampton T	L 0-3		10,206
3	Sep	2	(h)	Walsall	W 3-0	Rudd 2, Wilson	4,989
4		6	(h)	Stockport C	W 3-1	Wilson, Martin, Rudd	5,711
5		9	(a)	Gillingham	L 0-1		4,568
6		16	(h)	Scunthorpe U	W 2-1	Collins, Moore	7,825
7		23	(h)	Torquay U	D 1-1	Cockerill (pen)	5,465
8		25	(a)	Stockport C	D 1-1	Cockerill (pen)	8,747
9		30	(a)	Reading	L 0-3		7,784
10	Oct	4	(h)	Brighton & HA	W 4-2	Moore, Boylen, Cockerill (pen), Templeman (og)	4,933
11		7	(a)	Bristol R	L 0-3		6,626
12		14	(h)	Barrow	L 0-1		4,453
13		21	(a)	Oxford U	L 1-2	Rathbone	6,202
14		23	(a)	Brighton & HA	L 1-3	Wilson	13,185
15		28	(h)	Bury	W 3-1	Martin, Moore, Ross (pen)	4,307
16	Nov	4	(a)	Bournemouth	L 0-1		4,237
17		11	(h)	Colchester U	L 1-2	Moore	3,964
18		14	(a)	Walsall	L 0-2		13,354
19		18	(a)	Peterborough U	L 2-3	Moore, Linnell (og)	7,243
20		25	(h)	Mansfield T	D 0-0		3,263
21	Dec	2	(a)	Watford	L 1-7	Ross	9,074
22		16	(a)	Leyton O	L 0-1		3,690
23		23	(h)	Northampton T	D 0-0		3,595
24		26	(a)	Shrewsbury T	L 2-3	Worthington, Gregory (og)	7,208
25		30	(h)	Shrewsbury T	L 0-1		3,116
26	Jan	20	(a)	Scunthorpe U	W 3-0	Moore 2, Wilson	6,881
27	Feb	3	(a)	Torquay U	L 0-1		7,499
28		10	(h)	Reading	D 1-1	Moore	3,800
29		24	(h)	Bristol R	W 3-2	Moore, Taylor, Boylen	3,512
30		27	(a)	Swindon T	L 0-5		12,962
31	Mar	2	(a)	Barrow	L 0-2		6,009
32		13	(h)	Gillingham	D 1-1	Wilson	3,504
33		16	(h)	Oxford U	L 0-1		3,070
34		20	(h)	Tranmere R	W 3-0	Wilson 2, Boylen	2,805
35		23	(a)	Bury	L 0-2		7,718
36		30	(h)	Bournemouth	W 2-1	Wilson, Boylen	2,458
37	Apr	6	(a)	Colchester U	W 3-1	Wilson 2, Moore	3,231
38		12	(h)	Oldham A	L 0-1		7,048
39		13	(h)	Peterborough U	D 1-1	Boylen	4,101
40		16	(a)	Oldham A	L 1-2	Wilson	4,821
41		20	(a)	Mansfield T	D 1-1	Ross (pen)	6,277
42		24	(h)	Southport	W 2-0	Collins, Martin	2,750
43		27	(h)	Watford	L 0-1		3,027
44		29	(a)	Tranmere R	W 2-1	Worthington 2	5,187
45	May	3	(a)	Southport	W 1-0	Smith	4,788
46		11	(h)	Swindon T	W 3-2	Wilson, Housley, Collins	4,798

FINAL LEAGUE POSITION: 22nd in Division Three

Appearances
Sub Appearances
Goals

FA Cup

1	Dec	9	(h)	Bradford	D 1-1
R		11	(a)	Bradford	L 1-4

League Cup

1	Aug	23	(h)	Chesterfield	W 1-0
2	Sep	12	(h)	Bury	D 2-2
R		19	(a)	Bury	L 0-2

Wainman	Worthington	Taylor Graham	Ross	Rathbone	Cockerill	Collins	Boylen	Wilson	Rudd	Martin	Harker	Bloomer	Smith	Davidson	Jobling	Moore G	Housley	Wilkinson	Bartlett T	
1	2	3	4	5	6	7	8	9	10	11										1
1	2	3	4	5	6	7	8*	9	10	11			12							2
1	2	3	4	5	6	7		9	8	11			10							3
1	2	3		5	6	7		8	10	11			4			9				4
1	2	3		5	6	7		10	8	11			4			9				5
1	2	3	4	5	6	7		10	8	11						9				6
1	2	3	10	5	6	7			8	11				4		9				7
1	7	3	10	5	6				8	11		2	9	4						8
1	2	3	10	5	6	12		7	8*	11*			9	4						9
1	2	3	8		6		10	7		11				4	5	9				10
1	2	3	8		6		10	7		11				4	5	9				11
	2		8		6		10	7	12	11	1		3	4*	5	9				12
	2		4	5		7		8	10	11	1		3			9		6		13
	2	9	4	5	12	7		8	10	11	1		6					3*		14
	2	3	4	5		7		8	10	11	1		6			9				15
	2	3	4	5		7		8	10	11	1		6			9				16
	2	3	4	5		7		8	10	11	i		6			9				17
	2	3	4	5		11		8	10		1		6			9	7			18
	2	3	4	5			10	7	11		1		6			9	8			19
		3	4	5		9	10	8	11		1	2	6				7			20
	2	3	8	5			11*	9			1		10	4	6	12	7			21
1	9	3	6				11	8				2	12	4	5*	10	7			22
1	8	3	6	5		7		10		11		2		4		9				23
1	9	3	6	5		7	10	8		11		2		4						24
1	9	3	10	5		7	8			11		2	6	4						25
1	2	3	6	5		7	10	8		11			4			9				26
1	2	3	6	5		7	10	8		11			4			9				27
1	2	3	6	5		7	10	8		11			4			9				28
1	2	3	6	5		7	10	8		11			4			9				29
1	2	3	6	5		7	10	8		11			4			9				30
1	2	3	6	5		7	10	8		11			4			9				31
1	2	3	6	5		7	10	8		11			4			9				32
1	2	3	4	5		7	10	8		11			6			9				33
1	2	3	4	5			10	8		11					6	9			7	34
1	2	3	4	5			10	8		11			7		6	9				35
1	2	3	4	5		7	10	8		11					6	9				36
1	2	3	4	5		7	10	8		11					6	9				37
1	2	3	4	5		7	10	8		11		12			6	9*				38
1	7	3	4	5		8	10	9		11		2			6					39
1	2	3	6			8	10	9		11				4	5		7			40
1	2	3	6			7		9		11			10	4	5		8			41
1	2	3	4	5		10		9		11				8	6		7			42
1	2	3	10	5		8		9		11			12	6*	4		7			43
1	4	3	8	5		10		9		11		2			6		7			44
1	4	3*	8	5		10		9		11		2	12		6		7			45
1	4	3	8	5		10		9		11		2			6		7			46
36	45	44	44	40	12	36	26	43	17	41	10	10	26	15	18	28	12	2	1	
					1	1			1			1	4			1				
	3	1	3	1	3	3	5	12	3	3			1			10	1			

3 own-goals

1968-69

1	Aug	10	(h)	Newport C	W	3-0	Wilson 2, Moore	4,943
2		17	(a)	Darlington	D	0-0		5,024
3		24	(h)	Swansea T	L	1-2	Wilson	4,878
4		27	(h)	Workington T	L	0-1		3,717
5		31	(a)	Wrexham	L	0-2		6,866
6	Sep	7	(a)	Bradford	D	1-1	Hardie (og)	2,263
7		10	(h)	Aldershot	L	0-2		3,146
8		17	(h)	Notts C	W	2-0	Worthington, Moore	2,361
9		21	(a)	Lincoln C	L	0-3		9,140
10		28	(h)	Southend U	D	0-0		2,368
11	Oct	4	(a)	Colchester U	L	1-2	Housley	7,543
12		9	(a)	Workington T	L	0-2		3,055
13		12	(h)	Chesterfield	L	1-2	Rathbone	3,177
14		19	(a)	Peterborough U	D	1-1	Ross (pen)	5,783
15		26	(h)	Chester	D	0-0		2,828
16	Nov	2	(a)	Exeter C	D	2-2	Hickman, Ross	5,180
17		6	(a)	Scunthorpe U	W	2-1	Oates, Housley	5,368
18		9	(h)	York C	W	3-0	Worthington, Boylen, Brace	3,627
19		23	(h)	Port Vale	D	1-1	Walker	3,313
20		29	(a)	Doncaster R	L	1-2	Brace	8,935
21	Dec	7	(h)	Rochdale	W	2-0	Walker 2	2,714
22		14	(a)	Chesterfield	D	0-0		4,674
23		21	(h)	Peterborough U	D	2-2	Walker, Davidson	3,609
24		26	(h)	Colchester U	L	2-4	Oates, Hickman	5,990
25	Jan	4	(a)	Rochdale	L	1-6	Ross (pen)	2,038
26		11	(h)	Exeter C	L	1-2	Cockburn	3,073
27		18	(a)	York C	W	5-2	Brace 3, Rathbone, Kelly (og)	3,807
28		25	(h)	Scunthorpe U	L	0-1		5,983
29	Feb	1	(h)	Bradford C	L	1-5	Brace	2,844
30		22	(a)	Brentford	L	2-4	Brace, Walker	5,697
31		28	(a)	Newport C	L	0-2		1,846
32	Mar	8	(h)	Darlington	D	1-1	Moor (og)	5,007
33		12	(a)	Bradford C	D	1-1	Hickman	5,034
34		15	(a)	Swansea T	D	1-1	Brace	3,380
35		22	(h)	Wrexham	D	1-1	Rathbone	3,895
36		26	(a)	Chester	W	1-0	Turner (og)	4,051
37		29	(h)	Bradford	W	2-0	Rathbone, Ross (pen)	4,540
38	Apr	4	(h)	Halifax T	L	0-1		7,844
39		5	(a)	Southend U	W	1-0	Brace	9,934
40		7	(a)	Notts C	L	1-2	Cockburn	6,307
41		12	(h)	Lincoln C	D	1-1	Brace	5,113
42		15	(a)	Halifax T	D	0-0		6,492
43		19	(a)	Aldershot	L	1-3	Kennedy	4,001
44		21	(a)	Port Vale	L	0-1		2,679
45	May	3	(h)	Brentford	L	0-2		1,833
46		5	(h)	Doncaster R	L	1-3	Boylen	5,310

FINAL LEAGUE POSITION: 23rd in Division Four

Appearances
Sub Appearances
Goals

FA Cup

1	Nov	16	(a)	Darlington	L	0-2

League Cup

1	Aug	14	(h)	Notts C	D	0-0
R		21	(a)	Nott C	W	1-0
2	Sep	4	(h)	Burnley	D	1-1
R		10	(a)	Burnley	L	0-6

Wainman	Worthington	Duncliffe	Hickman	Rathbone	Jobling	Ross	Wilson	Moore G	Boylen	Collins	Macey	Bloomer	Davidson	Kennedy	Campbell F	Wigginton	Housley	Brace	Oates	Walker	Cockburn	
1	2	3	4	5	6	7	8	9	10	11												1
1	2	3	4	5	6	7	8	9	10	11												2
1	2	3	4	5	6	7	8*	9	10	11		12										3
1	4	3	8	5	6	7		9	10	11*		2	12									4
1	7	3	4	5	6	8	9			11		2	10									5
1	4	3		5	6			8		11		2	10		9		7					6
	4	3		5	6			9	10	11	1	2	8				7					7
	4	3		5	6			9	10	11	1	2	8				7					8
	4*	3	12	5	6			9	10	11	1	2	8				7					9
	4	3	8	5	6			9	10		1	2	11				7					10
	2	3	8	5	6	4		9	10		1		11				7					11
	2	3	8	5	6	4		9	10*		1	12	11				7					12
	2	3	8	5	6	4		9*			1	12	10				7		11			13
	2	3	8	5	6	4		9	12		1		10*				7		11			14
	2	3	9	5	6	4			10		1		8				7		11			15
	4	3	9	5		6			10		1	2	12				11*	7	8			16
	4	3	9	5	6				10		1	2					11	7	8			17
	4	3	9	5	6				10		1	2					11	7	8			18
	4	3	8	5	6				10		1	2						7	11	9		19
	2	3	8	5	6	4			10		1							7	11	9		20
	2	3	8	5	6				10		1		4					7	11	9		21
	2	3	8	5	6						1		4				11	7	10	9		22
	2	3	8	5	6						1		4				11	7	10	9		23
	2	3	8	5		6			10		1		4					7	11	9		24
	2	3	8	5	6	4			12		1		10					7	11*	9		25
	2	3		5	6	8			10		1		4					7		9	11	26
	4	3	8*	5	6				12		1	2						7	10	9	11	27
	4	3	8*	5	6				12		1	2						7	10	9	11	28
	2	3	6	5					8		1		4					7	10	9	11	29
1	2	3	12	5		6			8*				4					7	10	9	11	30
1	10	3				6			8			2	4			5		7	11	9		31
	2	3	10		5	6					1		8	4				7	11	9		32
	2	3	8	6	5	10					1			4				7	11	9		33
	2	3	8	6	5	10					1		12	4				7	11	9*		34
	2	3	9	6	5	10			12		1		8*	4				7	11			35
	2	3	9	6	5	10			8		1			4				7	11			36
	2	3	9	6	5	10			8		1			4				7	11			37
	2	3	10		5	6			8		1			4				7		9	11	38
	2	3	9*		5	6			10		1		8		4			7		12	11	39
	4	3			5	6			10		1	2	8					7		9	11	40
	2	3	8		6	4			10		1					5		7		9	11	41
1	2	3	9	5	6	10			8						4		11	7				42
1	2		9	5	6	10						3	8	4				7	11			43
	2	3	9	5	6	10			8		1			4				7			11	44
	2	3	4	5	6				8		1		12					7*	10	9	11	45
	2	3	9	5	6				8		1		10		4				7		11	46
10	46	45	38	40	41	30	4	13	32	9	36	16	26	9	4	2	16	30	27	20	12	
			2						5			3	4							1		
	2		3	4		4	3	2	2				1	1			2	10	2	5	2	

4 own-goals

1969-70

1	Aug	9	(a)	Workington T	D	0-0		2,344
2		16	(h)	Hartlepool	W	2-0	Hickman, Brace	3,507
3		23	(a)	Bradford	D	1-1	Ross (pen)	3,384
4		25	(a)	Southend U	W	3-1	Brace 3	11,826
5		30	(h)	Wrexham	D	0-0		5,986
6	Sep	6	(a)	Notts C	L	1-2	Brace	4,991
7		13	(h)	Scunthorpe U	D	1-1	Brace	7,161
8		16	(h)	Chester	W	4-1	Brace 2, Fletcher, Hickman	4,186
9		20	(a)	Port Vale	L	0-1		8,787
10		27	(h)	Lincoln C	L	0-2		6,718
11		30	(h)	Newport C	D	1-1	Hickman	3,672
12	Oct	4	(a)	Crewe A	L	0-3		2,616
13		6	(a)	Hartlepool	W	1-0	Hickman	2,758
14		11	(h)	Darlington	L	0-1		3,427
15		18	(h)	Peterborough U	D	0-0		3,869
16		25	(a)	Exeter C	W	1-0	Brace	5,459
17	Nov	1	(h)	Oldham A	W	4-1	Brace 2, Oates, Worthington	4,463
18		8	(a)	Chesterfield	W	2-1	Brace, Hickman	9,254
19		22	(a)	Colchester U	L	2-3	Brace, Hickman	3,474
20		24	(a)	Brentford	L	0-3		7,630
21	Dec	13	(a)	Scunthorpe U	D	1-1	Brace	7,340
22		26	(h)	Bradford	D	2-2	Hickman 2	6,805
23	Jan	3	(h)	Notts C	W	2-1	Worthington, Brace	3,791
24		10	(h)	Port Vale	W	2-0	Hickman, Brace	4,654
25		17	(a)	Lincoln C	L	0-2		7,269
26		24	(h)	Swansea T	L	0-2		4,460
27		31	(h)	Crewe A	L	0-2		4,252
28	Feb	7	(a)	Darlington	D	0-0		2,371
29		14	(h)	Workington T	D	1-1	Brace	3,228
30		21	(h)	Exeter C	W	2-0	Lewis, Boylen	2,093
31		28	(a)	Oldham A	W	2-0	Brace, Lewis	5,530
32	Mar	2	(a)	York C	D	1-1	Lewis	3,090
33		10	(h)	Aldershot	D	2-2	Rathbone, Oates	4,399
34		14	(a)	Northampton T	L	1-3	Brace	4,537
35		17	(a)	Swansea T	L	0-2		10,633
36		21	(h)	York C	D	0-0		3,335
37		27	(h)	Chesterfield	W	1-0	Lewis	7,801
38		28	(a)	Aldershot	D	2-2	Brace, Wigginton	7,740
39		30	(a)	Peterborough U	L	0-1		4,715
40	Apr	4	(h)	Southend U	D	2-2	Hickman, Brace	3,202
41		7	(h)	Brentford	W	2-1	Brace 2	3,793
42		15	(a)	Chester	L	1-3	Brace	2,186
43		18	(h)	Northampton T	L	0-1		3,445
44		20	(a)	Wrexham	L	2-3	Boylen, Brace	8,671
45		25	(a)	Newport C	L	0-1		998
46		28	(h)	Colchester U	W	5-3	Hickman 3, Oates 2	2,393

FINAL LEAGUE POSITION: 16th in Division Four

Appearances
Sub Appearances
Goals

FA Cup

1	Nov	15	(a)	Bradford C	L	1-2

League Cup

1	Aug	13	(h)	Doncaster R	L	0-2

Wainman	Worthington	Mobley	Kennedy	Rathbone	Ross	Brace	Fletcher	Walker	Hickman	Oates	Boylen	Wiggington	Duncliffe	Lewis	Chapman	Cockburn	Williams Ben	Marsden	Macey	
1	2	3	4	5	6	7	8	9	10	11										1
1	2	3	4	5	6	7	9		10	8	11									2
1	2	3	4	5	6	7	9		10	8	11									3
1	2	3	4	5	6	7	9		10	8	11									4
1	2	3	4	5	6	7	9		10	8	11*		12							5
1	2	3	4	5	6	7	9	11	10*	8						12				6
1	2	3	4	5	6	7	9		10	8	11									7
1	2	3	4	5	6	7	9		10	8	11									8
1	2	3	4	5	6	7	9		10	8	11									9
1	2	3	4		6	7	9	12	10	8	11*	5								10
1	2	3	4	5	6	7		9	10	8	11									11
1	2	3	4	5	6	7	9		10	8	11									12
1	2	3	4	5	6	7		9	8		10				11					13
1	2	3	4	5	6	7		9	8		10				11					14
1	2	3	4		6	7			9	8	10	5			11*	12				15
1	2	3	4		6	7			9	8	10	5	11							16
1	2	3	4		6	7			9	8	10	5	11							17
1	2	3	4		6	7			11	8	10	5						9		18
1	2	3	4		6	7			11	8	10	5						9		19
1	2	3	4		6	7			9	8	10	5				11				20
1	2	3	4		6	7			9	8	10	5	11							21
1	2	3	4		6	7			9	8	10	5				11				22
1	2	3	4	5	10	7			9	8*	11	6				12				23
1	2		6*	5	8	7			9		10	4	3			12	11			24
1	4	2		5		8			9		11	6	3		10		7*		12	25
1	10	2*		5	4	7			9	8	11	6	3		12					26
1	2			5	4	7			9	8	11	6	3	10						27
1	2			5	4	7			9	8	11	6	3	10						28
1	2		4	5	6	7			9	8	11		3	10						29
1	2		4	5	6	7			9	8	11	12	3	10*						30
1	2		4	5	6	7			9	8	11		3	10						31
1	2		4	5	6	7			9	8	11		3	10						32
1	2		4	5	6	7			9	8	11		3	10						33
1	2		4	5	6	7			9	8	11		3	10						34
1	2		10	5	4	7			9	8	11	6	3							35
1	2		4	5	6	7			9	8	11		3	10						36
1	2		4	5	10	7				8	11	6	3	9						37
1	2		4	5	10	7				12	11	6	3	9	8*					38
1	2		6	5	8	7					10	4	3	9	11					39
1	2		4	5	6	7			9	11	10		3	8						40
1	2		4	5	6	7			9	11	10		3	8						41
1	2		4	5	6	7			9	11	10		3	8						42
1	2		4	5	6	7			9	11	10		3	8						43
1	2	12	6	5	8*	7				11	10	4	3	9						44
1	4	2	6			7			9	10		5	3	8		11				45
1	2		4	5		7			9	11	10	6	3	8						46
46	46	26	42	36	43	46	11	5	42	40	43	22	26	19	6	3	2	2		
		1						1		1		1	1		1	4			1	
	2			1	1	25	1		13	4	2	1		4						

1970-71

1	Aug	15	(h)	Oldham A	W 4-1	Ross (pen), Boylen, Brace, Woodward	4,301
2		22	(a)	Bournemouth	L 1-2	Brace	7,029
3		29	(h)	Hartlepool	D 1-1	Woodward	4,500
4	Sep	1	(a)	Newport C	W 1-0	Ross (pen)	2,569
5		8	(a)	Southport	L 0-1		3,790
6		12	(h)	Northampton T	L 0-2		4,483
7		19	(a)	Peterborough U	D 1-1	Woodward	5,473
8		23	(a)	Lincoln C	L 0-3		8,844
9		26	(h)	Southport	L 1-2	Hickman	3,469
10		29	(h)	Southend U	W 2-0	Oates, Hickman	3,824
11	Oct	3	(a)	Scunthorpe U	W 2-1	Oates 2	6,945
12		7	(a)	Chester	L 0-5		4,596
13		10	(h)	Notts C	W 2-1	Boylen, Brace	5,384
14		17	(a)	Oldham A	L 0-1		9,100
15		21	(a)	Exeter C	L 0-4		4,087
16		24	(h)	York C	W 3-1	Boylen (pen), Woodward, Brace	4,052
17		31	(a)	Workington T	L 0-1		2,025
18	Nov	7	(h)	Cambridge U	W 2-0	Tees, Boylen (pen)	7,295
19		10	(h)	Barrow	W 3-1	Woodward, Rathbone, Tees	6,661
20		14	(a)	Brentford	L 0-2		5,490
21		28	(a)	Aldershot	L 2-3	Lewis, Tees	4,540
22	Dec	5	(h)	Stockport C	L 1-2	Tees	3,862
23		19	(h)	Bournemouth	W 1-0	Brace	2,968
24		26	(a)	Darlington	L 1-5	Tees	4,265
25	Jan	8	(a)	Southend U	D 1-1	Woodward	6,805
26		16	(h)	Exeter C	L 1-2	Lewis	2,926
27		30	(h)	Aldershot	L 0-2		1,955
28	Feb	5	(a)	Stockport C	L 0-1		1,777
29		20	(a)	Barrow	W 1-0	Hickman	1,825
30		22	(a)	Colchester U	L 0-1		7,253
31		27	(h)	Workington T	W 1-0	Tees	2,295
32	Mar	5	(a)	York C	L 1-4	Lewis	3,514
33		9	(h)	Lincoln C	D 1-1	Tees	4,217
34		13	(h)	Brentford	L 1-5	Lewis	3,167
35		17	(a)	Crewe A	L 0-4		2,827
36		20	(a)	Cambridge U	W 3-2	Hickman, Boylen, Lewis	3,929
37		27	(h)	Chester	D 2-2	Brace, Pountney (og)	2,591
38	Apr	3	(a)	Hartlepool	D 2-2	Green (og), Lewis	1,764
39		9	(h)	Scunthorpe U	W 1-0	Rathbone	7,639
40		10	(h)	Darlington	D 1-1	Woodward	3,059
41		13	(a)	Northampton T	W 4-0	Boylen, Woodward, Brace, Tees	6,538
42		17	(a)	Notts C	L 0-1		12,182
43		20	(h)	Colchester U	W 3-1	Brace, Lewis, Ross (pen)	4,166
44		24	(h)	Peterborough U	W 2-1	Brace, Tees	3,012
45		27	(h)	Newport C	W 2-0	Boylen, Woodward	4,710
46	May	4	(h)	Crewe A	W 2-0	Ross, Tees	4,739

FINAL LEAGUE POSITION: 19th in Division Four

Appearances
Sub Appearances
Goals

FA Cup

1	Nov	21	(h)	Bury	L 0-1

League Cup

1	Aug	14	(a)	Lincoln C	L 1-2

Wainman	Worthington	Kirkland	Ross	Rathbone	Kennedy	Woodward	Brace	Hickman	Lewis	Boylen	Gray S	Tees	Campbell A	Oates	Short	Wigginton	Moore A	Gadsby	Crampton	Carroll	
1	2	3	4	5	6	7	8	9	10	11											1
1	2	3	4	5	6	7	8	9*		11				10		12					2
1	2	3	8	5	6	9	7			10				11		4					3
1	2	3	4	5	6	7	8	9		10				11							4
1*	2	3	4	5	10		7	9		11				8		6			12		5
	2	3	10	5	6	7	8	9		11	4							1			6
	2	3		5	10	7	8	9		11	4					6		1			7
1	2	3		5	10	7	8	9		11	4					6					8
1	2	3		5	6	7	8	9		10	4			11							9
1	2		3	5	6	7	8	9		10	4			11							10
1	2		3	5	6	7	8	9		10	4			11							11
1	2		3		6	7	8	9		10	4			11		5					12
1	2		3	5	6	7	8	9		10	4			11							13
1	2		3	5	6	7	8	9		10	4			11							14
1	2		3	5	6	7	8	9		10	4			11							15
1	2			5	6	8	7	9		10	4		3	11							16
1	2			5	6	8	7	9		10	4		3	11							17
1	2			5	6	11	7	8		10	4	9	3								18
1	2			5	6	11	7	8		10	4	9	3								19
1	2		12	5	6	7		8	11	10*	4	9	3								20
1	2			5	6	7	11	4	8		10	9	3								21
1	2		4	5	6	7	11		8		10	9	3								22
1	2		6	5		7	11	9	12	10*	4	8	3								23
1	2		6	5		7	11		9	10	4	8	3								24
1	2		6	5		7	11	9*	12	10	4	8	3								25
1	2		6	5		7	11	8	9	10	4		3								26
	4		6	5	8	7	11		9	10	2		3		1						27
	2			5	4	7	11	9		10	6	8	3		1						28
	2	3		5	4	7	11	9		10	6	8			1						29
	2	3		5	4	7	11	9		10	6	8			1						30
	2			5	4*	7	11	8	12	10	6	9	3		1						31
	2	3*	12	5	4	7	11	8	9	10	6				1						32
	2		3	5	4	7	12	8	11	10*	6	9			1						33
	2		3	5	4	11*		8	10		6	9			1	12	7				34
	2			5	4		7*	8	11	10	6	9	3		1		12				35
	2			5	4		7	9	11	10	8		3		1	6					36
1	2			5	4	8	7	9	11	10	6		3								37
1	2		3	5		8	7	4	11	10	6	9									38
1	2			5		7	11	4	9	10	6	8	3								39
1	2		12	5		9	7	4	11*	10	6		3				8				40
1	2		8	5		11	7	4		10	6	9	3								41
1	2		8	5		11	7	4*		10	6	9	3			12					42
1	2		4	5		11	7		8	10	6	9	3								43
1	2		4	5		11	7		8	10	6	9	3								44
1	2		4	5		11	7		8*	10	6	9	3			12					45
1	2		4			11	7	8		10	6	9	3*			5				12	46
34	46	12	27	44	33	43	43	39	19	43	41	23	25	13	10	7	2	2			
			3				1		3							4	1		1	1	
			4	2		9	9	4	7	7		10		3							

2 own-goals

1971-72

1	Aug	14	(h)	Scunthorpe U	W	4-1	Tees 3, Lewis	7,497
2		21	(a)	Exeter C	W	4-3	Stacey (og), Brace, Tees, Crawford (og)	4,052
3		28	(h)	Workington T	D	1-1	Tees	8,427
4		31	(h)	Doncaster R	W	3-1	Woodward 2, Lewis	10,236
5	Sep	4	(a)	Barrow	D	0-0		2,686
6		11	(h)	Brentford	W	3-1	Rathbone, Brace, Hickman	11,529
7		17	(a)	Southend U	L	1-3	Hickman	6,310
8		25	(h)	Stockport C	W	4-1	Hickman, Tees, Woodward 2	9,658
9		29	(a)	Lincoln C	L	0-3		15,015
10	Oct	2	(a)	Reading	W	3-1	Boylen, Hickman, Tees	5,183
11		9	(h)	Gillingham	W	2-1	Hickman, Tees	10,381
12		16	(a)	Scunthorpe U	W	2-1	Tees 2	11,510
13		19	(h)	Crewe A	L	2-3	Brace, Tees	11,010
14		23	(h)	Southport	L	0-1		10,640
15		30	(a)	Northampton T	L	0-3		6,220
16	Nov	6	(h)	Hartlepool	W	3-2	Tees, Brace, Lewis	8,589
17		13	(a)	Darlington	L	2-3	Tees, Hickman	2,284
18		27	(a)	Aldershot	D	1-1	Brace	4,000
19	Dec	4	(h)	Bury	W	4-1	Thomson 2 (pens), Hickman, Tees	6,779
20		18	(h)	Barrow	W	2-0	Tees, Hickman	6,890
21		27	(a)	Cambridge U	L	1-3	Thomson	8,691
22	Jan	1	(h)	Southend U	W	4-1	Thomson (pen), Lewis, Brace, Hickman	9,137
23		8	(a)	Workington T	D	0-0		2,460
24		15	(h)	Newport C	W	4-2	Brace 2, Smith (og), Rathbone	8,112
25		22	(h)	Lincoln C	D	2-2	Worthington, Brace	15,564
26		29	(a)	Crewe A	W	1-0	Brace	1,960
27	Feb	5	(h)	Chester	W	1-0	Brace	9,431
28		12	(a)	Southport	L	0-1		2,670
29		19	(h)	Northampton T	W	4-2	Hickman, Brace 2 (1 pen), Tees	10,000
30		26	(a)	Hartlepool	W	1-0	Tees	5,194
31	Mar	4	(h)	Darlington	W	2-0	Gauden, Tees	10,388
32		11	(a)	Gillingham	W	1-0	Brace	4,279
33		13	(a)	Newport C	L	1-2	Gauden	2,870
34		21	(h)	Colchester U	W	3-0	Gauden, Tees, Brace	13,288
35		25	(a)	Brentford	L	0-2		14,620
36		27	(a)	Peterborough U	W	2-0	Hickman, Tees	4,961
37		31	(h)	Reading	W	2-0	Boylen, Tees	16,567
38	Apr	1	(h)	Cambridge U	W	2-1	Tees, Hickman	12,583
39		3	(a)	Stockport C	W	2-0	Brace 2 (1 pen)	4,026
40		8	(a)	Chester	W	2-1	Tees 2	2,823
41		15	(h)	Aldershot	D	3-3	Tees 2, Gauden	13,414
42		17	(a)	Colchester U	W	1-0	Chatterley	5,086
43		22	(a)	Bury	D	1-1	Wigginton	4,977
44		25	(a)	Doncaster R	L	1-2	Brace (pen)	12,320
45		29	(h)	Peterborough U	W	3-2	Wigginton, Brace (pen), Gauden	14,143
46	May	2	(h)	Exeter C	W	3-0	Tees, Hickman, Chatterley	22,489

FINAL LEAGUE POSITION: 1st in Division Four

Appearances
Sub Appearances
Goals

FA Cup

1	Nov	20	(a)	York C	L	2-4

League Cup

1	Aug	17	(h)	Doncaster R	W	4-3
2	Sep	7	(h)	Shrewsbury T	W	2-1
3	Oct	5	(a)	Gillingham	D	1-1
R		12	(h)	Gillingham	W	1-0
4		26	(h)	Norwich C	D	1-1
R	Nov	3	(a)	Norwich C	L	1-3

Wainman	Worthington	Campbell	Thomson JA	Rathbone	Gray	Brace	Lewis	Tees	Boylen	Woodward	Wigginton	Hickman	Chatterley	Gauden	Smith Bob	Simpson	Cuff	Ferguson	Turner	Czuczman	
1	2	3	4	5	6	7	8	9	10	11											1
1	2	3	4	5	6	7	8	9	10*	11		12									2
1	2	3	4	5	6	7	8	9	10	11											3
1	2	3	4	5	6	7	8	9*	10	11		12									4
1	2	3	4	5	6	7	8		10	11		9									5
1	2	3	4	5	8	7			10	11	6	9									6
1	2	3	4	5	8	7			10	11	6	9									7
1	2	3	4	5	6	7		9	10	11		8									8
1	2	3	12	5	6	7		9	10	11		8*				4					9
1	2	3		5	6	7		9	10	11		8				4					10
1	2	3		5	6	7		9	10	11		8				4					11
1	2	3	4	5	6	7		9	10			8				11					12
1	2	3	4	5	6	7		9	10		12	8				11*					13
1	2	3*	12	5	6	7	8	9	10			4				11					14
1	2		4*		6	7	10	9	11		5	8			3					12	15
	2				6	7	8	9	11		5	10			3		1	4			16
	2			5	3	7*	8	9	11		6	10			4		1	12			17
1	2	3*	4		6	7	10	9	12		5	8			11						18
1	2	3	4		6	7	10	9			5	8			11						19
1	2	3	4		6	7	8	9			5	11			10						20
1	2	3*	4		6	7	8	9	12		5	10			11						21
1	2	3	4*		6	7	8	9	12		5	10			11						22
1	2	3	4	5	6	7		9	10			8			11						23
1	2	3	4	5	6	7	8	9	10						11						24
1	2	3	4	5	6	7	8	9	10			11									25
1	2	3	4	5	6	7	8	9	10			11									26
1	2	3	4	5	6	7	8	9	10			11									27
1	2	3	4	5	6	7	8*	9	10		12	11									28
1	2	3	4*	5	6	7		9	10			8		11		12					29
1	2	3		5	6	7		9	10*		12	8	4	11							30
1	2	3		5	6	7		9	10		12	8	4	11*							31
1	2	3		5	6	7	8	9	10			11	4								32
1	2	3		5	6	7	11	9	10		8		4								33
1	2	3			6	7	12	9	10*		5	8	4	11							34
1	2	3			6	7	12	9	10		5	8	4	11*							35
1	2	3			6	7		9	10		5	8	4	11							36
1	2	3			6	7		9	10		5	8	4	11							37
1	2	3			6	7		9	10		5	8	4	11							38
1	2	3			6	7		9	10		5	8	4	11							39
1	2	3			6	7		9	10		5	8	4	11							40
1	2	3	12		6		8	9	10		5	11	4*	7							41
1	2	3			6		7	9	10		5	8	4	11*	12						42
1	2	3			6	11	7	9	10		5*	8	4	12							43
1	2	3			6	7		9	10		5	8	4	11							44
	2	3			6	7	12	9*	10		5	8	4	11					1		45
1	2	3			6	7		9	10		5	8	4	11							46
43	46	43	23	26	46	44	24	43	41	11	24	40	17	15	10	6	2	1	1		
			3				3		3		4	2		1	1	1		1		1	
	1		4	2	1	19	4	27	2	4	2	13	2	4							

3 own-goals

1972-73

1	Aug	12	(a)	York C	D 0-0		6,827
2		19	(h)	Rotherham U	W 2-1	Brace (pen), Lewis	11,969
3		26	(a)	Bristol R	L 1-2	Gauden	9,095
4		29	(a)	Plymouth A	L 1-3	Hickman	8,472
5	Sep	2	(h)	Watford	W 2-0	Brace 2	8,992
6		9	(a)	Walsall	L 0-1		4,174
7		16	(h)	Bolton W	W 2-0	Tees, Gauden	8,858
8		19	(a)	Oldham A	W 2-1	Tees, Brace	5,596
9		23	(a)	Scunthorpe U	W 2-1	Gray, Chatterley	10,768
10		26	(h)	Blackburn R	W 2-0	Boylen, Brace	12,994
11		30	(h)	Rochdale	W 1-0	Worthington	12,173
12	Oct	7	(a)	Swansea C	L 2-6	Chatterley, Booth	3,071
13		10	(a)	Shrewsbury T	L 2-3	Gauden 2	1,763
14		14	(h)	Charlton A	L 0-2		8,646
15		21	(a)	Halifax T	D 1-1	Lewis	3,068
16		24	(h)	Southend U	W 3-1	Hickman 2, Gauden (pen)	9,964
17		28	(h)	Bournemouth	L 0-1		12,370
18	Nov	4	(a)	Blackburn R	D 0-0		7,676
19		11	(h)	Oldham A	W 6-2	Brace 4 (1 pen), Tees, Hubbard	9,893
20		25	(a)	Wrexham	L 2-3	Brace 2 (1 pen)	3,656
21	Dec	2	(h)	Notts C	W 3-1	Hubbard 3	8,963
22		16	(h)	Brentford	W 4-0	Wigginton, Hickman, Chatterley, Worthington	8,926
23		23	(a)	Chesterfield	L 1-2	Brace	5,003
24		26	(h)	Scunthorpe U	W 1-0	Chatterley	16,580
25		30	(a)	Rotherham U	L 0-2		5,691
26	Jan	6	(h)	Bristol R	W 2-0	Hubbard, Booth	8,975
27		20	(a)	Watford	W 2-1	Tees 2	5,864
28		27	(h)	Walsall	W 6-2	Chatterley 3, Gauden 2, Hubbard	11,142
29	Feb	10	(a)	Bolton W	L 0-2		16,588
30		13	(h)	Shrewsbury T	W 3-2	Hubbard 2, Gaulden	11,382
31		17	(h)	York C	L 1-2	Hubbard	12,899
32		24	(a)	Brentford	W 1-0	Brace	9,300
33	Mar	3	(h)	Swansea C	W 2-0	Brace 2	11,701
34		6	(h)	Port Vale	L 0-1		13,896
35		10	(a)	Charlton A	D 1-1	Goldthorpe (og)	5,423
36		12	(a)	Southend U	L 0-2		4,813
37		17	(h)	Halifax T	D 0-0		10,836
38		19	(a)	Tranmere R	D 1-1	Czuczman	5,366
39		24	(a)	Bournemouth	D 1-1	Brace	11,393
40		31	(h)	Wrexham	L 0-1		9,040
41	Apr	7	(a)	Notts C	L 0-4		16,208
42		14	(h)	Tranmere R	W 2-0	Hickman, Farrimond (og)	7,211
43		20	(h)	Chesterfield	W 2-1	Brace, Hickman	10,353
44		21	(a)	Port Vale	L 0-3		3,772
45		23	(a)	Rochdale	L 2-3	Hubbard, Brace	1,911
46		28	(h)	Plymouth A	D 1-1	Booth	7,361

FINAL LEAGUE POSITION: 9th in Division Three

Appearances
Sub Appearances
Goals

FA Cup

1	Nov	18	(h)	Wigan A	W 2-1
2	Dec	9	(h)	Chesterfield	D 2-2
R		13	(a)	Chesterfield	W 1-0
3	Jan	13	(h)	Preston NE	D 0-0
R		15	(a)	Preston NE	W 1-0
4	Feb	3	(a)	Coventry C	L 0-1

League Cup

1	Aug	16	(a)	Barnsley	D 0-0
R		22	(h)	Barnsley	W 2-0
2	Sep	5	(a)	Bury	L 0-1

Wainman	Worthington	Booth	Wiggington	Rathbone	Gray	Brace	Hickman	Tees	Lewis	Gauden	Turner	Campbell	Chatterley	Hubbard	Lynch	Boylen	Czuczman	Hooks	
1	2	3	4	5	6	7	8	9	10	11									1
1	2	3	4	5	6	7	8	9	10	11									2
1	2	3	4	5	6	7	8	9	10	11									3
1	2*	3	4	5	6	7	8	9	10	11						12			4
	2	3		5	6	7	9		8	11	1		4			10			5
	2	3		5			7	9		11	1	12	4		6	10	8*		6
	2	3		5	8		7	9		11	1		4		6	10			7
	2	3		5	8	7		9	12	11	1		4		6	10*			8
	2	3		5	8	7	11	9	12		1		4		6*	10			9
	2	3		5	7	9		8*	12	11	1		4		6	10			10
	2	3	9	5	8*	7			12	11	1		4		6	10			11
	2	3	9	5	8	7			12	11*	1		4		6	10			12
	2	3	9*	5	8	7				11	1		4		6	10		12	13
	2	3		5	6	7	9*		8	11	1		4		12	10			14
		3	5		8	7			9	11*	1	2	4		6	10	12		15
		3	5		6	7*	8		9	11	1	2	4		12	10			16
		3	5		6		8		7	11	1	2	4	9		10			17
	12	3	5	4	6		8		7*	11	1	2		9		10			18
		3	5	12	6	7	4	9*		11	1	2		8		10			19
		3*	5		6	7	8		12	11	1	2	4	9		10			20
1	2		5		6	7	8		12	11		3	4	9		10*			21
1	2	3	5		6	7	8*		12	11			4	9		10			22
1	2	3	5		6	7	8			11			4	9		10			23
1	2	3	5		6	7	8			11			4	9		10			24
1	2	3	5	4	6	7	8		12	11				9*		10			25
1	2	3	5		6	7	8			11			4	9		10			26
1	2	3	6		5	7		10				4	8	9		11			27
1	2	3	5		6	7		9		11			4	8		10			28
1	2	3	5		6	7	8	9		11*			4	12		10			29
1	2	3	5		6		8		7	11			4	9		10			30
1	2	3	5		6		8		7	11			4	9		10			31
	2	3	5		6	7	8			11	1		4	9		10			32
	2*	3	5		6	7	8		12	11	1		4	9		10			33
		3	5		6	7		10	8	11	1	2	4	9					34
		3	5		6	7		9	8	11	1	2	4*	10			12		35
		3	5		6	7	8		10	11*	1	2		9	12		4		36
		3	5		6	7	4		8	11	1	2		9		10			37
		3	5		6	7	8		12	11	1	2		9*		10	4		38
		3	5		6	7	8		12	11	1*	2		9		10	4		39
1	2		5		6	7	8*		12	11		3		9		10	4		40
1	2		5		6	7	8		10			3		9	12	11	4*		41
1	2	3*	5		6	7	8		10				4	9		11	12		42
1	2	3	5		6	7	8		10				4	9		11			43
1	2	3	5		6	7	8		10				4	9		11*	12		44
1	2	3	5		6	7	8	10					4*	9	11	12			45
1	2	3	5		6		7*	9	12	11			4	8		10			46
22	34	43	39	16	45	39	36	17	20	39	24	16	33	29	10	38	6		
	1			1					14			1		1	4	2	4	1	
	2	3	1		1	18	6	5	2	8			7	10		1	1		

2 own-goals

1973-74

1	Aug	25	(h)	Hereford U	L 1-3	Chatterley	10,709
2	Sep	1	(a)	Chesterfield	L 0-1		4,977
3		8	(h)	Bristol R	D 1-1	Chatterley (pen)	7,640
4		11	(h)	Halifax T	W 4-1	Chatterley 2 (1 pen), Wigginton, Barton	7,860
5		14	(a)	Tranmere R	D 0-0		6,872
6		19	(a)	Blackburn R	L 0-1		7,975
7		22	(h)	Brighton & HA	D 0-0		7,797
8		29	(a)	Shrewsbury T	D 1-1	Chatterley	2,306
9	Oct	2	(h)	Blackburn R	W 4-2	Chatterley 2, Hubbard, Czuczman	7,608
10		12	(a)	Southport	W 1-0	Hubbard	2,294
11		20	(h)	Aldershot	W 1-0	Barton	7,644
12		27	(a)	Rochdale	D 1-1	Hubbard	1,849
13	Nov	3	(h)	Cambridge U	W 1-0	Sharp	7,011
14		6	(h)	Walsall	W 1-0	Sharp	7,869
15		10	(a)	Wrexham	D 1-1	Lewis	5,066
16		13	(a)	Plymouth A	L 0-1		7,700
17		17	(h)	Bournemouth	D 1-1	Lewis	8,194
18	Dec	8	(a)	Port Vale	D 1-1	Lewis	3,157
19		22	(h)	Shrewsbury T	L 1-2	Hubbard	5,071
20		26	(a)	York C	D 1-1	Lewis	5,527
21		29	(a)	Bristol R	D 1-1	Lewis	14,317
22	Jan	1	(h)	Chesterfield	D 1-1	Lewis	9,308
23		12	(h)	Tranmere R	W 5-0	Hickman 2, Barton, Hubbard, Boylen	5,200
24		19	(a)	Hereford U	L 1-2	Booth	10,287
25		26	(h)	Rochdale	W 5-1	Lewis, Hickman 2, Hubbard 2	5,548
26	Feb	2	(h)	Huddersfield T	W 2-1	Boylen 2	7,013
27		9	(a)	Brighton & HA	D 1-1	Lewis	10,469
28		16	(h)	Southport	W 2-1	Boylen, Ross (og)	7,240
29		23	(a)	Walsall	L 1-3	Hubbard	4,071
30	Mar	2	(h)	York C	L 1-2	Fletcher	7,410
31		16	(a)	Aldershot	L 0-1		4,005
32		20	(a)	Huddersfield T	L 0-1		4,473
33		23	(h)	Wrexham	D 1-1	Lumby	5,383
34		26	(h)	Southend U	W 2-1	Lumby, Hubbard	5,933
35		30	(a)	Cambridge U	W 1-0	Lewis	3,638
36	Apr	2	(a)	Oldham A	L 1-3	Lewis	12,338
37		6	(h)	Plymouth A	W 3-0	Lumby 3	5,102
38		9	(a)	Halifax T	W 2-1	Hubbard, Lumby	1,624
39		12	(h)	Charlton A	W 5-0	Lumby 2, Brown, Wigginton, Barton	8,168
40		13	(a)	Bournemouth	D 1-1	Boylen (pen)	6,223
41		15	(a)	Charlton A	L 1-2	Hickman	3,366
42		20	(h)	Port Vale	W 2-0	Lumby, Boylen	6,166
43		22	(a)	Southend U	L 1-4	Hickman	5,335
44		24	(h)	Oldham A	W 2-1	Hickman 2	7,820
45		27	(a)	Watford	W 2-1	Lewis, Hickman	6,935
46		29	(h)	Watford	D 2-2	Lewis 2	8,813

FINAL LEAGUE POSITION: 6th in Division Three

Appearances
Sub Appearances
Goals

FA Cup

1	Nov	14	(a)	Runcorn	W 1-0
2	Dec	15	(h)	Blyth Spartans	D 1-1
R		18	(a)	Blyth Spartans	W 2-0
3	Jan	5	(h)	Burnley	L 0-2

League Cup

1	Aug	28	(h)	Northampton T	W 2-1
2	Oct	10	(a)	Luton T	D 1-1
R		16	(h)	Luton T	D 0-0
2R		23	(h)	Luton T	L 0-2

Wainman	Beardsley	Booth	Chatterley	Wigginton	Gray	Brace	Barton	Hubbard	Hickman	Sharp	Boylen	Czuczman	Lewis	Lumby	Fletcher	Freeman	Brown	Turner	
1	2	3	4	5	6	7*	8	9	10	11			12						1
1	2	3	4	5	6	7	8	9	10	11									2
1	2	3	4	5	6	7	8	9	10	11*	12								3
1	2	3	4	5	6		7	9	8	11	10								4
1	2	3	4	5	6		7	9*	8	11	10	12							5
1	2	3	4	5	6		7	9	8	11	10								6
1	2	3	4	5	6		7	9	8	11	10*		12						7
1	2	3	4	5	6		7	9	8*	11	12	10							8
1	2	3	4	5	6		7	9	8	11		10							9
1	2	3	4	5	6		7	9	8	11		10							10
1	2	3	4	5	6		7	9	8	11		10							11
1	2	3	4	5	6		7	9	8	11		10							12
1	2	3	4	5	6		7	9	8*	11		10	12						13
1	2*	3	4	5	6		7	9		11		10	12		8				14
1		3	4	5	6		7	9		11	12	10	2		8*				15
1	2	3	4	5	6		7	9		11	10		8						16
1	2	3	4	5	6		7	9		11*		10	8		12				17
1	2	3	4	5	6		7*	9	8	11	10		12						18
1	2	3	4*	5	6		7	9	8	11	10		12						19
1	2	3	4	5	6		7		8	11	10		9						20
	2	3	4	5	6		7		8	11	10		9					1	21
1	2	3	4	5	6		7		8	11	10		9						22
1	2	3		5	6		7	4	8	11	10		9						23
1	2	3		5	6		7	4	8	11	10		9						24
1	2	3	12	5	6*		7	4	8		10		9		11				25
1	2	3		5	6		7	4	8		10		9		11				26
1	2	3		5	6		7	4	8		10		9		11				27
1	2	3		5	6		7	4	8		10		9		11				28
1	2	3		5	6		7	4	8		10		9		11				29
1	2	3		5	6		7	4	8	12	10		9		11*				30
1	2	3		5			7		4	11	10	6	9*	8	12				31
1	2	3		5			7		4	11	10	6	9	8					32
1	2	3		5			7	4	8		11	6	9	10					33
1	2	3		5			7	4	8		11	6	9	10					34
1	2	3		5			7	4	8		11	6	9	10					35
1	2	3		5			7	4	8	12	11	6	9	10*					36
1	2	3		5			7	4	8		11	6	9	10					37
1	2	3		5			7	4	8		11	6	9	10					38
1	2	3		5			7	4		12	8	6	9	10*			11		39
1	2	3		5			7	4			8	6	9	10*	12		11		40
1	2	3		5			7	4	8		11	6	9	10					41
	2	3		5			7	4	8		11	6	9	10		1			42
	2	3		5			7	4	8		11	6	9	10		1			43
	2	3		5			7	4	8		11	6	9	10		1			44
	2	3		5			7	4	8		11	6	9	10		1			45
	2	3		5			7	4	8		11	6	9	10		1			46
40	45	46	22	46	30	3	46	41	40	26	34	25	30	16	8	5	2	1	
			1							3	3	1	6		3				
		1	7	2			4	10	9	2	6	1	13	9	1		1		

1 own-goal

1974-75

1	Aug	17	(h)	Blackburn R	L 1-2	Lewis	7,293
2		24	(a)	Plymouth A	L 1-2	Lewis	8,531
3		31	(h)	Port Vale	W 3-0	Lumby, Lewis, Boylen (pen)	5,200
4	Sep	7	(a)	Bury	D 1-1	Lewis	3,428
5		14	(h)	Peterborough U	L 1-2	Hubbard	6,379
6		17	(h)	Watford	D 2-2	Czuczman, Lewis	5,003
7		21	(a)	Chesterfield	L 0-2		4,364
8		28	(h)	Aldershot	W 2-0	Lewis 2	4,342
9	Oct	1	(a)	Crystal P	L 0-3		19,105
10		5	(h)	Huddersfield T	L 1-2	Boylen (pen)	4,901
11		8	(h)	Brighton & HA	W 3-2	Barton 2, Hubbard	4,795
12		12	(a)	Wrexham	W 3-2	Brown 2, Hubbard	5,415
13		16	(a)	Brighton & HA	L 1-3	Lewis	8,172
14		19	(h)	Gillingham	W 2-1	Lewis 2	5,131
15		23	(a)	Bournemouth	W 1-0	Hubbard	4,254
16		26	(a)	Preston NE	L 0-2		9,934
17	Nov	2	(a)	Swindon T	L 2-3	Hubbard (pen), Lewis	7,198
18		9	(h)	Tranmere R	W 3-2	Barton 2, Hubbard	4,723
19		15	(a)	Colchester U	L 0-5		4,489
20		29	(a)	Southend U	L 0-3		4,992
21	Dec	7	(h)	Halifax T	W 2-1	Hubbard, Lewis	4,331
22		21	(h)	Charlton A	D 1-1	Barton	4,991
23		26	(a)	Peterborough U	W 3-1	Oakes (og), Lumby, Hubbard	10,163
24		28	(h)	Walsall	D 0-0		6,051
25	Jan	4	(a)	Watford	L 2-3	Coyle, Lewis	5,669
26		11	(a)	Halifax T	D 1-1	Lewis	2,063
27		14	(a)	Walsall	L 0-2		5,036
28		18	(h)	Southend U	D 0-0		4,904
29		31	(a)	Tranmere R	L 1-3	Wigg	2,940
30	Feb	8	(h)	Swindon T	W 2-0	Barton, Hubbard	5,121
31		15	(a)	Hereford U	L 2-3	Lewis 2	5,445
32		22	(h)	Colchester U	D 1-1	Lewis	5,608
33	Mar	1	(a)	Port Vale	L 0-1		3,335
34		4	(h)	Hereford U	D 0-0		5,445
35		8	(h)	Bournemouth	D 0-0		5,781
36		15	(a)	Aldershot	D 0-0		3,499
37		19	(a)	Blackburn R	D 1-1	Czuczman	13,062
38		22	(h)	Bury	W 2-0	Young, Hubbard	5,432
39		28	(h)	Chesterfield	W 2-0	Lewis, Brown	8,693
40		29	(a)	Charlton A	D 1-1	Boylen (pen)	11,277
41	Apr	5	(h)	Preston NE	W 2-1	Lewis, Hubbard	6,211
42		8	(h)	Crystal P	W 2-1	Brown, Lumby	8,381
43		12	(a)	Huddersfield T	L 0-1		3,961
44		19	(h)	Wrexham	W 2-0	Lewis 2	5,837
45		22	(h)	Plymouth A	D 1-1	Boylen	9,052
46		26	(a)	Gillingham	L 0-2		5,165

FINAL LEAGUE POSITION: 16th in Division Three

Appearances
Sub Appearances
Goals

FA Cup

1	Nov	23	(h)	Huddersfield T	W 1-0
2	Dec	14	(h)	Bury	D 1-1
R		17	(a)	Bury	L 1-2

League Cup

1	Aug	31	(a)	Chesterfield	L 0-3

Wainman	Beardsley	Cumming	Hubbard	Wigginton	Czuczman	Gray	Hickman	Lewis	Lumby	Boylen	Freeman	Booth	Govier	Marley	Young M	Coyle	Barton	Partridge	Wigg	Fletcher	Brown	
1	2	3	4	5	6	7	8	9	10	11*											12	1
1	2		4	5		7	8	9		6		3					11			10		2
1	2		4	5	8	6		9	10	11		3					7					3
1	2		4	5	10	6	8	9		11		3					7					4
1	2		4	5	10	6	8	9	12	11*		3					7					5
1	2		4	5	6		8	9	10	11		3					7					6
1	2		4*	5	6		8	9	10	11		3			12		7					7
1	2			5	6		8	9	12	11*		3			4		7				10	8
1	2			5	6	12	8	9*		11		3			4		7				10	9
1	2			5	6		8		9*	10		3			12	4	7				11	10
			8	5	2	6			9	10	1	3				4	7				11	11
			8	5	2	6		9		10	1	3				4	7				11	12
			8	5	2	6		9		10	1	3				4	7				11	13
			8	5	2	6		9		10	1	3				4	7				11	14
			8	5	2	6		9		10	1	3				4	7				11	15
			8	5	2	6		9		10	1	3				4	7				11	16
			8	5	2	6	12	9		10	1	3				4*	7				11	17
1			8	5	2	6		9		10		3				4	7				11	18
1		3	8	5	2	6	4	9		10							7				11	19
	7		8	5	2	6	4			10	1	3					9				11	20
	11		8	5	2	6		9		10	1	3				4	7					21
	2		8		6			9	10	11	1	3	5			4	7					22
	2		8		6		12	9	10*	11	1	3			5	4	7					23
	2		8		6			9	10*	11	1	3			5	4	7				12	24
	2		8		6			9		10	1	3			5	4	7				11	25
	2		8		6		12	9		10*	1	3			5	4	7				11	26
	2		8		6			9		10	1	3			5	4	7				11	27
	2		8		6		10*	9		11	1	3			5	4	7				12	28
	2	3	8		6			9			1				5	4	7		10		11	29
		3	10	5	2			7		11	1		6			4	8		9			30
1		3	8	5	2			7		10		11	6				4		9			31
1			10	5	2			7		11		3	6			4*	8		9		12	32
1	2		10		8	6		7				3			5	4	11		9*		12	33
1			9		2	6		7		10		3			5	4	8				11	34
1			9		2	6		7		10		3			5	4	8		12		11*	35
1			8		2	6				10		3			5	4*	7	9	12		11	36
1			4		2	6		8		10		3			5		7	9			11	37
1			4		2	6		7		10		3			5		8	9			11	38
1			4*		2	6		7		10			3	12	5		8	9			11	39
1			4		2	6		7		10			3		5		8	9			11	40
1			4		2	6		7		10			3		5		8	9			11	41
1			4		2	6		7*	12	10			3		5		8	9			11	42
1			4		2	6			7	10			3		5		8	9			11	43
1			4			6		7	9	10			3	2			5	8			11	44
1			4			6		7	9*	10		11	3	2			5	8			12	45
1			4			6		7		10		11	3	2			5	8			9	46
28	21	5	43	24	42	30	12	41	12	44	18	36	12	3	20	24	45	11	5	1	29	
						1	3		3					1	2				2		6	
			11		2			21	3	4					1	1	6		1		4	

1 own-goal

1975-76

1	Aug	16	(h)	Cardiff C	W	2-0	Lewis, Hubbard	6,283
2		23	(a)	Gillingham	L	0-3		4,407
3		30	(h)	Shrewsbury T	W	3-2	Lewis 2, Barton	4,709
4	Sep	6	(a)	Chester	W	2-1	Lewis, Boylen	4,902
5		13	(h)	Millwall	W	2-1	Czuczman, Wigg	6,466
6		20	(a)	Sheffield W	L	0-4		11,345
7		23	(h)	Halifax T	D	2-2	Hubbard, Lewis	6,130
8		27	(h)	Aldershot	W	1-0	Partridge	5,139
9	Oct	4	(a)	Walsall	L	0-2		4,113
10		11	(a)	Crystal P	L	0-3		15,552
11		18	(h)	Brighton & HA	W	2-1	Wigg, Lewis	4,938
12		25	(a)	Swindon T	L	0-3		5,873
13	Nov	1	(h)	Bury	D	0-0		5,189
14		4	(a)	Peterborough U	L	2-4	Partridge 2	7,646
15		8	(a)	Hereford U	L	2-3	Wigg, Barton	6,391
16		11	(h)	Wrexham	W	3-2	Boylen, Young, Lewis	4,850
17		15	(h)	Mansfield T	W	4-1	Partridge 2, Wigg, Lewis	4,659
18		29	(h)	Preston NE	D	0-0		4,519
19	Dec	5	(a)	Southend U	L	2-5	Partridge, Lewis	2,925
20		20	(a)	Port Vale	L	3-4	Lewis, Ridley (og), Wigg	2,789
21		26	(h)	Rotherham U	W	4-1	Partridge, Boylen, Lewis, Oldridge	6,919
22		27	(a)	Colchester U	L	0-1		3,136
23	Jan	3	(h)	Chesterfield	W	3-0	Boylen (pen), Walton, Marley	4,024
24		10	(a)	Shrewsbury T	L	0-1		3,334
25		17	(h)	Sheffield W	D	1-1	Wigg	7,167
26		24	(a)	Millwall	D	1-1	Waters	5,486
27		31	(a)	Wrexham	L	0-1		2,808
28	Feb	7	(h)	Peterborough U	D	1-1	Partridge	5,482
29		14	(h)	Hereford U	W	1-0	Lewis	5,944
30		21	(a)	Mansfield T	L	0-1		6,094
31		24	(a)	Halifax T	L	1-2	Czuczman (pen)	2,229
32		28	(h)	Swindon T	W	1-0	Partridge	5,218
33	Mar	6	(a)	Bury	D	1-1	Barton	4,821
34		9	(h)	Walsall	L	1-2	Partridge	4,942
35		13	(h)	Crystal P	L	1-2	Hubbard	8,412
36		17	(a)	Brighton & HA	L	2-4	Marley, Hubbard	17,384
37		20	(a)	Preston NE	D	0-0		6,586
38		27	(h)	Southend U	D	2-2	Waters, Booth	4,518
39		30	(h)	Port Vale	D	1-1	Lewis	4,322
40	Apr	3	(a)	Cardiff C	L	1-2	Lewis	9,645
41		7	(a)	Aldershot	W	3-0	Barton 2, Booth	3,069
42		10	(h)	Chester	W	2-0	Hubbard, Cumming	4,644
43		16	(a)	Chesterfield	L	3-4	Booth, Hubbard, Lewis	5,483
44		17	(a)	Rotherham U	L	0-3		4,414
45		19	(h)	Colchester U	L	0-1		4,682
46		24	(h)	Gillingham	W	2-1	Cumming, Booth	4,415

FINAL LEAGUE POSITION: 18th in Division Three

Appearances
Sub Appearances
Goals

FA Cup

1	Nov	22	(h)	Gateshead	L	1-3	

League Cup

1	Aug	19	(a)	Doncaster R	L	1-3
		25	(h)	Doncaster R	D	0-0

Grimsby Town lost on aggregate scores.

Freeman	Booth	Govier	Gray	Young	Cumming	Lewis	Partridge	Wigg	Boylen	Hubbard	Wainman	Baker	Czuczman	Marley	Barton	Walton	Waters	Ford	Parkin	Brown	Oldridge	
1	2	3*	4	5	6	7	8	9	10	11										12		1
	3		4*	5	12	7	8	9	10	11		1	2		6							2
			4	5	3	11	8	9	10	7	1		2		6							3
			4	5	3	7	8	9	10	11	1		2		6							4
			6	5	3	7	8	11	10	9	1		2		4							5
	11		6	5	3	7			10	9	1		2	8	4							6
	8		6	5	3	7			10	9	1			2	4					11		7
	8		6	5	3	7	11		10	9	1			2	4							8
	10		6	5	3	7	11	9		8*	1			2	4			12				9
	8		6	5	3	7	9	11	10		1		2	4								10
	8		6	5	3	7		11	10*	9	1		2	4				12				11
	3	12	6		11	8		9		10*	1		5	2	4			7				12
	10		6		3*	8	9	11		12	1		5	2	4			7				13
	3		6			8	9	11	10		1		5	2	4			7				14
1	3		6	5		8	9	11	10					2	4			7				15
1	3		6	5		8	9	11	10	4				2	7							16
1	3		6	5		7	9	11	10	8				2	4							17
1	3	6		4		7	9	11	10	8			5	2								18
1	3	6		4		7	9	11	10	8*			5	2				12				19
1	3	6		5	4	7	9	11	10	8			2									20
	3	6		5	4*	7	9	11	10	8	1		2								12	21
	3	6		5		7	9	11	10	8	1		2			4						22
	3		6		12	7		9	10	8	1		5	2		4*					11	23
	3		6		11	7		9	10	8	1		5	2	4							24
	3		6		12	7	8	9	10		1		5	2	4						11*	25
	3		6		11*	7	9	12	10		1		5	2	4		8					26
	3	6			11	7	9	10			1		5	2	4		8					27
	3		6			7	9	11	10		1		5	2	4		8					28
	3		6		12	7*	9	11	10		1		5	2	4		8					29
	3		6		12	7	9	11	10	8*	1		5	2	4							30
	3		6	4	11	7	9	12	10		1		5	2*	8							31
	3		6			7	9	11	10		1		5	2	4		8					32
	3		6			7	9	11	10		1		5	2	4		8					33
	3		6			7	9	11	10*		1		5	2	4		8	12				34
	3		6			7	8	11	10	9	1		5	2			4					35
	10	3	6	4		7	11	12		9*	1		5	2			8					36
		3	6	4		7	11	12	10	9	1		5	2*			8					37
	3		6		12	8	11*		10	9	1		5	2			4	7				38
	3		6	4	11*	10		12		9	1		5	2			8	7				39
	3		6	5	12	10*				9	1		2		4		8	7	11			40
	3		6	5	11					9	1			2	4		8	7	10			41
	3		6	5	11					9	1			2	4		8	7	10			42
	3*		6	5	11	7	12			9	1			2	4		8		10			43
1		3	6	5	11*	9		12						2	4		8	7	10			44
1	3		6	5	11*	10		12		9				2	4		8	7				45
1	3		6	5*	11	10	9	12					2		4		8		7			46
10	41	10	40	30	25	44	33	30	33	31	35	1	34	36	32	2	19	11	6	1	2	
		1			7		1	8		1								4		1	1	
	3			1	2	15	10	7	4	6			2	2	5	1	2				1	

1 own-goal

1976-77

1	Aug	21	(a)	Bury	L 0-2		4,107
2		24	(h)	Crystal P	L 0-1		5,841
3		28	(h)	Peterborough U	D 2-2	Partridge, Waters (pen)	4,057
4	Sep	4	(a)	Mansfield T	L 0-3		5,220
5		11	(h)	Brighton & HA	W 2-0	Partridge, Waters	4,481
6		18	(a)	Oxford U	L 2-5	Brolly, Waters (pen)	3,791
7		25	(h)	Preston NE	W 1-0	Boylen	3,896
8	Oct	2	(a)	Rotherham U	L 2-3	Partridge, Lewis	3,925
9		9	(h)	Chester	D 0-0		3,910
10		16	(h)	York C	W 1-0	Lewis	4,237
11		22	(a)	Tranmere R	L 0-2		3,580
12		30	(a)	Port Vale	L 0-2		3,714
13	Nov	2	(a)	Gillingham	D 1-1	Partridge	4,279
14		6	(h)	Chesterfield	L 1-2	Partridge	3,131
15		13	(a)	Shrewsbury T	L 1-2	Lewis	4,639
16		27	(h)	Portsmouth	W 1-0	Lewis	3,836
17		30	(h)	Wrexham	W 3-0	Donovan 2, Wigg	4,820
18	Dec	18	(h)	Reading	W 2-1	Waters, Lewis	3,080
19		27	(a)	Lincoln C	L 0-2		11,645
20		28	(h)	Sheffield W	D 1-1	Donovan	8,000
21	Jan	3	(h)	Port Vale	L 2-4	Partridge, Wigg	5,666
22		15	(a)	Crystal P	L 1-2	Wigg	13,638
23		22	(h)	Bury	W 2-0	Donovan, Wigg	3,638
24		29	(h)	Northampton T	L 0-1		3,676
25	Feb	1	(a)	Walsall	L 0-1		4,405
26		5	(a)	Peterborough U	L 1-3	Brolly	5,753
27		12	(h)	Mansfield T	L 0-1		5,322
28		16	(a)	Chesterfield	W 1-0	Donovan	3,250
29		19	(a)	Brighton & HA	L 0-3		20,412
30		26	(h)	Oxford U	L 1-2	Partridge	3,865
31	Mar	5	(a)	Preston NE	L 1-2	Young	7,278
32		8	(a)	Swindon T	L 1-4	Lewis	6,980
33		12	(h)	Rotherham U	D 1-1	Liddell	5,792
34		19	(a)	Chester	L 0-2		3,246
35		26	(a)	York C	D 1-1	Lewis	2,798
36	Apr	2	(h)	Tranmere R	W 1-0	Partridge	2,690
37		8	(h)	Lincoln C	L 1-2	Partridge (pen)	8,506
38		9	(a)	Sheffield W	L 0-1		10,182
39		11	(h)	Gillingham	D 1-1	Partridge	2,820
40		16	(a)	Wrexham	L 2-3	Drinkell 2	7,878
41		19	(a)	Northampton T	D 0-0		5,699
42		23	(h)	Shrewsbury T	W 2-1	Donovan, Brolly	2,430
43		30	(a)	Portsmouth	W 2-1	Liddell, Viney (og)	10,155
44	May	3	(h)	Walsall	D 2-2	Waters, Partridge (pen)	2,500
45		7	(h)	Swindon T	W 2-0	Lewis, Liddell	3,027
46		14	(a)	Reading	L 0-2		3,816

FINAL LEAGUE POSITION: 23rd in Division Three

Appearances
Sub Appearances
Goals

FA Cup

1	Nov	10	(a)	Droylsden	D 0-0
R		12	(h)	Droylsden	W 5-3
2	Dec	11	(h)	Chester	L 0-1

League Cup

1	Aug	14	(h)	Sheffield W	L 0-3
		18	(a)	Sheffield W	D 0-0

Grimsby Town lost 3-0 on aggregate.

Wainman	Cumming	Moore K	Young	Blant	Govier	Whitehead	Waters	Lewis	Booth	Oldridge	Batch	Yates	Harper	Partridge	Donovan	Harding	Hanvey	Gray	Ford	Liddell	Wigg	Drinkell	Boylen	Brolly	
1	2	3	4	5	6*	7	8	9	10	11				12											1
1	2	3	4	5		7	8	11	6*	12				9									10		2
1	2	3	5	6		7	4	9		11				8									10		3
1	2*	3	6	5		12	4	9		10				8	11				7						4
1	2	3	4	5			8	7						9		6							10	11	5
1	2	3	4	5			8	7						9		6							10	11	6
1	2	3	4	5			8	7						9		6					12		10*	11	7
1	2	3	4	5*			8	7		12				9		6							10	11	8
1	2	3	4	5			8*	7		12				9		6							10	11	9
1		3	5				2	9		7*				4	8			6			12		10	11	10
1	2	3	5				4	7		12				8				6			9		10*	11	11
1	2	3	4							8				10	7	5		6			9			11	12
1	3		4				2			8				10	7	5		6			9			11	13
1	3		4*				2	12		8				10	7	5		6			9			11	14
1	3	6	4				2	7						8				5			9		10	11	15
1	2	3	5				4	7*						8	12			6			9		10	11	16
1	2	3	5				4							8	7			6*	12		9		10	11	17
1	2*		6				4	7					3	8	12			5			9		10	11	18
1	3		4				2	7					6	8				5	12		9		10*	11	19
			5				2	7			1		3	8	4			6			9		10	11	20
	2		5				4	7*	3		1			8	12			6			9		10	11	21
	2		5				4		3		1			8	7			6			9		10	11	22
	2		5				4		3		1			8	7			6			9		10	11	23
	2		5				4		3	12	1			8	7			6			9		10*	11	24
	2	10	5				4		3		1			8	7			6			9			11	25
	2	12	5				4		3		1			8	7			6			9*		10	11	26
	2		12				4	7	3		1			8	9*		5	6					10	11	27
1	2		10				4	7	3					8	9		5	6						11	28
1	2		10				4	7	3					8	9		5	6						11	29
1	2		12				4	8	3					9			5	6	7*				10	11	30
1			12				4	7	3			2		8	9*		5	6					10	11	31
1			9				4	7	3			2		8			5	6					10	11	32
1		3					4	7				2		8			5	6		9			10	11	33
1	3						4	7				2		8			5	6		9			10	11	34
1	10	3	6				4	7	12			2		8			5*			9				11	35
1	7	3					4	8	6			2		9			5			10				11	36
1	10	3					4	7	6			2		8			5			9				11	37
1	10	3					4		6			2		8	7		5			9				11	38
1	10	3					4		6			2		8			5			7		9		11	39
1	10	3					4		6			2*		8			5			7		9	12	11	40
1	2						4	7	3					8			5	6		11		9	10		41
1	2						4	7	3*					8	12		5	6		9			10	11	42
1	2	3					4	7						8			5	6		9			10	11	43
1	2*	3					4	7						8			5	6	12	9			10	11	44
1	2	3					4	7*						8			5	6	12	9			10	11	45
1	2	3					4	7						8			5	6		9		12	10*	11	46
38	41	27	30	9	1	3	45	34	21	7	8	10	3	45	17	8	20	31	2	14	16	3	32	41	
		1	3			1		1	1	5				1	4				4		2	1	1		
			1				5	8						11	6					3	4	2	1	3	

1 own-goal

1977-78

1	Aug	20	(h)	Darlington	W 2-0	Donovan 2	3,182
2		26	(a)	Stockport C	L 0-2		3,054
3	Sep	3	(h)	Rochdale	W 2-1	Partridge (pen), Waters	2,516
4		6	(a)	Watford	L 0-1		6,850
5		10	(a)	York C	W 2-1	Liddell, Brolly	1,872
6		13	(h)	Hartlepool U	W 2-1	Liddell, Drinkell	3,790
7		16	(a)	Swansea C	L 0-2		7,402
8		24	(h)	Doncaster R	D 0-0		4,758
9		27	(a)	Southport	D 2-2	Drinkell, Waters	1,843
10	Oct	1	(a)	Newport C	L 0-3		2,746
11		4	(h)	Wimbledon	W 3-1	Drinkell 2, Liddell	4,048
12		8	(h)	Scunthorpe U	D 0-0		5,249
13		14	(a)	Barnsley	W 2-1	Liddell, Cumming	6,151
14		22	(h)	Aldershot	W 1-0	Cumming	4,283
15		29	(a)	Huddersfield T	W 3-1	Donovan 2, Liddell	5,871
16	Nov	5	(a)	Torquay U	L 1-3	Donovan	2,301
17		12	(h)	Reading	L 0-1		3,762
18		19	(a)	Crewe A	W 2-0	Ford, Liddell	2,227
19	Dec	3	(h)	Bournemouth	L 0-2		3,767
20		10	(a)	Brentford	L 1-3	Liddell	5,760
21		26	(h)	Halifax T	D 0-0		6,051
22		27	(a)	Northampton T	L 1-2	Liddell	3,518
23		31	(h)	Torquay U	W 3-1	Partridge (pen), Donovan 2	3,707
24	Jan	2	(a)	Southend U	D 1-1	Waters	9,973
25		14	(a)	Darlington	W 2-1	Cumming, Liddell	2,265
26		21	(h)	Stockport C	D 0-0		4,716
27	Feb	4	(h)	York C	W 3-2	Hanvey, Donovan 2	3,282
28		25	(h)	Newport C	W 1-0	Liddell	3,937
29		28	(a)	Doncaster R	W 1-0	Waters	4,280
30	Mar	3	(a)	Scunthorpe U	L 1-2	Donovan	7,612
31		7	(a)	Hartlepool U	L 1-3	Liddell	2,554
32		11	(h)	Barnsley	W 1-0	Brolly	5,005
33		17	(a)	Aldershot	L 2-4	Brolly, Donovan	3,606
34		20	(a)	Rochdale	W 3-1	Drinkell, Waters, Ford	1,042
35		24	(h)	Huddersfield T	W 1-0	Hanvey	7,718
36		25	(h)	Northampton T	L 0-1		4,835
37		27	(a)	Halifax T	D 0-0		2,481
38	Apr	1	(h)	Southend U	W 2-0	Brolly, Donovan	3,505
39		4	(a)	Wimbledon	D 2-2	Partridge, Lester	2,380
40		8	(a)	Reading	D 0-0		3,378
41		11	(h)	Watford	D 1-1	Partridge	7,189
42		15	(h)	Crewe A	D 2-2	Donovan, Lester	3,826
43		18	(h)	Swansea C	W 2-1	Donovan, Waters	5,692
44		22	(a)	Bournemouth	L 0-1		2,515
45		25	(h)	Southport	W 2-0	Waters, Lester	3,966
46		29	(h)	Brentford	W 2-1	Waters, Brolly	4,469

FINAL LEAGUE POSITION: 6th in Division Four

Appearances
Sub Appearances
Goals

FA Cup

1	Nov	26	(a)	Workington T	W 2-0
2	Dec	17	(h)	Barnsley	W 2-0
3	Jan	17	(h)	Southampton	D 0-0
R		11	(a)	Southampton	D 0-0
2R		17	(n*)	Southampton	L 1-4

*Played at Filbert Street, Leicester.

League Cup

1	Aug	13	(h)	Hartlepool U	W 3-0
		16	(a)	Hartlepool U	W 2-1
2		30	(h)	Watford	L 1-2

Wainman	Cooper	Moore K	Waters	Barker	Partridge	Brolly	Liddell	Drinkell	Donovan	Batch	Mawer	Cumming	Booth	Hanvey	Lester	Ford	Boylen	
1	2	3	4	5	6	7*	8	9	10			12					11	1
1	2	3	4	5	6	7	8	9	10								11	2
1	2	3	4	5	6	7	8	9	10			11*				12		3
1		3	4	5	6	12	7*	9	8		2	10				11		4
1		3	4	5	6	11	8	9			2	10				7		5
1		3	4	5	6	11	8	9			2	10				7		6
1		3*	4	5	6	11	8	9	12		2	10				7		7
1		3	4	5	6	11	8*	9	12		2	10				7		8
1		3	4	5	6	11	8*	9	12		2	10				7		9
1		3	4	5	6	11	8	9			2	10				7		10
1		3	4	5	6	11	8	9			2	10				7		11
1		3	4	5	6	11	8	9*	12		2	10				7		12
1		3	4	5	10	7	8	9			2	11		6				13
1		3	4	5	10	7	8	9	12		2	11*		6				14
1		3	4	5	10	7	8		9		2	11		6				15
1		3*	4	5	10	7	8		9		2	11		6		12		16
1		3	4	5	10	7	8		9*		2	11		6		12		17
		12	4	5	10*	11	8	9		1	2	3		6		7		18
			4	5	10	11	8	9	12	1	2	3*		6		7		19
		3	4	5	10	7	8	9*		1	2	11		6	12			20
1		3	4	5	10	11	8*	12	9		2			6	7			21
1		3	4	5	10	11	8		9		2			6	7			22
1		3	4	5	10	11	8	12	9		2			6	7*			23
1		3	4	5	10	11	8		9		2			6		7		24
		3	4	5	9	11	10	12	8*	1	2	7		6				25
		3	4	5		11	10	9*	12	1	2	7		6	8			26
		3	4	5	10	7	8*	12	9	1	2	11		6				27
		3	4	5	10	7	8		9	1	2			6		11		28
		3	4	5	10	7	8		9	1	2			6		11		29
		3	4	5	10	7	8		9	1	2			6		11		30
		3	4	5	10	7	8		9	1	2			6		11		31
1		3	4	5	10	7	8		9		2			6		11		32
1		3	4	5	10	7	8		9		2			6		11		33
1			4	5		7		8	9		2		3	6	10	11		34
1			4	5		7		8	9		2		3	6	10	11		35
1			4	5	10*	7	8	12	9		2		3	6		11		36
1		10	2	5*		11	8	12	9				3	6	4	7		37
1		5	4			11	8		9		2	10	3	6		7		38
1		5	4		12	11			9*		2	10	3	6	8	7		39
1		5	4		10	11	8				2		3	6	9	7		40
1		5	4		10	11			8		2		3	6	9	7		41
1		5	4		10	11			8		2		3	6	9	7		42
1		5	4		10	11			8		2		3	6	9	7		43
1		5	4		10	11*			8		2	12	3	6	9	7		44
1		3	4	5		11			8		2	10		6	9	7		45
1		5	4			11	12		8		2	10	3*	6	9	7		46
36	3	41	46	38	38	45	37	20	31	10	42	25	12	34	15	31	2	
		1			1	1	1	6	7			2			1	3		
			8		4	5	11	5	14			3		2	3	2		

1978-79

1	Aug	19	(h)	Reading	L 1-2	Lester	3,918
2		23	(a)	Wigan A	W 3-0	Donovan 2, K.Moore	9,227
3		26	(a)	Halifax T	W 2-1	Donovan, Ford	2,038
4	Sep	2	(h)	Torquay U	W 3-0	Darke (og), Brolly, K.Moore	3,934
5		9	(a)	Darlington	W 1-0	Brolly	2,220
6		12	(h)	Wimbledon	D 2-2	Waters (pen), Bryant (og)	6,974
7		16	(h)	Hartlepool U	L 0-1		4,729
8		23	(a)	Crewe A	W 3-0	K.Moore, Liddell 2	2,000
9		26	(a)	Huddersfield T	L 0-2		4,238
10		30	(h)	Rochdale	W 4-0	Brolly 2, Liddell 2	3,681
11	Oct	7	(a)	Port Vale	D 1-1	Liddell	3,433
12		14	(h)	Portsmouth	W 1-0	K.Moore	5,141
13		17	(h)	Northampton T	W 4-3	Drinkell 2, Young, Brolly	5,529
14		21	(a)	Bournemouth	D 0-0		3,399
15		28	(h)	Hereford U	D 1-1	Drinkell	5,349
16	Nov	4	(a)	Aldershot	L 0-2		3,536
17		11	(a)	Torquay U	L 1-3	Drinkell	3,136
18		18	(h)	Halifax T	W 2-1	Cumming, K.Moore	4,128
19	Dec	4	(a)	Stockport C	L 1-2	K.Moore	3,300
20		9	(h)	Newport C	W 1-0	Barker	3,667
21		23	(h)	York C	W 3-0	Cumming 3 (1 pen)	4,339
22		26	(a)	Scunthorpe U	L 1-2	Cumming	8,165
23	Jan	9	(h)	Bradford C	W 5-1	Ford 3, Mitchell, Cumming	4,995
24		16	(h)	Darlington	W 7-2	Lester 4, Ford, Waters, K.Moore	5,387
25		20	(a)	Hartlepool U	L 0-1		2,212
26	Feb	3	(h)	Huddersfield T	W 2-1	Waters, Ford	4,921
27		24	(a)	Portsmouth	W 3-1	Ford 2, Brolly	12,782
28		27	(h)	Crewe A	D 2-2	Ford, Cumming	6,598
29	Mar	3	(h)	Bournemouth	W 1-0	Waters	5,428
30		10	(a)	Hereford U	W 1-0	Price (og)	2,939
31		13	(a)	Rochdale	W 5-2	Ford, Brolly, Liddell, Waters (pen), Mitchell	2,395
32		17	(h)	Aldershot	D 0-0		6,121
33		20	(a)	Wimbledon	W 1-0	Waters	3,452
34		24	(h)	Wigan A	W 3-1	Waters, Brolly, Ford	8,252
35		28	(a)	Reading	L 0-4		8,394
36		31	(a)	Doncaster R	W 1-0	Ford	4,707
37	Apr	3	(h)	Port Vale	W 1-0	Ford	7,815
38		7	(h)	Stockport C	W 2-1	Cumming, Ford	7,495
39		13	(a)	York C	D 0-0		5,500
40		14	(a)	Scunthorpe U	D 1-1	Drinkell	10,197
41		16	(h)	Bradford C	W 3-1	Waters, Ford, Drinkell	4,505
42		21	(a)	Barnsley	W 2-0	Crombie, Lester	15,585
43		24	(a)	Northampton T	W 2-1	Cumming, Waters	3,450
44		28	(a)	Newport C	D 1-1	Waters	3,049
45	May	5	(h)	Doncaster R	L 3-4	Drinkell, Ford, Cumming	10,243
46		8	(a)	Barnsley	L 1-2	Lester	21,261

FINAL LEAGUE POSITION: 2nd in Division Four

Appearances
Sub Appearances
Goals

FA Cup

1	Nov	25	(a)	Hartlepool U	L 0-1

League Cup

1	Aug	12	(h)	York C	W 2-0
		15	(a)	York C	W 3-0
2		29	(a)	Manchester C	L 0-2

Batch	Mawer	Moore K	Waters	Barker	Crombie	Ford	Donovan	Lester	Mitchell	Cumming	Moore D	Wigginton	Brolly	Liddell	Drinkell	Young	Partridge	
1	2	3	4	5	6	7	8	9	10*	11				12				1
1	2	3	4	5	6	7	8	9	10	11*				12				2
1	2	3	4	5	6	7	8	9	10				11					3
1	2	3	4	5	6	7	8	9		10*			11	12				4
1	2	3	4	5	6	7		9					11	8		10		5
1	2	3	4	5	6	7*		9					11	8		10	12	6
1		3	2	5	6	7		9*	10				11	8	12	4		7
1	2	3	4	5	6	7							11	8	9		10	8
1	2	3	4	5	6	7							11	8	9		10	9
1	2	3	4	5	6	7							11	8	9	12	10*	10
1	2	3	4	5	6	7							11	8	9		10	11
1	2	3	4	5	6	7							11	8	9	12	10*	12
1	2	3	4	5	6	7							11	8	9	10		13
1	2	3	4	5	6	7				12			11	8	9	10*		14
1	2	3	4	5	6*	7				12			11	8	9	10		15
1	2	3	4	5	6	7				12			11	8*	9	10		16
1		3	4	5	6				11	10	2		7		9		8	17
1		3	4	5	6	12			11	10	2		7		9		8*	18
1		3	4	5	6	12		8	10	11	2		7		9*			19
1		3	4	5	6	7		9	8	10	2		11					20
1		3	4	5	6	7		9	8	10	2		11					21
1		3	4	5	6	7		9	8	10	2		11*		12			22
1		3	4	5	6	7		9	8	10	2		11*		12			23
1		3	4	5	6	7		9	8	10	2		11					24
1		3	4	5	6	7		9	8	10*	2		11		12			25
1		3	4	5	6	8		9	10	11	2		7					26
1		3	4	5	6	8		9	10	11*	2		7		12			27
1		3	4	5	6	8		9*	10	11	2		7		12			28
1		3	4		6	8		9	10	11	2	5	7*		12			29
1		3	4		6	8			10	11	2	5	7		9			30
1		3	4		6	8			10	11	2	5	7	9				31
1		3	4		6	8			10	11	2	5	7	9				32
1		3	4		6	8			10	11	2	5	7	9				33
1		3	4		6	8		11	10		2	5	7	9				34
1		3	4		6	8		11	10*		2	5	7	9	12			35
1		3	4		6	8		10		11	2	5	7	9*	12			36
1		3	4		6	8		10		11	2	5	7	9				37
1		3	4		6	8		10		11	2	5	7	9*	12			38
1		3	4		6	8		10		11	2	5	7	9				39
1		3*	4		6	8	12		10	11	2	5	7		9			40
1		3	4		6	8		10*		11	2	5	7	12	9			41
1		3	4		6	8		10		11	2	5	7		9			42
1		3	4		6	8		10		11	2	5	7		9			43
1		3	4		6	8		10		11	2	5	7		9			44
1		3	4		6	8		10		11	2	5	7		9			45
1		3	4		6	8		10*		11	2	5	7	12	9			46
46	15	46	46	28	46	43	4	30	24	31	30	18	44	21	20	7	7	
						2	1			3				5	10	2	1	
		7	10	1	1	16	3	7	2	10			8	6	7	1		

3 own-goals

1979-80

1	Aug	18	(h)	Exeter C	W	4-1	Cumming, Liddell 2, Waters (pen)	5,937
2		22	(a)	Chester	L	1-3	K.Moore	3,779
3		25	(h)	Blackpool	W	4-3	Waters (pen), Cumming 2, K.Moore	7,306
4	Sep	1	(a)	Blackburn R	D	0-0		8,877
5		8	(h)	Plymouth A	W	1-0	Cumming	7,244
6		15	(a)	Brentford	L	0-1		7,121
7		18	(a)	Bury	D	1-1	Kilmore	3,176
8		22	(h)	Colchester U	L	1-2	Kilmore	6,962
9		29	(a)	Swindon T	L	0-3		6,825
10	Oct	2	(h)	Bury	W	1-0	Cumming	7,109
11		6	(a)	Millwall	L	0-2		5,057
12		9	(h)	Chester	L	0-2		8,007
13		13	(h)	Chesterfield	D	1-1	Kilmore	6,559
14		20	(a)	Gillingham	W	1-0	Kilmore	6,378
15		23	(a)	Sheffield W	L	0-2		13,885
16		27	(h)	Rotherham U	W	2-0	Waters, Cumming	7,702
17	Nov	3	(a)	Exeter C	W	2-1	Ford, Hatch (og)	4,356
18		6	(h)	Sheffield W	W	3-1	Drinkell, Wigginton, Ford	14,900
19		9	(a)	Southend U	L	0-1		4,119
20		17	(h)	Wimbledon	W	1-0	Waters (pen)	6,716
21	Dec	1	(a)	Oxford U	W	1-0	Kilmore	3,361
22		8	(h)	Mansfield T	W	2-1	Ford, Waters (pen)	7,663
23		21	(a)	Carlisle U	W	2-0	Kilmore, K.Moore	4,663
24		26	(h)	Barnsley	W	3-0	Kilmore 2, Cumming	14,153
25		29	(a)	Sheffield U	D	1-1	Cumming	21,800
26	Jan	12	(h)	Blackburn R	L	1-2	Brolly	10,965
27		15	(h)	Reading	W	2-1	Drinkell, Kilmore	8,532
28		19	(a)	Plymouth A	D	1-1	Cumming	6,310
29		26	(a)	Blackpool	W	3-0	Drinkell 2, Cumming	4,932
30	Feb	2	(h)	Brentford	W	5-1	Brolly, Drinkell 2, Kilmore, Waters	9,669
31		8	(a)	Colchester U	L	1-2	Dowman (og)	5,149
32		16	(h)	Swindon T	W	2-0	Cumming, Ford	12,675
33		23	(a)	Chesterfield	W	3-2	Drinkell, Cumming, Kilmore	13,867
34	Mar	1	(h)	Gillingham	W	1-0	Drinkell	11,246
35		8	(a)	Rotherham U	D	0-0		9,032
36		15	(h)	Millwall	W	2-0	Kilmore, Drinkell	10,923
37		22	(h)	Southend U	W	1-0	Ford	10,532
38		25	(a)	Hull C	D	2-2	Brolly, Drinkell	14,176
39		29	(a)	Wimbledon	W	6-3	Kilmore 3, Cumming, Drinkell, Mitchell	2,485
40	Apr	4	(h)	Carlisle U	W	2-0	Mitchell, Drinkell	15,121
41		5	(a)	Barnsley	W	1-0	Brolly	16,433
42		7	(h)	Hull C	D	1-1	Cumming	18,363
43		12	(a)	Reading	D	1-1	Waters	9,549
44		19	(h)	Oxford U	W	2-0	K.Moore, Drinkell	11,735
45		26	(a)	Mansfield T	D	0-0		10,100
46	May	3	(h)	Sheffield U	W	4-0	Drinkell 3, Waters	19,276

FINAL LEAGUE POSITION: 1st in Division Three

Appearances
Sub Appearances
Goals

FA Cup

1	Nov	24	(h)	Chesterfield	D	1-1
R		27	(a)	Chesterfield	W	3-2
2	Dec	15	(h)	Sheffield U	W	2-0
3	Jan	5	(a)	Liverpool	L	0-5

League Cup

1	Aug	11	(h)	Scunthorpe U	W	2-0
		14	(a)	Scunthorpe U	D	0-0
2		28	(h)	Huddersfield T	W	1-0
	Sep	4	(a)	Huddersfield T	W	4-1
3		25	(h)	Notts C	W	3-1
4	Oct	30	(h)	Everton	W	2-1
5	Dec	4	(h)	Wolves	D	0-0
R		11	(a)	Wolves	D	1-1
2R		18	(n*)	Wolves	L	0-2

*Played at the Baseball Ground, Derby.

	Batch	Moore D	Moore K	Waters	Wigginton	Stone	Brolly	Ford	Liddell	Mitchell	Cumming	Crombie	Kilmore	Drinkell	Cawthorne	Crosby	Mawer	Lester
1	1	2	3	4	5	6	7	8	9	10	11							
2	1	2	3	4	5	6	7	8	9	10	11							
3	1	2	3	4	5	6	7	8	9	10	11							
4	1	2	3	4	5	6	7	8	9	10	11							
5	1	2	3	4	5	6	7	8	9*	10	11							12
6	1	2	3	4	5	6	7	8*	9	10	11	12						
7	1	2	3	4	5		7		9	10	11	6	8					
8	1	2	3	4	5	6*	7		9	10	11		8					12
9	1	2	3	4	5		7	8*	9	10	11	6	12					
10	1	2	3	4	5		7		8	10	11*	6	9	12				
11	1	2	3	4	5		7		9	10	11	6	8*	12				
12	1	2	3	4	5		7	8	9	10*	11	6	12					
13	1	2	3	4	5			7		10	11	6	8	9				
14	1	2	3	4	5		7		12	10	11	6	8*	9				
15	1	2	3	4	5		7			10	11	6	8	9				
16	1		3	4	5	2	7	8	12	10*	11	6		9				
17	1		3	4	5	2	7	8*	12	10	11	6		9				
18	1		3	4	5	2	7	8		10	11	6		9				
19	1		3	4	5	2	7	8		10	11	6		9				
20	1		3	4	5	2	7	11	8	10		6	9					
21	1		3	4	5	2	7		12	10	11	6	8	9*				
22	1		3	4	5	2	7	11	12	10		6	8*	9				
23	1		3	4	5	2	7			10	11	6	8	9				
24	1		3	4	5	2	7	8*	12	10	11	6	9					
25	1	2	3	4	5		7	8	9	10	11	6						
26	1			4	5	2	7	11		10		6	8*	9		3	12	
27	1		3	4	5*	2	11	7		10		6	8	9			12	
28	1		3	4	5	2	7	8		10	11*	6	12	9				
29	1	2	3	4	5	6	7			10	11		8	9				
30	1		3	4	5	2	8	12		10	11*	6	7	9				
31	1		3	4	5	2	11	7		10		6	8	9				
32	1		3	4	5	2	7	12		10	11	6	8*	9				
33	1		3	4	5	2	7	12		10	11	6	8	9*				
34	1	2		4	5		7	11		10	3	6	8*	9			12	
35	1	2	3	4	5		7	12		10	11	6	8*	9				
36	1	2	3	4	5		7	12		10	11*	6	8	9				
37	1	2	5	4			7	11		10	3	6	8	9				
38	1		3*	4			7	11		10	2	6	8	9	5	12		
39	1	2		4	5		7	11		10*	3	6	8	9		12		
40	1	2		4	5		7	11		10	3	6	8	9				
41	1	2		4	5		7	11		10	3	6	8*	9		12		
42	1	2	3	4	5		7	8		10	11	6		9				
43	1	2	3	4	5	12	7	8		10	11*	6		9				
44	1	2	3	4	5	12	7	8		10	11*	6		9				
45	1	2	3	4	5	11	7	8		10		6		9				
46	1	2	3	4	5	12	7	8		10*	11	6		9				
	46	29	41	46	44	25	45	32	14	46	40	38	27	31	1	1		
						3		5	6			1	3	2		3	3	2
			4	8	1		4	5	2	2	14		15	16				

2 own-goals

1980-81

1	Aug	16	(a)	Shrewsbury T	D 1-1	Drinkell	4,998
2		19	(h)	Preston NE	D 0-0		10,461
3		23	(h)	Wrexham	W 1-0	Ford	9,175
4		30	(a)	Bristol R	D 2-2	Cumming 2	4,461
5	Sep	6	(a)	Orient	L 0-2		4,506
6		13	(h)	Derby C	L 0-1		15,502
7		20	(a)	Blackburn R	L 0-2		10,838
8		27	(h)	Luton T	D 0-0		9,044
9	Oct	4	(h)	Bristol C	W 1-0	Drinkell	8,781
10		7	(a)	Notts C	D 0-0		8,017
11		11	(a)	Chelsea	L 0-3		15,206
12		18	(h)	Watford	D 1-1	K.Moore	8,906
13		21	(h)	Sheffield W	D 0-0		10,298
14		24	(a)	Swansea C	L 0-1		12,928
15	Nov	1	(h)	Queen's Park R	D 0-0		10,015
16		8	(a)	West Ham U	L 1-2	Stone	15,468
17		15	(h)	Shrewsbury T	W 1-0	Cumming	8,737
18		22	(a)	Bolton W	D 1-1	Stone	9,031
19		29	(h)	Cambridge U	W 3-1	Waters, Brolly, Cumming	7,592
20	Dec	2	(a)	Preston NE	W 4-2	Cumming, Ford, Brolly 2	5,209
21		6	(a)	Cardiff C	D 1-1	Waters (pen)	6,023
22		13	(h)	Chelsea	W 2-0	Whymark, Ford	14,708
23		20	(a)	Watford	L 1-3	Kilmore	10,209
24		26	(h)	Newcastle U	D 0-0		17,623
25		27	(a)	Oldham A	W 2-1	Waters, Ford	7,183
26	Jan	10	(h)	Bolton W	W 4-0	Cumming, Drinkell 2, Waters (pen)	9,320
27		17	(h)	Bristol R	W 2-0	Cumming, Drinkell	9,601
28		21	(a)	Wrexham	W 2-0	Cumming 2	5,619
29	Feb	7	(a)	Derby C	L 1-2	Waters (pen)	19,691
30		14	(h)	Orient	W 2-0	Waters 2 (2 pens)	10,190
31		21	(a)	Luton T	W 2-0	Cumming, Waters	9,217
32		28	(h)	Blackburn R	D 0-0		12,210
33	Mar	10	(a)	Bristol C	D 1-1	Cumming	5,881
34		14	(h)	Notts C	W 2-1	Whymark, Brolly	12,184
35		28	(h)	Swansea C	W 1-0	Whymark	12,166
36	Apr	4	(a)	Queen's Park R	L 0-1		8,906
37		11	(h)	West Ham U	L 1-5	Waters (pen)	17,924
38		18	(h)	Oldham A	D 0-0		10,634
39		20	(a)	Newcastle U	D 1-1	Drinkell	13,215
40		25	(h)	Cardiff C	L 0-1		7,377
41		28	(a)	Sheffield W	W 2-1	Drinkell, Kilmore	16,747
42	May	2	(a)	Cambridge U	L 1-5	Waters (pen)	4,528

FINAL LEAGUE POSITION: 7th in Division Two

Appearances
Sub Appearances
Goals

FA Cup

3	Jan	3	(a)	West Brom A	L 0-3

League Cup

1	Aug	9	(h)	Notts C	L 0-1
		12	(a)	Notts C	L 0-3

Anglo Scottish Cup (Qualifying Competition)

Q1	Jul	16	(a)	Hull C	L 0-1
Q2	Aug	2	(h)	Chesterfield	D 3-3
Q3		5	(h)	Sheffield U	W 1-0

Grimsby failed to qualify for the quarter-finals.

Batch	Stone	Moore K	Waters	Wigginton	Crombie	Brolly	Ford	Drinkell	Mitchell	Cumming	Crosby	Whymark	Kilmore	Czuczman	Moore D	Liddell	Steeples	Beacock	
1	2	3	4	5	6	7	8	9	10	11									1
1	2	3	4	5	6	7	8	9	10	11									2
1	2	3	4	5	6	7	8		10	11			12			9*			3
1	2	3	4	5	6	7	8	9	10	11									4
1	2	3	4	5	6	7	8*	9	10	11						12			5
1	2	3	4	5	6	7		9	10	11			8*			12			6
1	2	3	4	5	6	7*	12	9	10	11						8			7
1		6	4	5			7	9	10	11	3			2		8			8
1		6	4	5		12	7	9	10	11	3		8*	2					9
1		6	4	5		12	7	9	10	11	3		8*	2					10
1		6	4	5		12	7	9	10	11*	3		8	2					11
1	2	6	4	5		12	7*	9	10	11	3		8						12
1	2	6	4	5		7	8	9	10	11	3								13
1	2	6	4	5		7	8	9	10	11	3								14
1	2	6	4	5		7*	8	9	10	11	3		12						15
1	2	6	4	5		7		9	10		3		8			11*	12		16
1	2	6	4	5	3	7	8*	9	10	11			12						17
1	2	6	4	5	3	7*	8	9	10	11			12						18
1	2	6	4	5	3	7	8*	9	10	11			12						19
1	2	6	4	5	3	7	8	9	10	11*			12						20
1	2	6	4	5	3	7	11	9	10			8*	12						21
1		6	4	5	3	7	11	9	10			8*	12		2				22
1		6	4	5	3	7	11*	9	10			8	12		2				23
1	2	6	4		3	7	11*	9	10	12		8		5					24
1	2		4		6	7*	8	9	10	11	3	12		5					25
1	2	6	4	5	3	7	8	9	10	11*						12			26
1	2	6	4	5	3	7*	8	9	10	11		12							27
1	2	6	4	5	3	7		9	10	11		8							28
1	2	6	4	5	3	7*		9	10	11		8	12						29
1	2	6	4	5	3	7		9	10	11		8							30
1	2	6	4	5	3	7		9*	10	11		8	12						31
1		6	4	5	3	7		9	10	11		8			2				32
1		6	4	5	3	7		9	10	11		8			2				33
1	2	6	4	5	3	7		9	10			8	11*				12		34
1	2	6	4	5	3	7		9	10			8	12				11*		35
1	2	6	4	5	3	7*		9	10	11		8	12						36
1	2	6	4	5	3	7	12	9	10	11		8							37
1	2	6	4	5	3*	7	12	9	10			8					11*		38
1	2	6	4	5	3	11	7	9	10			8*	12						39
1	2	6	4	5	3			9	10	11		8	12				7*		40
1	2	6	4	5	3	11		9*	10			8	7					12	41
1		6	4	5	3	11		9	10			8	7*		2			12	42
42	33	41	42	40	33	36	25	41	42	31	10	19	9	6	5	4	3		
						4	3			1		2	15			3	2	2	
	2	1	10			4	4	7		11		3	2						

1981-82

1	Aug	29	(h)	Leicester C	D 2-2	Kilmore, Drinkell	11,032
2	Sep	1	(a)	Watford	W 2-0	Ford 2	11,257
3		5	(a)	Orient	W 2-1	Ford, Kilmore	3,764
4		12	(h)	Queen's Park R	W 2-1	Cumming 2	9,490
5		19	(a)	Charlton A	L 0-2		6,875
6		22	(h)	Norwich C	L 1-2	Whymark	10,185
7		26	(h)	Sheffield W	L 0-1		13,110
8	Oct	3	(a)	Bolton W	W 2-1	Drinkell, Mitchell	7,217
9		10	(h)	Cambridge U	L 1-2	Ford	7,450
10		17	(a)	Luton T	L 0-6		9,090
11		24	(h)	Blackburn R	D 1-1	Wigginton	7,159
12		31	(a)	Derby C	D 1-1	K.Moore	11,706
13	Nov	7	(a)	Wrexham	L 0-2		3,351
14		21	(a)	Chelsea	D 1-1	Ford	11,931
15		28	(h)	Newcastle U	D 1-1	Mitchell	9,256
16	Dec	5	(a)	Oldham A	L 1-3	Ford	5,907
17	Jan	9	(h)	Orient	L 1-2	Waters	6,877
18		30	(h)	Charlton A	D 3-3	Drinkell 2, K.Moore	7,088
19	Feb	6	(a)	Queen's Park R	L 0-1		8,753
20		9	(h)	Rotherham U	L 1-2	Waters (pen)	8,629
21		20	(a)	Sheffield W	D 1-1	Waters (pen)	14,654
22		27	(a)	Cambridge U	D 2-2	Brolly, Drinkell	3,542
23	Mar	2	(h)	Bolton W	D 1-1	Waters (pen)	6,525
24		6	(h)	Luton T	D 0-0		7,733
25		13	(a)	Blackburn R	L 0-2		8,676
26		16	(h)	Watford	L 0-2		6,146
27		20	(h)	Derby C	W 1-0	Kilmore	7,573
28		23	(a)	Barnsley	L 2-3	Drinkell, Whymark	15,383
29		27	(h)	Wrexham	D 1-1	Kilmore	6,216
30		30	(a)	Cardiff C	L 1-2	Whymark (pen)	3,924
31	Apr	3	(a)	Crystal P	W 3-0	Kilmore, K.Moore, Whymark	7,541
32		9	(h)	Barnsley	W 3-2	Whymark, K.Moore, Waters	12,218
33		10	(a)	Rotherham U	D 2-2	Whymark, Ford	10,011
34		17	(h)	Chelsea	D 3-3	D.Moore, Cooper, Kilmore	9,164
35		20	(h)	Crystal P	L 0-1		7,696
36		24	(a)	Newcastle U	W 1-0	Brolly	14,011
37		27	(h)	Shrewsbury T	W 5-1	Whymark, Waters (pen), Crosby, Brolly, D.Moore	7,051
38	May	1	(h)	Oldham A	W 2-1	Whymark, Waters (pen)	7,656
39		5	(a)	Norwich C	L 1-2	Whymark	18,360
40		8	(a)	Shrewsbury T	L 0-2		4,036
41		12	(a)	Leicester C	W 2-1	Whymark 2	13,941
42		15	(h)	Cardiff C	L 0-1		8,148

FINAL LEAGUE POSITION: 17th in Division Two

Appearances
Sub Appearances
Goals

FA Cup

3	Jan	5	(a)	Millwall	W 6-1
4		23	(a)	Newcastle U	W 2-1
5	Feb	13	(a)	Queen's Park R	L 1-3

League Cup

2	Oct	6	(h)	Watford	W 1-0
		27	(a)	Watford	L 1-3

League Group Cup (preliminary rounds played in groups of four)

C1	Aug	15	(h)	Chesterfield	W 1-0
C2		18	(h)	Sheffield U	W 2-0
C3		22	(a)	Doncaster R	W 2-0
QF	Dec	8	(a)	Newport C	W 2-0
SF		19	(h)	Shrewsbury T	W 2-1
F	Apr	6	(h*)	Wimbledon	W 3-2

Final played at Blundell Park, Cleethorpes.

Batch	Stone	Crombie	Waters	Wigginton	Moore K	Brolly	Whymark	Drinkell	Mitchell	Kilmore	Moore D	Crosby	Cooper	Ford	Cumming	Beacock	Czuczman	O'Dell	Ward	Steeples	
1	2	3	4	5	6	7*	8	9	10	11				12							1
1	2	3	4	5	6	7	8*	9	10	11				12							2
1	2	3	4	5	6	7		9	10	11*				8	12						3
1	2	3	4	5	6	7		9	10*	12				8	11						4
1	2	3*	4	5	6		8	9	10	12				7	11						5
1	2	3*	4	5	6	7	8	9	10	12					11						6
1		3	4	5	6	7	8	9	10	12	2				11*						7
1		3	4	5	6	7	8	9	10		2			12	11*						8
1		3	4		6	7	8	9*	10		2			12	11		5				9
1		3	4		6	7	8	9	10	12	2			11*			5				10
1	2*	3	4	5	6		9		10	12				8	11					7	11
1		3	4*	5	6	12	9		10		2			7	11				8		12
1		3		5	6	4	9		10	8	2			7	11*	12					13
1				5	3	7	9	12	10		2			11			6	4*	8		14
1		3		5	6	7	9		10		2			8	11			4*	12		15
1		3		5	6	7	9	12	10		2			8	11			4*			16
1		3	4	5	6	7*	9		10	12	2			8	11						17
1	4	3			5	12		9	10	8	2	6		7		11*					18
1	4		12	5	6	11		9	10	8	2	3		7*							19
1	7		4	5	6	11*		9	10	8	2	3		12							20
1	7	3	4	5	6	11		9	10		2			8							21
1	7	3	4	5	6	11		9	10		2			8							22
1		3	4	5	6	11		9	10		2*			8		7				12	23
1		3	4		6	7		9	10		2		5	8	11						24
1		3	4		6	7	12	9			2		5	8*	11	10					25
1		3	4		6	7	12	9		8	2		5		11*	10					26
1		3	4		6	7	12	9		8*	2		5		11	10					27
1		3	4		6	7	12	9		8	2		5		11*	10					28
1		3	4		6	7	12	9		8	2		5		11	10*					29
1	4	3			6	7	9		10	8	2		5*	12	11						30
1	5	3*	4		6	7	9		10	8	2	12			11						31
1	5		4		6	7*	9		10	8	2	3		12	11						32
1		6	4			11	9*		10	8	2	3	5	7		12					33
1		6	4			11	9	12	10	8	2*	3	5	7							34
1		6	4			11	9	12	10*	8	2	3	5	7							35
1	7	6	4			11	9			8*	2	3	5	12		10					36
1	7	6	4		10*	11	9			8	2	3	5	12							37
1	7	6	4		10	11*	9			8	2	3	5	12							38
1	2	6	4		10*	11	9			8		3	5	7		12					39
1	10	6	4			12	9	8			2	3	5	7	11*						40
1	7	6	4				9			8	2	3	5	11		10					41
1		6	4		5		9	12		8	2	3		7	11	10*					42
42	21	38	35	20	36	35	28	23	30	23	34	14	16	25	23	10	3	3	2	1	
			1			3	5	5		7		1		10	1	3			1	1	
			7	1	4	3	11	6	2	6	2	1	1	7	2						

1982-83

1	Aug	28	(h)	Leeds U	D 1-1	Kilmore	16,137
2	Sep	4	(a)	Carlisle U	W 3-2	Waters (pen), Drinkell 2 (1 pen)	4,683
3		7	(h)	Blackburn R	W 5-0	Drinkell, Kilmore 2, Waters, Ford	7,567
4		11	(h)	Shrewsbury T	W 2-0	Drinkell, Waters (pen)	7,599
5		18	(a)	Charlton A	W 1-0	Kilmore	4,361
6		25	(h)	Bolton W	W 1-0	Cumming	7,583
7		28	(a)	Middlesbrough	W 4-1	Waters 2 (2 pens), Cooper, Crombie	5,927
8	Oct	2	(a)	Chelsea	L 2-5	Drinkell, Cumming	10,019
9		9	(a)	Leicester C	L 0-2		9,640
10		16	(h)	Derby C	D 1-1	Waters	7,572
11		23	(a)	Sheffield W	L 0-2		17,904
12		30	(h)	Cambridge U	W 1-0	Drinkell	5,738
13	Nov	6	(a)	Wolves	L 0-3		12,701
14		13	(h)	Fulham	L 0-4		6,952
15		20	(h)	Barnsley	L 1-2	Whymark	7,219
16		27	(a)	Oldham A	D 1-1	Ford	5,508
17	Dec	4	(h)	Crystal P	W 4-1	Drinkell 3, Cumming	5,295
18		11	(a)	Queen's Park R	L 0-4		9,811
19		18	(h)	Burnley	W 3-2	Cumming, Bonnyman, Drinkell	5,448
20		27	(a)	Rotherham U	L 0-3		9,231
21		28	(h)	Newcastle U	D 2-2	Drinkell 2	14,983
22	Jan	1	(a)	Barnsley	L 0-4		12,318
23		3	(h)	Carlisle U	W 2-1	Drinkell, Ford	6,377
24		15	(a)	Leeds U	L 0-1		13,583
25		22	(h)	Charlton A	D 1-1	Wilkinson	5,990
26	Feb	5	(a)	Blackburn R	L 1-2	Cumming	4,724
27		12	(h)	Chelsea	W 2-1	Drinkell 2	6,711
28		19	(h)	Leicester C	W 2-0	Ford, Drinkell	6,963
29		26	(a)	Derby C	L 0-2		12,775
30	Mar	5	(h)	Sheffield W	D 1-1	Cumming	9,472
31		12	(a)	Cambridge U	L 0-1		3,337
32		19	(h)	Wolves	D 1-1	Waters (pen)	7,600
33		26	(a)	Fulham	L 0 4		8,906
34	Apr	2	(a)	Newcastle U	L 0-4		20,143
35		4	(h)	Rotherham U	L 1-2	Waters	7,117
36		8	(a)	Shrewsbury T	D 0-0		4,446
37		16	(h)	Middlesbrough	L 0-3		5,985
38		23	(a)	Crystal P	L 0-2		5,909
39		30	(h)	Oldham A	L 0-2		4,755
40	May	2	(a)	Bolton W	D 0-0		5,866
41		7	(a)	Burnley	D 1-1	Drinkell	7,083
42		14	(h)	Queen's Park R	D 1-1	Cumming	9,590

FINAL LEAGUE POSITION: 19th in Division Two

Appearances
Sub Appearances
Goals

FA Cup

3	Jan	8	(a)	Scunthorpe U	D 0-0
R		11	(h)	Scunthorpe U	W 2-0
4		29	(a)	Ipswich T	L 0-2

League Cup

1	Aug	31	(a)	Scunthorpe U	W 2-1
	Sep	14	(h)	Scunthorpe U	D 0-0
2	Oct	12	(h)	Sheffield U	D 3-3
		26	(a)	Sheffield U	L 1-5

League Trophy

Aug	14	(a)	Sheffield U	W 3-1
	18	(a)	Lincoln C	L 1-2
	21	(h)	Scunthorpe U	W 2-0

The first matches were played in eight groups of four, the top team from each group going into the quarter-finals. Lincoln City were top of this group (eight points), Grimsby finishing second (seven points). A bonus point was awarded to each team scoring three or more goals.

Batch	Moore D	Crombie	Waters	Cooper	Moore K	Ford	Kilmore	Drinkell	Bonnyman	Whymark	Groiter	Speight	Crosby	Cumming	Stone	Whitlock	Saxby	Wilkinson	O'Dell	Beacock	
1	2	3	4	5	6	7*	8	9	10	11										12	1
1	2	3	4	5	6	7*	8	9	10	11		12									2
1		3	4	5	6	7	8	9	10	11		2									3
1			4	5	6	7	8	9	10	11*		2	3	12							4
1	2	3	4	5	6		12	9	10	8*		11		7							5
1	2	3	4	5	6			9	10	8		11		7							6
1	2	3	4	5	6		12	9	10	8*		11		7							7
1	2*	3	4	5	6		12	9	10	8		11		7							8
1		3*	4	5	6	7	8	9	10			2		11						12	9
	2		4	5	6		8	9	10	12	1	11*	3	7							10
	2		4	5	6	12	8	9	10	11	1		3*	7							11
	2					11	7	9	10	8	1	6		3	5	4					12
	2					11	7*	9	10	8	1	6	12	3	5	4					13
1	2		4	7		11		9	10	8			3		5	6					14
1	2		4	5		11	12	9	10*	8		7		3		6					15
1	2		4	5	3	7		9	10	8				11*	12	6					16
1	2		4	5	3	7		9	10	8				11		6					17
1	2		4	5	3	7		9	10	8					11	6					18
1	2	3	4		6	7		9	10	8				11	5						19
1	2	3	4		6	7		9	10	8				11	5						20
1	2	3	4	5	6	7		9	10	8				11*		12					21
1	2	3	4	5	6	7		9		8				11					10		22
1	2	3	4	5	6	7		9		8				11					10		23
1	2	3	4		6	7		9	11	8					5				10		24
1	2	3	4		6	7		9	11*	8					5			12	10		25
1	2	3	4	5	6	7		9	10			11		8							26
1	2	3	4	5	6	7		9	10					8					11		27
1	2	3	4	5	6	7		9	10					8					11		28
1	2	3	4	5	6	7		9	10					8					11		29
1	2	3	4		6	7		9	10				5	8					11		30
1	2	3	4		6	7			9				10*	8	12		5		11		31
1	2	3	4		6	7			8				5	11	10*			9	12		32
1	2	12	4		6	7			8				3	11			5*	9	10		33
1	2	3	4		6	7	12	9	8*				5	11					10		34
1		12	4		6	7	8	9	10					3	2*		5		11		35
1	2	3	4		6	7		9	8					11			5		10		36
1	2	3	4		6	7		9	8					11			5*	12	10		37
1	2	3	4	7*	6	11	12	9	8								5		10		38
1	2	3	4		6	7	11*	9	10	8							5		12		39
1	2	3	4		6	7		9	10	8				11			5				40
1	2	3	4		6	7		9	10	8				11			5				41
1	2	3	4		6	7	12	9	10	8*				11			5				42
38	38	30	40	24	38	36	11	39	40	27	4	12	9	32	10	7	10	2	15		
		2				1	7			1		1	1	1	2	1		2	2	2	
		1	8	1		4	4	17	1	1				7				1			

1983-84

1	Aug	27	(h)	Shrewsbury T	D 1-1	Drinkell	5,177
2	Sep	3	(a)	Cardiff C	L 1-3	Waters	5,135
3		6	(h)	Leeds U	W 2-0	Drinkell, Waters (pen)	7,797
4		10	(h)	Newcastle U	D 1-1	Speight	9,000
5		17	(a)	Middlesbrough	D 1-1	Waters	10,239
6		24	(h)	Fulham	W 2-1	Wilkinson, Emson	5,769
7		27	(a)	Barnsley	L 1-3	Wilkinson	10,966
8	Oct	1	(a)	Manchester C	L 1-2	Emson	25,080
9		8	(a)	Huddersfield T	D 0-0		8,897
10		15	(h)	Brighton & HA	W 5-0	Wilkinson 2, Ford, Lund, Emson	5,969
11		22	(h)	Crystal P	W 2-0	Waters, Ford	6,075
12		29	(a)	Derby C	W 2-1	Drinkell 2	11,531
13	Nov	5	(a)	Portsmouth	L 0-4		12,906
14		12	(h)	Charlton A	W 2-1	Drinkell, Whymark	5,584
15		19	(a)	Swansea C	W 1-0	K.Moore	6,178
16		26	(h)	Carlisle U	D 1-1	Waters (pen)	5,665
17	Dec	4	(a)	Blackburn R	D 1-1	Bonnyman	6,409
18		13	(h)	Oldham A	W 3-0	Ford, Speight, Wilkinson	4,825
19		17	(a)	Chelsea	W 3-2	Waters, Emson, Ford	13,151
20		26	(h)	Sheffield W	W 1-0	Wilkinson	16,197
21		28	(a)	Cambridge U	D 2-2	Emson, Ford	4,319
22		31	(h)	Cardiff C	W 1-0	Emson	7,164
23	Jan	2	(a)	Fulham	D 1-1	Drinkell	7,351
24		14	(a)	Shrewsbury T	W 2-1	Drinkell, Wilkinson	3,343
25		21	(h)	Middlesbrough	D 0-0		7,342
26	Feb	4	(h)	Manchester C	D 1-1	Wilkinson	11,986
27		11	(a)	Newcastle U	W 1-0	Drinkell	28,526
28		21	(h)	Derby C	W 2-1	Wilkinson, Drinkell	8,530
29		25	(a)	Crystal P	W 1-0	Ford	5,956
30	Mar	3	(h)	Portsmouth	L 3-4	Drinkell, Ford, Cumming	8,729
31		10	(a)	Charlton A	D 3-3	Drinkell 2, Ford	7,626
32		17	(a)	Leeds U	L 1-2	Wilkinson	14,412
33		31	(h)	Huddersfield T	W 2-1	Waters (pen), Bonnyman	7,541
34	Apr	7	(a)	Brighton & HA	L 0-2		10,610
35		10	(h)	Barnsley	W 1-0	Wilkinson	6,769
36		14	(h)	Swansea C	W 3-0	Drinkell 3	5,851
37		21	(a)	Sheffield W	L 0-1		25,828
38		23	(h)	Cambridge U	D 0-0		5,828
39		28	(a)	Carlisle U	D 1-1	Wilkinson	3,512
40	May	5	(h)	Blackburn R	W 3-2	Bonnyman (pen), Lund 2	4,826
41		7	(a)	Oldham A	L 1-2	Lund	4,156
42		12	(h)	Chelsea	L 0-1		13,000

FINAL LEAGUE POSITION: 5th in Division Two

Appearances
Sub Appearances
Goals

FA Cup

1	Jan	7	(a)	Portsmouth	L 1-2

League Cup

1	Aug	30	(a)	York C	L 1-2
	Sep	13	(h)	York C	W 2-0*
2	Oct	4	(h)	Coventry C	D 0-0
		25	(a)	Coventry C	L 1-2

*After extra-time

Batch	Cumming	Crombie	Waters	Nicholl	Moore K	Ford	Wilkinson	Drinkell	Bonnyman	Emson	Speight	Whymark	Moore A	Cooper	Lund	Henshaw	Agnew	Shearer	
1	2	3	4	5	6	7	8	9	10	11									1
1	2	3	4		6	7	8*	9	10	11		12		5					2
1		3	4	5	6	7		9	10	11		8		2					3
1		3	4	5	6	7		9		11	10	8		2					4
1		3	4	5	6	7	8	9		11	10			2					5
1	12	3	4	5	6	7	8	9*		11	10			2					6
1	12	3	4	5	6	7	9			11	10			2	8*				7
1	12	3	4*	5	6	7	8	9		11	10			2					8
1	2	3	4	5	6	7	8	9		11	10								9
1	2	3	4	5	6	7	9			11	10*				8	12			10
1	2	3	4	5	6	7	8	9	10	11									11
1	2	3	4	5	6	7	8	9		11	10								12
1	2	3	4	5	6	7		9		11*	10	12						8	13
1	2	3	4		6	7	8	9		11	10	5							14
1	2	3	4	5	6	7	8	9		11	10								15
1	2	3	4	5	6	7	8	9		11	10								16
1	2	3	4	5	6	7	8*	9	12	11	10								17
1	2	3	4	5	6	7	8		12	11	10*	9							18
1	2	3	4	5	6	7	8		10	11		9							19
1	3		4	5	6	7	8		10	11		9	2						20
1	3		4	5	6	7	8	12	10	11		9*	2						21
1	2	3	4	5	6	7		9	10	11		8							22
1	2	3	4	5	6	7		9	10	11		8							23
1		3	4	5	6	7	8	9	10	11			2						24
1	2	3	4	5	6	7	8	9	10	11									25
1	2*	3	4	5	6	7	8	9	10	11	12								26
1	2	3	4	5	6	7	8	9	10	11									27
1	2	3	4	5	6	7	8	9	10	11									28
1	2	3	4	5	6	7	8	9	10	11									29
1	2	3	4	5	6	7	8	9	10	11									30
1	2	3	4	5	6	7	8	9	10	11*	12								31
1		3	4	5	6	7	8	9	10	11	2								32
1		3	4	5	6	7	8	9	10	11			2						33
1		3	4	5	6	7	8*	9	10	11			2					12	34
1		3	4	5	6	7	8	9	10*	11	2							12	35
1		3	4	5	6	7	8	9	10	11*	2							12	36
1		3	4*	5	6	7	8		10	11	2		12		9				37
1	2	3		5	6*	7	8	9		11	4				12	10			38
1	2	3		5	6	7	8	9	10	11	4								39
1	2*	3			6	7	8	9	10		4		5		12	11			40
1		6		5		7	8	9	10		4		2		11		3		41
1		3		5	6	7	8	9	10		4		2		12	11*			42
42	27	40	37	39	41	42	37	35	27	39	23	9	8	7	4	3	1	1	
	3							1	2		2	2	1		3	1		3	
		1	7		1	8	12	15	3	6	2	1			4				

1984-85

1	Aug	25	(h)	Barnsley	W 1-0	Wilkinson	6,190
2		27	(a)	Manchester C	L 0-3		21,137
3	Sep	1	(a)	Middlesbrough	W 5-1	Drinkell 2, Emson, Wilkinson, Ford	5,179
4		4	(h)	Charlton A	W 2-1	Drinkell, Ford	5,692
5		8	(h)	Leeds U	L 0-2		13,290
6		15	(a)	Blackburn R	L 1-3	Wilkinson	5,203
7		22	(h)	Oxford U	L 1-2	Bonnyman	5,563
8		29	(a)	Sheffield U	W 3-2	Lund 3	12,438
9	Oct	6	(h)	Oldham A	W 4-1	Emson 2, Wilkinson, Foley	5,072
10		13	(a)	Portsmouth	L 2-3	Wilkinson 2	13,624
11		20	(h)	Carlisle U	W 1-0	Lund	4,832
12		27	(a)	Cardiff C	W 4-2	Lund, Wilkinson, Emson, Drinkell	4,500
13	Nov	3	(a)	Notts C	D 1-1	K.Moore	5,750
14		10	(h)	Wolves	W 5-1	Wilkinson, Barnes (og), Ford, Bonnyman, Drinkell	7,220
15		17	(h)	Fulham	L 2-4	Ford, Lund	6,287
16		24	(a)	Wimbledon	D 1-1	K.Moore	3,314
17	Dec	1	(h)	Shrewsbury T	W 2-1	Wilkinson, Bonnyman	6,146
18		8	(a)	Brighton & HA	D 0-0		9,367
19		15	(h)	Crystal P	L 1-3	Wilkinson	5,814
20		22	(h)	Middlesbrough	W 3-1	K.Moore, Wilkinson, Drinkell	5,650
21		26	(a)	Birmingham C	L 1-2	Drinkell	14,168
22		29	(a)	Charlton A	L 1-4	K.Moore	3,853
23	Jan	1	(h)	Huddersfield T	W 5-1	Cumming 2, Lund, Foley, Wilkinson	8,790
24		12	(h)	Blackburn R	D 1-1	Lund	7,851
25	Feb	2	(h)	Sheffield U	L 0-2		7,261
26		9	(a)	Leeds U	D 0-0		12,517
27		23	(h)	Notts C	W 2-0	Drinkell 2	4,966
28	Mar	2	(h)	Cardiff C	W 6-3	Bonnyman 2 (2 pens), Drinkell 2, Ford, Lund	4,285
29		5	(a)	Wolves	W 1-0	Ford	6,127
30		9	(a)	Carlisle U	D 1-1	Wilkinson	3,218
31		16	(h)	Portsmouth	L 2-3	Cumming, Wilkinson	6,197
32		23	(a)	Oldham A	L 0-2		3,388
33		30	(a)	Oxford U	L 0-1		8,587
34	Apr	5	(h)	Birmingham C	W 1-0	Henshaw (pen)	6,926
35		9	(a)	Huddersfield T	D 0-0		5,834
36		13	(h)	Manchester C	W 4-1	Drinkell, Lund 2, Cumming	8,362
37		20	(a)	Fulham	L 1-2	Lund	3,632
38		27	(h)	Wimbledon	W 2-1	Cumming, Bonnyman (pen)	4,283
39		30	(a)	Barnsley	D 0-0		3,261
40	May	4	(a)	Shrewsbury T	L 1-4	Bonnyman	3,450
41		7	(h)	Brighton & HA	L 2-4	Bonnyman, Matthews	4,034
42		11	(a)	Crystal P	W 2-0	Drinkell 2	4,923

FINAL LEAGUE POSITION: 10th in Division Two

Appearances
Sub Appearances
Goals

FA Cup

3	Jan	5	(a)	Notts C	D 2-2
R		8	(h)	Notts C	W 4-2
4		26	(h)	Watford	L 1-3

League Cup

2	Sep	25	(h)	Barnsley	W 3-0
	Oct	9	(a)	Barnsley	D 1-1
3		30	(a)	Rotherham U	D 0-0
R	Nov	6	(h)	Rotherham U	W 6-1
4		20	(a)	Everton	W 1-0
QF	Jan	16	(h)	Norwich C	L 0-1

Batch	Cumming	Crombie	Foley	Nicholl	Moore K	Ford	Lund	Wilkinson	Bonnyman	Emson	Drinkell	Seagrave	Robinson	Moore A	Felgate	Agnew	Hine	Henshaw	Grotier	Matthews	Rowbottom	Dawson	
1	2	3	4	5	6	7	8*	9	10	11	12												1
1	2*	3	4	5	6	7		8	10	11	9	12											2
1		3	4	5	6	7		8	10	11	9	2											3
1		3	4	5	6	7		8	10	11	9	2											4
1		3	4	5	6	7		8	10	11	9	2											5
1		3	4	5	6	7		8	10	11	9	2*						12					6
1		3	4	5	6	7	12	8	10		9		2					11*					7
1		3	4	5	6	7	9	8	10	11			2										8
1		3	4	5	6	7	9	8	10	11			2										9
1		3	4	5	6	7		8	10	11			2							9			10
1		3	4	5	6	7	9	8	10	11		2											11
1		5	4		6	7	9	8	10	11*	12	2				3							12
1			4	5	6	7	9*	8	10	11	12	2				3							13
1		3	4	5	6	7	9	8*	10	11	12	2											14
1		3	4	5	6	7	9	8	10	11	12	2*											15
1		3	4	5	6	7		8	10	11	9	2											16
1		3	4	5	6	7		8	10	11	9	2											17
1		3	4	5	6	7		8	10	11	9	2											18
1		3	4	5	6	7	12	8	10	11	9	2*											19
1			4	5	6	7	12	8*	10	11	9	2				3							20
1	12	3	4	5	6	7		8	10	11*	9	2											21
1	12	3	4	5	6	7		8	10	11	9*	2											22
1		5	4		6	7	9	8	10	11		2				3							23
		5	4		6	7	9	8	10	11		2				3			1				24
	12	5	4		6	7	9	8	10	11*			2			3			1				25
		3	4*		6	7	12	8	10	11	9		2	5								1	26
	12	3	4	5		7	8*		10	11	9		2	6	1								27
	12	3	4	5		7*	8		10	11	9		2	6	1								28
	11	3	4	5	6	7		8	10		9		2		1								29
	11	3	4	5	6*	7		8	10	12	9		2		1								30
	11	3	4	5	6*	7		8	10	12	9		2		1								31
	11	6		5		7	12	8			9		2		1	3	10*				4		32
	11	3		5		7	8				9	2		6	1		4	10					33
	11	3		5		7	8				9	2		6	1		4	10					34
	11*	3		5		7	8			12	9	2		6	1		4	10					35
	11	3		5		7	8				9	2		6	1		4	10					36
	11	3			6	7	8		10	12	9		2*	5	1		4						37
	11				6	7	8*		10	12	9		2	5	1	3	4						38
	11	6				7			10	8	9		2	5		3	4*		1		12		39
	11	6				7			10		9		2	5		3	12		1	8*	4		40
		6				7			10	11	9		2	5		3			1	8	4		41
	2	6				7			10	11	9			5		3		4	1	8			42
23	15	39	31	31	31	42	19	30	37	30	30	22	17	13	12	12	8	6	6	4	3	1	
	5						5			5	5	1					1	1			1		
	5		2		4	6	12	14	8	4	14							1		1			

1 own-goal

1985-86

1	Aug	17	(a)	Brighton & HA	D 2-2	Lund, Hobson	9,787
2		20	(h)	Huddersfield T	D 1-1	Lund	6,180
3		24	(h)	Charlton A	D 2-2	Lund, Hobson	4,260
4		26	(a)	Fulham	L 1-2	Lund	4,873
5		31	(h)	Wimbledon	L 0-1		3,476
6	Sep	4	(a)	Stoke C	D 1-1	Lund	7,362
7		7	(a)	Sunderland	D 3-3	Ford, Gilligan, Lund	14,985
8		13	(h)	Carlisle U	W 1-0	Peake	4,099
9		21	(a)	Barnsley	L 0-1		5,356
10		28	(h)	Bradford C	W 2-0	Peake, Emson	5,158
11	Oct	5	(a)	Oldham A	L 1-2	Gilligan	5,301
12		12	(h)	Sheffield U	L 0-1		5,935
13		19	(a)	Leeds U	D 1-1	Hobson	11,244
14		26	(h)	Middlesbrough	W 3-2	Hobson, Gilligan 2	4,454
15	Nov	2	(h)	Millwall	W 5-1	Hobson 3, A.Moore, Bonnyman	3,658
16		9	(a)	Crystal P	L 1-2	Emson	4,620
17		16	(h)	Portsmouth	W 1-0	Bonnyman (pen)	6,436
18		23	(a)	Norwich C	L 2-3	Culverhouse (og), Emson	12,018
19		30	(h)	Blackburn R	W 5-2	Ford, Hine, A.Moore, Hobson 2	5,016
20	Dec	7	(a)	Huddersfield T	D 2-2	Lyons, Hobson	4,811
21		14	(h)	Brighton & HA	L 0-2		5,320
22		21	(a)	Charlton A	L 0-2		3,525
23		26	(a)	Hull C	L 0-2		12,824
24	Jan	1	(h)	Shrewsbury T	W 3-1	Lyons 2, Lund	4,750
25		11	(a)	Carlisle U	W 2-1	Hobson, Emson	2,483
26		18	(a)	Wimbledon	L 0-3		2,770
27		25	(h)	Stoke C	D 3-3	Emson, Bonnyman, Ford	4,523
28	Feb	1	(h)	Fulham	W 1-0	Peake	3,576
29		8	(h`	Leeds U	W 1-0	Hobson	6,382
30	Mar	1	(a)	Bradford C	W 1-0	Cumming	5,185
31		4	(a)	Middlesbrough	L 1-3	Crombie	4,496
32		8	(h)	Oldham A	L 1-4	Hobson	4,178
33		15	(a)	Sheffield U	D 1-1	Henshaw	9,165
34		22	(h)	Sunderland	D 1-1	Lund	5,339
35		29	(a)	Shrewsbury T	W 2-0	Lyons, Henshaw (pen)	3,097
36	Apr	1	(h)	Hull C	L 0-1		9,121
37		5	(a)	Millwall	L 0-1		3,612
38		12	(h)	Crystal P	W 3-0	Henshaw 2 (1 pen), Peake	4,222
39		19	(a)	Portsmouth	L 1-3	Cumming	12,967
40		22	(h)	Barnsley	L 1-2	Hobson	4,009
41		26	(h)	Norwich C	W 1-0	Hobson	8,090
42	May	5	(a)	Blackburn R	L 1-3	K.Moore	7,600

FINAL LEAGUE POSITION: 15th in Division Two

Appearances
Sub Appearances
Goals

FA Cup

3	Jan	4	(h)	Arsenal	L 3-4

League Cup

2	Sep	24	(h)	York C	D 1-1
	Oct	8	(a)	York C	W 3-2
3		29	(h)	Ipswich T	L 0-2

Full Members Cup (Northern group mini league 3)

NG	Sep	17	(h)	Sunderland	W 3-2
NG	Oct	1	(a)	Sunderland	L 1-2

Aggregate 4-4, Sunderland won 3-2 on penalties. Oldham Athletic and Middlesbrough withdrew from this group; only Grimsby and Sunderland competed.

Felgate	Robinson	Agnew	Peake	Moore A	Crombie	Ford	Lund	Gilligan	Bonnyman	Emson	Hobson	Moore K	Lyons	Cumming	Hine	Henshaw	Barratt	Batch	Matthews	Grocock	
1	2	3	4	5	6	7	8	9	10	11*	12										1
1	2	3	4	5	6	7	8*	9	10	11	12										2
1	2	3	4	5		7	8	9	10	11	6										3
1	2	3	4	5	6	7	8	9	10		11*				12						4
1			4	5	3	7	8	9	10		11	6					2				5
1	2		4	5	3	7	8	9	10		11	6									6
1	2*		4	5	3	7	8	9	10	12	11	6									7
1	2*		4	5	3	7	8	9	10	12	11	6									8
1		3	4	5		7	8	12	10	11*	9	6					2				9
1		3	4	5		7		8		11	9	6			10		2				10
1		3	4	5		7	12	8		11*	9	6			10		2				11
			4	5	3	7*	12	8		11	9	6			10		2	1			12
			4	5	3*	7	12	8	10		9	6		11			2	1			13
			4	5	3	7		8	10	11	9	6					2	1			14
			4*	5	3	7	8		10	11	9	6		12			2	1			15
			4	5	3	7	8*		10	11	9	6		12			2	1			16
			4		3	7		8	10	11	9	6	5				2	1			17
		3	4			7		8	10	11	9	6	5				2	1			18
				4		7		8	10		9	6	5	3	11		2	1			19
		12		4		7		8*	10		9	6	5	3	11		2	1			20
				4	12	7		8*	10		9	6	5	3	11		2	1			21
				4	3	7		12	10	11*	9	6	5	8			2	1			22
				4	3	7	12		10		9	6	5*	11	8		2	1			23
					3	7	8		10		9	6	5	11	4		2	1			24
1		3	4		6	7	8	12		11	9		5		10*		2				25
		3	4		6	7*	8	12	10	11	9		5				2	1			26
	2		4		6	7	8		10	11	9		5	3				1			27
	2		4		6	7	8		10	11	9		5	3				1			28
	2		4		6	7	8*	12	10	11	9		5	3				1			29
	2	3	4	5	6	7			10	11	9			8				1			30
	2	3	4	5	6	7			10	11	9			8				1			31
	2	3	4		6	7			10*	11	9	12	5	8				1			32
	10		4	2	3	12		8			9	6	5	11*		7		1			33
	10		4	2	3	12	8				9	6	5	11		7*		1			34
	10	3	4	2			8				9	6	5		7*	11	12	1			35
			4	2	3		8				9	6	5	11	10	7*	12	1			36
	2		4	12	3		8					6	5	11	10	9*	7	1			37
	10		4	2	3		8				9	6	5	11*		7		1	12		38
	10	12	4	2	3		8*				9	6	5	11		7		1			39
	10		4	2	3		8*				9	6	5	11		7		1	12		40
	10		4	2	3		12				9	6	5	11		7		1	8*		41
	10		4		3				2		9	6	5	11*		7		1	8	12	42
12	22	14	36	31	33	32	24	19	29	21	39	30	24	22	12	10	20	30	2		
		2		1	1	2	5	5		2	2	1		2	1		2		2	1	
			4	1	1	3	8	4	3	5	15	2	4	2	1	4					

1 own-goal

1986-87

1	Aug	23	(a)	Ipswich T	D 1-1	Walsh	12,455
2		30	(h)	Bradford C	D 0-0		6,393
3	Sep	6	(a)	Brighton & HA	W 1-0	Hobson	7,791
4		13	(h)	Derby C	L 0-1		7,305
5		20	(a)	Sheffield U	W 2-1	Hobson, K.Moore	9,840
6		27	(h)	Barnsley	L 0-1		4,789
7	Oct	1	(a)	Reading	W 3-2	Henshaw, Turner, Walsh	6,130
8		4	(a)	Shrewsbury T	L 1-4	Walsh (pen)	2,451
9		11	(h)	Plymouth A	D 1-1	K.Moore	4,155
10		18	(a)	West Brom A	D 1-1	Rawcliffe	8,618
11		25	(h)	Leeds U	D 0-0		7,168
12	Nov	1	(h)	Millwall	W 1-0	K.Moore	3,757
13		8	(a)	Crystal P	W 3-0	Walsh, Hobson, O'Riordan	5,052
14		15	(h)	Sunderland	D 1-1	Walsh (pen)	7,065
15		22	(a)	Portsmouth	L 1-2	Hazel	9,517
16		29	(h)	Birmingham C	L 0-1		4,734
17	Dec	2	(h)	Blackburn R	W 1-0	O'Riordan	3,483
18		6	(a)	Hull C	D 1-1	Hazel	7,217
19		13	(h)	Stoke C	D 1-1	Rawcliffe	4,642
20		21	(a)	Derby C	L 0-4		14,440
21		26	(h)	Oldham A	D 2-2	O'Riordan, Henshaw	6,469
22		27	(a)	Sunderland	W 1-0	Walsh	13,769
23	Jan	1	(a)	Huddersfield T	D 0-0		7,530
24		3	(h)	Brighton & HA	L 1-2	Henshaw	4,729
25		17	(a)	Blackburn R	D 2-2	Walsh 2 (1 pen)	4,654
26		24	(h)	Ipswich T	D 1-1	Robinson	4,981
27	Feb	7	(a)	Bradford C	L 2-4	K.Moore 2	8,413
28		14	(h)	Reading	W 3-2	Robinson 2, Turner	3,579
29		24	(a)	Barnsley	L 0-1		5,136
30		28	(h)	Sheffield U	W 1-0	O'Riordan	5,051
31	Mar	7	(a)	Leeds U	L 0-2		14,270
32		14	(h)	West Brom A	W 3-1	Henshaw, O'Riordan, Cumming	5,024
33		21	(a)	Plymouth A	L 0-5		2,671
34		28	(h)	Shrewsbury T	L 0-1		3,437
35	Apr	4	(h)	Crystal P	L 0-1		3,071
36		11	(a)	Millwall	L 0-1		3,881
37		18	(h)	Huddersfield T	L 0-1		4,198
38		21	(a)	Oldham A	D 1-1	O'Riordan	7,032
39		25	(h)	Portsmouth	L 0-2		5,085
40	May	2	(a)	Birmingham C	L 0-1		4,457
41		5	(h)	Hull C	D 2-2	Walsh, Turner	6,757
42		9	(a)	Stoke C	L 1-5	McGarvey	6,407

FINAL LEAGUE POSITION: 21st in Division Two

Appearances
Sub Appearances
Goals

FA Cup

3	Jan	10	(h)	Stoke C	D 1-1
R		26	(a)	Stoke C	D 1-1
2R		28	(a)	Stoke C	L 0-6

The second replay was played at Stoke after Grimsby lost the toss of a coin.

League Cup

1	Sep	2	(a)	Carlisle U	L 0-1
		9	(h)	Carlisle U	W 2-0
2		23	(a)	Hull C	L 0-1
	Oct	7	(h)	Hull C	D 1-1

Full Members Cup

Oct	21	(h)	Hull C	L 1-3

Batch	Burgess	Cumming	Peake	Lyons	Moore K	Robinson	Walsh	Hobson	O'Riordan	Turner	Agnew	Felgate	Prudhoe	Halsall	Crombie	Rawcliffe	Henshaw	Bonnyman	McDermott	McGarvey	Hazel	Straw	Rice	Grocock	Moore A	Horwood	Dixon	Matthews	Moore D	Pratt	
1	2	3	4	5	6	7	8	9	10	11																					1
1	2	3	4	5	6	7	8	9	10	11																					2
1	2	3	4	5	6		8	9	10	11							7*					12									3
1	2	12		5	6	4*	8	9	10	11					3		7														4
1	2			5	6		8	9	10	11	3						7					4									5
1	2	3		5			8	9*	10	11					6		7					4				12					6
1	2	3		5*		9	8		10	11					6	12	7					4									7
1	2	3				9	8		10	11					6	12	7					4*					5				8
1	2	3		5*	6		8	9	10	11						12	7	4													9
1	2			5*	6		8		10	11	3					9	7	12				4									10
	2			5	6		8	9	10		3	1				12		11*			7	4									11
	2			5	6			9	10		3	1				8					7	4	11								12
	2			5	6	4	8	9	10		3	1						12			7*		11								13
	2			5	6	4	8	9			3	1				12		10			7		11*								14
	2			5	6	4	8		10		3	1				9		11*			7	12									15
1	2			5	6	4	8		10		3					9					7		11*	12							16
1	2			5	6	4	8		10		3					12					7			11				9*			17
1				5	6	4	8		10	11	3						9				7								2		18
				5	6	4	8		10	7	3	1				12	9							11*					2		19
	2			5*	6	4	9		10	11	3	1				8	7					12									20
		11		5	6	2	8		10	4	3	1					9				7										21
		11		5	6	2	8		10	4	3	1					7	9													22
	12	11*		5	6	2	8		10	4	3	1					7	9													23
	8			5	6	2			10	4	3	1				12	7							11				9*			24
	2	11*			6	7	8		10	4	3	1			5	12		9													25
1	2			5	6	7	8		10*	4	3					12	11	9													26
1	2			5	6	11	8			4	3						10	9	7												27
1					6	7			10	4	3					8	11	9	2						5						28
1				9		7			10	4	3				6	11	8		2						5						29
1		11				7			10	4	3			6	5	12	8		2									9*			30
1	11					7			10	4	3			6	5		8		2	9											31
1		11				7	12		10	4	3			6	5		8*		2	9											32
1	12	11				7	9*		10	4	3			6	5		8		2												33
	12	11				7	8*		10		3		1	6	5		4		2	9											34
		11*				7			10	4			1	6	5		8			9				12	3				2		35
		12				2			10	4	3*		1	11	6	8	7			9					5						36
		11							10	4	3*		1	2	6	8	7	12		9					5						37
	3	11							10	4			1	7	6			8	2	9					5						38
	3	11							10	4			1	7	6		12	8*	2	9					5						39
	3	11				4	12		10	8			1	7*	6				2	9					5						40
	3	7					8		10	4			1		6				2	9				11	5						41
	2								10	4	3			8*	6		12	11	7	9					5					1	42
21	28	21	3	26	25	30	28	11	40	34	29	12	8	12	19	9	27	13	13	11	9	7	4	4	10		1	3	3	1	
	3	2					2									11	2	3				3		2		1					
		1			5	3	9	3	6	3						2	4			1	2										

1987-88

1	Aug	15	(a)	Doncaster R	L 0-1		2,482
2		22	(h)	Gillingham	W 2-0	Walsh 2	2,901
3		29	(a)	Notts C	D 0-0		5,322
4		31	(h)	Brentford	L 0-1		3,361
5	Sep	5	(a)	Preston NE	W 3-1	Saunders, Walsh, O'Riordan	5,522
6		12	(h)	Mansfield T	L 2-3	O'Riordan, Grocock	3,410
7		15	(a)	Bury	W 2-0	McGarvey 2 (1 pen)	1,899
8		19	(a)	Chester C	L 0-1		1,897
9		26	(h)	Walsall	L 0-2		3,314
10		29	(a)	Rotherham U	D 0-0		3,375
11	Oct	3	(h)	Southend U	L 1-3	O'Riordan	2,544
12		10	(a)	Chesterfield	W 3-0	North, Walsh 2 (1 pen)	2,072
13		17	(h)	Bristol C	L 1-4	McGarvey	3,100
14		20	(h)	Blackpool	D 1-1	Turner	2,260
15		24	(a)	Northampton T	L 1-2	Turner	5,388
16		31	(h)	Brighton & HA	L 0-1		2,711
17	Nov	3	(a)	Fulham	L 0-5		3,493
18		7	(a)	Sunderland	D 1-1	North	18,197
19		21	(h)	York C	W 5-1	North 2, Robinson 2, O'Riordan	2,973
20		28	(a)	Bristol R	L 2-4	O'Riordan 2 (1 pen)	2,787
21	Dec	12	(h)	Wigan A	L 0-2		2,196
22		19	(a)	Aldershot	L 2-3	Turner, Saunders	2,405
23		26	(a)	Walsall	L 2-3	McGarvey, North	6,272
24		28	(h)	Port Vale	W 3-1	North 3	3,043
25	Jan	1	(h)	Notts C	D 0-0		5,297
26		2	(a)	Mansfield T	L 0-1		3,315
27		16	(h)	Chester C	W 2-1	McGarvey 2	2,594
28		26	(h)	Bury	W 2-0	Turner, O'Riodan	2,525
29	Feb	2	(a)	Gillingham	D 1-1	McDermott	2,993
30		6	(h)	Preston NE	L 0-1		3,790
31		13	(a)	Port Vale	L 0-2		3,417
32		20	(h)	Doncaster R	D 0-0		3,890
33		23	(a)	Brentford	W 2-0	Jobling, Saunders	3,534
34		26	(a)	Southend U	D 0-0		3,409
35	Mar	5	(a)	Bristol C	D 1-1	O'Riordan	8,343
36		8	(h)	Rotherham U	W 2-1	Cunnington, North	3,423
37		12	(h)	Chesterfield	D 1-1	Stubbs	3,464
38		19	(a)	Brighton & HA	D 0-0		7,269
39		26	(h)	Northampton T	D 2-2	Cunnington, Robinson	3,406
40	Apr	2	(h)	Sunderland	L 0-1		7,001
41		4	(a)	York C	W 2-0	Stubbs, Agnew	3,315
42		9	(h)	Fulham	L 0-2		3,123
43		23	(a)	Blackpool	L 0-3		2,555
44		30	(h)	Bristol R	D 0-0		2,505
45	May	2	(a)	Wigan A	W 1-0	North	2,705
46		7	(h)	Aldershot	D 1-1	North	5,639

FINAL LEAGUE POSITION: 22nd in Division Three

Appearances
Sub Appearances
Goals

FA Cup

1	Nov	14	(a)	Scarborough	W 2-1
2	Dec	5	(h)	Halifax T	D 0-0
R		8	(a)	Halifax T	L 0-2

League Cup

1	Aug	18	(h)	Darlington	W 3-2
		26	(a)	Darlington	L 1-2*

*After extra-time (Darlington won on away-goals rule)

Sherpa Van Trophy

P	Oct	13	(a)	Scunthorpe U	L 0-2
P		27	(h)	Halifax T	W 2-1
P	Dec	15	(h)	Scunthorpe U	L 1-2†

†Play-off

Sherwood	McDermott	Agnew	Turner	Slack	Burgess	Robinson	Walsh	North	O'Riordan	McGarvey	Toale	Saunders	Dixon	Cunnington	Jobling	Watson	Curran	Grocock	Stubbs	Rawcliffe	Lever	Moore D	
1	2	3	4	5	6	7	8*	9	10	11		12											1
1	2*	3	7	5	6	4	8	9	10	11	12												2
1		3	4	5		7	8	9	10	11	2	6											3
1		3	4	5	6	7	8	9	10	11	2												4
1		3	4	5	6		8		10	11	2	7				9							5
1	12	3	4	5	6		8*	9	10	11†	2					7		14					6
1		3	4	5	6	9	12	8*	10	11	2					7							7
1		3	4	5	6	9	12	8	10	11*	2					7*		14					8
1	2	3	4	5	6			8	10	11	7	9*						12					9
1	2		4	5	6			8	10	11		9	3			7							10
1	2	3	4	5			12	8†	10	11	6	9				7*		14					11
1	2		4	5		6	8	9	10	11	3					7							12
1		3	4	5	6	8	9*		10	11	2					7		12					13
1		3	4	5	6	9		8	10	11	2					7*		12					14
1		3	4†	5	6	8		9	10	11	2*		14			7		12					15
1	2			5	6†	8		9	10	11		3	14			7*		4		12			16
1	2			5		4		9	10	11		8	3			6†	7	12					17
1	2			5				9	10	11		8	3			4	7*	6		12			18
1	2		4	5		6		9	10	11*		8	3				7	12					19
1	2		4			6		9	10	11	7*	8	3					5				12	20
1	2	3	4		5	6		9	10	11	7*	8					12						21
1	2*	3	4	5		6			10	11	12	8	9				7†	14					22
1		3	4	5*	6	7		9	10	11	14	8	2†				12						23
1		3	4		5	6		9	10	11		8	2				7						24
1		3	4		5	6		9*	10	11		8	2			12	7						25
1		3	4		5	6			10	11	7†	8	2			12	9*	14					26
1		3	4		5	6		9	10	11		8	2			12	7*						27
1		3	4		5	6			10	11*		8	2			12	7	9					28
1	7	3	4		5	6		9	10	11		8	2										29
1	7	3	4		5	6		9†	10	11		8	2*			14		12					30
1	3		4		5	7		9†	10		6*	8	2			12		11			14		31
1		3			5	11		9	10			8	2	4	6		7*	12					32
1	12	3			5	7		9*	10	11		8	2	4	6								33
1	9	3			5	7			10	11		8	2	4	6								34
1	14	3			5	7		9*	10	11		8†	2	4	6				12				35
1		3			5	7		9	10	11		8	2	4	6								36
1	14	3			5	7		9*	10	11		8	2†	4	6				12				37
1	14	3			5	7		9*	10	11		8†	2	4	6				12				38
1	12	3			5	7		9	10			8	2	4*	6			11					39
1	14	3			5	7		9†	10			8*	2	4	6			11	12				40
1	8	3			5	7			10				2	4	6			11	9				41
1	9	3			5	7			10		12		2*	4	6			11	8				42
1		3			5	7		9*	10	11		8	2	4	6				12				43
1		3			5	7		9	10	12		8	2	4	6			11*					44
1	9*	3			5	7		12	10	11†		8	2	4	6			14					45
1	11	3			5	7		9	10			8	2*	4	6			12					46
46	21	38	28	21	38	40	8	37	46	38	16	34	30	15	15	13	10	10	2				
	7						3	1		1	4	1	2			6	2	15	5	2	1	1	
	1	1	4			3	5	11	8	6		3		2	1			1	2				

1988-89

1	Aug	27	(a)	Cambridge U	L 1-4	Stoutt	2,290
2	Sep	3	(h)	Torquay U	W 1-0	North	2,889
3		10	(a)	Scunthorpe U	D 1-1	Alexander	6,037
4		17	(h)	Rotherham U	L 0-4		3,697
5		20	(a)	Wrexham	W 2-1	Jobling, North	2,267
6		24	(h)	Rochdale	L 1-3	North	2,939
7	Oct	1	(a)	Hereford U	L 1-2	O'Kelly	1,888
8		4	(h)	Tranmere R	D 0-0		2,288
9		8	(h)	Peterborough U	D 0-0		2,822
10		15	(a)	Exeter C	L 1-2	Alexander	2,232
11		22	(h)	York C	W 2-0	Cockerill, Alexander	2,829
12		25	(a)	Crewe A	D 2-2	Saunders 2	2,311
13		29	(h)	Halifax T	W 3-2	Saunders 2, O'Kelly	3,260
14	Nov	5	(a)	Stockport C	L 1-3	McDermott	2,064
15		8	(h)	Doncaster R	W 5-0	Watson 2 (1 pen), Alexander, Saunders, Cockerill	3,382
16		12	(a)	Hartlepool U	L 1-2	Watson (pen)	1,782
17		26	(a)	Carlisle U	L 1-2	Cockerill	2,195
18	Dec	3	(h)	Scarborough	W 2-1	Alexander, Cockerill	3,887
19		17	(h)	Leyton O	D 2-2	Lever, Saunders	3,445
20		26	(a)	Lincoln C	D 2-2	Watson, Alexander	8,038
21		31	(a)	Burnley	L 0-1		7,367
22	Jan	2	(h)	Colchester U	D 2-2	O'Kelly, Alexander	4,472
23		14	(a)	Torquay U	D 2-2	North, Alexander	2,251
24		21	(h)	Cambridge U	W 4-0	O'Kelly, Saunders, Cunnington, Tillson	3,644
25	Feb	4	(h)	Wrexham	L 0-1		5,058
26		11	(a)	Rochdale	W 2-0	Alexander 2	1,621
27		14	(h)	Darlington	D 0-0		4,628
28		25	(h)	Exeter C	W 2-1	O'Kelly, Lever	4,684
29		28	(h)	Crewe A	D 0-0		5,404
30	Mar	4	(a)	York C	W 3-0	Saunders, O'Kelly, North	3,481
31		7	(a)	Rotherham U	L 0-1		4,888
32		11	(h)	Stockport C	W 2-0	North, Jobling	4,685
33		14	(a)	Halifax T	L 1-2	O'Kelly	1,609
34		18	(h)	Scunthorpe U	D 1-1	O'Kelly	9,796
35		24	(a)	Colchester U	D 0-0		4,507
36		27	(h)	Lincoln C	W 1-0	O'Kelly	8,618
37	Apr	1	(a)	Leyton O	L 0-5		4,149
38		4	(a)	Darlington	D 1-1	Jobling	1,840
39		8	(h)	Burnley	W 1-0	Saunders	4,856
40		15	(h)	Hereford U	D 1-1	Gilbert	4,036
41		25	(a)	Peterborough U	W 2-1	Alexander, Jobling (pen)	2,937
42		29	(h)	Carlisle U	D 0-0		3,833
43	May	1	(a)	Doncaster R	W 3-2	Banton, Tillson, O'Kelly	2,183
44		6	(a)	Scarborough	W 3-2	Alexander 2, Saunders	3,923
45		9	(a)	Tranmere R	L 2-3	Cockerill, Gilbert	6,938
46		13	(h)	Hartlepool U	W 3-0	Cockerill, Alexander, Gilbert	3,801

FINAL LEAGUE POSITION: 9th in Division Four

Appearances
Sub Appearances
Goals

FA Cup

1	Nov	19	(h)	Wolves	W 1-0
2	Dec	10	(h)	Rotherham U	W 3-2
3	Jan	7	(a)	Middlesbrough	W 2-1
4		28	(h)	Reading	D 1-1
R	Feb	1	(a)	Reading	W 2-1
5		18	(a)	Wimbledon	L 1-3

League Cup

1	Aug	30	(h)	Rotherham U	L 0-1
	Sep	6	(a)	Rotherham U	L 0-1

Sherpa Van Trophy

P	Nov	29	(h)	Rotherham U	W 1-0
P	Dec	6	(a)	Doncaster R	D 1-1
P	Jan	17	(h)	Huddersfield T	L 1-3

Sherwood	Dixon	Agnew	Williams	Cunnington	Cockerill	Jobling	McDermott	O'Kelly	Stoutt	North	Tillson	Reece	Lever	Alexander	Saunders	Caldwell	Grocock	Watson	Stephenson	Banton	Gilbert	Smaller	
1	2*	3	4	5	6	7	8	9	10	11	12												1
		3	4	6		7	12	9	10	8	5	1	2	11*									2
		3	4	6		7		9		8	5	1	2	11	12	10*							3
		3	4	8	6	7	12	9*			5	1		11	14	10†	2						4
	2	3	4	6		7		9		8	5	1		11			10						5
	2	3	4	6		7		9		8	5	1		11		12	10*						6
1	2*	3	4	6	14	7	10	9		8	5			11†	12								7
1		3		6		7	2	9		8	4		5	11*	10		12						8
1		3		6		7*	2	9		8	4		5	11	10		12						9
1	14	3		6	12	7*	2	9		8†	4		5	11			10						10
1		3	2*	6	10		7	9		12	4		5	11	8								11
1		3		6			2	9		7	4		5	11	8			10					12
1		3	2	6			7	9			4		5	11	8			10					13
1			2*	6	3		7	9			4		5	11	8		12	10					14
1				6	10		2	9			4		5	11	8			7	3				15
1		12		6	10		2*	9†			4		5	11	8		14	7	3				16
		3		6	10		2	9		7	4	1	5	11*	8			12					17
1		3		6	10		2	9		7	4		5	11	8								18
1		3		6	10	12	2	9*		7	4		5	11	8								19
		3				10	2	9		7*	4	1	5	11	8		12	6					20
		3				10	2	9*		7	4	1	5	11	8		12	6					21
		3		6	14	10†	2	9		12	4	1	5	11*	8			7					22
		3		6	10	7*	2			9	4	1	5	11	8			12					23
		3		6	10		2	9		7	4	1	5	11	8								24
		3		6	10	2		9		7	4	1	5*	11	8			12					25
1		3		6	10	7		9		2	4		5	11	8								26
1		3		6	10	7*		9		2	4		5	11	8			12					27
1		3		6	10		2	9		7	4		5	11	8								28
1		3		6		10	2	9		7	4		5	11*	8			12					29
1				6		10	2	9		7	4		5		8			11	3				30
1				6		10	2	9		7	4		5	12	8			11*	3				31
1				6		10	2	9		7	4		5	11	8				3				32
1				6		10	2	9		7	4		5	11	8			12	3*				33
1		12		6		10	2	9		7	4		5	11	8				3*				34
1		3		6	10	7	2	9			4		5	11	8								35
1		3		6	10	2		9			4		5	11	12					7*	8		36
1		3		6	10	7	2	9*		7	4		5†	11	12				14		8		37
1			5	6	10	7	2				4			11	9				3		8		38
			2	6		10					4	1	5	11	7			12	3	9*	8		39
			2	6	14	10	9*				4	1	5†	11	7				3	12	8		40
1		3	5	6	12	10	2	9*			4			11	7						8		41
1		3	5†	6	10	7*	2	12			4			11	9					14	8		42
1		3*	5	6	10		2	9			4			14	7†			12		11	8		43
1			2	6	10		9				4		5	11	7			12	3*	14	8†		44
1			2	6	10		3				4†		5	11	9			7*	14	12	8		45
1			4	6	10		2						5†	11	9			7*	3	12	8	14	46
32	4	32	19	44	24	31	36	38	2	27	44	14	37	42	36	2	4	12	12	3	11		
	1	2			5	1	2	1		2	1			2	5	1	6	9	2	5		1	
				1	6	4	1	10	1	6	2		2	14	10			4		1	3		

Grimsby Against Other League Clubs

Grimsby Town have played 120 clubs in the Football League since 1888-89. Below is their record against each club. Some clubs changed their names (eg Small Heath became Birmingham then Birmingham City) and some clubs modified their titles (eg Leicester Fosse became Leicester City). In all cases the current name used by each club covers all games under previous names.
*Signifies that the total includes a game played in the abandoned 1939-40 season.

		HOME					AWAY				
	P	W	D	L	F	A	W	D	L	F	A
ACCRINGTON	22	11	0	0	36	6	5	0	6	14	17
AFC BOURNEMOUTH	26	6	4	3	14	9	3	4	6	12	16
ALDERSHOT	20	4	4	2	11	10	1	3	6	13	19
ARSENAL	42	11	6	4	31	26	1	4	16	18	76
ASHINGTON	10	4	0	1	21	9	1	0	4	5	8
ASTON VILLA	20	4	1	5	20	16	2	3	5	19	29
BARNSLEY	78	23	8	8	82	39	9	9	21	50	73
BARROW	26	12	0	1	30	4	2	4	7	11	22
BIRMINGHAM C	52	16	5	5	40	27	7	5	14	36	59
BLACKBURN R	50	12	6	7	54	38	0	8	17	18	54
BLACKPOOL	56	15	9	4	56	29	7	6	15	44	66
BOLTON W	40	9	8	3	34	18	7	3	10	25	42
BOOTLE	2	1	0	0	3	0	0	0	1	1	3
BRADFORD	44	13	5	4	42	18	6	3	13	23	41
BRADFORD C	38	9	3	7	25	26	6	6	7	23	26
BRENTFORD	46	14	4	5	52	27	9	0	14	23	46
BRIGHTON & HA	28	6	3	5	27	20	4	4	6	15	22
BRISTOL C	36	10	3	5	33	24	1	5	12	12	44
BRISTOL R	24	6	5	1	20	12	1	3	8	20	29
BURNLEY	34	12	1	4	27	13	0	3	14	8	41
BURTON TS	18	8	0	1	38	9	4	1	4	12	16
BURTON U	8	3	1	0	7	1	1	0	3	3	5
BURTON W	6	3	0	0	12	3	0	1	2	2	7
BURY	48	18	3	3	49	19	4	9	11	29	49
CAMBRIDGE U	16	6	1	1	14	4	2	2	4	11	19
CARDIFF C	24	4	4	4	18	13	2	2	8	17	29
CARLISLE U	24	8	3	1	20	9	5	3	4	19	21
CHARLTON A	36	6	7	5	34	33	4	5	9	20	29
CHELSEA	40	10	5	5	28	21	3	2	15	19	52
CHESTER C	26	8	4	1	27	13	5	1	7	13	20
CHESTERFIELD	66	17	11	5	60	33	11	6	16	48	54
COLCHESTER U	26	6	3	4	26	18	3	3	7	12	22
COVENTRY C	16	5	0	3	17	9	1	3	4	5	11
CREWE A	40	12	4	4	42	18	7	6	7	22	28
CRYSTAL P	22	5	1	5	14	10	4	0	7	12	18
DARLINGTON	36	11	3	4	32	13	7	5	6	20	22
DARWEN	12	5	0	1	25	6	1	1	4	8	17
DERBY C	54	13	6	8	45	35	5	5	17	33	64
DONCASTER R	28	8	4	2	31	15	6	2	6	23	21
DURHAM C	10	4	1	0	11	4	3	1	1	7	7
EVERTON	22	4	3	4	12	14	2	1	8	16	32

		HOME					*AWAY*				
	P	W	D	L	F	A	W	D	L	F	A
EXETER C	18	6	1	2	18	8	3	2	4	12	19
FULHAM	42	10	3	8	28	34	5	3	13	26	47
GAINSBOROUGH T	26	6	4	3	22	16	4	2	7	19	25
GATESHEAD	10	3	2	0	8	2	0	1	4	2	13
GILLINGHAM	22	8	3	0	21	7	2	3	6	7	15
GLOSSOP	26	9	4	0	24	3	1	3	9	7	25
HALIFAX T	42	13	5	3	48	18	6	6	9	23	28
HARTLEPOOL U	32	13	1	2	32	7	3	4	9	14	25
HEREFORD U	10	1	3	1	4	5	1	0	4	7	10
HUDDERSFIELD T	56	14	9	5	50	34	8	7	13	30	38
HULL C	46	10	7	6	29	21	7	5	11	32	50
IPSWICH T	6	0	1	2	3	6	0	1	2	4	6
LEEDS C	18	4	1	4	16	13	2	0	7	11	29
LEEDS U	38	10	5	4	35	21	2	5	12	11	34
LEICESTER C	60	20	6	4	77	31	6	5	19	23	51
LEYTON O	44	11	7	4	45	22	6	5	11	21	35
LINCOLN C	76	18	12	8	86	51	14	9	15	64	63
LIVERPOOL	36	8	5	5	26	23	0	5	13	21	64
LOUGHBOROUGH T	10	5	0	0	25	1	3	1	1	9	4
LUTON T	22	4	4	3	22	14	2	4	5	12	26
MANCHESTER C	46	13	6	4	60	35	4	2	17	28	53
MANCHESTER U *	37	10	4	4	37	26	4	2	13	26	42
MANSFIELD T	28	6	3	5	23	17	1	5	8	12	28
MERTHYR T	2	0	1	0	1	1	0	0	1	1	3
MIDDLESBROUGH	50	15	3	7	55	45	6	3	16	27	52
MIDDLESBROUGH I	2	1	0	0	2	1	1	0	0	6	2
MILLWALL	18	7	1	1	21	7	3	1	5	6	11
NELSON	8	3	0	1	8	3	0	2	2	2	6
NEW BRIGHTON	6	1	1	1	3	3	1	1	1	6	4
NEW BRIGHTON T	6	1	1	1	8	6	0	0	3	1	9
NEWCASTLE U	32	8	6	2	27	13	5	2	9	17	34
NEWPORT C	20	7	2	1	16	6	3	2	5	9	12
NORTHAMPTON T	22	5	2	4	19	15	3	1	7	12	26
NORTHWICH V	4	2	0	0	9	1	1	0	1	4	5
NORWICH C	12	2	2	2	7	7	0	3	3	4	8
NOTTINGHAM F	30	7	5	3	22	14	4	2	9	19	29
NOTTS C	48	14	7	3	41	25	7	3	14	25	45
OLDHAM A	54	17	5	5	60	31	9	5	13	37	43
OXFORD U	12	2	1	3	6	6	1	0	5	5	13
PETERBOROUGH U	26	5	7	1	20	13	3	3	7	18	23
PLYMOUTH A	24	3	8	1	21	14	2	2	8	11	25
PORTSMOUTH	42	11	3	7	26	26	3	2	16	26	51
PORT VALE	66	20	8	5	78	35	8	5	20	38	70
PRESTON NE *	49	9	10	6	43	39	3	3	18	21	50
QUEEN'S PARK R	26	6	7	0	24	13	2	2	9	9	31
READING	34	9	4	4	33	18	5	5	7	19	34
ROCHDALE	32	11	4	1	36	13	7	2	7	27	30
ROTHERHAM C	6	1	1	1	4	3	0	0	3	2	8
ROTHERHAM T	6	3	0	0	15	2	0	0	3	5	8
ROTHERHAM U	28	7	2	5	25	21	0	4	10	7	23
SCARBOROUGH	2	1	0	0	2	1	1	0	0	3	2
SCUNTHORPE U	40	10	5	5	33	19	9	6	5	30	22
SHEFFIELD U	34	6	1	10	23	24	3	4	10	20	37

		HOME						AWAY				
	P	W	D	L	F	A	W	D	L	F	A
SHEFFIELD W	38	9	4	6	34	23	1	2	16	10	47
SHREWSBURY T	36	11	3	4	32	21	5	3	10	23	34
SOUTHAMPTON	24	6	4	2	26	16	2	3	7	9	32
SOUTHEND U	34	11	5	1	27	12	2	4	11	13	37
1921 SOUTHPORT – 1978	30	10	1	4	24	12	3	2	10	14	32
SOUTH SHIELDS X	6	2	1	0	8	3	1	0	2	4	6
1921 STALYBRIDGE C – 1923 X	4	1	1	0	4	1	0	0	2	2	6
STOCKPORT C	48	18	2	4	54	19	5	10	9	23	34
STOKE C	40	7	7	6	33	31	2	5	13	11	43
SUNDERLAND	36	3	6	9	27	29	2	4	12	20	48
SWANSEA C	42	12	3	6	38	23	3	5	13	19	35
SWINDON T	24	8	1	3	25	13	0	3	9	7	29
1927 TORQUAY U	14	5	1	1	15	7	1	2	4	7	13
TOTTENHAM H	14	4	1	2	14	8	1	0	6	10	19
TRANMERE R	36	13	5	0	46	9	6	4	8	29	32
WALSALL	50	16	4	5	55	27	1	4	20	16	50
WATFORD	26	5	4	4	20	18	3	2	8	16	29
WEST BROMWICH A	32	9	3	4	33	26	3	1	12	24	50
WEST HAM U	24	6	2	4	20	15	2	0	10	14	28
1978 WIGAN ATHLETIC	4	1	0	1	3	3	2	0	0	4	0
1921 WIGAN BOROUGH – 1931 X	10	1	4	0	7	3	0	2	3	4	11
1977 WIMBLEDON	10	3	1	1	8	5	2	2	1	10	9
WOLVERH'TON W *	49	13	5	7	38	24	6	3	15	23	71
1951 WORKINGTON – 1977	24	6	2	4	17	8	1	5	6	10	17
WREXHAM	42	11	6	4	27	12	5	3	13	22	42
1929 YORK C	34	12	3	2	36	14	6	9	2	27	21
	3495	961	411	376	3318	1893	391	353	1003	1950	3497

Grimsby Town's Whittaker takes a goal-kick in the match against Stoke at Blundell Park on 4 October 1902. Note that goalkeepers did not wear distinguishing jerseys in those days.

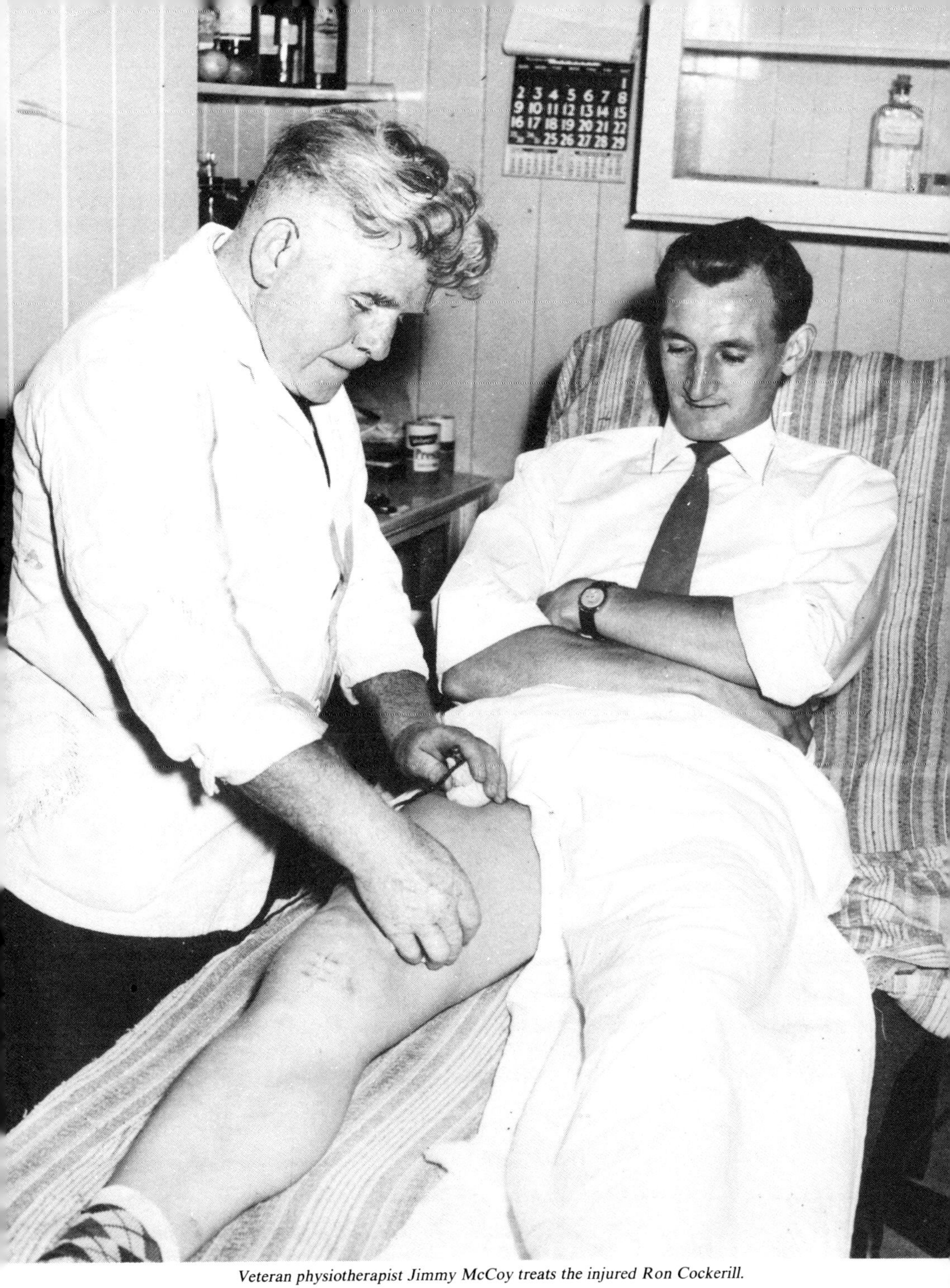

Veteran physiotherapist Jimmy McCoy treats the injured Ron Cockerill.

PRICE TWOPENCE

MANCHESTER UNITED FOOTBALL CLUB

F.A. CHALLENGE CUP: SEMI-FINAL TIE

WOLVERHAMPTON

WANDERERS

VERSUS

GRIMSBY

TOWN

SATURDAY, MARCH 25th, 1939 KICK-OFF 3-0 P.M.

OLD TRAFFORD - MANCHESTER

Mariners in the FA Cup

1882-83
Round 1
Bye: drawn at home to Queen's Park (Glasgow) who refused to travel.
Round 2
Nov 25 v Phoenix Bessemer (h) 1-9
H.Monument
H.Evans; Revd J.F.Flowers, W.Jenkinson, T.Warner, R.C.Hall, S.Noble, B.Tonge, C.Chapman, C.France, H.Monument, R.Ousley.

1983-84
Round 1
Nov 3 v Hull Town (a) 3-1
Scorers unknown
H.Evans; Revd J.F.Flowers, W.Asling, R.C.Hall, G.Kimpson, A.H.Read, S.Noble, T.Garnham, T.Atkinson, H.Monument, G.Atkinson.
Round 2
Nov 26 v Grantham (a) 0-4
H.Evans; W.Asling, W.Jenkinson, G.Atkinson, G.Kimpson, A.H.Read, S.Noble, T.Garnham, T.Atkinson, Lowe, Gunner.

1884-85
Round 1
Oct 25 v Grantham (a) 1-1
H.Mundahl
W.Asling; J.H.Taylor, H.Taylor, R.C.Hall, G.Kimpson, H.Chambers, S.Noble, T.Garnham, R.Raynes, H.Mundahl, A.H.Read.
Replay
Nov 8 v Grantham (h) 1-0
Garnham
Asling; J.H.Taylor, H.Taylor, Hall, Kimpson, Chambers, Noble, Garnham, Raynes, Read, Monument.
Att: 2,000
Round 2
Dec 6 v Redcar (h) 3-1
Garnham 2, Raynes
Asling; J.H.Taylor, H.Taylor, Hall, Kimpson, Chambers, Noble, Garnham, Raynes, Read, Monument.
Att: 2,000
Round 3
Jan 3 v Lincoln City (h) 1-0
Mundahl
Asling; J.H.Taylor, H.Taylor, Hall, Kimpson, Chambers, Noble, Mundahl, Raynes, Read, Monument.
Att: 3,000
Round 4
Jan 24 v Old Carthusians (a) 0-3
Asling; J.H.Taylor, H.Taylor, Hall, Kimpson, Chambers, Noble, Garnham, Raynes, Read, Monument.

1885-86
Round 1
Oct 31 v Lincoln City (a) 2-0
R.Sharman, Monument
G.Atkinson; H.Taylor, J.H.Taylor, Hall, Kimpson, W.Hopewell, H.Atkinson, Garnham, T.Seal, R.Sharman, Monument.
Att: 2,000
Round 2
Nov 21 v Darlington (h) 8-0
H.Atkinson, Seal 3, Monument 4
G.Atkinson; J.H.Taylor, H.Taylor, Hall, Kimpson, Hopewell, H.Atkinson, Garnham, Seal, Sharman, Monument.
Att: 2,000
Round 3
Dec 19 v Middlesbrough Ironopolis (a) 1-2
Monument
G.Atkinson; J.H.Taylor, H.Taylor, Read, Kimpson, Hopewell, H.Atkinson, Garnham, Seal, Sharman, Monument.
Att: 3,000

1886-87
Round 1
Oct 30 v Sheffield Heeley (a) 4-1
T.Chapman, S.Pearson 3
G.Atkinson; Mundahl, H.Taylor, J.H.Taylor, Seal, Hopewell, H.Atkinson, Garnham, T.Chapman, S.Pearson, C.Atkinson.
(Heeley were actually drawn at home but the match was played at Grimsby).
Round 2
Nov 13 v Nottingham Forest (a) 2-2
Garnham, Caborn (og)
G.Atkinson; H.Taylor, Mundahl, J.H.Taylor, Seal, Hopewell, H.Atkinson, Garnham, Chapman, Pearson, C.Atkinson.
Att: 3,500
Replay
Nov 20 v Nottingham Forest (h) 0-1
G.Atkinson; Mundahl, H.Taylor, J.H.Taylor, Seal, Hopewell, H.Atkinson, Garnham, Chapman, Pearson, C.Atkinson.
Att: 3,000

1887-88
Round 1
Oct 15 v Cleethorpes (a) 4-0
Lundie, H.Smith, Lee, C.Atkinson (og)
H.Smith; Lundie, H.Taylor, Seal, H.Smith, Hopewell, H.Atkinson, Lee, Morton, Riddoch, Monument.
Att: 200
Round 2
Nov 26 v Lincoln City (h) 2-0
Lundie, Lee
G.Atkinson; Lundie, H.Taylor, J.H.Taylor, H.Smith, Hopewell, H.Atkinson, Lee, Morton, Riddoch, Soames.
Att: 5,000

Round 3
Dec 17 v Old Foresters (a) 2-4
H.Atkinson, Lee
Christian; Lundie, H.Taylor, J.H.Taylor, H.Smith, Hopewell, H.Atkinson, Lee, Morton, Riddoch, McBeth.

1888-89
1st Qualifying Round
Oct 6 v Lincoln City (h) 1-1
Sutherland
Holtby; Lundie, H.Taylor, J.H.Taylor, H.Smith, Ogilvie, Sutherland, Lee, Riddoch, McBeth, Hunt.
Att: 2,500
Replay
Oct 13 v Lincoln City (a) 1-1
McBeth
Holtby; Lundie, Doyle, J.H.Taylor, H.Smith, Ogilvie, Mudie, Sutherland, Riddoch, McBeth, Hunt.
Att: 4,000
2nd Replay
Oct 24 v Lincoln City (n) 3-1 (at Bramall Lane)
McBeth, Hunt, (other scorer not known)
Holtby; Lundie, J.H.Taylor, Ogilvie, H.Smith, Child, Mudie, Sutherland, Riddoch, McBeth, Hunt.
Att: 1,500
2nd Qualifying Round
Oct 27 v Newark (a) 4-4
Lee, McBeth, (Other scorers not known)
Holtby; Lundie, J.H.Taylor, Ogilvie, Smith, Child, Lee, Mudie, Riddoch, McBeth, Hunt.
Att: 1,500
Replay
Nov 3 v Newark (h) 9-0
Sutherland 2, Lee 2, Riddoch, Hunt (Other scorers not known)
Holtby; Lundie, J.H.Taylor, Ogilvie, Smith, Mudie, Lee, Sutherland, Riddoch, McBeth, Hunt.
Att: 2,000
3rd Qualifying Round
Nov 17 v Cleethorpes Town (h) 5-0
McBeth (Other scorers not known)
Holtby; Doyle, J.H.Taylor, Ogilvie, H.Smith Lundie, Lee, Sutherland, Riddoch, McBeth, Hunt.
Round 1
Dec 15 v Sunderland Albion (h) 3-1
J.Taylor, McBeth 2
Holtby; Lundie, Doyle, J.H.Taylor, H.Smith, Reid, J.Taylor, Sutherland, Riddoch, McBeth, Hunt.
Round 2
Feb 16 v Preston North End (h) 0-2
Holtby; Lundie, Doyle, J.H.Taylor, H.Smith, Reid, J.Taylor, Sutherland, Riddoch, McBeth, Hunt.
Att: 8,000

1889-90
Round 1
Jan 18 v Newcastle West End (a) 2-1
McBeth, Black
Ogilvie; Lundie, Reid, J.Taylor, H.Smith, Ross, Sutherland, McBeth, McKnight, Riddoch, Black.
Round 2
Feb 1 v Blackburn Rovers (a) 0-3
Ogilvie; Lundie, Reid, J.H.Taylor, H.Smith, Sutherland, McKnight, McBeth, Findley, Riddoch, Black.

1890-91
1st Qualifying Round
Oct 11 v Ecclesfield (a) 2-8
Smith 2
Holtby; Winter, T.Frith, Harvey, Waring, Walton, W.Smith, Hollingsworth, C.Frith, Haines, Hughes.
Att: Unknown

1891-92
1st Qualifying Round
Oct 3 v Long Eaton Rangers (h) 2-1
Devlin, Ackroyd
Ogilvie; Lundie, Gray, Murrell Reid, Walker, Devlin, H.Rose, Riddoch, Ackroyd, MacBeth.
Att: Unknown
2nd Qualifying Round
Oct 24 v Boston Town (h) 10-0
Reid 3, Haines, Ackroyd, Riddoch 2, H.Rose 2, Devlin
Ogilvie; Lundie, Gray, Murrell, Reid, Walker, Haines, Ackroyd, Riddoch, H.Rose, Devlin.
Att: Unknown
3rd Qualifying Round
Nov 14 v Sheffield United (h) 1-2
Haines
Ogilvie; Lundie, Gray, Walker, Reid, C.Frith, H.Rose, A.Rose, Hughes, Ackroyd, Haines.
Att: Unknown

1892-93
1st Qualifying Round
Oct 15 v Attercliffe (a) 2-0
Higgins, Mullen
Whitehouse; Lundie, Reid, Murrell, Walker, Ogilvie, Higgins, H.Rose, Mullen, Riddoch, Ackroyd.
Att: Unknown
2nd Qualifying Round
Nov 10 v Doncaster Rovers (a) 2-1
Higgins 2
Whitehouse; Lundie, Frith, Murrell, Walker, Ogilvie, Higgins, Henderson, Mullen, Fletcher, Riddoch.
Att: 1,500
Abandoned because of bad light on 29 October and replayed on 10 November
3rd Qualifying Round
Nov 19 v Gainsborough Trinity (h) 1-0
Higgins
Holtby; Lundie, Reid, Murrell, Walker, Ogilvie, Higgins, Henderson, Mullen, Ackroyd, Riddoch.
Att: Unknown
4th Qualifying Round
Dec 10 v Lincoln City (h) 5-0
Higgins, Mullen 3, Fletcher
Whitehouse; Lundie, Ogilvie, Murrell, Walker, Fairley, Ackroyd, Higgins, Mullen, Riddoch, Fletcher.
Att: 3,000
Round 1
Jan 21 v Stockton (h) 5-0
Ackroyd, Higgins, Mullen 2
Whitehouse; Lundie, Reid, Murrell, Ogilvie, Fairley, Ackroyd, Higgins, Mullen, Fletcher, Riddoch.
The remaining goal awarded after Stockton's goalkeeper was charged into the net
Att: 3,000
Round 2
Feb 3 v Darwen (a) 0-2
Whitehouse; Lundie, Reid, Murrell, Walker, Ogilvie, Ackroyd, Higgins, Mullen, Fletcher, Riddoch.
Att: Unknown

1893-94
1st Qualifying Round
Oct 14 v Kilnhurst (h) 5-1
Ackroyd, Crawford, McCairns 2, Cleator
Whitehouse; West, Frith, Russell, Graham, Riddoch, Ackroyd, Crawford, McCairns, Cleator, Jones.
Att: 1,500
2nd Qualifying Round
Nov 4 v Lincoln City (a) 5-2
Riddoch 2, McCarins 3
Whitehouse; Lundie, Frith, Murrell, Graham, Russell, Ackroyd, Riddoch, McCairns, Fletcher, Jones.
Att: Unknown
3rd Qualifying Round
Nov 22 v Grantham Rovers (a) 6-2
Ackroyd 2, McCairns 2, Fletcher 2
Whitehouse; Lundie, Frith, Higgins, Graham, Russell, Ackroyd, Riddoch, McCairns, Fletcher, Jones.
Att: 1,000
4th Qualifying Round
Dec 16 v Gainsborough Trinity (h) 6-1
Riddoch 2, McCairns 2, Fletcher, Jones
Whitehouse; Lundie, Frith, Higgins, Graham, Russell, Ackroyd, Riddoch, McCairns, Fletcher, Jones.
Att: 1,500
Round 1
Jan 27 v Liverpool (a) 0-3
Whitehouse; Lundie, Frith, Higgins, Graham, Russell, Ackroyd, Rose, McCairns, Riddoch, Jones.
Att: Unknown

1894-95
1st Qualifying Round
Oct 13 v Lincoln City (a) 3-0
Stott, Fletcher, Frost
Whitehouse; Lindsay, Frith, Higgins, Stott, Waterson, Rose, Eccleston, McCairns, Fletcher, Frost.
Att: 5,000
2nd Qualifying Round
Nov 3 v Attercliffe (h) 2-2
Higgins, Riddoch
Waterson; Frith, Lindsay, Higgins, Stott, Graham, Rose, Eccleston, Riddoch, Fletcher, Frost.
Att: 2,000
Replay
Nov 5 v Attercliffe (h) 8-0
Higgins, Stott, Eccleston, Riddoch 2, Frost 3
Whitehouse; Frith, Lindsay, Higgins, Stott, Graham, Rose, Eccleston, Riddoch, Fletcher, Frost.
Att: 1,000
3rd Qualifying Round
Nov 24 v Worksop (h) 0-1
Whitehouse; Lundie, Lindsay, Waterson, Stott, Graham, Rose, Eccleston, Higgins, Fletcher, Riddoch.
Att: 2,500

1895-96
1st Qualifying Round
Oct 12 v Staveley (a) 5-0
McCairns 3, Gray 2
Whitehouse; Lindsay, Hudson, Davis, Munn, Graham, Bell, Pratt, McCairns, Fletcher, Gray.
Att: 1,000
2nd Qualifying Round
Nov 2 v Kilnhurst (a) 4-1
Davis, Graham, McCairns 2
Whitehouse; Higgins, Frith, Davis, Blair, Graham, Bell, Pratt, McCairns, Fletcher, Gray.
Att: 1,000
3rd Qualifying Round
Nov 23 v Lincoln City (a) 4-2
McCairns 3, Fletcher
Whitehouse; Lindsay, Frith, Munn, Higgins, Graham, Bell, Pratt, McCairns, Fletcher, Gray.
Att: 5,000
4th Qualifying Round
Dec 14 v Rotherham (h) 4-0
Munn, Bell 2, (opp og)
Whitehouse; Lindsay, Frith, Munn, Higgins, Graham, Bell, Pratt, McCairns, Fletcher, Gray.
Att: 3,000
Round 1
Feb 1 v Darwen (a) 2-0
Graham, Pratt
Whitehouse; Lindsay, Davis, Munn, Higgins, Graham, Bell, Pratt, McCairns, Fletcher, Gray.
Att: 4,000
Round 2
Feb 15 v West Bromwich Albion (h) 1-1
Gray
Whitehouse; Lindsay, Davis, Munn, Higgins, Graham, Bell, Pratt, McCairns, Fletcher, Gray.
Att: 7,500
Replay
Feb 20 v West Bromwich Albion (a) 0-3
Whitehouse; Lindsay, Davis, Munn, Higgins, Graham, Bell, Pratt, McCairns, Fletcher, Gray.
Att: 11,000

1896-97
Round 1
Jan 28 v Bolton Wanderers (h) 0-0
Wallace; Lindsay, Frith, Munn, Higgins, Chapman, Rogers, Morris, McCairns, Fletcher, Gray.
Att: 10,000
Replay
Feb 3 v Bolton Wanderers (a) 3-3
Rogers, Bell, McCairns
Wallace; Lindsay, Frith, Munn, Higgins, Chapman, Rogers, Bell, McCairns, Fletcher, Gray.
Att: 7,000
2nd Replay
Feb 11 v Bolton Wanderers (n) 2-3 (at Bramall Lane)
Fletcher, (opp og)
Wallace; Lindsay, Frith, Munn, Higgins, Chapman, Rogers, Bell, McCairns, Fletcher, Gray.
Att: 10,000

1897-98
Round 1
Jan 29 v Nottingham Forest (a) 0-4
Leaning; Lindsay, McLean, Mountain, Bell, Chapman, Rogers, Goldie, McCairns, Fletcher, Gray.
Att: 7,000

1898-99
1st Qualifying Round
Oct 29 v Mexborough (h) 5-0
Greenwood 2, Cockshutt, Griffiths 2
Bagshaw; Mountain, Nidd, Bell, Gray, Nelmes, Jenkinson, Greenwood, Cockshutt, Ratcliffe, Griffiths.
Att: 4,000
2nd Qualifying Round
Nov 19 v Lincoln City (h) 2-1
Gray, Griffiths
Bagshaw; Mountain, Nidd, Bell, Gray, Nelmes, Jenkinson, Greenwood, Cockshutt, Ratcliffe, Griffiths.
Att: 8,000

3rd Qualifying Round
Dec 10 v Barnsley (a) 0-0
Bagshaw; Nidd, Frith, Cherry, Gray, Nelmes, Jenkinson, Greenwood, Cockshutt, Chapman, Griffiths.
Att: Unknown
Replay
Dec 14 v Barnsley (h) 2-1
Jenkinson, Cockshutt
Bagshaw; Nidd, Frith, Cherry, Gray, Nelmes, Jenkinson, Greenwood, Cockshutt, Chapman, Griffiths.
Att: 2,000
Round 1
Jan 28 v Preston North End (a) 0-7
Bagshaw; Mountain, Nidd, Griffiths, Gray, Nelmes, Richards, Jenkinson, Cockshutt, Ratcliffe, Greenwood.
Att: Unknown

1899-1900
3rd Qualifying Round
Oct 28 v Doncaster Rovers (h) 3-1
Jenkinson, Richards, Cockshutt
Whitehouse; Mountain, Nidd, Griffiths, Gray, Nelmes, Jenkinson, Richards, Cockshutt, Ratcliffe, Hemingfield.
Att: Unknown
4th Qualifying Round
Nov 21 v Barnsley (h) 3-2
Richards, Cockshutt, Ratcliffe
Whitehouse; Mountain, Nidd, Greenwood, Gray, Nelmes, Jenkinson, Richards, Cockshutt, Hemingfield, Ratcliffe.
Att: 3,000
5th Qualifying Round
Dec 9 v Chesterfield (h) 3-2
Jenkinson 2, Hemingfield
Whitehouse; Finlayson, Nidd, Griffiths, Gray, Nelmes, Jenkinson, Richards, Greenwood, Ratcliffe, Hemingfield.
Att: 5,000
Round 1
Jan 27 v Nottingham Forest (a) 0-3
Whitehouse; McAvoy, Mountain, Griffiths, Gray, Nelmes, Jenkinson, Richards, Cockshutt, Ratcliffe, Hemingfield.
Att: 7,000

1900-01
Extra Qualifying Round
Jan 5 v Middlesbrough (h) 0-1
MacFarlane; Mountain, McAvoy, Griffiths, Hemingfield, Nelmes, Jenkinson, Fletcher, Leigh, Mellor, Lakey.
Att: 5,000

1901-02
Round 1
Jan 25 v Portsmouth (h) 1-1
Appleyard
Whittaker; Mountain, A.McConnell, Griffiths, Gray, Nelmes, Fletcher, Ronaldson, Appleyard, Harper, Gardner.
Att: 10,000
Replay
Jan 29 v Portsmouth (a) 0-2
Whittaker; Mountain, A.McConnell, Griffiths, Gray, Nelmes, Fletcher, Ronaldson, Appleyard, Harper, Gardner.
Att: 12,000

1902-03
Round 1
Feb 7 v Newcastle United (h) 2-1
Fletcher, Ronaldson
Spendiff; Mountain, Gardner, Hemingfield, Hall, Dunn, Fletcher, Ronaldson, Appleyard, Glen, Singleton.
Att: 7,000
Round 2
Feb 21 v Notts County (h) 0-2
Spendiff; Mountain, Gardner, Hemingfield, Hall, Dunn, Fletcher, Ronaldson, Appleyard, Glen, Singleton.
Att: 9,000

1903-04
Preliminary Round
Dec 12 v Barnsley (h) 2-0
Hodgkinson, Wilkinson
Spendiff; A.McConnell, Gardner, Dunn, Roberts, McDiarmid, Long, Hodgkinson, Rouse, Wilkinson, Williams.
Att: Unknown
Round 1
Feb 6 v Preston North End (a) 0-1
Spendiff; A.McConnell, Dunn, McDiarmid, Roberts, Nelmes, Nichol, Rouse, Elkins, Long, Lappin.
Att: 10,000

1904-05
Qualifying Round
Jan 14 v Gainsborough Trinity (h) 2-0
Reynolds, Baker
Spendiff; Morley, Mochan, McGregor, McDiarmid, Nelmes, Reynolds, Baker, Phillips, Higgins, Ross.
Att: 3,000
Round 1
Feb 4 v Stoke (a) 0-2
Spendiff; Morley, Mochan, McGregor, McDiarmid, Nelmes, Reynolds, Baker, Phillips, Hunter, Ross.
Att: 10,600

1905-06
Round 1
Jan 16 v Newcastle United (h) 0-6
Cartledge; Butler, McConnell, McGregor, Morley, Higgins, Fletcher, Baker, Padley, Burnett, Swarbrick.

Town were drawn at home but the match was actually played at Newcastle

1906-07
Jan 12 v Woolwich Arsenal (h) 1-1
Hooper
Carmichael; Morley, Butler, McGregor, T.H.Morris, Higgins, Hooper, Rodger, Burnett, R.Morris, Swarbrick.
Att: 9,000

Replay
Jan 16 v Woolwich Arsenal (a) 0-3
Carmichael; Morley, Butler, McGregor, T.H.Morris, Higgins, Hooper, Rodger, Burnett, R.Morris, Swarbrick.
Att: 13,500

1907-08
Round 1
Jan 11 v Bristol City (a) 0-0
Scott; Wheelhouse, Vincett, Lee, Higgins, Hatton, Stokes, Kilbourne, Blanthorne, Hakin, Fletcher.
Att: 10,000
Replay
Jan 15 v Bristol City (h) 2-1
Lee, Blanthorne
Scott; Wheelhouse, Vincett, Lee, Higgins, Hatton, Stokes, Kilbourne, Blanthorne, Hakin, Fletcher.
Att: 7,000
Round 2
Feb 1 v Carlisle United (h) 6-2
Kilbourne, Blanthorne 5
Carmichael; Wheelhouse, Vincett, Higgins, Bowden, Hatton, Stokes, Kilbourne, Blanthorne, Hakin, Fletcher.
Att: 6,000
Round 3
Feb 22 v Crystal Palace (h) 1-0
Blanthorne
Carmichael; Wheelhouse, Vincett, Lee, Bowden, Hatton, Stokes, Kilbourne, Blanthorne, Higgins, Fletcher.
Att: 9,000
Round 4
Mar 7 v Newcastle United (a) 1-5
Kilbourne
Scott; Wheelhouse, Vincett, Lee, Bowden, Higgins, Stokes, Kilbourne, Blanthorne, Hakin, Fletcher.
Att: 45,000

1908-09
Round 1
Jan 20 v Stockport County (h) 0-2
Scott; Wheelhouse, Henderson, Lee, Davidson, Hatton, Springthorpe, Bradley, Owens, Satterthwaite, Coxon.
Att: 5,000
Replay of the match abandoned 15 January

1909-10
Round 1
Jan 15 v Bristol Rovers (h) 0-2
Scott; Wheelhouse, Henderson, Lee, Davidson, Hargreaves, Rowston, Coulbeck, Gates, Kilbourne, Coxon.
Att: 5,000

1910-11
Round 1
Jan 26 v Croydon Common (h) 8-1
Hubbard 2, Leonard 3, Springthorpe, Worth 2
Lonsdale; Wheelhouse, Arrowsmith, Lee, Gordon, Kelly, Hobson, Hubbard, Leonard, Springthorpe, Worth.
(Replay of match declared void 14 January)
Att: 5,000
Round 2
Feb 4 v Crewe Alexandra (a) 5-1
Gordon, Hubbard 2, Leonard (pen), Springthorpe
Lonsdale; Wheelhouse, Arrowsmith, Lee, Gordon, Kelly, Hobson, Hubbard, Leonard, Springthorpe, Worth.
Att: 10,000
Round 3
Feb 25 v Bradford City (a) 0-1
Lonsdale; Wheelhouse, Arrowsmith, Lee, Gordon, Kelly, Hobson, Hubbard, Young, Springthorpe, Worth.
Att: 24,000

1911-12
1st Qualifying Round
Nov 18 v Lincoln City (a) 2-3
Hubbard, Mayson
Bradley; Wheelhouse, Arrowsmith, Seeburg, Gordon, Martin, Staniforth, Hubbard, Mounteney, Mayson, Worth.
Att: 8,000

1912-13
Round 1
Jan 18 v Sheffield Wednesday (a) 1-5
Rippon
Lonsdale; Wheelhouse, Arrowsmith, Andrews, Gordon, Martin, Staniforth, Rippon, Rampton, Mayson, Birch.
Att: 26,442

1913-14
Round 1
Jan 10 v West Bromwich Albion (a) 0-2
Spendiff; Wheelhouse, Arrowsmith, Andrews, Gordon, Martin, Quinn, Gregson, Rampton, Mayson, Scott.
Att: 14,000

1914-15
Round 1
Jan 9 v Northampton Town (h) 0-3
Summers; Atkin, Arrowsmith, Andrews, Gordon, Martin, Spink, Rippon, Rampton, Mayson, Scott.
Att: 8,000

1915-16 season to 1918-19 season inclusive there was no competition because of World War One.

1919-20
Round 1
Jan 10 v Bristol City (h) 1-2
Thompson
Jennings; Dawson, McEachran, Battiste, Kenny, Martin, Smith, Thompson, Clarke, Storer, Huxford.
Att: 10,000

1920-21
6th Qualifying Round
Dec 18 v Kettering Town (a) 4-2
Storer, Sankey, Smith (2 pens)
Whalley; Affleck, McEachran, Gillow, Carmichael, Storer, Collier, Morrall, Sankey, Macauley, Smith.
Att: Unknown

Round 1
Jan 8 v Norwich City (h) 1-0
Smith (pen)
Whalley; Affleck, McEachran, Gillow, Deacey, Storer, Collier, Morrall, Clarke, Macauley, Smith.
Att: 11,000
Round 2
Jan 29 v Southampton (h) 1-3
Storer
Whalley; Affleck, McEachran, Gillow, Carmichael, Storer, Spink, Collier, Sankey, Morrall, Smith.
Att: 14,000

1921-22
5th Qualifying Round
Dec 3 v Kettering Town (h) 1-1
J.Miller
Moody; Stevenson, H.Millar, Coupland, Deacey, Bradford, Spink, Carmichael, J.Miller, Morrall, Smith.
Att: 7,000
Replay
Dec 8 v Kettering Town (a) 2-0
A.Smith, own goal
Jones; Affleck, H.Millar, Coupland, Deacey, Bradford, F.Smith, Carmichael, J.Miller, Raby, A.Smith.
Att: 7,850
6th Qualifying Round
Dec 17 v Tufnell Park (h) 1-1
Spink
Jones; Afflect, H.Millar, Coupland, Deacey, Bradford, Spink, Carmichael, Talks, Raby, Smith.
Att: Unknown
Replay
Dec 22 v Tufnell Park (a) 2-1
Coupland, Collier
Jones; Affleck, H.Millar, Coupland, Deacey, Bradford, Spink, Collier, Carmichael, Morrall, Laws.
Att: Unknown
Round 1
Jan 7 v Notts County (h) 1-1
Carmichael
Jones; Affleck, Felton, Gillow, Deacey, Bradford, Collier, Coupland, Carmichael, J.Miller, A.Smith.
Att: 12,000 (£811)
Replay
Jan 12 v Notts County (a) 0-3
Jones: Affleck, Felton, Gillow, Deacey, Bradford, Collier, Marshall, Carmichael, J.Miller, A.Smith.
Att: 16,381 (£1,274)

1922-23
5th Qualifying Round
Dec 22 v Worksop Town (h) 0-2
Harrison; H.Millar, Felton, Coupland, Deacey, Hilton, Kirsopp, McKenna, Graver, J.Miller, Laws.
Att: Unknown

1923-24
5th Qualifying Round
Dec 1 v Hinckley (a) 3-0
Thomson, Miller 2
Archibald; Arch, Affleck, Wilson, Hilton, Bradford, Honeyman, Thomson, Carmichael, Miller, Marshall.
Att: Unknown
6th Qualifying Round
Dec 15 v Chesterfield (a) 0-0
Archibald; Arch, Affleck, Wilson, Hilton, Bradford, McKenna, Thomson, Carmichael, Miller, Marshall.
Att: 10,000
Replay
Dec 18 v Chesterfield (h) 2-0
Carmichael (pen), Miller
Archibald; Arch, Affleck, Wilson, Hilton, Bradford, McKenna, Thomson, Carmichael, Miller, Marshall.
Att: 12,176
Round 1
Jan 12 v Exeter City (a) 0-1
Archibald; Arch, Affleck, Wilson, Hilton, Bradford, McKenna, Thomson, Carmichael, Miller, Marshall.
Att: 8,250

1924-25
5th Qualifying Round
Nov 29 v Chesterfield (h) 1-2
Carmichael
Atter; Arch, Affleck, Wilson, Hilton, Field, Thompson, Cooper, Carmichael, Dent, Marshall.
Att: Unknown

1925-26
Round 1
Nov 28 v Walsall (a) 1-0
McKenna
Archibald; Pearson, Jacobson, Wilson, Hardy, Pugsley, Devan, Cooper, Carmichael, McKenna, Marshall.
Att: 4,982
Round 2
Dec 12 v Kettering Town (a) 1-1
Carmichael
Archibald; Pearson, Jacobson, Wilson, Hardy, Pugsley, Devan, Cooper, Carmichael, McKenna, Marshall.
Att: 7,074
Replay
Dec 15 v Kettering Town (h) 3-1
Devan, Carmichael, McKenna
Archibald; Pearson, Jacobson, Wilson, Hardy, Pugsley, Devan, Gardner, Carmichael, McKenna, Marshall.
Att: 7,000
Round 3
Jan 9 v Birmingham (a) 0-2
Archibald; Wilson, Jacobson, McLachlan, Hardy, Pugsley, Devan, Gardner, Robson, McKenna, Marshall.
Att: 36,000

1926-27
Round 1
Nov 27 v Halifax Town (h) 3-2
Pugsley (pen), McKenna, Marshall
Prout; Jackson, Jacobson, McLachlan, Wrack, Pugsley, Devan, Cooper, Robson, McKenna, Marshall.
Att: 8,500
Round 2
Dec 11 v York City (h) 2-1
Bestall, Robson
Archibald; Jackson, Jacobson, McLachlan, Wrack, Pugsley, McKenna, Bestall, Robson, Cooper, Marshall.
Att: 10,000

Round 3
Jan 8 v Burnley (a) 1-3
Hardy
Archibald; Jackson, Jacobson, Newton, Hardy, Pugsley, Ferguson, Bestall, Carmichael, Cooper, Marshall.
Att: 19,556

1927-28
Round 3
Jan 14 v Reading (a) 0-4
Cowell; Harris, Jacobson, Wilson, Wrack, Powell, Meikle, Bestall, Robson, Coglin, Marshall.
Att: 19,007

1928-29
Round 3
Jan 12 v West Bromwich Albion (h) 1-1
Cooper
Read; Calderwood, Jacobson, Wilson, Swaby, Powell, Prior, Bestall, Robson, Cooper, Marshall.
Att: 16,000
Replay
Jan 16 v West Bromwich Albion (a) 0-2
Read; Calderwood, Jacobson, Wilson, Swaby, Powell, Prior, Bestall, Robson, Cooper, Marshall.
Att: 21,190

1929-30
Round 3
Jan 11 v Brighton & Hove Albion (a) 1-1
Prior
Read; Wilson, Jacobson, Priestley, Wrack, Buck, Prior, Bestall, Coleman, Coglin, Marshall.
Att: 10,000
Replay
Jan 14 v Brighton & Hove Albion (h) 0-1
Read; Wilson, Jacobson, Priestley, Wrack, Buck, Prior, Bestall, Coleman, Coglin, Marshall.
Att: Unknown

1930-31
Round 3
Jan 10 v Scarborough (a) 2-1
Prior, Bestall
Read; Bell, Jacobson, Wilson, Swaby, Buck, Prior, Bestall, Glover, Coleman, Marshall.
Att: 8,000
Round 4
Jan 24 v Manchester United (h) 1-0
Marshall
Read; Bell, Jacobson, Priestley, Swaby, Buck, Prior, Bestall, Coleman, Cooper, Marshall.
Att: 15,000
Round 5
Feb 14 v Everton (a) 3-5
Bestall, Coleman, Marshall
Read; Wilson, Jacobson, Hall, Priestley, Buck, Prior, Bestall, Coleman, Cooper, Marshall.
Att: 65,534

1931-32
Round 3
Jan 9 v Exeter City (h) 4-1
Glover 4
Read; Wilson, Jacobson, Hall, Priestley, Buck, Prior, Bestall, Glover, Cooper, Marshall.
Att: 12,000

Round 4
Jan 23 v Birmingham (h) 2-1
Bestall 2
Read; Wilson, Jacobson, Hall, Priestley, Buck, Fielding, Bestall, Coleman, Cooper, Marshall.
Att: 18,000
Round 5
Feb 13 v Liverpool (a) 0-1
Read; Wilson, Jacobson, Hall, Priestley, Buck, Fielding, Bestall, Coleman, Cooper, Marshall.
Att: 49,479

1932-33
Round 3
Jan 14 v Portsmouth (h) 3-2
Dyson, Glover 2
Read; Wright, Jacobson, Hall, Betmead, Buck, Dyson, Bestall, Glover, Craven, Fielding.
Att: 9,200
Round 4
Jan 28 v Bolton Wanderers (a) 1-2
Craven
Tweedy; Wright, Jacobson, Hall, Betmead, Buck, Ponting, Bestall, Glover, Craven, Fielding.
Att: 25,866

1933-34
Round 3
Jan 13 v Clapton Orient (h) 1-0
Glover
Tweedy; Kelly, Jacobson, Hall, Betmead, Buck, Jennings, Bestall, Glover, Craven, Holmes.
Att: 13,500
Round 4
Jan 27 v Portsmouth (a) 0-2
Read; Kelly, Jacobson, Hall, Betmead, Buck, Jennings, Bestall, Glover, Craven, Holmes.
Att: 34,565

1934-35
Round 3
Jan 12 v Everton (a) 3-6
Glover 2, Craven
Tweedy; Kelly, Wright, Hall, Hodgson, Buck, Dyson, Bestall, Glover, Craven, Jennings.
Att: 44,850

1935-36
Round 3
Jan 11 v Hartlepools United (a) 0-0
Tweedy; Kelly, Hodgson, Hall, Betmead, Buck, Baldry, Bestall, Glover, Craven, Lewis.
Att: 15,064
Replay
Jan 14 v Hartlepools United (h) 4-1
Buck, Bestall, Glover 2
Tweedy; Kelly, Hodgson, Hall, Betmead, Buck, Baldry, Bestall, Glover, Craven, Lewis.
Att: 11,500
Round 4
Jan 25 v Port Vale (a) 4-0
Baldry 2, Bestall, Craven
Tweedy; Kelly, Hodgson, Hall, Betmead, Buck, Baldry, Bestall, Glover, Craven, Lewis.
Att: 13,350

Round 5
Feb 15 v Manchester City (h) 3-2
Glover, Lewis 2
Tweedy; Kelly, Hodgson, Hall, Betmead, Buck, Baldry, Bestall, Glover, Craven, Lewis.
Att: 28,000
Round 6
Feb 29 v Middlesbrough (h) 3-1
Glover, Craven, Smailes
Tweedy; Kelly, Hodgson, Hall, Betmead, Buck, Baldry, Bestall, Glover, Craven, Smailes.
Att: 21,000
Semi-Final
Mar 21 v Arsenal (n) 0-1 (at Leeds Road, Huddersfield)
Tweedy; Vincent, Kelly, Hall, Hodgson, Buck, Baldry, Bestall, Glover, Craven, Smailes.
Att: 63,210

1936-37
Round 3
Jan 16 v Cardiff City (a) 3-1
Glover, Craven, Lewis
Tweedy; Vincent, Kelly, Hall, Hodgson, Buck, Dyson, Bestall, Glover, Craven, Lewis.
Att: 36,245
Round 4
Jan 30 v Walsall (h) 5-1
Buck, Glover 3, Lewis
Tweedy; Vincent, Kelly, Hall, Hodgson, Buck, Dyson, Bestall, Glover, Craven, Lewis.
Att: 11,000
Round 5
Feb 20 v Wolverhampton Wanderers (h) 1-1
Craven
Tweedy; Kelly, Hodgson, Hall, Betmead, Buck, Dyson, Bestall, Glover, Craven, Lewis.
Att: 31,651

Replay
Feb 24 v Wolverhampton Wanderers (a) 2-6
Craven, Lewis
Tweedy; Kelly, Hodgson, Hall, Betmead, Buck, Dyson, Bestall, Glover, Craven, Lewis.
Att: 56,799

1937-38
Round 3
Jan 8 v Swindon Town (h) 1-1
Tomlinson
Tweedy; Vincent, Kelly, Dyson, Hodgson, Buck, Bestall, Hinchcliffe, Tomlinson, Craven, Coulter.
Att: 14,000
Replay
Jan 12 v Swindon Town (a) 1-2
Tomlinson
Tweedy; Vincent, Hodgson, Hall, Betmead, Buck, Dyson, Bestall, Tomlinson, Craven, Coulter.
Att: Unknown

1938-39
Round 3
Jan 10 v Tranmere Rovers (h) 6-0
Vincent (pen), Beattie 2, Howe 2, Lewis
Tweedy; Vincent, Hodgson, Hall, Betmead, Buck, Boyd, Beattie, Howe, Jones, Lewis.
Att: 10,000
Round 4
Jan 21 v Millwall (a) 2-2
Howe 2
Tweedy; Vincent, Hodgson, Hall, Betmead, Buck, Boyd, Beattie, Howe, Jones, Lewis
Att: 38,447

Town's reserve goalkeeper George Moulson (left) is knocked unconscious after diving at the feet of Wolves' Dorsett (also on ground, right) during the 1939 FA Cup semi-final.

Replay
Jan 24 v Millwall (h) 3-2
Boyd, Howe, Jones
Tweedy; Vincent, Hodgson, Hall, Betmead, Buck, Boyd, Beattie, Howe, Jones, Swain.
Att: 14,400
Round 5
Feb 11 v Sheffield United (a) 0-0
Tweedy; Vincent, Hodgson, Hall, Betmead, Buck, Boyd, Beattie, Glover, Jones, Bartholomew.
Att: 62,022
Replay
Feb 14 v Sheffield United (h) 1-0
Howe
Tweedy; Vincent, Hodgson, Hall, Betmead, Buck, Boyd, Beattie, Howe, Jones, Crack.
Att: 14,500
Round 6
Mar 4 v Chelsea (a) 1-0
Crack
Tweedy; Vincent, Hodgson, Hall, Betmead, Buck, Boyd, Beattie, Howe, Jones, Crack.
Att: 45,409
Semi-Final
Mar 25 v Wolverhampton Wanderers (n) 0-5 (at Old Trafford, Manchester)
Moulson; Vincent, Hodgson, Hall, Betmead, Buck, Boyd, Beattie, Howe, Jones, Crack.
Att: 76,962

1939-40 season to 1944-45 season inclusive there was no competition because of World War Two.

1945-46
Round 3 (1st leg)
Jan 5 v Sunderland (h) 1-3
Rodi
Moulson; Mouncer, J.V.Hodgson, Hall, S.Hodgson, Jones, Chadwick, Moore, Jas.Johnson, Rodi, Wardle.
Att: 12,000
2nd leg
Jan 9 v Sunderland (a) 1-2
Moore
Moulson; Vincent, J.V.Hodgson, S.Hodgson, Charlesworth, Blenkinsopp, Harvey, Rodi, Moore, Jones, Wardle.
Att: 9,000
1946-47
Round 3
Jan 11 v Reading (a) 2-2
Cairns 2
Tweedy; Vincent, Fisher, Hall, R.E.Taylor, Blenkinsopp, Jno.W.Johnson, Clifton, Cairns, Jones, Wardle.
Att: 20,000
Replay
Jan 14 v Reading (h) 3-1
Cairns 2, Keeble
Tweedy; Vincent, Fisher, Hall, R.E.Taylor, Blenkinsopp, Wallbanks, Whitfield, Cairns, Keeble, Wardle.
Att: Unknown
Round 4
Jan 25 v Liverpool (a) 0-2
Tweedy; Mouncer, Fisher, Hall, R.E.Taylor, Blenkinsopp, Wallbanks, Clifton, Cairns, Keeble, Wardle.
Att: 42,000

1947-48
Round 3
Jan 10 v Everton (h) 1-4
Whitfield
Tweedy; Sibley, Fisher, Galley, R.E.Taylor, F.Reeve, Burnett, Whitfield, Briggs, Cairns, Wardle.
Att: 19,000

1948-49
Round 3
Jan 8 v Exeter City (h) 2-1
Whitfield, Cairns
Chisholm; Moody, Fisher, McKenna, Sibley, Forrest, McStay, Whitfield, Briggs, Cairns, Lloyd.
Att: 15,210
Round 4
Jan 29 v Hull City (h) 2-3
Forrest, Briggs
Chisholm; Moody, Fisher, McKenna, Sibley, Forrest, McStay, Whitfield, Briggs, Cairns, Lloyd.
Att: 26,505

1949-50
Round 3
Jan 7 v Luton Town (a) 4-3
Briggs 4
Bircham; Fisher, Harnby, Johnston, McMillan, Duthie, McStay, Shearer, Briggs, Cairns, Hair
Att: 18,843
Round 4
Jan 28 v Portsmouth (a) 0-5
Bircham; Fisher, Harnby, Johnston, McMillan, Duthie, McStay, Barney, Briggs, Cairns, Hair.
Att: 39,364

1950-51
Round 3
Jan 16 v Exeter City (h) 3-3
Scotson, Bloomer, M.L.Mackenzie
Turnbull; Mouncer, W.B.Taylor, Scotson, Duthie, Barratt, Lloyd, Squires, Bloomer, M.L.Mackenzie, Maddison.
Att: 13,823
Replay
Jan 10 v Exeter City (a) 2-4
Squires, Bloomer
Turnbull; Harnby, W.B.Taylor, Scotson, Duthie, Barratt, Lloyd, Squires, Bloomer, M.L.Mackenzie, Maddison.
Att: 18,177

1951-52
Round 1
Nov 24 v Darlington (h) 4-0
Bloomer, Cairns 3
Hayhurst; Brown, Galbraith, Scotson, McMillan, Johnston, Campbell, Bloomer, Cairns, Hernon, McCue.
Att: 14,309
Round 2
Dec 15 v Lincoln City (a) 1-3
Cairns
Hayhurst; Brown, Galbraith, Scotson, McMillan, Johnston, Campbell, Bloomer, Cairns, Hernon, Maddison.
Att: 21,757

1952-53
Round 1
Nov 22 v Darlington (a) 3-2
Johnston, Rayner, Millar
Hayhurst; Brown, Galbraith, Scotson, McMillan, Johnston, McCue, Bloomer, Rayner, Millar, Maddison.
Att: 9,452
Round 2
Dec 6 v Bath City (h) 1-0
Johnston
Hayhurst; Brown, Galbraith, Scotson, McMillan, Johnston, McCue, Millar, Smith, Hernon, Maddison.
Att: 15,175
Round 3
Jan 10 v Bury (h) 1-3
McCue
Hayhurst; Freeburn, Galbraith, Scotson, McMillan, Johnston, Lloyd, McCue, Smith, Hernon, Maddison.
Att: 15,291

1953-54
Round 1
Nov 21 v Rochdale (h) 2-0
Smith, Maddison
Williams; Brown, Robson, Scotson, McMillan, Walker, Stroud, Bloomer, Smith, Wright, Maddison.
Att: 8,509
Round 2
Dec 12 v Witton Albion (a) 1-1
Rayner
Williams; Brown, Robson, Scotson, McMillan, Walker, Stroud, Bloomer, Rayner, Wright, Maddison.
Att: 7,573
Replay
Dec 15 v Witton Albion (h) 6-1
Bloomer, Rayner 3, Wright, Maddison
Williams; Brown, Robson, Scotson, McMillan, Walker, Stroud, Bloomer, Rayner, Wright, Maddison.
Att: 5,564
Round 3
Jan 9 v Fulham (h) 5-5
Scotson, Bloomer 3, (opp og)
Williams; Brown, Robson, Scotson, McMillan, Walker, Stroud, Johnston, Bloomer, Wright, Maddison.
Att: 14,772
Replay
Jan 18 v Fulham (a) 1-3
Stroud
Williams; Brown, Robson, Scotson, McMillan, Walker, Stroud, Smith, Bloomer, Wright, Maddison.
Att: 18,729
(This replay was originally started on January 13th but abandoned at half-time because of a waterlogged pitch).

1954-55
Round 1
Nov 20 v Halifax Town (h) 2-1
Hughes, Maddison
Williams; Brown, Higgins, Conner, Player, Jobling, Stroud, Bloomer, Harbertson, Hughes, Maddison.
Att: 10,174
Round 2
Dec 11 v Southampton (h) 4-1
Harbertson 2, Harrison 2
Williams; Brown, Higgins, Conner, Player, Johnston, Stroud, Harbertson, Harrison, Hughes, Maddison.
Att: 10,075
Round 3
Jan 8 v Wolverhampton Wanderers (h) 2-5
Harrison, Stokes
Williams; Brown, Higgins, Conner, Johnston, Walker, Stroud, Harbertson, Stokes, Harrison, Maddison.
Att: 25,964

1955-56
Round 1
Nov 19 v Netherfield (a) 5-1
Evans, Crosbie 2, Reeson 2
Williams; Brown, De Gruchy, Conner, Chilton, Richardson, Priestley, Evans, Crosbie, Reeson, Maddison.
Att: 5,161
Round 2
Dec 10 v Southport (a) 0-0
Williams; Brown, De Gruchy, Conner, Chilton, Richardson, Priestley, Evans, Pell, Reeson, Maddison.
Att: 9,000
Replay
Dec 13 v Southport (h) 3-2
Priestley, Crosbie (pen), Reeson
Williams; Brown, De Gruchy, Conner, Chilton, Richardson, Priestley, Evans, Crosbie, Reeson, Maddison.
Att: 6,960
Round 3
Jan 7 v Portsmouth (a) 1-3
Maddison
Williams; Brown, De Gruchy, Conner, Chilton, Richardson, Priestley, Evans, Crosbie, Reeson, Maddison.
Att: 34,598

1956-57
Round 3
Jan 5 v West Ham United (a) 3-5
Conner, Priestley, Rafferty
Williams; Brown, Richardson, Conner, Tucker, Johnston, Priestley, Evans, Rafferty, Reeson, Maddison.
Att: 24,500

1957-58
Round 3
Jan 4 v Sheffield United (a) 1-5
Evans
Williams; Brown, Richardson, Conner, Player, Whitefoot, Scott, Priestley, Rafferty, Evans, Fell.
Att: 27,459

1958-59
Round 3
Jan 10 v Manchester City (h) 2-2
Cullen, Stockin
Barnett; Donovan, Richardson, Welbourne, Jobling, Cockerill, Scott, Cullen, Rafferty, Stockin, Fell.
Att: 14,964

Replay
Jan 24 v Manchester City (a) 2-1
Cockerill 2
Barnett; Donovan, Richardson, Welbourne, Jobling, Cockerill, Scott, Cullen, Rafferty, Stockin, Fell.
Att: 35,000
Round 4
Jan 28 v Nottingham Forest (a) 1-4
Scott
Barnett; Bratley, Richardosn, Welbourne, Jobling, Cockerill, Scott, Cullen, Rafferty, Stockin, Fell.
Att: 39,289

1959-60
Round 1
Nov 14 v Rhyl (a) 2-1
(2 opp og)
Barnett; Keeble, Richardson, Donovan, Joblin, Birbeck, Scott, Cullen, Rafferty, Stockin, Fell.
Att: 4,405
Round 2
Dec 5 v Wrexham (h) 2-3
Rafferty, Hunt
Barnett; Keeble, Richardson, Donovan, Jobling, Birbeck, Scott, Cullen, Rafferty, Hunt, Fell.
Att: 11,472

1960-61
Round 1
Nov 5 v Darlington (a) 0-2
White; Donovan, Keeble, Pearce, Jobling, Welbourne, Marklew, Rafferty, Cullen, Williams, Fell.
Att: 12,357

1961-62
Round 1
Nov 4 v Mansfield Town (a) 2-3
Portwood, Rafferty
Barnett; Donovan, Keeble, Welbourne, Jobling, Cockerill, Scott, Portwood, Rafferty, Cullen, Fidler.
Att: 10,127

1962-63
Round 3
Jan 5 v Leicester City (h) 1-3
Scott (pen)
Barnett; Donovan, Keeble, Rafferty, Jobling, Cockerill, Scott, Portwood, McLean, Foster, Hill.
Att: 15,325

1963-64
Round 3
Jan 25 v Blackburn Rovers (a) 0-4
Wright; Donovan, Taylor, Cockerill, Jobling, Knights, Pennington, Portwood, McLean, Foster, Hill.
Att: 22,887

1964-65
Round 1
Nov 14 v Barrow (a) 1-1
Barratt
Wright; Thompson, Donovan, Cockerill, Clifton, Jobling, Pennington, Barratt, McLean, Foster, Hill.
Att: 3,675
Replay
Nov 17 v Barrow (h) 2-2
Cockerill (pen), Foster
Wright; Thompson, Donovan, Cockerill, Clifton, Jobling, Pennington, Barratt, Young, Foster, Hill.
Att: 4,193
2nd Replay
Nov 23 v Barrow (n) 2-0 (at Old Trafford)
Pennington, Tees
Wright; Thompson, Taylor, Donovan, Clifton, Jobling, Pennington, Cockerill, Tees, Foster, Hill.
Att: 9,292
Round 2
Dec 7 v Stockport County (a) 0-1
Wright; Thompson, Taylor, Cockerill, Jobling, Donovan, Pennington, Tees, Young, Foster, Hill.
Att: 10,163
(First match, 5 December, abandoned through fog)

1965-66
Round 1
Nov 13 v Barrow (a) 2-1
Tees, Foster
Wright; Thompson, Taylor, Morgan, Jobling, Clifton, Collins, Tees, Green, Foster, Hill.
Att: 8,656
Round 2
Dec 4 v Barnsley (a) 1-1
Green (pen)
Wright; Thompson, Taylor, Davidson, Jobling, Clifton, Collins, Tees, Green, Foster, Hill.
Att: 8,112
Replay
Dec 8 v Barnsley (h) 2-0
Tees 2
Wright; Thompson, Taylor, Ross, Jobling, Clifton, Collins, Tees, Green, Foster, Hill.
Att: 10,664
Round 3
Jan 22 v Portsmouth (h) 0-0
Wright; Thompson, Taylor, Ross, Jobling, Cockerill, Collins, Tees, Green, Foster, Hill.
Att: 10,204
Replay
Jan 26 v Portsmouth (a) 3-1
Tees, Green 2
Wright; Thompson, Taylor, Ross, Jobling, Cockerill, Collins, Tees, Green, Foster, Hill.
Att: 23,735
Round 4
Feb 12 v Manchester City (a) 0-2
Wright; Thompson, Taylor, Ross, Jobling, Cockerill, Collins, Tees, Green, Foster, Hill.
Att: 37,918

1966-67
Round 1
Nov 26 v Crewe Alexandra (a) 1-1
Tees
Wainman; Thompson, Taylor, Jobling, Rathbone, Cockerill, Worthington, Tees, Green, Rudd, Martin.
Att: 6,000
Replay
Nov 30 v Crewe Alexandra (h) 0-1
Wainman; Thompson, Taylor, Jobling, Rathbone, Cockerill, Collins, Tees, Green, Rudd, Martin.
Att: 5,414

1967-68
Round 1
Dec 9 v Bradford (Park Avenue) (h) 1-1
Ross (pen)
Wainman; Bloomer, Taylor, Ross, Rathbone, Smith, Housley(Boylen), Wilson, Worthington, Rudd, Collins.
Att: 2,388

Replay
Dec 11 v Bradford (Park Avenue) (a) 1-4
Worthington
Wainman; Bloomer, Wilkinson, Davidson, Jobling, Smith, Wilson, Moore, Worthington, Ross, Taylor.
Att: 5,243

1968-69
Round 1
Nov 16 v Darlington (a) 0-2
Macey; Bloomer, Duncliffe, Worthington, Rathbone, Jobling, Brace. Hickman, Oates, Boylen, Housley.
Att: 6,082

1969-70
Round 1
Nov 15 v Bradford City (a) 1-2
Boylen
Wainman; Worthington, Mobley, Kennedy, Wigginton, Ross, Brace, Oates, Hickman, Boylen, Cockburn.
Att: 8,134

1970-71
Round 1
Nov 21 v Bury (h) 0-1
Wainman; Worthington, Campbell, Gray, Rathbone, Kennedy, Brace, Hickman, Tees, Boylen, Woodward.
Att: 7,191

1971-72
Round 1
Nov 20 v York City (a) 2-4
Thomson (2 pens)
Wainman; Worthington, Smith, Thomson, Rathbone, Gray, Hickman, Lewis, Tees, Boylen, Simpson(Brace).
Att: 6,578

1972-73
Round 1
Nov 18 v Wigan Athletic (h) 2-1
Brace, Boylen
Turner; Campbell, Booth, Hickman, Wigginton, Gray, Brace, Hubbard, Tees(Lewis), Boylen, Gauden.
Att: 11,560
Round 2
Dec 9 v Chesterfield (h) 2-2
Hickman, Gauden
Wainman; Worthington, Campbell, Chatterley, Wigginton, Gray, Brace, Hickman, Hubbard, Boylen, Gauden(Lewis).
Att: 10,646
Replay
Dec 13 v Chesterfield (a) 1-0
Brace
Wainman; Worthington, Booth, Chatterley, Wigginton, Gray, Brace, Hickman, Hubbard, Boylen, Gauden.
Att: 9,658
Round 3
Jan 13 v Preston North End (h) 0-0
Wainman; Worthington, Booth, Chatterley, Wigginton, Gray, Brace Hickman, Hubbard, Boylen, Gauden(Lewis).
Att: 16,000
Replay
Jan 15 v Preston North End (a) 1-0
Gauden
Wainman; Worthington, Booth, Hickman, Wigginton, Gray, Brace, Chatterley, Hubbard, Boylen, Gauden.
Att: 13,175
Round 4
Feb 3 v Coventry City (a) 0-1
Wainman; Worthington, Booth, Chatterley, Wigginton, Gray, Brace, Hickman, Tees, Boylen, Gauden.
Att: 38,104

1973-74
Round 1
Nov 14 v Runcorn (a) 1-0
Barton
Wainman; Beardsley, Booth, Chatterley, Wigginton, Gray, Barton, Fletcher, Hubbard, Czuczman, Sharp.
Att: 3,934
Round 2
Dec 15 v Blyth Spartans (h) 1-1
Hickman
Wainman; Beardsley, Booth, Chatterley, Wigginton, Gray, Barton, Hickman, Hubbard(Lewis), Boylen, Sharp.
Att: 5,724
Replay
Dec 18 v Blyth Spartans (a) 2-0
Hickman, Hubbard
Wainman; Beardsley, Booth, Chatterley, Wigginton, Gray, Barton, Hickman, Hubbard, Boylen, Sharp.
Att: 2,500
Round 3
Jan 5 v Burnley (h) 0-2
Wainman; Beardsley, Booth, Chatterley, Wigginton, Gray, Barton, Hickman, Lewis, Boylen, Sharp (Hubbard).
Att: 14,152

1974-75
Round 1
Nov 23 v Huddersfield Town (h) 1-0
(opp og)
Freeman; Czuczman, Booth, Hickman, Wigginton, Gray, Barton, Hubbard, Lewis, Boylen, Brown.
Att: 5,541
Round 2
Dec 14 v Bury (h) 1-1
Barton
Freeman; Czuczman, Booth, Coyle, Wigginton, Gray, Barton, Hubbard, Lewis, Boylen, Beardsley.
Att: 5,927
Replay
Dec 17 v Bury (a) 1-2
Lewis
Freeman; Czuczman, Booth, Coyle, Wigginton, Gray, Barton, Hubbard, Lewis, Boylen, Beardsley.
Att: 4,546

1975-76
Round 1
Nov 22 v Gateshead (h) 1-3
Booth
Freeman; Marley, Booth, Barton, Young, Gray, Hubbard, Partridge, Brown(Ford), Boylen, Lewis.
Att: 5,120

1976-77
Round 1
Nov 20 v Droylsden (a) 0-0
Wainman; Waters, Cumming, Young, K.Moore, Gray, Partridge, Wigg, Lewis, Boylen, Brolly.
Att: 5,000
Replay
Nov 23 v Droylsden (h) 5-3
Gray, Lewis, Partridge 2 (1 pen), Wigg
Wainman; Waters, Cumming, Young, Gray, K.Moore, Lewis, Partridge, Wigg, Boylen, Brolly.
Att: 4,464
Round 2
Dec 11 v Chester (h) 0-1
Wainman; Cumming, K.Moore, Waters, Young, Gray, Partridge, Donovan, Wigg, Boylen, Brolly(Lewis).
Att: 5,729

1977-78
Round 1
Nov 26 v Workington (a) 2-0
Waters, Liddell
Batch; Mawer, Cumming, Waters, Barker, Hanvey, Ford, Liddell, Drinkell, Partridge, Brolly.
Att: 1,200
Round 2
Dec 17 v Barnsley (h) 2-0
Donovan 2
Wainman; Mawer, K.Moore, Waters, Barker, Hanvey, Brolly, Donovan, Partridge, Liddell, Cumming.
Att: 6,171
Round 3
Jan 7 v Southampton (h) 0-0
Batch; Mawer, K.Moore(Drinkell), Waters, Barker, Hanvey, Cumming, Liddell, Donovan, Partridge, Brolly.
Att: 16,582
Replay
Jan 11 v Southampton (a) 0-0
Batch; Mawer, K.Moore, Waters, Barker, Hanvey, Cumming, Donovan, Partridge, Liddell(Drinkell), Brolly.
Att: 22,462
2nd Replay
Jan 17 v Southampton (n) 1-4 (at Leicester)
Waters
Batch; Mawer, K.Moore, Waters, Barker, Hanvey, Cumming, Partridge, Donovan(Drinkell), Liddell, Brolly.
Att: 11,556

1978-79
Round 1
Nov 25 v Hartlepool United (a) 0-1
Batch; D.Moore, K.Moore, Waters, Barker, Crombie, Ford, Mitchell, Drinkell, Cumming, Brolly(Lester).
Att: 3,584

1979-80
Round 1
Nov 24 v Chesterfield (h) 1-1
Waters
Batch; Stone, K.Moore, Waters, Wigginton, Crombie, Brolly, Ford, Kilmore(Drinkell), Mitchell, Cumming.
Att: 8,406
Replay
Nov 27 v Chesterfield (a) 3-2
K.Moore, Drinkell
Batch; Stone, K.Moore, Waters, Wigginton, Crombie, Brolly, Ford(Kilmore), Drinkell, Mitchell, Cumming.
Att: 7,820
Round 2
Dec 15 v Sheffield United (h) 2-0
Waters, Crombie
Batch; Stone, K.Moore, Waters, Wigginton, Crombie, Ford, Kilmore, Drinkell(Liddell), Mitchell, Brolly.
Att: 14,849
Round 3
Jan 5 v Liverpool (a) 0-5
Batch; D.Moore, Crombie, Waters, Wigginton, Stone, Brolly, Kilmore(Ford), Drinkell, Mitchell, Cumming.
Att: 49,706

1980-81
Round 3
Jan 3 v West Bromwich Albion (a) 0-3
Batch; Stone, Crombie, Waters, Wigginton, K.Moore, Brolly(Ford), Whymark, Drinkell, Mitchell, Cumming.
Att: 22,477

1981-82
Round 3
Jan 5 v Millwall (a) 6-1
Brolly, Whymark, Drinkell 2, Cumming 2
Batch; D.Moore, Crombie, Waters(Ford), Wigginton, K.Moore, Brolly, Whymark, Drinkell, Mitchell, Cumming.
Att: 5,824
Round 4
Jan 23 v Newcastle United (a) 2-1
Kilmore, Drinkell
Batch; D.Moore, Crombie, Stone, K.Moore, Crosby, Ford, Kilmore, Whymark(Drinkell), Mitchell, Beacock.
Att: 25,632
Round 5
Feb 13 v Queen's Park Rangers (a) 1-3
K.Moore
Batch; D.Moore, Crombie, Waters, Wigginton, K.Moore, Brolly, Ford, Drinkell, Mitchell(Beacock), Stone.
Att: 13,334

1982-83
Round 3
Jan 8 v Scunthorpe United (a) 0-0
Batch; D.Moore, Crombie, Waters, Cooper, K.Moore, Ford, Whymark, Drinkell, O'Dell, Cumming.
Att: 11,010
Replay
Jan 11 v Scunthorpe United (h) 2-0
Waters (pen), Ford
Batch; D.Moore, Crombie, Waters, Stone, K.Moore, Ford, Whymark, Drinkell(Wilkinson), O'Dell, Bonnyman.
Att: 9,509
Round 4
Jan 29 v Ipswich Town (a) 0-2
Batch; D.Moore, Crombie, Waters, Cooper, K.Moore, Ford, Whymark(Wilkinson), Drinkell, Bonnyman, Speight.
Att: 21,455

1983-84
Round 3
Jan 7 v Portsmouth (a) 1-2
Drinkell
Batch; Cumming, Crombie, Waters, Nicholl, K.Moore, Ford, Wilkinson, Drinkell, Bonnyman, Emson.
Att: 12,707

1984-85
Round 3
Jan 5 v Notts County (a) 2-2
Ford, Lund
Batch; Seagraves, Agnew, Foley, Crombie, K.Moore, Ford, Wilkinson, Lund, Bonnyman, Cumming (Emson).
Att: 6,202
Replay
Jan 8 v Notts County (h) 4-2
Wilkinson, Lund 3
Batch; Seagraves, Agnew, Foley, Crombie, K.Moore, Ford, Wilkinson, Lund, Bonnyman, Cumming.
Att: 6,743
Round 4
Jan 26 v Watford (h) 1-3
Foley
Grotier; Seagraves(Cumming), Agnew, Foley, Crombie, K.Moore, Ford, Wilkinson, Lund, Bonnyman, Emson.
Att: 12,989

1985-86
Round 3
Jan 4 v Arsenal (h) 3-4
Lund, Lyons, Peake (pen)
Batch; Barratt, Agnew, Peake, Lyons, Crombie, Ford, Lund, Hobson, Hine, Emson(Gilligan).
Att: 12,829

1986-87
Round 3
Jan 10 v Stoke City (h) 1-1
Walsh
Felgate; Burgess, Agnew, Turner, Lyons, K.Moore, Robinson, Walsh, Bonnyman, O'Riordan, Cumming.
Att: 7,367
Replay
Jan 26 v Stoke City (a) 1-1
Moore
Batch; Burgess, Agnew, Turner, Lyons, K.Moore, Robinson, Walsh, Bonnyman(Rawcliffe), O'Riordan, Henshaw.
Att: 14,340
2nd Replay
Jan 28 v Stoke City (a) 0-6
Batch; Burgess, Agnew, Turner, Lyons, K.Moore, Robinson, Walsh, Bonnyman, O'Riordan, Henshaw (Rawcliffe).
Att; 12,087

1987-88
Round 1
Nov 14 v Scarborough (a) 2-1
McGarvey, North
Sherwood; McDermott, Dixon, Turner, Slack, Robinson, Curran(Grocock), Saunders, North, O'Riordan, McGarvey.
Att: 3,764
Round 2
Dec 5 v Halifax Town (h) 0-0
Sherwood; McDermott, Agnew, Turner, D.Moore, Robinson, Grocock, Saunders, North, O'Riordan, McGarvey.
Att: 3,239
Replay
Dec 8 v Halifax Town (a) 0-2
Sherwood; McDermott, Agnew, Turner, Burgess, Robinson, Toale(Grocock), Saunders, North, O'Riordan, McGarvey.
Att: 2,633

1988-89
Round 1
Nov 19 v Wolverhampton Wanderers (h) 1-0
Cockerill
Sherwood; McDermott, Agnew, Tillson, Lever, Cunnington, North, Saunders, O'Kelly, Cockerill, Alexander.
Att: 7,922
Round 2
Dec 10 v Rotherham United (h) 3-2
North, Cunnington, Russell (og)
Sherwood; McDermott, Agnew, Tillson, Lever, Cunnington, North, Saunders, O'Kelly, Cockerill, Alexander.
Att: 5,676
Round 3
Jan 7 v Middlesbrough (a) 2-1
North 2
Reece; McDermott, Agnew, Tillson, Lever, Cunnington, Jobling, Saunders, O'Kelly(North), Cockerill, Alexander.
Att: 19,190
Round 4
Jan 28 v Reading (h) 1-1
North
Reece; McDermott, Agnew, Tillson, Lever, Cunnington, North, Saunders, O'Kelly, Cockerill, Alexander.
Att: 9,401
Replay
Feb 1 v Reading (a) 2-1
Cunnington, Jobling
Reece; McDermott(Jobling), Agnew, Tillson, Lever, Cunnington, North, Saunders, O'Kelly, Cockerill, Alexander.
Att: 8,541
Round 5
Feb 18 v Wimbledon (a) 1-3
Alexander
Sherwood; North, Agnew, Tillson, Lever, Cunnington, Jobling, Saunders, O'Kelly(Dixon), Cockerill, Alexander.
Att: 12,517

Hungarian coach Emilio Berkessy gives some tips to Grimsby's Ray De Gruchy.

YARWOOD SUPPLY CO., LTD.

SELF-DRIVE HIRE. WEDDING CARS. YARWOOD MOTOR SCHOOL.
CARS BOUGHT, SOLD and EXCHANGED. Hire Purchase Arranged.

146 BRADSHAWGATE, BOLTON

TELEPHONE: BOLTON 1262

LESLIE M. SOULSBY

FOR YOUR BETTER SERVICE

REMEMBER "SOULSBY SUITS"

BOLTON WANDERERS

Colours—Shirts: White. Shorts: Blue.

HOPKINSON

2—HARTLE 3—COOPER

4—HENNIN 5—EDWARDS (B.) 6—STANLEY

8—STEVENS 10—DEAKIN

7—HOLDEN 9—LOFTHOUSE 11—HILL

Kick-off 7-30 p.m.

THIS SATURDAY SAY "BUFF" SATURDAY'S GREAT SPORTS PAPER

Referee: Mr. A. JOBLING (Morecambe).

11—FELL 9—CULLEN 7—MARKLEW

10—WILLIAMS 8—RAFFERTY

6—WELBOURNE 5—JOBLING 4—PEARCE

3—KEEBLE 2—DONOVAN

WHITE

GRIMSBY TOWN

Colours—Shirts: Black and White Stripes. Shorts: Red.

Linesmen—Mr. G. Earnshaw (Huddersfield)—Red Flag.
Mr. F. W. Gallop (Halifax)—Yellow Flag.

YOUR PERSONAL TAILOR—45 BRIDGE ST.

MILLS & SEDDON LTD.

MOTOR COACH and TAXI PROPRIETORS—FARNWORTH and RADCLIFFE
Enquiries: 39, ALBERT ROAD, FARNWORTH Tel. 530/1
or WHARF GARAGE, RADCLIFFE. Tel. 2020

YOUR ENQUIRIES ARE SOLICITED FOR SPORTS MEETINGS, DANCES, THEATRES, etc. EARLY BOOKINGS ARE ADVISABLE

Sheffield Wed. v Bolton W. Saturday October 29. Depart 12-30 p.m. Return fare 7/-.

Printed by Pendlebury & Sons Ltd., Victoria Street, Bolton,
for Bolton Wanderers F. & A. Co. Ltd.

Mariners in the Football League Cup

(Milk Cup & Littlewoods Cup)

1960-61
Round 1 Bye
Round 2
Oct 26 v Bolton Wanderers (a) 2-6
Rafferty 2
White; Donovan, Keeble, Pearce, Jobling, Welbourne, Marklew, Rafferty, Cullen, D.Williams, Fell.
Att: 7,992

1961-62
Round 1
Sep 13 v Doncaster Rovers (a) 2-3
Scott (pen), Rafferty
Barnett; Wealthall, Keeble, Welbourne, Jobling, Cockerill, Scott, Portwood, Rafferty, Cullen, Jones.
Att: 4,000

1962-63
Round 2
Sep 25 v Barnsley (a) 2-3
Rafferty, Young
White; Donovan, Keeble, Pearce, Jobling, Knights, Jones, Rafferty, Young, Cullen, Hill.
Att: 5,408

1963-64
Round 2
Sep 25 v Rotherham United (h) 1-3
Young
Wright; Thompson, Taylor, Donovan, Jobling, Cockerill, Pennington, Foster, Young, Tees, Portwood.
Att: 6,829

1964-65
Round 2
Sep 23 v Oldham Athletic (h) 3-1
Young 2, McLean
Wright; Thompson, Keeble, Cockerill, Clifton, Jobling, Pennington, Young, McLean, Foster, Hill.
Att: 5,775
Round 3
Oct 19 v Leicester City (h) 0-5
Wright; Thompson, Lakin, Cockerill, Clifton, Jobling, Pennington, Barrett, McLean, Foster, Hill.
Att: 7,270

1965-66
Round 2
Sep 22 v Crystal Palace (a) 1-0
Green
Wright; Thompson, Taylor, Clifton, Jobling, Cockerill, Ross, Tees, Green, Foster, Hill.
Att: 13,285
Round 3
Oct 13 v Bolton Wanderers (h) 4-2
Ross, Green 2, Foster
Wright; Thompson, Taylor, Ross, Jobling, Cockerill, Collins, Tees, Green, Foster, Hill.
Att: 8,844
Round 4
Nov 3 v Preston North End (h) 4-0
Tees 3, Foster
Wright; Thompson, Taylor, Ross, Jobling, Clifton, Collins, Tees, Green, Foster, Hill.
Att: 10,340
Round 5
Nov 17 v West Ham United (h) 2-2
Tees, Green
Wright; Thompson, Taylor, Davidson, Jobling, Clifton, Collins, Tees, Green, Foster, Hill.
Att: 16,281
Replay
Dec 15 v West Ham United (a) 0-1
Wright; Thompson, Taylor, Davidson, Jobling, Clifton, Collins, Tees, Green, Foster, Hill.
Att: 17,500

1966-67
Round 1
Aug 24 v Barnsley (a) 2-1
Worthington, Hill
Wainman; Bloomer, Taylor, Thompson, Jobling, Cockerill, Fielding, Ross, Worthington, Rudd, Hill.
Att: 2,495
Round 2
Sep 14 v Bradford Park Avenue (a) 0-0
Wainman; Thompson, Taylor, Ross, Jobling, Cockerill, Worthington, Tees, Green, Rudd, Hill.
Att: 3,384
Replay
Sep 21 v Bradford (h) 3-1
Worthington, Tees, Green
Wainman; Thompson, Taylor, Ross, Lancaster, Cockerill, Worthington, Tees, Green, Rudd, Hill.
Att: 6,877
Round 3
Oct 5 v Workington (h) 3-0
Cockerill (pen), Worthington, Hill
Wainman; Bloomer, Taylor, Ross, Jobling, Cockerill, Worthington, Tees, Green, Rudd, Hill.
Att: 6,104
Round 4
Oct 26 v Birmingham City (h) 2-4
Cockerill, Tees
Wainman; Thompson, Taylor, Ross, Jobling, Cockerill, Worthington, Tees, Green(Collins), Rudd, Hill.
Att: 11,298

1967-68
Round 1
Aug 23 v Chesterfield (h) 1-0
Rudd
Wainman; Worthington, Taylor, Ross, Rathbone, Cockerill, Collins, Boylen, Wilson, Rudd, Martin(Smith).
Att: 5,354

Round 2
Sep 12 v Bury (h) 2-2
Worthington, Collins
Wainman; Worthington, Taylor, Ross, Rathbone, Cockerill, Collins, Rudd, Moore, Wilson, Martin.
Att: 7,017
Replay
Sep 19 v Bury (a) 0-2
Wainman; Worthington, Graham, Taylor, Davidson, Rathbone, Cockerill, G.J.Taylor, Rudd, Moore, Smith, Martin.
Att: 6,564

1968-69
Round 1
Aug 14 v Notts County (h) 0-0
Wainman; Worthington, Duncliffe, Hickman, Rathbone, Jobling, Ross, Wilson, Moore, Boylen, Collins.
Att: 4,627
Replay
Aug 21 v Notts County (a) 1-0
Hickman
Wainman; Worthington, Duncliffe, Hickman, Rathbone, Jobling, Ross, Wilson, Moore, Boylen, Collins.
Att: 6,082
Round 2
Sep 4 v Burnley (h) 1-1
Hickman
Wainman; Worthington, Duncliffe, Ross(Bloomer), Rathbone, Jobling, Housley, Hickman, Moore, Davidson, Collins.
Att: 8,762
Replay
Sep 10 v Burnley (a) 0-6
Macey; Bloomer, Duncliffe, Worthington, Rathbone, Jobling, Housley, Collins, Moore, Davidson, Boylen.
Att: 5,926

1969-70
Round 1
Aug 13 v Doncaster Rovers (h) 0-2
Wainman; Worthington, Mobley, Kennedy, Rathbone, Ross, Brace, Fletcher, Walker, Boylen, Oates.
Att: 6,243

1970-71
Round 1
Aug 14 v Lincoln City (a) 1-2
Hickman
Wainman; Worthington, Kirkland, Ross, Rathbone, Kennedy, Woodward, Brace, Hickman, Lewis(Oates), Boylen.
Att: 7,665

1971-72
Round 1
Aug 17 v Doncaster Rovers (h) 4-3
Brace, Lewis, Tees, Woodward
Wainman; Worthington, Campbell, Thomson, Rathbone, Gray, Brace, Lewis, Tees, Boylen, Woodward.
Att: 8,836
Round 2
Sep 7 v Shrewsbury Town (h) 2-1
Brace 2
Wainman; Worthington, Campbell, Thomson, Rathbone, Gray, Brace, Lewis(Simpson), Hickman, Boylen, Woodward.
Att: 13,596
Round 3
Oct 6 v Gillingham (a) 1-1
Brace
Wainman; Worthington, Campbell, Simpson, Rathbone, Gray, Brace, Hickman, Tees, Boylen, Woodward.
Att: 9,038
Replay
Oct 12 v Gillingham (h) 1-0
Boylen (pen)
Wainman; Worthington, Campbell, Simpson, Rathbone, Gray, Brace, Hickman, Tees, Boylen, Woodward(Thomson)
Att: 15,801
Round 4
Oct 26 v Norwich City (h) 1-1
Gray
Wainman; Worthington, Simpson, Thomson, Wigginton, Gray, Brace, Hickman, Tees, Lewis, Boylen.
Att: 22,408
Replay
Nov 3 v Norwich City (a) 1-3
Tees
Wainman; Worthington, Gray, Smith, Wigginton, Rathbone, Brace, Lewis, Tees, Hickman(Thompson), Boylen.
Att: 27,531

1972-73
Round 1
Aug 16 v Barnsley (a) 0-0
Wainman; Worthington, Booth, Wigginton, Rathbone, Gray, Brace(Boylen), Hickman, Tees, Lewis, Gauden.
Att: 4,292
Replay
Aug 22 v Barnsley (h) 2-0
Tees 2
Wainman; Worthington, Booth, Wigginton, Rathbone, Gray, Hickman(Boylen), Tees, Lewis, Gauden.
Att: 12,383
Round 2
Sep 5 v Bury (a) 0-1
Turner; Worthington, Booth, Chatterley, Rathbone, Gray(Wigginton), Brace, Lewis, Hickman, Boylen, Gauden.
Att: 3,096

1973-74
Round 1
Aug 28 v Northampton Town (h) 2-1
Brace, Sharp
Wainman; Beardsley, Booth, Chatterley, Wigginton, Gray, Brace, Barton, Hubbard, Hickman, Sharp.
Att: 7,829
Round 2
Oct 10 v Luton Town (a) 1-1
Chatterley
Wainman; Beardsley, Booth, Chatterley, Wigginton, Gray, Barton, Hickman, Hubbard, Czuczman, Sharp(Lewis).
Att: 9,656
Replay
Oct 16 v Luton Town (h) 0-0
Wainman; Beardsley, Booth, Chatterley, Wigginton, Gray, Barton, Hickman, Hubbard, Czuczman, Sharp(Lewis).
Att: 13,643

2nd Replay
Oct 23 v Luton Town (h) 0-2
Wainman; Beardsley, Booth, Chatterley, Wigginton, Gray, Barton, Hickman, Hubbard, Czuczman, Sharp(Lewis).
Att: 15,365
Town won choice of venue by the toss of a coin.

1974-75
Round 1
Aug 21 v Chesterfield (a) 0-3
Wainman; Beardsley, Booth, Hubbard, Wigginton, Czuczman, Gray, Hickman, Lewis, Lumby(Barton), Boylen.
Att: 4,159

1975-76
Round 1 (1st leg)
Aug 19 v Doncaster Rovers (a) 1-3
Wigg
Freeman*; Czuczman, Booth, Gray, Young, Cumming, Hubbard(Walton), Partridge, Wigg, Boylen, Brown.
*Hubbard went in goal for the injured Freeman, Walton replacing Hubbard in the attack.
Att: 3,218
Round 1 (2nd leg)
Aug 25 v Doncaster Rovers (h) 0-0 (agg 1-3)
Wainman; Czuczman, Booth, Gray, Young, Barton, Hubbard, Partridge, Wigg, Boylen, Lewis.
Att: 5,552

1976-77
Round 1 (1st leg)
Aug 14 v Sheffield Wednesday (h) 0-3
Wainman; Cumming, K.Moore, Young, Govier, Booth, Ford, Waters, Partridge, Gray, Lewis.
Att: 6,222
Round 1 (2nd leg)
Aug 18 v Sheffield Wednesday (a) 0-0 (agg 0-3)
Wainman; Cumming, K.Moore, Young, Blant, Govier, Oldridge, Waters(Ford), Partridge, Booth, Lewis.
Att: 10,207

1977-78
Round 1 (1st leg)
Aug 13 v Hartlepool United (h) 3-0
Waters (3 inc. a pen)
Wainman; Cooper, K.Moore, Waters, Barker, Partridge, Donovan, Drinkell, Liddell, Boylen, Brolly.
Att: 2,318
Round 1 (2nd leg)
Aug 16 v Hartlepool United (a) 2-1 (agg 5-1)
Drinkell, Donovan
Wainman; Cooper, K.Moore, Waters, Barker, Partridge, Brolly, Liddell, Drinkell, Donovan, Boyden.
Att: 2,733
Round 2
Aug 30 v Watford (h) 1-2
Donovan
Wainman; Cooper, K.Moore, Waters, Barker, Partridge, Brolly, Liddell, Drinkell(Ford), Donovan, Cumming.
Att: 4,345

1978-79
Round 1 (1st leg)
Aug 12 v York City (h) 2-0
Waters (pen), Lester
Batch; Mawer, K.Moore, Waters, Barker, Crombie, Ford, Donovan, Cumming, Lester, Mitchell.
Att: 3,051
Round 1 (2nd leg)
Aug 15 v York City (a) 3-0 (agg 5-0)
Donovan, Mitchell, Cumming
Batch; Mawer, K.Moore, Waters, Barker, Crombie, Ford, Donovan, Lester(Liddell), Mitchell, Cumming.
Att: 2,668
Round 2
Aug 29 v Manchester City (a) 0-2
Batch; Mawer, K.Moore, Waters, Barker, Crombie, Ford, Donovan, Lester, Mitchell, Cumming(Liddell).
Att: 21,481

1979-80
Round 1 (1st leg)
Aug 1 v Scunthorpe United (h) 2-0
Ford 2
Batch; D.Moore, K.Moore, Waters, Wigginton, Stone, Brolly, Ford, Liddell, Mitchell, Cumming(Drinkell).
Att: 5,083
Round 1 (2nd leg)
Aug 14 v Scunthorpe United (a) 0-0 (agg 2-0)
Batch; D.Moore, K.Moore, Waters, Wigginton, Stone, Ford, Liddell, Drinkell, Mitchell, Brolly.
Att: 3,908
Round 2 (1st leg)
Aug 28 v Huddersfield Town (h) 1-0
Cumming
Batch; D.Moore, K.Moore, Waters, Wigginton, Stone, Brolly, Ford, Liddell, Mitchell, Cumming.
Att: 7,803
Round 2 (2nd leg)
Sep 4 v Huddersfield Town (a) 4-1 (agg 5-1)
Lester, Ford, Cumming 2
Batch; D.Moore, K.Moore, Waters(Lester), Wigginton, Stone, Brolly, Ford, Liddell, Mitchell, Cumming.
Att: 5,550
Round 3
Sep 25 v Notts County (h) 3-1
Ford, Liddell, Cumming
Batch; D.Moore, K.Moore, Waters, Wigginton, Crombie, Brolly, Ford, Liddell(Drinkell), Mitchell, Cumming.
Att: 11,881
Round 4
Oct 30 v Everton (h) 2-1
Brolly 2
Batch; Stone, K.Moore, Waters, Wigginton, Crombie, Brolly, Ford, Drinkell, Mitchell, Cumming.
Att: 22,043
Round 5
Dec 4 v Wolverhampton Wanderers (h) 0-0
Batch; Stone, K.Moore, Waters, Wigginton, Crombie, Brolly, Ford, Drinkell, Mitchell, Cumming.
Att: 23,115
Replay
Dec 11 v Wolverhampton Wanderers (a) 1-1
(opp og)
Batch; Stone, K.Moore, Waters, Wigginton, Crombie, Ford, Liddell, Drinkell, Mitchell, Brolly.
Att: 28,455
2nd Replay
Dec 18 v Wolverhampton Wanderers (n) 0-2 (at the Baseball Ground, Derby)
Batch; Stone, K.Moore, Waters, Wigginton, Crombie, Brolly, Ford(Liddell), Drinkell, Mitchell.
Att: 16,475

1980-81
Round 1 (1st leg)
Aug 9 v Notts County (h) 1-0
Waters
Batch; Stone, K.Moore, Waters, Wigginton, Crombie, Brolly, Ford, Drinkell, Mitchell, Cumming.
Att: 7,402
Round 1 (2nd leg)
Aug 12 v Notts County (a) 0-3 (agg 1-3)
Batch; Stone, K.Moore, Waters, Wigginton, Crombie, Brolly, Ford, Drinkell, Mitchell, Cumming.
Att: 4,718

1981-82
Round 2 (1st leg)
Oct 6 v Watford (h) 1-0
K.Moore
Batch; D.Moore, Crombie, Waters, Wigginton, K.Moore, Brolly, Whymark, Drinkell, Mitchell, Cumming(Ford).
Att: 7,044
Round 2 (2nd leg)
Oct 27 v Watford (a) 1-3 (agg 2-3)
Whymark
Batch; Cumming, Crombie, Waters, Wigginton, K.Moore, Brolly, Whymark, Drinkell, Mitchell, Kilmore(O'Dell).
Att: 13,213

1982-83
Round 1 (1st leg)
Aug 31 v Scunthorpe United (a) 2-1
Drinkell 2
Batch; D.Moore, Crombie, Waters, Cooper, K.Moore, Ford, Kilmore, Drinkell, Bonnyman, Whymark.
Att: 2,620
Round 1 (2nd leg)
Sep 14 v Scunthorpe United (h) 0-0 (agg 2-1)
Batch; Speight(Cumming), Crosby, Waters, Cooper, K.Moore, Ford, Kilmore, Drinkell, Bonnyman, Whymark.
Att: 3,347
Round 2 (1st leg)
Oct 12 v Sheffield United (h) 3-3
Drinkell 3
Grotier; D.Moore, Crosby, Waters, Cooper, K.Moore, Cumming, Kilmore, Drinkell, Bonnyman, Speight.
Att: 5,295
Round 2 (2nd leg)
Oct 26 v Sheffield United (a) 1-5 (agg 4-8)
K.Moore
Grotier; D.Moore, Crosby, Waters, Cooper(O'Dell), K.Moore, Cumming, Whymark, Drinkell, Stone, Ford.
Att: 13,367

1983-84
Round 1 (1st leg)
Aug 30 v York City (a) 1-2
Wilkinson
Batch; Cumming, Crombie, Waters, Nicholl, K.Moore, Ford, Wilkinson, Drinkell, Bonnyman, Emson.
Att: 3,505
Round 1 (2nd leg)
Sep 13 v York City (h) 2-0 (agg 3-2)
Drinkell 2
Batch; Cooper(Cumming), Crombie, Waters, Nicholl, K.Moore, Ford, Wilkinson, Drinkell, Speight, Emson.
Att: 3,529
Round 2 (1st leg)
Oct 4 v Coventry City (h) 0-0
Batch; Cumming, Crombie, Waters, Nicholl, K.Moore, Ford, Wilkinson, Drinkell, Henshaw, Emson.
Att: 6,088
Round 2 (2nd leg)
Oct 25 v Coventry City (a) 1-2 (agg 1-2)
Wilkinson
Batch; Cumming, Crombie, Waters, Nicholl, K.Moore, Ford, Wilkinson, Drinkell, Bonnyman, Emson.
Att: 8,705

1984-85
Round 2 (1st leg)
Sep 25 v Barnsley (h) 3-0
K.Moore, Wilkinson, Bonnyman (pen)
Batch; Seagraves, Crombie, Foley, Nicholl, K.Moore, Ford, Wilkinson, Lund, Bonnyman, Emson.
Att: 3,577
Round 2 (2nd leg)
Oct 9 v Barnsley (a) 1-1 (agg 4-1)
Foley
Batch; Seagraves, Crombie, Foley, Nicholl, K.Moore, Ford, Wilkinson, Lund(Rowbotham), Bonnyman, Emson.
Att: 5,578
Round 3
Oct 30 v Rotherham United (a) 0-0
Batch; Seagraves, Agnew, Foley, Crombie, K.Moore, Ford, Wilkinson, Lund, Bonnyman, Emson.
Att: 8,413
Replay
Nov 6 v Rotherham United (h) 6-1
Foley, Ford, Wilkinson, Lund, Bonnyman, Emson
Batch; Seagraves, Crombie, Foley, Nicholl, K.Moore, Ford, Wilkinson(Drinkell), Lund, Bonnyman, Emson.
Att: 7,649
Round 4
Nov 20 v Everton (a) 1-0
Wilkinson
Batch; Seagraves, Crombie, Foley(Drinkell), Nicholl, K.Moore, Ford, Wilkinson, Lund, Bonnyman, Emson.
Att: 26,298
Round 5
Jan 16 v Norwich City (h) 0-1
Batch; Seagraves, Agnew, Foley(Henshaw), Crombie, K.Moore, Ford, Wilkinson, Lund, Bonnyman, Emson.
Att: 15,050

1985-86
Round 2 (1st leg)
Sep 24 v York City (h) 1-1
Gilligan
Felgate; Barratt, Agnew, Peake, A.Moore, K.Moore, Ford, Gilligan, Hobson, Bonnyman, Emson.
Att: 2,908
Round 2 (2nd leg)
Oct 8 v York City (a) 3-2 (agg 4-3)
Hobson 2, Gilligan
Felgate; Barratt, Crombie, Peake, A.Moore, K.Moore, Ford, Gilligan, Hobson, Hine, Cumming(Lund).
Att: 5,030
Round 3
Oct 29 v Ipswich Town (h) 0-2
Batch; Barratt, Crombie, Peake, A.Moore, K.Moore, Ford, Gilligan(Lund), Hobson, Bonnyman, Emson.
Att: 6,684

1986-87
Round 1 (1st leg)
Sep 2 v Carlisle United (a) 0-1
Batch; Burgess, Cumming, Peake, A.Moore, K.Moore, Robinson(Henshaw), Walsh(Horwood), Hobson, O'Riordan, Turner.
Att: 2,861
Round 1 (2nd leg)
Sep 9 v Carlisle United (h) 2-0 (agg 2-1)
Walsh 2
Batch; Burgess, Crombie, Peake, Lyons, K.Moore, Henshaw, Walsh, Hobson, O'Riordan, Turner.
Att: 3,902
Round 2 (1st leg)
Sep 23 v Hull City (a) 0-1
Batch; Burgess, Agnew, Straw, Lyons, K.Moore(Cumming), Henshaw, Walsh, Hobson, O'Riordan, Turner.
Att: 5,115
Round 2 (2nd leg)
Oct 7 v Hull City (h) 1-1 (agg 1-2)
Walsh
Batch; Burgess, Cumming, Robinson, Lyons, Crombie, Henshaw, Walsh, Hobson(Rawcliffe), O'Riordan, Turner.
Att: 5,471

1987-88
Round 1 (1st leg)
Aug 18 v Darlington (h) 3-2
Walsh, McGarvey, North
Sherwood; McDermott, Agnew, Turner, Slack, Burgess, Robinson, North, Walsh, O'Riordan, McGarvey.
Att: 2,248
Round 2 (2nd leg)
Aug 26 v Darlington (a) 1-2 (aet) (agg 4-4)
North
Sherwood; Toale, Agnew, Turner, Slack, Burgess, Robinson, Walsh(Saunders), North, O'Riordan, McGarvey.
Att: 1,237
Score at 90 minutes 1-2 Darlington go through on away goals rule.

1988-89
Round 1 (1st leg)
Aug 30 v Rotherham United (a) 0-1
Reece; Dixon(McGarvey), Agnew, Williams, Tillson, Cunnington, Jobling, McDermott, O'Kelly, Stoutt, North.
Att: 2,517
Round 1 (2nd leg)
Sep 6 v Rotherham United (a) 0-1 (agg 0-2)
Reece; Lever, Agnew, Williams, Tillson, Cunnington, Jobling, North, O'Kelly, Stoutt(McDermott), Alexander(Saunders).
Att: 3,381

Ian Walsh (left) and Scott McGarvey scored against Darlington in the 1987-8 Milk Cup but the Quakers eventually went through on away goals.

Grimsby in the Football League Trophy

1982-83
Group Match
Aug 14 v Sheffield United (a) 3-1
Dinkell 3
Batch; D.Moore, Crombie, Waters, Cooper, K.Moore, Ford(Steeples), Whymark, Drinkell, Bonnyman(Beacock), Speight.
Att: 5,831
Group Match
Aug 18 v Lincoln City (a) 1-2
Drinkell
Batch; D.Moore, Crosby, Waters, Cooper, K.Moore, Kilmore, Whymark(Ford), Drinkell, Bonnyman, Crombie.
Att: 1,430
Group Match
Aug 21 v Scunthorpe United (h) 2-0
K.Moore, Waters (pen)
Batch; D.Moore, Crombie, Waters, Cooper, K.Moore, Ford(Cumming), Whymark(Kilmore), Drinkell, Bonnyman, Speight.
Att: 2,334

Sherpa Van Trophy

1987-88
Preliminary Round
Oct 13 v Scunthorpe United (a) 0-2
Sherwood; Toale, Stephenson, Turner, Slack, Burgess, Robinson, Walsh, North(Rawcliffe), Dixon, McGarvey(Grocock).
Att: 1,710
Preliminary Round
Oct 27 v Halifax Town (h) 2-1
Grocock, McGarvey
Sherwood; Rawcliffe, Agnew(Dixon), Grocock, Slack, Burgess, Watson, Robinson, North(Saunders), O'Riordan, McGarvey.
Att: 1,316
Preliminary Round
Play-Off
Dec 15 v Scunthorpe United (h) 1-2
Turner
Sherwood; McDermott, Agnew, Turner, Curran, Robinson, Toale, Saunders, North(Watson), O'Riordan, McGarvey.
Att: 970

1988-89
Preliminary Group Match
Nov 29 v Rotherham United (h) 1-0
Saunders
Reece; McDermott(Jobling), Agnew, Tillson, Lever, Cunnington, North, Saunders, O'Kelly, Cockerill, Alexander.
Att: 1,192
Preliminary Group Match
Dec 6 v Doncaster Rovers (a) 1-1
Saunders
Sherwood; McDermott, Agnew, Watson, Lever, Cunnington(Jobling), North, Saunders, O'Kelly, Cockerill, Alexander.
Att: 681
1st Round
Jan 17 v Huddersfield Town (h) 1-3
North
Reece; McDermott, Agnew, Tillson, Lever(Jobling), Cunnington, Watson(O'Kelly), Saunders, North, Cockerill, Alexander.
Att: 2,116

The Full Members' Cup

1985-86
Round 1 (1st leg)
Sep 17 v Sunderland (h) 3-2
Bonnyman, Hobson 2
Batch; Barratt(Cumming), Agnew, Hine, A.Moore, Crombie, Ford, Lund, Gilligan(Emson), Bonnyman, Hobson.
Att: 2,435
Round 1 (2nd leg)
Oct 2 v Sunderland (a) 1-2 (agg 4-4 Sunderland won 3-2 on penalties.)
Lund
Batch; Barratt, Agnew, Peake, A.Moore, K.Moore, Ford, Lund, Gilligan, Hine, Emson.
Att: 11,571

1986-87
Round 1
Oct 21 v Hull City (h) 1-3
Walsh
Batch; Burgess, Agnew, Straw, Bonnyman, K.Moore, Henshaw(Horwood), Walsh, Rawcliffe, O'Riordan, Turner(Robinson).
Att: 2,460

The Football League Group Cup

1981-82
Group Match
Aug 15 v Chesterfield (h) 1-0
Waters
Batch; Stone, Crombie, Waters, Wigginton, Czuczman, Brolly, Whymark(Kilmore), Drinkell, Mitchell, Cumming(Ward).
Att: 1,772

Action from the Group Cup match against Chesterfield on 15 August 1981.

Group Match
Aug 18 v Sheffield United (h) 2-0
Whymark, Mitchell
Batch; Stone, Crombie, Waters, Wigginton, Czuczman(D.Moore), Brolly, Whymark, Drinkell(Ford), Mitchell, Kilmore.
Att: 2,314
Group Match
Aug 22 v Doncaster Rovers (a) 2-0
K.Moore, Brolly
Batch; Stone, Crombie, Waters, Wigginton, K.Moore, Brolly(Czuczman), Whymark, Drinkell, Mitchell, Kilmore.
Att: 4,097

Quarter-Final
Dec 8 v Newport County (a) 2-0
Beacock, Drinkell
Batch; D.Moore, Crombie, Waters, Wigginton, K.Moore, Brolly, Whymark(Ward), Drinkell, Beacock(Mitchell), Cumming.
Att: 2,206
Semi-Final
Jan 19 v Shrewsbury Town (h) 2-1
Kilmore 2
Batch; D.Moore, Crombie, Waters(Beacock), Czuczman, K.Moore, Stone, Kilmore, Whymark, Mitchell, Ford.
Att: 3,253
Final
Apr 6 v Wimbledon (h) 3-2
Cumming, Ford 2
Batch(Grotier); Waters, Crosby, O'Dell, D.Moore, K.Moore, Steeples(Brolly), Ford, Whymark, Mitchell, Cumming.
Att: 3,423

The Anglo-Scottish Trophy

1980-81
Group Match
Jul 28 v Hull City (a) 0-1
Batch; Stone, K.Moore(Crosby), Waters, Wigginton, Crombie, Brolly, Ford, Drinkell(Liddell), Mitchell, Cumming.
Att: 4,848
Group Match
Aug 2 v Chesterfield (h) 3-3
Brolly, Drinkell, Ford
Batch; Stone, K.Moore, Waters, Wigginton, Crombie, Brolly, Ford, Drinkell, Mitchell, Cumming.
Att: 3,148
Group Match
Aug 5 v Sheffield United (a) 1-0
Waters
Batch; Stone, Cumming, Waters, Wigginton, Crombie, Brolly, Ford, Drinkell, Mitchell, Liddell(Kilmore).
Att: 4,921

Mariners in the Lincolnshire Cup

1881-82
Round 1
Jan 14 v Brigg Ancholme (a) 6-3
Atkinson 2, Marshall 2, Unknown 2
Round 2
Feb 18 v Louth District (a) 2-2
Earle, Atkinson
Replay
Feb 25 v Louth District (h) 3-0
Scorers unknown
Semi-final
Mar 25 v Brigg Town (a) 0-5

1882-83
Round 1
Nov 11 v Brigg Britannia (h) 2-1
Monument, Tonge
Round 2
Jan 6 v Manchester Sheffield & Lincolnshire Railway Steamship Dep. (h) 2-1
Read, Marshall
Semi-final
Mar 17 v Brigg Town (a) 0-3

1883-84
Round 1
Nov 25 v Market Rasen (h) 10-1
Noble 2, Monument, T.Atkinson 3, G.Atkinson 2, Garnham 2
Round 2
Jan 5 v Brigg Town (a) 3-1
Garnham 2, Monument
Round 3
Mar 8 v Barton (h) 2-0
Noble, France
Semi-final
Mar 22 v Gainsborough Trinity (h) 4-2
Garnham, France, T.Atkinson, Monument
Final
Apr 5 v Spilsby (at Brigg) 2-4
Noble, Monument

1884-85
Round 1
Oct 1 v Manchester Sheffield & Lincolnshire Railway Steamship Dep. (h) 3-1
Read, 2 Unknown
(the MS & LR team left the field before full time. Result stood)
Round 2
Nov 29 v Barton (h) 2-0
Noble, Raynes
Round 3
Jan 10 v Louth and District (a) 2-1
Monument, Garnham
Semi-final
Jan 31 v Gainsborough Trinity (a) 1-2
Garnham

1885-86
Round 1
Nov 7 v Grantham Victoria (h) 2-0
H.Atkinson, Seal
Round 2
Nov 28 v Lincoln Rangers (h) 5-0
Seal 3, H.Atkinson, (opp og)
Round 3
Jan 23 v Grantham Town (a) 3-1
Monument, Garnham, H.Atkinson
Semi-final
Mar 13 v Lincoln City (h) 1-1
Monument
Lincoln refused to play extra-time. Grimsby were awarded the match.
Final
Apr 3 v Lincoln Lindum (at Grantham) 2-0
H.Atkinson 2
(Trophy withheld)

1886-87
Round 1
Nov 27 v Lincoln St Swithin's (h) 15-0
Seal 3, Pearson 3, H.Atkinson 2, Garnham 2, H.Taylor 2, C.Atkinson, Hall, J.H.Taylor
Round 2
Jan 19 v Morton St Paul's (n) 19-0
Scorers unknown
(on Grimsby Rangers Ground)
Round 3
Bye
Round 4
Feb 19 v Grantham Town (h) 5-1
Seal 2, Monument, Pearson, Chapman
Semi-final
Mar 12 v Brigg Town (h) 4-0
Monument 3, Seal
Final
Apr 2 v Lincoln City (n) 2-2
Chapman, H.Atkinson
(at Gainsborough)
Replay
Apr 23 v Lincoln City (n) 0-2
(at Gainsborough)

1887-88
Round 1
Oct 29 v Lincoln Rangers (h) 10-0
Soames 3, Seal 2, Monument 2, Smith, J.Chapman, 1 Unknown
Round 2
Dec 8 v Horncastle United (a) 2-1
McBeth, H.Atkinson

Round 3
Jan 14 v Gainsborough Trinity (h) 5-0
Lee 2, H.Atkinson, Soames, Monument
Semi-final
Feb 18 v Cleethorpes Town (a) 3-0
H.Atkinson 2, Lee
Grimsby Town resigned from the Lincolnshire FA and the final was not played.

1888-89
Round 1
Jan 26 v Grantham Town (h) 2-1
J.Taylor, Lundie

Semi-final
Mar 2 v Lincoln Ramblers (a) 5-0
McBeth 2, Smith, Riddoch, Hunt
Final
Apr 13 v Grantham Rovers (n) 3-1
Hunt 2, Doyle
(at Boston)

1889-90
Grimsby Town scratched from the competition.

1890-91
Semi-final
Feb 14 v Gainsborough Trinity (h) 1-2
Reid

Grimsby Town did not participate for the next five seasons.

1896-97
Round 1
Mar 16 v Gainsborough Trinity (h) 2-1
McCairns 2
Semi-final
Apr 1 v Grimsby All Saints (?) 2-1
Scorers unknown
Final
Apr 29 v Lincoln City (h) 6-2
Fletcher 3, Gray, McCairns, Higgins

1897-98
Round 1
Feb 19 v Grismby All Saints (h) 4-0
McCairns 2, Gray, Goldie
Match declared void as Town included an ineligible player.
Replay
Mar 28 v Grimsby All Saints (?) 7-0
Emmerson 2, Rogers, McCairns, 2 Unknown, Leaming (og)
Semi-final
Apr 13 v Lincoln Adelaide (a) 0-4

1898-99
Round 2
Mar 1 v Horncastle United (a) 6-1
Scorers unknown
Semi-final
Apr 19 v Grimsby All Saints (h) 5-2
Cockshutt 3, Jenkinson, Richards
Final
Apr 27 v Gainsborough Trinity (n) 4-0
Scorers unknown
(at Lincoln)

1899-1900
Semi-final
Apr 5 v Gainsborough Trinity (h) 0-0
Replay
Apr 19 v Gainsborough Trinity (h) 4-1
Hemingfield 2, Ratcliffe 2
Final
Apr 24 v Lincoln Adelaide (h) 6-4
Hemingfield 2, Ratcliffe 2, Griffiths, Richards

1900-01
Semi-final
Mar 21 v Gainsborough Trinity (h) 3-1
Fletcher, Mellor, Richards
Final
Apr 29 v Lincoln City (a) 1-0
Watkins

1901-02
Semi-final
Apr 7 v Lincoln City (a) 1-1
Fletcher
Replay
Apr 17 v Lincoln City (h) 3-0
Dean, Ronaldson, Hemingfield
Final
Apr 24 v Gainsborough Trinity (h) 1-0
Fletcher

1902-03
Semi-final
Mar 5 v Gainsborough Trinity (h) 2-2
Gray, Mountain
Replay
Mar 30 v Gainsborough Trinity (a) 2-1
Hall, 1 unknown
Final
Apr 29 v Lincoln City (a) 1-1
Scorer unknown
Replay
Apr 30 v Lincoln City (h) 3-2
Wilkinson 2, Rouse

1903-04
Semi-final
Mar 16 v Lincoln City (a) 1-2
Scorer unknown

1904-05
Semi-final
Mar 30 v Grimsby Rangers (h) 2-2
Baker, Reynolds
Replay
Apr 11 v Grimsby Rangers (a) 2-1
Baker 2
Final
Apr 26 v Gainsborough Trinity (a) 0-1

1905-06
Semi-final
Mar 28 v Lincoln City (h) 1-0
Padley
Final
Apr 24 v Gainsborough Trinity (h) 4-1
Bisley, Robinson, Baker, Hooper

1906-07
Semi-final
Feb 2 v Lincoln Adelaide (h) 6-1
R.Morris 3, Burnett, Rodger, Hooper
Final
Apr 17 v Gainsborough Trinity (a) 0-1

1908-09
Semi-final
Nov 13 v Gainsborough Trinity (a) 0-3

1908-09
Semi-final
Sep 29 v Gainsborough Trinity (h) 5-0
Leonard 2, Davidson, Coxon, Bradley

Final
Dec 28 v Lincoln City (a) 2-1
Appleyard, Satterthwaite

1909-10
Semi-final
Nov 24 v Gainsborough Trinity (a) 1-0
Blackburn
Final
Feb 5 v Lincoln City (a) 0-4

1910-11
Semi-final
Mar 7 v Lincoln City (h) 2-1
Springthorpe, Hubbard
Final
Mar 21 v Gainsborough Trinity (h) 0-1

1911-12
Semi-final
Jan 13 v Grimsby Rovers (h) 6-0
Seeburg 3, Hubbard 2, Rippon
Final
Mar 6 v Lincoln City (h) 0-1

Semi-final
Mar 8 v Boston United (a) 7-1
Andrews 3, Mayson 2, Gordon, Duncan
Final
Apr 28 v Lincoln City (a) 3-2
Rippon 3

1913-14
Semi-final
Jan 31 v Lincoln City (a) 1-2

1919-20
Semi-final
Mar 29 v Gainsborough Trinity (a) 4-0
Storer 4
Final
May 3 v Lincoln City (a) 0-7

1920-21
Semi-final
Apr 6 v Gainsborough Trinity (a) 0-0
Replay
Apr 12 v Gainsborough Trinity (h) 1-0
Smith
Final
Apr 27 v Lincoln City (h) 4-1
Smith, McAuley, Collier, Deacey

1921-22
Semi-final
Mar 16 v Lincoln City (a) 2-2
Carmichael, Miller
Replay
Mar 22 v Lincoln City (h) 0-1

1922-23
Round 4
Jan 11 v Grimsby Rovers (h) 3-0
J.Miller 3
Semi-final
Mar 15 v Boston United (a) 1-0
J.Miller
Final
Apr 30 v Lincoln City (h) 2-1
Carmichael 2

1923-24
Round 4
Feb 7 v Scunthorpe United (h) 2-0
Carmichael 2
Semi-final
Mar 6 v Cleethorpes Town (h) 6-0
Casson 4, Marshall, Dent
Final
Apr 14 v Lincoln City (a) 0-1

1924-25
Round 4
Jan 22 v Grantham Town (a) 1-1
Thain
Replay
Feb 19 v Grantham Town (h) 6-1
Carmichael 4, Burley 2
Semi-final
Mar 19 v Scunthorpe United (h) 2-2
Carmichael 2
Replay
Apr 2 v Scunthorpe United (h) 1-1
Marshall
2nd Replay
Apr 20 v Scunthorpe United (a) 3-0
Carmichael 2, Marshall
Final
Apr 23 v Boston United (a) 1-0
Carmichael

1925-26
Round 4
Jan 12 v Scunthorpe United (h) 6-3
Robson 3, McKenna, Carmichael, Devan
Semi-final
Jan 26 v Lincoln City (h) 0-1

1926-27
Round 3
Feb 1 v Lincoln City (h) 1-3
Devan

1927-28
Round 3
Jan 24 v Gainsborough Trinity (h) 2-0
Coglin, Powell
Semi-final
Feb 28 v Scunthorpe United (h) 7-1
Robson 6, Prior
Final
Apr 24 v Lincoln City (a) 3-1
Robson 3

1928-29
Semi-final
Mar 12 v Gainsborough Trinty (h) 5-0
Coglin 2, Twell, Marshall, Prior
Final
May 11 v Lincoln City (a) 1-0
Robson

1929-30
Semi-final
Feb 25 v Gainsborough Trinty (h) 5-1
Glover 3, Prior, Coleman
Final
May 10 v Lincoln City (h) 7-1
Robson 6, Marshall

1930-31
Semi-final
Mar 14 v Gainsborough Trinity (h) 4-1
Coleman 2, Bestall, Hall
Final
May 9 v Lincoln City (a) 2-2
Glover, Prior
Replay
Sep 22 v Lincoln City (h) 0-1

1931-32
Semi-final
Mar 15 v Gainsborough Trinity (h) 7-1
Chalmers 3, Moralee 2, Craven 2
Final
May 14 v Lincoln City (a) 1-1
Holmes
Replay
Sep 13 v Lincoln City (h) 3-4
Glover 2, Dodsworth

1932-33
Semi-final
Mar 16 v Scunthorpe United (h) 4-1
Moralee 2, Wilson, Glover
Final
Apr 25 v Lincoln City (h) 3-1
Craven 2, Glover

1933-34
Semi-final
Mar 20 v Scunthorpe United (h) 7-1
Craven 3, Glover 2, Jennings, Young (og)
Final
Apr 26 v Lincoln City (h) 2-2
Glover, Craven
Replay
May 3 v Lincoln City (a) 1-2
Holmes

1934-35
Final
Sep 24 v Lincoln City (a) 0-5

1935-36
Final
Sep 24 v Lincoln City (h) 4-0
Craven 2, Jennings, Moulson (og)

1936-37
Final
Sep 23 v Lincoln City (a) 6-1
Tomlinson 3, Lewis 2, Hinchcliffe

1937-38
Final
Sep 28 v Lincoln City (h) 4-1
Bestall 2, Hinchcliffe, Tomlinson

1938-39
Withdrew

1945-46
Final
May 1 v Lincoln City (h) 1-1
N.Moore
Replay
May 11 v Lincoln City (a) 1-4
Vincent

1946-47
Final
May 21 v Lincoln City (a) 2-1
Clifton 2

1947-48
Final
May 8 v Lincoln City (h) 0-2

1949-50
Final
May 14 v Lincoln City (a) 1-2
Cairns

1949-50
Final
May 13 v Lincoln City (h) 2-1
Cairns 2

1950-51
Final
May 19 v Lincoln City (a) 0-3

1951-52
Semi-final
Mar 31 v Scunthorpe United (a) 0-1

1952-53
Semi-final
Apr 15 v Lincoln City (a) 3-0
Maddison 2, Lord
Final
May 9 v Scunthorpe United (h) 1-0
Hernon

1953-54
Final
May 8 v Scunthorpe United (a) 2-4
Wright, Smith

1954-55
Semi-final
Oct 19 v Lincoln City (a) 0-2

1955-56
Semi-final
Oct 18 v Lincoln City (h) 1-2
Evans

1956-57
Semi-final
Oct 16 v Boston United (h) 0-2

1957-58
Semi-final
Oct 8 v Boston United (a) 3-1
Rafferty, Evans, Reeson

Final
May 5 v Scunthorpe United (h) 2-3
Rafferty 2

1958-59
Semi-final
Oct 9 v Scunthorpe United (a) 1-2
Fell

1959-60
Semi-final
Oct 27 v Boston United (a) 1-2
Rafferty

1960-61
Semi-final
Nov 7 v Lincoln City (h) 8-3
Rafferty 6, Scott, Williams
Final
Mar 6 v Scunthorpe United (h) 0-4

1961-62
Semi-final
Oct 17 v Scunthorpe United (h) 0-1

1962-63
Not contested for.

1963-64
Semi-final
Apr 28 v Scunthorpe United (a) 0-3

1964-65
No evidence of participation found.

1965-66
Semi-final
Mar 29 v Lincoln City (a) 1-1
Green
No replay date could be agreed. Lincoln City went through on toss of a coin.

1966-67
Semi-final
Nov 7 v Scunthorpe United (h) 2-3
Collins, Worthington

1967-68
Semi-final
Nov 7 v Gainsborough Trinity (h) 3-1
Collins, Boylen, Knights (og)
Final
Mar 26 v Lincoln City (a) 3-2
Boylen, Collins, Wilson

1968-69
Semi-final
Oct 23 v Lincoln City (h) 0-0
Replay
Oct 29 v Lincoln City (a) 1-1 (aet)
Rathbone
No trace of 2nd replay found.

1969-70
Round 1
Sep 22 v Gainsborough Trinity (a) 2-3
Fletcher, Oates

1970-71
Semi-final
Mar 1 v Lincoln City (h) 3-1
Brace 2, Lewis
Final
May 11 v Gainsborough Trinity (a) 0-1

1971-72
Semi-final
May 3 v Grantham (a) 1-2
Rathbone

1972-73
Round 1
Oct 17 v Grantham (h) 3-2
Lewis, Brace, Gauden
Semi-final
Dec 20 v Gainsborough Trinity (h) 1-0
Chatterley
Final
May 1 v Boston United (h) 2-1
Brace, Hubbard

1973-74
Quarter-final
May 7 v Scunthorpe United (a) 1-2
Hubbard

1974-75
Quarter-final
Jan 7 v Grantham (h) 2-1
Barton, Lewis
Semi-final
Mar 11 v Gainsborough Trinity (h) 2-0
Hubbard, Boylen
Final
Apr 29 v Lincoln City (a) 0-2

1975-76
Quarter-final
Aug 2 v Lincoln City (h) 3-2
Wigg 3
Semi-final
Aug 7 v Scunthorpe United (a) 4-1
Partridge, Lewis, Money (og), Wigginton (og)
Final
Aug 12 v Gainsborough Trinity (a) 1-0
Partridge
From here on the early stages are played in qualifying groups.

1976-77
Group match
July 31 v Lincoln City (h) 1-2
Waters
Group match
Aug 7 v Scunthorpe United (h) 1-3
Lewis

1977-78
Group match
Jul 30 v Lincoln City (h) 2-2
Cumming, Drinkell
Group match
Aug 6 v Scunthorpe United (a) 1-4
Liddell

1978-79
Group Match
Aug 1 v Scunthorpe United (a) 0-1
Group Match
Aug 5 v Lincoln City (h) 0-1

1979-80
Group match
Jul 31 v Scunthorpe United (h) 2-1
Liddell, K.Moore
Group Match
Aug 6 v Lincoln City (a) 0-0
Final
Oct 16 v Gainsborough Trinity (h) 1-0 (aet)
Brolly

1980-81
Group match
Jul 29 v Lincoln City (a) 0-1
Group match
Jul 30 v Scunthorpe United (a) 2-1
Cumming, Drinkell

1981-82
Group match
Aug 11 v Scunthorpe United (h) 1-1
K.Moore
Group Match
Aug 12 v Lincoln City (a) 0-1

1982-83
Group match
Aug 7 v Scunthorpe United (h) 1-1
Kilmore
Group match
Aug 9 v Lincoln City (h) 0-4

1983-84
Group Match
Jan 30 v Lincoln City (h) 5-0
Drinkell 2, K.Moore 2, Emson
Group match
Mar 19 v Boston United (a) 3-2
Shearer 2, Drinkell
Final
May 14 v Gainsborough Trinity (h) 2-2
Lund, Bonnyman
No extra-time. Grimsby won 5-3 in penalty shoot-out.

1984-85
Group Match
Jul 31 v Gainsborough Trinity (a) 2-4
Lund, Wilkinson
Group match
Aug 7 v Scunthorpe United (h) 1-1
Wilkinson

1985-86
Group match
Aug 3 v Boston United (a) 3-5
Gilligan 2, Crombie
Group Match
Aug 12 v Grantham Town (h) 1-0
Peake

1986-87
Back to knock-out rounds.
Semi-final
Aug 13 v Boston United (a) 4-0
Walsh 2, Horwood 2
Final
Nov 11 v Scunthorpe United (h) 2-1
Rawcliffe 2

1987-88
Semi-final
Aug 4 v Lincoln City (h) 1-3
Turner

1988-89
Semi-final
Aug 10 v Boston United (a) 0-0
Boston won 4-2 on penalties

Ron Rafferty (left) scored six goals against Lincoln City in the 1960-61 Lincolnshire Cup. Neil Horwood (right) was on target twice against Boston United in the 1986-7 competition.

Charity Cups

During the inter-war years charity matches were common. These were usually in aid of the local hospit. and were played between the local League club and another club on an invitation basis.

Grimsby Hospital Cup

All matches played at Blundell Park.

1927
May 3 v Hull City 3-1
Coglin 2, Pugsley

1928
May 3 v Leicester City 4-5 (aet; 90 min 3-3)
Robson 3, Marshall

1929
May 6 v Leicester City 1-2 (aet; 90 min 1-1)
Coglin

1930
Apr 29 v Leicester City 1-2
Glover
Grimsby fielded a reserve eleven because of League commitments.

1931
Apr 20 v Notts County 2-4
Coleman, Bestall

1933
May 3 v Northampton Town 6-2
Glover 4, Dyson, Craven

1934
May 1 v Norwich City 3-0
Craven, Moralee, Jennings

1935
May 6 v Sheffield Wednesday 3-0
Bestall 2, Glover

1936
May 9 v Bolton Wanderers 1-0
Crack

1937
May 4 v Leicester City 5-2
Craven 2, Tench, Kelly, Dyson

1938
May 9 v Hull City 7-3
Kurz 3, Shaw 2, Crack 2

1939
May 8 v Newcastle United 3-2
Beattie, Crack, Glover

Wilson Lincoln Hospital Cup

1922
Mar 27 v Lincoln City (a) 3-3
Miller, Laws, Carmichael

Replay
Apr 4 v Lincoln City (h) 5-1
Carmichael 3, Morrall, Miller

Spalding Nursing Cup

Played at Black Swan ground, Spalding

1931
Apr 28 v Sheffield United 6-0
Coleman 3, Craven 2, Bestall

1932
Sep 27 v Leicester City 2-7
C. Wilson, Glover

Norwich Hospital Cup

1934
May 7 v Norwich City (a) 2-7
Glover, Lewis

Boston Hospital Cup

1924
Apr 28 v Boston (a) 1-0
Dent

1925
Apr 30 v Boston (a) 0-0

1927
Apr 25 v Boston (a) 2-1
Cooper, Robson

1928
Apr 19 v Boston (a) 3-1
Cooper, Robson, Marshall

1929
May 5 v Boston (a) 2-2
Marshall, Robson

East Riding County FA Invitation Trophy

1946-47
Final
May 26 v Hull City (a) 0-1

1947-48
Final
May 3 v Hull City (a) 3-1 (aet; 90 min 1-1)
Briggs, McGowan, Wardle

1953-54
Final (1st leg)
Apr 26 v Hull City (h) 1-0
Stroud
Final (2nd leg)
Apr 29 v Hull City (a) 1-0 (agg 2-0)
Hernon

Yorkshire & Humberside Cup

1988-89
Group match
Aug 13 v Halifax Town (h) 0-1
Group match
Aug 16 v Sheffield United (h) 1-1
Cunnington
Group match
Aug 20 v Rotherham United (a) 1-0
O'Kelly

Grimsby Town Reserves

MIDLAND LEAGUE

	P	W	D	L	F	A	Pts	Pos
1901-02	28	16	3	9	76	38	35	4th
1902-03	32	12	4	16	51	47	28	13th
1903-04	34	15	4	15	55	62	34	8th
1904-05	Did not compete							
1905-06	34	24	6	4	88	31	54	2nd
1906-07	38	25	7	6	92	46	57	2nd
1907-08	38	18	8	12	68	57	44	5th
1908-09	38	16	5	17	70	71	37	11th
1909-10	42	20	4	18	107	81	44	7th
1910-11	The first team played in the Midland League. No reserve side.							
1911-12	36	17	5	14	68	84	39	5th
1912-13	38	15	9	14	66	66	39	7th
1913-14	34	16	6	12	68	56	38	6th
1914-15	38	21	3	14	73	54	45	7th
1919-20	34	14	5	15	66	64	33	10th
1920-21	38	12	5	21	45	70	39	18th
1921-22	42	24	9	9	81	82	57	2nd
1922-23	42	21	9	12	77	59	51	5th
1923-24	42	25	6	11	98	46	56	2nd

MIDLAND COMBINATION

	P	W	D	L	F	A	Pts	Pos
1924-25	22	8	6	8	37	31	20	7th

MIDLAND COMBINATION SUBSIDIARY

	P	W	D	L	F	A	Pts	Pos
1924-25	10	6	2	2	28	10	14	1st

MIDLAND COMBINATION

	P	W	D	L	F	A	Pts	Pos
1925-26	24	14	5	5	72	26	33	1st

COMBINATION CUP

	P	W	D	L	F	A	Pts	Pos
1925-26	12	9	2	1	40	15	20	1st

MIDLAND COMBINATION

	P	W	D	L	F	A	Pts	Pos
1926-27	24	13	1	10	48	43	27	5th

MIDLAND COMBINATION SUBSIDIARY

	P	W	D	L	F	A	Pts	Pos
1926-27	12	7	4	1	29	12	18	2nd

MIDLAND LEAGUE

	P	W	D	L	F	A	Pts	Pos
1927-28	44	20	8	16	93	88	48	12th
1928-29	54	24	6	20	109	96	54	10th
1929-30	50	28	9	13	160	86	65	4th
1930-31	46	32	6	8	174	73	70	1st
1931-32	46	36	3	7	178	60	75	2nd
1932-33	46	36	1	9	189	66	73	1st
1933-34	32	25	4	3	127	47	54	1st
1934-35	38	20	8	10	114	54	48	3rd
1935-36	40	16	8	16	89	70	40	4th
1936-37	42	23	70	12	108	61	53	3rd
1937-38	42	22	5	15	88	57	49	5th
1938-39	42	23	6	13	120	74	52	5th
1946-47	42	29	8	5	133	54	66	1st
1947-48	42	18	10	14	101	88	46	10th

MIDLAND LEAGUE

	P	W	D	L	F	A	Pts	Pos
1948-49	42	21	9	12	87	65	51	5th
1949-50	46	29	7	10	98	58	65	2nd
1950-51	42	23	5	14	84	61	51	4th
1951-52	42	15	7	20	73	73	37	14th
1952-53	46	27	8	11	115	56	62	3rd
1953-54	46	20	8	18	74	64	48	10th
1954-55	46	16	9	21	89	98	41	17th
1955-56	46	19	6	21	88	76	44	12th
1956-57	46	18	7	21	108	86	43	15th
1957-58	46	22	10	14	88	75	54	5th

NORTH REGIONAL LEAGUE

	P	W	D	L	F	A	Pts	Pos
1958-59	36	12	10	14	58	58	34	11th
1959-60	42	13	8	21	58	67	34	19th
1960-61	40	14	8	18	62	81	36	14th
1961-62	28	14	3	11	70	50	31	5th
1962-63	32	16	3	13	68	53	35	14th
1963-64	32	15	9	8	67	49	39	6th
1964-65	30	14	4	12	60	63	52	12th

NORTHERN INTERMEDIATE LEAGUE

	P	W	D	L	F	A	Pts	Pos
1965-66	32	18	8	6	84	44	44	4th

(This was the youth side. No reserve squad this season)

MIDLAND COUNTIES LEAGUE

	P	W	D	L	F	A	Pts	Pos
1966-67	42	14	5	23	70	83	33	6th
1967-68	40	10	11	19	53	61	31	16th

NORTH MIDLANDS LEAGUE

	P	W	D	L	F	A	Pts	Pos
1968-69	26	8	4	14	36	51	20	11th
1969-70	28	8	2	18	31	53	18	14th
1970-71	26	3	9	14	30	56	15	13th
1971-72	28	10	6	12	40	52	26	9th
1972-73	28	7	11	10	42	58	25	10th
1973-74	28	15	4	9	48	37	34	4th
1974-75	28	10	7	11	38	39	27	7th
1975-76	24	8	6	10	32	40	22	7th
1976-77	22	7	5	10	25	42	19	7th
1977-78	28	11	6	11	38	32	28	8th
1978-79	30	15	7	8	60	37	37	2nd
1979-80	28	14	4	10	44	46	32	6th
1980-81	28	13	7	8	68	49	33	5th
1981-82	24	9	4	11	39	41	22	9th
1982-83	16	5	4	7	16	23	14	4th

CENTRAL LEAGUE (Division Two)

	P	W	D	L	F	A	Pts	Pos
1983-84	30	10	8	12	53	46	38	12th
1984-85	34	11	10	13	50	57	43	12th
1985-86	34	18	2	14	58	59	56	7th
1986-87	32	17	5	10	63	43	56	3rd

CENTRAL LEAGUE (Division One)

	P	W	D	L	F	A	Pts	Pos
1987-88	34	6	3	25	29	100	21	17th
1988-89	34	12	15	17	47	61	41	10th

Mariners' Scoring Feats

Grimsby Town players have scored three or more goals in a single match in senior competitive football (League FA Cup or League Cup) 155 times to the end of the 1987-8 season.

Most goals in a single match were scored by Tommy McCairns, who netted six times in a Second Division match against Leicester Fosse at Abbey Park on 11 April 1896.

Five goals have been scored on two occasions: by Pat Glover in a League match against Sunderland on 12 April 1937; and in the FA Cup by Bob Blanthorpe against Carlisle United on 1 February 1908, both at Blundell Park.

Four goals have been scored on 30 occasions (27 League and three Cup). Twenty players have achieved this feat, with Pat Glover being the most regular, having scored four in four League matches and one Cup match.

Hat-tricks have been scored in 122 matches; 105 League, 14 FA Cup and three League Cup. Sixty-seven players have been involved. Both Joe Robson and Pat Glover scored hat-tricks in eight matches, Robson's were all in the League and Glover's included one FA Cup match. Pat Glover is the leading multi-goal scorer, having scored three or more in 14 matches, four of them in the 1935-6 season.

The first hat-tricks in senior competitive football were in an FA Cup match against Darlington on 21 November 1885, when Harry Monument scored four and J.Seal three in an 8-0 victory.

The first hat-trick in League football was by Sandy Higgins, against Small Heath on 1 October 1892.

The fastest hat-trick is attributed to Joe Robson, who scored three in just over three minutes (reports vary) against Preston North End on 5 May 1928, when Town fought back from a 6-0 defecit in the last ten minutes to lose 6-4.

Fred Smith scored four in seven minutes (14, 17, 19, 21) against Hartlepools United on 15 November 1952. Town won 7-0.

Three or more goals in one match for the Mariners.

Six Goals

League

McCairns, Tommy v Leicester Fosse (h) .... 11 April 1896

Five Goals

League

Glover, Pat v Sunderland (h) .... 12 April 1937

FA Cup

Blanthorne, Bob v Carlisle United (h) .... 1 February 1908

Four Goals

League

Bestall, Jackie v Blackpool (a) ....2 January 1928
Bloomer, Jimmy v Southampton (h) ....28 October 1950
Brace, Stuart v Oldham Athletic (h)....11 November 1972
Carmichael, Jimmy v Halifax Town (h)....24 December 1921
Carmichael, Jimmy v Barrow (h) ....28 January 1922
Carmichael, Jimmy v Ashington (h)....24 February 1923
Coglin, Steve v Clapton Orient (h)....15 September 1928
Coleman, Tim v Leicester City (h) ....1 November 1930
Crosbie, Bob v Chester (h) ....23 August 1955
Crosbie, Bob v Crewe Alex (h) ....31 March 1956
Fletcher, Harry v Loughborough (h) ....4 December 1897
Glover, Pat v Preston NE (h) ....15 October 1932
Glover, Pat v Huddersfield Town (n) ....15 September 1934
Glover, Pat v Aston Villa (a)....2 November 1935
Glover, Pat v Middlesbrough (h) ....3 October 1936
Howe, Fred v Leicester City (h) ....17 December 1938
Lester, Mike v Darlington (h)....16 January 1979
Lewis, Cyril v Preston North End (h) ....31 October 1936
McCairns, Tommy v Lincoln City (h) ....7 September 1895
McCairns, Tommy v Burton Town Swifts (h) ....5 February 1898
McClean, George v Bury (h)....18 August 1963
McClean, George v Oldham Athletic (a)....22 August 1964
Rafferty, Ron v Lincoln City (a) ....3 September 1958
Robson, Joe v Wolverhampton Wanderers (h)....7 May 1927
Robson, Joe v Everton (a) ....12 April 1930
Smith, Fred v Hartlepools United (h) ....15 November 1952
Williams, Derek v Tranmere Rovers (a) ....29 October 1960

FA Cup

Briggs, Tommy v Luton Town (a) ....7 January 1950
Glover, Pat v Exeter City (h) ....9 January 1932
Monument, Harry v Darlington (h)....21 November 1885

Three Goals

League

Appleyard, Willie v Aston Villa (h)....12 April 1902
Bell, Thomas v Birmingham (a) ....5 March 1910
Bloomer, Jimmy v Brentford (h) ....11 November 1950
Brace, Stuart v York City (a) ....18 January 1969
Brace, Stuart v Southend United (a) ....25 August 1969
Briggs, Tommy v Coventry City (h)....23 October 1948
Briggs, Tommy v Lincoln City (a) ....5 March 1949
Briggs, Tommy v Coventry City (h)....27 August 1949
Briggs, Tommy v Luton Town (h) ....31 December 1949
Briggs, Tommy v Middlesbrough (h) ....4 April 1958
Cairns, Billy v Leeds United (h) ....17 May 1947
Cairns, Billy v Manchester United (a) ....11 October 1947
Cairns, Billy v Southport (h) ....1 March 1952

Carmichael, Jimmy v Lincoln City (a)........................22 September 1923
Carmichael, Jimmy v Ashington (h)............................8 April 1924
Carmichael, Jimmy v Wigan (h)................................25 April 1925
Carmichael, Jimmy v Accrington Stanley (h)...................30 January 1926
Chatterley, Lew v Walsall (h)................................27 January 1973
Cockshutt, James v Newton Heath (h)..........................4 March 1899
Cockshutt, James v Darwen (h)................................15 April 1899
Coglin, Steve v Reading (h)..................................30 August 1927
Coglin, Steve v Liverpool (h)................................1 February 1930
Coleman, 'Tim' v West Ham United (a).........................7 February 1931
Coleman, 'Tim' v Birmingham City (h).........................28 March 1931
Coleman, 'Tim' v Blackpool (h)...............................25 April 1931
Coleman, 'Tim' v Liverpool (h)...............................6 February 1932
Cooper, Joe v Tranmere Rovers (h)............................14 September 1925
Craven, Charlie v Oldham Athletic (h)........................18 February 1933
Craven, Charlie v Aston Villa (h)............................6 October 1934
Cumming, Bobby v York City (h)...............................23 December 1978
Crosbie, Bob v Chesterfield (h)..............................24 December 1955
Crosbie, Bob v Oldham Athletic (h)...........................18 February 1956
Dent, George v Barrow (h)....................................26 April 1924
Drinkell, Kevin v Sheffield United (h).......................3 May 1980
Drinkell, Kevin v Crystal Palace (h).........................4 December 1982
Drinkell, Kevin v Swansea Town (h)...........................14 April 1984
Dyson, Jimmy v West Bromwich Albion (a)......................30 April 1932
Fielding, Horace v Derby County (a)..........................12 December 1931
Fletcher, Harry v Crewe Alexandera (h).......................10 March 1894
Fletcher, Harry v Glossop (h)................................28 September 1907
Ford, Tony v Bradford City (h)...............................9 January 1979
Glover, 'Pat' v Oldham Athletic (a)..........................2 September 1933
Glover, 'Pat' v Manchester United (a)........................25 December 1933
Glover, 'Pat' v Millwall (h).................................17 March 1934
Glover, 'Pat' v Derby County (a).............................13 October 1934
Glover, 'Pat' v Sunderland (h)...............................12 October 1935
Glover, 'Pat' v Brentford (h)................................7 December 1935
Glover, 'Pat' v Derby County (h).............................18 April 1936
Green, Rod v Scunthorpe United (h)...........................7 September 1966
Gray, Bob v Lincoln City (h).................................2 October 1897
Hickman, Mike v Colchester United (h)........................28 April 1970
Higgins, 'Sandy' v Small Heath...............................1 October 1892
Higgins, 'Sandy' v Burslem Port Vale (h).....................26 January 1895
Hill, Brian v Scunthorpe United (h)..........................7 September 1966
Hobson, Gordon v Millwall (h)................................2 November 1985
Holmes, Maxey v West Bromwich Albion (a).....................30 April 1932
Holmes, Maxey v Blackpool (h)................................28 April 1934
Hubbard, Phil v Notts County (h).............................2 December 1972
Hunt, Ralph v Colchester United (h)..........................1 September 1959
Hunt, Ralph v Torquay United (h).............................15 April 1961
Jenkinson T. v Darwen (h)....................................15 April 1899
Jennings, Dennis v Lincoln City (h)..........................11 February 1933
Kilmore, Kevin v Wimbledon (a)...............................29 march 1980
Lewis, Cyril v Manchester United (h).........................14 November 1936
Leigh, Walter v Lincoln City (h).............................1 December 1900
Leonard, Harry v Glossop (h).................................26 February 1910

Leonard, Harry v Burnley (h) . . . . . 9 April 1910
Lloyd, Stan v Sheffield Wednesday (h) . . . . . 8 October 1949
Lumby, Jimmy v Plymouth Argyle (h) . . . . . 6 April 1974
Lund, Gary v Sheffield United (a) . . . . . 29 September 1984
Mayson, Tommy v Stockport County (h) . . . . . 22 February 1913
McCairns, Tommy v Loughborough (h) . . . . . 17 October 1896
McCairns, Tommy v Darwen (h) . . . . . 6 March 1897
McKenna, Frank v Accrington Stanley (h) . . . . . 25 December 1922
McKenna, Frank v Walsall (h) . . . . . 31 August 1925
Miller, James v Ashington (h) . . . . . 3 September 1921
Miller, James v Durham City (h) . . . . . 11 February 1921
Mounteney, 'Pecker' v Fulham (a) . . . . . 20 April 1912
North, Marc v Port Vale (h) . . . . . 28 December 1987
Portwood, Cliff v Lincoln City (h) . . . . . 7 October 1961
Rafferty, Ron v Barnsley (h) . . . . . 20 December 1960
Rafferty, Ron v Tranmere Rovers (h) . . . . . 18 March 1961
Rafferty, Ron v Reading (h) . . . . . 26 September 1961
Rampton, George v Stockport County (h) . . . . . 20 February 1915
Rampton, George v Lincoln City (h) . . . . . 3 April 1915
Ratcliffe, George v Lincoln City (a) . . . . . 8 April 1899
Reeson, Tony v York City (a) . . . . . 22 October 1955
Richards, Charles v Loughborough (h) . . . . . 11 February 1899
Richards, Charles v Luton Town (a) . . . . . 30 December 1899
Richards, Charles v Burton Swifts (h) . . . . . 7 April 1900
Robinson, 'Hervey' v Rotherham Town (h) . . . . . 10 February 1894
Robson, Joe v New Brighton (a) . . . . . 19 December 1925
Robson, Joe v Bradford Park Avenue (h) . . . . . 25 December 1925
Robson, Joe v Middlesbrough (h) . . . . . 8 February 1927
Robson, Joe v Fulham (a) . . . . . 19 February 1927
Robson, Joe v Barnsley (a) . . . . . 14 April 1928
Robson, Joe v Preston North End (h) . . . . . 5 May 1928
Robson, Joe v Bradford Park Avenue (h) . . . . . 6 October 1928
Robson, Joe v Port Vale (h) . . . . . 10 November 1928
Rodger, Thomas v Stockport County (h) . . . . . 30 March 1907
Rouse, Frederick v Burton United (h) . . . . . 1 April 1904
Russell, James v Northwich Victoria (h) . . . . . 2 September 1893
Tees, Matt v Scunthorpe United (h) . . . . . 14 August 1971
Wilson, Dave v Gillingham (h) . . . . . 6 May 1967
Young, Dick v Derby County (a) . . . . . 22 September 1962

FA Cup

Bloomer, Jimmy v Fulham (h) . . . . . 9 January 1954
Cairns, Billy v Darlington (h) . . . . . 24 November 1951
Frost, Walter v Attercliffe (h) . . . . . 5 November 1894
Glover, Pat v Walsall (h) . . . . . 30 January 1937
Leonard, Harry v Croydon Common (h) . . . . . 26 January 1911
Lund, Gary v Notts County (h) . . . . . 8 January 1985
McCairns, Tommy v Lincoln City (a) . . . . . 4 November 1893
McCairns, Tommy v Staveley (a) . . . . . 12 October 1895
McCairns, Tommy v Lincoln City (a) . . . . . 23 November 1895
Mullen, Matthew v Lincoln City (h) . . . . . 10 December 1892
Pearson, S v Sheffield Heeley (h) . . . . . 30 October 1886
Rayner, Jimmy v Witton Albion (h) . . . . . 15 December 1953

Reid, Walter v Boston Tour (h) ....24 October 1891
Seal J. v Darlington (h) .... 21 November 1885

Football League Cup

Drinkell, Kevin v Sheffield United (h) ....12 October 1982
Tees, Matt v Preston North End (h) ....3 November 1965
Waters, Joe v Hartlepool United (h) ....13 August 1977

Two of the Mariners' hat-trick heroes, from widely differing eras. Kevin Drinkell (left) hit four hat-tricks in the 1980s. Charlie Craven (right) netted two in the 1930s.

Grimsby Town Internationals

The following is a list of Grimsby Town players who gained international caps whilst on the club's books. Before 1925 there was only one 'Ireland' team. Thereafter the Republic of Ireland began separate international matches. In this list, appearances for the Ireland team before 1925 appear in the Northern Ireland section.

ENGLAND

BESTALL, Jackie (1)
6 February 1935 v Northern Ireland (Goodison Park).

BETMEAD, Harry (1)
20 May 1937 v Finland (Helsinki).

TWEEDY, George (1)
2 December 1936 v Hungary (Highbury).

WALES

CHAPMAN, Thomas (1)
29 March 1897 v England (Sheffield).

COLLIER, David (1)
12 February 1921 v Scotland (Aberdeen).

GLOVER, 'Pat' (7)
31 October 1931 v Scotland (Wrexham).
4 November 1933 v Northern Ireland (Belfast) *1 goal.*
5 October 1935 v Scotland (Cardiff).
17 October 1936 v England (Cardiff) *1 goal.*
2 December 1936 v Scotland (Dundee) *2 goals.*
17 March 1937 v Northern Ireland (Wrexham) *2 goals.*
15 March 1939 v Northern Ireland (Wrexham) *1 goal.*

MORRIS, Hugh (1)
29 March 1897 v England (Sheffield).

MORRIS, Richard (1)
3 March 1906 v Scotland (Edinburgh).

NORTHERN IRELAND

ANDREWS, William (2)
15 February 1913 v England (Belfast).
15 March 1913 v Scotland (Dublin).

COULTER, John (1)
16 March 1938 v Wales (Belfast).

NICHOLL, Chris (2)
21 September 1983 v Austria (Belfast).
12 October 1983 v Turkey (Ankara).

SCOTT, Johnny (2)
17 June 1958 v Czechoslovakia (Malmö).
19 June 1958 v France (Norrköping).

REPUBLIC OF IRELAND

WATERS, Joe (2)
13 October 1976 v Turkey (Ankara).
21 November 1979 v Northern Ireland *(sub)* (Belfast).

ENGLAND 'B'

BRIGGS Tommy (1)
18 January 1950 v Switzerland (Hillsborough).

NORTHERN IRELAND 'B'

SCOTT, Johnny (1)
24 October 1957 v Rumania (Belfast).

UNDER-23 INTERNATIONALS
WALES

LEWIS, Jack (1) (over age player)
4 February 1976 v Scotland (Wrexham).

UNDER-21 INTERNATIONALS
ENGLAND

LUND, Gary (1)
13 November 1984 v Turkey (Bursa).

WILKINSON, Paul (2)
25 March 1985 v Eire (Portsmouth) *1 goal.*
30 April 1985 v Rumania *(sub)* (Brasow).

AMATEUR INTERNATIONALS
ENGLAND

BLANCHARD, William (1)
7 February 1912 v Wales (Bishop Auckland).

SPRINGTHORPE, Harold (1)
19 February 1910 v Wales (Huddersfield).

FOOTBALL LEAGUE

BESTALL, Jackie (3)
23 September 1931 v Irish League (Belfast).
7 November 1931 v Scottish League (Glasgow).
23 September 1936 v Irish League (Belfast).

HIGGINS, Sandy (1)
7 November 1896 v Irish League (Belfast).

McCAIRNS, Tommy (1)
9 November 1895 v Irish League (Stoke)

Grimsby Town in 1897-8. Back row (left to right): Leach (trainer), Lindsay, Whittaker, Mount, Mr Coulson (president), Richardson. Middle row: Munn, Johnston, Chapman. Front row: Rogers, Goldie, McCairns, Fletcher, Gray.

Grimsby Town in 1977-8. Back row (left to right): Michael Brolly, Bob Cumming, Gary Liddell, Terry Donovan, Tony Ford. Middle row: Paul Cooper, David Booth, Geoff Barker, Harry Wainman, Nigel Batch, Malcolm Partridge, Keith Hanvey, Martin Young. Front row: Kevin Moore, Joe Waters, John Newman (manager), David Boylen, Kevin Drinkell.

• Grimsby Town Career Records •

This list contains every player who has appeared in a first-class match for the club since 1882. 'League debut' indicates full League debut except where the player made only substitute appearances. An asterisk (*) by a debut date indicates that the player has made previous appearances as substitute. A dagger (†) indicates a player scoring on his debut. The three matches in the abandoned 1939-40 season are not included.

Player	Seasons	League debut	Result	League App	League Gls	FA Cup App	FA Cup Gls	FL Cup App	FL Cup Gls	Total App	Total Gls
Abbott WA	1919-20	27-3-1920 (h) Port Vale	W 2-0	5	0					5	0
Ackroyd J	1892-94	3-9-1892 (h) Northwich Victoria	W 2-1	38	16	13	6			51	22
Ackroyd JW	1923-24	25-8-1923 (a) Tranmere Rovers	L 1-2	6	0					6	0
Affleck G	1919-25	1-11-1919 (a) Hull City	L 1-4	197	0	13	0			210	0
Agnew P	1983-	7-5-1984 (a) Oldham Athletic	L 1-2	126/4	1	15	0	8	0	149/4	1
Ainsworth C	1909-10	16-10-1909 (a) Glossop	L 0-3	3	0					3	0
Alexander K	1988-	3-9-1988 (h) Torquay United	W 1-0	42/2	14	6	1	1	0	49/2	15
Allen K	1964-65	6-3-1965 (h) Reading †	D 1-1	6	1					6	1
Anderson JE	1955-56	15-10-1955 (h) Halifax Town	W 4-0	3	0					3	0
Anderson TD	1938-39	1-4-1939 (h) Bolton Wanderers	D 1-1	1	0					1	0
Andrews W	1912-15	3-9-1912 (h) Blackpool	D 1-1	105	2	3	0			108	2
Annables W	1932-35	17-4-1933 (a) Bradford	D 1-1	6	0					6	0
Appleyard W	1901-03 1908-09	25-12-1901 (a) Blackburn Rovers	L 0-2	57	21	4	1			61	22
Arch WH	1923-26	22-9-1923 (a) Lincoln City	W 3-1	91	0	5	0			96	0
Archer JC	1954-55	21-8-1954 (a) Rochdale	W 3-0	10	0					10	0
Archibald J	1923-27	20-10-1923 (a) New Brighton	D 0-0	111	0	10	0			121	0
Armitage LC	1947-48	17-1-1948 (a) Sheffield United	L 0-4	8	2					8	2
Armstrong JB	1912-13	21-9-1912 (a) Barnsley	L 0-3	4	1					4	1
Arrowsmith JT	1911-15	2-9-1911 (h) Wolverhampton W	D 0-0	137	0	7	0			144	0
Ashton E	1911-13	8-4-1912 (h) Glossop	D 0-0	8	0					8	0
Asling W	1883-85					7	0			7	0
Atherton TH	1902-03	25-10-1902 (a) West Bromwich A	L 0-1	2	0					2	0
Atkin FW	1914-15	26-9-1914 (h) Glossop	W 1-0	12	0	1	0			13	0
Atkinson C	1886-87					3	0			3	0
Atkinson G	1883-88					9	0			9	0
Atkinson H	1885-88					9	2			9	2
Atkinson T	1883-84					2	0			2	0
Atter JT	1922-26	17-3-1923 (a) Stalybridge Celtic	L 2-3	48	0	1	0			49	0
Ayre HW	1904-05	1-10-1904 (a) Blackpool	D 1-1	3	0					3	0
Bache JW	1920-21	28-8-1920 (h) Northampton Town	W 2-0	5	1					5	1
Bacon GC	1908-12	3-4-1909 (h) Tottenham Hotspur	L 1-2	11	0					11	0
Bagshaw JE	1898-99	3-9-1898 (a) Manchester City	L 2-7	34	0	5	0			39	0
Bailey W	1895-96	7-9-1895 (h) Lincoln City	W 4-2	2	0					2	0
Baker K	1975-76	23-8-1975 (a) Gillingham	L 0-3	1	0					1	0
Baker L	1903-06	1-4-1904 (h) Burton United	W 4-0	59	16	3	1			62	17
Baldry GW	1935-36	30-11-1935 (a) Preston North End	L 0-1	20	7	6	2			26	9
Banton D	1988-89	27-3-1989 (h) Lincoln City	W 1-0	3/5	1					3/5	1
Barker GA	1977-79	20-8-1977 (h) Darlington	W 2-0	66	1	6	0	6	0	78	1
Barley HF	1929-31	30-11-1929 (a) Bolton Wanderers	W 3-2	5	1					5	1
Barnett GAS	1958-63	25-12-1958 (h) Sheffield United	L 1-2	116	0	7	0	1	0	124	0
Barney VC	1949-50	3-9-1949 (a) Luton Town	D 0-0	7	0	1	0			8	0
Barr J	1906-07	30-3-1907 (h) Stockport County	W 3-1	2	1					2	1
Barrass C	1921-22	1-10-1921 (h) Wigan Borough	D 1-1	4	0					4	0
Barratt AG	1950-51	28-10-1950 (h) Southampton	W 4-1	23	0	2	0			25	0
Barratt LE	1964-65	24-10-1964 (a) Workington †	D 2-2	4	1	2	1	1	0	7	2
Barratt T	1985-86	31-8-1985 (h) Wimbledon	L 0-1	20/2	0	1	0	3	0	24/2	0
Barrett RH	1958-59	24-2-1959 (a) Bristol City	L 0-1	3	0					3	0
Bartholomew R	1938-39	27-8-1938 (h) Aston Villa	L 1-2	12	4	1	0			13	4
Bartlett TR	1967-68	20-3-1968 (h) Tranmere Rovers	W 3-0	1	0					1	0
Barton F	1973-76	25-8-1973 (h) Hereford United	L 1-3	123	15	8	2	5/1	0	136/1	17
Barton H	1897-98	16-10-1897 (a) Darwen	L 0-1	3	1					3	1
Batch NA	1976-87	28-12-1976 (h) Sheffield Wednesday	D 1-1	348	0	22	0	33	0	403	0

Player	Seasons	League debut	Result	League App	League Gls	FA Cup App	FA Cup Gls	FL Cup App	FL Cup Gls	Total App	Total Gls
Bateman A	1929-33	2-11-1929 (a) Leeds United	L 0-6	18	0					18	0
Battiste W	1919-20	30-8-1919 (h) Stockport County	L 0-3	31	0	1	0			32	0
Beacock GC	1980-83	*30-1-1982 (h) Charlton Athletic	D 3-3	10/7	0	1/1	0			11/8	0
Beadling W	1908-10	21-11-1908 (h) Barnsley	D 0-0	35	5					35	5
Beardsley DT	1973-75	25-8-1973 (h) Hereford United	L 1-3	66	0	6	0	5	0	77	0
Beattie JM	1937-39	12-2-1938 (h) Birmingham †	W 4-0	56	13	7	2			63	15
Beckers P	1964-65	24-4-1965 (a) Southend United	L 0-4	1	0					1	0
Bell AS	1958-59	26-8-1958 (h) Lincoln City	W 4-2	8	0					8	0
Bell J	1895-99	2-9-1895 (a) Woolwich Arsenal	L 1-3	76	14	12	3			88	17
Bell JJ	1920-21	19-3-1921 (h) Newport County	D 1-1	3	0					3	0
Bell TD	1909-12	1-9-1909 (h) Bradford	L 0-1	32	9					32	9
Bell WT	1930-32	1-1-1931 (a) Middlesbrough	L 1-2	11	0	2	0			13	0
Bellas WJ	1951-52	18-8-1951 (a) Chesterfield	L 1-3	5	0					5	0
Bellingham J	1901-02	3-9-1901 (h) Derby County	D 1-1	4	0					4	0
Bemrose FE	1959-61	28-3-1959 (a) Fulham	L 0-3	2	0					2	0
Bestall JG	1926-38	4-12-1926 (a) Clapton Orient †	W 4-2	427	76	30	7			457	83
Betmead HA	1931-47	15-9-1931 (h) Bolton Wanderers	W 2-0	296	10	19	0			315	10
Beveridge D	1899-1900	2-9-1899 (h) Luton Town	D 3-3	5	2					5	2
Bidmead WH	1908-09	1-9-1908 (h) Stockport County	W 3-0	1	0					1	0
Binks L	1922-23	3-2-1923 (h) Barrow	W 2-0	3	0					3	0
Birbeck J	1959-60	22-8-1959 (h) Chesterfield	W 5-1	18	0	2	0			20	0
Birch W	1912-14	3-9-1912 (h) Blackpool	D 1-1	34	1	1	0			35	1
Bircham B	1949-50	10-12-1949 (a) Brentford	L 0-1	8	0	2	0			10	0
Bird WS	1919-20	28-2-1920 (a) Lincoln City	L 0-2	7	2					7	2
Bisby F	1905-08	16-12-1905 (a) Hull City	W 1-0	12	1					12	1
Bisby JC	1906-08	24-11-1906 (a) Stockport County	L 0-3	7	1					7	1
Black D	1889-91					2	1			2	1
Blackburn R	1909-10	1-9-1909 (h) Bradford	L 0-1	6	0					6	0
Blair J	1895-96	2-9-1895 (a) Woolwich Arsenal	L 1-3	1	0	1	0			2	0
Blake E	1920-21	6-9-1920 (a) Southend United	L 1-3	7	0					7	0
Blanchard WS	1907-13 1913-15	4-1-1908 (h) Lincoln City	L 0-2	11	0					11	0
Blant C	1976-77	21-8-1976 (a) Bury	L 0-2	9	0			1	0	10	0
Blanthorne R	1907-08	26-10-1907 (h) Blackpool † (2)	D 2-2	28	14	5	7			33	21
Blenkinsopp TW	1946-48	3-9-1946 (h) Wolverhampton W	D 0-0	74	10	4	0			78	10
Bloomer J (Sen)	1949-55	3-12-1949 (h) Blackburn Rovers	L 1-2	109	42	11	7			120	49
Bloomer JM (Jnr)	1965-69	9-4-1966 (h) Mansfield	L 0-1	48/4	0	3	0	3/1	0	54/5	0
Blythe TH	1897-99	2-4-1898 (h) Newton Heath	L 1-3	4	1					4	1
Bogie M	1963-64	28-9-1963 (h) Derby County	L 1-3	1	0					1	0
Bonnyman P	1982-87	28-8-1982 (h) Leeds United	D 1-1	146/6	16	9	0	13	2	168/6	18
Booth D	1972-78	12-8-1972 (a) York City	D 0-0	199/1	7	13	1	12	0	224/1	8
Boulton R	1947-49	24-4-1948 (h) Charlton Athletic	L 1-3	3	0					3	0
Bowden JW	1907-08	3-9-1907 (h) Gainsborough T	L 1-4	19	0	3	0			22	0
Boyd JM	1938-39	27-8-1938 (h) Aston Villa	L 1-2	37	9	7	1			44	10
Boylen D	1966-78	6-5-1967 (h) Gillingham	W 4-0	370/14	34	20/1	2	18/2	1	408/17	37
Boylen J	1923-24	19-1-1924 (a) Chesterfield	L 2-4	4	0					4	0
Brace SC	1968-74	2-11-1968 (a) Exeter City	D 2-2	205/1	81	9/1	2	12	5	226/2	88
Brader A	1960-61	6-9-1960 (h) Bradford City	W 1-0	2	0					2	0
Bradford J	1920-24	18-9-1920 (h) Bristol Rovers	W 3-1	108	0	10	0			118	0
Bradley M	1907-08	18-4-1908 (h) Hull City	D 1-1	28	6	1	0			29	6
Bradley P	1911-13	11-11-1911 (a) Blackpool	W 2-1	6	0	1	0			7	0
Bratley A	1958-59	4-10-1958 (a) Barnsley	L 1-3	2	0	1	0			3	0
Brayshaw E	1892-93	3-9-1892 (h) Northwich Victoria	W 2-1	2	0					2	0
Briggs TH	1947-50 1958-59	23-8-1947 (h) Aston Villa	W 3-0	135	87	5	5			140	92
Brocklesby HE	1897-98	9-4-1898 (a) Loughborough	L 1-2	3	0					3	0
Brolly MJ	1976-82	11-9-1976 (h) Brighton & HA	W 2-0	246/8	27	16	1	16	2	278/8	30
Brooks AF	1909-10	8-2-1910 (a) Bradford †	L 1-6	4	2					4	2
Brooks JE	1919-20	20-9-1919 (a) Huddersfield Town	L 0-3	3	0					3	0
Broom W	1919-20	4-10-1919 (a) Blackpool	L 0-2	3	2					3	2
Broome TA	1920-21	28-8-1920 (h) Northampton Town	W 2-0	7	0					7	0

Player	Seasons	League debut	Result	League App	League Gls	FA Cup App	FA Cup Gls	FL Cup App	FL Cup Gls	Total App	Total Gls
Browell G	1911-12	4-12-1911 (a) Leeds City	W 2-1	23	0					23	0
Brown K	1973-76	12-4-1974 (h) Charlton Athletic †	W 5-0	32/7	5	2	0	1	0	35/7	5
Brown WF	1951-58	18-8-1951 (a) Chesterfield	L 1-3	265	1	18	0			283	1
Brumley E	1900-03	16-2-1901 (h) Burton Town Swifts†	W 5-2	5	2					5	2
Buck T	1929-39	25-12-1929 (h) Leicester City	L 1-4	354	4	32	2			386	6
Burgess D	1986-88	23-8-1986 (a) Ipswich Town	D 1-1	66/3	0	4	0	6	0	76/3	0
Burkinshaw JD	1907-08	29-2-1908 (h) Burnley	L 0-1	5	3					5	3
Burley B	1934-35	1-9-1934 (h) Portsmouth	W 3-0	22	5					22	5
Burley WRE	1924-25	30-8-1924 (h) Darlington	L 0-2	5	0					5	0
Burnett J	1958-59	25-10-1958 (h) Scunthorpe United	D 1-1	1	0					1	0
Burnett JJ	1905-07	2-9-1905 (a) Chesterfield	W 4-1	51	13	3	0			54	13
Burnett WJ	1947-48	29-11-1947 (h) Bolton Wanderers	L 0-2	10	0	1	0			11	0
Burton R	1919-20	20-12-1919 (h) Birmingham	L 0-3	13	0					13	0
Bush G	1907-08	14-3-1908 (h) Oldham Athletic	W 2-0	12	2					12	2
Butler J	1904-07	11-3-1905 (h) Bristol City † (2)	W 4-0	44	2	3	0			47	2
Cadden JY	1952-53	21-2-1953 (a) Workington Town	L 1-3	1	0					1	0
Cain T	1896-97	2-9-1896 (a) Loughborough Town	W 4-1	2	0					2	0
Cairns WH	1946-54	26-10-1946 (h) Portsmouth †	W 3-2	221	120	10	9			231	129
Calderwood JC	1927-30	14-9-1927 (a) Reading	D 2-2	74	0	2	0			76	0
Caldwell A	1988-89	10-9-1988 (a) Scunthorpe United	D 1-1	2/1	0					2/1	0
Campbell D	1951-52	27-10-1951 (a) Gateshead	D 1-1	6	0	2	0			8	0
Campbell F	1968-69	7-9-1968 (a) Bradford	D 1-1	4	0					4	0
Campbell TA	1970-73	24-10-1970 (h) York City	W 3-1	84/1	0	3	0	4	0	91/1	0
Carmichael HW	1906-08	26-12-1906 (h) Gainsborough T	W 2-0	36	0	4	0			40	0
Carmichael J	1920-27	28-8-1920 (h) Northampton Town	W 2-0	227	137	17	5			244	142
Carrington AS	1959-61	28-12-1959 (a) Bradford City	D 2-2	4	0					4	0
Carroll M	1971-72	4-5-1971 (h) Crewe Alexandra	W 2-0	0/1	0					0/1	0
Cartledge SH	1904-07	19-11-1904 (h) Manchester United	L 0-1	52	0	1	0			53	0
Cassidy PG	1912-13	26-4-1913 (a) Birmingham	L 1-2	1	0					1	0
Casson W	1921-24	11-3-1922 (h) Nelson †	W 3-1	19	5					19	5
Catley JW	1962-63	16-2-1963 (a) Middlesbrough	W 1-0	2	0					2	0
Cawthorne GJ	1979-80	25-3-1980 (a) Hull City	D 2-2	1	0					1	0
Chadwick H	1945-46					1	0			1	0
Chalmers A	1913-15	4-4-1914 (h) Birmingham	L 0-2	5	0					5	0
Chalmers W	1931-32	29-8-1931 (a) Huddersfield Town	D 1-1	6	1					6	1
Chambers H	1883-85					5	0			5	0
Chantry H	1906-07	17-11-1906 (a) Gainsborough T	L 1-2	4	0					4	0
Chapman C	1882-83					1	0			1	0
Chapman JE	1886-87					3	1			3	1
Chapman H	1898-99	3-9-1898 (a) Manchester City † (2)	L 2-7	10	4	2	0			12	4
Chapman KFR	1969-70	6-10-1969 (h) Hartlepool	W 1-0	6/1	0					6/1	0
Chapman T	1896-98	2-9-1896 (a) Loughborough Town	W 4-1	50	0	4	0			54	0
Charlesworth F	1938-47	19-4-1939 (a) Portsmouth	L 1-2	2	0	1	0			3	0
Chatburn FW	1897-99	22-1-1898 (h) Luton	L 1-3	2	1					2	1
Chatterley LC	1971-74	26-2-1972 (a) Hartlepool	W 1-0	72/1	16	9	0	5	1	86/1	17
Cherry T	1898-99	3-9-1898 (a) Manchester City	L 2-7	7	0	2	0			9	0
Child A	1888-89					2	0			2	0
Chilton AC	1954-57	19-3-1955 (h) Workington Town	L 0-1	63	0	4	0			67	0
Chisholm W	1946-51	5-4-1947 (h) Blackburn Rovers	W 2-1	92	0	2	0			94	0
Christian F	1887-88					1	0			1	0
Clarke J	1919-21	30-8-1919 (h) Stockport County	L 0-3	39	12	2	0			41	12
Cleator	1893-94					1	1			1	1
Clifton B	1962-66	27-10-1962 (h) Stoke City	D 1-1	104	5	6	0	6	0	116	5
Clifton H	1946-49	31-8-1946 (a) Manchester United	L 1-2	69	23	2	0			71	23
Clutterbuck HJ	1901-02	23-11-1901 (h) Sunderland	D 3-3	1	0					1	0
Cockburn K	1968-70	11-1-1969 (h) Exeter City †	L 1-2	15/4	2	1	0			16/4	2
Cockerill R	1958-68	23-8-1958 (a) Liverpool	D 3-3	293/1	28	15	3	14	2	322/1	33
Cockerill J	1988-	27-8-1988 (a) Cambridge United	L 1-4	24/5	6	6	1			30/5	7
Cockshutt JW	1898-1900	3-9-1898 (a) Manchester City	L 2-7	61	21	8	4			69	25
Coglin S	1926-31	8-2-1927 (h) Middlesbrough	L 4-7	118	39	3	0			121	39
Coleman E	1928-32	30-3-1929 (h) Oldham Athletic †	W 1-0	87	57	7	1			94	58

Player	Seasons	League debut	Result	League App	League Gls	FA Cup App	FA Cup Gls	FL Cup App	FL Cup Gls	Total App	Total Gls
Coles FG	1904-08	3-9-1904 (h) Barnsley	D 0-0	44	0					44	0
Collier DJ	1920-22	28-8-1920 (h) Northampton Town	W 2-0	44	13	6	1			50	14
Collins JD	1963-69	2-10-1963 (a) Cardiff City	D 0-0	96/7	9	8	0	10/1	1	114/8	10
Conner RJ	1953-59	30-1-1954 (h) Workington Town	W 1-0	186	8	9	1			195	9
Cook J	1906-08	2-3-1907 (h) Chelsea	W 2-1	8	0					8	0
Cook RJ	1922-23	30-3-1923 (h) Darlington	L 0-1	5	0					5	0
Cooper J	1924-32	27-9-1924 (h) Chesterfield	D 0-0	154	47	13	1			167	48
Cooper N	1981-84	6-3-1982 (h) Luton Town	D 0-0	47	2	2	0	5	0	54	2
Cooper PT	1977-78	20-8-1977 (h) Darlington	W 2-0	3	0			3	0	6	0
Cooper R	1894-99	8-9-1894 (a) Walsall	L 3-4	2	0					2	0
Coulbeck T	1907-10	9-9-1907 (a) Stockport County	L 0-3	13	4	1	0			14	4
Coulter J	1937-38	16-10-1937 (a) Huddersfield Town †	W 2-1	25	11	2	0			27	11
Coupland C	1921-23 1927-28	17-9-1921 (h) Stalybridge Celtic	D 1-1	56	2	6	1			62	3
Coverdale R	1924-25	4-10-1924 (a) Accrington Stanley	W 3-0	30	1					30	1
Cowell W	1926-28	19-2-1927 (a) Fulham	W 5-0	39	0	1	0			40	0
Cowper PP	1927-28	27-8-1927 (h) Clapton Orient	D 2-2	4	0					4	0
Coxon T	1908-10	1-9-1908 (h) Stockport County	W 3-0	61	6	2				63	6
Coyle R	1974-75	5-10-1974 (h) Huddersfield Town	L 1-2	24	1	2	0			26	1
Crack FW	1935-39	2-5-1936 (h) Manchester City	W 3-1	28	7	3	1			31	8
Crampton P	1968-71	8-9-1970 (a) Southport	L 0-1	0/1	0					0/1	0
Crapper C	1907-08	3-9-1907 (h) Gainsborough T	L 1-4	3	0					3	0
Craven C	1930-38	13-9-1930 (h) Sheffield Wednesday	L 2-3	256	95	17	7			273	102
Crawford W	1893-94	2-9-1893 (h) Northwich Victoria	W 7-0	7	6	1	1			8	7
Crombie DM	1978-87	19-8-1978 (h) Reading	L 1-2	316/4	3	17	1	27	0	360/4	4
Crosbie RC	1955-57	20-8-1955 (h) Rochdale	D 1-1	65	45	3	3			68	48
Crosby PA	1979-83	12-1-1980 (h) Blackburn Rovers	L 1-2	34/5	5	1	0	3	0	38/5	5
Crozier J	1922-23	21-10-1922 (h) Rochdale	D 1-1	14	0					14	0
Cuff PJ	1971-72	6-11-1971 (h) Hartlepool	W 3-2	2	0					2	0
Cullen MJ	1958-63	23-8-1958 (a) Liverpool	D 3-3	178	35	7	1	3	0	188	36
Cumming DD	1922-23	26-8-1922 (h) Wrexham	W 4-0	6	0					6	0
Cumming R	1974-87	17-8-1974 (h) Blackburn Rovers	L 1-2	338/27	58	19/1	2	26/3	5	383/31	65
Cunnington S	1987-	20-2-1988 (h) Doncaster Rovers	D 0-0	59	1	6	2	2	0	67	3
Curran ET	1987-88	3-11-1987 (a) Fulham	L 0-5	10/2	0	1	0			11/2	0
Czuczman M	1971-76 1980-81	9-9-1972 (a) Walsall	L 0-1	116/6	6	4	0	6	0	126/6	6
Daley TE	1951-54	29-8-1951 (a) Lincoln City	W 2-0	14	0					14	0
Dart E	1909-10	11-9-1909 (h) Clapton Orient	W 2-0	3	0					3	0
Davidson AC	1908-10	1-9-1908 (h) Stockport County	W 3-0	59	0	2	0			61	0
Davidson AG	1965-69	20-11-1965 (h) Reading	D 3-3	46/5	1	2	0	5	0	53/5	1
Davies GA	1923-25	6-10-1923 (a) Hartlepools United	D 1-1	12	1					12	1
Davis FC	1895-97	2-9-1895 (a) Woolwich Arsenal	L 1-3	29	1	5	1			34	2
Daw EC	1896-97	5-12-1896 (a) Leicester Fosse	L 2-4	2	0					2	0
Dawson R	1984-85	9-2-1985 (a) Leeds United	D 0-0	1	0					1	0
Dawson S	1919-21	30-8-1919 (h) Stockport County	L 0-3	48	0	1	0			49	0
Deacey C	1920-23	27-12-1920 (a) Norwich City	D 0-0	90	4	8	0			98	4
Dean A	1901-02	3-9-1901 (h) Derby County	D 1-1	17	1					17	1
De Gruchy R	1954-58	21-8-1954 (a) Rochdale	W 3-0	74	2	4	0			78	2
Delvin	1891-92					2	2			2	2
Dent GH	1923-25	10-11-1923 (h) Wolverhampton W	W 2-0	24	12	1	0			25	12
Devan GF	1925-27	14-9-1925 (h) Tranmere Rovers	W 8-0	50	12	5	1			55	13
Dixon A	1986-89	4-10-1986 (a) Shrewsbury Town	L 1-4	35/3	0	1/1	0	1	0	37/4	0
Dixon WH	1923-26	26-4-1924 (h) Barrow	W 5-0	9	0					9	0
Dodds LS	1931-34	2-4-1932 (a) Everton	L 2-4	14	1					14	1
Dodsworth VE	1932-33	10-9-1932 (h) Stoke City	L 0-1	4	1					4	1
Donaldson DE	1931-32	9-9-1931 (a) Bolton Wanderers	L 3-5	1	0					1	0
Donovan DC	1958-65	23-8-1958 (a) Liverpool	D 3-3	238	1	12	0	3	0	253	1
Donovan TC	1976-79	4-9-1976 (a) Mansfield Town	L 0-3	52/12	23	5	2	6	3	63/12	28
Dow HC	1931-32	9-9-1931 (a) Bolton Wanderers	L 3-5	2	0					2	0
Doyle D	1888-89					4	0			4	0
Drinkell KS	1976-85	11-4-1977 (h) Gillingham	D 1-1	242/30	89	12/5	5	20/4	8	274/39	102

Player	Seasons	League debut	Result	League App	League Gls	FA Cup App	FA Cup Gls	FL Cup App	FL Cup Gls	Total App	Total Gls
Dubois JM	1953-54	9-9-1953 (h) Accrington Stanley	W 2-0	6	1					6	1
Duff WFA	1959-60	13-10-1959 (h) Queen's Park R	W 3-1	3	1					3	1
Duke J	1919-21	10-4-1920 (h) Clapton Orient	W 2-0	6	0					6	0
Duncan AL	1912-13	22-2-1913 (h) Stockport County	W 4-1	2	0					2	0
Duncliffe MJ	1968-70	10-8-1968 (h) Newport County	W 3-0	71/1	0	1	0	4	0	76/1	0
Dunn A	1902-04	6-12-1902 (a) Liverpool	L 2-9	45	1	4	0			49	1
Duthie J	1948-51	30-4-1949 (a) Bury	L 1-5	40	0	4	0			44	0
Dyson JM	1931-38	19-3-1932 (a) Portsmouth	L 0-2	139	38	8	1			147	39
Eccleston W	1894-95	1-9-1894 (h) Leicester Fosse	W 4-3	29	13	4	1			33	14
Elkins A	1903-05	23-1-1904 (a) Bolton Wanderers	L 0-4	18	7	1	0			19	7
Emson P	1983-86	27-8-1983 (h) Shrewsbury Town	D 1-1	90/7	15	3/1	0	12	1	105/8	17
Evans CJH	1925-26	26-9-1925 (h) Durham City	W 3-1	5	0					5	0
Evans H	1882-84					3	0			3	0
Evans WE	1955-58	20-8-1955 (h) Rochdale †	D 1-1	102	28	6	2			108	30
Fairbairn J	1894-95	10-11-1894 (h) Lincoln City †	W 3-0	2	2					2	2
Fairley W	1892-93	26-9-1892 (a) Sheffield United	L 0-2	17	0	2	0			19	0
Faulkner AA	1954-55	5-3-1955 (h) Accrington Stanley	W 2-1	5	1					5	1
Felgate DW	1984-87	23-2-1985 (h) Notts County	W 2-0	36	0	1	0	2	0	39	0
Fell JI	1956-61	23-2-1957 (h) Fulham †	W 3-1	166	35	7	0	1	0	174	35
Felton W	1921-23	24-9-1921 (a) Wigan Borough	D 1-1	43	0	3	0			46	0
Ferguson EB	1971-72	6-11-1971 (h) Hartlepool	W 3-2	1/1	0					1/1	0
Ferguson JJ	1926-27	6-11-1926 (a) Bradford City	D 2-2	3	0	1	0			4	0
Fidler DJ	1961-62	14-10-1961 (a) Northampton Town	L 0-7	9	3	1	0			10	3
Field R	1924-25	1-9-1924 (h) Hartlepools United	W 2-1	32	0	1	0			33	0
Fielding H	1930-33	27-9-1930 (a) Manchester United †	W 2-0	69	12	4	0			73	12
Fielding JA	1965-67	27-12-1965 (h) Swindon Town †	D 2-2	29/1	8			1	0	30/1	8
Findley J	1889-90					1	0			1	0
Finlayson E	1899-1900	9-9-1899 (a) Burslem Port Vale	W 3-2	5	0	1	0			6	0
Fisher FT	1938-51	4-2-1939 (a) Brentford	W 2-1	166	0	8	0			174	0
Flanaghan HN	1923-24	25-8-1923 (a) Tranmere Rovers	L 1-2	3	0					3	0
Fleet A	1906-07	15-9-1906 (h) Burton United	D 1-1	4	0					4	0
Fleming BJ	1957-61	4-9-1957 (a) Cardiff City	W 3-1	22	0					22	0
Fletcher HH	1892-98 1900-03 & 1905-10	5-11-1892 (h) Ardwick	W 2-0	273	92	33	8			306	100
Fletcher JM	1969-70	9-8-1969 (a) Workington Town	D 0-0	11	1			1		12	1
Fletcher JR	1973-75	6-11-1973 (h) Walsall	W 1-0	9/3	1	1	0			10/3	1
Flowers (Rev) J	1881-84					2	0			2	0
Foley S	1984-85	25-8-1984 (h) Barnsley	W 1-0	31	2	3	1	6	2	40	5
Ford T	1975-88	*25-10-1975 (a) Swindon Town	L 0-3	321/34	55	15/4	2	31/3	5	367/41	62
Forrest E	1948-49	21-8-1948 (h) Fulham	L 2-3	33	1	2	1			35	2
Forester W	1908-09	1-9-1908 (h) Stockport County	W 3-0	5	0					5	0
Foster JF	1925-26	29-8-1925 (h) Doncaster Rovers	W 3-0	10	1					10	1
Foster RE	1962-66	1-12-1962 (a) Luton Town	D 2-2	129	24	12	2	8	2	149	28
France C	1882-83					1	0			1	0
Freeburn W	1951-53	12-4-1952 (h) Bradford City	W 2-1	34	0	1	0			35	0
Freeman N	1973-76	20-4-1974 (h) Port Vale	W 2-0	33	0	4	0	1	0	38	0
Frith C	1893-94	16-9-1893 (h) Burton Town Swifts	W 2-1	9	1	2	0			11	1
Frith T	1892-99	3-9-1892 (h) Northwich Victoria	W 2-1	125	0	18	0			143	0
Frost W	1894-95 1898	1-9-1894 (h) Leicester Fosse	W 4-3	16	5	3	4			19	9
Fulljames W	1911-12	24-2-1912 (a) Bristol City	L 0-3	1	0					1	0
Gadsby MD	1970-71	12-9-1970 (h) Northampton Town	L 0-2	2	0					2	0
Galbraith WM	1951-53	1-9-1951 (a) Halifax Town	L 0-3	77	0	5	0			82	0
Gallacher HK	1937-38	26-1-1938 (a) Leeds United	D 1-1	12	3					12	3
Galley T	1947-49	22-11-1947 (a) Portsmouth	L 0-4	32	2	1	0			33	2
Gardner A	1901-02	3-9-1901 (h) Derby County	D 1-1	31	4	2	0			33	4
Gardner DA	1902-04	9-9-1902 (h) Nottingham Forest	L 0-1	51	0	3	0			54	0
Gardner T	1931-32	15-9-1931 (h) Bolton Wanderers	W 2-0	13	0					13	0
Gardner W	1925-27	31-10-1925 (h) Coventry City	W 2-0	20	4	2	0			22	4
Gardham T	1883-87					12	4			12	4
Garland D	1965-66	26-3-1966 (a) Bournemouth	L 0-1	2	0					2	0

Player	Seasons	League debut	Result	League App	League Gls	FA Cup App	FA Cup Gls	FL Cup App	FL Cup Gls	Total App	Total Gls
Gates GJ	1909-10	18-9-1909 (a) Blackpool	L 0-1	17	2	1	0			18	2
Gauden A	1971-73	19-2-1972 (h) Northampton Town	W 4-2	54/1	12	6	2	3	0	63/1	14
Gilbert D	1988-	27-3-1989 (h) Lincoln City	W 1-0	11	3					11	3
Gildea H	1909-10	1-9-1909 (h) Bradford	L 0-1	3	0					3	0
Gilligan J	1985-86	17-8-1985 (a) Brighton & HA	D 2-2	19/5	4	0/1	0	3	2	22/6	6
Gillow WB	1919-22 1923-25	7-2-1920 (h) Nottingham Forest	W 1-0	103	5	5	0			108	5
Gimblett A	1913-14	13-12-1913 (a) Leeds City	L 1-4	4	0					4	0
Glen A	1902-03	9-9-1902 (h) Nottingham Forest	L 0-1	13	1	2	0			15	1
Glennon JE	1907-09	7-12-1907 (h) Bradford City	L 0-1	10	0					10	0
Glover EM	1929-39	8-2-1930 (a) West Ham United	L 0-2	227	180	18	17			245	197
Godwin V	1951-52	12-1-1952 (a) Wrexham	L 0-2	1	0					1	0
Goldie E	1897-98	4-9-1897 (h) Gainsborough T	W 4-2	26	5	1	0			27	5
Golightly M	1919-20	30-8-1919 (h) Stockport County	L 0-3	9	0					9	0
Gordon JT	1909-15	26-2-1910 (h) Glossop	W 4-0	126	7	7	1			133	8
Govier S	1974-77	21-12-1974 (h) Charlton Athletic	D 1-1	23/1	0			2	0	25/1	0
Graham J	1893-97	2-9-1893 (h) Northwich Victoria	W 7-0	84	2	15	2			99	4
Grant EA	1952-54	1-1-1953 (a) Tranmere Rovers	L 1-2	15	5					15	5
Grant W	1903-06	12-3-1904 (a) Burton United	L 0-1	9	2					9	2
Graver F	1922-23	26-8-1922 (h) Wrexham	W 4-0	6	1	1	0			7	1
Gray JR	1891-92					3	0			3	0
Gray AE	1924-27	18-10-1924 (a) New Brighton †	L 2-3	5	1					5	1
Gray GJP	1950-51	7-10-1950 (a) Barnsley	L 1-3	3	0					3	0
Gray M	1919-20	11-10-1919 (h) West Ham United	L 0-1	1	0					1	0
Gray P	1898-1903	3-9-1898 (a) Manchester City	L 2-7	121	5	11	1			132	6
Gray RSM	1895-98	2-9-1895 (a) Woolwich Arsenal	L 1-3	69	25	11	3			80	28
Gray S	1970-77	12-9-1970 (h) Northampton Town	L 0-2	263/1	2	19	1	17	1	299/1	4
Green HR	1965-67	21-8-1965 (h) Bristol Rovers	D 1-1	65	20	8	3	9	5	82	28
Green K	1951-52	2-2-1952 (h) Wrexham	W 1-0	1	0					1	0
Greenwood W	1898-1900	3-9-1898 (a) Manchester City	L 2-7	57	13	7	2			64	15
Greetham H	1950-51	14-4-1951 (a) Leeds United	L 0-1	4	0					4	0
Gregory G	1893-94	9-12-1893 (a) Ardwick	L 1-4	1	0					1	0
Gregson A	1913-15	13-9-1913 (a) Leicester Fosse	L 0-2	49	12	1	0			50	12
Griffiths JE	1898-1902	3-9-1898 (a) Manchester City	L 2-7	85	5	11	3			96	8
Grocock C	1985-89	*2-12-1986 (h) Blackburn Rovers	W 1-0	18/24	1	1/2	0			19/26	1
Grotier P	1982-85	16-10-1982 (h) Derby County	D 1-1	10	0	1	0	2	0	13	0
Gunner	1883-84					1	0			1	0
Haines W	1890-92					3	2			3	2
Hair G	1948-51	5-2-1949 (a) Queens Park R	W 2-1	68	8	2	0			70	8
Hair W	1928-29	10-11-1928 (h) Port Vale	W 3-1	6	2					6	2
Hakin JT	1906-08	1-9-1906 (h) Nottingham Forest	W 3-1	58	16	4	0			62	16
Hall AF	1929-48	12-4-1930 (a) Everton	W 4-2	358	4	31	0			389	4
Hall B	1900-03	12-1-1901 (h) Leicester Fosse †	W 4-1	39	4	2	0			41	4
Hall RC	1882-86					9	0			9	0
Halsall M	1986-87	28-2-1987 (h) Sheffield United	W 1-0	12	0					12	0
Ham RS	1963-64	21-3-1964 (a) Leeds United †	L 1-3	2	1					2	1
Hansen E	1946-47	26-12-1946 (a) Charlton Athletic	D 0-0	1	0					1	0
Hanvey K	1976-78	12-2-1977 (h) Mansfield Town	L 0-1	54	2	5	0			59	2
Harbertson R	1954-55	18-9-1954 (a) Gateshead	L 0-1	26	6	3	2			29	8
Hardie G	1896-97	27-2-1897 (a) Walsall	W 1-0	6	0					6	0
Harding SJ	1976-77	11-9-1976 (h) Brighton & HA	W 2-0	8	0					8	0
Hardy JJ	1925-27	29-8-1925 (h) Doncaster Rovers	W 3-0	46	4	5	1			51	5
Hargreaves WV	1908-10	17-10-1908 (a) Bradford	W 2-0	18	1	1	0			19	1
Harker CJ	1967-68	14-10-1967 (h) Barrow	L 0-1	10	0					10	0
Harmsworth F	1903-04	30-1-1904 (h) Burnley	D 0-0	5	0					5	0
Harnby RR	1949-52	10-12-1949 (a) Brentford	L 0-1	34	0	3	0			37	0
Harper GC	1976-77	18-12-1976 (h) Reading	W 2-1	3	0					3	0
Harper G	1901-03	3-9-1901 (h) Derby County	D 1-1	21	3	2	0			23	3
Harris CV	1926-28	30-8-1926 (h) Swansea Town	L 0-1	47	1	1	0			48	1
Harris G	1900-01	1-9-1900 (a) Burnley	L 0-3	13	0					13	0
Harrison P	1921-22	24-12-1921 (h) Halifax Town	W 4-1	8	0	1	0			9	0

Player	Seasons	League debut	Result	League App	League Gls	FA Cup App	FA Cup Gls	FL Cup App	FL Cup Gls	Total App	Total Gls
Harrison RW	1954-55	21-8-1954 (a) Rochdale	W 3-0	38	7	2	3			40	10
Hart H	1952-53	25-12-1952 (h) Chesterfield	D 0-0	13	3					13	3
Harvey W	1945-46					1	0			1	0
Harvey W	1890-91					1	0			1	0
Hatton A	1907-10	7-9-1907 (a) Lincoln City	L 0-1	74	2	5	0			79	2
Haydock WE	1964-65	12-12-1964 (h) Oldham Athletic †(2)	W 3-1	21	4					21	4
Hayhurst S	1950-53	20-1-1951 (h) Preston North End	L 0-4	62	0	5	0			67	0
Hazel D	1986-87	25-10-1986 (h) Leeds United	D 0-0	9	2					9	2
Hemingfield WE	1899-1900	23-9-1899 (a) Middlesbrough	L 0-1	94	9	7	1			101	10
Henderson C	1892-93	3-9-1892 (h) Northwich Victoria	W 2-1	12	0	2	0			14	0
Henderson CG	1908-10	5-9-1908 (h) West Bromwich A	D 1-1	65	0	2	0			67	0
Henderson WP	1911-12	23-9-1911 (a) Burnley	D 1-1	4	0					4	0
Henshaw G	1883-87	23-4-1984 (h) Cambridge United	D 0-0	46/4	9	2	0	4/2	0	52/6	9
Hernon J	1951-54	22-8-1951 (h) Lincoln City	L 2-3	91	23	4	0			95	23
Hickman MFT	1968-75	10-8-1968 (h) Newport County	W 3-0	247/7	48	14	3	17	3	278/7	54
Higgins G	1954-57	21-8-1954 (a) Rochdale	W 3-0	47	0	3	0			50	0
Higgins M	1904-12	24-9-1904 (a) Bolton Wanderers	L 1-4	95	8	9	0			104	8
Higgins W	1892-97 1911-12	3-9-1892 (h) Northwich Victoria	W 2-1	127	27	22	8			149	35
Hill B	1960-67	15-4-1961 (h) Torquay United †	W 4-2	180	26	12	0	13	2	205	28
Hilton F	1922-25	24-2-1923 (h) Ashington	W 7-4	71	0	6	0			77	0
Hinchcliffe T	1936-38	7-11-1936 (a) Sheffield Wednesday	L 0-2	27	5	1	0			28	5
Hine M	1984-86	23-3-1985 (a) Oldham Athletic	L 0-2	20/2	1	1	0	1	0	22/2	1
Hobson G	1985-87	*24-8-1985 (h) Charlton Athletic †	D 2-2	50/2	18	1	0	7	2	58/2	20
Hobson J	1910-11					3	0			3	0
Hodgkinson AV	1903-04	21-11-1903 (a) Bristol City	L 0-4	16	4	1	1			17	5
Hodgkinson JC	1911-12	9-9-1911 (a) Leicester Fosse	W 2-0	12	3					12	3
Hodgson BG	1956-57	27-10-1956 (a) West Ham United †	W 1-0	7	1					7	1
Hodgson J	1913-14	25-4-1914 (a) Clapton Orient	D 0-0	1	0					1	0
Hodgson JV	1932-48	31-8-1932 (a) Plymouth Argyle	L 0-4	212	2	22	0			234	2
Hodgson S	1946-48	31-8-1946 (a) Manchester United	L 1-2	21	0	2	0			23	0
Hogan W	1896-97	12-9-1896 (a) Burton Wanderers	L 1-5	1	0					1	0
Hogg R	1902-03	6-12-1902 (a) Liverpool †	L 2-9	3	1					3	1
Hollingsworth	1890-91					1	0			1	0
Holmes MM	1931-35	12-3-1932 (h) Blackburn Rovers †	W 4-3	37	17	2	0			39	17
Holtby J	1888-92					10	0			10	0
Honeyman JW	1923-24	3-9-1923 (a) Bradford	L 1-2	21	1	1	0			22	1
Hooks VA	1972-73	10-10-1972 (a) Shrewsbury Town	L 2-3	0/1	0					0/1	0
Hooper W	1905-07	30-9-1905 (a) Barnsley	L 0-2	33	6	2	1			35	7
Hopewell W	1885-88					9	0			9	0
Horner J	1903-07	23-4-1904 (a) Barnsley	L 1-3	14	0					14	0
Horwood N	1986	27-9-1986 (h) Barnsley	L 0-1	0/1	0			0/1	0	0/2	0
Housley S	1966-69	24-2-1967 (a) Oldham Athletic	W 1-0	34	3	2	2			38	3
Howe F	1938-39	8-10-1938 (a) Arsenal	L 0-2	29	15	6	6			35	21
Howells WM	1963-64	19-10-1963 (a) Bury	D 1-1	6	0					6	0
Hubbard A	1911-12	2-9-1911 (h) Wolverhampton W	D 0-0	25	13	4	5			29	18
Hubbard PJ	1972-76	28-10-1972 (h) Bournemouth	L 0-1	144/2	37	12/1	1	7	0	163/3	38
Hudson CH	1895-96	14-9-1895 (a) Darwen	D 3-3	5	0	1	0			6	0
Hughes A	1954-55	21-8-1954 (a) Rochdale † (2)	W 3-0	25	11	2	1			27	12
Hughes J	1921-23	14-1-1922 (h) Tranmere Rovers	W 5-1	31	0					31	0
Hughes H	1890-91					2	0			2	0
Hunt J	1888-89					8	1			8	1
Hunt RA	1959-61	22-8-1959 (h) Chesterfield † (2)	W 5-1	53	39	1	1			54	40
Hunter R	1904-05	17-12-1904 (h) Lincoln City	W 1-0	8	1	1	0			9	1
Hunter W	1926-28	29-1-1927 (h) Notts County	L 1-4	6	0					6	0
Huxford AT	1909-20	30-4-1910 (a) Gainsborough T	D 1-1	18	2	1	0			19	2
Hyde LJ	1897-98	11-9-1897 (h) Darwen	W 5-0	4	0					4	0
Irvine AW	1920-21	23-10-1920 (a) Merthyr Town	L 1-3	3	0					3	0
Jack S	1907-08	3-9-1907 (h) Gainsborough T	L 1-4	1	0					1	0
Jackson E	1925-27	19-12-1925 (a) New Brighton	W 4-1	20	0	3	0			23	0
Jacobson H	1925-35	29-8-1925 (h) Doncaster Rovers	W 3-0	360	1	22	0			382	1

Player	Seasons	League debut	Result	League App	League Gls	FA Cup App	FA Cup Gls	FL Cup App	FL Cup Gls	Total App	Total Gls
Jenkin K	1950-54	17-2-1951 (h) Queens Park R	D 2-2	23	6					23	6
Jenkinson T	1898-1901	10-9-1898 (h) Glossop North End †	D 1-1	66	24	10	4			76	28
Jenkinson W	1882-84					2	0			2	0
Jennings DB	1932-36	1-10-1932 (a) Lincoln City	L 3-6	99	29	3	0			102	29
Jennings W	1919-20	1-1-1920 (h) Coventry City	L 0-1	2	0	1	0			3	0
Jewel W	1907-08	3-9-1907 (h) Gainsborough T	L 1-4	19	2					19	2
Jobling KA	1953-69	13-2-1954 (h) Barrow	W 1-0	450	5	24	0	19	0	493	5
Jobling K	1987	20-2-1988 (h) Doncaster Rovers	D 0-0	46/1	5	2/1	1	2	0	50/2	6
Johnson J	1946-50	31-8-1946 (a) Manchester United	L 1-2	6	1					6	1
Johnson JW	1946-48	31-8-1946 (a) Manchester United	L 1-2	44	2	2	0			46	2
Johnson Jos	1905-06	2-9-1905 (a) Chesterfield	W 4-1	19	3					19	3
Johnson NV	1912-13	1-2-1913 (a) Lincoln City	L 0-3	1	0					1	0
Johnston CP	1948-57	5-2-1949 (a) Queens Park R	W 2-1	250	16	11	2			261	18
Johnston H	1920-21	2-4-1921 (a) Gillingham	L 1-2	1	0					1	0
Johnston H	1897-98	6-11-1897 (h) Newcastle United	W 2-0	8	0					8	0
Jones FG	1961-63	19-8-1961 (a) Newport County	W 2-0	58	9			2	0	60	9
Jones JL	1893-94	2-9-1893 (h) Northwich Victoria	W 7-0	28	6	5	1			33	7
Jones T	1921-22	17-9-1921 (h) Stalybridge Celtic	D 1-1	3	0	5	0			8	0
Jones TW	1938-47	27-8-1938 (h) Aston Villa †	L 1-2	48	8	10	1			58	9
Keeble BB	1959-65	29-9-1959 (h) York City	D 2-2	172	1	5	0	4	0	181	1
Keeble WFW	1946-47	12-10-1946 (a) Leeds United	L 0-1	7	1	2	1			9	2
Kelly JE	1932-38	18-3-1933 (a) Millwall	W 1-0	160	3	14	0			174	3
Kelly T	1908-10	3-4-1909 (h) Tottenham Hotspur	L 1-2	26	3	3	0			29	3
Kemp G	1919-20	24-1-1920 (h) Barnsley	D 1-1	9	1					9	1
Kennedy R	1968-71	8-3-1969 (h) Darlington	D 1-1	84	1	2	0	2	0	88	1
Kenny D	1913-20	6-9-1913 (h) Notts County	D 0-0	58	0	1	0			59	0
Kent PW	1920-21	25-9-1920 (a) Reading	L 1-4	1	0					1	0
Kerry BP	1964-67	18-12-1965 (h) Oldham Athletic	W 3-1	0/1	0					0/1	0
Kettle WW	1922-23	11-11-1922 (a) Crewe Alexandra	L 0-3	16	3					16	3
Kilbourne A	1907-10	3-9-1907 (h) Gainsborough T †	L 1-4	66	16	6	2			72	18
Kilmore K	1979-83	18-9-1979 (a) Bury †	D 1-1	70/32	27	4/1	2	4	0	78/33	29
Kimpson G	1883-86					10	0			10	0
Kirkland JW	1970-71	15-8-1970 (h) Oldham Athletic	W 4-1	12	0			1	0	13	0
Kirsopp WHJ	1922-23	30-9-1922 (a) Wigan Borough	L 0-1	6	2	1	0			7	2
Kitching H	1923-24	22-9-1923 (a) Lincoln City	W 3-1	16	1					16	1
Knights AF	1959-64	12-12-1959 (h) Bury	D 2-2	75	1	1	0	1	0	77	1
Kurz FJ	1938-39	17-9-1938 (h) Derby County	D 1-1	3	0					3	0
Lakey T	1899-1900	9-9-1899 (a) Burslem Port Vale	W 3-2	30	12	1	0			31	12
Lakin J	1964-65							1	0	1	0
Lancaster R	1964-67	12-12-1964 (h) Oldham Atheltic	W 3-1	16/2	0			1	0	17/2	0
Lappin HH	1903-04	1-9-1903 (h) Bradford City	W 2-0	20	4	1	0			21	4
Laverick PH	1957-61	1-3-1958 (h) Ipswich Town	L 0-2	4	0					4	0
Laws JM	1921-23	29-10-1921 (h) Southport	D 0-0	53	5	2	0			55	5
Leafe AR	1909-10	9-10-1909 (h) Stockport County	L 0-1	1	0					1	0
Leaning J	1897-98 1900-01	16-10-1897 (a) Darwen	L 0-1	5	0	1	0			6	0
Leddy H	1923-24	25-8-1923 (a) Tranmere Rovers	L 1-2	13	0					13	0
Lee A	1906-10	10-11-1906 (a) Clapton Orient	L 0-1	86	0	9	1			95	1
Lee JA	1913-15	6-9-1913 (h) Notts County	D 0-0	15	0					15	0
Lee J	1887-89					7	6			7	6
Leigh W	1900-03	1-9-1900 (a) Burnley	L 0-3	48	12	1	0			49	12
Leiper J	1900-02	1-9-1900 (a) Burnley	L 0-3	46	0					46	0
Leonard HD	1908-11	12-9-1908 (a) Birmingham	L 1-3	53	23	2	4			55	27
Lester MJ	1977-80	*26-12-1977 (h) Halifax Town	D 0-0	45/3	10	0/1	0	3/1	2	48/5	12
Lever M	1988-	*3-9-1988 (h) Torquay United	W 1-0	37/1	2	6	0	1	0	44/1	2
Lewis AC	1933-39	24-3-1934 (a) Lincoln City	D 3-3	75	31	10	6			85	37
Lewis FJ	1969-77	31-1-1970 (h) Crewe Alexandra	L 0-2	231/27	74	8/5	2	12/3	1	251/35	77
Liddell G	1976-81	12-3-1977 (h) Rotherham United †	D 1-1	90/15	22	5/1	1	9/3	1	104/19	24
Lindsay W	1894-98	1-9-1894 (h) Leicester Fosse	W 4-3	106	1	14	0			120	1
Linton J	1892-93	31-3-1893 (h) Sheffield United	L 0-1	1	0					1	0
Lloyd S	1948-53	21-8-1948 (h) Fulham	L 2-3	148	23	5	0			153	23

Player	Seasons	League debut	Result	League App	League Gls	FA Cup App	FA Cup Gls	FL Cup App	FL Cup Gls	Total App	Total Gls
Lockie J	1898-99	11-3-1899 (a) New Brighton Tower	L 0-2	6	0					6	0
Long J	1901-04	11-2-1902 (a) Sheffield United †	D 2-2	57	13	2	0			59	13
Lonsdale TS	1908-14	5-12-1908 (h) Hull City	D 0-0	87	0	4	0			91	0
Lord W	1952-54	11-4-1953 (h) Carlisle United †	L 2-3	7	1					7	1
Lowe GLW	1883-84					1	0			1	0
Lowe WC	1898-99	10-9-1898 (h) Glossop North End	D 1-1	2	0					2	0
Lowry BT	1954-56	28-8-1954 (h) Tranmere Rovers	D 2-2	12	1					12	1
Lumby JA	1973-75	16-3-1974 (a) Aldershot	L 0-1	28/3	12			1	0	29/3	12
Lumby WCW	1937-38	25-12-1937 (h) Stoke City	L 1-5	3	0					3	0
Lund GT	1983-86	27-9-1983 (a) Barnsley	L 1-3	47/13	12	4	5	6/2	1	57/15	18
Lundie J	1892-95	3-9-1892 (h) Northwich Victoria	W 2-1	50	0	27	2			77	2
Lynch BJ	1972-73	9-9-1972 (a) Walsall	L 0-1	10/4	0					10/4	0
Lynn F	1948-49	25-9-1948 (a) Luton Town	D 1-1	2	0					2	0
Lyons M	1985-87	16-11-1985 (h) Portsmouth	W 1-0	50	4	4	1	3		57	5
Macauley JL	1920-21	28-8-1920 (h) Northampton T † (2)	W 2-0	16	4	2	0			18	4
McAvoy J	1899-1901	6-1-1900 (h) Burslem Port Vale	D 1-1	26	0	2	0			28	0
MacBeth G	1891-92					1	0			1	0
McBeth R	1887-90					11	7			11	7
McCairns T	1893-98	23-9-1893 (a) Lincoln City	W 2-1	137	86	17	18			154	104
McClennon JW	1923-25	5-4-1924 (a) Southport	L 0-3	11	0					11	0
McConnell A	1901-05	7-9-1901 (a) Sheffield Wednesday	L 1-3	84	0	4	0			88	0
McConnell J	1903-06 1907-08	16-1-1904 (h) Chesterfield	W 1-0	55	0	1	0			56	0
McCue AB	1951-53	18-8-1951 (a) Chesterfield	L 1-3	37	15	4	1			41	16
McDermott J	1986-	7-2-1987 (a) Bradford City	L 2-4	70/9	2	8	0	2/1	0	80/10	2
McDiarmid G	1903-05 1907-08	19-9-1903 (a) Chesterfield	W 1-0	71	1	4	0			75	1
MacDonald J	1906-07	1-9-1906 (h) Nottingham Forest	W 3-1	16	0					16	0
McEachran G	1919-22	30-8-1919 (h) Stockport County	L 0-3	66	0	4	0			70	0
Macey JRT	1968-70	14-9-1968 (h) Aldershot	L 0-2	36/1	0	1	0	1	0	38/1	0
MacFarlane R	1900-01	15-12-1900 (a) Glossop	D 0-0	18	0	1	0			19	0
McGarvey S	1986-88	7-3-1987 (a) Leeds United	L 0-2	49/1	7	3	1	2/1	1	54/2	9
McGowan J	1946-49	31-8-1946 (a) Manchester United †	L 1-2	34	4					34	4
McGregor J	1904-07	12-11-1904 (a) Bristol City	L 0-5	93	3	5	0			98	3
McHardy G	1892-93	31-3-1893 (h) Sheffield United	L 0-1	3	0					3	0
McKenna FC	1922-27	25-11-1922 (a) Walsall	L 0-1	114	31	10	3			124	34
McKenna T	1948-50	21-8-1948 (h) Fulham	L 2-3	50	2	2	0			52	2
McKenna TP	1913-15	13-12-1913 (a) Leeds City	L 1-4	16	0					16	0
McKenzie DC	1951-52	18-8-1951 (a) Chesterfield	L 1-3	4	0					4	0
McKenzie ML	1949-51	24-9-1949 (h) Sheffield United	W 4-0	58	11	2	1			60	12
MacKnight H	1889-90					2	0			2	0
McLachlin F	1925-27	19-12-1925 (a) New Brighton	W 4-1	52	0	3	0			55	0
McLatchie C	1902-03	6-12-1902 (a) Liverpool	L 2-9	9	1					9	1
McLean GR	1962-65	15-9-1962 (h) Newcastle United	L 0-1	91	41	3	0	2	1	96	42
McLean JC	1897-98	1-9-1897 (a) Woolwich Arsenal	L 1-4	30	2	1	0			31	2
McMillan D	1948-55	9-4-1949 (h) Brentford	W 3-0	188	2	12	0			200	2
McStay JG	1948-51	21-8-1948 (h) Fulham	L 2-3	61	2	4	0			65	2
Maddison JP	1950-59	7-10-1950 (a) Barnsley	L 1-3	272	40	19	4			291	44
Marklew RK	1960-61	29-10-1960 (a) Tranmere Rovers †	W 6-3	6	1	1	0	1	0	8	1
Marley A	1974-76	19-4-1975 (h) Wrexham	W 2-0	39/1	2	1	0			40/1	2
Marlow F	1951-52	25-8-1951 (h) Bradford †	W 3-0	12	6					12	6
Marsden AJ	1969-70	8-11-1969 (a) Chesterfield	W 2-1	2	0					2	0
Marshall WE	1923-32	3-9-1923 (a) Bradford	L 1-2	340	60	23	3			363	63
Martin F	1911-21	2-9-1911 (h) Wolverhampton W	D 0-0	159	1	5	0			164	1
Martin G	1966-68	5-11-1966 (h) Shewsbury Town	D 1-1	71	5	2	0	3	0	76	5
Matthews N	1984-87	13-10-1984 (a) Portsmouth	L 2-3	9/2	1					9/2	1
Mawer SK	1977-80	6-9-1977 (a) Watford	L 0-1	57/3	0	5	0	3	0	65/3	0
Mayson T	1911-15	21-10-1911 (h) Bristol City	W 3-0	85	28	4	1			89	29
Meikle AML	1927-28	8-10-1927 (h) Oldham Athletic	L 1-2	13	2	1	0			14	2
Mellor H	1900-01	1-9-1900 (a) Burnley	L 0-3	33	4	1	0			34	4
Millar H	1921-24	10-12-1921 (a) Walsall	L 1-2	26	0	5	0			31	0

Player	Seasons	League debut	Result	League App	League Gls	FA Cup App	FA Cup Gls	FL Cup App	FL Cup Gls	Total App	Total Gls
Millar JW	1952-53	15-11-1952 (h) Hartlepools United †	W 7-0	5	2	2	1			7	3
Millar J	1913-14	6-9-1913 (h) Notts County	D 0-0	6	1					6	1
Miller J	1921-24	27-8-1921 (a) Ashington	L 0-1	89	32	9	4			98	36
Miller WL	1903-04	1-9-1903 (h) Bradford City	W 2-0	4	0					4	0
Mills KD	1960-61	22-4-1961 (a) Walsall	L 1-2	2	0					2	0
Milnes C	1905-07	4-11-1905 (h) Bradford City	W 1-0	35	1					35	1
Mitchell R	1978-82	19-8-1978 (h) Reading	L 1-2	142	6	9	0	16	1	167	7
Mobley DA	1969-70	9-8-1969 (a) Workington Town	D 0-0	26/1	0	1	0	1	0	28/1	0
Mochan C	1904-05	19-11-1904 (h) Manchester United	L 0-1	12	0	2	0			14	0
Monument H	1882-86					10	7			10	7
Moody JH	1920-22	6-9-1920 (a) Southend United	L 1-3	33	0	1	0			34	0
Moody KG	1943-51	17-3-1948 (h) Manchester United	D 1-1	114	0	2	0			116	0
Moore AR	1983-87	26-12-1983 (h) Sheffield Wednesday	W 1-0	62/2	1			4	0	66/2	0
Moore AP	1970-71	13-3-1971 (h) Brentford	L 1-5	2/1	0					2/1	0
Moore D	1978-83 1986-88	11-11-1978 (a) Torquay United	L 1-3	139/1	2	9	0	9	0	157/1	2
Moore G	1966-69	28-2-1967 (a) Swindon Town	L 1-3	52/1	15	1	0	6	0	59/1	15
Moore KT	1976-87	21-8-1976 (a) Bury	L 0-2	397/3	28	25	3	41	3	463/3	34
Moore NW	1946-47	14-9-1946 (a) Sheffield United	D 1-1	7	1	2	1			9	2
Moore TR	1948-50	4-12-1948 (h) Bury	L 2-3	3	0					3	0
Moralee M	1931-36	23-4-1932 (h) Derby County	W 2-1	27	5					27	5
Morgan AN	1902-03	1-11-1902 (h) Notts County	D 1-1	1	0					1	0
Morgan D	1965-66					1	0			1	0
Morley H	1904-07	3-9-1904 (h) Barnsley	D 0-0	93	3	5	0			98	3
Morrall GR	1920-22	18-9-1920 (h) Bristol Rovers †	W 3-1	65	8	6	0			71	8
Morris H	1896-97	2-9-1896 (a) Loughborough Town	W 4-1	23	1	1	0			24	1
Morris R	1906-07	1-9-1906 (h) Nottingham Forest †	W 3-1	24	7	2	0			26	7
Morris TH	1906-07	3-9-1906 (a) Leicester Fosse	L 0-2	28	0	2	0			30	0
Morton H	1887-88					3	0			3	0
Moulson GB	1936-47	4-4-1947 (h) Stoke City	L 2-5	1	0	3	0			4	0
Mouncer FE	1946-49	23-9-1946 (a) Wolverhampton W	L 0-2	22	0	3	0			25	0
Mount E	1897-98	11-9-1897 (h) Darwen	W 5-0	4	0					4	0
Mountain G	1895 1897-1903	26-10-1895 (a) Manchester City	L 1-2	152	4	12	0			164	4
Mounteney A	1911-13	2-9-1911 (h) Wolverhampton W	D 0-0	45	17	1	0			46	17
Mudie H	1888-89					4	0			4	0
Mulholland JR	1949-51	10-12-1949 (a) Brentford	L 0-1	2	0					2	0
Mullen M	1892-93	22-10-1892 (a) Walsall	L 1-3	16	6	6	6			22	12
Mundahl H	1884-91	9-11-1889 (a) Crewe Alexandra	L 0-6			5	2			5	2
Munn S	1895-98	7-9-1895 (h) Lincoln City	W 4-2	63	0	9	1			72	1
Murray J	1894-95	9-2-1895 (a) Crewe Alexandra	L 1-2	2	0					2	0
Murrell AJ	1892-95	3-9-1892 (h) Northwich Victoria	W 2-1	35	1	9	0			44	1
Nelmes A	1898-99	3-9-1898 (a) Manchester City	L 2-7	219	14	15	0			234	14
Newton B	1953-54	3-10-1953 (h) Bradford City	W 1-0	3	0					3	0
Newton W	1926-27	4-9-1926 (h) Manchester City	D 2-2	14	0	1	0			15	0
Nichol J	1903-04	1-9-1903 (h) Bradford City	W 2-0	16	3	1	0			17	3
Nicholl CJ	1983-85	27-8-1983 (h) Shrewsbury Town	D 1-1	70	0	1	0	8	0	79	0
Nicholson GH	1953-54	16-9-1953 (a) Accrington Stanley	L 1-3	17	0					17	0
Nidd GF	1898-1900	1-10-1898 (a) Burslem Port Vale	L 0-2	50	1	8	0			58	1
Noble S	1882-85					8	0			8	0
North M	1987-89	15-8-1987 (a) Doncaster Rovers	L 0-1	64/3	17	8/1	5	4	2	76/4	24
Oakes F	1904-05	4-3-1905 (a) Burslem Port Vale	L 0-2	1	0					1	0
Oakley N	1966-67	10-12-1966 (a) Gillingham	L 0-2	15	0					15	0
Oakton AE	1924-25	14-3-1925 (h) Nelson	W 2-0	2	0					2	0
Oates G	1968-71	12-10-1968 (h) Chesterfield	L 1-2	80/1	9	2	0	1/1	0	83/2	9
O'Dell A	1981-83	21-11-1981 (a) Chelsea	D 1-1	18/2	0	2	0	0/2	0	20/4	0
Ogilive A	1892-93	3-9-1892 (h) Northwich Victoria	W 2-1	21	0	17	0			38	0
O'Kelly R	1988-	27-8-1988 (a) Cambridge United	L 1-4	38/1	10	6	0	2	0	46/1	10
Oldridge AR	1975-77	*3-1-1976 (h) Chesterfield †	W 3-0	9/6	0			1	0	10/6	0
Openshaw W	1905-07	30-9-1905 (a) Barnsley	L 0-2	5	0					5	0
O'Riordan D	1986-88	23-8-1986 (a) Ipswich Town	D 1-1	86	14	6	0	6	0	98	14

Player	Seasons	League debut	Result	League App	League Gls	FA Cup App	FA Cup Gls	FL Cup App	FL Cup Gls	Total App	Total Gls
Ousey A	1882-83					1	0			1	0
Owens I	1908-09	1-9-1908 (h) Stockport County †	W 3-0	6	3	1	0			7	3
Padley G	1904-06 1915	22-4-1905 (h) Leicester Fosse † (2)	W 2-0	18	8	1	0			19	8
Pangborn T	1898-99	10-9-1898 (h) Glossop North End	D 1-1	3	0					3	0
Parker A	1897-98	5-3-1898 (h) Walsall	L 1-2	1	0					1	0
Parkin TA	1975-76	3-4-1976 (a) Cardiff City	L 1-2	6	0					6	0
Parry FT	1926-27	16-10-1926 (h) Hull City	L 0-1	1	0					1	0
Partridge M	1974-79	15-3-1975 (a) Aldershot	D 0-0	134/4	25	9	2	7	0	150/4	27
Paterson P	1902-03	25-10-1902 (a) West Bromwich A	L 0-1	2	0					2	0
Pattinson JB	1907-08	3-9-1907 (h) Gainsborough T	L 1-4	19	2					19	2
Paul T	1958-59	25-10-1958 (h) Scunthorpe United	D 1-1	1	0					1	0
Peake A	1985-87	17-8-1985 (a) Brighton & HA	D 2-2	39	4	1	1	5	0	45	5
Pearce JA	1958-62	30-3-1959 (a) Rotherham United	L 1-2	48	0	1	0	2	0	51	0
Pearson JC	1924-26	6-12-1924 (a) Durham City	L 1-6	5	0	3	0			8	0
Pearson S	1886-87					3	3			3	3
Pearson WGA	1946-49	14-9-1946 (a) Sheffield United	D 1-1	35	8					35	8
Pell D	1955-57	18-2-1956 (h) Oldham Athletic †	W 5-1	3	1	1	0			4	1
Pennington A	1898-99	3-9-1898 (a) Manchester City	L 2-7	1	0					1	0
Pennington J	1962-65	6-4-1963 (h) Swansea Town	W 1-0	89	8	5	1	3	0	97	9
Penrose N	1946-48	14-12-1946 (a) Derby County	L 1-4	9	0					9	0
Phillips H	1903-05	1-4-1904 (h) Burton United	W 4-0	21	9	2	0			23	9
Phillips MS	1954-55	8-3-1955 (h) Carlisle United	W 2-0	6	1					6	1
Pickering FC	1912-13	8-2-1913 (h) Wolverhampton W	W 2-1	2	0					2	0
Player PRI	1952-59	6-4-1953 (a) York City	L 0-2	57	0	3	0			60	0
Ponting WT	1930-36	26-12-1930 (a) Liverpool	D 1-1	12	3	1	0			13	3
Porter J	1909-10	1-9-1909 (h) Bradford	L 0-1	1	0					1	0
Portwood C	1961-64	19-8-1961 (a) Newport County	W 2-0	92	35	3	1	2	0	97	36
Poskett TW	1928-31	4-5-1929 (a) Middlesbrough	L 0-3	2	0					2	0
Powell WMP	1927-30	27-8-1927 (h) Clapton Orient	D 2-2	78	1	3	0			81	1
Pratt L	1986-89	9-5-1987 (a) Stoke City	L 1-5	1	0					1	0
Pratt TP	1895-96	2-9-1895 (a) Royal Arsenal	L 1-3	29	15	7	1			36	16
Priestley G	1955-59	20-8-1955 (h) Rochdale	D 1-1	110	11	6	2			116	13
Priestley J	1928-32	25-8-1928 (a) Bristol City	D 2-2	139	7	7	0			146	7
Pringle WA	1954-55	21-8-1954 (a) Rochdale	W 3-0	2	0					2	0
Prior J	1926-32	8-2-1927 (h) Middlesbrough	L 4-7	160	34	8	2			168	36
Prout GW	1926-27	18-12-1926 (a) Wolverhampton W	W 4-3	4	0	1	0			5	0
Prudhoe M	1986-87	28-3-1987 (h) Shrewsbury Town	L 0-1	8	0					8	0
Pugsley J	1925-27	29-8-1925 (h) Doncaster Rovers	W 3-0	80	6	7	1			87	7
Purvis WY	1961-63	23-12-1961 (a) Southend United	L 0-2	7	2					7	2
Pynegar A	1905-06	25-11-1905 (a) Burton United	L 0-1	2	0					2	0
Quigley D	1936-39	3-3-1937 (a) Brentford	W 3-2	23	2					23	2
Quin JJ	1912-15	3-9-1912 (h) Blackpool	D 1-1	61	5	1	0			62	5
Raby WL	1921-22	29-10-1921 (h) Southport	D 0-0	2	1	2	0			4	1
Rafferty R	1956-63	12-1-1957 (a) Leyton Orient	D 1-1	264	145	10	3	3	4	277	152
Rampton G	1911-15	9-9-1911 (a) Leicester Fosse †	W 2-0	73	30	3	0			76	30
Ramsden E	1909-10	18-12-1909 (h) Gainsborough T	W 2-1	5	0					5	0
Rankin J	1949-51	10-4-1950 (a) Leeds United	L 0-1	5	1					5	1
Ratcliffe GA	1898-1900	3-9-1898 (a) Manchester City	L 2-7	57	19	7	1			64	20
Rathbone GC	1966-73	16-11-1966 (a) Reading	L 0-6	232/1	11	6	0	17	0	255/1	11
Rawcliffe P	1986-88	*18-10-1986 (a) West Bromwich A †	D 1-1	9/13	2	0/2	0	0/1	0	9/16	2
Rayner JP	1952-54	20-12-1952 (a) Wrexham	L 1-3	12	3	3	5			15	8
Raynes R	1884-85					5	1			5	1
Read AH	1882-86					8	0			8	0
Read TA	1927-34	21-1-1928 (a) Bristol City	D 0-0	247	0	12	0			259	0
Reay H	1924-25	20-12-1924 (a) Wigan Borough	L 1-3	1	0					1	0
Redding TR	1954-57	27-12-1954 (a) Barnsley	W 3-1	4	0					4	0
Reid W	1892-93	17-9-1892 (h) Darwen	L 0-1	10	0	11	3			21	3
Reece P	1988	3-9-1988 (h) Torquay	W 1-0	14	0	3	0	2	0	19	0
Reeson MA	1955-58	20-8-1955 (h) Rochdale	D 1-1	76	20	5	3			81	23
Reeve FW	1946-48	31-8-1946 (a) Manchester United	L 1-2	46	0	1	0			47	0

Player	Seasons	League debut	Result	League App	League Gls	FA Cup App	FA Cup Gls	FL Cup App	FL Cup Gls	Total App	Total Gls
Reeve KE	1946-48	12-2-1947 (a) Liverpool	L 0-5	24	5					24	5
Reynolds J	1904-05	3-9-1904 (h) Barnsley	D 0-0	29	3	2	1			31	4
Reynolds W	1905-06	30-12-1905 (h) Chesterfield	W 2-0	6	0					6	0
Rice B	1986-87	1-11-1986 (h) Millwall	W 1-0	4	0					4	0
Richards CH	1898-1901	7-1-1899 (a) Glossop North End	L 2-4	80	42	5	2			85	44
Richardson D	1955-60	20-8-1955 (h) Rochdale	D 1-1	175	1	11	0			186	1
Richardson W	1897-99	1-9-1897 (a) Woolwich Arsenal	L 1-4	2	0					2	0
Riddoch D	1892-95	3-9-1892 (h) Northwich Vic † (2)	W 2-1	59	18	29	10			88	28
Rippon T	1911-20	27-1-1912 (h) Burnley †	W 1-0	121	37	2	1			123	38
Rippon W	1913-14	25-10-1913 (a) Lincoln City	W 3-1	23	12					23	12
Ritchie T	1958-59	20-9-1958 (a) Cardiff City	L 1-4	1	0					1	0
Ritchie W	1922-23	7-10-1922 (h) Chesterfield	W 3-1	25	4					25	4
Roberts C	1903-04	1-9-1903 (h) Bradford City	W 2-0	31	4	2	0			33	4
Robertson AC	1935-38	19-2-1936 (a) Sunderland	L 1-3	5	0					5	0
Robinson A	1909-10	2-4-1910 (a) Fulham	L 2-3	2	0					2	0
Robinson F	1905-07	16-12-1905 (a) Hull City	W 1-0	33	8					33	8
Robinson HJ	1893-99	13-1-1894 (h) Ardwick †	W 5-0	10	9					10	9
Robinson I	1936-37	23-1-1937 (a) Leeds United	L 0-2	3	0					3	0
Robinson JN	1948-49	24-8-1948 (h) Nottingham Forest	L 1-2	5	0					5	0
Robinson N	1984-88	22-9-1984 (h) Oxford United	L 1-2	109	6	6	0	4	0	119	6
Robinson RW	1921-22	17-9-1921 (h) Stalybridge Celtic	D 1-1	9	0					9	0
Robinson S	1899-1900	26-12-1899 (h) Newton Heath	L 0-7	1	0					1	0
Robson J	1924-31	13-9-1924 (h) Wrexham	L 0-1	161	123	6	1			167	124
Robson TR	1952-55	4-10-1952 (h) Workington Town	W 2-0	58	2	5	0			63	2
Rodger T	1906-07	1-9-1906 (h) Nottingham Forest	W 3-1	34	13	2	0			36	13
Rodi J	1945-46					2	1			2	1
Rogers J	1896-98	12-9-1896 (a) Burton Wanderers †	L 1-5	53	23	4	1			57	24
Ronaldson D	1901-03	3-9-1901 (h) Derby County	D 1-1	64	19	4	1			68	20
Rose A	1891-92					1	0			1	0
Rose THT	1892-96	10-9-1892 (a) Crewe Alexandra	L 0-1	34	7	9	2			43	9
Ross RC	1965-71	21-8-1965 (h) Bristol Rovers	D 1-1	208/4	18	7	1	15	1	230/4	20
Ross W	1889-90					1	0			1	0
Ross W	1904-05	3-9-1904 (h) Barnsley	D 0-0	32	7	2	0			34	7
Rouse FW	1902-04	14-3-1903 (a) Middlesbrough	L 0-2	37	15	2	0			39	15
Rowbotham M	1984-85	23-3-1985 (a) Oldham Athletic	L 0-2	3/1	0			0/1	0	3/2	0
Rowston CE	1909-10	11-9-1909 (h) Clapton Orient	W 2-0	15	1	1	0			16	1
Rudd AC	1907-08	17-4-1908 (h) Wolverhampton W	L 0-1	1	0					1	0
Rudd WT	1966-68	20-8-1966 (a) Workington Town	L 1-2	59/1	9	3	0	8	1	70/1	10
Rushby W	1912-14	18-1-1913 (h) Barnsley	D 1-1	5	0					5	0
Russell J	1893-94	2-9-1893 (h) Northwich Vic †(3)	W 7-0	25	4	5	0			30	4
Sankey T	1920-21	4-12-1920 (a) Southampton	W 1-0	4	0	2	1			6	1
Satterthwaite JN	1908-09	14-11-1908 (a) Leeds City	L 1-4	20	2	1	0			21	2
Saunders S	1987-	29-8-1987 (a) Notts County	D 0-0	70/6	13	9	0	0/2	0	79/8	13
Saxby MW	1982-83	12-3-1983 (a) Cambridge United	L 0-1	10	0					10	0
Scotson R	1950-55	9-12-1950 (h) Swansea Town	W 4-2	164	4	12	2			176	6
Scott J	1956-63	25-8-1956 (h) Notts County †	W 2-1	240	51	8	2	1	1	249	54
Scott JG	1913-15	13-9-1913 (a) Leicester Fosse	L 0-2	47	1	2	0			49	1
Scott W	1907-10 1920	16-11-1907 (a) Oldham Athletic	L 0-2	99	0	5	0			104	0
Seagraves CA	1984-85	1-9-1984 (a) Middlesbrough	W 5-1	22/1	0	3	0	6	0	31/1	0
Seal J	1885-88					7	3			7	3
Seddon WC	1931-33	2-4-1932 (a) Everton	L 2-4	20	1					20	1
Seeburg MP	1911-12	2-9-1911 (h) Wolverhampton W	D 0-0	20	0	1	0			21	0
Sharman R	1885-86					3	1			3	1
Sharp F	1973-74	25-8-1973 (h) Hereford United	L 1-3	26/3	2	4	0	4	1	34/3	3
Shaw AE	1923-24	5-4-1924 (a) Southport	L 0-3	5	0					5	0
Shaw H	1937-39	26-1-1938 (a) Leeds United	D 1-1	15	3					15	3
Shaw J	1937-39	26-1-1938 (a) Leeds United	D 1-1	7	0					7	0
Shaw JF	1909-10	23-10-1909 (h) Birmingham	L 0-2	6	0					6	0
Shearer DJ	1983-84	5-11-1983 (a) Portsmouth	L 0-4	1/3	0					1/3	0
Shearer JMM	1948-51	26-2-1949 (a) Bradford	W 1-0	34	7	1	0			35	7

Player	Seasons	League debut	Result	League App	League Gls	FA Cup App	FA Cup Gls	FL Cup App	FL Cup Gls	Total App	Total Gls
Sherwood S	1987-	15-8-1987 (a) Doncaster Rovers	L 0-1	78	0	6	0	2	0	86	0
Short M	1970-71	30-1-1971 (h) Aldershot	L 0-2	10	0					10	0
Sibley ES	1947-49	6-12-1947 (a) Charlton Athletic	W 3-2	23	0	3	0			26	0
Simpson O	1971-72	29-9-1971 (a) Lincoln City	L 0-3	6/1	0	1	0	3/1	0	10/2	0
Sinclair MJ	1957-61	26-4-1958 (h) Bristol Rovers †	W 3-2	6	1					6	1
Singleton HB	1902-03	13-9-1902 (a) Bury	L 1-2	18	2	2	0			20	2
Skinner H	1901-02	30-11-1901 (a) Newcastle United	L 1-5	1	0					1	0
Slack T	1987-88	14-8-1987 (a) Doncaster Rovers	L 0-1	21	0	1	0	2	0	24	0
Slater JB	1954-55	27-12-1954 (a) Barnsley	W 3-1	4	0					4	0
Smailes J	1935-36	21-9-1935 (h) Bolton Wanderers	W 3-1	10	0	2	1			12	1
Smaller P	1988-	*13-5-1989 (h)) Hartlepool	W 3-0	0/1	0					0/1	0
Smith A	1919-22	30-8-1919 (h) Stockport County	L 0-3	89	15	9	4			98	19
Smith DN	1952-54	30-4-1953 (a) Port Vale	L 0-4	4	0					4	0
Smith F	1920-22	6-9-1920 (a) Southend United	L 1-3	5	0	1	0			6	0
Smith FE	1952-54	17-9-1952 (h) Barrow † (2)	W 2-1	50	24	4	1			54	25
Smith H	1887-88					1	0			1	0
Smith H	1887-90					13	1			13	1
Smith RMS	1971-72	30-10-1971 (a) Northampton Town	L 0-3	10/1	0	1	0			11/1	1
Smith RW	1966-68	14-1-1967 (a) Torquay United	L 1-3	48/4	1	2	0	1/1	0	51/5	1
Smith W	1892-93	26-9-1892 (a) Sheffield United	L 0-2	2	1	1	2			3	3
Smith WE	1922-23	6-1-1923 (a) Bradford	L 1-2	10	0					10	0
Soames C	1887-88					1	0			1	0
Sowerby WHR	1953-55	13-2-1954 (h) Barrow	W 1-0	12	1					12	1
Speak G	1911-13	17-2-1912 (h) Clapton Orient	W 2-1	4	0					4	0
Speight M	1982-84	7-9-1982 (h) Blackburn Rovers	W 5-0	35/3	2	1	0	3	0	39/3	2
Speight W	1903-04	3-10-1903 (a) Burnley	L 0-2	6	1					6	1
Spendiff FM	1902-05 1913-20	27-9-1902 (a) Sunderland	L 1-5	123	0	7	0			130	0
Spink TW	1914-22	1-9-1914 (h) Preston North End	D 2-2	116	3	5	1			121	4
Springthorpe TH	1908-13	1-9-1908 (h) Stockport County †	W 3-0	25	6	4	2			29	8
Squires F	1950-51	19-8-1950 (h) Cardiff City	D 0-0	36	2	2	1			38	3
Staniforth FW	1911-13	2-9-1911 (h) Wolverhampton W	D 0-0	67	8	2	0			69	8
Steeples J	1980-82	*28-3-1981 (h) Swansea City	W 1-0	4/3	0					4/3	0
Stephenson G	1988-	8-11-1988 (h) Doncaster Rovers	W 5-0	12/2	0					12/2	0
Stevenson J	1901-02	28-9-1901 (h) Bury	W 2-0	8	1					8	1
Stevenson R	1921-23	24-9-1921 (a) Wigan Borough	D 1-1	8	0	1	0			9	0
Stewart T	1898-99	1-10-1898 (a) Burslem Port Vale	L 0-2	1	0					1	0
Stockin R	1957-60	24-8-1957 (h) Leyton Orient †	W 7-2	49	14	4	1			53	15
Stokes AW	1954-57	27-12-1954 (a) Barnsley †	W 3-1	16	3	1	1			17	4
Stokes P	1907-09	7-9-1907 (a) Lincoln City	L 0-1	14	2	5	0			19	2
Stone JG	1979-83	18-8-1979 (h) Exeter City	W 4-1	89/5	2	8	0	11	0	108/5	2
Storer H	1919-21	30-8-1919 (h) Stockport County	L 0-3	64	18	4	2			68	20
Stott J	1894-95	1-9-1894 (h) Leicester Fosse	W 4-3	29	4	4	2			33	6
Stoutt S	1988-	27-8-1988 (a) Cambridge United †	L 1-4	2	1			2	0	4	1
Straw I	1986-87	*20-9-1986 (a) Sheffield United	W 2-1	7/3	0			1	0	8/3	0
Stroud DNL	1953-55	29-8-1953 (a) Stockport County †	L 2-3	71	12	8	1		79	13	
Stubbs B	*1987-88	4-4-1988 (a) York City †	W 2-0	2/5	2					2/5	2
Summers P	1914-15	1-9-1914 (h) Preston North End	D 2-2	34	0	1	0			35	0
Sutherland D	1888-90					9	3			9	3
Swaby HN	1926-32	30-4-1927 (a) Notts County	L 0-3	44	2	4	0			48	2
Swain JS	1936-39	7-11-1936 (a) Sheffield Wednesday	L 0-2	22	6	1	0			23	6
Swarbrick J	1905-07	2-9-1905 (a) Chesterfield †	W 4-1	67	12	3	0			70	12
Sykes AB	1920-21	6-11-1920 (a) Swansea Town	L 1-3	1	0					1	0
Talks T	1920-22	5-2-1921 (h) Crystal Palace †	W 1-0	15	4	1	0			16	4
Taylor F	1897-88	16-4-1898 (a) Blackpool	D 1-1	1	0					1	0
Taylor GT	1965-68	5-10-1965 (a) Brighton & HA	W 2-1	0/1	0	1	0	1	0	2/1	0
Taylor G	1961-68	14-9-1963 (h) Newcastle United	W 2-1	189	2	12	0	14	0	215	2
Taylor H	1884-89					15	0			15	0
Taylor J	1888-89					2	1			2	1
Taylor JH	1884-90					23	0			23	0
Taylor RE	1938-48	22-10-1938 (h) Birmingham	W 1-0	36	0	4	0			40	0

Player	Seasons	League debut	Result	League App	League Gls	FA Cup App	FA Cup Gls	FL Cup App	FL Cup Gls	Total App	Total Gls
Taylor WB	1949-51	18-2-1950 (h) Hull City	W 1-0	21	0	2	0			23	0
Tees M	1963-67 1970-73	24-8-1963 (a) Swansea Town †	D 1-1	196	93	14	6	17	10	227	109
Temple W	1938-39	27-8-1938 (h) Aston Villa	L 1-2	2	0					2	0
Tennant W	1901-02	3-9-1901 (h) Derby County	D 1-1	13	0					13	0
Thain JW	1924-25	30-8-1924 (h) Darlington	L 0-2	26	4					26	4
Theaker CA	1935-39	7-3-1936 (h) Preston North End	D 0-0	5	0					5	0
Thompson AJ	1904-05	1-4-1905 (a) Chesterfield	D 0-0	2	0					2	0
Thompson A	1919-20	20-12-1919 (h) Birmingham	L 0-3	3	1	1	1			4	2
Thompson EG	1924-25	20-9-1924 (a) Rotherham County	L 0-3	7	0	1	0			8	0
Thompson JB	1962-67	23-3-1963 (h) Sunderland	L 1-2	156	2	12	0	12	0	180	2
Thompson RH	1913-15	4-4-1914 (h) Birmingham	L 0-2	12	0					12	0
Thomson D	1923-24	25-8-1923 (a) Tranmere Rovers	L 1-2	25	3	4	1			29	4
Thomson JA	1971-72	14-8-1971 (h) Scunthorpe United	W 4-1	23/3	4	1	2	3/2	0	27/5	6
Tillson A	1988-	*3-9-1988 (h) Torquay United	W 1-0	44/1	2	6	0	2	0	52/1	2
Tinsley C	1954-58	8-4-1955 (h) Bradford	W 1-0	24	0					24	0
Toale I	1987-88	29-8-1987 (a) Notts County	D 0-0	16	4	1	0	1	0	18	4
Tomlinson RW	1935-38	4-3-1936 (a) Wolverhampton W	L 0-1	20	2	2	2			22	4
Tonge J	1882-83					1	0			1	0
Tucker M	1953-58	19-4-1954 (a) Chesterfield	L 0-1	40	0	1	0			41	0
Turnbull GF	1950-51	26-12-1950 (a) Leicester City	D 0-0	2	0	2	0			4	0
Turner I	1971-74	29-4-1972 (h) Peterborough United	W 3-2	26	0	1	0	1	0	28	0
Turner P	1986-88	23-8-1986 (a) Ipswich Town	D 1-1	62	7	6	0	6	0	74	7
Turner PJ	1904-05	3-9-1904 (h) Barnsley	D 0-0	14	0					14	0
Tweedy GJ	1932-53	19-11-1932 (h) Bradford City	D 1-1	347	0	25	0			372	0
Twell B	1927-28	31-12-1927 (a) Clapton Orient	W 2-1	3	1					3	1
Tyler W	1927-28	6-3-1928 (h) Stoke City	L 1-2	1	0					1	0
Vincent NE	1934-47	19-1-1935 (h) Everton	L 1-3	144	2	15	0			159	2
Vincett JH	1907-08	14-9-1907 (h) Stockport County	W 2-1	32	0	5	0			37	0
Wainman WH	1964-78	16-1-1965 (a) Peterborough United	L 1-3	420	0	20	0	32	0	472	0
Wainwright AH	1919-20	1-11-1919 (a) Hull City †	L 1-4	8	2					8	2
Waite JA	1961-63	2-12-1961 (a) Hull City	W 1-0	8	1					8	1
Walker A	1950-58	14-4-1951 (a) Leeds United	L 0-1	65	0	6	0			71	0
Walker DH	1963-64	10-9-1963 (h) Charlton Athletic	L 0-2	15	1					15	1
Walker J	1892-93	3-9-1892 (h) Northwich Victoria	W 2-1	13	0	8	0			21	0
Walker JG	1968-70	*23-11-1968 (h) Port Vale †	D 1-1	25/2	5			1	0	26/2	5
Wallace AJJ	1896-97	12-9-1896 (a) Burton Wanderers	L 1-5	20	0	3	0			23	0
Wallbanks WH	1946-47	2-11-1946 (a) Everton	D 3-3	9	1	2	0			11	1
Walsh I	1986-88	23-8-1986 (a) Ipswich Town †	D 1-1	36/5	13	3	1	6	4	45/5	18
Walton IJ	1975-76	27-12-1975 (a) Colchester United	L 0-1	2	1					2	1
Walton R	1890-91					1	0			1	0
Ward JP	1981-82	31-10-1981 (a) Derby County	D 1-1	2	0					2	0
Wardle W	1939-48	31-8-1946 (a) Manchester United	L 1-2	73	11	6	0			79	11
Waring J	1933-34	10-3-1934 (a) Swansea Town	D 1-1	2	0					2	0
Waring T	1890-91					1	0			1	0
Warner T	1882-83					1	0			1	0
Warren RA	1909-10	1-9-1909 (h) Bradford	L 0-1	1	0					1	0
Waters JJW	1975-84	24-1-1976 (a) Millwall †	D 1-1	356/1	65	20	5	29	5	405/1	75
Watson T	1987-	5-9-1987 (a) Preston North End	W 3-1	25/15	4					25/15	4
Waterson J	1894-95	1-9-1894 (h) Leicester Fosse	W 4-3	20	3					20	3
Watkins AE	1900-01	16-2-1901 (h) Burton T Swifts † (2)	W 5-2	11	5					11	5
Wattam F	1932-39	27-12-1932 (a) Burnley	L 0-2	27	0					27	0
Wealthall BA	1961-63	30-8-1961 (a) Torquay United	L 2-3	9	0			1	0	10	0
Weatherall L	1954-56	8-4-1955 (h) Bradford	W 1-0	10	1					10	1
Welbourne D	1957-64	21-9-1957 (h) Huddersfield Town	W 4-1	130	3	5	0	2	0	137	3
Welsh W	1919-20	11-10-1919 (h) West Ham	L 0-1	5	0					5	0
West A	1893-94					1	0			1	0
Whalley F	1920-21	28-8-1920 (h) Northampton Town	W 2-0	23	0	3	0			26	0
Wheatley R	1951-52	18-8-1951 (a) Chesterfield	L 1-3	5	0					5	0
Wheaton GJ	1962-63	13-10-1962 (h) Rotherham United	L 1-2	7	0					7	0
Wheelhouse S	1907-15	3-9-1907 (h) Gainsborough T	L 1-4	234	3	13	0			247	3

Player	Seasons	League debut	Result	League App	League Gls	FA Cup App	FA Cup Gls	FL Cup App	FL Cup Gls	Total App	Total Gls
Whelpton JI	1913-14	4-4-1914 (h) Birmingham	L 0-2	1	0					1	0
Whitchurch E	1912-20	22-2-1913 (h) Stockport County	W 4-1	30	0					30	0
White M	1958-63	18-10-1958 (a) Sheffield Wednesday	L 0-6	65	0	1	0	2	0	68	0
Whitefoot J	1957-58	16-11-1957 (a) Barnsley	D 3-3	26	5	1	0			27	5
Whitehead NJ	1976-77	21-8-1976 (a) Bury	L 0-2	3	0					3	0
Whitehouse J	1892-96 1899-1900	3-9-1892 (h) Northwich Victoria	W 2-1	137	0	24	0			161	0
Whitfield J	1946-49	19-10-1946 (a) Sunderland	W 2-1	29	7	4	2			33	9
Whitlock M	1982-83	30-10-1982 (h) Cambridge United	W 1-0	7/1	0					7/1	0
Whittaker W	1897-98 1901-03	1-9-1897 (a) Woolwich Arsenal	L 1-4	75	0	2	0			77	0
Whymark TJ	1980-84	6-12-1980 (a) Cardiff City	D 1-1	83/10	16	6	1	5	1	94/10	18
Wigg RG	1974-77	31-1-1975 (a) Tranmere Rovers †	L 1-3	51/12	12	3	1	4	1	58/12	14
Wigginton CA	1968-75 1979-82	28-2-1969 (a) Newport County	L 0-2	286/9	8	21	0	22/1	0	329/10	8
Wilkinson F	1903-04	5-9-1903 (a) Lincoln City	L 1-2	16	2	1	1			17	3
Wilkinson J	1965-68	9-10-1965 (h) Watford	W 2-1	8/1	0	1	0			9/1	0
Wilkinson P	1982-85	*19-3-1983 (h) Wolverhampton W †	D 1-1	68/2	27	4/2	1	10	5	82/4	33
Williams BF	1969-70	10-1-1970 (h) Port Vale	W 2-0	2	0					2	0
Williams C	1952-60	29-4-1953 (a) Crewe Alexandra	W 2-1	188	0	14	0			202	0
Williams D	1953-54	20-2-1954 (a) Bradford City	L 0-3	5	0					5	0
Williams D	1956-62	12-1-1957 (a) Leyton Orient	D 1-1	44	19	1	0	1	0	46	19
Williams T	1903-04	5-12-1903 (a) Glossop	D 1-1	4	1	1	0			5	1
Williams T	1988-89	27-8-1988 (a) Cambridge United	L 1-4	19	0			2	0	21	0
Williamson J	1926-27	30-8-1926 (h) Swansea Town	L 0-1	1	0					1	0
Wilson A	1947-48	3-9-1947 (h) Wolverhampton W	L 0-4	17	1					17	1
Wilson C	1931-33	12-3-1932 (h) Blackburn Rovers	W 4-3	27	2					27	2
Wilson CH	1923-33	10-11-1923 (h) Wolverhampton W	W 2-0	273	2	19	0			292	2
Wilson DEG	1966-69	4-3-1967 (h) Oxford United	W 1-0	63	22	2	0	4	0	69	22
Winter J	1890-91					1	0			1	0
Wood K	1950-52	28-4-1951 (a) Swansea Town † (2)	W 3-1	3	2					3	2
Woodward A	1970-71	15-8-1970 (h) Oldham Athletic †	W 4-1	54	13	1	0	5	1	60	14
Worth A	1911-12	2-9-1911 (h) Wolverhampton W	D 0-0	20	2	4	2			24	4
Worthington D	1966-73	27-8-1966 (h) Walsall †	W 3-1	292/1	14	12	1	23	4	327/1	19
Wrack C	1925-31	31-8-1925 (h) Walsall	W 5-1	125	2	5	0			130	2
Wright AW	1953-54	19-8-1953 (h) York City	W 3-0	39	9	5	1			44	10
Wright CG	1962-66	16-2-1963 (a) Middlesbrough	W 1-0	129	0	11	0	8	0	148	0
Wright J	1932-35	22-10-1932 (h) Bury	W 1-0	27	0	3	0			30	0
Wright N	1927-30	10-3-1928 (h) Nottingham Forest	W 2-1	17	3					17	3
Yates D	1976-77	5-3-1977 (a) Preston North End	L 1-2	10	0					10	0
Young C	1905-11	3-3-1906 (h) Burnley † (2)	W 2-0	5	2	1	0			6	2
Young M	1974-79	*28-9-1974 (h) Aldershot	W 2-0	87/7	4	4	0	4	0	95/7	4
Young R	1962-65	8-9-1962 (a) Walsall	L 1-4	33	13	2	0	3	4	38	17

THE MARINER

The Story of the Grimsby Town Programme

OVER the years the Grimsby Town programme, which is the link between the supporters and the club, has changed its size, style and colour many times and, as programme collecting has increased in popularity, the publication has not been without its critics.

No definite date can be given as to when the first Grimsby Town programme was issued, but the oldest programme known to exist is a 'match card' for a Lincolnshire County Cup Final between Grimsby and Lincoln City, which was held at Gainsborough on 22 April 1887. It is a single card, printed on one side, showing the team line-ups and having space for the score and for the numbers of corners. The half-time and full-time scores have been added in pencil and there is a nice drawing in the centre, showing three players in the kit of the day, including caps.

Pre-1939 Grimsby Town home programmes are rarely seen these days, although a few keep appearing on the programme market. Published and printed by A. Windle in Grimsby, it was a large programme, approximately 9¾in x 7¼in, and of 12 pages. It featured the first Mariner emblem with a cat on the front cover and was a mixture of club gossip and advertisements. It sold at two old pence.

Wartime programmes, when issued, were very flimsy and because of a paper shortage were mostly a single folded sheet measuring 8¼in x 5¼in. Information was limited. The price was still 2d.

Immediate post-war programmes retained the 8¼in x 5¼in format but were increased to eight pages. Information was still restricted, with team line-ups, senior and reserve fixture lists and a brief history of the opponents. After a few issues, the cover of which showed two players in front of goal, the familiar 'trawling' cover was introduced,

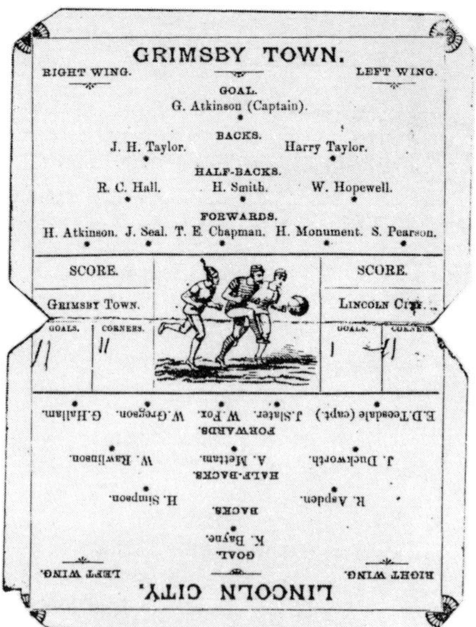
GRIMSBY TOWN.
RIGHT WING. LEFT WING.
GOAL.
G. Atkinson (Captain).
BACKS.
J. H. Taylor. Harry Taylor.
HALF-BACKS.
R. C. Hall. H. Smith. W. Hopewell.
FORWARDS.
H. Atkinson. J. Seal. T. E. Chapman. H. Monument. S. Pearson.
SCORE. SCORE.
GRIMSBY TOWN. LINCOLN CITY.
GOALS. CORNERS. GOALS. CORNERS.
FORWARDS.
E.D. Teesdale (capt.) J. Slater. W. Fox. W. Gregson. G. Hallam.
HALF-BACKS.
J. Duckworth. A. Mettam. W. Rawlinson.
BACKS.
R. Aspden. H. Simpson.
GOAL.
K. Bayne.
RIGHT WING. LEFT WING.
LINCOLN CITY.

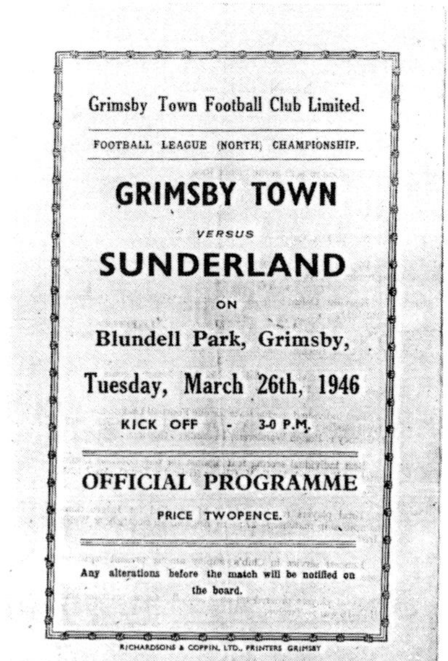
Grimsby Town Football Club Limited.
FOOTBALL LEAGUE (NORTH) CHAMPIONSHIP.
GRIMSBY TOWN
VERSUS
SUNDERLAND
ON
Blundell Park, Grimsby,
Tuesday, March 26th, 1946
KICK OFF - 3-0 P.M.
OFFICIAL PROGRAMME
PRICE TWOPENCE.
Any alterations before the match will be notified on the board.
RICHARDSONS & COPPIN, LTD., PRINTERS GRIMSBY

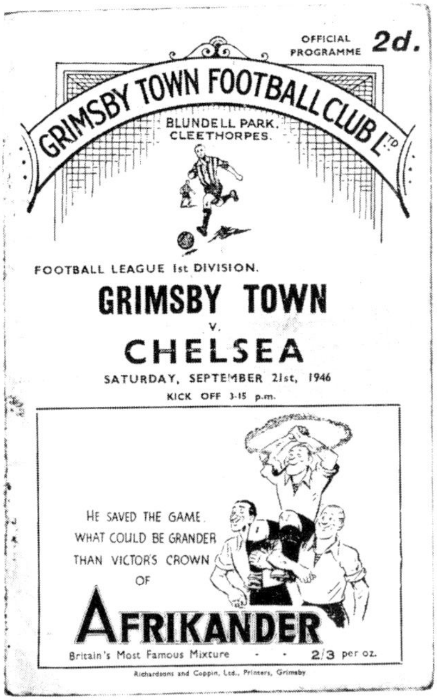

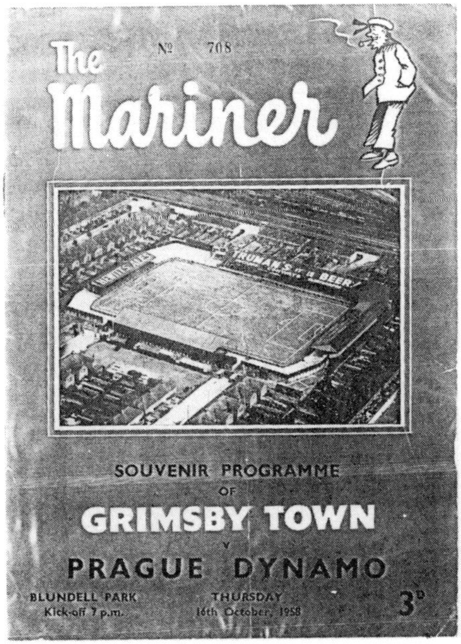

showing a fishing vessel towing a goal into which fish bearing the names of the clubs in the division in which the Mariners were competing — with a bigger fish for the FA Cup — were about to be trapped. A similar but smaller programme was issued for reserve matches. The title, *The Mariner* was dropped in favour of *Official Programme.*

This programme remained in use until the 1952-3 season which saw the introduction of the famous 'Orange Mariner', which collectors consider the best and most collectable of the programmes thus far. At 6½in x 9in in size, it featured a bright orange cover with an aerial view of Blundell Park in the centre. *The Mariner* re-appeared and the Mariner emblem, without his cat, returned to the top right-hand corner. Consisting of 12 pages, it was the first move towards the modern, more informative programme, with manager's note, a supporters' club column and a readers' letters page, as well as the usual team line-ups and fixture lists. This extravagant publication showed a 50 per cent price increase to 3d. The 'Orange Mariner' lasted three seasons under three managers, Bill Shankly, Billy Walsh and Allenby Chilton. It made one return appearance for the visit of Prague Dynamo on 16 October 1958.

The 1955-6 season saw the introduction of a famous Grimsby landmark with a photograph of the 312ft high Dock Tower and a fishing trawler on the front cover. The size was reduced to 8in x 5in. This programme consisted of 12 pages and saw the introduction of a crossword and a quiz. It featured a 'lucky number' on the front cover with a draw for the chance to purchase a Cup Final ticket.

This programme lasted a decade until the 1965-6 season, when a red and white cover was introduced. The Dock Tower and trawler remained but a drawing replaced the photograph. The dimensions and number of pages remained unchanged, but features now included a more comprehensive article on the opposing team and the first player 'profiles'. The price, however, had increased to 6d.

In 1970-71 the red disappeared and an aerial photograph of Blundell Park returned to the top right with the line drawing of the Dock Tower remaining. Dimensions were unchanged but the programme now consisted of 16 pages. The introduction of decimal currency in 1971 saw a 5p cover price, this being increased to 10p in 1973-4.

Between 1967-8 and 1973-4, the *Football League Review* was included as an insert. From the end of the war until 1977-8, the programme printers were Richardson & Coppin of Grimsby.

The 1978-9 season saw the first of the truly modern style programmes — a red and black cover with the familiar Dock Tower and trawler, separated by a drawing of two players. The size was 8¼in x 5¾in and there were now 20 pages, of which four were given over to the visiting team. For the first time the full match-by-match line-up chart was introduced. There was a similar programme in 1979-80 but the drawing of the two players was replaced by an action photograph. The price was 15p in 1978-9 and 20p in 1979-80. Printers for these seasons were the Graphic Press of Grimsby.

For the next five seasons the club turned to specialist programme contractors, Maybank Press of Leicester. A lavish, all-colour production with dimensions of 9½in x 6½in, the programme consisted of 16 pages of club programme, with an eight-page insert common to all programmes in the Maybank stable. Although not popular with some collectors, the British Programme Club voted it the most improved in Division Two. Cover style changed every season, with an action picture on the front changing two or three times a season.

The match against Luton Town on 6 March 1982 saw an unusual occurrence when Maybank used up a few old covers and some programmes bore a picture

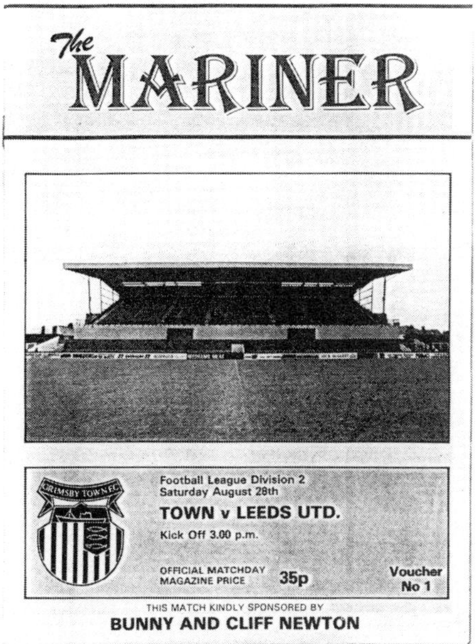

of a team line-up whilst the majority bore an action picture of Kevin Drinkell. The cover-price reflected the inflation of the 1980s, from 30p in 1980-81, through 35p in 1982-3 to 40p in 1983-5.

For the 1985-6 season the club severed their connections with Maybank Press and a smaller 6in x 8¼in programme was produced by Askew Design & Print of Doncaster. The number of pages was increased to 24, with no insert. The cover remained full-colour with a photograph of the docks in the top half and an aerial view of Blundell Park in the bottom half. A small photograph of a player or club official was inset and changed with each programme. The price was now 50p.

In 1986-7 the format remained the same but the cover showed a family of supporters encircled by a football and flanked by two floodlight pylons. Printing was now in the hands of Elvins of Hull.

The 1987-8 season started off with the same format and the cover now showed a new photograph of the docks with a football and an inset of a player superimposed.

Halfway through the season the financial decline of the club was reflected by a sudden decline in the quality of the programme. Elvins were discarded in favour of the Printing Press of Grimsby. The full-colour disappeared, to be replaced by a strange green and red design. Four pages were lost and the text appeared to have been set on a word processor.

In 1988-9 the sponsored programme was introduced, with chemical giants, Giba Geigy, putting up the money. Dimensions were still 6in x 8½in, but the programme was back to 24 pages. After two issues with a rather basic cover, the full-colour returned with an action shot. This refinement brought the first price increase in four seasons with a rise to 60p. The title was now *Mariners Review* and the programme was designed by Ian D.Grimshaw (Associates) of Grimsby, although no printer's imprint appeared.

THE MARINER,
Being the OFFICIAL PROGRAMME of the GRIMSBY TOWN F.C.
TWOPENCE.
SATURDAY, May 1st, 1926.
No. 36. Vol. IX.
The BEST OF LUCK in the Promotion Struggle
The EMPIRE
CLEETHORPES.
Continuance Performance from 6-15 p.m.
KING OF THE CASTLE
Entertainment of Merit
THE RAT
WE SMILE TO-NIGHT.
COLISEUM
CLEETHORPES.
WHO CARES
THE LOVE GAME
PLAYING WITH S
OFFICIAL PROGRAMME
2d.
GRIMSBY TOWN FOOTBALL CLUB LTD
BLUNDELL PARK, CLEETHORPES
FOOTBALL LEAGUE FIRST DIVISION.
BLACKPOOL
SATURDAY, MARCH 22nd. 1947.
Kick off 3-15 p.m.
HE SAVED THE GAME
WHAT COULD BE GRANDER
THAN VICTOR'S CROWN
OF
AFRIKANDER
Britain's Most Famous Mixture
2/3½ per oz.
The Mariner
OFFICIAL PROGRAMME
OF
GRIMSBY TOWN
FOOTBALL CLUB
3D.
ARINER
SATURDAY SEPTEMBER 11TH
35p
DIVISION 2
EWSBURY TOWN
WINTER GARDENS
RON RAMSD
THE
MARINER
CANON LEAGUE DIVISION TWO
40p
SATURDAY 13th APRIL
TOWN
TODAY' SPONSOR
Beechams Toiletries
THE
MARINER
OFFICIAL MATCHDAY MAGAZINE
PRICE 50p
Canon
CANON LEAGUE DIVISION TWO
FULHAM
Saturday, 1st February, 1986
Kick off 3.00 p.m.
SHIRT SPONSOR
THE
MARINER
PRICE 50p
OFFICIAL MATCHDAY MAGAZINE
Match Sponsors:
IMMINGHAM
MOTOR CO. LTD.
BARCLAYS LEAGUE
Division Three
Saturday, 17th October, 1987
Kick off 3.00 p.m.
BY TOWN v BRISTOL CI
OFFICIAL MATCHDAY MAGAZINE
The MARINER
GRIMSBY
TOWN
V
DONCASTER
ROVERS
Saturday
20th. Feb. 1988
Kick-Off 3.00 p.m.
BARCLAYS LEAGUE
Division 3
Today's MATCH SPONSORS
R.W. STAPLES (BUILDERS) Ltd
STALLINGBOROUGH Const
Match Sponsors
PRICE 5
GRIMSBY TOWN
V
TORQUAY UTD.
Barclay's League Division Four
Saturday 3rd September, Kick-off 3 p.m.
Grimsby Town F.C.
Selected items of
sponsorship still
available, please
contact Commercial
Dept. on 697111 for
further details.
MARINERS REVIEW
Sponsored by
CIBA-GEIGY CHEMICALS LTD.
OFFICIAL MATCHDAY MAGAZINE
FOOD TOWN
50p

SUBSCRIBERS

Presentation Copies
1 Grimsby Town Football Club
2 The Football League • 3 The Football Association

4 Les Triggs
5 David Hepton
6 Sid Woodhead
7 Terry Hall
8 Mr & Mrs R S Duggan
9 Mr & Mrs R Yorston
10 Michael Rice
11 Jane Teige
12 Tim Ward
13 R J Yeomans
14 Mr & Mrs A G Holmes
15 Graham Shepherd
16 J L Green
17 Kevin Prestwood
18 D A Herrett
19 S T Parker
20 J F Outhouse
21 J W Sleight
22 J Field (Grimsby Town Supporters Club)
23 Peter F Seed
24 David J Seed
25 Ray Glover
26 R J Sandy
27 Jonathan Bradshaw
28 Peter Gibson
29 David Webster
30 Raymond Ayre
31 Bill Meek
32 Paul Dodman
33 James Danby
34 J G Broughton
35 A W Sylvester
36 Jonathan R C Wray
37 M J Gascoigne
38 N W Mayne
39 M E Clover
40 T T Lingard
41 Mike Langmaid
42 James Pickett
43 Alan Quickfall
44 Philip S Fawcett
45 G Clayton
46 B Whittaker
47 Frank R Thompson
48 Nigel S Broddle
49 John William Stiles
50 Kevin Michael Parker
51 A J Roberts
52 Trevor John Martyn
53 Bryn Jones
54 B W Clark
55 Kathryn J Broadburn
56 Martin Copass
57 B Spittlehouse
58 Mark Liney
59 Norman Douglas
60 Malcolm Naulls
61 Tony I Robinson
62 W Cunningham
63 A C Carter
64 Kenneth Pike
65 Nick Durkin
66 J A Linfitt
67 Ron Boyd
68 Michael Alcock
69 D G Cockrill
70 Carl Rudd
71 J Hurst
72 Garry Freeman
73 Peter Townsend
74 M W Low
75 Jim Wardle
76 Giles Sudderick
77 Ashley Portlock
78 Brian Firth
79 Rachel & Martin Branson
80 D Wallwork
81 R Howden
82 Robert Moss-Waddell
83 G C Ostler
84 M Cavallini
85 R M Briggs
86 David Smith
87 Alan Gary Smith
88 David Charles Elsey
89 John Michael Warr
90 L G Warren
91 Charles Ekberg
92 D Poucher
93 J R Poucher
94 Michael White
95 Armas Best
96 Michael Smart
97 Dermot McKeown
98 Martin Gilbert
99 Paul Jackson
100 Michael Cardy
101 Neil Dickinson
102 Christine Kelley
103 Patrick Conway
104 Duncan Watt
105 D T Bryant
106 J A Harris
107 John Treleven
108 Brian H Hobbs
109 John Robinson
110 Petra Robinson
111 Stuart Walton
112 Peter Bradford
113 J S Pyke
114 Gerald Hill
115 J M Moore
116 A P J M Otten
117 Christopher Minchin
118 Esa Kautonen
119 Geir Juva
120 Lars-Olof Wendler
121 P W Stevenson
122 Simons Martin
123 Harald Lohr
124 Surapot Saengchote
125 Kåre M Torgrimsen
126 I Watts
127 David J Godfrey
128 M Swart
129 A Young
130 Keith Lowe
131 R G Woolman
132 Richard Stocken
133 Gordon Small

134 John Motson
135 S P Tomlin
136 P H Whitehead
137 Phil Soar
138 G D Painter
139 G Adams
140 J & C Wakefield
141 Michael K Hubbert
142 J N Darley
143 John Osgerby
144 Keith R Collins
145 C Eastwell
146 K A Eastwell
147 Harold John Kemp Hall
148 Phillip R Neary
149 John Jebson
150 Brian Woodhead
151 John & David Kirk
152 Vic Swann
153 Christine Harrison
154 David Stark
155 Paul McDonald
156 Norman L Lockwood
157 Clifford Gamble
158 A C Shephard
159 Harry Kay
160 Dcrek Hyde
161 Geoff Allman
162 R J Gamble
163 B H Standish
164 David Keats
165 Moira & Frederick Furness
166 Fred Lee
167 Graham & Janet Carter
168 Donald Noble
169 Peter Lunn
170 D A R H Webster
171 R D N Wells
172 David Robert Earnshaw
173 Dave Hillam
174 Colin Cameron
175 J Roberts
176 R A Kelly
177 George Foster
178 Ron Fisher
179 M Parker
180 Graeme Walster
181 Peter Linley
182 Ryan Linley
183 S K Saxby
184 D J Watford
185 R A Eley
186 Ron Bevers
187 J Lathan
188 Alan Hilditch
189 B Harrison
190 Frank Grande
191 Ian Appels
192 S R Winn
193 Peter Baxter
194 Arthur Frank Pearson Jnr
195 Peter Pickup
196 Malcolm Hartley
197 Ian Willott
198 Leslie A West
199 Barry Whittaker
200 David Needham
201 C A Thomas
202 Sidney Arnold
203 Geoffrey Edwin Milborn
204 Paul Carrick
205 John Bristow
206 Eric Heesom
207 Anders Johansson
208 J Gardiner
209 Ingvar Thomas
210 Ian Griffiths
211 W D Phillips
212 Harry Thompson
213 Dave Helliwell
214 Simon Byatt
215 L R Bradford
216 John Shaw
217 Angus W Rodger
218 Andrew Anderson
219 David G Wherry
220 P N Blake
221 Pete Farrell
222 Steve Mosley
223 Nigel A King
224 A Parrott
225 G N Forman
226 Andy Gibson
227 Alan Breese
228 W E Riggall
229 Raymond Shaw
230 David Gregg
231 J Ringrose
232 Rowena Jones
233 Joan Linnell
234 Moira Tabois
235 David James Robertson
236 Jim & Sandra Stearn
237 Alan John Waumsley
238 Ron Counte
239 Mike Purkiss
240 Trond Isaksen
241 George Odlin
242 S G Bacon
243 Sports Marketing (Australia)
244 David Colin Gregory
245 Andrew Bushell
246 M C Harrison
247 R K Larder
248 Cyril Marcussen
249 David M Dixon
250 William Needs
251 David Brown
252 Stephen Wright
253 Roger Wash
254 Brian Tabner
255 Paul B Jones
256 Steven Jones
257 Derek Baisbrown
258 B M Gould
259 Dr C J Morton
260 John Northcutt
261 Stanley A Robinson
262 Richard James Bridge
263 Derek Ringland
264 Jonathan S Pexman
265 E M Holmes
266 Alan Cross
267 Andrew M Alcock
268 Robert Jack
269 Paul Jerome
270 Keith L Scott
271 David Downs
272 Norman Green
273 David Burton
274 D M Potts
275 Ken Arnold
276 David Wagstaff
277 Matthew Wagstaff
278 Roger A Swindells
279 Robert Lingard
280 Gary M Chambers